CLIVE BARKER:
THE
DARK FANTASTIC

Also by Douglas E Winter

Fiction

RUN

Anthologies

PRIME EVIL (EDITOR)

REVELATIONS (US) / *MILLENNIUM* (UK) (EDITOR)

Non-fiction

STEPHEN KING: THE ART OF DARKNESS

FACES OF FEAR

CLIVE BARKER:
THE
DARK FANTASTIC

DOUGLAS E WINTER

HarperCollins*Publishers*

HarperCollins*Publishers*
77–85 Fulham Palace Road,
Hammersmith, London W6 8JB

www.**fire**and**water**.com

Published by HarperCollins*Publishers* 2001
1 3 5 7 9 8 6 4 2

Copyright © Douglas E Winter 2001

Chapter illustrations © Clive Barker

The Author asserts the moral right to
be identified as the author of this work

A catalogue record for this book
is available from the British Library

ISBN 0 00 255041 5

Set in Minion with Trajan display
Typeset by Rowland Phototypesetting Ltd,
Bury St Edmunds, Suffolk

Printed and bound in Great Britain by
Clays Ltd, St Ives plc

For Leonard Barker
and William E Winter
Fathers of lost boys

He looked at his own Soul with a Telescope.
What seemed all irregular, he saw and showed
to be beautiful Constellations; and he added
to the Consciousness hidden worlds within worlds.
— SAMUEL TAYLOR COLERIDGE, *Notebooks*

Peter did reach the Gardens at last . . .
as I am to tell you now.
— JM BARRIE, *Peter Pan in Kensington Gardens*
is available from the British Library

TABLE OF CONTENTS

FOREWORD

'Why me? ... Why should I have to tell it?'
'Because you're the best liar,' Jerichau replied with a tight smile.
'You can make it true.'

         – CLIVE BARKER, *Weaveworld*

Some books are written; others are lived.

The fable that follows – about the lives, real and imagined, of my friend Clive Barker – has its beginning, appropriately enough, at his birthplace of Liverpool. It was there, on an October night in 1983, that I met Clive – not in person, but in the way so many millions of people would meet him over the years to come: in his fiction.

My wife, Lynne, and I were visiting Ramsey and Jenny Campbell at their home in suburban Merseyside. With the enthusiasm of youth, I was intent on explicating the sudden surge of horror fiction and film into the popular culture – while offering, perhaps, an argument for its legitimacy. I was writing a biography/critique, *Stephen King: The Art of Darkness* (1984), and an oral history, *Faces of Fear* (1985); and Ramsey, whose wisdom was essential to both books, had agreed to an interview.

After hours of red wine and the deeper red of Italian horror videos, Ramsey disappeared into the shadows of his writing eyrie, only to emerge with a towering stack of manuscripts: the short stories of an unpublished playwright named Clive Barker. 'You're about to read the most important new horror writer of this decade,' Ramsey told me. After reading only fifty pages, I was convinced that he was right.

Here was a fiction of savage violence and sexual abandon that embraced, with breathtaking ferocity, the possibilities of horror, not its boundaries; that had the courage and strength to dream, to indulge the dark fantastic in all of its glory, and to explore the emotion perceived by the fabulist ER Eddison, writing so many years before: 'horror not of the unknown, but of the unknowable, the impossible, the unconceivable'.

The manuscripts were published in the UK in March 1984 as *Clive Barker's Books of Blood*. The rest, as they say, is history. In the blur of years that followed, this unknown author became one of contemporary literature's hottest properties, transcending the false premise of a horror genre and crafting a fiction that, in its insistent diversity, could be described only as his own. His prodigious talent and ambition, coupled with a tenacious work ethic, soon created screenplays, motion pictures, illustrated fiction, comic books, games, models, art and photographic exhibitions . . . an empire of enthusiasms.

Clive Barker proved himself a polymath of the perverse – an artist who was wilfully determined *not* to fulfil expectation, but to persist in offering a personal vision that, by the sheer force of its creativity, would delight and terrify, excite and repulse, confront and challenge, and ultimately enrapture an ever-growing audience. Perhaps inevitably, he became something of a *cause célèbre*, championed in magazines as diverse as *Fangoria, Penthouse, People* and *Out*; on talk shows from 'Larry King Live' to 'Late Night with David Letterman' and 'Politically Incorrect'; in television documentaries and internet websites and newsgroups. Like his infamous progeny Pinhead, Clive Barker was a citizen of the public imagination, attending the Academy Awards, directing music videos, autographing petitions for animal rights, modelling menswear for Saks Fifth Avenue; but despite this outward visibility, he remained, in a personal sense, an unknown – and hardly different from the shy young playwright I was to meet in London a few nights after reading his unpublished manuscripts. He is older and wealthier now, of course, more comfortable in his stance and his sexuality; but bright lights and video cameras are flat and reflective, like the television screen, and offer rare glimpses of his polite calm, his acute and articulate intelligence, his wicked humour, his boundless capacity for friendship and love.

On that evening, so long ago, so near, we descended into the basement of an Italian restaurant, and any semblance of small talk disintegrated as I described the visionary finale of the film my wife and I had seen the night before. 'Fulci!' he said, nearly shouting, with unbridled delight, the name of the Italian director who lensed *L'Aldila* ('The Beyond') (1981); and in that moment of shared enthusiasm for an ill-budgeted and obscure motion picture, a lifelong bond was formed, as if I had offered, and he had returned, the secret handshake of an outcast tribe. (Years later, when I met Lucio Fulci, his first words to me were: 'So . . . you know Clive Barker!')

The union forged in that evening's marathon of conversation would evolve with the years as I became Clive's friend – and, on occasion, confidant, interviewer, photographer, reviewer, critic and editor. I've been at his side during moments of triumph, as well as moments of despair (the wrenching aftermath of *Nightbreed*) and surreal wonder (declining the attentions of glamorous transsexuals in one of Manhattan's more curious clubs).

Perhaps it was destined that I would become his biographer; but the commission was accepted with reluctance. In the spring of 1990, I was living in Detroit, far from home, trying the lawsuit of my life. Northwest Airlines Flight 255 had crashed at Detroit Metropolitan Airport in 1987, leaving 156 people dead; the resulting litigation was consolidated into a federal jury trial that lasted nineteen gruelling months. In the midst of this madness, Ed Breslin, then Editor-in-Chief of HarperCollins*Publishers*, called and said: 'I'd like to take you to dinner.' A few nights later, we met at the Ritz Carlton in Bloomfield Hills; before our drinks arrived, he said: 'Let me cut to the chase. I've read your book on Stephen King. We'd like you to write one about Clive Barker.'

I was honoured, but I told him: it was too early. Certainly I had no time to write a book – the litigation, with a myriad of appeals, would continue until 1996 – and I felt that Clive, who was not yet forty, needed time to pursue his ambition further before a meaningful text, and not some pop artifice, could be constructed. And even then, I must admit, the prospect was daunting. To quote my subject: 'How can Gauguin and Goya keep such easy company with Karloff and King Kong? Or Barbarella with the Bible? Or William Blake with anyone?' These questions would haunt this memoir; and in finding answers, I would also find new questions to ask.

With the kind indulgence of HarperCollins, I wrote this book in my own way and in its own time, exploring the lives of Clive Barker with a patience and persistence that, I hope, will reward the reader with unique insight into the man and the artist. In authorizing this biography, Clive agreed to sit for many hours of taped interviews – and many more hours of simple conversation – in which his private self, rarely exposed in his public appearances (or, indeed, in his plays and his fiction) was coaxed, with increasing willingness, into the light.

There are many truths here, however mundane, that have been obscured by the culture industry and its machines of celebrity – muddled in the telling or, on occasion, polished to an impossible perfection. Clive knows the phenomenon too well; at times, he has contributed, intentionally or not, to a mythology that delighted but ultimately disturbed him. As he wrote in the novel *Imajica* (1991) about his mirror-self Gentle: 'The fact that he'd become a figment of the popular imagination amused Gentle at first, but after a time it began to weigh on him. He felt like a ghost among these living versions of himself, invisible among the listeners who gathered to hear tales of his exploits, the details of which were embroidered and embellished with every telling.'

With his participation, then, I present the man and not the ghost, offering a critical biography whose purpose, at heart, is to seek the origins of the tales. In tracing Clive's journey from his childhood in Liverpool to an apotheosis in Beverly Hills, it is impossible to ignore the transformation of the central facts from external realities (school days, friendships, frolics) to the internal fantasies that he, in turn, has brought to life in the theatre, on the printed page, on canvases and silver screens. The traditional focus of biography on the mundane realm of existence fades – and, at times, disappears – as I explore the more vivid lives of his imagination. After all, as Clive has written: 'What did it matter, what was true and what was false, what real and what invented? In his head all of it, the half-lies and the truths, were one continuum of personal history.'

The memoir offered here is indeed a continuum, a melding of facts and fiction with all the elements of a fable: a weaving of alternate histories, as spoken by family and friends and collaborators, with words from Clive's lips and pen, and my own critical assessment of his art. Unlike some biographers and critics, I make no claim of objectivity – a spurious conceit for any writer, but certainly for those who seek to reinvent the lives and creations of others. I write with an unequivocal enthusiasm for Clive Barker. I do not temper my criticism, when it is due; but I admit to a forgiving stance – and a belief in the power of the positive.

Frank Kermode once noted that '[i]t is not expected of critics as it is of poets that they should help us to make sense of our lives; they are bound only to attempt the lesser feat of making sense of the ways we try to make sense of our lives'.

In attempting this lesser feat, I have had the confidence and assistance of a number of people who deserve acknowledgment and my deepest appreciation.

For their willingness to participate in interviews on the record and/ or less formal conversations about Clive's life and work: David Armstrong, Nicole Armstrong, Peter Atkins, Len and Joan Barker, Roy and Lynne Barker, Alan Baumgarten, Eddie Bell, Julie Padget née Blake, Caitlin Blasdell, Barbara Boote, Doug and Lynne Bradley, Ginjer Buchanan, Ramsey and Jenny Campbell, Helen Clarke, Bill Condon, Bess Cutler, David Dodds, Nan du Sautoy, Jo Fletcher, Lucio Fulci, Neil Gaiman, Mick Garris, Charles Grant, James and Eileen Herbert, Jane Johnson, Stephen Jones, Stephen King, Angus MacKenzie, Kim Newman, Philip Nutman, George Pavlou, Ingrid Pitt, Joe Riley, Mary Roscoe, Bernard Rose, Norman Russell, David J Schow, John Silbersack, Malcolm Smith, Michael Marshall Smith, Peter Straub, Herbert Swartz and Kevin Yagher – as well as those who spoke in anonymity.

For providing research and bibliographic materials and other background information: John W Amberg, Andrew Armstrong, Michael Barry, Cheryl Bentzen-Green, Stephen R Bissette, Michael Brown, Joe Daley, Laura Cleveland, Lois Dombek, Stephen Dressler, Stefan Dziemianowicz, William C Edgar, Antonella Fulci, Michael Hadley,

June Hall, Stefan Jaworzyn, Alan Jones, Michael Lang, Tim and Donna Lucas, Denny McLain, Jeffrey W Morof, Michael A Morrison, Kim Newman, Steve Niles, Ana Osgood, Garrett Peck, Jo Anne Peele, Lindsay Sagnette, Anthony Timpone, William C Winter – and, of course, many of the interviewees noted above. The late James Blair Lovell deserves special note for his attention to bibliographic detail; Angus MacKenzie provided rare video footage and many helpful insights into the geography of Liverpool and Wales; David Christian, Barbara Hutchison, Debbie McGeady and Cindy Kolodner assisted in deciphering interview tapes; and Robb Humphreys and Anna Miller offered wisdom and warm food on the set of *Lord of Illusions*.

For her thoughtful insights on the manuscript, my editor at Harper-Collins, Jane Johnson.

For their friendship, guidance and, above all, patience, my agents in New York and London, Howard Morhaim and Abner Stein; and, as always, my wife and best friend, Lynne.

Douglas E Winter
Oakton, Virginia
June 2000

1

THE POOL OF LIFE

In the private storybook of her head this trip . . . was a return to the mire of childhood; a reminder not of blissful, careless years, but of an anxious, blinkered state from which adulthood had liberated her. And Liverpool had been that state's metropolis: a city of perpetual dusk, where the air smelled of cold smoke and a colder river. When she thought of it she was a child again, and frightened of dreams.
— CLIVE BARKER, *Weaveworld*

Early in the twentieth century, one of our great thinkers, wounded by depression, found healing in a dream. His 'black and opaque' emotions took physical form as he walked the streets of a foreign city, grey with soot and dirt. 'It was night, and winter, and dark, and raining.' His footsteps wound out of a harbour and into the 'real city . . . up above', which was arranged radially around 'a broad square dimly illuminated by street lights, into which many streets converged'. At the centre of the square, and the city, waited revelation: 'a round pool, and in the middle of it a small island. While everything round about was obscured by rain, fog, smoke, and dimly lit darkness, the little island blazed with sunlight. On it stood a single tree, a magnolia, in a shower of reddish blossoms. It was as though the tree stood in the sunlight and were at the same time the source of light.'

The dreamer was Swiss psychologist Carl Gustav Jung. From this poignant night-vision of a bleak but ultimately redeeming city emerged 'a first inkling of my personal myth' – and his theory of the 'collective unconscious'. He awoke not only from his sleep, but also from his depression: 'I had had a vision of unearthly beauty, and that was why I was able to live at all.'

The city of Carl Jung's dream was Liverpool. He called it 'the pool of life'.[1]

Fabled in the nineteenth century as the 'City of Ships', the dream and the reality of Liverpool are linked inextricably with water. One of England's principal ports – an apex of the slave triangle and the cotton triangle – Liverpool is located on the River Mersey, three miles inland from the Irish Sea. The natural gateway for the agriculture and industry of Lancashire, it prospered during the Victorian expansion; but despite its wealthy merchants and the splendour of their Georgian homes and magnificent churches, Liverpool was – and is – a working-class town.

The docks and landing stages on the tideless harbour of the Mersey once occupied seven miles of river frontage, and were filled with Alfred Holt's blue funnelled steamships and transports, ferries and dredges, the boats from Ireland and the transatlantic liners of Cunard and P&O and the Harrison Line. On the western bank of the river were the busy docks of Birkenhead, home of the Laird shipbuilding yard, famous for its battleships and passenger liners. The maritime trade brought heavy industry – shipbuilders, repair stations, steel mills, chemical works, automobile plants; and what Charles Dickens had described as one of England's most beautiful cities was shadowed by industrialization. The destruction inflicted by Luftwaffe bombers during the Second World War – and the dulling hand of time – sent Liverpool into decline. The shipping industry shifted to the Southampton Docks, and the factories fell victim to low capital investment and labour unrest.

By the 1970s, Liverpool was a working-class town without any work; and when Clive Barker wrote his autobiographical and autumnal novel *Weaveworld* (1987), he invoked its spectre: 'Once this waterway had been busy with ships, arriving weighed down with their cargo and riding high as they headed for faraway. Now, it was empty. The docks silted up, the wharfs and warehouses idle. Spook City; fit only for ghosts.'

Today, Liverpool seems a very good place to come from; its population, estimated at 450,000, is ageing and declining – and departing. The city centre is dark and imposing, and its two great churches, the Metropolitan Cathedral of Christ the King and the massive Anglican Cathedral, tower like artifacts of an ancient civilization. There is a third, and quite different, cathedral located on Matthew Street, where a rough-and-tumble beat club, the Cavern, was once the venue for a rock-and-roll band known as the Beatles. Demolished in the 1970s, the Cavern has been rebuilt in honour of the city's new industry: tourism. The mighty seaport no longer trades on shipping, but with its brief flirtation with global attention and a hundred metres of street.

As working people, Liverpudlians are hard and hearty, many of them descended from sailors and Irish emigrants. One certain way to escape the docks and the factories was popular entertainment and sports; and the city is known for its rock stars and comedians – the wit of the scouser is mythic – as well as legends of the football field (Ian St. John), the boxing ring (John Conteh) and the stage (Rex Harrison).

The Beatles, like others before them and since, left Liverpool and never really returned. But their music did return, time and again, evoking its landmarks, some real, others imagined – including the stretch of blacktopped road known as Penny Lane. It was there, on Penny Lane – twenty years before John Lennon and Paul McCartney immortalized the street in song – that music brought two Liverpudlians together, to find their own private island in the pool of life.

Near Penny Lane there was a barber (Bioletti's) and a banker and, yes, even a fireman with a clean machine, but there was also an imposing old family home called Cadby Hall, which in 1946 housed the Wavertree Community Centre. Operated by a sometime editor of the *Shanghai Times*, the Community Centre was a social club with a coffee bar – no alcohol was allowed – where servicemen returning from the War could meet and mingle, find new friends and, perhaps, even lovers.

One of its members was twenty-one-year-old Telegraphist [Special] Leonard Barker, a veteran of three years of duty with the Royal Navy.

3

Encouraged to join by his friend Terry Emery, Len spent many of his evening hours at the club, enjoying the big band music, the dancing and, most of all, his survival of the war.

Len was the only child of a sailor who was, in turn, the child of a sailor. He was fourteen years old when Great Britain declared war in 1939, and he enlisted in the Royal Navy as soon as he was eligible, in 1943. His service designation – Telegraphist [Special] – confirms that he was no ordinary wireless operator; although Len left school at age fourteen, he was deft mentally and mechanically. His earliest service was devoted to intercepting German radio transmissions; but he was soon dispatched to the Far East, where he was assigned to the complex Anglo-American code-breaking effort directed at Japan. He spent two and a half years in South Africa, Madagascar, Salaam, India, and finally Mauritius, based at listening stations that intercepted and monitored Japanese wireless signals. 'I had a good war,' he says. 'A lucky war. I was in the right place at the right time, when others were in the wrong places.'

Len Barker's good luck continued back home in Liverpool. With his dashing good looks and a penchant for ballroom dancing, he served as master of ceremonies for soirées at the Wavertree Community Centre, introducing and playing 78 rpm records by the likes of Tommy Dorsey, Benny Goodman and Glenn Miller. One evening he caught the attention of Joan Revill, an attractive and strong-willed twenty-one-year-old who visited the club with two girlfriends. Joan loved to dance, but she had definite opinions – usually negative – about the footwork of the men on the dance floor. Each evening, when the time came for Len to announce a 'ladies request' dance – during which he stopped the record, allowing the ladies to choose their partners – Joan would ask him to stop the record when she was close to one of the better dancers. It wasn't long before she realized that Len was the dancer of choice. 'Very posh,' Joan says; but Len demurs: 'I wasn't, really. All I did was put the records on and chat up the next girl who came in the door.'

The acquaintance soon grew into friendship, and then romance. Twelve months later, Len and Joan decided to marry; but the decision was troubling for their parents. Although each had been born in Liverpool, they were children of vastly different worlds.

4

Len's ancestors were Irish; like many other Liverpudlians, they had emigrated from County Cork during the potato famine, and decided that the port city was as fine a place as anything their original destination, America, might have to offer. 'Land didn't seem to interest them as much as the water,' Len says. 'It's probably something I inherited; I always had a love of it.'

Little wonder: Len's paternal grandfather, William Barker, was a riverman and sailor. Born in the 1850s, he owned a tugboat and barges that he sailed to Cheshire, returning to Liverpool and Birkenhead with salt mined at Norwich for export. The tug was christened after his wife, Mary Ellen. When a son was born to them in 1892, it seemed only right to name him after Queen Victoria's late husband.

Like his father, Albert Edward Barker was summoned by the water, although, as Len notes: 'There was not much choice in Liverpool between the wars. If you weren't sailing, you were shipbuilders, or stevedores, or working in offices for insurers . . .' Albert started work at a young age as a hand on his father's barges; but William was such a stern taskmaster that Albert quit, taking work as a riveter with Campbell Lewis, a large shipyard in Birkenhead.

With the First World War, Albert enlisted in the Army, but the pull of the water was relentless; he was transferred first to the Merchant Navy, and then the Royal Navy, and was believed lost at sea when his transport ship was sunk by a German U-boat. After the war, Albert joined Alfred Holt, the shipping line known as 'Blue Funnel' or 'Blue Flue' because of the distinctive cobalt blue of its ships' steam funnels. (Loyalty to the company was so strong in Birkenhead that employees would paint the front doors of their homes cobalt blue.) His peacetime voyages took him to the Far East – the same course that his son would follow, years later, in wartime – but one day, while gutting a fish, a frozen bone pierced the palm of his hand. When the ship's doctor, an alcoholic, stitched Albert's hand into a nearly useless claw, Alfred Holt, in its generosity, sacked him.

Back in Liverpool, Albert served as the cook on a river tender and finally returned to Alfred Holt and the sea just before the Second World War was declared. Summoned to duty in the Royal Navy, again his ship was sunk. 'He didn't have a great deal of time for the Germans as a consequence,' Len notes.

After the war, Albert completed a full circle, going back to work on river barges.

Albert and his wife, Florence, did not marry until late in their thirties; she had been engaged to marry another man, but he died in the First World War. Born in 1883, Florence Jones was the eldest daughter of a large Liverpool family; at the age of nine, her mother died of tuberculosis, and she left school to look after her brothers and sisters. She was later put into service for large families in Liverpool and London, Derbyshire and Kent, working as a housemaid or kitchen hand. Returning to Liverpool, she became the cook and then housekeeper for a well-regarded German-Jewish couple, Maximilian and Amanda Luwenthal. Max, a Prussian-born physician, was responsible for vetting German nationals who were recalled to the fatherland for military duty in the First World War. He was a stern man who refused bribes from those trying to avoid service, and he was known for having his chauffeur drive him south of the city, into the countryside, leaving Max there to walk the long miles home.

Luwenthal saved the life of the only child of Albert and Florence: Leonard Barker. Born on May 18, 1925, when Florence was 42, Len had chest and digestive problems; the attending nurse said: 'Oh, there's no hope.' Luwenthal picked him up and said, 'There's life in this baby' – he slapped him, and Len cried his way into life. The costs of Len's subsequent medical care were far beyond the Barkers' means; but Luwenthal looked after him for free – and Len survived, although his frailty delayed his entry into school. 'I was one of those seven-stone weaklings that Charles Atlas used to talk about.'

Len was an only child, and one with few men in his life: his father was always at sea, gone for months at a time, and his hard life, and penchant for cigarettes, saw him barely survive his own father, who died at the age of ninety: 'One of those hard men who sat in front of the fire, making little spills out of newspaper, then lighting this godawful pipe that would have killed all the bugs in the greenhouse.' Len's fondest memories of youth were of the times he was sent to buy his grandfather's plugs of tobacco – and the times his father returned home, smelling of the salt sea.

Joan Revill came from a more genteel and mysterious upbringing. Her maternal grandfather, Rocco Peverelli, was born in the 1880s at Lake Como in Italy. How this handsome young man came to meet and marry Grace Smith, a daughter of Liverpool, remains a mystery – Grace, Joan's grandmother, didn't believe in talking about the past, and she was tight-lipped about her own roots, and those of Rocco, noting only that he had served as a cavalryman in World War One.

Rocco and Grace operated the Rocket Hotel in the Broad Green district of Liverpool (a motorway now spans the site). Their only child was born in 1898 – a daughter with a lovely name: Ruby Angelina Theodora Peverelli. Although Ruby was given cuttings of bearded Italians, laden with medals from fighting the Austrians, she otherwise learned little of her parents' pasts, save an occasional story about one of Rocco's two sisters – her namesake, Angelina, who had three sons who never married.

Ruby shared her parents' disdain for revelations about the past. She married Frank Kitchen Revill, another only child. Born in 1896, Frank had a stepsister, Mary, and two stepbrothers, but none of them married. His calling was cotton; Lancashire was then the world's cotton-manufacturing centre, and Frank worked for Milligan & Mackintosh, a Liverpool cotton brokerage. When the First World War halted the cotton trade, the firm went out of business; Frank took up banking, then returned to cotton brokerage until the Second World War sent him back to banking.

Frank and Ruby had two daughters: Joan, born on December 3, 1925; and Brenda, born on July 13, 1930. Like Len Barker, Joan nearly succumbed to illness in her youth. Her grandfather Rocco nursed her through whooping cough, but then contracted it himself – which killed him, at the age of sixty-eight, when Joan was only four.

Joan and Brenda grew up in a large five-bedroomed house, on its own grounds, with a staircase in the middle and a huge cupboard beneath the stairs. During the Second World War, her father, too old for combat, served as an air raid warden as German bombers flew constant missions intended to cripple the port and destroy the ship-building and support infrastructure on the docks. With her mother, grandmother and sister, Joan would wait out the Blitz in the cupboard, studying her lessons. Soon, fearing that the air raids would grow in severity, Frank Revill moved his family twenty miles up the coast to a small hotel in Southport – from which Joan could see the Luftwaffe planes flying past, very low, just after dropping their bombs.

Joan was educated from the age of eight to seventeen at Huyton College, the premier girls' school in Liverpool; then she attended the SLCC College of Domestic Science, whose three-year curriculum – which ranged from cookery to child care to medicine – was compressed into two years during the war. She graduated at the age of eighteen and, because of the continued German bombing, moved in 1943 to Lake Windermere in the Lake District, where she took her first job as Deputy School Matron at Blackwell House, handling the infant department of Huyton College, which had been evacuated from Liverpool. When the war ended in 1945, she returned to Liverpool as the housekeeper for Belvedere High School, a large public school where she managed the catering and cleaning staff; at only twenty-one years of age, she was younger than everyone who worked for her.

When Joan took work at Belvedere, her mother turned against her – 'a difficult lady,' notes Joan. She befriended the school cook, Elsie McIntyre, who became like an elder sister.

Joan's mother was also disappointed in Joan's new boyfriend – and, it seemed, fiancé. Len Barker was decidedly working-class, and he lacked Joan's higher education and finesse; Ruby didn't find him adequate or acceptable for her daughter. Len's mother, in turn, became resentful that he wasn't being accepted by the Revills. She also tried to prevent the marriage, hoping that Len, who had lost his youth to the War, would explore life more fully before becoming tied down with marital responsibilities. 'We could have been parted, really,' Len says, 'had we not been the sort of people we are.'

Despite their parents' misgivings, Joan left her job at Belvedere High School to spend her life with Len. Their attraction was beyond endearment. He was the dashing dancer, to be sure, but he was also a dedicated, and very hard-working, man; and, as for Joan, Len tells me, with a delighted whisper: 'She made the most beautiful cakes.' Their marriage would last more than fifty years; and, indeed, until death.

Len Barker and Joan Revill married on April 9, 1949. A friend found them 'digs', one-half of a house on Glenmore Avenue that was owned by Captain and Mrs Weatherall – soon known as Uncle Billy and

Aunty Marie. William Weatherall was a commodore captain for the Harrison Line, the shipping company that employed Len as timekeeper for the stevedoring department. When Billy set sail, Marie would return to a cottage that she kept in Guernsey, her childhood home in the Channel Islands. The couple decided to take in full-time tenants, who would look after their house when Billy was at sea. Len and Joan paid one pound, twenty-five pence each week for rent (utilities included), and lived cheerfully at Glenmore Avenue until 1950.

The Weatheralls decided to sell the house, and the Barkers, who couldn't afford it, bought a large terraced house at 34 Oakdale Road, a hundred metres from its intersection with Penny Lane – and across a field from Cadby Hall, the site of their first encounter at Wavertree Community Centre. Although Len worked long, arduous hours at the Harrison Line, money was tight; and Joan considered returning to work. Len's mother suggested that they take in house-guests in order to supplement Len's income; one of her friends owned a guest house that was favoured by theatrical people, and she gave Len and Joan a steady stream of referrals. The first people who knocked on their door were the understudies for Vivien Leigh and Laurence Olivier; other guests included director Nicolas Roeg and actress Maureen Swanson. An unforeseen benefit was that the Barkers were given their first glimpse of the theatre, with free tickets and backstage visits.

The house on Oakdale Road was a busy place, never in need of tenants. Joan's success with keeping guests expanded to a contract with the Automobile Association, which brought a steady stream of men studying to become AA inspectors – and their little vans, parked on the street outside.

Soon enough, however, there was a different kind of guest: Joan was pregnant. On October 5, 1952, their first child, a son, was born.

His name was Clive Barker.[2]

2

OAKDALE ROAD

*Know what it is to be a child? . . . [I]t is to be so little that the elves
can reach to whisper in your ear.*

                   – FRANCIS THOMPSON, 'Shelley'

Joan and Len brought their baby boy home from 'Oxford Street' –
the Liverpool Maternity Hospital on Oxford Street – to 34 Oakdale
Road. It was a fortnight after Clive's birth; he was delivered by Caesarean section, an arduous procedure for mothers of the 1950s, and
although his health was perfect, Joan's recovery was slow.

    Clive attributes his fascination with, and terror of, the sight of blood
to the difficult circumstances of his birth. 'I was a Caesarean birth,
and Mother and I nearly died, and I was stuck, upside-down, for a
long time. And there was a series of traumatic first impressions of the
world, which I believe have become a *leitmotif* of terror for me. A lot
of noise. Panicked voices, even if they have nothing to do with me. I
think the first few minutes of my life were just horrible; and worse
for Mum, in that she was unable to hold me. And then, when we both

did survive, there was this fierceness, an absolute sort of *I'm never going to let you go* on both sides – still expressed. And the sight of blood makes my body change; I break into a cold sweat. I shake. Not all the time, but under the weirdest circumstances: there have been PG-13 movies in which something, a gunshot wound or a certain rhythm of the shot, just shock me, make me shake; and then, of course, there are elaborate Grand Guignol things where I don't give a flying fuck – I thoroughly enjoy them.

'There's something primal there, and the only thing I can figure out is that it's because of these terrible circumstances of the very, very beginning of my life.'

Clive spent his childhood years beneath the blue suburban skies off Penny Lane until his family moved in 1966, the same year that the Beatles brought it fame.[1] But for Clive, the skies above Oakdale Road seemed more grey than blue. It was a classic British working-class neighbourhood, the short road lined with identical brick-terraced houses. At the back of number 34 was a tiny yard of concrete, an alley, and then the playing field for Dovedale Road School.

The house on Oakdale Road is a haven of fond memories. 'I have very, very strong memories of being an infant there,' Clive says. 'I have memories of waking up at four on Christmas morning, at the age of five, in my room. I remember standing by the window on Christmas Day, and the place being completely snowed in, nothing moving in any direction, when I was six or seven. And carols playing on the radio, and I remember enchantments. My memory has been very kind to me in that regard, and I access it constantly for writing the benigner elements – the latter portions of *Weaveworld*, for instance. The pursuit, when Uriel comes after Cal in the snow, and the sense of ice stopping the clocks of England. The world comes to a halt, and in the snow, in the storm, something momentous and extraordinary is taking place. All of that absolutely comes from Oakdale, snow at Oakdale.'

Many of Clive's memories of Oakdale Road are textures and vague impressions. 'I remember burning summers. I remember seeing an eclipse from the back yard when I was a kid. And I write about summers a lot, and I do write about that very hot, ominous feeling – a foreboding that comes with summer.'

'So much else of it is texture, so much else of it is not about specific things, and you know this about your own childhood, it's not about things you can fix, it's about moments that you can't really name, it's about nuances, it's about the heat of summer and hearing the television when coming home, and it's so hot you daren't breathe, and all the curtains are closed, and my mother is watching this tiny black and white television and she's watching Wimbledon. And for me, when I think of the heat of summer in that house, I think of the sound of tennis balls. That's just completely fixed in my head as an eight- or nine-year-old's image. And it doesn't really mean anything. They're useful to the writer, because you use them and you massage them and you turn them into lots of other things. They're a place where my imagination lingers, and takes a kind of comfort.'

His upbringing on Oakdale Road was 'very normal, very healthy. I don't perceive it as being out of the ordinary'. He pauses in reflection, then laughs. 'Though that may say something about me.' Indeed, his youth seemed so mundane that, in time, Clive would feel that its most significant drama was his effort to co-exist with the sheer banality of life in a town that did not interest him.

Glimpses of Barker's youth occur rarely in his fiction, but he offers a poignant reverie on those years in the novel *Weaveworld* (1987):

> He'd always been a solitary child, as much through choice as circumstance, happiest when he could unshackle his imagination, and let it wander. It took little to get such journeys started. Looking back, it seemed he'd spent half his school days gazing out the window, transported by a line of poetry whose meaning he couldn't quite unearth, or the sound of someone singing in a distant classroom, into a world more pungent and more remote than the one he knew. A world whose scents were carried to his nostrils by winds mysteriously warm in a chill December; whose creatures paid him homage on certain nights at the foot of his bed, and whose peoples he conspired with in sleep.

In writing about writers, and particularly those who indulge the tropes of the grotesque and the fantastic, there is a tendency among journalists and biographers to pursue some first cause, an event –

typically a traumatic one – to which their subject's creativity, and its particular twist to the dark side, may be traced. Often, we are told, it is a question of escape; but in considering Clive's youth, the question – What was he trying to escape from? – remains unanswered. Indeed, it seems meaningless to him, and to his parents. 'It was a very unexceptional childhood,' he says, 'but that was part of its pleasure.' Those words suggest the superficiality of the inquiry; perhaps the question is not what a writer is escaping from, but what he is evolving to.

Despite his own ruminations on the implications of his difficult birth, Clive isn't interested in conventional psychological explanations of why he or anyone else creates words or images of fantasy and horror: 'Because it seems to me that, although they may not always be spurious, they're always going to be reductionist. Motives are more complicated than one could ever express – so all you end up doing is telling part of the truth. If you say, *Well, I had a terrible experience when my dog was run over, and I started writing horror fiction because of it*, that's never going to be the whole truth. I don't like the notion of hanging motive upon certain key events, as though the mind isn't – as I perceive it to be – a fluid, infinite series of associations.

'I wonder whether there are any ground rules about the way that minds are made. I don't feel that my taste was shaped by anything in particular that happened in my childhood. I remember strange things from my childhood, but there were no traumas. I was always an imaginative child, and my imagination had a considerable range – from very fanciful, light material to rather darker stuff. I know I had a reputation for being a dreamer; I had imaginary friends, and I liked monsters and drew monsters and so on. But I think lots of kids like monsters.'

Young Clive was Joan's pride and joy, and a very precocious – and definitely imaginative – child. 'Clive spoke perfectly at two,' Joan says, and his skill with words may be traced to her running conversations with him – and the stories she told and read to him. She and Len always spoke to Clive in adult voices, using adult words. His grandparents were also great conversationalists. Len's mother, who lived nearby, would sit and talk with him for hours, and she enjoyed telling him stories, some real, others invented, about her own childhood.

Joan was also a wonderful storyteller, and her stories opened his first window into the realm of the fantastic. She always had a bedtime story for Clive, but not necessarily from a book; many of the stories she would extemporize. Clive loved her readings from JM Barrie's *Peter Pan in Kensington Gardens* (1902) and *Peter and Wendy* (better known as *Peter Pan*) (1911); and Kenneth Grahame's *The Wind in the Willows* (1908). Joan adored the stories of Beatrix Potter; she knew them by heart, and could tell them without the books, often adding her own embellishments. Clive was a demanding listener; he would ask her to tell specific stories that she had told before, but Joan, having forgotten them, would reinvent them to his delight. One of his favourite stories, which she created in the style of Kenneth Grahame – and, at Clive's urging, retold in endless variations – was about a riverbank and all the animals who lived there. ('You could put a lot of animals into a riverbank,' Joan says.)[2]

Len, an avid craftsman, built a large playpen in the morning room, where Clive spent hours under Joan's watchful eye, happily talking with her or to himself. Soon his audience increased, when the Barkers adopted a small mixed-breed dog named Kemis, after Caemaes, the village in Wales where he was born (most people, including Len's father, mistakenly called him 'Chemist').

Clive was not yet three when Joan noticed, with increasing frequency, that he would talk about his 'friends'. His reports were so vivid and continual that, when relatives and neighbours visited, they would inevitably say: 'Tell us about your friends, Clive . . . What are your friends doing today, Clive?' And Clive, encouraged by their interest, would oblige, telling them about these imaginary friends and their adventures – 'simple things,' Joan recalls, 'like they'd been out shopping, or walking the dog, but it would go on and on.' His stories seemed remarkably complete, told with a beginning, middle and end.

On February 24, 1956, when Clive was nearly three-and-a-half, his younger brother, Roy, was born. Clive was delighted. 'He was absolutely wonderful in every way,' Joan says. 'He helped, he fetched and carried. Watched over him.' In Roy, Clive now had a regular and receptive audience in the morning room. He would talk with Roy, and dress Kemis in different clothes, and tell them both stories.

'As parents we always talked to them,' Joan says. 'We had long conversations. I would talk with Roy even though I couldn't understand a word he was saying. Funnily enough, Clive could.' As Len remembers it, 'Roy talked scribble. It was rubbish, hilarious rubbish; he was so pleased with himself. It was all about laughter, really. You couldn't help but join in his humour. Clive could be humorous also; but his diction, as a small child, was very, very good. I got the sense that at times, he didn't use a word unless he could say it properly.'

Although Clive adored Joan's riverbank tales, his first and true love among the books she read to him was *Peter Pan*. ('It's the book I want to be buried with,' he once told me.) He was so enamoured of *Peter Pan* that, at the age of six or seven, he imagined himself as one of the lost boys – and longed to fly away from Liverpool and into Never-Never Land.[3]

His introduction to *Peter Pan* as a story – in the form of text, and not a television or stage production – simply underscored its power. 'I don't have Sandy Duncan flying through my memories, and I'm grateful. What is essential about Peter Pan is his masculinity, because he is such a troubled little boy. The things which troubled Peter Pan are not things which would trouble a little girl . . . the things which trouble Peter Pan are *boy* things. He doesn't have a mother. He has this curious mingling of anger and sentimentality. He is deeply aggressive, and a leader of little lost boys. So the image of this boy being played by not only a girl, but a fully-grown girl, is doubly preposterous!'[4]

The boyish power of Peter Pan was irresistible to him, and became a mirror of his imagined self. 'The boy sexuality of Peter Pan is a very important part of who he is. The crowing, literally cock-crowing, aggressiveness is so much a part of who he is. So my Peter Pan is modelled after *me*; because I think every little boy who reads *Peter Pan* at the right age says: *It's me. That's absolutely me.* And a part of the power of the book is that, as a little boy you look at Peter and say, *Yes, I could be part of the lost boys, and I could completely save Tiger Lily in the nick of time, and Captain Hook would live in fear of me.* You know, at the right time, that's how you identify. And there wasn't anybody else in children's literature I identified with.'

Although he was entertained by other classic children's books, none seemed to connect with him. 'The closest would be Toad from *Wind in the Willows*, because he's such a sort of pompous little ass, full of enthusiasms . . . but *nothing* could compare with Peter. Because he was just everything I wanted to be. He could fly. He didn't belong to anybody. He was his own boy. And as a child I think you want that so much. All children want to be their own person, right? It's what you want as a child – to be your own thing, your own object, your own creature.

'I wanted to fly. I wanted to open the nursery windows and be gone. And the price Peter pays for that freedom didn't seem to me to be too bad a price at the age of eight. But I would always cry at the end of the book. I was acutely aware of how sad the book was. And I never quite worked that out.

'You buy into voices. I bought into JM Barrie's. I bought into his snobbishness. I bought into his pathos. I bought into his nostalgia. I bought into his sense of loss. I think it's a very sad book, and its sadness found me, even as a child; and that's what moved me, and that's what made me devoted to it, was its sadness. So it's as far from Sandy Duncan as you can get.'[5]

Clive also learned, however, the danger of his dreams of flight. In May 1956, the family, with four-year-old Clive and newborn Roy in tow, went to an air show at Speke Airport on the outskirts of Liverpool. Because they could not afford admission, Len parked the car at the edge of a nearby cornfield and the family, along with Clive's aunt and uncle and their young son, watched the airplanes fly past. The star of the event was Leo Valentin, a stunt parachutist who was making his final performance that day. Known as the 'Bird Man', Valentin would leap from an aeroplane, gliding on balsa wings until, at a certain altitude, he opened his parachute and descended safely to earth. Young Clive was tired and unimpressed; as he wrote, years later, in *The Essential Clive Barker* (1999): 'the spectacle, such as it was, seemed so remote, so undramatic. It required an adult's comprehension of the risk this man was taking to make the diminishing shape of the plane and Valentin's tumbling form seem significant.'

But something had gone wrong; the Bird Man's wings were broken, and he fell from the sky. 'Don't look,' Joan warned Clive, over and over again. 'Don't look. Don't look. Don't look.' He defied her words, but saw only his father and uncle, looking on helplessly at Valentin's impending, inescapable death. 'What I picture in my mind's eye,' Clive says, 'are two stoic witnesses to this terrible scene. This was maleness, this witnessing; or so in that moment I came to believe. And if my early work is marked by a certain hunger to see what should not be seen, to show what should not be shown, the beginning of that appetite may be here, at the edge of the cornfield with the men watching the sky, and me, struggling in my mother's arms because I was forbidden the sight.'[6]

Raising two boys became a full-time occupation for Joan, and the Barkers took in fewer house-guests. Len worked a gruelling five-and-a-half day week at the Harrison Line, labouring until seven p.m. on every evening except Sunday; he didn't arrive home until eight, and often he would simply collapse into sleep. He deeply regrets his absence from his sons during those early years. 'Like my own father – I don't think I ever thought of having one. Here was a man who appeared smelling of mothballs with his sea bag, who disappeared for months.' Forty years later, he expressed the misgivings familiar to all conscientious fathers, wishing that he could have spent more time with his children – and wrestling with a misdirected guilt, the unfortunate feeling that, if he had spent more time with Clive, he might have affected his son's sexual preferences. 'It's one of those odd things about life, really, that God gives you children when you're young. Really you should have them when you're old, because then you could spend more time with them.'

In time Len's persistent work ethic – which his sons would inherit – paid off. In 1957 he left the Harrison Line and the docks, taking a position as a personnel officer with British Insulated Callender's Cables Ltd ('BICC'), a leading international cable manufacturer and shipper. He then devoted himself to studying accounting and management, and qualified as a chartered secretary; in the 1960s he would become personnel manager for a sizeable element of the company – a position that he would hold until his retirement.

Len's long hours were a sign of the times: Liverpool was struggling in the aftermath of the war, with some rationing still in effect and unemployment rising. For his children, the grey landscape seemed the preview of an uncertain apocalypse; as he headed to work, toward the River Mersey, almost every street was scarred by bomb sites, and damaged and levelled houses. 'We were on the crest of a wave: the post-war boom. *Britain can make it* was the great phrase ... but it went on for quite a while. We were living off the back of a lot of work, but a lot of it was very basic, very coarse, because we had lost the niceties we had before the war, but we hadn't yet run into the post-war boom. We were still suffering from the housing shortage. There wasn't much choice in things like clothing. It wasn't easy.'

There was also little time for formal religion. Joan and Len were members of the Church of England, but rarely attended. They took Clive to services at a local church, but soon drifted away, leaving Clive to remark, in later years: 'I went to church once, when I was baptized, but the font water boiled. They took me out and decided never to take me in again. I go to church for other people's weddings, baptisms, and the occasional funeral, but that's really it.' Indeed, until his forties, when he experienced a profound spiritual awakening, he would express a belief only 'in system'.

While Len worked for most of his waking hours, Clive and Roy found occasional male guidance – and exposure to a remarkable diversity of races and cultures – in the boarders at the house, from Automobile Association and bank trainees to an increasing number of foreign employees of BICC and other local companies: Africans from the Gold Coast who dressed in tribal robes; Turks and Indians and so many others who shared their life stories with the boys when they joined them each evening at the meal table.

Another man who played an important role in Clive's early years was Captain William Weatherall. Uncle Billy and Aunty Marie were Clive's godparents; and Billy, a profoundly authoritarian ship's captain, mesmerized Clive with his stories of voyages to places far from Liverpool. 'When I was a kid, he was romance personified. In *Weaveworld*, Cal goes down to the Mersey and talks about how he was taken there and shown ships and that they were going to the great faraway. And Uncle Billy would do that. He would say, *That ship's going to Madagascar; and that ship's going to Jamaica.* And I adored him.'

The house on Oakdale Road had four bedrooms. Clive's bedroom was at the top of the stairs, and, like Roy's room, faced out onto the back and side of the house. It was long and narrow, and could barely fit his bed; as a result, when the Barkers had two lodgers, Clive would share Roy's room – and replace Joan as the bedtime storyteller; but, as Roy remembers, they weren't like any stories Roy had ever heard – they always left him wondering: 'What's going to happen next?'

Although Clive's storytelling continued at a rapid pace, he also found new ways to express himself – by drawing, constantly drawing. Indeed, Joan doesn't remember him ever *not* drawing: 'He always picked up a pencil and drew, sketched, even when he was in a high chair.' His artwork was part of a family tradition: Len was a 'great doodler' and would create caricatures, cartoony sketches of sailors and passers-by; Joan, like her own father, also loved to draw.

Clive's relentless desire to create then found another outlet, when he discovered that he could give his fantastic ideas three-dimensional form. One day he asked Joan for a piece of string. As she watched in awe, he took a discarded cigarette package – a hard box with a folding top – and created a puppet by drawing a face on the box, then tying the string so that the boxtop became a mouth that opened and closed. Soon he began making models out of papier-mâché and wire, and puppets out of discarded socks and clothing.

From the earliest age, Clive disliked conventional toys; he wanted only things that could be created. Len, who loved model railways, believed that there was a singular advantage to having two sons: 'I was going to get the most magnificent model railway.' He assembled the railway on the landing at the top of the stairs; and although Roy loved it, it wasn't for Clive. 'That was something ready-made, and probably functional, rather than imaginary. He wanted the Never-Never Land side of it.'

In September 1957, a month before his fifth birthday, Clive was enrolled in the infant department (5 to 7 years) of Dovedale Road School, where he also attended junior school (7 to 10 years). His fellow alumni include John Lennon and George Harrison, who attended almost a decade before.

Clive enjoyed those early years of school: 'I have really very good memories of Dovedale. And I dream about it constantly. I dream about school days constantly.' He hated the organized sports, but excelled in geography; although he found mathematics and the sciences less than interesting, he did well on all of his tests. His real success, however, came in the school plays and musical shows, which were usually presented as preludes to the Christmas and summer holidays.

Clive always performed in these events, practising hard, acting his heart out; and in one memorable show, he led the students in a march out of the auditorium as they sang: 'We're all going on a summer holiday.' His performances were so legendary that, when Roy attended rehearsals in later years, he found himself introduced as 'Clive's brother'. In Roy's words: 'Clive had made his mark even then.'

At home as well as school, Roy's early years seemed spent in his brother's shadow. 'Clive was verbally rather dominant,' Len says, and soon he offered words that 'even his mother wasn't terribly sure about'. Roy had his own creative qualities; he was a natural engineer and, like his father, capable with his hands. Len loved to tinker with his motorbike, and it was Roy who worked with him; but 'if you asked Clive for a spanner, he sort of picked it up like it was alien'. Clive could build, too, but he created less practical, more fanciful things; and he would draw, which seemed his solace: 'He drew on everything, including the walls.'

The boys often played together in the back yard and the alley behind the house – and in the street, since there were few cars. The community was close and protective; Clive knew the names of most of the people who lived on Oakdale Road, and never felt any fear in the neighbourhood – although, he notes, 'there were bullies'.

In Clive's third year at Dovedale, he staggered home one day with cuts and bruises. Another schoolboy had beaten him, and the attacks resumed when Clive walked to school the next day. When Joan looked out from the terraced house, over the back passage to Dovedale, she could see the boy pushing Clive. That night, at Joan's urging, Len told Clive: 'Look, if David goes for you again, just hit him.' But Clive said: 'Mum, you told me not to hit people.' Joan replied: 'This time, you've got my permission.' The following day, she watched as Clive walked to school; David went for him, and Clive hit him. 'And you know, that child never touched Clive again.'

But Clive didn't like the encounter: the physicality of it bothered him, and he was also squeamish. A few years earlier, he and Roy had been forbidden by their parents from entering the school's football field; but, tempted by taboo, they decided to sneak in. When Clive began to climb the fence, he cut his hand on a spike, and the sight of his blood seemed to hurt him more than the wound.

Even at an early age, Roy felt that Clive was somehow 'different'. He didn't have many pals in to play at the house, and seemed much more comfortable by himself. He spent hours alone, reading or drawing or simply thinking. At times, he wondered whether Never-Never Land might truly exist – perhaps just outside his little bedroom. 'I have a very clear memory of seeing a UFO over the house opposite, of seeing a bright light hovering over there,' Clive says of a day when he was eight or nine years old, 'which came back to me like a strange flash about ten years ago, and has stayed with me, very clearly, in my head. I think I was prone, in my imaginative way, to seeing shit constantly.'

Clive and Roy enjoyed playing marbles in the school playground and collecting bubblegum trading cards; but Roy liked the bubblegum, and the idea of assembling a set or sequence of cards, while Clive was interested in the imagery, the artwork of the cards, and interpreting and making sense of what they meant. He was fascinated by the infamous Topps 'Civil War News' trading cards, with their gory and glorified depictions of combat and death in the American Civil War.[7]

Clive also became an avid reader and collector of comic books, using most of his pocket money to buy them, mostly secondhand, from Bascombe's, a shop on Smithdown Road. 'I still dream about that place,' he says. It was a tiny store, with toffees and sweets in jars, as well as racks of magazines. On the floor, in a cardboard box, he found random, frayed issues of Marvel and DC Comics, whose bright colours and superheroic themes were far different from the black-and-white, more juvenile comic books then published in England.

Batman was the first American comic he purchased. Although he enjoyed *Superman* and other DC Comics, 'they never caught my imagination the way the Marvel Comics did'. He preferred Marvel's *Spiderman* and *The Incredible Hulk*, and anything illustrated by Jack Kirby (who, Clive notes, was 'one of the idols of my childhood'); and he went through countless cycles of collecting issues, then selling them, then regretting the decision and collecting them again.

Legend has it that American comic books were brought into Liverpool as ballast on transport vessels. 'There seemed no real order to the way they were distributed; you could not hope to get a series.

There's a run of Jack Kirby *Fantastic Fours*, which were, by general consensus, the greatest amongst the great comics of that period. And to see the covers advertised in other comics, but not be able to find them – it really was my childhood equivalent of the Holy Grail, finding this stuff. It would make my day if Bascombe's had one ... there'd be gravy stains on them, they'd been through so many hands, but I didn't give a shit.'

Inspired by their mingling of text and illustrations, Clive began to create his own cartoon strips and comic books, much like Marvel Comics in layout, and drawn in impressive detail entirely for himself and for Roy.

There was another room at Bascombe's, however, which featured, among other things, men's action magazines – 'they tended to have pictures of semi-clad girls being tortured by Nazis on the cover'– and the nudist magazine *Health & Efficiency*. 'I was always waiting for the little old lady who was there on Sunday to look the other way, so I could pop round the corner and take a look at this stuff. And she was always very forbidding when she found you there; certainly she added the sense of the forbidden to it. I was afraid that she would ban me from the place, because as interested as I was in *Health & Efficiency* and all this stuff, I would never have sacrificed my sole access to these comics, which were so important to me.'

Horror and fantasy became Clive's constant companions after his first exposure to Edgar Allan Poe: 'A two shillings and sixpence edition of *Tales of Mystery and Imagination*, which had a house and a lurid red sky and a skull glowering over it. "The Masque of the Red Death" was always my favourite. I had three horror books, and I'd read them over and over again. I came across a couple of EC Comics, but my parents didn't really approve too much of that. And then the movies. I think the posters affected me long before I actually saw any of the movies, and it came as a great disappointment that often the films were nowhere near as good as I had imagined from the posters. I remember the poster for *Frankenstein Created Woman* being Hot Stuff – capital H, capital S – and thinking, *This has got to be some kind of movie*! One of my school friends and I would have long debates on the implications of these posters.' ('Why do boys always love talking about ghosts and murders and hangings?' he wrote, years later, in his childhood fable *The Thief of Always* (1992); and then answered: 'Because it's exciting.')[8]

Clive's early reading in the realm of horror fiction was, for the most part, traditional and devoted to the classics: Mary Wollstonecraft Shelley's *Frankenstein; or the Modern Prometheus* (1818), Robert Louis Stevenson's *The Strange Case of Dr Jekyll and Mr Hyde* (1886) and Bram Stoker's *Dracula* (1897), as well as the fiction of Arthur Machen, MR James and Dennis Wheatley. But Poe remained his greatest childhood influence, as he found dread and delight in 'The Fall of the House of Usher', 'The Cask of Amontillado' and 'The Murders in the Rue Morgue'.

He was less interested in the stories of HP Lovecraft; the 'turgid, ornamental quality' of Lovecraft's prose seemed 'pretension getting in the way of good storytelling'. Yet Lovecraft's imagery sometimes affected him deeply, as reflected in the creatures of 'The Skins of the Fathers' (1984) and 'The Last Illusion' (1985) and his original screenplay *American Horror* (2000). The short fiction of Ray Bradbury appealed to him in adolescence – 'his work has the courage of poetry' – but as Clive grew older, Bradbury's nostalgic romanticism seemed overly sweet and sanguine.

Clive's earliest exposure to an anthology collecting stories by different writers was the *Pan Book of Horror Stories*, an annual mainstay of British publishing edited by Herbert van Thal. 'I shamelessly stole and embroidered the tales for retelling around scout camp-fires and on school treks. It was one of the few things I was actually good at as a kid; and I don't doubt that those retellings were the first experiences I had of the power the teller of horror stories feels as he holds his audience in a grip from which they might wish to wriggle but can't . . .'[9]

His parents were concerned about his reading habits, and his preoccupation with the grotesque and the fantastic, which carried over to his television viewing. Clive had first seen television in the mid-1950s, when his godparents, Billy and Marie Weatherall, invited Joan to bring the boys to their house to watch their new television set. Clive loved the children's show 'Andy Pandy', but he would burst into tears when it was finished. It seemed so traumatic to Joan that, after a time, she couldn't bear to take him back to watch.

In 1960, when Clive was eight, the Barkers bought their first television, a small black-and-white model. He watched 'Dr Who' religiously: 'I was a great Dalek fan. There were ten years in there when I never missed an episode.' Although he enjoyed 'The Avengers' and 'Adam Adamant', and recalls the BBC television production of *Quatermass and the Pit* and Peter Cushing in *1984*, 'I never liked television very much. There were these few things, but it was more out of a desperation.' His TV viewing became a source of family tension because Clive preferred programmes that his parents found gruesome and unappealing – particularly horror films. They reacted 'with difficulty,' Len says. 'I found it difficult to get on his wavelength. With hindsight – and there's no greater exact science, is there, than hindsight – I suppose I could have done better. I could have tried to involve myself with his thoughts, with his ideals; and it didn't happen.'

The power of his imagination gave Clive authority and self-assurance that was otherwise lacking in his life: he could tell stories to people, and they would listen. Then he experienced the excitement of performing – of enticing an audience and, on occasion, receiving a material reward. When Clive was nearing ten, he and Roy won a prize – a packet of sweets, as best as anyone can recall – by singing one of Cilla Black's hit songs on stage at Happy Valley, a concert park in Wales ('Roy, I must be fair, was the better of the two,' says Joan).[10]

The boys also collaborated on a performance for a children's Christmas party organized by local police; Clive created glove puppets, moulding their heads and attaching them to bodies sewn by their mother. Roy worked two puppets in silence, while Clive, working a third puppet, stood and spoke the story to the children.

Indeed, Clive's first real taste of working 'behind the footlights' was as a puppeteer. At the age of eleven, he had seen 'Punch and Judy' puppet shows at a local pier, and his enthusiasm was so intense that Len, ever the handyman, constructed a wooden stage and helped him paint several backdrops. 'One I remember with special clarity: a quay-side, with tall ships at anchor, sails unfurled or unfurling in preparation for a voyage.'[11] As Len recalls: 'It wasn't the greatest thing I've ever made ... If only I'd understood more about it. I think I didn't help, truly, over some of Clive's creating things, because I couldn't quite get onto his wavelength. Whilst Joan and I love the theatre, it's from the sitting in the stalls side of it, rather than what makes it tick behind.' But Len was very good at woodwork, and built an impressive theatre with an electric light inside. Joan sewed curtains, and the stage was set.

With his parents' help, Clive had constructed a cast of hand, rod and marionette puppets with papier-mâché heads; Joan dressed them, and Len stringed the marionettes. 'My cast was fairly generic, if memory serves. A sword-wielding hero, a princess, a skeleton, a devil, a hag-witch, a dragon. But they were all I needed to create exotic tales of midnight crimes and magic rituals, of horrendous jeopardies and last-minute escapes.'[12] Clive wrote elaborate scenarios for them to enact, with cruelty and humour typical of Punch and Judy shows.

The theatre was set up facing the back of the house, and the neighbourhood children gathered in the alleyway to watch – and to feast on the buns and lemonade that Joan offered them. Although Roy was dragooned into helping with the puppetry, Clive was the showman, operating puppets and voicing all the parts. The show was well-received – perhaps too well, as Len recalls:

'I remember saying to him, *Well, you're going to have this fine performance.* And Clive said, *Oh, not just this performance, there will be one at two o'clock, and it will be repeated at five, and then we've got the weekend coming* . . . and I wondered: *What have we started here?*'

3

IN A LONELY PLACE

'Then I shan't be exactly a human?' Peter asked.
'No.'
'Nor exactly a bird?'
'No.'
'What shall I be?'
'You will be a Betwixt-and-Between,' Solomon said, and certainly
he was a wise old fellow, for that is exactly how it turned out.
— JM BARRIE, *Peter Pan in Kensington Gardens*

'There are things that happen in your childhood which just give you a new sense of who you can be.' Clive Barker offers those words to me while gazing out of the window of his home in Beverly Hills to a place seen only in his memory: Tiree, a sere and seemingly deserted island in the Hebrides, off the northwest coast of Scotland. Although Carl Jung had dreamed of a journey to Liverpool in order to find a sense of self, Clive needed to escape that city for self-revelation and validation, which he found in the loneliest of places – remote, isolated, and by the sea. The experience would prove central to his occasionally autobiographical novel *Weaveworld* (1987), in which a Liverpool that seems 'grey from gutter to chimney stack' fades with one glimpse of a world beyond:

He'd lived here all his life; this had been his world. The television and the glossy magazines had shown him different vistas on occasion, but somehow he'd never believed in them. They were as remote from his experience, or indeed from what he would hope to know in his allotted seventy years, as the stars that were winking out above his head.

But the Fugue had been different. It had seemed, for a short, sweet time, a place he might truly belong.

Like one of the lost boys, Clive sought a magical island – that 'place he might truly belong' – and his parents, without realizing it, provided him with Never-Never Land in three distant, delightful locations, each discovered on holidays.[1]

The first of these trips took him to North Wales, and a small village in the Lleyn Peninsula – then, only three houses – named Tudweiliog. The location, far from an exotic one, was dictated by its proximity to Liverpool: it was the summer of 1956, just five months after Joan had given birth to Roy, and the family had little money to spend on travel; indeed, they could not afford a car, and relied on Len's motorbike for transportation.

Len booked the holiday at the recommendation of a friend. The family rode to Tudweiliog on Len's motorbike, which he had painted green to subdue its original red, and then outfitted with a sidecar that he built from scratch. The sidecar's front seat held Joan; in the back was a smaller seat for Clive and a special space where Roy lay in his carry-cot, wedged in with tins of food.

The motorbike took them through a maze of country lanes, and Len would sometimes drive off the road in search of isolated beaches. Once, on a particularly difficult track, a beautiful Jaguar followed them, but they reached a point where the car couldn't manoeuvre farther. As the Barkers drove on, the driver and his Jaguar had to back out. (Forty years later, Len remembers the moment as if it were yesterday. The driver said: 'You're fortunate.' Len offers me the loveliest smile and says: 'And we were.')

When the motorbike brought them to the ocean, the family walked down rocky paths to the tiny beaches, and Joan and Clive would venture together into the water. There was no one else – just the family in a splendid togetherness. Clive, ever the explorer, wandered around the rock pools; 'and if he couldn't see anything,' Len says, 'he'd make it up.'

Tudweiliog was defined by its isolation and calm. The Barkers stayed at an ancient farmhouse, its walls two feet thick and painted white, with deep windowsills. There were few conveniences – water was fetched from a nearby well – but there was a duck pond, an orchard (which would become a key locale in *Weaveworld*) and, as always, the sight of the sea.[2] Len and Joan loved the silence and simplicity – and they couldn't have afforded anything more.

At night, Clive and Roy slept together in what seemed like an enormous bed. To give them light, Joan placed little candles in saucers of water around the bed. 'The smell of an extinguished candle, and I'm there,' Clive says. 'It's like a time machine. I'm a seven-year-old, I'm lying in bed with Roy, I am *so* excited because we're on holiday, and the sea is just half a mile away.'

In those early years of Clive's life, the family returned again and again to Tudweiliog. When Len bought a car, their vacations into Wales became more adventurous, with visits to Tintern, site of the famous abbey, where the family stayed at the Royal Oak pub; and then farther south to Cornwall and Tintagel, the supposed home of King Arthur's Round Table.

As the boys grew older and Len's career advanced, the family travelled to more distant and fascinating places. The first of them was Guernsey in the Channel Islands, where Clive's godparents – Len and Joan's former landlords Billy and Marie Weatherall – now lived full-time. Clive's eyes were widened yet again by a strange new environment and its imaginative stimuli.

Marie was the daughter of minor nobility. When the Germans invaded the Channel Islands during the Second World War, her family home was appropriated as quarters for the commanding officers – who proceeded to stab the eyes out of the portraits and paintings with gramophone needles. When Clive first visited Guernsey, at the age of ten or eleven, the German barbed wire was still in place and parts of the house were in ruins. Aunty Marie showed them photos of the house that had been taken during the war, which showed bunting emblazoned with swastikas hanging from its windows. She also had a

German soldier's helmet, which she used to hold her gardening shovels and trowels; she would carry the helmet in one hand as she walked around the garden with a fork spade, digging to find other relics of the war. 'I wanted to wear this helmet,' Clive remembers. 'I passionately wanted to wear this helmet.' Indeed, a photograph shows the young, bespectacled Clive wearing the helmet and 'looking very, very scary because I'm a *bad* Nazi.'

Another attraction was the abandoned German defences: huge concrete fortifications and gun emplacements that had been installed in anticipation of an Allied invasion. (The island was instead blockaded into submission after D-Day.) Clive was fascinated by the ruins – vast concrete bunkers and, behind them, quarters and toilets built into the cliff. There was even an underground hospital, with a mortuary and operating rooms. Now they were empty, except for graffiti on the walls and a smell of mildew – 'a place where soldiers had stood and watched out the war, waiting for an invasion which came, but missed them, really. It was eerie but wonderful. Just the sense of presences. Things having come and gone. My imagination would go berserk.'

But for Clive, the most moving and inspiring of the family's vacation sites was Tiree. The remote island was the new home of Elsie MacKinnon née McIntyre, the cook whom Joan had befriended after taking her first job at Belvedere School. During the war, Elsie had married a soldier in the Royal Air Force, but he went missing in action six months later and was never found. As late as the mid-1950s, she held séances in an effort to contact him; when Joan mentioned the experiments in spiritualism to young Clive, he was disturbed and afraid. Finally Elsie met and fell in love with a 'Gaelic-speaking, hawknosed, gentle, ruddy crofter' named Hugh MacKinnon, married him, and moved to Tiree. (Clive and Roy were children-in-waiting at the wedding.)

Beginning in the early 1960s, the Barkers visited the MacKinnons regularly on family holidays, making the long drive by car north to Oban in Scotland, where a ferry would carry them through a chilly sound ('there's nothing more glorious than Scotland on a good day,' Clive notes, 'and nothing more grim on a bad one'); and, after two stops in the Hebrides, on to Tiree.

The island is a low-lying vista of white sand and sea; there is not a single tree. The population numbers in the very low thousands, and the house nearest to the MacKinnon's was a mile distant. Tiree offered vast, and usually chill, emptiness – and an overwhelming silence. 'You went out in the evening,' Joan says, 'and you could listen to the silence. You'd hear a bird cry, or a sheep, but that's all.'

For Clive, Tiree was an essential and life-changing experience. 'It was, for Roy and me, just amazing, because there was absolutely nobody. And it was a place of great romance, in a very Gaelic way. Very spartan, very spare, and tiny white houses and a lot of corn and a lot of *macchair* and sheep and oyster-catchers and terns and silence. No street lights. The Aurora Borealis at night. Shooting stars. Everything a little kid could want to move their heart. Just amazing. And amazing in an incredibly simple way – as far from Disneyland as it's possible to get. And one of the greatest gifts my mother and father ever gave to me was taking me there. Because it opened up this floodgate in my imagination of another way to life. It put me close to nature; it put me close to the sea.'[3]

Tiree was the first place where Clive could exist entirely on his own for long periods of time. 'There was no danger there, so I would leave in the morning and come back at night. Nothing could happen to you, you know?' He spent hours walking the island. Once he came upon a hole filled with the skulls of animals, bleached white; he brought several of them home, where he kept them in his room and lined them up on the staircase.

The island was also the first place where he truly interacted with animals, whether alive or dead, other than the family dog. There were cows and sheep, sheep dogs and nine cats. 'I loved being with Elsie when she was milking the cows. I loved going out at night and bringing the herd back in. It's a nine-year-old kid's dream. In a place where, once the lights go out, there are no lights.'

Tiree was an experience filled with stories, told and read. Clive slept alone, in a little bed downstairs; everyone else slept upstairs. There was no television, but there were books – some brought by Clive and others found at the house – and Hugh MacKinnon was a magnificent storyteller. At night, he would spin fanciful tales about the 'wee people', and at first Clive believed him; he would lie awake all night afterward – and read. 'The almost monastic simplicity of the life up there, and having lots of books, and just being there with books and the sky and the cows was just wonderful; and remains wonderful.'

On one visit, Clive discovered, in a sweetshop in Oban, a collection of Fritz Leiber's 'Fafhrd and the Grey Mouser' stories – 'it was a perfect companion on that island' – and it was on Tiree that Clive first read two novels that profoundly influenced his later fiction: ER Eddison's masterful epic *The Worm Ouroboros* (1926) and CS Lewis's metaphysical fantasy *Out of the Silent Planet* (1938). 'I sat on a beach with nothing in any direction but me and some cows and a lot of kelp, and some whales breaching out there, and read *The Worm Ouroboros*. Fucking perfect. I mean, just perfect.'

Although his early fiction, including the story 'Scape-Goats' (1984), would evoke its sere landscapes, Tiree haunts Clive's later novels. It is a constant of the novels of 'The Art' (its beaches are those that border the fantastic sea known as Quiddity); and it is the setting for the finale of *Sacrament* (1995). While writing the latter book, Clive offered me a lengthy reverie on the wonderland of Tiree:

'The first of any thing that you encounter in your life is always going to carry undue power. So that the first rollercoaster ride may not be the biggest rollercoaster ride you go on, but it's going to have considerable authority because it's the first one. And the first time I was all alone and wandered on a beach and spent an entire day not speaking to anybody and just spent my time with nature was in Tiree. And those are important moments for me, being alone with natural phenomena – the cold clichés, the sea and the sky.

'There was such poetry there. I was so moved by it. The first time I ever got an echo of what's going on was when I read the *Prelude*, when Wordsworth speaks about rowing across a lake and seeing a mountain. It's romantic pantheism at its best, and you don't have to know what it is to be moved by it, but landscape has always moved me profoundly. I have a stronger response to landscape, and particularly empty landscape – without even a sign of human presence – than I do, probably, to human beings. There is what Yeats calls the 'Egotistical Sublime' in Wordsworth: the idea that you find something of yourself echoed in the landscape; that the landscape offers up a vast dramatization of your inner self, your inner states. I know of no more amazing sight in all my life than thunderheads gathering over Tiree.

Just because it's so untouched. It's a yearning, which you see in fantastic writing, for the apocalypse – an apocalyptic desire, a desire to see the board, as it were, wiped clean. This urge to see the world cleansed of human detritus in order to allow the broad, sublime strokes of creation to make themselves manifest – that is to say, vast cloud formations.

'I'm not misanthropic at all, but I'm not very interested in the self-perpetuating manifestations of human obsession. Politics, for instance, with its endless round of manipulations and feints and counter-feints, bores the fuck out of me. Now it doesn't bore me in terms of its social application, in terms of how much it may apply to the justice system, or the way that we care for the mentally ill or the old; but more often than not, that's not what politics is about. More often than not, it's about posturing and positioning and so on. So politics with a small "p" has the same sickening effect on my belly as looking down a highway that is dominated by strip malls. If you show me a picture of a highway dominated by strip malls and you put that beside a picture of Tiree, and you say: *Where do you want to be*? I am going to shake my head in despair at the person who chooses the highway. I'm just not going to have anything to say to that person. And I know there are a lot of people like that, who are comforted by those signs for McDonald's and Blockbuster, and I just don't know where to begin with them; I just don't get it.'

After that first adventure on Tiree, however, he didn't know where to begin with anyone – his parents, his brother, his few friends. The wonders that he had found and that he had imagined in these distant places posed a terrible, and terrifying, dilemma – which he would express years later in *Weaveworld*: 'The question was: to tell or not to tell. To speak what he'd seen, and endure the laughter and the sly looks, or to keep it hidden. Part of him badly wanted to talk, to spill everything to somebody . . . and see what he made of it. But another part said: be quiet, be careful. Wonderland doesn't come to those who blab about it, only to those who keep their silence, and *wait*.'

He had found a physical reality that seemed somehow to mirror the emotional reality that, until Tiree, he had experienced only in his imagination. At the age of eleven, on the verge of adolescence, Clive felt a growing distance from the material world – and from his parents and brother. On these vacations, and indeed in life, Roy always stayed close to Len and Joan; but Clive would wander away, constantly looking, constantly exploring, constantly seeking. 'Our concern,' Len says, 'was losing sight of him.'

This finally happened, one day when Clive was fourteen or fifteen. The family took an Easter holiday in North Devon – as always, by the sea. It was sunny but cold as Len and Joan and Roy strolled along a beach at Ilfracombe, with Clive walking far ahead of them. Suddenly an enormous sea fret surged landward and over the beach. Clive disappeared, lost to view in the fog.

'He just walked into the mist,' Joan says, then adds, without irony: 'Like a film.'[4]

If any place could compete with the ethereal landscapes of these holiday wonderlands, it was the cool and dark interior of the cinema. There Clive experienced another reality, one in which his eyes might somehow witness the feverish creatures of his imagination. 'Certainly my two earliest memories of cinema are Ray Harryhausen and Disney. And they did what the cinema does so well: make stuff concrete that cannot be made concrete in any other form; it makes this stuff real.'

Another early, and lingering, film influence was Jean Cocteau, whom Clive discovered in the autumn of 1960, while seriously ill with the flu. He was watching the family's small black-and-white television set, and was transfixed by an interview with Cocteau and imagery from his final film, *Le Testament d'Orphée* ('The Testament of Orpheus') (1960). Clive soon pursued Cocteau in his many incarnations: painter, designer, illustrator, author, poet and film-maker. He saw Cocteau's cinematic masterworks, *La Belle et la Bête* ('Beauty and the Beast') (1946) and *Orphée* ('Orpheus') (1949), and 'by degrees, began to interpret his very particular code … it had in some measure to do with being homosexual, in some measure to do with his faith in mythic models, and a great deal to do with his fearless belief that he was a king in his own country, and could legislate freely there.'

'The lesson seems clear enough: make what your heart instructs, and don't let anyone persuade you to compromise with your own truth.'[5]

When Clive discovered horror films – principally through pro-motional posters – he was enthralled by the prospect of what visions might be seen inside the cinemas, and he found himself restlessly anticipating each new film of horror or the fantastic. The enthusiasm grew from his insistent love of monsters: 'It comes from seeing those Ray Harryhausen movies as a kid. I suspect that if you trace back the enthusiasm of an awful lot of people working in the cinema, you'll find Ray Harryhausen in their past somewhere.' There were no childhood nightmares, no frights, prompted by stories or films; instead he felt a growing identification with the monsters, an attraction to their glorious differences, and a sense that their state was somehow safe, and powerful – that the side of the monsters was a mighty one.

Often his hopes were soundly dashed when he saw a film whose posters or trailers had seemed enticing; but his imagination was more than fulfilled in his first experience with an adult horror film – Alfred Hitchcock's classic *Psycho* (1960): 'There is a small movie house at the back of my head where it's been running ever since.'

A local cinema – now a church called the Shrine of the Blessed Sacrament – featured a double bill of *Psycho* and George Pal's *The War of the Worlds*. The British Board of Film Classification (then known, more honestly, as the British Board of Film Censorship) had given both films X certificates, restricting attendance to those aged 18 and older. 'My friend Norman and I were then fourteen or fifteen, and we decided that this was coming-of-age time. We rolled up hand-kerchiefs and put them in our shoes so as to appear taller. Norman, whose weight added a certain credibility, bought the tickets. I slunk in behind him, but we had mistimed it, because as we were going in, the descent into the cellar was just beginning – you know, a quarter of an hour before the end of *Psycho*. So we sat down, sweaty-palmed because this was an X-movie, and we'd been in there a minute and a half when Mother Bates turns around.

'It was apocalyptic, of course; shrieks and screams filled the cinema. I'm thinking, *Are X-movies like this all the time?*

'We saw the end of the movie, and then the George Pal, and then *Psycho* started again. Four girls came in and sat in the row in front of us, giggling. And I remember thinking quite distinctly, *I am in control this time, because I know what's going to happen. And these poor creatures in front of us don't.* And the feeling of, yes, *power* built up, as eventually the story caught up with the section we had walked in on. And again the woman was going down into the cellar.

'I wasn't looking at the screen. I was looking at the girls. I couldn't wait for the moment when they leapt off their seats. There was a distinct sense of *frisson* – not with the movie, but with what it was doing. And looking back, there was something muttering in my head, saying, *I want to do this to people.'*

There were other favourite movie moments in his teenage years, including the infamous face-peeling scene and the redemptive liberation of the animals in Georges Franju's *Les Yeux Sans Visage* ('Eyes Without a Face'/'The Horror Chamber of Dr Faustus') (1959). He had (and still has) a special fondness for mummy films, and even today he finds a great scare in the moment in Terence Fisher's stylish remake, for Hammer Films, of *The Mummy* (1959), when the creature smashes through glass to attack Peter Cushing: '[T]his one, lumbering, three thousand-year-old heap of pure malice that couldn't be reasoned with, which couldn't say anything to you and to whom you could say nothing because it couldn't speak English, struck me as being a very scary idea. It's the only one of the conventional genre elements that I would like to commit a novel to doing.'

Clive's early adolescence seems defined by a growing sense of isolation, and distance, from the mundane machinations of the world. With his graduation from Dovedale Road School at the age of ten, he took his scholarship at Quarry Bank Grammar School; and his 'very normal, very healthy' childhood was at an end.

Early in the 1960s, the local bully – a boy in his late teens who lived with his aunt at nearby Rosedale Road – was accused of murder. An Army family – Sergeant Jones and his wife and children – had recently moved into the neighbourhood. One of their boys, little Tony, became friendly with the bully, who, in the past, had played football and games with Clive and Roy and other local children; indeed, he had been inside the Barkers' house on a few occasions.

One afternoon, Mrs Jones came running to the Barker house, crying: 'Oh God, Joan, somebody's been killed!' She had found bloodstained clothing under Tony's bed. The bully, it seemed, had taken Tony to his aunt's house, where the aunt was later found dead behind the door (according to gossip among the children, her corpse was in a state of advanced decay). Apparently the bully had killed her for money to take the tram to town. Although he was acquitted of the crime at trial, Joan says: 'We knew he'd done it.'

These unnerving events seemed like a sign: it was time to move. The neighbourhood was in transition, its houses being converted into flats. Len's success at BICC brought him an opportunity, at last, to have the one thing he had never had, even as a child: a garden.

In 1966, the Barkers moved to a lovely home on Rangemore Road, in a more bucolic and truly suburban area of Liverpool known as Mossley Hill. There, Len and Joan devoted many hours to a lovely garden, and they adopted a new dog – a mongrel named Buster – and a budgie. Clive often visited a nearby Victorian estate, Sudley, with its small collection of paintings, statuary and stuffed animals. But the sense of family closeness was disintegrating as Clive and Roy entered their teens. In Roy's view, a kind of 'armed neutrality' set in between Clive and the rest of the family, with difficult moments often settled by Clive's prodigious way with language. 'He used to blind me with words,' Roy recalls. 'If we ever got into an argument, he would always, invariably win.'

But conversations of any kind were rare. In an inversion of their younger days, Roy became the 'chatterbox' at home, while Clive was quiet and introverted – with only these 'odd moments' when, performing on stage, he seemed 'very extroverted, as if unleashed'. He had few friends and preferred being alone in his room. There, he brooded and bristled beneath what he calls 'the tyranny of the real', losing himself in thoughts and words and pictures.

He also began to assert himself on his living space. His tiny bedroom at Oakdale Road had been decorated and cleaned by Joan, but at Rangemore Road, his room was his own, stacked high with books, magazines and pictures, with his own sketches and artwork scattered everywhere. Sometimes Roy would rummage through the books Clive brought home from the library, many of them large volumes of art: William Blake in particular, but also Goya, Richard Dadd, Hieronymous Bosch. They seemed 'very boring' to Roy, but 'intensely significant', in unspoken ways, to Clive, who increasingly sought ways to recreate the potent emotional and spiritual impact these artists produced in him.

'It was just an artist's den,' his father recalls. 'It was the bane of Joan's life.'

Joan complained, with decreasing frequency, about the mess, until an agreement was reached that 'it was fine as long as he kept it in his bedroom'. Len tried to help by building Clive a worktop desk with bookshelves; for a moment the room seemed part of the house, with a chair for visitors, a knitted quilt on the bed, and a view out on the garden; but chaos quickly descended as Clive filled the room with sketches and half-finished models and candles, a constant flux of shapes and forms, melting and mutating in the throes of creation. 'He hadn't that same discipline over the things that he owned, the things he used, as Roy did,' notes Len. 'He wasn't a tidy sort of boy. But then he was always creating something, always writing or drawing or building models.'

With the expenses of the move, the family didn't go on holiday that year. Instead, Len bought the boys gifts while on a business trip to London. Roy received a guitar and two songbooks; he soon pursued his own creative ambitions, playing and singing folk-influenced songs in school concerts (he continues to perform today). His musical talent eluded Clive, who had a brief fling with the trombone in the school band, but preferred to whistle and sing for himself. Clive's musical tastes were defined by his parents, who enjoyed BBC Radio One and Hollywood musicals – and who always sang their favourite songs: 'I never liked the Rolling Stones; I never liked The Who. I could put up with The Beatles . . . just. I never liked, and to this day I do not like, aggression in music, unless it serves some dramatic purpose. I get that from Mom and Dad; they would sing to each other constantly. There are some songs which I will always consider *their* songs, because they would serenade one another with them: Cole Porter's 'True Love' from *High Society* and 'A Woman in Love' from *Guys and Dolls*.'[6]

Clive's real talent with music was as an organizer – and, indeed, as a teenaged producer and impresario who single-handedly saved a local Boy Scout troop from financial disaster.

Clive was a member, fleetingly, of the Cub Scouts while at Dovedale Road School, but at fourteen, bowing to peer pressure, he joined the

24th Picton Scout Troop. Formerly known as the First Wavertree, it is the second oldest Boy Scout troop in the world, and once counted Len Barker among its members. The walls of its Scout Hall – a brick building that Len helped build as a child – boasted a certificate signed in 1910 by Lord Anthony Baden-Powell, the founder of the Boy Scouts, honouring the troop's service.

Despite its fine pedigree, the 24th Picton was an 'open' or 'free' troop, not supported by a church or other community organization, and it had fallen heavily into debt. One evening, Len accompanied Joan as she met with other parents to try to sort out the problems; he ended up working with the troop for the next twenty-five years, first as its treasurer/secretary and then as its Scout Leader.

Clive's membership in the troop, however, was short lived; in Len's words, 'he wasn't a very happy scout'. Joan smiles, and explains: 'He wanted to turn the scout troop into a dramatic society.' Clive announced that he would stage a concert to relieve the financial difficulties. He gathered other willing scouts in a one-evening variety show that filled the Scout Hall to capacity – and then he delivered its show-stopping performance. Joan dressed him in a 'pink froo-froo dress' and a wig, and he bounced onto stage with a piece of wood and string as a microphone, lip-synching to Cilla Black's hit single 'You're My World'. It brought the house down. 'Tears were running down my face,' Joan says, 'and I always remember – we made two hundred pounds!'

Although he saved the troop, Clive didn't care for scouting. 'It wasn't him,' Len acknowledges. He organized one other fund-raising performance for the scouts, a play that he wrote and directed. 'It was a comedy, a hilarious farce. One of those mad things young boys do, running on and off the stage, that sort of thing.'

But the scouts, like school, team sports and other conventional social structures, seemed empty – championing formalities and rules, codes and conventions, without giving Clive any hope of experiencing (or, indeed, becoming) the things he could see while in the thrall of Tiree or books or films or art or the stage.

He was walking away from his youth and from his family on a cold beach known as adolescence; and he was lost.

4

QUARRY BANK

VOODOO (1967)
INFERNO (1967)
NEONGONEBONY (1968)

Out of this rock, you will find truth.
– Quarry Bank Grammar School Motto

'It's a vast, devouring world, especially if you're alone.'

These words, written by Clive Barker in his short story 'Jacqueline Ess: Her Will and Testament' (1984), echo his first experiences of adolescence and higher education.

When Clive passed his eleven-plus examination, he was one of only ten students from Dovedale Road School selected to enter Quarry Bank Grammar School in the fall of 1964. Quarry Bank, housed in a Tudor-style mansion constructed by a local timber merchant, was an all-male senior school (for boys aged 11 to 18). Entry was based strictly upon academic merit as measured by the eleven-plus, and only the most academically-gifted students attended Quarry Bank, which was considered Liverpool's premier grammar school.

The headmaster of Quarry Bank was William Ernest Pobjoy, an occasionally liberal-minded gentleman who had allowed a student named John Lennon to form his first skiffle band, the Quarry Men, on the school premises. Pobjoy managed Quarry Bank to the model of a traditional English public school, with a house system, gowned teachers, prefects and a head boy; there was strong orientation to a liberal education, sports and the arts. Although Quarry Bank had been hailed by some as 'the Eton of the Labour Party', the 1960s found the school in transition. By the end of the decade, it would merge with a neighbouring girls' school, doubling in size to over a thousand pupils under a new name, Calderstones Community Comprehensive School.

In Clive's early years at Quarry Bank, the school seemed insufferable – a model of the public school assembly line denounced in Lindsay Anderson's surreal motion picture *If . . .* (1968) and Pink Floyd's rock opus *The Wall* (1979). The first form of ninety new students was divided at the start of the school year into three classes of thirty pupils (at that time, over six hundred boys attended the school). Eleven-year-old Clive (who stood just over four feet ten inches tall and weighed seven stone and seven pounds) was assigned to Sefton House – not a physical structure, but, in emulation of the Etonian system, a division of students to which an internal allegiance was expected, typically when the school's several 'houses' were set against each other in sporting events. 'This is one of those schools where they set child against child from the very earliest experience. I hated it. I hated it, because everything about it was alien to my nature.' An 'overweight, spectacled youth, bullied by sixth-formers', Clive withdrew into books and art: 'It's the whole notion of commanding the world via what you created, and retreating toward a world where you knew the ground rules because you invented them. But it was also a world where I could work through the problems.

'For imaginative children,' Clive observes, 'the deprivation comes not at home, but in school.' He had loved Dovedale, but as he grew older, most of his studies seemed irrelevant: 'It seemed to me, from quite early on, that my formal education was not addressing the problems which I was really interested in. I didn't want to know the gross national product of Ghana. But I devoured books of mythology and books of paintings; I got something from those which I didn't get from school – a sense that I was delivered into a world where *ideas* had physical form.'

His father felt that the collision of worlds was inevitable, and frustrating: 'I don't think that Clive and school ever sat together terribly well. He's not a natural academic, I suppose. That which he chooses to do, he does well. That which he doesn't want to do, he's a bit dismissive of.' Although Clive excelled in literature and geography and social sciences, he was bored by mathematics and the sciences – although, as at Dovedale, he did well on most tests. On one memorable occasion, he completed a biology assignment simply by drawing beetles on a piece of paper; he earned no marks, only a lengthy scolding from the headmaster. Len realized the obvious: 'I don't think he accepted school.'

The mental sterility of those early years at Quarry Bank was made worse by the constant bullying of fellow students – and certain teachers. Clive had never been a physical boy, and Len and Joan had believed, naïvely, that the grammar school system was above bullying – when, in fact, administrators turned a blind eye to all but the more egregious cases. Calder High School, an all-girls school, was literally 'over the wall' from Quarry Bank: 'that strange nineteenth century idea that you separate the sexes,' Clive says. 'The great humiliation was to be debagged and your pants pulled off you and then to be thrown over the wall. And the girls just *loved* this. The great terror – if you were a little fat boy, as I was – was that you could not scramble back over the wall fast enough before one of these sort of Gorgonian women came marching out and you got thoroughly trashed. I lived in terror of that!' Far more serious was a reign of violence by three boys who brutalized younger students, injuring one quite seriously; they set upon Clive, hitting him and tearing up a scarf that Joan had knitted. Clive started running away from school, which only increased tensions with his father.

The most trying situation involved his Latin teacher – 'who is now dead,' Clive notes, 'and, I hope, rotting in Hell. Latin was a subject I was hopeless at, and he was a bastard; he was a vicious, sadistic man. He beat people mercilessly, he bullied people mercilessly – you could still do that. *If* . . . is a more extreme version, but that's what the world was like for the first two years of my life there. There were teachers who lined the sleeves of their robes with ball bearings, so they could sling them around and bring them down on your hand. Nobody complained – it was good for the child, you know. Things that, if you did them now, you'd be found insane or sent to gaol – and rightly so. Child abuse. Sexual stuff; homosexual stuff; pederasty built into the system.'

During the spring of Clive's first year he was absent thirty-seven times, effectively half of the term; academically, he ranked fifteenth among the thirty students in Sefton House: 'A bright, lively and intelligent boy,' one master noted in his Report Book. 'This form is the poorer when he is absent.' Clive observes: 'The old system, based on the Etonian model, was in decay. It was in decay for social reasons; I went into a class system, and the class system was falling apart. It was a very interesting time, because I was a working-class kid, and I was smart, and I went to the school that everybody wanted to go to – and I hated it! And Pobjoy, who was a pompous prick, called me into his office after several weeks of truancy, and said, *Look, if you don't want to be a member of the school, there are hundreds of boys who would take your place* – which, of course, was absolutely true. I knew I had mortified Mum and Dad; I knew it. They were very angry with me, and very disappointed in me. So I stuck it out.'

Clive also suffered the institutionalized bullying of the Mather Avenue Playing Fields, where students were expected to participate in cricket and football with Darwinian zeal. Since he was 'a classic wimp' with no talent for sports, he spent endless hours avoiding the agonies of athletics. As Joan recalls: 'I'm the mother in Liverpool who wrote more excuse letters for football than anyone else.'

For Clive, the compulsory games and athletics gave the playing fields the anxious quality of a prison yard. There he endured seemingly endless hours of fear and boredom, which, for a time, he escaped only through his imagination; but ironically, it was at the playing fields that, in his first year at Quarry Bank, he met his best friend and, for a time, alter ego. Phil Rimmer, a first-year student in another house, was also a self-styled 'wimp and dreamer', but with a deftness for creating things mechanical and electronic. 'Art was the option,' Rimmer says, 'the way out of the physical suffering the rest of the school had to offer.' When the two boys, each anxious to avoid another sporting event, met, a new kind of team was formed at Quarry Bank – one that exalted the imaginative above the physical, and that would, in time, embrace a wide range of talents and almost every category of the arts.

'Phil was this incredibly smart, frightened little guy,' Clive recalls, 'who had this wonderfully iconoclastic father who was an inventor. The father and Phil were these fabulously crazy guys; and I adored Phil, and respected him. He was an incredible influence on me, and I miss him still. I wish I knew where he was ... He knew science fiction; he was a great reader. I was the soft end – I was *The Lord of the Rings*. I wasn't into hard sf; he was, and he was very smart about it. And this marriage you find in some of my books of high fantasy with a desire to find some metaphysical/scientific model – most clearly in *Imajica* – came out of sitting for hours and hours with Phil when we were eleven or twelve. I turned him on to *The Lord of the Rings*; he turned me on to Arthur C Clarke.'

Clive found another ally – and his mentor – in Quarry Bank English instructor Norman Russell. Then in his early thirties, Russell was assistant master of the English Department; after Clive's graduation, he would become headmaster. He taught Clive in every year but one from the first through the sixth forms.[1] A single man utterly devoted to his profession, Russell was the teacher whom every student wishes he or she could have experienced – one who treated his wards with reality and dignity, as if they were his own children.

'He was the great validator,' Clive says. 'He was the guy who said, *This is all nonsense you're going through right now ... And you'll come out the other end and this won't mean anything at all.* And that was an important thing to hear from a teacher. He was so eloquent about his love of language and about his love of books and his love of art. The idea of art. He made me into a pretentious little bugger. He made me aim high. He made me look at the idea that storytelling was more than telling stories – that it was about what you believed about the world.'

Norman Russell was also the first person to say that Clive Barker was a writer. One day he handed an assignment back to Clive and said: 'I can't mark this paper.' Russell smiles as he remembers the moment. 'Oh, and the look of concern and worry on this little round face, as he said, *Why not?* And I told him that he was getting too good, that he was getting above the marking grade. *You've moved into a realm where your writing is a personal statement.'*

Clive's writing was intense and evocative – and often difficult for Russell to shake. 'I can remember going through a day where I had Clive first period, and I read one of his essays, and I carried it through my mind all that day. The imagery wouldn't go away . . . Very often his settings and his people seemed to merge. Can you imagine people with leaves growing on them? It was so hard at times. What do you do with something like that? How do you mark it? How do you give it a grade? And you think: *Is anybody apart from me ever going to value this? Or see that this boy is in the business of unlocking doors into other worlds?'*[2]

Norman Russell's recollections of Clive are eloquent and endearing, and his insights into the boy whom he mentored, and watched grow into a man, deserve to be offered here in his own voice:

'He had grace, and his bearing and the way he moved and the way he gave his attention to everybody who spoke to him, as though just for that moment, that was the person who mattered, really. He was a little chap, and even at that age you could see aspects of this world he was going to create. And the interesting thing is that it came, to a great extent, through his interest in drama and plays. I don't think he realized at that time what I knew: which was that he would one day be a writer, and that it would be through the medium of prose that he would make, I think personally, his greatest impact.

'One of the important things when you're a schoolmaster is to be able to spot ability and talent, not because they might necessarily be of use to the pupil in future years, but because they're there to be nurtured, which in my book is what teaching is about. And I was presented with this bright young fellow, quite irrepressible, very courteous but not servile – a very attractive boy to teach. He wore glasses in those days. Round glasses. Anything you put in front of him, he would attack with great delight. Anything you told him, he would remember. In those days we taught a lot of grammar and formal English, and you could teach Clive that, and he would understand it immediately. Now that's a sign of intelligence, obviously. You could tell him, and ever after that, he would apply the rule you'd taught him and it would be right. And on spelling tests, once I corrected his mistakes, they were always correct, ever after. So by the time he was fourteen, he was perfect from the point of view of the mechanics of writing English.

'Over and above that, though, I saw very early on that Clive had two worlds in which he lived. There was our world, in which, in the words of the poet, we didn't want him to interfere too much with our education; and there was also the world of his own. It was an intensely imaginative world.

'I would speak to him, as you do to boys; I would talk to him about what he liked, and things of this kind, and I found that he had, even at the age of fourteen, a highly-developed sense of a world of fantasy. I use this word advisedly, because it wasn't that he was reflecting modes of imagining that had been in the works he'd studied. He wasn't giving me another Rochester from *Jane Eyre*. They were things of his own; they were intensely-imagined stories, when he wrote stories. His essays would lift themselves off the paper and float away. It's very hard to explain what I mean by those words, because there are many people who could write a good essay, and you'd say, *Ten out of ten*. But Clive's work wasn't like that . . . you went on a journey. I could see that he had his own metaphors. Simile is an interesting art, but metaphor is more subtle, and he had his own metaphors. When he wrote, he could clothe a sentence in its own character, so that when you got to the end of it, you said, *A boy of fourteen can't write like this . . . he couldn't.*

'He didn't approach English Literature; he was *in* it. And he came out of it in a strange way. He shook hands, in passing, with the various literary figures we studied. He was one of them. He was always one of them himself. Now that could have ended up with Clive simply floating away on a sea of imagination. But he had faith in himself; he had a strong will. He was modest, and I must emphasize this point, he still is – but almost subconsciously he knew that he was a creative mind and that he needed to defend his creations.

'I thought he was a gift; he lightened the burden of my days. That boy was quite incredible. There were others, obviously, but he was a unique one – I will never forget him.'

Under Russell's tutelage, Clive became reconciled with life at Quarry Bank and swiftly excelled: at the conclusion of his second form, he had been absent only four times and ranked second in his house. He also discovered, through Russell, several of the texts that would form the inspirational backbone of his later work as a novelist, including Christopher Marlowe's *The Tragicall Historie of Doctor Faustus* (circa 1588) and William Shakespeare's *A Midsummer Night's Dream* (circa 1596) and *The Tempest* (circa 1611). He was intrigued by the homosexuality of Marlowe's *Edward II* (circa 1592), and the violence in the plays of John Webster ('partly because here was a poetry, a deeply perverse poetry and a deeply sick poetry'). But spurred on by experiencing Eddison's *The Worm Ouroboros* in Tiree, he continued to read voraciously outside the classroom, embracing the fantasies of Lord Dunsany and William Morris, and discovering Herman Melville ('*Moby Dick* was just this edifice') and the hardboiled private detective novels of Raymond Chandler.[3]

Russell soon encouraged Clive onto the stage, taking him to New Hayes, an adjoining school where the Merseyside Chamber of Commerce held public speaking competitions. 'They would give you a subject,' Clive recalls, 'and you had to write a three-minute speech that you had to deliver to an audience. And it helped if there was some morally-uplifting message to it, with an element of humour or whatever. It was very good for me, because it taught me to be confident in public. It taught me the essentials of keeping an audience. I remember a very galling one where we lost to some Catholic girls – these nuns won, and Norman was furious. He was high, high Anglican, and ... *How dare these damned Catholics win*? He was wonderful under those circumstances. He was the first teacher who sort of let his hair down for me.'[4]

Clive also found solace and vindication in his art classes, which were taught by an older head, Rodney Warbrick, and Alan Plent, in whom he found a different kind of mentor. Plent did not feel that Clive was the most talented artist he had taught, but his style was 'instantly appreciable' – and memorable. Plent lent affirmation to Clive's visions, whether sketched or inked or painted; unlike Clive's parents, and other teachers, he was never overly concerned about what Clive was putting on paper as long as it was created well.

'Clive had a storybook art,' Plent recalls. 'Even by the third year he was drawing and creating quite dramatic, exciting and – fairly strange for his age – quite sexually-oriented cartoons, which were all bizarre, which was Clive's prime word at that age ... He was rescuing fair maidens of the most "voluptuous kind" before most boys gave a thought to the "voluptuous kind", and that amazed me. It was not over-evident, but the fact that such sexuality appeared in such a young mind was quite surprising. But then it was the same high standards of understanding of life and its bizarre aspects that appeared in the females, the monsters, the landscapes and in the storms in the sky. He was, as far as his cartoons went, years ahead of his time.' Even at the age of thirteen or fourteen, Clive's artwork invited a story: 'You never looked at it and said, *Oh, well there's a lovely landscape,*' Plent says. 'You were inclined to say, *What's going on in there?*'

Plent, who was classically trained, encouraged his student to master the technicalities: 'He was very individual, but what I wanted him to do was to learn to draw. My whole intention was for him to practice and to improve his technique.' Teacher and student engaged in furious discussions as Plent stressed the importance of craft, while Clive proposed 'an art to support his imagination, on the level of horror and the monstrous'. Each benefited from the encounter: 'It was actually quite empty after he left,' Plent says, 'there was nobody to take his place.' As Plent and Warbrick noted, with remarkable foresight, in Clive's Report Book: 'He deserves success.'

Like Norman Russell, Plent's influence extended to opportunities outside the classroom, providing Clive with a sense of perspective – of the place of his imaginings in the greater realms of art: exhibitions and museums and the world itself. 'Plent took us down to London,' Clive recalls, 'and that was so important because I saw a scale of painting I had never seen before – huge, huge things.'

When Russell arranged for groups of students to visit Stratford and attend several plays, Clive's theatrical ambitions were heightened. In March 1967, during his third form, he was persuaded by Adrian Phillips, a friend from Dovedale, to act in the annual school play. Because Quarry Bank was an all-male school, younger boys whose voices had not yet broken were recruited to play female roles – 'often with humorous results,' Clive notes. This was his fate when he took to the stage in the absurdist and 'curiously joyless' *One Way Pendulum*; but the effect on him was profound.

'My almost instantaneous response to this was: *Let me grab the stage and give this a go.*' Soon he and Phil Rimmer mounted their own productions using Quarry Bank's facilities – and especially Morrison Hall, which stood separate from the school, built in the 1950s for assemblies and stage performances. It offered Clive and his friends their own Stratford. 'The Head got a bit tired of Clive always wanting the school hall,' Norman Russell recalls, 'and he tried to persuade him to do other things. And Clive was very courteous, and very obedient, but he got the hall.'[5]

The first play, *Voodoo* (1967), was a living horror film written by Clive and Phil Rimmer in 'one hectic weekend' that spring and per-formed on a Thursday and Friday night. It featured an insane German, Baron Von Strüker; a hunchback named Ygor (played by another student, Dave Fishel); and scenery constructed entirely out of card-board boxes. Through Phil's technical wizardry, some of those boxes were rendered into volcanoes that erupted on stage.

Producing and promoting these kinds of theatrics was unheard of for students at Quarry Bank, and it is a credit to Headmaster Pobjoy that he indulged the talents that were evolving within the school's walls. Like a pied piper, Clive brought his plays to life, and the plays, in turn, brought him a growing reputation and a growing circle of friends and fellow talents. At first there was a core group of four – Clive, Phil, Dave Fishel and Malcolm Sharp (who could regurgitate dialogue from films with remarkable ease); but soon there was a creative company of teenagers whose accomplishments would prove extraordinary.

In 1966, twelve-year-old Doug Bradley entered his first form at Quarry Bank, and quickly learned about a third-former named Clive Barker: 'He was a fairly flamboyant figure. He stood out from a crowd. He had a way of walking, and he had a blue silk scarf which he used to throw across his neck, over the school uniform – that was a statement.' Although Bradley saw Clive perform in that spring's school play, *One Way Pendulum*, he knew that the older student was up to something different when Clive later marched into his art class, leading Dave Fishel by a noose tied around his neck. Clive said, quite simply: 'Come and see my play.'

The new play, *Inferno* (1967), was also created in collaboration with

Phil Rimmer. A weird reinvention of Dante, *Inferno* was, in Clive's words, 'Hell and Nazis and God knows ... it was sort of Grand Guignol.' Like *Voodoo,* it took no notice of the traditional rhythms of the stage, and instead was 'basically Marvel Comics brought to life'. But these plays were also produced in reaction to the traditionalism (and occasional ineptitude) of the official school plays, including Quarry Bank's infamous rendition of *Macbeth*, which included dry-ice smoke effects that went out of control and a Macduff who led his entire army on stage during the wrong act.

Bradley was drawn to the audacity and eclecticism of *Inferno*, but he was truly moved, as were many of the students and faculty, by *Neongonebony* (1968), an earnest and sobering play about the end of the world that Clive, Phil, Dave and Malcolm developed entirely through improvisation. 'They were not *my* plays,' Clive insists. 'There were no leaders. It was a very democratic group of people. We were all directing, we were arguing all the time. They were collaborations in the truest sense of the word. They gave me a confidence that I've been able to bring to bear, many times, on a movie set – in just making shit up. This was a group of kids, isolated totally from the vocabulary of mainstream acting, but we found our own little solutions, which were really just from the heart. That informed, hugely, my method-ology as an artist – including films and painting. A sense that you just *go at it* – and sure, you're going to fuck up, but sometimes the fuck-ups will be very interesting.'

The play was performed before the Christmas break in Clive's fifth form, and he produced another inventive publicity campaign to drum up attendance. 'I remember getting a whole bunch of photographs of women, pouting and breathy and sweaty, and photocopying them and writing on them: *I'm coming ... to Neongonebony*. And I put the copies up all around the school. Now they didn't last very long, they lasted for probably an hour, but by the time they'd been up there, for that hour, everyone in the school was going to come to see the play!

'I remember people saying to me: *What does that mean?* And because I'd been reading erotica, I had a piece of vocabulary that they did not know. So much of my reputation came from knowing this stuff, all of which I'd got from books. I had no physical knowledge of this whatsoever, but everybody assumed I did.'

Neongonebony concerned a dying post-apocalyptic world, its title signalling the passage of the bright light of civilization into darkness. Folding chairs were arranged on the stage of Morrison Hall, where the audience was seated, facing out into a vast, cavernous darkness: the entire play took place on the floor. As Doug Bradley notes: 'That's the kind of very simple, but fundamentally devastating thing that he would do.' Candles held by the actors provided the only lighting.

'It was a ninety-minute, perhaps two-hour, play,' Clive recalls, 'improvised entirely by four fourteen- and fifteen-year-olds. Very pessimistic, but it had this really amazing, incredibly memorable ending; because none of us could sing, and we all sang.' The conceit of the play was that, with the onset of eternal darkness, the survivors of an unknown holocaust were slowly freezing to death. In the finale, the four actors, huddled together, sang one of Clive's favourite carols, 'In the Bleak Midwinter', whose lyrics were written by Christina Rossetti. 'As we sang this carol, one by one, the singers froze to death, until there was just Phil – who had the worst voice of the four of us – carrying the last verse of this hymn, holding a single candle. It was wonderful, because it was the first time I felt that I could really do something that wasn't campy and derived from comic books; there was something about Phil singing this incredibly forlorn song in this immense darkness, and then blowing out the candle. It was great.

'I was so lucky. I got to be with a lot of smart people who were constantly challenging my own beliefs, while at the same time, I had this very particular agenda about the *fantastique*, which was really strongly forming in me – and which would have manifested itself so much faster had I not gone to university.

'These plays were about fantastic things – Hell and voodoo and the end of the world – and they were pretty fearless. And the effect that we had upon our contemporaries was startling. The feeling was something special, and I think it fuelled a lot of what followed, in terms of our experiments – because we'd done it, we'd pulled it off, and it's hard when you're four fifteen-year-olds and you're taking on an audience of adults and our contemporaries, who are ready to tear us limb from limb, of course, if we fuck up – and making it up as we go along. To pull that off was very empowering. I felt a great surge of confidence in my own abilities after that.'

Clive had continued to perform in school productions, including *Spring 1600* by Emlyn Williams, in which he played the actor Ben Cook; and Jean Anouilh's *The Lark*, based on the life and death of Joan of Arc, in which he played the head inquisitor – 'which was a fucking wonderful role, because you had these huge metaphysical speeches'. The latter production, whose setting was a trial, probably influenced his later play *The History of the Devil* (1980); and its historical costuming also gave him a renewed sense of transformation from a child who imagined into an adult who acted on his imaginings. 'I remember being the baby-fat boy; I remember being very aware of the fact that I looked farcical in tights. By the time I got to *The Lark*, I had changed, and I felt like I could carry off the robes and all that.'

Doug Bradley befriended Clive in the spring of 1969 while acting in the school play, Nicolai Gogol's *The Government Inspector*. It was the end of Clive's fifth form, and he had passed his O-level examinations to gain admittance to the lower sixth. Students who performed in the school play were excused from classes for a week of preparation in Morrison Hall; which, Bradley observes, was a special kind of heaven, a 'week that seemed to go on forever', in which friendships and collaborations were formed that have continued for more than thirty years. 'What was really great,' Clive recalls, 'was that these things always happened in spring – the clocks had gone on, evenings were longer, exams were over, you were making plays, and summer was coming! Marvellous! I don't think I've ever felt happier than those times.'

Clive took a lead role as the Mayor, while Bradley played one of the twins. On opening night, Clive subverted the play, making it into his own. 'I was a terrible ham. I was terribly disrespectful that night, but I would do anything for a laugh. I was the bad version of Jim Carrey; I would just do anything.' Norman Russell recalls the evening vividly: 'It was a hilarious performance. I can still see him now on the stage. He put in words of his own that were not in the text – typical of Clive. There was one character with an enormous moustache, and Clive kept calling him *Brillo Pad Features* – not in the text, I hasten to add. And he had all kinds of gestures, like Groucho Marx . . . he was there one minute, over there the next, then back, incredibly energetic – and very popular, he got standing ovations from the boys and from us.

51

'This is the interesting thing about Clive Barker. He wasn't a traditional boring rebel. Every boy has to be a James Dean or whatever – he wasn't. Neither, incidentally, was John Lennon. He wasn't that kind of rebel, either, in the professional *go against the authority* vein. Clive enjoyed himself thoroughly, but he was clever, you see. Some people have resentment that arises from their ignorance or inability to do something; but Clive could do everything.'

After *The Government Inspector*, Clive invited Doug Bradley to join his growing circle of friends and participate in a new project, an ambitious play he had conceived called *The Holly and the Ivy*. 'I was absolutely terrified of them,' Bradley recalls. 'They were an extraordinary bunch of people. They were improvising the whole thing. I didn't even know improvisation existed. I wasn't up to this at all. But I knew that this was something I wanted.'

Like earlier productions, *The Holly and the Ivy* was prepared and presented with the benign indulgence (and occasional ignorance) of Quarry Bank, with rehearsals often held at lunchtime. Despite its epic length of three hours, the play was wholly improvised. Clive would describe each actor's character and what would happen in a scene, and the actors would then attempt to make up their lines and actions on the spot. These improvisations would evolve under Clive's direction and eventually become fixed as parts of the play, committed to memory without any written script.

Clive acted as the leader, guiding and shaping the play into its final form; in Bradley's words: 'He was absolutely the dominant individual in what was nevertheless a collaborative effort.' And, although only sixteen years of age, 'he was the most extraordinary person I've ever come across. He changed my life, there's no question about that. Had it not been for this experience that grew out of this accidental grouping of people in the school play, I wouldn't be an actor.

'He was a big personality – you couldn't miss him. He was tremendously friendly. He was two years senior to me – in senior school, that's a big gap, it's a convenient excuse for condescending to people; he never did that at all. Very funny. Tremendously witty. And a brilliant conversationalist. You wanted to be around him. And I was aware that there was a world, and a level of ideas, here that was a long way outside the world of the petty bourgeois from which we both came.'

The shared life moved quickly from school to home as the boys became great friends. Bradley lived about a half-hour's walk from Clive's home, but the distance seemed to shorten with each day as they did so many things together – going to films, theatre, art galleries, or simply visiting each other and talking. 'He redefined the word *eclectic*. There was nothing that was not grist to his mill. There was nothing that he wasn't interested in . . . apart from football.'

5

THE COMPANY OF DREAMERS

THE HOLLY AND THE IVY (1970)

> *Only connect...*
> – EM FORSTER, *Howards End*

The Holly and the Ivy was presented in Morrison Hall on three consecutive nights, a Wednesday through a Friday, in the autumn of 1970, during Clive's upper sixth, his final year at grammar school. The actors included Doug Bradley and the original foursome – Clive, Dave Fishel, Malcolm Sharp and Phil Rimmer (who devised an effect with a magnesium charge that literally exploded in his face, forcing him to play out a scene with a blackened face and singed eyebrows); but this was also the first of Clive's plays with actresses: Anne Taylor and the brilliant Jude Kelly – 'a force of nature', in Clive's words, 'and she was in love with me – and I was a little in love with Jude. She was an extraordinary woman – and, I gather, still is.' In her Clive had found another kindred spirit: 'What I recognized in her instantly was someone for whom no rules were ever going to apply.'

For the staid Quarry Bank, and particularly its faculty, the performance of *The Holly and the Ivy* was not merely avant-garde but also disturbing. Following the precedent of *Neongonebony*, the actors performed on the hall floor while the audience sat on-stage. Clive prepared special programmes, burned around the edges to look like timeworn manuscripts. Autumn leaves were scattered on the floor, incense was burned, a wind-up gramophone played 'This Is My Lovely Day', and the audience of teachers, staff, students and their invited guests witnessed a grand and solemn Arthurian fantasy – a mingling of the musical *Camelot* and its source, *The Once and Future King*, with Jean Anouilh's play *Becket* (1959) – whose final act, with its jarring revelation of a homosexual romance between the male leads, caused outrage and concern among the faculty.

Norman Russell sat next to Headmaster Pobjoy, and suffered through his sarcastic comments about the performance; but he could see that something genuine was happening on the floor: 'If only people listened to young people occasionally, if they would shut up and listen, or watch ... The theme was really marriage as conceived through the eyes of somebody who was too young to know anything about it; but he perceived things. It was a love story, and Clive had a happy ending *in the middle*. The marriage, and the vicar smiling; it was lovely, and then ... but *no*, that was only what *could* have happened. Here in fact was what happened, and we had a pretty nasty, tragic thing.'

The bride and groom walked forward to the strains of Bing Crosby singing 'White Christmas'. 'Since the play was vaguely Arthurian,' Doug Bradley notes, 'this was gloriously anachronistic, underlined by having the record player standing on a table in the acting area. Another actor then knocked the arm of the record player off the 78 rpm disc, looked at the audience and said, *Now* that's *a happy ending. If that's what you want, go home now.*'

The sudden twist, and the rejection of heterosexual marriage in favour of homosexual romance, moved Norman Russell: 'For me, as a teacher, it had great interest – and a certain feeling that it was very brave for a young fellow, in the context of a school, where you are committed to teach a certain moral stance, to use these images. Not to serve up the convention. And it was an age when people were starting to liberate themselves from whatever it was that held everybody in thrall.'

Times were changing with dramatic speed. Youth seemed in

rebellion – not only against America's war in Vietnam, but against the perceived tyranny of social, political and, indeed, educational institutions. In May 1968, a series of general strikes and student riots had shattered Paris, ultimately forcing the authoritarian government of Charles de Gaulle to concede to student demands for reform. 'I was very strongly aware of what happened in Paris in 1968,' Clive notes. 'That was very important. I never thought of myself as a communist, but I was aware of the foment, and the Vietnam War foment. I was hauled over the coals by my father for having an opinion. He said, *This has nothing to do with you – you don't understand the situation*. I was trying to make paintings about these things: Naïve does not begin to describe them, but I was trying to tackle these things. The school didn't like them, and Dad certainly didn't like them; and yet I feel blessed to have seen two sides of the organizational coin where education is concerned, because I think they both have their value. I'm not saying there's any value to ball bearings being brought down on children's hands, but I think I was given a very high level of education and I was then allowed to be an activist in the destruction of the system I had hated so much. And I was an activist in the sense that I was making plays, and the first and most obvious thing was my saying to the school: *I don't want to be in the school play any more, I'm going to write my own plays. Anybody going to stop me?* And Pobjoy said, *No, you can do anything*. It was like a little revolution. And there were signs of that everywhere . . .'

The sixth form, which comprised two years of instruction, was taught in small sets of eight to ten students, in preparation for A-level examinations and university.[1] Clive's lower sixth included a 'liberal studies' class taught by a new instructor in the Art Department, twenty-six-year-old Helen Clarke.[2] Like Norman Russell, she was smitten with Clive's creative powers. She invited one of her friends, William Scobie, then senior lecturer in Liberal Studies at Liverpool Polytechnic, to attend *The Holly and the Ivy*.

Scobie, who now owns an antique shop in Merseyside, recalls his first encounter with Clive Barker: 'Helen said, *Oh, you must come and see this play. It's done by one of our very best students, and he's very, very clever . . . you'll like it*. And I was dragged along very reluctantly – I *hate* school plays. It was a fairy story, probably the precursor of the mime series that Clive did later. It was beautifully done, but the basic story was of a prince who falls in love with a shepherd. This wasn't exactly clear until the end of the play, at least not entirely; and at the end of the play, when the prince finally meets the shepherd, the whole front row froze. I'm not sure if it was the Lord Mayor, but certainly someone of that stature, plus the headmaster. Nothing was said; it was too well-behaved a school for anyone to have actually said anything to me or anybody at the time.'

Norman Russell shakes his head when he recalls the controversy that followed: 'Clive's imagery impinged upon certain lifestyles which we were not encouraged to discuss. And I had a profound conviction that they were the private business of the people concerned. Some people made a fuss – there was talk in the staff room, and there's nothing worse than talk in the staff room. I think it was Sidney Smith who said there are three sexes: men, women and clergymen; but actually there are four: men, women, clergymen and schoolmasters. And the words went around and the shocked expressions and *What's the world coming to*?

'Why are people such hypocrites? Do they want to be hypocrites? Do they like being hypocrites? It was nothing more than sheer hypocrisy.

'You can become very intolerant if you teach young people; it's so easy just to crush and destroy, especially if you're a teacher, because you're in a position of authority. And one of the most awesome things about teaching is that your pupils believe you. If you put on an act, they believe you. And if you say this kind of thing is disgusting, and don't let me ever see it again, they believe you mean it. So you don't say it, because it's not true. This is how I was with my pupils, because people are different, and people are genetically predisposed to be what they are ... and to interfere with that is to say, *I'm not going to let you grow*. It's like putting weed killer on a rose. And the older you are, the more disinclined you are to join in the charade – the charade that we must all conform to a certain way.'[3]

Helen Clarke later commissioned a painting by Clive, 'A Midsummer Night's Dream', and organized the first exhibition of his artwork as part of a party at her home. She also introduced Clive to the poetry of William Butler Yeats, which affected him profoundly. 'I was given a collection by Helen Clarke, *Selected Poems*, in which she had written the famous Forster quote: *Only connect*. I still have it here, among the shelves. Of all the books of poetry I have from my childhood, the only book that I still have in its original edition is my Yeats. I was just completely transported by it. The melancholy of it. *When you are old and full of sleep, take down this book and read . . .*[4]

'What Yeats taught me was that there was a tougher way to do this . . . Yeats's early stuff is about faeries, but by the time you get to "The Circus Animals" or "Sailing to Byzantium", which is one of the great poems, what I learned was that these romantic tools could be used in a harder, crisper way. Whenever I write fantasy, the great teacher, still, is Yeats. If you want to learn everything you need to know about writing fantasy, you should read the seven verses of "Sailing to Byzantium".

'Yeats then led me to the Golden Dawn, and from the Golden Dawn to Aleister Crowley – and to a whole metaphysical system based on magic. Which I took terribly, terribly seriously. I was trying these experiments, putting things under my pillow in the belief they would influence my dreams in a certain direction. For a couple years there, Mom was saying, *What are these things I keep finding under your pillow?* And not really admitting them to anybody except Phil.

'Magic, and the idea of magic – that the will works upon the world in some way to change it – is really interesting, isn't it? Because it's what we're hoping we do with our words.'

Bill Scobie had a flat in the city centre where Huskisson Street (named for the first victim of a railway accident) met Hope Street, overlooking the Anglican Cathedral. Its doors were always open to his students and friends. One day Helen Clarke brought Clive by for a visit. To this day, Clive recalls Scobie's first words to him: 'So. Helen Clarke tells me you're a combination of Michelangelo and Edgar Allan Poe. What else do you do?'

There, surrounded by Scobie's collections of Ruskin pottery and art deco, the student and the professor became friends, and traded thoughts on topics dear to Scobie: Ezra Pound and John Cage, Wittgenstein and theatre (particularly Eastern theatre and Kabuki). Curiously, the two rarely discussed art, and Scobie did not view any of Clive's artwork until years later, when Clive gave him some drawings and photographs as remembrances before departing for London.

For Clive, these discussions were tinged with something that was distinctly uncomfortable, and yet eye-opening. Scobie was the first man he met who was open about his homosexuality, and it frightened him: 'Not the sexuality but the attitude. It was a very courageous thing then. And it was a new world to me. I turned away from it for a long time. It was like I knew I was out of my depth.'

Scobie was taken with Clive's intellect: 'Active is the word ... Enquiring. Argumentative, quite rightly. I think he had an exciting mind. What you hoped was going to turn into something even more exciting. What surprised me – the first surprise I had from Clive – was the later experiment with mime. Because there was a calm, an absolute peace, about those performances. And I thought, *How on earth had Clive managed to exude this calm when he himself isn't calm?*

'One of the reasons we got on so well is that we were both anti-establishment. I don't mean that in a political sense; I mean that in a much deeper, more important sense. If somebody, with long-established authority, says, *This is so*, my first reaction is always to say: *Why?* Or: *Prove it*. And to a great extent, Clive was doing what a lot of less gifted but quite clever students would like to do, which is to kick authority quite gently in the shins, in an intelligent manner. I think most of them do it in silly ways, like not going to school, or blowing up the science lab.'[5]

Clearly Clive believed in creation rather than destruction. One of his more memorable antics came in the sixth form assembly, in which a department head would read, to an audience of some two hundred sixth formers collected in Morrison Hall, from a book deemed appropriate. Alan Plent had been reading from a political volume, and he offered the stage to any student; Clive immediately took to the stage and announced: 'I will now read to you from ... *Winnie the Pooh*' – which he then did, performing the parts of the characters as he read.

The next target of his subversion was the school magazine, known as *The Quarry*. In Norman Russell's fine description, 'It consisted of a certain amount of fictional material provided by the boys, interspersed with long accounts of football matches and other interhouse competitions and chess problems. It was a very fine magazine designed totally to crush the spirit of anyone who read it. And it cost sixpence.'

Clive produced an alternative magazine of his own using the school mimeograph; it was named *Humphri*. 'The name itself was subversive for its time,' Scobie notes. 'How could you name a magazine *Humphri?*' Its single issue consisted of loose mimeographed sheets of handwritten text and illustrations (including nudes), some of them burned at the edges. The sheets were placed, along with leaves, twigs and other artifacts, into clear plastic bags and given to friends with a handwritten note. Scobie's copy, for example, included a trading card from the gory 'Civil War News' series that Clive had collected as a child, along with pages clipped from comic books.

Headmaster Pobjoy was upset – by now, predictably – when he reviewed his copy with its nude drawings and provocative fiction. He called Norman Russell aside: 'Norman, why can't Clive's magazines be like everyone else's magazines?' Russell replied: 'Sir, it's because they're *Clive's* magazines.' *Humphri* was, to Russell's thinking, one of the earliest examples of a multimedia 'package', but its intrinsic themes and emotions were traditional, with echoes of Tennyson and the paintings of George Frederick Watts. There was also a radical sensuality to the presentation. 'In those days,' Russell notes, 'you were not supposed to exist below the neck.'

'Making art,' Clive reflects, 'empowers you because you start to feel very special – because, as Norman rightly observed to Pobjoy, only one person can make that thing, and that's you. It may not be a very good thing, but hey, it's mine. And when I was making those things at school, I was thinking the same thing. Maybe I was thinking about beginning to have a consciousness of being a gay man. Obviously, I don't remember. I don't think so, but maybe I was. I was certainly aware that my imagination was one of the few things which distinguished me. I was not a distinguished scholar. I had little patience with the business of school. I was a lousy school politician. I was not very good with the politics of prefects and head boys and all that stuff. I was a lousy sportsman. And I was a little iconoclast. I wasn't proudly or arrogantly an iconoclast; I was just made that way, it was like it was the colour of my hair . . . it was just who I was. I have to put that down to genetics. I have to put that down to Mom and Dad, who were both iconoclastic, marrying in spite of their parents, and being brought up in this household that always had that iconoclastic thing going on.'

Clive's decision to publish *Humphri* found its roots in another epiphany of his sixth form: Helen Clarke invited a local writer, Ramsey Campbell, to speak at Quarry Bank about his career in horror fiction. Then in his early twenties, Campbell had published his first book at the age of eighteen and was acclaimed even then as one of contemporary horror fiction's foremost stylists.

After English instructor Bruce Prince introduced their guest to the eager students, Campbell stood in silence for several moments. Then he said: 'What is horror?' His eclectic presentation included the playing of Frank Zappa's album *Absolutely Free*, during which a few of the teachers got up and left; but Clive and his friends stayed to talk. 'This bunch of snotty-nosed little kids all gathered around, and this guy came in, and I thought he was marvellous. For one thing, he was *weird* and that was great. And he did it – he did it, for God's sake! There were people out there who actually *wrote* these things for a living!'

Twenty years later, Clive would recall the vivid impact of that evening: 'The talk was called, I believe, *Why Horror?* The question needed no answer as far as I was concerned (except possibly: *Why Not?*) but he talked with a warmth and wit which left many amongst the audience mightily impressed. Though there were only a handful of years between he and me, *he* stood in the outside world while I still laboured in the salt-mines of State-supplied education, and it was wonderful to hear somebody from that other world express such an unalloyed love of all things dark and disturbing. The pride he took in the genre contrasted forcibly with my own slightly furtive passion. Horror fiction has rarely been viewed as an intellectually credible area of endeavour and I – with one eye on Oxford and the other on Edgar Allan Poe – didn't have the courage of my enthusiasms. I may say he changed that, simply by demonstrating that horror fiction could be spoken of with as much aesthetic insight as any other fiction – with the added bonus that it gave you apocalyptic dreams.'[6]

Campbell invited Clive and other Quarry Bank students to join him on 'Close Up', an arts programme that he hosted on Radio Merseyside. He spoke about horror film and fiction for the first half hour, and when the students joined in: 'Clive had more to say than anyone else.' Clive encountered Campbell again in the early seventies, usually at parties at Helen Clarke's flat, where Ramsey would recommend books and films; but, as the years passed, they lost touch – for a time.

In 1969, fifteen-year-old Julie Blake, a student at Liverpool's High School for Girls, was transferred from her third form to the newly consolidated, co-educational school formerly known as Quarry Bank. The change was breathtaking, especially for female students. Her school's motto had been 'Courage – Honour – Service'. Academic achievement was paramount, and discipline strict, to the point of a requirement that girls wear indoor shoes and outdoor shoes.

The new comprehensive school was 'a time bomb going off, basically' – and the classrooms seemed suddenly liberal and relaxed. The Quarry Bank boys were an inviting distraction, and among them, Julie learned, was one named Clive Barker, who was known for inventing and reciting poems about butterflies. He was pointed out to her one day on the playing field, wearing a loose overcoat that billowed around him as he walked. Then, in the winter of 1970, she attended *The Holly and the Ivy*, and was struck by its sombre tone: 'It was quite solemn . . . a funeral procession, all very atmospheric and intense.'

Although Clive was studying for his A-levels, he busily pursued his true enthusiasms. *The Holly and the Ivy* was followed by a brief revival of *Neongonebony*; and, in the spring of 1971, he acted in his last school play, the John Chapman farce *Dry Rot*. 'I have no idea how well we did it,' Doug Bradley says. 'But we had tremendous fun doing it.' Clive played the role of a false vicar, and Julie Blake, who was interested in acting, also earned a part. In rehearsals, Clive was a dynamo, 'always incredibly busy, dashing off somewhere – people to see, drawings to do – and charismatic'. He was 'very friendly, outgoing, and he would always challenge anyone, he would challenge the status quo, challenge assumptions. He thought a lot. He thought about things that people didn't usually talk about – mortality and what one was going to do with one's life. He thought about things more deeply than most people.'

To Julie, this young man, although only seventeen, seemed dedicated to the idea of art and of his life being devoted to art. 'His mind never stopped. I always got the impression that he was looking at things from an artist's point of view, or he was being a theatre director next, and then suddenly he was a film cameraman, and always he was working things out . . . asking, *What do you think of this for an idea?*' She was particularly impressed by his artwork, which he typically rendered in black fountain pen, often while he talked – 'and, if you were lucky, he would give you the drawing . . . To know Clive was to know his work.'

Julie quickly formed a friendship with Clive that moved beyond the creative. 'We were confidants,' she notes. 'We were able to talk quite honestly with each other. We were able to talk about intimate things – about relationships, and his feelings about his sexuality.' She joined the ever-evolving informal circle of friends – Clive, Phil, Doug, Lynne Darnell, Anne Taylor, Sue and Graham Bickley – who now decided to pursue their collective impulses for creativity on a more formal basis. There was a sudden sense of companionship on a journey that was not yet charted, but that lay somewhere in Clive's imagination – which he began to share with them more fully, taking Julie and Lynne to the locale that had so enchanted him: Tiree. 'I wanted to show them this emptiness. This glorious emptiness.'

The friends also shared favourites from literature and painting and film – Clive championed older black and white films and musicals – and attended movies and plays together. Sometimes they created special occasions, gathering around bonfires to hold celebratory readings from poems and stories.

It was at one of these get-togethers that Clive suggested that they form a theatre company. 'It seemed,' he says, 'to be a place where I could use several skills, where I could satisfy my desire to make pictures *and* my desire to write.'

His years at Quarry Bank were at an end. He had entered the school as a boy, lonely and often afraid; he was leaving as a man, with a circle of friends and a confidence in his abilities – and the knowledge, expressed by Norman Russell, that he was, indeed, a writer.

'I felt that Clive had the work ethic,' says Russell. 'I knew that he wouldn't stop. But for a while I wondered if he'd not gone up the wrong path when he did these plays. I thought to myself, *Oh, Clive, when are you going to put pen to paper?* I was waiting for him to do that. Clive was a bit of an exhibitionist, and he liked to do those things, and that led him into drama and the experimental type theatre, which I felt was pulling him away from what he should have been doing . . . which was writing.'

6

HYDRA RISING

THE HYDRA THEATRE COMPANY (1972–74)
SALOME (1973) and THE FORBIDDEN (1975–78)
THE THEATRE OF THE IMAGINATION (1974)
A CLOWN'S SODOM (1976)

> 'There are lives lived for love,' said Lichfield to his new company,
> 'and lives lived for Art. We happy band have chosen the latter
> persuasion.'
>
> — CLIVE BARKER, 'Sex, Death and Starshine'

Graduation from Quarry Bank brought Clive to another crossroads.
In his mind, the next step was clear: he had secured a place at the
Liverpool College of Arts. His parents, however, had different plans.
Len had left school at fourteen, and laboured for long hours to find
advancement; and, as a personnel manager at BICC, he knew that
employment opportunities were denied to those without a university
education. Concerned that art school would prove a hotbed of decadence – the very reason that Clive wanted to attend – Len and Joan

encouraged him to attend university instead, insisting that his studies would place him on the right path to a useful livelihood.

'I was trying to do it in the best interests of Clive,' says Len. 'The simple problem with Clive was that he didn't want to work, in the sense of being employed. He was his own man.' Surprisingly, Helen Clarke shared their point of view.[1]

In an effort to help Clive understand his perspective, Len arranged for Clive to sit for mock job interviews at BICC, playing the part of a recent grammar school graduate in sessions that were videotaped for the training of company job interviewers. Clive was interviewed by the man who became Len's director, and in answering questions, Len says, 'Clive's views were so very strange.' When asked about what he had done at school, Clive talked about creating *Humphri*, and the ivy leaves pressed between its pages. The tape was among those shown for years in training, and Len would say: 'For God's sake, don't tell them it's my son.'

'My Dad's a practical man,' says Roy Barker. 'And having an "arty-farty" son, to use a phrase he would have used at the time, he didn't see him as a son who was going to do so well. And Clive was clearly of the opinion that he didn't care whether he made it or not. The fact was this was what he wanted to do. He never gave the impression of being career-minded then. That seemed to come later.'

Bowing to his parents' pressure, Clive agreed to attend the University of Liverpool, at first studying Philosophy but then switching to a degree in English Literature. Several of his teachers, including Norman Russell, lament that he did not attend Oxford; but Clive still wishes that he had attended art school. 'I was an okay scholar, but not a great one by any means. No real application, the way that people who got into Oxford and Cambridge had application; you really saw that in their lives. I didn't see that in my life, or if I saw it, I didn't care for it. Much to Norman's disappointment. Norman wanted me in Oxford. And I just couldn't get my shit together. Why? That wasn't what I was going to be. I didn't know what I was going to be, but it wasn't going to be that. I didn't want to join the BBC; I didn't want to be an MP, justice of the peace, or any of the number of things that Oxford turns out – I wasn't going to do that. I think that's one of the reasons why Blake is so important to me. I believe in art and artists most when they follow their own instincts wherever their instincts lead, however ill-equipped they are for the journey.'

Clive could not countenance the strictures of formal education; in Bill Scobie's words: 'The problem with universities is that they do tie you into a straightjacket, so that they become very rigid. He really needed people to bring him alive.' As Joan puts it, quite simply: 'He got bored.'

Clive's experience would be reflected in stories like 'Dread' (1984), in which a university student is tormented by a would-be guru. Classes bored him, and most of his time was spent working in theatre and mime with his friends and fellow students. 'I never took much notice of my courses. I got on with writing plays and making pictures and doing all the other things I had done beforehand. Academe didn't suit me at all. I was biding my time. I was preparing for whatever I was going to do when I got out.' As Doug Bradley recalls: 'He didn't talk much about university; he seemed simply to really get through with it . . . He was quite determined that he wouldn't work for anybody else, that he would be his own master and his own man.'[2]

Clive felt that he had been placed on a treadmill from O-levels into A-levels into university; but now he and his friends were maturing, becoming more self-aware, less interested in school than in their newfound social life, underground culture and experimental art. The political current had shifted: England was going liberal at a breakneck speed. A Labour government was in power for the first time in more than a decade, and there was a Year Zero mentality – that this was a moment to be seized, particularly in the creative realm.

As Doug Bradley puts it: 'It wasn't until I got to university that, for the first time in my life I said, *Who am I doing this for*? And it certainly wasn't for me.' He dropped out of the University of Liverpool, left home and began living with Lynne Darnell; but Clive held on, if only to satisfy his parents.

'If I were quite honest,' Len says, years later, 'I wish I had understood what he was driving at better. My wife would be the first to say I lack imagination. To try to get on Clive's wavelength was difficult. I'm basically a practical sort of man, with all the problems that brings. Joan has got one of those imaginations that causes her anguish, unnecessarily. But I could have helped Clive more, had I understood better what he was driving at. You see, Roy I could follow: he played football – I can understand that. He taught himself, with the help of a schoolmaster, to play guitar – I could follow that. Clive's weird drawings and his writings – I found it difficult to share his ability. I still do, to some extent.'

Joan, on the other hand, found it easy – 'I've got too much imagination,' she says – and she was at home, with Clive, during the day. (Throughout his years at university, Clive lived at home; as Len explains it: 'Teachers asked him, *Does your mum make good apple pie*? When he said *yes*, they said, *What the hell are you leaving home for*?')

Before beginning university, Clive penned a short novel dedicated to, and based upon, his friends and constant companions. Originally called *The Company of Dreamers*, its final title was *The Candle in the Cloud* (1971). Clive wrote its final draft in longhand in one of his father's BICC wiring installation notebooks. Also kept in a folder labelled 'The Company of Dreamers' were several shorter manuscripts, including an early draft of *The Candle in the Cloud* and a short story, written in pencil, called 'The Three Red Sails'.

Dedicated to 'Julie, Sue, Anne, Lynne, Phil, Doug, and Graham, being a book for you all', *The Candle in the Cloud* is eighty-six hand-written pages, single-spaced and with corrections, comprising a novel for young adults in twenty chapters – with song lyrics and an illustration by Clive. Its story involves the fantastic quest of a group of children to overcome dark forces, with a weighty role played by a magician named Daraph. Influenced by the fantasies of CS Lewis, its finale offers the poignant image of a dark thundercloud that eats the sun, reducing it to grey ash, from which the world is rebuilt, but in a new and better way. On a whim, Clive submitted a typed manuscript of the novel to the prestigious Bodley Head – 'and they damned near bought it'. An editor responded very positively, but requested certain changes in the text. 'I was about to go into university,' Clive says, 'and I just wasn't up for it.' He wrote back, asking the publisher to wait until he was integrated into the rhythm of university life; but he soon lost interest in the book. *The Candle in the Cloud* makes clear that, even in his earliest efforts at fiction, Clive eschewed the Tolkien model of an abstract fantasy world in favour of the realms of ER Eddison and *Peter Pan*, where characters could step (or dream) from reality into fantasy, and vice versa.

His lingering obsession, however, was to take that step himself: to walk from the drab reality of his studies into the dreamworld that he had found while on the theatre stage. During his first year at university, he returned to Quarry Bank as a member of the audience for that spring's school play, Bertolt Brecht's *The Caucasian Chalk Circle* (1944). 'I hated Brecht, I hated his politics; but it's a great play – and it was one of those big influences. I learned so much from that play. I was jealous as hell; because it felt like my moment had passed. I was now in another area of endeavour, and I was a new boy again. And having been the shining light at my school, I was now reduced to this . . . I didn't want to go to university, but Mum and Dad – it was the last request they were going to make of me. And in many regards I was intellectually outclassed, because I don't have a good academic mind. I'm a chaotic thinker, not an organized academic thinker. The philosophy stuff was an agony, and I had all this eagerness to be doing my own thing. I didn't want to be sitting there studying Shakespeare, I wanted to be writing. It was the worst.'

He found an escape by returning to the stage, taking a lead role as Thomas à Becket in an independent production of TS Eliot's *Murder in the Cathedral* (1938). The play was staged at Liverpool's All Hallow's Church under the direction of Jude Kelly, then in her final year at Quarry Bank. When Len and Joan attended, Joan was reduced to tears when Becket died at the hands of his assassin – played by none other than Doug Bradley. Clive lay sprawled on the altar steps through the remainder of the scene; and, in homage to their acting skills, Joan says, 'I was furious at Dougie for ages, for doing that to my son!'

The play, which Kelly had mounted without the assistance of Quarry Bank, convinced Clive and his friends that it was possible to present independent productions – and not of classic plays, but using their own original material. 'It was still a vague thing that we wanted,' Doug Bradley says, 'but we knew that we didn't want to let go of what we had at school.' This sense was confirmed in the friends' first performance outside Quarry Bank, which was, at heart, a rip-off of a Whitehall farce – *Dry Rot* revisited – called *Is There Anybody There?* (1971).

Bradley laughs at the memory: 'The only four-and-a-half hour farce in the history of theatre.'

The Everyman Theatre on Hope Street, co-founded by Terry Hands (who later managed the Royal Shakespeare Company), included a famous bistro, staged intriguing plays, and had served as a venue for various Merseybeat groups in the sixties. In 1974, Willy Russell's play *John, Paul, George, Ringo ... & Bert* made its world première there (Russell would later write *Shirley Valentine*, *Educating Rita* and *Blood Brothers*). Because the Everyman had a youth theatre, Clive and his friends were allowed access to the premises for rehearsals on Monday nights. 'We went in and built the set in twenty-four hours. We were still putting curtains up on the set when Clive's mother arrived at the auditorium. This was like twenty past seven, curtain up at half past, and we were still finishing the set.'

Is There Anybody There? was written principally by Clive and Phil Rimmer, with input from the other actors (including Jude Kelly, as well as Les Heseltine – now television game show host Les Dennis – and his wife-to-be, Lynne Webster). Directed by Clive, the performance had a fair element of improvisation: 'It wasn't always four-and-a-half hours long,' Bradley says. 'It was probably three hours long when we started; but it just kept getting longer each time we did it, because there was more and more and more business going on. There was no hard taskmaster director saying, *You can't do this!*'

Clive's parents were very enthusiastic: 'It was totally and utterly ridiculous,' Len says, 'but it worked!' When they urged Clive to continue with this kind of entertainment, however, he declined, taking his theatrical endeavours into a realm that confused Len and Joan, who summarize his later plays in five words: 'What was that all about?'

In 1973, Julie Blake and Anne Taylor entered IM Marsh College of Dance and Drama (now part of the John Moores University). Julie obtained permission to use the drama studio, where, over the next three years, the nascent acting company rehearsed, constantly improvising, and also made their masks and costumes.

The circle of friends assembled an evening of more serious entertainments, staged at a small pavilion in Childwall which, according to Julie Blake, 'people used for elocution lessons and changing for their tennis.' The main feature was Clive's adaptation of Oscar Wilde's

Salomé, along with Noel Coward songs, a Joyce Grenfell sketch and a dramatization of Clive's short story 'The Wood on the Hill' (which is published, for the first time anywhere, as the Appendix to this book). Audience members were shocked by the sight of John the Baptist's head in a bloody white bucket that Clive had found, marked 'Soiled Dressings'. (The bucket became an icon of the formative troupe, and would appear in many of its productions.) Doug Bradley played the role of the beheaded prophet, and since John is blind in Wilde's rendition, Bradley had his first experience with prosthetic make-up, with Clive constructing and painting papier-mâché covering for his eyes. A rope was tied backstage and measured out to the front, then secured around Bradley's stomach so that he could move freely on stage without fear of falling.

Clive and Phil Rimmer decided to make a short silent film of *Salomé* (1973). The would-be film-makers worked with the oft-repeated dictum of Orson Welles: 'Have the confidence of ignorance.' It was their fifth or sixth attempt to create a short film; earlier, Clive and Phil had acquired a Super 8 millimetre camera that allowed for stop-action photography, and thus some rudimentary animation and other effects. Their first collaboration, whose title is long forgotten, found them creating footage of murky atmospheres, shot in stop-motion, with an Action Man figure as their hero. 'It was a violent, nasty little Lovecraftian thing in which our Action Man went up against some terrible plasticine monster,' Clive says. 'It was set in a graveyard, and there was this terrible monster and a lot of fire and destruction.' The film involved 'a lot of sludge dripping down steps,' Julie Blake remembers. 'It was difficult to make out things.'

The budding film-makers then pursued a more ambitious project, *Jack O Lant* (circa 1972). Although never completed, the short film included a wedding scene shot in a church in Woolton. Sue Bickley played the bride, draped in lace curtains for a wedding gown that seemed to convince some older ladies who were passing by. 'One of us also ran semi-naked through the graveyard, which owed something to Hammer,' Blake recalls, 'and every couple of minutes Phil had to climb into the boot of the car to change the film.'

Jack O Lant was followed by another incomplete film, *The Dark Tower* (circa 1972). The new project was an experiment in stop-motion animation whose putative star was another Action Man figure, which Julie Blake and Lynne Darnell dressed as a prince with a sword. They constructed an eight-foot-long dragon, which Phil rigged to breathe fire. Clive created two plasticine harpies with grotesque faces, pendulous breasts, clawed feet, large flapping wings and writhing snakes for hair. Anne Taylor's sister owned a florist's shop on Smithdown Road, and an entire forest was constructed in its cellar by mingling real twigs and bushes with large plasticine rocks modelled with faces that would speak. Clive and Phil spent hours filming the prince as he moved through the enchanted forest. 'This was done out of a profound affection for Harryhausen,' Clive notes; but, in Julie Blake's words, 'we outgrew the project long before it was completed ... It was just not quite weird enough to maintain the interest of any of us.'

One day the friends went to Hale Beach with an assortment of costumes and masks, filming ideas for the planned production of the most sincere of these efforts: *Salomé*, a black-and-white expressionist nightmare shot in darkness with one hand-held light. Clive directed Anne Taylor in the title role, with Doug Bradley as King Herod. The cellar of the florist's shop was their stage, if only because it was the only place they knew where they could use smoke. 'It was damp and cold and half the time people were semi-naked,' Julie Blake recalls. 'We had to bend double, but we all spent days doing continuity or waiting to be filmed. Somehow we managed to maintain our enthusiasm. Clive and Phil did a lot of the camera work but Clive would get excited about a shot and everybody would have to have a look through the viewfinder which would hold things up further. We all had our moments of glory when we were beautifully lit, but sometimes we were also required to be ugly, this being essentially Clive's film. Clive had a thing about smoke and he also loved chiaroscuro. Getting the lighting right took hard work and the smoke sometimes got us into trouble; he wanted lots of it. Walls were painted with faces and demons. Next door flowers wilted.'

The footage was developed in the bathroom of Phil's house and edited by hand; Clive later decided to reshoot the execution scene at the IM Marsh drama studio. The finished film was screened occasionally for friends, including Helen Clarke, at the house on Broughton Drive where Doug Bradley and Lynne Darnell lived – and once at a special invited showing at IM Marsh. 'Screenings were always fun,' Bradley recalls, 'because we used to play music to it – in real time on the record player.' Salomé's dance was accompanied by Pink Floyd's 'Sisyphus' and cues from the soundtracks of *King of Kings* and *A Fistful of Dollars*. Helen Clarke's reaction to Clive's directorial debut on film was unequivocal: 'It has to be one the best things he's ever done – Bergman, eat your heart out.' But with the abandon that typified these years of his creative life, *Salomé* was put aside and effectively forgotten until 'The South Bank Show' unearthed and aired footage as part of a 1994 television special.

Clive wrote another play, *The Scream of the Ape* (circa 1974), whose cast would consist entirely of actors playing monkeys. The company travelled to Chester Zoo to observe the caged animals, then returned to the drama studio, where Clive encouraged them to lose their inhibitions and act the part of apes. Perhaps the first of his works explicitly to confront the theme of evolution, *The Scream of the Ape* was performed once, at IM Marsh, for an invited audience.

To confirm their collective approach to their art, the group began to call themselves the Hydra Theatre Company. Because a musical influence was strong, their next adventure was the creation of a fully-fledged musical named (for the Brueghel painting) *Hunters in the Snow* (circa 1974), which, according to the *Liverpool Echo*, was produced for eight pounds. Although written in the collective, Clive and Phil produced most of the words and music – with the able assistance of Julie Blake, who played piano, worked with Clive on several songs and contributed some of her own – and, for the first and only time, Roy Barker, who played guitar and composed additional music. Presented at the Everyman Theatre, *Hunters in the Snow* concerned the conflicting lives of a visionary artist named Jerusalem, played by Clive, and a salt-of-the-earth farmer played by Les Heseltine: 'A kind of life of Giotto with songs,' Doug Bradley says. 'I don't know why.' Bradley played Jerusalem's persecutor, the Dutchman, an undead witchfinder 'who is an early incarnation of Pinhead. He didn't sing any songs.' (Bradley also believes he received the 'best note *ever* from a director when I was the Dutchman; Clive said, *Dougie, I want you to say this line as if the North Wind was blowing through your eyes . . .*')

Rehearsals were all-consuming. Although the friends met at different homes and different places, the Barker house became, to Len's dismay, the fulcrum of an 'ever-expanding group of people who would come into the house, and eat the place out of biscuits and drink the place out of coffee'. It was stressful at times; Len didn't welcome the constant intrusion, or the noise. 'I don't know whether we're quite fair in this,' he says, 'but we felt we were more open house to Clive's friends than Clive's friends' parents were in reverse. You'd come in and there would be two or three lads writing something, building something, debating something. Which was good, it was an opportunity to discuss and debate.' But their hospitality soon reached its limits. In Joan's words: 'Because Clive was the leader, Clive's friends always came here. Which is lovely, I accept that, but after a while, when the coffee tin and the biscuit tin are completely empty, you feel something different.'

Clive graduated from the University of Liverpool in 1974 with a Bachelor of Arts Degree (with Honours) in English Literature. He skipped the graduation ceremony and moved fully into a life of creativity. Almost a year before, he had decided, perhaps in response to the rigid literary analysis he experienced in the classroom, to create a series of theatrical performance pieces that were liberated from tradition – and, indeed, even the spoken word. He decided to rent the Everyman Theatre for a week and present a series of original, experimental plays and performances that would be named after a troupe: the Theatre of the Imagination.

In June 1974, Graham Bickley, then playing drums in a rock-and-roll band, introduced Clive to Peter Atkins, the band's eighteen-year-old guitarist and singer. In Graham's view, Clive and Pete shared a common interest: they both read books. 'And that,' Atkins notes, 'was deemed sufficiently odd to make us soulmates.'

They met, appropriately, at Liverpool's Allerton Community Library. Atkins arrived alone, and as he browsed through the books, he noticed a young man staring at him. 'We sneered at each other. At each other's pretension. There was me – desperately attempting to be hip, a pathetic slave to fashion, a Bryan Ferry clone, prissy and preened. And there was this other guy, equally dreadful in a different way: round John Lennon glasses, stubbly bum-fluff beard, long black coat, straggly hair, the starving student – what I used to call the wannabe-Russian-poet look.' At that moment, Graham arrived and said: 'Oh, I see that you've found each other!'

The two seeming opposites found an immediate attraction: 'Half the reason for the contemptuous stare was that we recognized, in the pretension of the other, something that we, too, wanted to pretend to,' Atkins says. 'I actually wanted to pretend to be a Russian poet, and Clive actually wanted to pretend to be a pop star, so we had a lot in common right from the off.' (Indeed, both had regularly frequented the cardboard box of American comic books at Bascombe's.)

That very day, Clive introduced Atkins to Doug Bradley and Lynne Darnell, and the series of plays that the Theatre of the Imagination intended to mount with professional aspirations. By late afternoon, Atkins was rehearsing with them in the drama studio at IM Marsh.

Doug Bradley describes their haphazard technique: 'We would arrive one evening, and decide that we wanted to perform a twenty-minute mime based on themes to be found in the work of Edgar Allan Poe. And we'd kind of start, like kids playing in the playground: *You do this* and *You do that*, and at the end of the evening we had a twenty-minute mime called *Poe*, which was a mixture of "The Fall of the House of Usher" and "The Black Cat" and "The Tell-Tale Heart".' Rumours circulated at the college that the actors practised some kind of witchcraft; and Julie Blake was called to the principal's office when a caretaker found the remnants of a cigar in a toilet and thought the friends had been smoking marijuana.

Drugs were not an inspiration – the company had far too many creative influences, from Peter Brooks's adaptation of *The Tempest* to the offerings of the local film society, which screened 'art' films – where they discovered Bunuel, Fellini and Pasolini, as well as classic silent films and underground films from America, including *The Brig*, Mapplethorpe's *Robert Having His Nipple Pierced* and Andy Warhol's *Flesh*. ('Joe D'Allesandro became a kind of fantasy role model for me,' Doug Bradley says.)

The cinema brought a startling revelation, however, when some of the friends went to see Roman Polanski's *Chinatown* (1974), and Clive left in the middle, unnerved by the scene in which Jack Nicholson's nose is slit. 'I had a tough time with that scene,' he admits, 'and I still do.' Early in his years at Quarry Bank, he had been required to give blood – and he passed out. On the table next to him 'was a classically-beautiful boy athlete with flopping blond hair who I just adored from afar. So it wasn't bad enough to pass out, but to pass out beside this boy; because if there was any kid I wanted to be sure I looked butch in front of, it was this guy . . . and here I was passing out.

'On a day to day basis,' he says, 'I'm not a fearful person; but anyone smart knows that the world is a fearful place – and not just fearful to the body, but to the psyche. It's possible for the mind to get itself into a place in which the very business of being conscious is an agony. And I got that fairly quickly. I'm amazed that we're a species that can even approach the level of sanity that we do – because we have so little control over, or comprehension of, what the world is, and what our place in it is and what our purpose is; and that never leaves me. I feel as though I've spent most of my life walking a tight-rope, and that does not go away at all.

'The fear of blood is far less important, and far less significant in my life, than the fear of being insane, or the fear of losing control of one's sanity. And I'm playing constantly with fictional moments in which characters step over the boundary into a territory where they lose a little control – because things are too terrible, too unruly, too chaotic, too wild – and still come out the other side.'

The friends also began invading London for what Julie Blake calls 'feasts of culture'. Constantly short of cash, they sometimes hitchhiked and stayed in hostels – and, later, with friends from school – seeing six films in a day. 'There was nothing else that London had to offer that we were remotely interested in – but fringe theatre, West End theatre, mainstream movies, avant-garde movies, it didn't matter; if it was something that was interesting, we'd go see it.' London offered theatre unlike anything they had ever seen: the Lindsay Kemp Company at the Institute of Contemporary Arts performing *Flowers: A Pantomime for Jean Genet*; and at the Roundhouse, *The History of the World from Moses to Mao* by Jerome Savary's Le Grande Magique Circus. Mime appealed to them, and the idea that mime could collide with Genet was fascinating, if only because it seemed so forbidden. 'It was heavily homosexual,' Bradley recalls. 'We could come down to London, and we'd feel that we were in touch with something different, original and dangerous. Again, the feeling of being in touch with a subculture.'

Another epiphany came when, in 1973, the friends travelled to Paris for ten days to visit Sue Bickley, who was working there for a year as an *au pair*, and who had an empty flat available. Crowding together in the flat at night, they spent their days in cemeteries and museums and theatres; for Clive, his first experience of the continent was intoxicating and influential. 'There were a number of revelations,' he notes. 'The Louvre, and Gericault's painting *The Raft of the* Medusa. It is a massive painting, a cinemascope painting, and it's just so morbid and overwhelming – and that was very important.'

There was also something in these experiences that seemed to challenge the Liverpool of the 1970s; Clive and his friends felt excluded from the artistic life of the city, which seemed trapped in the grip of a socialist ethos; in Pete Atkins's words, 'a ten-years-too-late, post-Alan Sillitoe notion that art could only be about the struggle of the proletariat.' But there was no conscious feeling – not yet – about London as a destination of their ambition. It was 'a kind of Babylon' for the friends: a nice place to visit, but not a goal of their lives. Yet the latest direction of the troupe – mime – was doomed to failure in Liverpool, where there was no fringe or alternative theatre circuit. 'We were in the right time, but the wrong place,' Bradley says. 'We should have been in London.'

The Theatre of the Imagination rehearsed for almost a year, including the period of Clive's final exams at university. 'I think he was going slowly crazy,' Bradley says. 'Words were becoming almost meaningless to him.' In Lindsay Kemp he had seen something totally other, unique – and, in theatrical terms, very pure. 'So inevitably, when we came back to Liverpool, the influence of what we had seen came on strong.' At the beginning of the year, Bradley was living at home and a university student. 'By the end of the year, I had left home, I was unemployed, and my world had changed forever.'

The Theatre of the Imagination took to the stage on three consecutive nights at the Everyman, where the company performed a full-length 'theatre piece', *A Dream*, followed by *An Evening of Four Shorts*, and then a lengthy play, *The Wolfman*. 'This was going to be our putting childhood behind us,' says Julie Blake. In anticipation of the rigours of the week, the company performed the four shorts in a room above Brook House, a pub in Smithdown Road, as a trial run. As with earlier performances, every element of the production – promotion, handbills, lighting, costumes, props – was handled by the company on a budget of nothing.

A Dream, performed on the first night at the Everyman, was conceived by Clive as 'an atheist's *Pilgrim's Progress*'; it was influenced by comic books, Robert E Howard's *Conan the Barbarian* and mime, but included words – and the music of Wagner and Sibelius, which was meant to invoke its mythic emotions. Interaction and spectacle were vital, as Clive urged the strength of the visual, encouraging the actors to take inspiration from silent films, where expression and movement conveyed unspoken words. *A Dream* offered the company's first true epiphany, and one of its most memorable anecdotes. Julie Blake played a hermaphroditic angel. Nude with false male genitalia, painted yellow-gold, and wearing a headdress built on the spot from a wire frame embellished with bits of colour lighting gel, she materialized at the moment when Doug Bradley, playing a pilgrim known as the Warrior, lay at the front of the stage, having just battled a minotaur played by Clive. Another actor walked behind Julie, shining a hand-held light through the headdress.

When she appeared on stage, everything stopped – and a disembodied voice, someone in the balcony, a member of the audience, said, 'Oh my God, how beautiful.'

'It seemed that was entirely what we were driving for,' Doug Bradley says, 'to get somebody to involuntarily say, in a voice loud enough to be heard on stage, *Oh my God, how beautiful.*'

An Evening of Four Shorts, held the following night, focused on darker, more grotesque and, indeed, surreal subjects. *Poe* was a sinister enactment of the horror master's more grisly moments in mime. *The Fish Bride* was a short play with dialogue about a mermaid in a fairground freak show. In the quasi-science-fictional *The Egg*, Doug Bradley played a man on an operating table, with bulging papier-mâché eyes; he was skinned, and his guts spread around him. *Grünewald's Crucifixion* was a re-enactment, in mime, of the eponymous painting, with Clive playing Christ descending from the cross – 'all done very slowly,' Julie Blake notes, with lengthy rehearsals intended to find the right poses, paying infinite attention to detail.

The mime performances were akin to silent films, although the actors' lips did not move; someone once told Bradley it was like watching theatre with the sound turned down. It was certainly not people in white faces and black leotards, pretending to walk against the wind. 'That stuff we hated,' says Bradley. 'I remember us all going to see Marcel Marceau, and we were bored to tears. It's tremendously clever, and it leads you nowhere, it doesn't do anything at all. We were doing physical comedy; it was like a cross between silent movies and circus clowns.'

The final evening was devoted to *The Wolfman*, a wordy, poetic play written by Clive without the collaborative improvisation that marked the other pieces. Despite its title, it was only vaguely a werewolf tale, and had developed out of a non-musical version of *Hunters in the Snow* called *A Private Apocalypse* (circa 1974), which the company had performed for another invited audience at IM Marsh and which Clive entered, without success, in a drama competition. 'A play often horrific, sometimes blasphemous, occasionally very beautiful,' its poster declared. 'Men into wolves, women into visions, bishops into crustacea.' Perceived by some as avant-garde and others as incomprehensible, Clive refused to explain its content. A rabbit was skinned on stage during the performance, which only added to the controversy. Despite the fine audience reaction to the other performances, *The Wolfman* was generally disliked, and (in Clive's words) 'thoroughly trashed' by the *Daily Telegraph*. Even Len and Joan Barker felt that the diverse performances were 'way out ... we came away totally confused'. Roy remembers his parents being disturbed: 'I didn't feel comfortable because they didn't feel comfortable; I couldn't quite see what it was all about.'

After a year of work to put on three nights of performances, the company felt confused and defeated. 'We couldn't get people to see the things, in the first place,' Bradley says, 'and we couldn't get critics along. We'd get disillusioned, and disheartened. In a way, we didn't know what we were doing. The work was extraordinary, and it had an audience, I'm sure of that; but we didn't have an idea how to reach that audience – none whatsoever. As a consequence, we had an audience that was completely wrong.'

None of the pieces was ever performed again, with the exception of *The Fish Bride*. There was an emotional lull. Doug Bradley became a kind of administrator, attempting to obtain bookings, but between his lack of knowledge of the business and the nature of their material, the Theatre of the Imagination was getting nowhere. In retrospect, Bradley feels that they were simply careless – that the pieces could have been performed further and perfected into commercial projects. 'It was all a rollercoaster. We didn't care where we were or what we were doing or where we were going or where we were doing it or why we were doing it. But it had this kind of inexorable energy that carried us all along.'

Bradley felt that he and the company should belong to the world of theatre, but Clive's perception was different: although he believed strongly in the idea of a theatre company, he thought that the imaginative life of the work was more important. 'He was always looking for something else, for something new. Because today's ideas are bubbling up, so what was yesterday? And I do genuinely believe that his internal life, his imaginative life, is more important to him than what's immediately going on around him in his environment. So he tends to remember the one and forget the other.'

By then the friends were living together. A closely-knit group who worked together constantly, and hard, it was the inevitable next step; and Len and Joan Barker felt that it was time for Clive to leave Rangemore Road. Clive, Phil, Sue, Doug, Lynne and Julie crowded into a run-down rented house on Lidderdale Road, off Smithdown Road in a poor district of Liverpool, for one very miserable winter. Pete Atkins was their semi-permanent house-guest: 'They obviously had electricity, but it feels, in memory, as if they didn't. It feels Dickensian, that there were candles burning and things dripping from the ceiling. And it almost was that miserable.'

The house, with cockroaches stirring in the fireplace, 'frightened the socks off of me,' says Len Barker. 'The drabness of it all. I'd done my spell in life of pigging it in a low-grade place, and you sort of want more for your sons, don't you?'

'It was quite trying,' says Julie Blake, 'because it was a terraced house, which was falling down, basically. The electricity would go out; plaster would fall from the ceiling.' The bathroom walls were white plaster, which they didn't bother to decorate; in time, everyone began writing and drawing on the walls – Julie suspects that Clive started the practice – until one was completely covered in graffiti, including the phrase 'Shit light upon the heads of the damned' (which later would feature in the *Books of Blood*).

The friends adopted a small mongrel dog, Anu, and drew up vague rosters of who would handle the day-to-day chores, taking turns cooking. Clive could make a good curry, but more often Lynne and Sue would prepare the food. There were terrible arguments about house-cleaning, and about people not pulling their weight, which was complicated because some of them were at home all day while others were at college.

While living at Lidderdale Road, Clive wrote another book-length manuscript: *The Adventures of Mr Maximillian Bacchus and His Travelling Circus* (circa 1974–75), four interconnected fantasies for children, illustrated with detailed pen-and-ink drawings, about the eponymous troupe and their conflicts with Maximillian's sworn enemy, Dr Jozabiah Bentham. The book was a 'love song' to his friends, says Pete Atkins: 'An idealized wish of what the Theatre of the Imagination might become. Clive thought he was Maximillian Bacchus, and we were his travelling circus – although, in the illustrations, Max looked more like Phil Rimmer, and Jozabiah Bentham, the villain, looked like Clive.' The manuscript was so good that his friends believed a breakthrough – and possible bestsellerdom – was imminent. 'It was the first time that I'd seen the commercial possibilities in what Clive was doing,' recalls Julie Blake; but several publishers passed on the manuscript, and Clive, as always, moved on to the next creative project.

In 1975, the friends abandoned the house on Lidderdale Road and moved 'over the water', across the Mersey to a ranch-style white bungalow in Irby on the Wirral called the 'Ponderosa' – and soon known affectionately as the 'Pond' or the 'Ranch'. This modern detached house, and its distance from urban Liverpool, seemed to relieve the domestic pressures confronting the friends, and it became a 'creative den'.

Their personality was soon stamped upon the place; its occupants, Len Barker reports, included 'a great run-down, salivating St Bernard dog that the previous owner left behind, and a monitor lizard that found its way into the central heating duct'. (Len was summoned to get it out.) 'You see, other people get cats, dogs . . . our son has to get a bloody monitor lizard.' Clive donated the lizard, who they named El Greco, to the Chester Zoo, but the plaque acknowledging the donorship was stolen from the zoo in the wake of Clive's success. Another member of the menagerie, introduced to Clive by Helen Clarke, was Paul O'Grady – now the celebrated drag artist and game show host(ess) Lily Savage, but then an infamous female impersonator known as 'Lily LaDouche' (he once walked to the local off-licence dressed as Margot Fonteyn).

At the Ponderosa, the friends tried to transform themselves into what Doug Bradley calls 'the Merseyside Branch of Warhol's Factory'. Clive lived in the moment, constantly creating ('just being and doing,' Bradley says) and his encouragement was boundless. 'You *can* achieve your dreams,' he told them. Living together seemed to expand their creative potential, and life at the Ponderosa was a non-stop exercise in writing poetry, children's stories, fiction, scripts. Plays were prepared and rehearsed; films were planned and made; paintings were constantly in progress; photographs were taken – and everything was created for their own entertainment. 'The end product didn't matter,' Bradley notes. 'It was the *doing* that was important.' They supported themselves in various ways: Bradley worked at a library; others taught or modelled; some were still at university.

Although they tried to obtain grants and subsidies, they found them-selves coming up against what Pete Atkins describes as 'committees and panels of very upper-middle-class people who nevertheless thought that money should only be given to people who were making art about the struggles of the working-class – socially- or sociologically-based art, rather than philosophically- or psychologically- or metaphysically-based art, which is what we were trying to do. Having made ourselves sound like martyrs there, we were also snotty little bastards. I mean, we really thought we were the best there had ever been, and that soon, when we moved to London, when we played the West End, when the world succumbed to us . . . that was the attitude. And meanwhile, we would play to audiences of eight or whatever, and not get any money. All living on welfare.

'In one way or another, we all started to go slowly bats. And I'm sure that was to no small extent a reflection of this crazy house we had chosen to live in.'

There was one very special outlet for the anxieties and pressures of the house, says Julie Blake: their dog Anu and the footpath leading to Thurstaston Common. 'What kept us all sane at times was that there was a beautiful common at the end of the road, and the dog was a very *walked* dog; because we always used that for relaxation.'

Clive's room at the Ponderosa was an extension of his room at Rangemore Road, filled with books and artwork, rough sketches and photographs. There were constant, and very spontaneous, drawing sessions (which, as Julie Blake notes, usually began with the words: 'all right, take your clothes off'); but Clive also began to experiment with still photographs, which Phil Rimmer would sometimes develop and manipulate in the darkroom.

Although his friends seemed happy and productive, Clive experienced an agonizing episode of depression – a disease that would return to haunt him much later in life. His emotions and, indeed, his sanity seemed in crisis; every emotional contact, whether personal or in film or music or television shows, and however mundane, brought him pain. His theatrical project had failed, and he had reached a strange plateau; there were things he wanted to express, but he could not seem to find the medium to convey the subversive content of his work to many people. He feared the grandness of his ambition, and in his years at the Ponderosa, he contemplated how he might reinvent himself to accomplish the things he wanted so much.

The most moving and mature of Clive's experimental films, *The Forbidden*, was started at the Ponderosa, and shot haphazardly between 1975 and 1978, without being truly completed. It began as a straightforward adaptation, as a screenplay, of Christopher Marlowe's *The Tragicall Historie of Doctor Faustus*, which Doug Bradley worked on with Clive. 'Had we shot it as it was written then, what we would have turned out would have been very much *Doctor Faustus* as made by Derek Jarman. But Clive being Clive, as soon as the ink was dry on that, everything was moving on. He'd left Marlowe behind, and there were specific ideas that he was interested in, and he didn't want to make Marlowe's *Faustus*, he wanted to make his own *Faustus*. So he was off and running with that. It had rapidly become something quite, quite other.'

One of Clive's drawings from that time, titled 'The Forbidden', depicts a surgical incision; he soon talked about filming Pete Atkins as a skinned man. He was fascinated by a book of photographs of anatomy and surgery, and the anatomical etchings of Vesalius. After several intermediate drafts of a screenplay, the friends pooled their money to buy a new camera – a 16-millimetre Bolex – and Clive began shooting the silent film, which presents extraordinary images that clearly presage his motion picture *Hellraiser* (1987). Pete Atkins plays a Faustian seeker who is flayed alive for his trangressions, then stalks a wounded landscape as an anatomical etching given life. Despite its powerful and provocative content, the film was abandoned; as Doug Bradley notes: 'Clive would outgrow things while he worked on them, or thought he'd come to the end of them before they were completed, and he was off on another angle by then, doing something else.' *The Forbidden* was unfinished and unedited until 1994, when its existing footage was assembled under Clive's supervision and screened, along with *Salomé*, at the National Film Forum in July 1995. Redemption Video subsequently released both films on commercial videotape and DVD.

Another unfinished short film, *Soiled Dressings* (circa 1975), was inspired by the hospital bucket Clive found, which had become a mascot of sorts for the friends. Written and directed by Doug Bradley, and shot on Super 8 film, it featured Pete Atkins as a vampire and Clive as a vampire slayer, but that is all that anyone recalls about its content: 'I can't remember details,' Bradley says, 'but it was all about sex. Everything I was doing was about sex at that point.'

Under the influence of Pasolini, Bradley also drafted a screenplay for an eponymous film about Dionysus; and he and Lynne Darnell managed to obtain a grant from the Merseyside Arts Association to make a puppet film called *Children of Pride*, based on Alistair Graham's book *Eyelids of Morning: The Mingled Destinies of Crocodiles and Men* (1973). The film joined the growing ranks of incomplete projects.

'There were an awful lot of things begun in that period that didn't get finished,' Bradley says, 'until – and I think this is significant – suddenly, around 1975 or 1976, Clive said, *I think we should do some theatre again*. And it was almost like there was a collective sigh of relief.'

The relief was personal as well as professional. The communal living relationship was disintegrating, and Julie Blake moved out, soon followed by Clive, who went to live with a lover, John Gregson, in a flat in Liverpool overlooking Sefton Park. 'Clive went from strength to strength there,' notes Julie Blake. 'He started to structure his day around his writing and making sure that nothing interfered with that. He started to see himself and to treat himself as a writer. He started to learn how to like himself, for there were ways in which he didn't very much. Almost symbolically he dyed his hair blond.'

In 1976, fulfilling Clive's vision of a theatrical company based on the Italian Commedia dell'Arte, the friends reinvented themselves as a mime troupe called the Mute Pantomime Theatre. They had no training – merely, as always, ambition; and, in Pete Atkins's words, 'We just decided it would be cool.' Clive was the writer and director of record, but it was workshop theatre, originating in his concepts and then interpreted and transformed in rehearsal. 'He didn't believe in the sanctity of the text,' says Bradley. 'And that readiness to mutate, readiness to transform, has been very useful for him.'

The result, *A Clown's Sodom* ('A Herlequinade') (1976), was their first real breakthrough to popular success. Unlike the earlier, experimentally-constructed mimes, Clive prepared a written scenario – a play without dialogue but best summarized by his programme notes:

> *The First Act*: the Seduction.
> It is the dog-days, in Sodom, the city of the plains. Against the abattoir wall Pulcinella guards the bulls for the slaughter, while his brother Lot sweats and calculates his profits. Herlequin, pursued and hungry, attempts to steal meat, is caught and punished by Lot. In the shade of the wall, Pierrot courts Columbine, while Herlequin sows his revenge.
>
> It is afternoon in the garden of the Patriarch and Lot's dalliance is interrupted by the arrival of a beautiful, veiled woman. Lot proposes and is accepted. The couple leave to be married.
>
> The Wedding Night. In the street outside Lot's house, Pulcinella reveals the secret of the veil to Pierrot, while within, the Patriarch serves his bride.

The Second Act: the Suckling.
It is the following spring in the garden, and Herlequin furthers his revenge, while Pulcinella transforms behind the wall.

Again the dog-days. In her bedroom, Lot's wife dreams of a child, and Pierrot is blind with love.

It is the hottest day of the year, and Lot prepares for the slaughter, but Herlequin burns down the abattoir, and in the conflagration his brother is burned to Death.

The Third Act: the Slaughter.
The following night, Columbine is stalked on the streets of Sodom and meets her death. Lot and his wife, homeless and begging, are also on the streets and the Patriarch is executed for the murder. Herlequin and Pierrot must bury the corpses.

In the garden, Herlequin is filling in the graves when the Angel of Death appears and destroys Sodom. The earth splits and Lot and Columbine are resurrected to claim their beloveds. The couples are saved from the Apocalypse.

In the desert, the Patriarch and his family flee, averting their eyes from the burning city. Lot's wife becomes salt and Herlequin returns to the ruins.

Beside the last wall standing in Sodom, the Surgeon prepares to officiate at the wedding of Pierrot and Columbine . . .

After months of rehearsal, the first – and only – performances took place on April 26 and 27, 1976, at the Eleanor Rathbone Theatre at the University of Liverpool. It was a collision of stories: the Biblical tale of Sodom and Gomorrah told with Commedia dell'Arte characters, using a Commedia dell'Arte scenario in which Harlequin (tellingly renamed 'Herlequin') changed sex by trickery, but convincingly enough to have a baby. Stylish moments would diverge suddenly into silent-film slapstick, when cast members would literally 'kick the bucket' (using, of course, the familiar 'Soiled Dressings'). The performance was praised highly in local and regional newspaper reviews – and, for the first time, the company received a guarantee-against-loss for a night's performance. The shows were sold out.

Bill Scobie, who saw *A Clown's Sodom*, felt that the mimes were 'very much in the tradition of Marcel Marceau, but the classical mime company rather than Marceau himself. It depended on fluidity of movement and expression, very much like the ballet – and simple but highly-expressive costumes. The language of the gestures was very clear, and you could read the story rather like a ballet. There were moments in it that gave you a *frisson*. Clive succeeded in his mimes – and in many ways in his literature, particularly in his novels – by doing the classic thing: if you want to do a telling piece of theatre or literature, you fulfil all the expectations of your audience, and then push them one bit forward – not two bits forward, like *Finnegans Wake*, but one bit forward, like *Ulysses*. That's what he did in his mimes; they did what you expected, but there was a twist always, something happened you weren't expecting. In one of them, there was a feeling almost that there was going to be speech but it didn't happen – and to that extent, they were very exciting.'

Although the company received an offer from Northwest Arts to take *A Clown's Sodom* on tour, they declined, with some disagreement. Doug Bradley comments: 'The notion of getting in the back of a van and touring around the northwest of England to do this show was of no interest to Clive at all. It was of interest to me as a burgeoning actor, but to Clive I think there was an element of casting pearls before swine. Which reflects my own sense of frustration, that we were doing it in Liverpool and not in London.'

A slow boil began within the group; each of them, for their own particular reasons, was looking south, toward London. Sue Bickley left the company, and Julie Blake, unhappy with the pursuit of mime, followed. They were becoming frustrated, and the frustration was becoming an issue. Despite their fiery talent and ambition, nothing was being achieved. 'The belief in what we were doing was absolute,' Bradley says, 'but we were doing it in a small corner where no one was watching. And I think that became an issue for the first time.'

It was another new beginning. Clive had learned a crucial lesson of the theatre: that success was measured by the number of seats that were filled. He could not be boring. He had to acknowledge that his audience had paid good money to experience what he offered, and that he had an obligation to deliver:

'What the theatre does is that you are made very painfully aware, very quickly, when you are boring. You have no recourse when the theatre is empty. It breaks your heart. It really does. People leave, shaking their heads. And of course that happens, lots of times. And I'm a quick study. I realized that if you do certain things, you can start to hook people. Mystery will do it. *Who was that person? Why did that person say that?* You learn very simple rules of seeding the narrative, so that you give the audience information by increments, coaxing them along – at the same time, giving them the most elaborate and interesting emotional rollercoaster that you possibly can.'

London – and fame – was calling.

7

LONDON CALLING

DOG (1978)

NIGHTLIVES (1979)

THE HISTORY OF THE DEVIL (1980)

On the whole, he had enjoyed himself very much down there in
Hell, and he insisted that the devils were not such bad fellows after
all.

—FRANÇOIS RABELAIS, *Gargantua and Pantagruel*

There was no turning back: London called to the friends, and over a
period of two years, in 1976 and 1977, they heeded its call, migrating
south in pursuit of their dreams.

Earlier, when Doug Bradley and others had suggested that the company should seek its fortune in London, Clive resisted, arguing that
Liverpool offered not only a familiar and comfortable home, but also
a certain cachet, distant and aloof from the stages of the capital city.
But his views soon changed – as the result of romance.

Just after his graduation from university in 1974 – according to the 'official' version that Clive would later offer to his parents and certain friends – Clive met John Gregson at Kirkland's, a Liverpool wine bar. In fact, they met at Sadie's, a small, late-night gay bar. 'It was the first time I had ever been to a gay bar,' Clive confesses. 'I went at Julie Blake's behest.'

John, a bright and handsome mathematician from Lytham St Anne's, worked for a local insurance company and had a sincerity that matched his good looks. The son of a butcher, he was 'unpretentious, down-to-earth, a solid man – fearless in lots of regards, and much more comfortable in that world than I was . . . He treated me very well and very kindly and gave me confidence I had not had.' For the first time in his life, Clive had fallen in love. 'He was a very bewitching fellow. He was very handsome. Although we were essentially the same age, he was very *old*. He was very determined to have me in his life – and he pursued me with a relentlessness which surprised the hell out of me, because I'd never had that before; it was a new experience.'

In his teenage years, Clive had wrestled with a growing understanding that he was a homosexual. It was not a matter of sexual conduct, however, but of sensibility: his imagination celebrated sexuality in all its aspects, while physically he lived in a place and time that urged the repression of desires for persons of the same sex. Even after his graduation from university, 'I was not devoted to the idea of making a choice,' he says. 'I was making a lot of erotic art. Most of it was gay, and I was selling a lot of it. But it was mostly from imagined things. I was very sexually anxious. I was anxious about how attractive I was; I was very insecure about it. I had been a fat, short-sighted, round-spectacled kid; and I'd grown out of that. I'd gotten myself some contact lenses, again at Julie Blake's suggestion. I think I was sufficiently comfortable that I felt that, whatever I am – and in whatever proportion, I'm going to discover in time – I'm certainly, in some measure, a gay man. And I was very unbothered by it. In a way, it felt like, *Well, it'll sort itself out.* I was a lot more concerned, honestly, about my art and my storytelling and my picture-making.

'I remember, for instance – and this is one of those sort of regrets – there was this beautiful man, Tim. He was one of Scobie's protégés, and he was designing a set for an opera, and he wanted me to come and paint with him. He made overtures to me, and I just fled them. I was seventeen or eighteen. I wasn't ready. I just wasn't ready for being drawn into gay life. Gay life still doesn't interest me, actually.

'When John and I were together, we would go out on a Saturday night, and we would go down to the same bars and see the same people, and it would get very boring very quickly. The dinner parties . . . it was just not interesting – and it's never been interesting to me.'

Although his circle of friends from Quarry Bank was a mingling of boys and girls, Len and Joan soon realized that the attraction was not love, but art: 'It wasn't the sort of group where people were pairing off, with girlfriends or boyfriends' – although Doug Bradley and Lynne Darnell did fall in love and eventually married. 'There was nobody that he used to bring home for tea or anything,' Joan notes.

Clive's one romance with a girl was shortlived. Dyan was eighteen, while he was only fifteen, and Joan was quick to express her disapproval: 'Dyan came up, and it was a rough day, and she took off her tights, which I remember were black, and put them over the lounge radiator. And when I went in with coffee for them, she had her feet up on the radiator. I went right off her. Straightaway.' As did Clive: on another day, while in Dyan's bedroom in a state of entanglement, he looked over at the bureau and saw a photograph of the young man from Rosedale Road who had been accused of murdering his aunt. In a fabulous twist, Dyan turned out to have slept with the alleged killer. 'She was mischief,' Clive recalls. 'No question.'

By the time of his graduation from university, Clive was open to his friends, and in his social existence, about his sexual orientation. He had had several dalliances, including one that had lasted a year; and then lived with John Gregson for almost two years in Liverpool. 'I enjoyed, for a period of time with John, that sort of growing into being a gay man, and part of a couple; but I found that stultifying, very quickly.' On a whim – and a desire to see America – Clive left for Boston at the invitation of William A Henry III – the late culture critic for *Time* magazine, and great-nephew of a neighbour in Rangemore Road. Henry, an influential thinker who twice won the Pulitzer Prize, 'kept' Clive for several months, which nearly ended his relationship with John Gregson. 'I loved Bill deeply,' Clive says. 'I still do. I value his contribution to my growth as an artist. He was an extraordinary guy, and totally original. We argued; we disagreed about every-thing. But he was a marvellous man.'

In 1977, after Clive moved to London with John, he took his brother Roy aside during a visit home, looked at him 'very seriously' and told him that he was gay. Roy answered: 'We guessed that.' He was testing the waters, preparing to tell their parents; but Roy tried to reassure him: 'I think they already know.'

'To me,' Len says, 'it was one of those unspoken things. It was an awareness that all wasn't as I would have wished it to be.' Finally Clive told Joan, in the kitchen of the house on Rangemore Road: 'He had some silly idea that I didn't know about it.' Len recalls: 'One day he said to me, *You know, I'm gay, Dad*. And I said, *Look, I recognized it*. I shouldn't have said *I feared it*, I should have said *I anticipated it*. And that was the end of the matter.'

'We were sorry,' Joan says, 'because we would have liked him to have been married and have a family. But it's just part of your life. As long as Clive is all right, that's all that matters.'

'My Dad went through a lot of tortured thinking,' Roy says: '*Well, could it be my fault?* That's the sort of thing he went through then, be that right or wrong now.' Len would never escape his discomfort, or his awkward feelings of guilt; but with time, he would reconcile his emotions with an undoubted love for his son. Indeed, in my last conversation with Len, he talked at length about his feelings about his son's sexuality, and concluded with this simple statement: 'I personally am most grateful that Clive is what he is.'

Soon after Clive began living with John Gregson, they decided to leave Liverpool, moving in 1976 when John took employment with an insurance firm in London. 'We both got, from each other, the courage to leave Liverpool. We would not have gone to London with-out each other.' Doug Bradley and Lynne Darnell followed, staying for a time with Clive and John; then Julie Blake came and stayed with Lynne and Doug. By 1978, like dominoes falling, Phil Rimmer, Sue Bickley and Pete Atkins arrived, and the company was again complete – although Julie soon decided to retire from acting, and instead devote herself to helping with lighting, set designs and administration, becom-ing a 'general dogsbody'.

Clive and John found a modest flat at 29 Mountview Road in

Crouch End, a section of North London with a reputation for horror in fiction and fact. It was here where Peter Straub wrote his break-through novel *Ghost Story* (1979), and it was here where, after a visit to Straub's house, Stephen King wrote the short story 'Crouch End' (1980), which immortalized the perplexing 'ladder' of the area's parallel streets. It was also here, in nearby Cranley Gardens, where the infamous Dennis Nielson murdered male prostitutes and drifters, burying their corpses in his drain. And here Clive Barker would write his famous *Books of Blood*.

In the late seventies, however, Clive was as distant from stardom (or, indeed, financial well-being) as anyone could imagine. London was an exciting place, but money was in short supply. He had no job and no income. A DHSS official considered him unemployable when he listed his occupation as 'writer'. His earliest earnings came on a lark, when, for a minimal fee, he illustrated a few centrefolds for gay S&M magazines that Scotland Yard seized from the publisher, along with his original artwork, and consigned to the flames ('which,' he notes, 'I always thought was the ultimate compliment. It was real confirmation that the stuff worked and they needed to burn it'). Like most of his friends, he lived 'on the dole', collecting welfare cheques while devoting his attention, with John's kind support, to the stage.

London was the place of greater opportunity; in Pete Atkins's words, 'we eventually realized that it was the only place to be in England' for their theatrical pursuits. The mood of the company was strong: 'We were all committed to art, whatever it may be. And it was a collective endeavour; it was fun. Life was good.' But it was also harsh, and occasionally Dickensian: 'It was sort of warming-your-mittened-hands-over-the-single-ring-in-a-bedsit,' Atkins says. 'I remember some very cold nights, and misery. But the potential of London more than outweighed any temporary living discomforts.'

The flat in Crouch End became a regular gathering place. John was very neat, tidy and domestic – the kitchen was his domain – and, despite Clive's talent with curry, he probably never cooked a meal. In the evenings, the friends would visit, sitting crosslegged on the floor with coffee, talking about plays and films and fiction – and their ambitions. Idle time was spent in every imaginable creative pursuit: writing sonnets, dabbling with artwork and experiencing all that the city had to offer, indulging what Atkins calls a 'complete breadth of taste as consumers, and therefore this great breadth of taste as practitioners'. But each day, they rehearsed for hours and hours, in apartments, even outdoors – and didn't worry about money. 'We were poor,' Atkins notes, 'but it was a very strange time in England – everyone we knew was poor. Everybody I knew was on the dole. There was a huge recession, and there was a wilful desire to be on the dole: *What, you mean the state is going to give me money? Great, I'll get on with what I want to do . . .*'[1]

The seventies were a time of renaissance in British theatre, with an increasing influx of diversity and populism in stage productions. In 1976, the National Theatre (since 1988, the Royal National Theatre) occupied its new facilities on the south bank of the Thames, and in 1982, the Barbican Centre opened as home to the Royal Shakespeare Company. By 1980, more than three hundred small repertory theatre troupes were active in England, performing in pubs, private clubs, fringe theatres, colleges and outdoor venues – and London was the epicentre of this movement, the place where careers could be made, and broken.

Over the next few years, the collective of friends would evolve into a full-fledged professional acting troupe known as the Dog Company. London brought them a new sense of purpose, and an attitude and ambition that were increasingly professional. Doug Bradley recaptures their motivation: 'Okay, in the past we've had a lot of fun, we've spent a year rehearsing stuff that's only been performed once. This is clearly nonsense, and it has to stop. If we're going to carry on doing theatre work, we have to form ourselves into a proper theatre company, we have to have proper rehearsal times and proper scripts, we have to have proper bookings, and we have to treat ourselves as professionally as possible. Which is what we then proceeded to do with the Dog Company.'

The first step on the path to professional triumph was the creation of new and provocative material. As Bradley recalls: 'After sitting us down and saying, *The word is dead – we're a mime company*, Clive now said, *we can't quite express what we want to express, and we need words to take us that extra mile.*'

Clive had found words again, and he was intent on bringing his unique visions to the stage as a playwright and director. The brief but evocative experiment with mime was abandoned in a series of new and ever-more-ambitious plays that he penned between 1977 and 1982. The grammar school actors who became the mature talents of the Dog Company proved themselves astonishingly versatile: they started with farce, then moved to musicals, then straight theatre, then became a mime company before returning to straight theatre, with occasional performances for children, all in a period of five years and without extensive professional training or supervision.

The playwright's art is a tenuous thing. Plays, unlike most other contemporary forms of writing, are protean texts – the stuff of the living word. The stage is a place of performance rather than posterity, where a play, true to its name, is enacted each time in a different way. Unless a performance is captured on film or video, the text, if one exists at all, exists in eternal flux. Even when recorded, a play is subject to grand revisions in production, design, casting and direction; thus Shakespeare has enjoyed renditions with New York street gangs (*West Side Story*), Nazis (*Richard III*) and mafiosi (*Men of Respect*). The subtle essence of acting – the whim of vocal expression, gesture, and stance, and even an arched eyebrow, a curl of the lip, a well-timed breath – can add to, or subtract from, a play's substance. Unless written by a master – a definition that, more often than not, requires the author's death – most plays live only in weathered typescripts and in the memories of their performers and audiences, as ephemeral and as difficult to reconstruct on paper as an opera, a rock concert, a political rally.

The stagecraft of Clive Barker survived for decades in this midnight realm. His early pantomimes, many created through improvisation, were typically performed without scripts. The texts of several early plays have been lost to time. His mature plays passed through a series of texts, none of which he intended as definitive or to be recreated with certitude on stage: each was thought of as a draft, a work in progress, that would evolve with each new performance. Those who witnessed Barker's plays on stage thus saw, perhaps unknowingly, to the heart of his dilemma and challenge as a creator: his constant striving to create new and diverse means of expressing his ideas.

With his later success in fiction and film, Barker's career as a playwright was memorialized in two collections, *Incarnations* (1995) and *Forms of Heaven* (1996), whose titles underscore his avowed addiction to storytelling as a 'process of putting on skins; of living lives and dying deaths that belong to somebody else'. They also assert the common themes of his seminal plays: the rending and healing of flesh; death and resurrection; and the Christian paradox of god in man, or man in god. These extant texts offer entertaining and provocative reading, and an opportunity for a detailed consideration and critique of an evolving talent.

Barker's first new play was *The Magician* (1977), a farce in the style of the Commedia dell'Arte about Caliogstro the Alchemist. Although written and rehearsed in London, it was performed only in Liverpool – on December 1, 1977, at the Liverpool Academy of Arts, and later, for grant money, at Quarry Bank's Morrison Hall. The friends also performed *The Magician* as street theatre, with great success, in a tough Liverpool neighbourhood, Netherley, with an audience that Pete Atkins describes (again in Dickensian terms) as 'hardened housewives and street urchins'.

Several months later, the company returned to Liverpool and the Everyman Theatre with another new play, *The Sack* (1978). In this tragicomedy, women tie up a man and place him into a sack, obtaining their revenge on him and on mankind – imagery that would be resurrected in *Paradise Street* (1981). All concerned agree that *The Sack* was the least of Clive's plays – and best forgotten; indeed, its sole performance was at the Everyman on June 26, 1978.

The homecoming was a disaster. Bill Scobie was chairman of the Hope Street Festival that year. Not realizing that Clive had again taken a new direction, he invited the Dog Company to perform at the Festival on an evening devoted to mime; its performance would be followed by a major Kathakali ensemble. Clive contacted Scobie before the performance and said, 'By the way, we're putting in some words.' Scobie replied: 'Well, this is supposed to be mime, but all right, if you like . . . I trust you.' When the Dog Company performed what Scobie felt was 'a stylized spoken-word play based on Jean Genet's *Querelle*', he was stunned. 'It was all words . . . The mime had gone,' Scobie recalls, baffled and disappointed to this very day. 'The mime had been replaced by what happens when mime artists try to talk. It's not ham acting, it's something . . . different. It just doesn't work. And it's interesting that they ultimately tried to do the same thing on the London stage, and it didn't work there, either. I didn't mind, it was great fun, but the language was obscene – some of the words were not suitable for the audience of ten-year-old girls and their fathers. It was a Genet story, so it was very dubious in its content. And all these mums had brought their children to see this mime company. We had a terrible to-do afterward.'

The Festival Committee refused to pay the Dog Company, and left them sitting in the foyer for an hour; Scobie had to intervene, finally threatening to compensate the performers from his own pocket. 'The people who didn't rush away with their children ten minutes after it opened might well have realized it was interesting to see, because once again some of the themes of the novels came out. But it didn't have the quality of the mimes. The Dog Company was a superb mime company, it really was; it could have travelled in its own right. I thought the Dog Company was the best mime company I have ever seen. Absolutely the best.'

Scobie did see, however, that Clive was now a more mature, more involved person: 'I think the Dog Company had made him into a more sophisticated person. Certainly he had become more laid-back. And that's probably what enabled him to write, really; that he'd become more involved with things, with more of a clinical eye.'

The Dog Company also planned to stage, in collaboration with local composer Joe Riley, a multimedia performance at Liverpool's Anglican Cathedral; but their application for a council grant was rejected. 'A crying shame, this one,' Doug Bradley says. 'A life of Christ complete with dancing Chinese dragons. I would have played Christ (has anyone ever played him and the Devil?), and for the crucifixion Clive planned to have me suspended in multi-coloured cloths from the central arch over the nave.' The grant committee included Alan Bleasdale, a successful Liverpool writer and proponent of the politically-driven theatre of the time. When Clive appeared before the committee to appeal its decision, he felt genuine antagonism. Bleasdale said: 'I've read this thing, and it seems like a prime candidate for Pseud's Corner' (a feature of the satirical magazine *Private Eye* that skewered bad writing). When Clive responded, 'Ah, you'd prefer a social tract,' Bleasdale replied: 'Quick, aren't you?' The appeal was rejected.

Dog (1978) was the first full-length play rehearsed and performed in London, and it gave the company its name.[2] It was a transitional work – from Liverpool to London, and from mime to the spoken word. While the friends still lived in Liverpool, Clive had revised their successful mime, *A Clown's Sodom*, into a darker version, *The Day of the Dog* ('L'Abattoir d'Amour') (1977), excising much of the humour; it was performed in London at the Cockpit Theatre as part of a mime festival. Staged in three parts, *The Day of the Dog* is set outside a mythic abattoir, its Commedia dell'Arte antics best summarized by Barker's production notes:

The Morning
It is dawn, and the working day begins: the cleaning of the tiles; the sharpening of the knives; the preparations for the slaughter. To the Abattoir wall comes Dog, in search of meat. He is punished for attempted theft and instigates his revenge. The Lovers meet in the rising heat of the day, party and go their ways. Dog dresses in offal and seduces the Butcher. All retire for a light lunch.

The Afternoon
It is getting hotter. The Butcher sleeps and dreams of the evening. Dog produces the second part of the revenge and goes on to wound the Lover. As the heat becomes unbearable, the Hunchback seems to see Dog transformed and the Butcher goes mad.

The Evening
The heat has soured and thunder threatens as Dog dines. There is no rain. The whore falls in love with Dog and remembers herself too late. The Butcher wakes, the unveiling takes place and there is slaughter outside the Abattoir. Dog plays his third trick, the Lovers are reunited, the Hunchback exists.

Night and rain.

In London, Clive transformed *The Day of the Dog* into the stageplay *Dog* – a four-hour opus, if played in its entirety. As its duration alone suggests, the Dog Company was not only ambitious, but also high-minded in pursuit of their art. 'We thought we were too big for the league we were in,' Bradley notes. In retrospect, it is an extraordinary tribute to the character and resourcefulness of the friends that they were able to stage Clive's imaginings. At four hours, with two intervals, *Dog* was written like grand opera, and required operatic staging; but the company performed without a budget. When the play premiered at the British Council, Bradley recalls, 'the sets weren't finished, the costumes weren't finished, and we were playing to an international audience, lots of whom didn't speak English . . . and they loved it.'

Barker's script for *Dog* was intentionally complex and dense, and is without doubt the most daunting of his plays: 'I wrote the plays as source text that would be sampled; none of the texts was ever played in their entirety, nor were they intended to be. Maybe in my dream arena, I wanted every word and every comma and every dot played; but I was always very keen on the malleability, the protean quality of the theatre experience, and *Dog* is almost the perfect example of that, because it is very, very dense. You can't play the first pages of this; I mean, the first pages are a long speech, it's something where maybe you end up playing ten lines of the sixty. Now, this was in some sense a counter-response to Stoppard, to Beckett, to Shaw – and I mention three disparate writers who are nevertheless obsessive about the fact that every word will have to be in place. I always liked the idea of an abundance – that, when you first go to *Weaveworld* or *Imajica*, or Quarrel's speech at the beginning of *Dog*, you probably won't get it all. But I want the drama to be driven by very accessible feelings: desire and revenge and love and the desire for justice, all those things which drive the characters on a page-by-page basis.'

In the dog days of English summer, bucket-carrying Thomas Quarrel (played by Phil Rimmer) confronts local citizens and, in time, Louis Erasmus Sugarman, whom he serves as dogsbody. Although sweetly named – 'genealogy has its little jokes' – Sugarman is a former politician and Member of Parliament who has retired to domestic tyranny, where he 'brings out the bawling baby in everyone who crosses him'. He lives above the law, on an enclave named Sugarman Street, his fantasy of an island in the churning sea of reality: 'Plato on his bookshelves, and blood on his stoop . . .' (Doug Bradley played

Sugarman, padded out to a bulky sixty inches at the waist. 'I used to have terrific fun with him. And I used to enjoy upsetting Clive enormously, because I would go and sit on his knee, in this vast costume, in character, and start talking to him: *I think you need a monologue here, Clive. I think you can write this for me.* And he used to get very upset – *Get this thing away from me!*'[3])

Although Quarrel notes that canines have been behaving like humans – standing, dancing, conversing – Sugarman Street is visited by Daniel Beard (played by Clive), a man who has taken the name of 'Dog'. He is soon followed by his would-be master, John Palmer (Peter Atkins), an otherwise rational banker who has muzzled Dog, and who fails to see that he is a man who walks on all fours. 'If Palmer finds his dog, he'll go back to his insipid wife and they'll die together.'

Dog eludes Palmer, leading the banker into revelation. '[T]his dog was thinking more than canine thoughts: watching us, smiling at our foibles, encouraging us in our idiocies.' He wishes to 'lie down in Sugarman's house', usurping the politico and his paternal authority.

The shapeshifting, genderbending Dog is 'naturally what all men want to be; he's helpless to be anything but coarse and gruff, his delicacy, out of that hide, couldn't be prettier. After the beast itself, I wouldn't be content with limitations.' Palmer, entrenched in domesticity, tells his wife (Lynne Darnell, who played all three of the play's female roles) that he desires the state of the dog – and liberation from the flesh, and family, and the finite fiction of humanity:

> I'll only be a dog 'til this season is over; after that, I'll be a fish for a while, it'll be cool in the water; you can come and see me in the ocean, I'll be a whale perhaps; after that, what's it to be, with a whole Protean world in front of me: perhaps a lizard, how would that suit you, dear? or a bird, or a cat, or a tortoise, an otter, rhinoceros, antelope, flea, fly. I'm out of my skin, Eloise, and flayed into life; I never want to see my children, or you, or my work, or my mother, or my father, or my history, or my future again. I am indefinite, and you have no part of me.

The play indulges romantic dalliances and diversions as it circles on itself, the comic absurdities and metamorphoses creating a chaotic whirlpool that, at last, summons revolution. An army of dog-men charges into a pitched battle on Sugarman Street and finds victory, pillaging Sugarman's residence. But during the fracas, Dog is shot, and as his dying body reverts to human form, his army of canines disperses, leaving him – having had his day – to die.

In the finale, the survivors debate the meaning of the play's events:

PALMER:	It makes a peculiar story; how in God's name do I tell it?
JACQUELINE:	I would have thought that was obvious, John. Tell it as an allegory.
PALMER:	What of?
JACQUELINE:	Whatever you like: political instability.
PALMER:	Dog would turn over in his grave.
JACQUELINE:	If he had one.
QUARREL:	No, it's not about politics.
JACQUELINE:	What then?
QUARREL:	The frailty of human endeavour.
PALMER:	What endeavour?
QUARREL:	A good question.
PALMER:	What about a savage indictment of human stupidity?
JACQUELINE:	Or a hymn to the senses.
PALMER:	Or a critique of corruption by power.

Quarrel concludes for them all: 'Rubbish.' By tweaking the audience and critics with these inevitable interpretations of the play, Barker urges them to remember that the essence of his 'peculiar story' is entertainment. Although *Dog* ranks moderately in the hierarchy of Barker's works for the stage, it marks another significant step in his evolution as a creator. From this time forward, art was not an isolationist impulse, shared and understood by Clive and his friends and collaborators; it was intrinsic to a dialogue with an audience. With his return to the word, Barker was intent on becoming a communicator.

Dog took the young playwright and his actors onto the rough-and-tumble stages of the London fringe circuit, premiering in a cellar theatre-space near Leicester Square; it also provided the centrepiece of the company's first true 'season' of performances in 1979.

The Dog Company's reputation and audiences began to grow with another new play, *Nightlives*, which was performed in several venues, notably on May 14–17, 1979, at the York and Albany, a pub theatre on Parkway in Camden. In the words of a Dog Company solicitation: '*Nightlives* [is] a thriller about identical twins, one a major political figure, the other an underworld boss, who meet and exchange lives for one unforgettable evening. Designed in black and white, the production recreates the style and hard-boiled wit of early gangster films.' As its title suggests, the play concerned the 'secret selves' of its characters, and their transformation, at night, from one life into another – transvestites, prostitutes and their clients, politicians and their mistresses. 'If this play is anything to go by,' the *Camden Journal* reported, 'Mr Barker and his company are sure to be around for a very long time. It is fringe theatre at its most entertaining and best. Don't miss it.'

Although the cultural climate was increasingly receptive to the diverse and original productions offered by the Dog Company, the political climate was changing. After Margaret Thatcher and the Tories regained power in 1979, London's fringe theatre began to wither beneath the tightening fist of the British Arts Council; and considerations of public morality accompanied many funding decisions.

Every effort to obtain funding from the Arts Council met with failure. The Council's Jonathan Lamede – known to the Dog Company as 'La Merde' ('a Thatcherite toad of the first order,' Bradley says with a smile) – came to see *Dog*, but left at the first interval. He later called Bradley and said, 'Have you seen the People Show? You should go look at what the People Show are doing and copy them.' (Lamede later told Bradley that he felt Clive had nothing more to say than George Bernard Shaw. 'I still don't know whether that's a compliment or not. I don't think he meant it to be.')[4]

Between 1977 and 1979, Clive wrote what his friends consider 'the great lost Clive Barker work': a monumental stage play, *The Comedy of Comedies*. Intended as the final flowering of the Dog Company's collective obsession with Commedia dell'Arte characters, the play would have been performed over three consecutive nights, at an estimated total length of seventeen hours. It was never rehearsed, but there was one reading by the actors, without stage action: 'It took us an entire day, and it was extremely good,' says Pete Atkins, who fondly remembers its 'typically Barkerian' finale, in which a patriarch burns his possessions in the face of death.

By 1980, however, the Dog Company was experiencing fundamental changes in its relationships on and off the stage. Although Clive lived comfortably with John in a new flat on Hillfield Road (just thirteen houses from where Peter Straub wrote *Ghost Story*), and Doug Bradley and Lynne Darnell lived together happily, rehearsals seemed increasingly volatile. As Atkins notes, 'We were a bunch of relatively young, untried people, so we hated each other half the time, as much as we loved each other. There were rows: people would quit, people wouldn't quit.'

Of the original six members of the Dog Company, Phil Rimmer was the first to announce he was leaving, although he stayed for another year; Pete Atkins was the first to depart, in September 1980. 'I had been swept up into this very intellectually-rigorous world when I was seventeen, and I'd missed out on a bad boy adolescence.' He returned to Liverpool 'to form a rock-and-roll band, drink beer and chase women . . . I think I needed to get out from under Clive's wing for a time.'

Clive also felt the need to move forward; he yearned for the 'single signature' respect that only being a painter or composer or novelist – or, indeed, playwright – could produce. His friends and, increasingly, others recognized that his talent was singular, and he felt a growing need to be paid for his work, with money and recognition. As Atkins puts it: 'He was looking for a way to get people to know his name.'

In 1980, Clive decided to retire from acting and devote his full attention to writing and directing the plays – and, hopefully, to making the Dog Company into a successful professional endeavour. The decision surprised Clive's family, but not the members of the company. Although he was an effective and very idiosyncratic actor, he was not a great one; and the time was right. 'It was necessary for the company, necessary for the productions,' Doug Bradley says, 'that we had a director who was standing entirely outside.' Later, in the short story 'Sex, Death and Starshine' (1984), Clive would ruminate on the peculiar fate of the stage director: 'A director is the loneliest creature on God's earth. He knows what's good and bad in a show, or he should if he's worth his salt, and he has to carry that information around with him and keep smiling ... The job isn't about succeeding ... it's about learning not to fall on your sodding face.'

For the first time, the Dog Company sought out new actors to join its ranks – a move that transformed its identity for the better, proving that the troupe was defined by professional ability, not personal relationships. The initial recruit was Oliver Parker, a recent drama school graduate who was introduced to Clive by a mutual friend. Parker had earned a place at Cambridge, but he was intent on a career in theatre and film, and he decided to join the Dog Company instead.

Later that summer, twenty-one-year-old Mary Roscoe, a drama student at the Rose Bruford College, noticed a small advertisement in the trade magazine *Stage* seeking an actress for the Dog Company. She 'did something that no other actor from my drama school did: I accepted a job which had no Equity card, no money and no future whatsoever ... but it did have Clive Barker – and Doug Bradley, Lynne Darnell, Julie Blake and Oliver Parker.' Her first meeting with the company was a day-long audition – 'it was the most intense audition I've ever had in my life, ridiculously long, really.' Clive showed her a painting by Goya and asked her to improvise her feelings. 'When you're that young, it's quite rare to meet people you feel have something really important to say. I didn't even know who they were; it wasn't like meeting Stephen Sondheim, so it was a question of just being true to the intuition of it ... It didn't feel like I had to impress them, it felt like I was on a journey with them – that we were going on an extraordinary journey, which, of course, we were. It was a huge risk, and it was about taking a great leap of faith, really – for them as well as me.'

Mary soon took charge of finding venues for the performances. 'In those days you could hire a room above a pub for sixty pounds a week – the same rooms are twelve hundred pounds a week now. It gave me a terrible grounding in not being an actor who waits for their agent to ring – a spirit of *go out there and find it and ring someone up and make it happen*.'

The company was working on a new play called *The History of the*

Devil, or Scenes from a Pretended Life (1980),[5] with rehearsals taking place, as they had for several years, in an upstairs room of the Earth Exchange, an old house operated as a co-operative in Archway, North London. After each day's rehearsals, Doug Bradley and Lynne Darnell earned money downstairs making soup. (All of the company members were still living on the dole, receiving about forty pounds a week for food and rent, which left little money for clothes, and certainly less for costuming, props and promotion.)

Although Clive was now a full-time writer and director, the rehearsals – surrounded by the smell of baking lentils and bread – proceeded with the improvisational quality of earlier productions. Once a scene was written and learned, its words and textures would be explored, with the actors encouraged to suggest alternatives and embellishments. 'Clive was rushing in every day with rewrites,' Roscoe says. 'There were fierce discussions about the characters, and arguments about what was happening. When I say arguments, I mean debate. I don't remember anyone having a big tantrum or storming out or anything like that; it had to do with really understanding what we were trying to say with this material.' The collaborative spirit continued: everything from design and construction of props and sets to costumes, make-up, transportation, publicity, was done by the company members. 'Members of the company were not simply actors,' Roscoe says, 'they did everything. The philosophy was: *I'm not just an actor; I make this company happen.*'[6]

After nearly ten weeks of rehearsals, *The History of the Devil* premiered at the York and Albany in Camden. The pub's empty upstairs room, painted black, could be hired as a makeshift stage and, in the best tradition of fringe theatre, people would pay a small sum to come up from the bar with a pint of lager and sit in folding chairs, hoping to be entertained. Within a week, word of mouth brought in sell-out audiences of sixty people a night (which is good for fringe theatre, as Roscoe notes: 'You quite often and still do play to three people a night if it's not getting good publicity').

The play opened to a tape of the Rolling Stones' 'Sympathy for the Devil'. Clive had sculpted a devil's head out of papier-mâché, and it was wired so that it rotated and looked at the audience as they arrived. 'We had a mixture of comic-book brilliance,' Bradley says. 'The scenes were very short and very fast; changes in location all the time. The audience was whisked through about twelve centuries of history, and certainly they had no idea of what we were going to be doing next.' Bradley played the Devil; it was his favourite Dog Company role – and one that belongs in the same stable as the Dutchman and Sugarman and Bradley's most famous incarnation, Pinhead of the *Hellraiser* films.

'The Devil's tale,' Clive writes in the play's production notes, 'is the tale of our own confusion, ego and inability to live without hope for Heaven.'

> His wings removed, Satan is dropped into the world wounded, and though he conceals his frailty well enough, putting on a fine show of dispassion, he's never far from throwing back his head and raging like an abused child. If the play persuades its audience to look at what this mirage of external evil is – in short, an excuse; a brushing off – then it has done something of what I intended.

Created with the company's financial limitations in mind, *The History of the Devil* required only six actors and a minimalist stage, decorated with words instead of sets.[7] Its storyline, however, is as epic as its title portends. Lucifer himself stands trial, and the evidence spans thirty centuries and the globe, with characters, locations and atmospheres changing with the mesmeric quality of a newsreel.

'History always begins with a cry,' we are told, 'of anger perhaps, of jubilation, of panic–' A scream echoes, and a frightened woman staggers onto the stage, telling of a hole that has opened in the earth, birthing a howling beast. 'A shout, yes. And finally, silence. But in between? (*Expansively*) The great panorama: the triumphs, the casual atrocities. Love, death. The spectacle of the world cut open.' In these few lines, Barker states his précis: that history is like life, and that the history of that eternal bogeyman Satan – a 'pretended life', indeed – offers lessons crucial to our own existence.

To the London home of barrister Samuel Kyle comes the Demon Verrier – 'Less than an angel, more than a man' – who summons Kyle to defend the greatest criminal in history: the Devil. He flies the lawyer to Kenya and Lake Turkana – 'jade with stagnation, stinking in the sun' – where a primitive courtroom has been erected in the black sand, '[s]ixty miles east of where Eden stood'.[8]

Enter Catharine Lamb and Jane Beck, lawyers for the prosecution. Catharine is an aggressive, ambitious barrister, while Jane is a subdued pragmatist whose research suggests a simple conclusion: 'When it comes down to it, he's an unexotic thug like all the others you've put behind bars. Five thousand years old, but a thug.' Cue Lucifer: '*ENTER THE DEVIL, SMILING. HE IS A STAR IN HIS OWN ROTTED FIRMAMENT. AS GLAMOROUS – AND AS ARTIFICIAL – AS ANY HOLLYWOOD ICON. A COAT OVER HIS SHOULDER, PERHAPS. SUNGLASSES, PERHAPS. PERHAPS NOTHING.*' He seeks the mercy of the court with words that echo Jane's prediction: 'I come before you a supplicant already tried by history: treat me as the pickpocket I am. It's my only crime . . . No Leviathan. I'm so remarkably . . . unremarkable.'

The issue is whether the Devil may at last return to Heaven. Dyspeptic octogenarian Felix Popper, the only jurist willing to hear the case, summarizes the law:

> [B]y the terms of his exile, his appeal for a return to the City of God is to be judged by us, the humanity whose world he's shared. If it's found that his ministry tended more to evil than to good, he'll be condemned to earth indefinitely. If, however, his Advocate can prove his time on earth hasn't adversely affected mankind, he must be judged innocent and returned to Heaven. Whatever the jury – whose pure and invisible souls are watching us even now, twelve just ghosts and true – whatever they decide, to that judgment the defendant is bound.

The witnesses are summoned, one by one: 'This is not a dream-play; not a medieval mystery play, parading semi-symbolic figures for a moral purpose. It's a history.' When the Archangel Michael proves unavailable, Catharine calls a peasant woman, Ulla Shim, as her first witness, and the scene is transported to 1212 BC and a snowy wasteland in what is now Russia. Ulla sees angels – Lucifer and his allies – falling from the sky. He is wounded, wingless and apparently insane. 'There were tears on his face. Human tears.'

The defence summons Yapshi Kanishka, a twelve-year-old boy from 88 BC, living in a Greek settlement besieged by barbarians. There, the Devil persuades Callimachus, despondent over his wife's adultery, to open a gate for the invaders. He has orchestrated the massacre for a simple reason: 'Curiosity . . . If you were given power over a species, wouldn't you want to examine their passions? It was my sentimental education.' Underscoring the play's subtext about the evil of passivity, Kyle argues: 'It demonstrates my client's . . . impartiality. At no time was he responsible for an act of violence. He has always been a spectator.'

Catharine then calls Jesus Christ to the stand; but he, too, is unavailable, and the Devil offers Christ's diary, 'given to me at Golgotha, by his far from virginal mother'. The passage describing Christ's temptation in the wilderness proves far different from the New Testament version, with Christ persuading the Devil to arrange for his crucifixion. 'I was the dupe,' says the Devil.

> Here was me, thinking I was getting rid of a competitor, and in fact I was stage managing his apotheosis. I tell you, when I saw them fall down on their knees at Golgotha, I wept. I was tricked, tricked! – and you called me the Father of Lies. You put me on trial while he goes free. He gets a cult to himself, but my synagogue is blasphemy . . .
>
> The earth was given to me: remember that. I was to be Prince of the World. But now, it was Christian. Though I was an exile, they found me everywhere. Here's the Devil, they said, possessing pigs and small boys. Ha! Here's the Devil, they said, in everything diseased and putrescent. The world rose against me. Everywhere: slandered, my works twisted, my ambitions destroyed and my face dragged in fear and loathing.

And so it goes: with each new witness, a story of betrayal and death and damnation – and, in time, the Devil's alienation from humanity. He devises a simulacrum: 'To a creature such as myself, rejected by all and sundry, what better solution than to construct a companion of my own, without will except my word?' He brings the man-machine to England in 1799, to box the 'Star of Israel', prizefighting champion

Mendoza. Although invulnerable, the machine begins to cry, and Mendoza bests him. The machine tells its maker:

> You're frightened because there's something you haven't taken account of, that makes me dream, that makes me bow my head to little Israel. You'll never be Prince of the World, you know that: because there's a mystery here you can't fathom. And if I dreamt it, who was never in a womb, who had no childhood, how much more certain is it that flesh has it in its head, this nostalgia? Can you explain, engineer? How is it an engine, mere mechanics, aches to hold in its works a half-remembered beauty?

The Devil destroys his machine – 'it had no life, so there was no murder ... it was mine to kill' – and broods in Hell for a century. His wife, Lilith, demands to testify, recalling the excitement stirred in him by Darwin's *The Origin of the Species*, and Nietzsche's proclamation of the death of God. 'He said he had the opportunity to tread the earth now as its master ... He said he'd hold a war, and it would be called the Twentieth Century ...'

Seemingly defeated, the lawyer Kyle rises to offer his own evidence. His real name is Keipenhauer, and his grandfather Georg, a German soldier, met Lucifer on the Russian front at the end of World War Two. Georg holds a baby he has rescued from a mass grave, and the Devil confronts him: 'Germany, why do you look so unhappy? All the engineers of Hell couldn't conceive of this. I'm humbled. The teacher, taught. You've set the standard for a coming generation.'

KEIPENHAUER: It wasn't me –
THE DEVIL: It never is, Germany, that's the trick of it.
How shall we ever stop it when we can't
find the culprit? Owning up to evil takes the
courage of an innocent: an unresolvable state
of affairs.

He offers Kyle's grandfather safe passage in exchange for the baby. 'I let her go,' Georg confesses, 'to my shame I let him take the living child and bury her. Criminals I've known, always apparent; brutal men. I've showered with them. They were flesh enough. But this bland evil, so reasonable, so understanding. I never knew it. But it's The Devil himself.'[9]

The testimony is concluded. During a brief recess, Jane and Catharine ponder the fate of the men sent to Heaven to bring the Archangel Michael and Jesus Christ to the witness stand. One slit his own throat, while the other hanged himself after delivering a delirious message: 'Sleep: remember? – he told us he counted sheep going through the gates of Heaven so he could get to sleep. When he came back from Heaven, he hadn't slept. No more sheep, he said. Why? No shepherd, he said. Why?'

Catharine realizes then that the prosecution must lose and allow the Devil to return to Heaven. 'He's a vacuum. He belongs where there's nothing. Nothing to nothing.' In her summation, she argues:

> This creature came to us with a reputation so foul, that his name stood for depravity. But what have we found, when we look a little closer? That time and time again he is cheated by those he trusts, rejected by those he loves, and far from being the Great Manipulator, he's limped from one mincing failure to the next, crippled, loveless and defeated.
>
> Can we convict him? Any more than we can kick a dog with its bowels out, dying in a gutter? Look at him – wounded, and out of his season. Doesn't he look, in his confusion, in his cowardice, and in the profundity of his misery, a little like us? Let him go to Heaven – and never come back.[10]

The jury finds the defendant not guilty. The Devil abandons his minions and ascends to Heaven, but returns with an enraged scream: 'The City of God's empty! Do you hear me? ... She's put me in Heaven, locked me away forever, and it's empty! That's why your miserable warrant carriers slit their Christian throats! *God has gone.* I'm alone!' As the play ends, he implores the assembled audience: 'Don't let them send me away ... You need me, for justification. What will you tell your children to keep them quiet? What will you hang your crimes on? There's no harm in me. No harm in all the world ...'

*

With its strong central concept and clever internal history of errant human nature, *The History of the Devil* was the Dog Company's first attempt to take a play beyond a handful of performances and signalled another change in direction for both the company and Clive Barker. Oliver Parker and Mary Roscoe influenced their professionalism and gave them a sense of long-term potential. 'I think we injected a sense of a future for them,' Roscoe says. Ollie's family became their resident cheering section, attending as many performances as possible; his younger brother, Nat, would sit in the front row and laugh uproariously even though he had seen the play endless times. 'The Parkers became our patron,' Roscoe notes, 'and certainly gave us money. We probably wouldn't have got some of our performances on if it hadn't been for them being in the audience. Very often we felt we were doing the show *for* the Parkers; that if they hadn't been there, we wouldn't have been doing it.'

The History of the Devil was performed throughout London, in arts centres and church halls and pub theatres, before reaching its apotheosis in Amsterdam and the Edinburgh Fringe Festival. In total, the Dog Company would enact the play more than a hundred times, a number that exceeded the sum of all other performances in its history. Given Clive's evolutionary and improvisational approach to his material – and differing venues – it was rendered in several forms: 'There was the two-hour form for Edinburgh,' he says, 'because you only had two hours to play it in and be frazzled. There was the two-and-a-half hour version, and then a three-and-a-half hour version in Amsterdam because everyone was high as kites.'

In 1981, the Dog Company was invited to perform for a week at Amsterdam's legendary De Melkweg, an extraordinary 'artistic department store' where, for the price of admission, visitors might find a rock-and-roll band, improvisational theatre, performance art, and a cafe and a tea room (featuring *tee mit rum,* thick black tea with a liberal dose of liquor). Marijuana could be purchased openly; and on an upper floor, people gathered, smoking dope on scattered cushions, to watch the Dog Company perform. On opening night, the play was well-attended, but soon a group of four people left; later, nearly twenty people departed. Backstage, the actors huddled in confusion – *What are we doing wrong? Is it only because it's in English? What's happening?*

– but by the close of the performance, the room was packed. Only then did the company realize that this was the way of De Melkweg: 'An artistic understanding,' Roscoe explains, 'that allows *anything* to happen – avant-garde ballet, dance, music, theatre … Everyone's smoking dope, and they make this lovely tea with rum, and you watch whatever's happening. We performed this play to a bunch of dopeheads, basically, who walked in and out and treated it like a television – and then came back and cheered very loudly and afterward came up and were very earnest about what it all meant.' This curious but wonderful reception was bettered only by the company's pay: a flat fee, when the best that they had obtained in London was a box-office split.

The Dog Company gave the play its grand finale at the 1981 Edinburgh Fringe Festival – the mecca of British fringe theatre, which offered the company a vital opportunity for exposure, despite its legendary rigours. The three-week-long Festival, held in late August, is well known for actors working around the clock, sleeping on floors, building sets, distributing handbills and fliers, and then performing for an audience of one. Hundreds of plays compete for attention, and the company had to join the Fringe Society, find and hire their venue (St Patrick's Primary School, on Drummond Street), handle every aspect of their production and publicity, and, as Doug Bradley notes: 'Everything had to be fireproofed – we'd never bothered with that before. So every bit of scenery had to be fireproofed. And they weren't joking. The night before we opened, the fire department came round with big cigarette lighters and tried to set fire to our scenery.'

The History of the Devil was staged at 7:30 pm on Tuesday through Saturday from August 18 through September 5, 1981, followed by a 10:15 pm performance of *Dangerous World*, a one-hour play directed by Barker but 'devised' by Doug Bradley and Oliver Parker using the words and visions of William Blake. Parker played Blake in his final hour, while Bradley and others played characters Blake had written and painted, indulging, as promised by the Company's flier, 'an extraordinary range of theatrical effects: choral techniques, exquisite masks, mime, music and high comedy'.

The History of the Devil was a breathtaking success in Edinburgh and won a 'Twelve Best' award from the *Festival Times*. Within the first week, word of mouth and reviews brought hundreds of people to its performances. 'Few Fringe productions are at once so entertaining and so profound,' noted *The Scotsman*, while the *Guardian* described the play, to Clive's delight, as 'a mixture of *Decline and Fall, Paradise Lost, Perry Mason* and *Flash Gordon*'.

The effect of the popular and critical reception on the actors was extraordinary. 'The penny finally dropped for me,' Doug Bradley says. 'The idea was in my mind that *this* is what I wanted to be.'

Hailed by *Stage* as 'an artistic team full of interesting, intelligent ideas and with the courage to try them out', the Dog Company had become a fully professional organization, using solicitors to register as a non-profit making company with charitable objects. Its board of directors was headed by Oliver Parker's mother, and its patrons included his father, Sir Peter Parker; film actress Gayle Hunnicutt; and *Time* magazine culture critic William A Henry III. The company prepared an ambitious schedule for their 1982 season, developing promotional and fund-raising materials intended to allow them to sustain a series of performances in London and Europe through the spring and summer, culminating in a planned nine-week autumn tour of the United States and Canada, in which the company would perform and present workshops at different universities. Clive wrote furiously, creating three new and strikingly diverse plays – a historical fantasia, a blood-soaked Grand Guignol and a frolicking farce.

In 1981, the *Kensington Post* had written, quite prophetically: 'Playwright Clive Barker, still in his twenties, is already a master of his craft and clearly destined for success.'

That success was imminent; but it was not the success that anyone – save Norman Russell – had anticipated.

8

DOG DAYS

PARADISE STREET (1981)
FRANKENSTEIN IN LOVE (1981)
THE SECRET LIFE OF CARTOONS (1982)

In the lonely streets, unseen by man,
A little dog danced. And the day began . . .
— RUPERT BROOKE, 'The Little Dog's Day'

Despite the Dog Company's triumphs in Holland and Edinburgh, the experience did little to improve their lot in London. The running battle with the Arts Council continued, and repeated requests for grants suffered because the company declined to perform classics and proposed staging original work – written by Clive Barker – instead. After mounting seven original productions in five years without financial backing of any kind, Clive applied for, and finally obtained, a three-month bursary to write a new play, *Paradise Street* (1981); but ironically, the Council refused to provide the Dog Company with funds to perform it.

Paradise Street premiered at the York and Albany Pub in July 1981.[1] The play is set in Liverpool, on the street immortalized in the opening line of the sea shanty 'Blow the Man Down': 'As I was a-wal-kin' down Paradise Street' – a path that leads a traveller to the 'Holy Crossroads', where Paradise Street intersects with Lord Street, Whitechapel and Church Street. The play, a vague successor to *The Sack*, and precursor of the novel *Weaveworld*, is a funereal yet funny hymn to Barker's birthplace, imagining (in the words of the production notes) 'what it would be like if, in the depths of [winter], magic were to transform the city, replacing the grey with green blossom, and lending the people trapped in its streets a new perspective and a new purpose'.

The play proposes that Queen Elizabeth I, '[t]ime-travelling on the beatific light of her own glorious presence', arrives in present day Liverpool along with Ben Jonson and other members of her court (including an ape named Benny Butterblood). Gloriana desperately wants to know whether she has venereal disease – which Barker pre-sents as the fundamental concern of her reign (in Doug Bradley's words, 'did she or did she not have the clap, and if so, who gave it to her?'). A miraculous spring is unleashed on the city, and Paradise Street, haunted by a mad Irish poet named Mulrooney (who would resurface in *Weaveworld*, as 'Mad Mooney'), is the site of a complex intrigue. Bradley played the Earl of Essex, Robert Devereaux, as well as an archetypal scouser, Quinn Bonner. Oliver Parker played Quinn's brother, Shay, while a newcomer, Konni Burger, was Elizabeth I – since Mary Roscoe, impoverished, had left: 'None of us were paid, and I needed to earn some money – and I had to go get this ridiculous thing called an Equity card. In those days, you couldn't work in tele-vision or film without it. So it was me being practical, really. My heart wanted to be there, and it still is . . .'[2]

At the play's centre was a clash of cultures and perspectives – and, indeed, of dramatic styles. Framed by a masque, *Paradise Street* shifts briefly to contemporary urban realism before evolving into a feverish mingling of historical drama, farce and fantasia.[3] As the play opens – to the sound of that famous hauling song – a masquer announces: 'The subject's love.' But love, although simply stated, is extraordinarily complex, as a series of subplots demonstrate. Shay Bonner, a soldier and lout, has returned from a posting overseas to find his family home on Paradise Street demolished. Reunited with his former lover, Georgia Vaux, and his brother, Quinn, he cruelly breaks their hearts – and not for the first time. But this is the realm of Clive Barker, not the soap opera of 'Coronation Street', and petty passions soon succumb to far greater forces.

Like a divine presence, Queen Elizabeth I, although dead for four hundred years, descends upon Liverpool. With Gloriana's arrival, the chill and clouded city blossoms with warmth and vegetation, a garden flourishing in the midst of winter. She exists beyond space and time as an angelic creature of light – and because of her femininity. 'Men make these distinctions . . . it's their territorial instincts misplaced. They divide existence as they do land. Life here, death there, and a border between. They guard it with the Church, with science . . . only poets defy the divide, and even they can be sentimental about it. It's taken us four hundred years to realize that if the Golden World is to be won, and kept, it must be won with ambiguity.'

On Christmas Day, Gloriana queries a local nurse, Jude Colquohon, about the possibility that she has inherited syphilis. She proposes to mate and then travel back in time, bearing daughters who will establish a matriarchy and cure England of the twentieth century. Only one man makes sense: Jack Mulrooney, a displaced professor of mathematics and devotee of Charles Fort, who wants more than anything to witness a miracle. In his seeming madness, he offers a telling homage to the power of the imagination: 'I don't distrust the internal vision. I don't say what the mind sees is less than what the eye sees. I say there's a threshold, where one becomes the other. Where the fruit of the mind becomes edible, where the waters of the imagination become available to wash in. The rest is politics, the rest is sociology, the rest is commerce with dissolution and I want none of it.'

When Essex, still fixated on resolving the Irish question, kills Mulrooney, Gloriana resurrects him as her consort – it is, after all, Paradise Street – and life, and love, return to a forbidding normalcy.

Paradise Street was another transitional work – for the first time, the company worked with a professional set designer – but, despite good reviews, it was the least satisfactory of their major productions. An effective staging – one that was realistic rather than in the company's traditional symbolic mode – required funds that simply weren't available. 'It was a complicated play,' Doug Bradley observes. 'It was a difficult play; it was in many ways an unsatisfactory and unrewarding play, both for actors and for audiences. It had some extraordinary stuff in it – some extraordinary moments, extraordinary characters, extraordinary dialogue, language, sure; but it didn't quite all add up.'

The Dog Company performed *Paradise Street* for two weeks at London's Cockpit Theatre in October 1981, but by then, they were preparing another new play, the provocatively titled *Frankenstein in Love, or The Life of Death* (1981).[4] With this project came a significant decision: the company believed that this play should be directed by someone other than Clive. The decision, Bradley notes, was partly political: 'We thought, in terms of wooing the Arts Council, that it would look better – that Clive did not appear to be the great poobah in the company. It certainly changed a lot of things again.' Malcolm Edwards, who directed *Frankenstein in Love*, 'came at it with a completely different attitude. The attitude had always been an unwritten law about how the company perceived its work and went about producing it. Whereas Clive had always taken the approach of throwing everything up into the air – far too many balls for everybody to catch, but if people caught two of them, fine – what we had now was someone who was determined that the audience were going to see one ball go into the air, and they were going to be entirely focused on catching that one ball'. Many who saw *Frankenstein in Love* felt that its acting was the company's tightest, which may have resulted from Edwards's more conventional approach.

As its title suggests, *Frankenstein in Love* is the play that most clearly anticipated the horror fiction and film on which Clive Barker's fame would be based (indeed, its subtitle, 'The Life of Death', was used for the lead story in *Books of Blood Volume Two*). The text was 'designed to disturb and scare its audience; to take them by their clammy hands and lead them into distressing spaces, there to show them sights that they will not readily forget . . . plainly I was in pursuit of an experience that would push the audience to its limits.'[5]

It is a brilliant yet bleak affair that melds Jacobean masque, Grand Guignol and low-budget horror film into a unique rendition of the

Frankenstein myth while tweaking Andrew Lloyd Webber's West End stalwart *Evita* along the way. 'In its obsessive way,' report Barker's production notes, 'the play creates a kind of alternative world, where everybody is corrupted or corrupt, dead or dying; monstrous in form, deed, or both. A fantasia, if you will, on taboo themes, which refuses to offer much in the way of comfort to its audience. In that singularity of intention lies both its limitation and its potential for theatrical power.'

The curtain opens to a tableaux of crisis and carnage: '*THE PER-FORMANCE SPACE IS PART ABATTOIR, PART CARNIVAL, DEC-ORATED WITH BANNERS ILLUSTRATING VIOLENT SCENES FROM HISTORY AND FICTION. LOOPS OF COLOURED LIGHTS HANG OVER THE SPACE, MINGLING WITH BLOODY CHAINS AND BUTCHERS HOOKS.*' There are two scenic necessities: '*THE HEAD OF A MAN, IMPALED ON A POLE AND COVERED WITH STAINED CLOTH. A COLLECTION OF SURGICAL SAWS, DRILLS AND SCALPELS, LAID OUT AS IF FOR AN INTERRUPTED OPERATION.*'

After a blackout to explosions and screams, a spotlight offers up the shrouded figure of a dead woman (Lynne Darnell), who introduces the play:

> It is the last, long night of the world. The last, the very last. Tomorrow ... (*Shrugs*). Expect an apocalypse. How should I know this? Well, my name is Maria Reina Duran. I was, until recently, a palm reader, a fan-dancer, and alive. I'm now none of those. I came here tonight a walking corpse, to show you the story I read on my murderer's palms. I call it *Frankenstein in Love, or The Life of Death*. Some of this story has already happened, but the worst is yet to come. I can see the future. I know there are monsters out there tonight, roaming around, looking for love. And when they find it ... endless night.

This introduction – in darkness, heat and passion – signals Barker's inversion of Mary Shelley's classic novel, whose framing story was set in an arctic whose white sterility symbolized the cold rationality of science. The central character of the play is not Dr Frankenstein (here known by the first name Joseph) but his creation.[6] Maria is a victim (like her namesake, the child who died at Shelley's monster's hands) who acts as a mediator between the realms of the living and the dead.

The time shifts to the previous day, when Maria was still alive, in the nameless capital of a banana republic. The gruesome setting is a vault beneath the palace of deposed President Garcia Heliodoro Perez: the operating room of Frankenstein, its walls 'slimy with human grease ... Atrocities were committed here in the name of God and Science, acts so obscene they beggar words.'[7] Onto the stage marches a parade of bloody and bloodthirsty penitents whose words and deeds enact a horrific romance. In the words of Barker's production notes: 'Just as long as the audience feels trapped in an asylum with a cast of wicked, and occasionally inspired, poet psychotics, then the endeavour will be off in the right direction.'

The first to arrive is the cruel dictator Perez (played by Doug Bradley, who reappeared in the roles of Cardinal Armitano and Dr Frankenstein). 'They say he ate babies,' Maria notes, in one of Barker's self-parodic asides. 'Now don't look so shocked. Eating babies is the least of tonight's entertainments.' Overthrown by insurgents, Perez is a frightened fugitive, seeking refuge in Frankenstein's surgery but denying knowledge of the doctor's experiments. 'The dead don't stay dead down here,' Maria tells him. 'What's a mortuary to some was a cradle to him ... He was their mother; he kissed them into life, he suckled them, rocked them–' Frankenstein's work has expanded from creation to evolution, invoking the latter-day mythology of HG Wells's *The Island of Dr Moreau* (1896).

One of the revolutionaries, a dandy nicknamed Cockatoo, discovers Perez. The rebel leader, Cesar Guerrero – El Coco, the Bogey-Man, but in fact, Frankenstein's monster (played by Oliver Parker) – joins them: '*HIS FLESH IS A PATCH-WORK – PART RED, PART BLACK, PART WHITE, AND BADLY SCARRED. HIS LONG, BLACK HAIR IS KNOTTED. HE WEARS CLOTHES ALL OF ONE COLOUR, IN AN ATTEMPT TO UNIFY A BODY THAT SEEMS AT WAR WITH ITSELF. HIS GAIT IS UNEASY, HIS TORSO CROOKED. HIS ARMS AND FINGERS TWITCH; ONLY HIS FACE IS STILL.*' Barker's rendition of the monster (described in the cast list as 'a visionary') is more true to Shelley than to popular film precedents: he is an intelligent, loquacious being whose monstrosity is purely physical. In a compelling twist, the monster walks on fire, trumping the myth of his maker, whom Shelley termed 'The Modern Prometheus'.

Perez claims shock at the carnage of the vault – 'It's profane' – but El Coco disagrees: 'No. Quite the contrary. I think God probably approves.' A wild-eyed political prisoner, Veronique Flecker, emerges from her captivity in the mortuary, where she was violated sexually and scientifically. 'We had a Cardinal down here,' she tells them. 'He used to come to bless the scalpels, and then watch Frankenstein at work. He liked vivisections best.' She points to Perez. 'And him too–' With El Coco's blessing, she stabs the dictator to death. As Veronique exits, El Coco injects himself with heroin, calling out: 'Father . . .'

Cockatoo soon reveals the rational skin beneath his gaudy plumage. Divination, he tells Maria, will be outlawed: 'We're not having any more of that – no more superstitious stuff like that. It's one of the first articles of the Revolutionary Manifesto: liberation of the people from all sources of metaphysical conditioning. Everything from palm readers to the Pope.' But she reads El Coco's palms and finds senseless contradictions. 'Your hands, they're odd. They don't match . . . The life line stops and starts again. (*Left hand*) Success. (*Right hand*) Violent death. (*Left hand*) And yet success. (*Right hand*) Horrors, pain, murder. You commit murder. Many murders. (*Left hand*) Joy, marriage, love forever . . . There's no pattern to it. Just chaos.'

In a scene that anticipates the short story 'The Body Politic' (1984) and that underscores Barker's embrace of the subtext of social repression and class struggle in Shelley's novel, El Coco reveals that he is the ultimate revolutionary: even his body parts are in revolt. 'They don't belong to me,' he tells Maria, 'but I belong to them.'

EL COCO: This (*The left*) is a writer's hand. He died old and blind. He wants nothing better than to hold a pen and write fictions. He obeys me, sometimes.

MARIA: And the other one?

EL COCO: A dice-player. He shot his children, then himself.

MARIA: A young man?

EL COCO: Twenty-three. Impulsive, proud, angry. He wants freedom. He wants to be away, off like a spider to find a grave ... They hate each other, the writer and the dice-player. And you know what's worst about that? I can't pray (*Brings his hands together, they fight*) because they hate each other so much. (*Pulls them apart*) Is there salvation for a man whose hands won't pray?

As El Coco contemplates his rebellious body, the right hand grips Maria's throat and, with her blessing, strangles her. He eulogizes over the dead body, then offers up a telling dream:

> I dreamt last night, Maria. I dreamt all the men and women on earth were one huge beast ... It had a billion arms, this beast, and a billion eyes, and it was roaming through the stars like a wild thing peering behind planets, putting its head into the hearts of suns. Then it turned its head towards me, and its eyes rested on me, and I knew its look. It was searching for love, Maria, for another like itself, aching not to be left alone. It's the only thing we have in common – a lack of love.

At the altar of a pillaged cathedral, Cardinal Armitano kneels, praying for a miracle – 'a well-fuelled Ford sedan' – as he waits for Dr Frankenstein. Veronique arrives instead, offering what she says is a farewell gift from the doctor: a curious box. When the Cardinal places his hands inside, they are skewered by blades. He does not recognize Veronique, but she knows him too well: 'I was in Hell last time we met; naked under his needle, faceless. But I have friends you may remember.'

An unlikely pair of monsters – Follezou and Mattos – enter. One is skeletal, while the other is pulpy-fat and carries a bundle of tools.[8] 'You offend us, with that look of horror on your face ... Just because we've been tampered with, are we any less reasonable, less sensitive?' – or, in the famous words of *The Island of Dr Moreau*: 'Are we not men?' The Cardinal had witnessed their creation in the doctor's laboratory. 'You blessed the scalpels,' Veronique reminds him as the monsters close in. 'The slab was washed down with Holy Water ... You used to watch. Smiling. Why?' The Cardinal admits his hatred for all living things; but Frankenstein was different: 'Oh dear Joseph, he always loved humanity.'

> Oh yes. He had a passion for its intricacies, its strength, its elasticity. So he wanted to stretch it, shape it, remake it by his own rules. To make a law for the flesh, a physical morality, he called it. I just saw a blood-letter, a tormentor. And it pleased me, watching him silence their complaints, sluice out their minds with agonies. I'd put my finger sometimes, into their hot heads, buried in thought up to the knuckle, and see their lives go out a little further with each prod. That pleased me too. He worked out of love, I out of loathing.

Veronique was Frankenstein's special plaything: 'He tampered with you endlessly. You're just a jug, full of him ... He's changing you from inside.' Indeed, her body is sprouting wings, fur, feathers, and summoning strange appetites for sex and blood. Her predecessor in scientific shenanigans, El Coco, arrives, seeking the doctor: 'Each of these parts has a different father and mother, but he assembled me.' The creature was given life eight years earlier in a charnel-house in Prague: 'An abattoir and me its fruit, its marvellous boy ... I was a clean slate, with no memory of what this brain had been, but I knew my condition. Living corruption, a crowd sewn together in one skin. Anarchy in every limb, and bones that ached to go to dust.' When the house was raided, the creature made his way into the world, learning to play the part of a natural man and pursuing the doctor, 'faithful as only a son can be who longs to see his father's face ... Sons are always like their fathers, however deeply the resemblance is buried. I wanted to see him once more, know the miseries I'd inherit, then kill him.'

EL COCO: I've precious little control left over my
              appetites. I have to finish him off and forget I
              was a monster, make a new world.
VERONIQUE: Without monsters.

121

EL COCO: They [repulse] me. Magic, miracles, the pursuit
             of the impossible – it all repulses me. Give me
             order; give me calm, law, reason.
VERONIQUE: And what will you do with the freaks, lunatics,
             visionaries?
EL COCO: Purge them, for their own sakes. As Plato
             wanted to drive out the poets for the order of
             the state.

The monster aspires to humanity, but Veronique gainsays him: 'You'll never be human. Look at yourself. You're a walking cemetery, a paradox, a contradiction.' He laments: 'I can't live with my condition; and my condition is death, so I can't die from it. All I can do is try to forget.' In a scene that anticipates Lori's entreatment of sympathetic monster-in-the-making Aaron Boone in Barker's short novel *Cabal* (1988), Veronique urges the creature to accept his monstrosity and find hope in love, not in death.

El Coco joins Follezou and Mattos as they feast on the Cardinal's corpse. Then he adjures his adoring public: 'A free man knows he is free because his hands can do good or bad, and he is at peace only when he chooses to do good. If you are beside me and with me and in me, if you will be my face I will teach you to walk on fire, teach you to find that part of you which is without humanity, is strong and wise and deadly. And then my friends, we fire-walkers will take the world!'

The political problems of having an undead cannibal as the head of state are obvious. Even as President-Elect El Coco meets with American and Russian ambassadors, Maria counsels Cockatoo: 'You can't suffer monsters to live.' El Coco and Veronique are given over to Dr Frankenstein, who wants only to destroy his creation: 'I would have forgiven you but – *you never loved me!* You never loved me! I damned myself for you, and yet you never loved me.' He orders his lackeys to flay El Coco, and the creature's skin, stripped from his body, is hung on display; so ends Act 1.

Act 2 opens with the corpse of El Coco, wrapped in stained canvas and hessian, at centre-stage.[9] Maria returns to address the audience:

Of course, this isn't the end of the world. The end of the world was yesterday. You are already dead, you just remember having tickets to the theatre tonight and as your brain cools it dreams you're here. Soon you'll hear a hammering as they nail down the lid on you, and the only sound left will be the whine in your head. Frightened? No? I'll have to try harder. I know I promised a romance and I swear, there'll be love in the second act, albeit love in a grave.

A tailor, Camilo Bozuffi, seeks out cross-dressing pathologist Doctor Fook, who oversees the victims of the revolution and the plague of cholera that has followed in its wake. Bozuffi's shop was gutted in the rebellion, and he blackmails Fook into supplying him with cloth from the dead. When Fook argues that death is a commonplace – merely an absence – El Coco, skinned of his flesh, rises from beneath his bloodstained shroud with an argument of his own: 'I live by my will, and I will continue to live until my will is done.'

He seeks vengeance upon Frankenstein, and vindication of his people: 'The dead. The great, silent majority. The powerless nation. Well that changes from tonight. From tonight the dead will walk . . . they will get up from their pits and you will wish you had never been born.' He calls upon Bozuffi to make him a new skin, finely tailored from the flesh of the living: 'I want to seem a perfect gentleman.'

In homage to another classic horror story, Edgar Allan Poe's 'The Masque of the Red Death', Frankenstein and his puppet dictator, the drugged Cockatoo, hide in the Presidential Palace, fearing the taint of the people outside. Veronique is with them, quaffing blood, her face transformed with scales. 'Until we are without death,' Frankenstein urges, 'we will be beasts . . .'

[W]e predict our deaths, that's the unbearable part. We know it's coming. When we're children we think death's a kind of sleep, curable in a while. Gradually the truth dawns: death is a permanent complaint. We look at our bodies and we see them putrefying around our living minds and we know, finally, that the enemy is our flesh. The body is a prison and must be escaped by metaphysics, or changed by wit and knife and courage.

123

Freedom from death, Frankenstein contends, would mean freedom from fear and taboo: 'We could act and love and never think of darkness.' It is love, of course, that is on his mind: a love for Veronique, as the intended mother of an undying race of his children: 'I do it all of the same, indivisible love. For you, for them, for the future.'

Veronique has no choice but marriage, and asks Maria to gather skeletons and mummified corpses as the wedding guests.[10] When the ceremony goes awry, Frankenstein tears at Veronique's clothes and tells her of his mad ideal of love: 'Love has many faces, a smile is just one. A bloody sheet is no less lovely. A bare back, a lost life . . . all signs of love. Love is a wound, and a shaft that makes a wound. An emptiness suddenly filled to brimming.'

El Coco interrupts the assault: 'I've learned all I need to learn. I understand your nature, father. The selfless pursuit of life against all reason. I won't repeat your error . . . Look at me. Couldn't I pass for a man? Look! And so, appearing to be a man, I claim the right of every natural son to murder his father.' When he touches Frankenstein, however, blood blossoms in his hands. The doctor warns: 'That is the first law I taught you, son . . . To touch me in anger is to bleed.' Echoing Pygmalion's final words to Galatea – 'I have given you all my being, I only live in you' – Frankenstein tells his creation:

> You are my beauty, my body, perfected. All I was, drained off into you. When you went, my health went with you – leaving a moral morbidity I smell in my sleep. The acts I committed for the love of you. Acts I can never forget. I crawled into the bellies of the dead to fish out a little life . . . I have an appetite for it now. I have an unrelenting lust for death.

'I have a heart,' the doctor tells Veronique. 'Capable of feeling.' She clutches at his shirt – 'Show me your heart' – and tears the organ from his chest.

Fire surges into the Palace, but a waltz begins, and the lovers, reunited, dance into the sudden dark. Only Maria is left, and she has her own romantic rendezvous: 'If the world fails, so what? If sin disappoints, never mind. He will come, and at his arrival the trap is sprung . . .' Her consort, Death, enters and embraces her. She melts into his arms as the lights slowly fade to black.

Awash in blood, *Frankenstein in Love* is an unrepentant cavalcade of the grotesque that succeeds through its sheer audacity and a calculated strategy of distancing, and then entertaining, the audience. From Maria's opening monologue, which carefully announces that what follows is a *fantastique*, to its coy gallows humour, the play insists that it is a play, and, like the best of Grand Guignol, invites the audience's outrage and complicity. By its embrace of the Frankenstein mythology, it reassures and yet intrigues, and in its finale, Barker resurrects the moral centre of Shelley's masterwork, diluted by story and stage and screen: the need to acknowledge one's progeny.[11] It is a theme he would develop further in works as diverse as *Imajica* (1991) and *Lord of Illusions* (1995), and one that is central to an understanding of his aesthetic of artistic responsibility.

The life of death – the hideous progeny that Frankenstein dared to create but could not, in its imperfection, accept – offers a lesson both simple and sublime for the living: '[A]fter death, love is the only hope we have.'

Frankenstein in Love opened at the Cockpit Theatre from April 14 to May 1, 1982, and the Dog Company then travelled to the continent, performing the play in Belgium and Holland, where it was warmly received. Termed 'bloodcurdling' by the *London Evening Standard* and 'magnificent' by *Stage*, the neo-Grand Guignol (and not, as originally planned, *Paradise Street*) took pride of place as the company's lead performance at the 1982 Edinburgh Fringe Festival, where it was staged for three weeks, from August 17 through September 4, at the St Patrick's Primary School.

In a reprise of the hectic but rewarding programme pursued by the company a year before, the 7:30 pm performances of *Frankenstein in Love* were followed, at 10:15 pm, by a play that Clive wrote specifically for the Festival. As Doug Bradley recalls, 'We literally said to Clive: *We want another late night show to do. Write us something, please*' – and 'almost before breakfast', a new play appeared.

The Secret Life of Cartoons (1982), an hour-long twist of fantasy and farce, had been developed by Clive under the working title *Live*

Sex on Radio. Its plot centred on a film studio animator whose zany creations – the stuff of Warner Brothers cartoons, including Bradley in the lead role of the Rabbit – invade his home. Its rollicking premiere at Edinburgh was so well-received – garnering the *Festival Times* 'Ten Best' award – that it proved to be the swan song of the Dog Company.

After further performances of the comedy at the Cockpit Theatre in London on November 10–13, 1982, the members of the company agreed, over a series of discussions, that their efforts as a collective had reached the end of the line – ironically, as the result of success. Doug Bradley explains: 'The response to *The Secret Life of Cartoons* in Edinburgh was so strong that we realized, for the first time, that we had a commercial property on our hands. But we also knew – and at the time Clive was trying to fight this – that, in order to make this work as a commercial property, the Dog Company had to let it go, and Clive had to let us go with it. Because if it was going to happen on the West End, it couldn't work under the Dog Company umbrella; it would have to have names in it, and none of us were that.'[12]

Suddenly there was a serious possibility that Clive Barker's words would be given voice on a major stage and with considerable financial backing. He retained Vernon Conway as his theatrical agent – and, in time, *The Secret Life of Cartoons* would open in London's West End (*see* Chapter 16). But before that day, Clive Barker would find fame – not as a playwright, but as a writer of fiction.

Although its members would move on to different pursuits – and considerable successes – the Dog Company felt united by their early experiences: 'rather like people who have survived something,' Mary Roscoe says with a laugh.

The heritage of the small circle of friends who first acted in school plays at Quarry Bank, then declared themselves artists and actors as the Hydra Theatre Company, the Theatre of the Imagination and even the Mute Pantomime Theatre before finding professional fame, if not fortune, as the Dog Company, is extraordinary. Some have suggested, jokingly, that there was something in the water in the Liverpool of the 1960s – or, perhaps, that Carl Jung was right, and Liverpool is indeed the pool of life.

Consider: Pete Atkins now lives and works in Hollywood as a novelist and screenwriter; Graham Bickley starred in the television series

'Bread' and performed in West End musicals, including *Les Miserables*;
Sue Bickley is a highly-regarded opera singer; Julie Blake became a
Senior Examiner for the British Board of Film Classification, a writer
and a mother; Doug Bradley gained world renown as Pinhead in the
Hellraiser films and has a well-established career as an actor, and with
his wife, Lynne Darnell, has two lovely children; Dave Fishel managed
the Liverpool Playhouse; Les Heseltine adopted the name Les Dennis
and is a popular comedian and television game show host; Jude Kelly is
a prominent director of regional theatre and for the Royal Shakespeare
Company; Oliver Parker earned repute as a screenwriter and director
with motion picture adaptations of *Othello* (1995), starring Kenneth
Branagh and Lawrence Fishburne, and Oscar Wilde's *An Ideal Husband*
(1999); Mary Roscoe joined the David Glass Ensemble, and plans to
bring *The History of the Devil* back to the stage. Only Phil Rimmer,
Clive's first collaborator and constant friend, seems, as of this writing,
missing in action.

'That was a troubled group,' Clive says. 'We were troubled by sexual
questions, we were troubled by artistic questions – it was a stew,
constantly. There was never stability. There was always drama. And
looking back, I think a lot of it had to do with deeply held emotions
about one another; I think we felt emotional about one another, and
we were just trying to find ways to express it. Because we were all
joined together by common artistic themes. Instead of being couples,
we were this milling group; and I've always liked that . . . I've always
enjoyed being with groups of artists.'

The man at their centre, Clive Barker, insists that his success is
rooted in this company of dreamers – 'in this kid who, with a bunch
of other kids, said:

'*We can do it all. We can have it all.*'

9

THE PLAY'S THE THING

CRAZYFACE (1982)
SUBTLE BODIES (1982)
COLOSSUS (1983)

'[Y]ou know the paradox of this profession . . . To play life . . . what a curious thing it is. Sometimes I wonder, you know, how long I can keep up the illusion.'

— CLIVE BARKER, 'Sex, Death, and Starshine'

With the end of the Dog Company, Clive Barker focused his attention on writing new plays, and found an immediate patron in Alasdair Cameron, the artistic director of London's Cockpit Theatre. The Cockpit, located on Gateforth Street off Church Street near the Edgware Road tube station, had served as the venue for several of the Dog Company's performances. Cameron, impressed with Clive's talent, commissioned him to write three major plays as workshop projects for the Cockpit Youth Theatre, which provided dramatic experience for sixteen- to twenty-three-year olds.

The first of these plays, written in 1982, was the dizzying *Crazyface*, sometimes subtitled 'A Comedy (with Lions)'.[1] With multiple settings and more than thirty speaking roles, *Crazyface* is one of Barker's more complex plays; it is also the most classical in form and feel. Freed from the constraints of writing for an ensemble, he gloried in the prospect of a sizable cast and ambitious staging, unleashing an epic picaresque whose hero is Tyl Eulenspiegel, a 'sweet-natured, virgin fool' better known as 'Crazyface'.[2]

'[P]erhaps the only kind of truth relevant to this tale and its telling,' report the production notes, 'is a clown's truth: the truth of laughter, though its source may be cruel and unsavoury.' The play evolves through a series of brief set-pieces, much like the performances of a variety show or circus, in which Tyl Eulenspiegel, ever the fool, discovers a world that is even more foolish – and at last finds salvation. His journey begins in innocence but descends into vitriol and violence – the currency of both comedy and crime – and, like the best of clowns, Tyl proves an object of affection and derision, happy in his sadness, sad in his happiness.

Crazyface opens at dawn, at the edge of a forest somewhere in the Low Countries. It is the Renaissance, at the height of Spanish exploration and conquest, and the wane of the Inquisition. Enter Ella Eulenspiegel and her daughters-in-law Sheba, Irvette and Annie – all married to the same polygamist, Ella's prodigal son Lenny. The women carry all their worldly possessions. With them is Ella's other son, Crazyface, who carries nothing, and simply trails a large silver fish behind him on a string. When Irvette, exasperated, asks why he pulls the fish, he replies: 'Well, I can't *push* it, can I?'

Crazyface, properly known as Tyl, is a mooncalf – a simpleton who sees, and converses with, angels. His antics have forced the ragged family into exile from city after city, and now they come upon bloody confusion at a place called, appropriately, Loon. The town idiot, Wormwood, has donned homemade wings and leapt from the church spire, hoping to fly but finding only the hard and unforgiving earth. Crazyface (like young Clive, after his vision of the plummeting 'Bird Man' Valentin) is fascinated by the fallen man and his broken wings – and his instant of flight, almost that of an angel. In that instant, the dying Wormwood reveals, he saw that the world was 'all vision . . .

nothing real at all'. He urges the wings upon Crazyface: 'You look like a man with Heaven in his hair. Take them.'

Crazyface takes the wings but hides them, since the townspeople, tasting blood, seem only to want more. Dragooned into burying Wormwood, Crazyface is met at a crossroads by a mysterious foursome of conspirators and spies: Alvarez, the 'Spanish Fly', who is pursued by Alvin, the Englishman; Alfonso, the Italian; and Allegro, the Frenchman. Alvarez is set upon and murdered by masked assassins – 'BLOOD POURS DOWN HIS FACE LIKE YOLK FROM A CRACKED EGG' – but he bequeaths Crazyface a puzzle box that contains 'the glory of the world'.

Annie arrives, warning that the townspeople have declared Crazyface a heretic for giving succour to the dying Wormwood. With his mother's blessing, he and Annie set off into the world, carrying the mysterious secret – which will provoke war and endless suffering – with them.

In Spain, the King and a priest, Mengo, consult a witch in order to raise Alvarez from the dead. Learning that the traitor has given the secret – 'the birthright of the Spanish nation . . . the salvation of Spain' – to Crazyface, the King orders that Tyl be found and silenced, and the secret returned to Spain. Mengo has the perfect assassin: Tyl's trigamist brother, Lenny, who is a prisoner of the Inquisition; after all, 'a clown knows the best working of other clowns'.

As the English, French and Italians raze the countryside, murdering and pillaging in search of the puzzle box, Crazyface – wearing a rudimentary clown disguise – plans to deliver its secret to Rome and the Pope. He and Annie are set upon by bandits – all of them women – and their leader takes the treasure box. She masters its puzzle, and it grinds open to reveal nothing but a handful of seeds. Annie joins the bandits, leaving Tyl with the curious treasure. He meets the grieving remnants of a wedding party – a pig-breeder and his wife consoling their pregnant daughter, whose husband-to-be was allegedly eaten by lions just moments before the ceremony. At the urging of the parents, Crazyface weds the bereaved girl; but his brother Lenny interrupts the wedding meal, demanding the box and its secret. A melee ensues, and the errant groom arrives, alive and well, to make amends for his folly.

Act 2 opens in darkness – 'WE'VE MOVED FROM THE

BREATHLESS DAWN OF PART ONE INTO A DARKER WORLD, A HAUNTED WORLD.' In escaping the riotous reception, Crazyface has lost the puzzle box to Lenny; he is set upon by the trio of surviving 'Als' – English, French and Italian – but is rescued again by Annie, who is now dressed like a man, with an eyepatch and cropped hair. She has usurped his plan to travel to Rome: 'I've got a few secret ambitions ... [and] an audience with the Pope ... He doesn't know it yet.'

Meanwhile, Lenny returns the prized box to Spain. 'It's a Chinese design,' Mengo tells him, solving its puzzle to reveal the mysterious seeds inside:

> Of all the treasures Spain found in the New World, this is the greatest. Consider it. So small, so unprepossessing. Yet this humble seed, when ground to powder and mixed with a few spices into paste, makes chocolate.
>
> And Spain has it. Only Spain. We own the land where it grows, we own the savages who have farmed it for centuries, and until Alvarez stole it, we owned this – (*He waves the piece of paper*) – the definitive recipe, the one perfect balance of cocoa and sugar, and milk and spice.

Lenny is stunned: 'The Lowlands are ash. Thousands have died. For ... chocolate?' He offers Mengo proof of his murder of Crazyface, but it is pig meat; and Mengo, fearing that the clown has memorized the recipe, intercepts the pilgrimage to Rome and takes him prisoner. But when Crazyface, sentenced to death, gives a persistent angel his coat, the angel is mistaken for him and taken to the gallows instead. Crazyface escapes, but not before freeing Lenny, who forces Mengo to eat chocolate until he dies. 'You're the genius,' Mengo calls out to Crazyface. 'I'm the fool.'

Back on the road to Rome, Crazyface meets the three warring schemers – Englishman, Frenchman, Italian – and gives them identical boxes whose contents, unknown to them, are rat faeces. The schemers, intent on sole possession of the secret, stab each other furiously to death.

Finally Crazyface arrives in Rome, and circumvents the throng of

CLIVE BARKER: THE DARK FANTASTIC

pilgrims seeking audience with the Pope by sneaking through the sewers and into the Vatican. He fears for his soul, having caused the death of an angel. Lenny arrives, brandishing his knife with the verve of a western gunslinger: 'The world isn't big enough for the two of us.' As the only person who believed his brother could see angels, he wants to see them too: 'I cursed. I prayed. I even committed murder to make them come and fetch me.' Hoping that his threat will provoke the angels to appear, he rushes at Crazyface but stabs himself and dies.

The Cardinals, believing that Crazyface has committed fratricide, condemn him to death; but as the sword is about to fall, the Pope enters. It is Annie, her face hidden beneath shaving soap, spectacles and a cap. She urges everyone away and reveals herself to Crazyface: 'It's a long story. I told a few lies, I arranged a few miracles. Really, getting here was not so difficult. Staying here may be another matter. And I haven't yet got the knack of pissing standing up.' She concludes: 'I'm the best man for the job; really I am.'

Crazyface confesses to his murder of the angel and asks if he will go to the Devil. 'How the hell should I know?' Her Holiness replies. Then she forgives him. Finding redemption, Crazyface is magically flown back to his beginnings, and his mother: 'I saw a bird yesterday, hovering over the side of a hill . . . it was standing still in the air. I thought then, all he needed was to catch the right wind . . . the right wind can take you anywhere, more or less . . . anywhere you want . . . Even home.'

In a garden at Loon, almost nine years after the dawn on which the play opened, Ella, nearly blind, waits: 'Why don't I die, I wonder?' Crazyface greets her, and his mother cries for the first time in fifty years. 'Am I crazy?' he asks her, then adds: 'Is that so bad?'

As the wind rises, he goes to find the long-buried wings of Wormwood: 'All the birdman needed was an up-draught.' Ella asks Sheba to watch the sky, and with the growing sound of gulls, Sheba sees 'another bird' flying '[h]igher and higher, wheeling around' the sky until he's 'almost disappeared'. Ella sits, smiling, as her son ascends like an angel into the heavens.

The comic optimism of *Crazyface* – leavened, to be sure, by its episodic violence – would be invoked the following year, when Barker wrote his second Cockpit Youth Theatre play specifically in service of a theme proposed by Alasdair Cameron: gay sexuality in the context of family. Determined to downplay sexual politics in favour of characterization, Barker merged the familiar template of the English farce with elements of fantasy and the surreal in *Subtle Bodies* (1983), which became renowned for its scene in which a ship sinks on stage.[3] 'This is a dream play,' state the production notes, 'a comedy of altered states in which images that have been shaped by the private rages, frustrations and desires of the characters take public, or at least semi-public, form.'

Somewhere on the northwest coast of England is the small, aged Atlantic Hotel: '*THE BUILDING IS ALMOST TRANSPARENT, A DREAM HOTEL, HOVERING ON THE BRINK OF EXISTENCE.*' Its architecture is fragmented – the frame of a front door, a balcony, windows with venetian blinds, a rear exit leading to a patio and a view of certain dreamscapes: the ever-encroaching sand dunes and, later, a beach, a ship, the sea. These spaces are isolated by lighting effects, '*BUT OFTEN THE HOTEL CAN BE SEEN IN ITS STRANGE ENTIRETY, WITH VARIOUS EVENTS (OR NON-EVENTS) RUNNING SIMULTANEOUSLY BUT DISCREETLY. CAUSE AND EFFECT, OR SIMPLY EFFECT.*' The hotel and its environs seem descended from the entropic science fictional villa of JG Ballard's *Vermilion Sands* (1971), a realm of imaginative degeneration and regeneration.

The plot, like those of most farces, is a complex web of romantic intrigue; in Clive's most memorable summation of the play: 'Carys loves Dex who loves Rob who fancies Sean who's an object of lust for Edward Lear who ends up marrying a gorilla, while Vince is in drunken pursuit of Rose who has deeply repressed feelings for Phoebe whose husband Lindberg once had an unforgettable night of lust with a transsexual in Bangkok.'[4]

The play begins as a young couple, Carys Skinner and Dexter Juffs, arrive at the hotel – a fond memory from Dex's youth. They have decided that their marriage, scheduled for the next day, will not take place – they need time to talk. In the lobby they meet Sean, an employee who busily brushes sand out of the hotel, a ritual that continues throughout the play; and Mrs Corcoran, the widowed proprietor.

Suddenly a gorilla enters, shattered shackles at its wrists, carrying a screaming virgin over its shoulder; essentially unnoticed by the players, it wanders back offstage with its hostage.

The love-lorn gorilla, we soon learn, is the dream of watercolourist and nonsense poet Edward Lear, dead author of 'The Owl and the Pussycat' (1871), whose afterlife is spent lounging at the hotel under the name of Mr Foss. As the tragicomedy of the doomed engagement of Dex and Carys unfolds, a more curious tragicomedy – the dreamlife of Mr Foss – is revealed.

Foss is an agent of the Dream Bureau, stationed at the hotel by a conspiracy that nurtures the dream-life of the nation; but he is running out of dreams:

> Did you know there were tides in a glass of water? Oh certainly. Dominion of the moon, this tumble glass. And the waters of my eyes. Tides there, even. And what do I do, surrounded by such wonders? I dream banalities. Loveless, the soul goes to dust ... I wish once in a while my empty head could drum up a few terrors. Floating cities, rains of fire, men with hooks for hands scratching at the back door. I tried to conjure up a dream of pure energy, pure sexuality. Pure life. Something to prove my potency. And what do I get? An adhesive and love-lorn Gorilla.

'We possess two bodies,' Foss advises. 'The physical and the subtle ... The subtle body is our dream-self. By day, it is discreet. Like a flame in sunlight, burning yet invisible ... But by night, the subtle body goes, at the speed of thought' to the place where all things are possible. That evening, as if to confirm this wisdom, a young man, his nearly-nude body painted, enters with bow in hand and shoots an arrow into Dex's back.[5] It is another dream – although, like all dreams, evocative of truth – and Carys wakes the sleepwalking Dex, who has fallen in the hallway of the hotel.

Act 2 brings a new day and the unexpected arrival of the wedding party – parents (Lindberg and Phoebe Skinner, Frank and Melba Juffs), the best man (Rob Kidd) and others (including family friend Rose Giddy) – who, unaware of the romantic rift, believe that Carys and Dex have decided to elope rather than endure the formal ceremony at Manchester. In the midst of the hubbub, we learn that Dex and Rob have slept together – which is why Dex brought Carys to the hotel: 'I couldn't marry her without explaining.' Rob challenges him: 'What's to explain, Dex? You're not gay. You just sleep with men.' But Dex admits his love for Rob, and kisses him, not realizing that Rose has witnessed their encounter.

When Rose promptly drinks herself to near-suicide, the story is made public. Lindberg Skinner, like his daughter Carys, rants at Rob, accusing the best man of fomenting trouble: 'You don't care, your type never does. Lower form of humanity . . . You make me want to puke.' Rob tries to console Carys: 'Nothing was going on. Nothing was going to go on. It was in the past.' But she won't listen; no one will listen.

Foss, who watches the proceedings with grim disappointment, determines to create one last dream – a mighty, apocalyptic dream that echoes the sinking of the *Titanic*: 'All of us on one final cruise into frenzical waters.' With the sounds of the sea rising in the background, Act 3 finds the hotel transformed into a subtle ship – the luxury liner *Bear of Amsterdam*, sailing the dark Arctic Ocean under the command of none other than Mr Foss.[6] On deck, the wedding party strolls, most of them in costume: Rob in a tuxedo; Dex as a groom, with shirt and tie painted on his torso; Carys as the Bride of Dracula; Lindberg and Phoebe Skinner as Napoleon and Josephine; and at last Foss, swathed in bandages as the Invisible Man.

Phoebe Skinner mistakes Foss for her husband; after her insistent come-on, he abducts her. This is the final straw for Lindberg, who pulls his pistol, threatening to kill Rob: 'I'm shooting the sodomite.' But there's something in the fog; the ship grates against an iceberg and, in the panic that follows, Lindberg shoots the Invisible Man. When the dead man is revealed as Foss – the Captain – they ignore impending doom and pose for a photograph. The ship rams into a second iceberg and begins to sink.

'This is like some bad dream,' Carys says. The passengers make for the lifeboats, women and children first – although one of the men steals on board in drag. Lindberg tries bribery and then fights his way onto the lifeboat as most of the other male leads cling to its side and escape the sinking ship – but not the cold, dark waters below. One by one the characters are lost, with Lindberg blaming Rob and his homosexuality for the disaster.

Finally Dex pushes his own father overboard, and Carys shouts at Rob: '[Y]ou say it's all right? It isn't! It's never been all right! The lullabies are wrong!' But Rob sees through the madness and into the reality of the dream: 'I hope you remember this. God, I hope we *all* remember this . . . when it's over.' He notes the absence of stars, the presence of sharks in arctic water. 'The illusion's almost perfect . . . but not perfect enough . . . There's solid ground under here, some-where. Just over the edge of my bed. I wouldn't sink. Not if I didn't believe it.' He steps off the boat and onto solid ground; he is alive, and awake. Foss arrives and announces that the dream was 'my swanish song . . . After tonight I am a legendary poet and nothing more.'

With Act 4, morning light summons the cast from their bedrooms, with only vague memories of the night's long dream-voyage. The social strands weave back together in curious ways, with new pairings of lovers and strange confessions. Lindberg tells Dex about the night he made love to a transvestite in Bangkok; and although Dex still wants to marry Carys, she declines: 'Last night, drifting along, I thought, it's all right. If I drown, I drown. It's my life.'

Slowly the memories of the night – the lifeboat, the dark water – emerge. The joys and terrors of the dreamworld supplant the mundane banter; but Lindberg, a rationalist to the bitter end, insists: 'They're just dreams.' He argues that they should agree to forget – that we should learn to compromise with the truth – but Carys demurs: 'Wait. For a while we were in each other's heads. One mind; all of us. Isn't that a wonderful thought?' Still Lindberg refuses: 'We all have our little secrets. We have to respect that in each other. That's how we get on in the world, isn't it? I don't go meddling in your mind and you stay out of mine . . . That's how we keep control.'

The 'we' of Lindberg's worldview is implicit; and in chaotic response, Edward Lear, formerly known as Mr Foss, reappears with his own wedding party – and his bride, unveiled, is revealed as . . . the gorilla of his dreams.

'The glory of dream-plays,' Barker notes, 'is that they carry us past the superfice of behaviour, into the maelstrom of motive.'[7] The whimsical and, indeed, nonsensical Lear/Foss skewers a social fabric based on triviality and the artifice of convention; but Barker declines to deliver a tidy finale that champions the politically correct, refusing to pair Dex and Rob and instead leaving the romantic entanglements as confused as they were at the outset.

The issue of sexuality is secondary; what is crucial, Barker insists, is love, in its many incarnations. Thus, when Rob inquires about the gorilla's sex, Lear tells him: 'I didn't ask. It seemed impertinent. It loves my nose. That's all that matters. For that I could love it, whatever it was.' And in closing, Barker, again through Lear, offers a lingering insight: 'Significance does seem to lie in insignificant places, doesn't it? In an arrangement of clouds, in the ink stain on my thumb . . . in dreams. There most of all.'

The resilient optimism of *Crazyface* and *Subtle Bodies* was blunted in the grim world of *Colossus* (1984), Barker's third and final play for the Cockpit Youth Theatre.[8] Performed at the Cockpit under the direction of Geoff Gillham, the play is arguably his best, an ambitious mingling of farce and fable in a tale of forsaken and mistaken identity whose title, setting, characters and tableaux are derived from the artwork of the Spanish master Francisco José Goya y Lucientes (1746–1828). Indeed, its central character is Goya, who, true to his print *Yo Lo Vi* ('I Saw This'), bears witness to a vortex of bloody events.[9]

Goya has been called 'the *éminence gris* of modern painting'. His artwork forced the question of the function that painting should fulfil in the absence of religious, dynastic or decorative purpose. The eighty etchings known as *Los desastres de la guerra* ('The Disasters of War') reflect his personal witness to the atrocities of the Napoleonic invasion of Spain, and provide a profound expressionistic condemnation of war that remains vital today. It has been argued that these etchings, which were not published in Goya's lifetime, signalled the shift to the modern perception of history as a sequence of events rather than the unfolding of a superior destiny.[10]

Written in four acts, each moving deeper into night, *Colossus* is classic historical drama, probably the most traditional and certainly the most naturalistic of Barker's stage repertoire, eschewing supernatural events in favour of the casual brutality that Goya chronicled in *Los desastres de la guerra*. It is also the most complex of Barker's works for the theatre, with a cast of nearly fifty characters – and, preferably, many supernumeraries – moving on and off stage as several mysteries evolve through a performance that, according to Barker's production notes, 'must be as urgent and mesmeric as a news bulletin'.

Set outside Madrid in June 1811, during the Peninsular War (which pitted the British and their Portuguese and Spanish allies against the royalist puppet government of Joseph Bonaparte), the play opens in crisis. A barrage of artillery shells demolishes the sumptuous country house of Duke Damaso: '*ONCE SO CAREFULLY ORGANIZED, AND NOW CHAOS, ITS HIERARCHIES A CONTINUUM OF HEAPED RUBBLE AND COLLAPSED ROOF TIMBERS.*' Several of the occupants are killed instantly, while others are buried in the ruins. Among the missing is the deaf artist Goya, who had been commissioned to paint a portrait of the Duke's trophy bride, eighteen-year-old Sofia. Unseen by everyone but the audience and a mad woman, Goya rises, bloody and dazed, from the debris and staggers offstage.

By literally demolishing the physical world in the opening scene, then contrasting that world with one seen through the eyes of the artist – who becomes a kind of moral searchlight – Barker challenges his audience to distrust the ordinary and the expected, to see with eyes that, like those of Goya, have been freed of the blinkers of everyday existence. It is an aesthetic that he would explore so powerfully in his later fiction: 'We live, the play suggests, in more than one world. It's only when events shatter our simple constructs – when the order we have imposed on reality falters – that we sense this multiplicity. The revelation may drive us crazy, or help us better understand ourselves. The choice is ours.'

Santiago, the Duke's officious major-domo, searches through the gory detritus of the house, more concerned about the stylish French furnishings than the guests and staff whose bodies, alive and dead and dismembered, now decorate the estate. As the aristocrats, who escaped the bombardment while touring the Duke's stables, return to view the destruction, the carnage is downplayed: 'Tell her it's not real; just Signor Goya, spilling the paint.' They picnic while watching the exhumations, and the inquiry shifts to whether Duchess Sofia went willingly or by force to the garden, where she was seen in the comfort of a stranger.

The mystery man is the actor Castropol, who entered the house a thief and emerged as the Duchess's paramour. 'I can play anything you ask me. I can be a doctor, a priest, a lover. I can be death itself if it seems appropriate.' Disguised as a doctor, he returns boldly to attend to the Duchess, who tells the Duke she was raped. (In suitably ironic commentary, Castropol notes: 'This is a highly moral play. If we're going to have sex in it, it's rape or nothing. That way we can claim we disapprove, however pornographic the content.')

The ruins offer up the artist's glasses, then his sketchbook and palette, and finally a body in his paint-flecked coat, its head crushed beyond recognition. 'Goya was more than flesh and blood,' the Duke pronounces. 'He was a great man.'

DUKE:	Where's it gone, Nicholas?
GENERAL GUYE:	Where's what gone?
DUKE:	His greatness.
GENERAL GUYE:	Into history, I suppose.
DUKE:	Perhaps that's the safest place to be.

In Act 2, nuns arrive with Goya wrapped in cloth. 'The man in the coffin is a thief. He stole my clothes; just as his companion stole the subject of this very painting [of Duchess Sofia]. Believe me or not, it's of no consequence. Am I the only significant corpse?' He is not. Rafael, the Duke's gardener, has found his pregnant wife in the rubble. In his sorrow, he tears their baby from her womb and begins to eat it: 'Better he be in me, safe in me, and wrapped up, than in the ground.'

Goya embraces his sudden anonymity, maintaining the fiction of his death. He salvages a sketchbook and a change of clothes from the ruins: 'Painters never steal. We may pay homage to, we are influenced by, but we never steal. I am now going to pay homage to somebody else's coat.' He draws compulsively as events continue to unfold around him: 'I think perhaps the dead see more than we do. I envy that.'

Other men have to fill their mouths all day, I have to cram my eyes. Looking's a vice with me. I have to devour everything I so much as glance at, what the angels and the fallen angels made, it's the same to me. And when I've got the sights in here I want to make them all over again, in paint, and sign them, yes sign the world and say: 'Goya saw this!'

As the Duchess plots her getaway with Castropol, unkind epitaphs are spoken over Goya's 'corpse'. First come the words of Santiago: 'I was always indifferent to your conspicuous shows of suffering on behalf of humanity. Well yes. I thought it undignified to be frank, a man of your age, sweating and wringing his hands about the facts of life. Tomorrow, you see, things will be different: we won't waste time agonizing over how to save our vile souls.' Goya's son arrives and claims to recognize the body – 'He always loved dirt and desolation' – then disparages his father's artwork. 'I'm not simply deaf,' Goya realizes. 'I'm completely senseless, not to have known. They never loved me!' His despair summons up memories of a childhood fear that echoes El Coco's dream in *Frankenstein in Love*:

> When I was a child, I thought our town was built on the back of a giant. In the night, I was certain I heard this Colossus breathe, and I fretted that someone in their ignorance would wake him, and he'd rise up, not knowing what he did, and the hills, the town, our house, my bed, would fall off his back and roll away into the dark. Now I'm sixty-five, and still I think maybe he's there, underground. Maybe I could wake him, if I only could find his face, and there'd be an end to us all.[11]

He descends into a hole in the earth, seeking his Colossus. When he returns, he has found only the corpse of Rafael's wife:

> The shock made me drop the lamp. It went out. I was in absolute darkness; and for the first time since I went deaf I heard something other than the whines and moans that fill my head. I heard my heart.
> The hot darkness, the smell of a woman's blood, the heartbeat, suddenly I was a baby again, wanting to be born. There was no Colossus underground, just this memory, so strong I remembered how it felt, being spat into the world. The ache of separation and

the beginning of love. Mourning begins there, doesn't it? It's the dawn of grief.

That despair, he realizes, is his Colossus: 'He's that baby, grown fat on sorrow, grown angry and monstrous like you.'

Act 3 opens in the full of night, lit only by distant stars and the campfire of the French soldiers who guard the ruins. Out of the darkness emerges a vast, shrouded replica of a human head, with long hair and beard but empty eye sockets, accompanied by cloaked and masked figures with bells and drums.[12] It is a troupe of actors seeking Castropol, who played their Don Juan but stole their money and costumes and disappeared.

The plot thickens like the deepening night: as the *conte heroique*, Castropol has been blackmailed by the major-domo Santiago to seduce Duchess Sofia and break her heart, so that Santiago, who lusts for her, may pick up the pieces. When Goya presents the Duchess with her finished portrait, it is a warning. 'Is this me?' she asks. 'And the monster leaning over me, with its claws in my breast, what's that?' Goya responds: 'It's the future ... It may kill you.' When she asks, 'What do you see in me?' he replies: 'Oh the old lie. Beauty as truth ... As if in your perfection there might be some signal from the far side of Hell.'

Castropol talks the troupe into staging a performance for the French soldiers; it is another deception. When the actors return, costumed as bandits, the infantrymen mistake them for guerrillas and massacre them with bullets and blades. 'What a world of wonders,' Goya says, taking up his sketchbook to record the bloody scene. 'It's the only way I can stop my hand shaking.'

Then it is the full of night, and the final act. The Duke hangs himself when Castropol, disguised as the doctor, reveals the Duchess's infidelity. A remorseful Santiago confesses his scheme to the Duchess, and asks for forgiveness – and marriage. 'Is that the beast you painted, Signor Goya? You didn't tell me it would be so subtle.' Goya offers her his thoughts on evil:

GOYA: There's a beast called Basilisk, ever heard of it?
            THE DUCHESS SHAKES HER HEAD. This thing

is supposedly so unspeakable that if you see it,
you turn to stone. But nobody can tell if it exists
or not, because if you've seen it, you're dead.

DUCHESS: Do you believe in it?

GOYA: I think maybe the worst monsters are almost
invisible, just seen out of the corner of the eye.
And I think the future will be full of them.

When the soldiers prepare to execute Rafael's friend Felipe, Goya
bids the Duchess to look away. She insists on watching: 'I think I
could learn to look at the worst thing in the world with practice. Even
your Basilisk. Wouldn't that defeat it? To look with open eyes at it
and see it clearly, in all its detail, and know it utterly?'

As the firing squad takes aim, all is plunged into darkness, and
Rafael the child-eater emerges from the earth, covered in muck and
holding pieces of human flesh. The soldiers are routed, and Felipe
escapes. When the soldiers rally, their pursuit tracks Castropol instead;
he hides inside the huge eyeless head, a pretender to godhood. The
Duchess gives him away to the soldiers, who bayonet the head, killing
Castropol as she utters her final word: 'Blind.'

This epitaph is not simply a self-condemnation of her embrace of
deception, but also signals the metaphysical dilemma that powers the
play. In *Colossus*, as in Goya's art, darkness is a visual equivalent of
nothingness, and in the darkest hour of night, the Duchess and Goya
– and Clive Barker – confront the ultimate horror: the horror of not
seeing. The great eyeless head is the symbol of Colossus, of a universe
created by an unseeing and uncaring god who does nothing as the
tiny race called humanity lives out its arbitrary and often cruel existence. And the ultimate horror, Barker tells us, is for us to refuse to
look upon its empty face, and to live and love without knowledge of
the worst of things.

It is also a savage critique of the artist's function. In the entwined
stories of Castropol and Goya, art's potential for pernicious deception
is contrasted with its potential for penetrating truth. Notably both
artists indulge the tropes of realism and fantasy, and the distinction
proves irrelevant: the message is that their art, and not its medium,
is important.

The artist teaches us to see the world. In the vacuous entertainments of Castropol, we are distracted, misled, deluded and ultimately betrayed; but in the revelations of Goya, we are given truth, even if it is not entirely welcome.

Despite his dire musings on the Colossus, Barker's finale is optimistic. Goya's wife, the frail Josefa, arrives and realizes immediately that the corpse is not that of her husband. Goya, certain of her love, reveals himself and embraces her. Felipe is freed from his own hiding place among the dead. When, at last, dawn approaches, Goya accepts its promise of redemption: 'Look at the light. I thought it would never come. Ribbons of it; just look ... Coming through the smoke like this. Coming down on all this ruin. So confident, as though it's never heard of night. As if it's here forever.'

Colossus is the last stageplay that Clive Barker has completed to date. By the time it was performed at the Cockpit Youth Theatre in 1984, his writing had evolved, once again, but this time to a different medium: the short story.

The date remains vague, but it was in 1981, probably as the Dog Company headed north to perform for the first time at the Edinburgh Fringe Festival, that Clive hopped into the van and showed Doug Bradley a handwritten manuscript. It was a horror story, written for his own amusement and that of his friends. He asked Doug what he thought about the story, and wondered aloud whether horror fiction might bring him some money.

The answer would be known as *Clive Barker's Books of Blood*.

10

AFTER THE DANSE

[M]an is become as one of us, to know good and evil . . .
                              – The Book of Genesis 3:22

One of the seminal short story collections of this generation, *Clive Barker's Books of Blood* (1984), was written as a diversion. In 1981, playwriting consumed Clive's working hours with an intensity that demanded relief; on a whim, he began to compose stories at night. 'I was writing them at odd moments and just enjoyed doing them for the benefit of friends or my own pleasure.'

The texts blended the evolving personal and social philosophy of his plays with his childhood enthusiasm for Edgar Allan Poe and other masters of the grotesque and the supernatural, as embellished by the increasingly ferocious horror cinema of the late 1970s. In London, Clive and his friends avidly attended the crimson wave of gory special-effects films that followed William Friedkin's explosive rendition of *The Exorcist* (1973). His favourites included the motion pictures of David Cronenberg, particularly *Shivers* ('They Came from Within') (1975); Brian De Palma's *Carrie* (1976); George A Romero's 'Living Dead' films; and the visionary and violent Italian horror films of Dario Argento, Mario Bava and Lucio Fulci.

Because his stories were imaginative exercises, written only for

144

himself – and for the occasional pleasure of his friends – Clive pursued their ideas and images without apology or self-censorship. He did not imagine them seeing print, and did not even consider submitting the manuscripts to magazines or anthologies for publication. Then, while browsing through a bookstore one day, he came across a hefty new anthology of original horror fiction called *Dark Forces* (1980).[1] 'It had Isaac Bashevis Singer and Stephen King and Ramsey Campbell and Joyce Carol Oates – all these people doing completely different things, but they could all fit in one book. This was something of a revelation. I had been bound by what I thought were the conventions of the genre. Now I thought, *The options are wide open. Let's see how far we can press this.*'

Impressed by the breadth of what could be published in the name of horror, Clive realized that his 'diversion' might offer a commercially viable form for the expression of the ideas he was exploring on stage. Intoxicated by this revelation, he turned to writing horror stories with eagerness and audacity; but the mere idea of creating a story collection displayed his naïveté about the business of publishing: short stories are typically an anathema to major book publishers, who insist that anthologies and collections do not sell as well as novels. His timing, however, was impeccable; in the 1980s, horror briefly supplanted science fiction as the last great preserve of the short story, producing a renaissance of the series anthology and an unprecedented number of single-author story collections.[2]

By 1983, Clive was ready: he gave his manuscripts – more than six hundred pages typed by Mary Roscoe and titled *The Book of Blood* – to his theatrical agent, Vernon Conway, who was equally naïve in the ways of publishing. Conway offered the manuscript, without success, to Livia Gollancz at Victor Gollancz, a major hardcover imprint. Then he submitted the sixteen stories to Sphere Books, an independent paperback publisher with offices on the Gray's Inn Road in London. Editor Barbara Boote read the stories and was suitably impressed; she passed them along to Rights Director Nan du Sautoy.

Boote and du Sautoy concluded that Sphere would be interested – for an appropriate price. Although horror fiction had evolved, through a series of bestselling novels by Stephen King, James Herbert and Peter Straub, into what British and American publishers considered a profitable marketing category, it seemed to have reached a commercial zenith in the early 1980s. Faced with an apparently shrinking readership and the overpayment of advances to certain writers, it was a cautious moment for publishers; indeed, Sphere was then cutting back its list of horror titles. Ten thousand copies of any given novel could be sold easily in the United Kingdom; but anything more required luck or exceptional quality.

Sphere considered Clive's stories with cautious optimism. 'Everybody knows that horror stories don't sell,' says Barbara Boote, now an editor with Little Brown UK, where du Sautoy is Rights Director. 'They're lovely to read, but they're usually by terribly famous people, and here was an unknown with sixteen stories. They were so original that we thought long and hard about them. Then we got another two stories in, and we thought they were original as well. We were trying to think how to do them. In the end, we thought about doing them as *Sphere Books of Blood*, because we thought that this was a bit of a selling point – Sphere being more of a name than Clive Barker at the time.'

With du Sautoy's help, Boote overcame opposition in editorial and sales meetings, and persuaded Managing Director Nick Webb to publish the stories in three volumes. 'We bought eighteen stories relatively cheaply,' Boote says. 'So it was three books for £1,000 each for world rights. Which has turned out to make a fortune for us, and not done Clive badly, either, because of the royalties . . .' (Under the agreement, Sphere licensed the exclusive right to publish the first three *Books of Blood* in any language throughout the world – or to sublicense those rights to others – in exchange for paying an advance to Barker of £1,000 per book. The agreement remains in effect for as long as Sphere or its successor keeps the volumes in print.)

Boote and du Sautoy then met Clive, Vernon Conway and Conway's assistant, Bryn Newton, for a celebratory lunch. They were ecstatic upon meeting their new author: 'Clive was obviously young, handsome, chatty and exciting – and British,' Boote says. 'Which always helps in terms of promotion. We clicked with him, socially as much as anything else. If you're a self-publicist, in a nice way, an agreeable way, and you have that sort of rapport, you're much more likely to succeed.'

At the lunch, it became obvious to Boote and du Sautoy that Conway had submitted the manuscript to Sphere out of 'a complete misunderstanding of what we published'. He turned to Boote and said: 'We sent them to you because you publish Stephen King.' The contracts had been signed, the advance had been paid, and, in Boote's words: 'I didn't bother to say, *Well, we don't . . .*'[3]

Although conceived by Clive as a single book, Sphere believed that consumers would be unwilling to risk money on a large (and thus more expensive) collection of stories by an unknown author. Working with Boote, Clive arranged the stories into three volumes, although he has always viewed the texts as an integrated work (and, indeed, more recent editions of the *Books of Blood* have been issued as a single volume).

On the strength of the fiction – and in order to stir interest – Sphere decided to take two dramatic steps: Clive Barker's name was added to the title and the three volumes were published simultaneously. As Boote recalls: 'We could have done one volume at a time, one a year or every six months, but we decided to do all three volumes in one go, which again is quite dodgy, because when the reps are selling three books in one go, for one author, the shops are going to reduce their orders for each one.' By issuing the three volumes together, however, Sphere would obtain more space than it would for a single book – 'and that's what we wanted to do, to get the shelf space for them'.

Clive, concerned by the intricacies and ramifications of the contracts, turned to the only professional writer he knew – the man who had uttered the words 'Why Horror?' to a roomful of delighted Quarry Bank students: Ramsey Campbell. The assistance soon spiralled beyond friendly advice; on March 24, 1983, Campbell wrote a provocative letter to Barbara Boote, intended to offer 'a few of my thoughts on the books':

> I think Clive Barker is the most important new writer of horror fiction since Peter Straub. He's the first writer to write horror fiction in Technicolor – the first to take the gruesome horror movie and make it work as prose. I think he is, in the best sense, the most deeply shocking writer now working in the field. He's given horror fiction a few hefty jolts to get it moving again. Yet in

the midst of his unparalleled gruesomeness there's a poetry and sensitivity rare in the field. I thought I was past being profoundly disturbed by horror fiction, but these books proved me wrong.[4]

At Boote's request, Campbell then wrote an astute and gracious formal introduction to the first volume of the *Books of Blood*, which urged readers to 'rejoice as I did to discover that Clive Barker is the most original writer of horror fiction to have appeared for years, and in the best sense, the most deeply shocking writer now working in the field'.

Sphere published *Clive Barker's Books of Blood* in March 1984, without any advertising, promotion, or expectations. 'They were category publishing,' Boote notes, 'and we never saw them as leads.' It was hoped that the books would sell through their ten-thousand-copy first printing; and, for a time, it seemed that Sphere's perspective was correct. Although well-received critically, the books were not an immediate commercial success; several of Sphere's established writers of horror fiction, particularly Graham Masterton, outsold Barker in significant numbers. But within months, propelled almost entirely by word of mouth and an occasional review, these stories, originally published for a small niche audience, rose from the shadows and into the mainstream to become one of the true publishing phenomena of the 1980s.

Little wonder: *Clive Barker's Books of Blood* represent the ideal that so often eludes writers and publishers – a moment in which talent and timing entwine and enrapture an audience eager to read and learn and then read more.

By 1984, the literature of horror had reached an unprecedented level of popularity in England and America. In the aftermath of Ira Levin's *Rosemary's Baby* (1967), William Peter Blatty's *The Exorcist* (1971) and Thomas Tryon's *The Other* (1971) and *Harvest Home* (1973), Stephen King and James Herbert had published a series of novels that made their names synonymous with horror – and bestsellerdom. The Year of Fear was 1979, when *The Dead Zone* first took the name of Stephen King onto the *New York Times* hardcover bestseller list; Peter Straub's *Ghost Story* followed weeks later, while James Herbert's *The Spear* and the first novel by Virginia (VC) Andrews, *Flowers in the Attic*, dominated paperback bestseller lists on both sides of the Atlantic. *Dawn of the Dead* and *Alien* brought violent special effects mayhem and magic onto motion picture screens, and a burgeoning technology – the videocassette recorder – opened a new market for private, at-home viewing that was ripe for films that were transgressive or merely exploitative. For the first time in decades, the supernatural was a staple of mass market entertainment.

Seemingly overnight, fear obtained commercial, if not critical, respectability. It was a fiction for a new decade, a violent *fantastique* of apparently limitless possibilities, powered by an exhilarating sense of liberation – the feeling that horror, like punk and new wave music and art, was a means of casting off the safe seventies shroud of disco, mindless sitcoms, and the wishful science fiction of George Lucas and Steven Spielberg. In the aftershock of Vietnam, energy crisis, deficit economy, citizens held hostage in foreign lands, America had entered an era of imperial decline, presided over by an aging actor. England suffered in the grip of unemployment and industrial devastation, with a widening poverty gap whose seeming solution in Thatcherism would indulge economic hedonism and a hypocritical pursuit of Victorian family values. What better window on our existential dilemma than the literature and cinema of the horrific?

Stephen King was a perfect poet for this imperfect time. A child of the 1950s, he had witnessed every errant step of the American descent – from Sputnik to Love Canal, Dealey Plaza to Watergate, southeast Asia to Watts – all told, a grand and violent loss of innocence. Unerring in his instinct for the visceral, King was the campfire storyteller; his effortless, colloquial prose took our collective hands and walked with us through the ever-darkening shadows toward the millennium. By the early 1980s, he had won the hearts and minds (and wallets) of the United States and UK – tens of millions of his books were in print, and he was not simply the bestselling horror writer of all time but also an icon of popular culture, appearing in television commercials, parodied on 'Saturday Night Live', inescapable in bookshops and theatres.

In 1982, King published *Danse Macabre*, an anecdotal history of contemporary horror in fiction, television and film. Two years later, my own *Stephen King: The Art of Darkness* (1984) assessed his crucial role in returning the literature of horror to the cultural mainstream.

Both books acknowledged the rich bloodline that powered King's success, and particularly the cadre of writers who had carried the torch during the lean years of the sixties and the seventies: the successors to Robert Bloch, Ray Bradbury, Richard Matheson and Rod Serling who had worked in virtual anonymity to set the stage for the new decade of darkness. Principal among them were Ramsey Campbell, John Farris, Charles L Grant – and, of course, James Herbert and Peter Straub. If King was the heart of contemporary horror fiction, then Straub was its head, the premier stylist of the field; and Herbert was its fist, liberating its imagery from the cozy atmospheres of ghost stories and into a naturalistic realm of violence whose enduring colour was red.

As these writers took centre stage in the early 1980s, other potent talents joined them. Each year brought new novels, new adventures, new canvases for an ever-growing art of darkness.[5] The reason, as Clive Barker noted in the opening line of the second volume of his *Books of Blood*, was simple: 'There is no delight the equal of dread.'

> If it were possible to sit, invisible, between two people on any train, in any waiting room or office, the conversation overheard would time and again circle on that subject. Certainly the debate might appear to be about something entirely different; the state of the nation, idle chat about death on the roads, the rising price of dental care; but strip away the metaphor, the innuendo, and there, nestling at the heart of the discourse, is dread. While the nature of God, and the possibility of eternal life go undiscussed, we happily chew over the minutiae of misery. The syndrome recognizes no boundaries; in bath-house and seminar-room alike, the same ritual is repeated. With the inevitability of a tongue returning to probe a painful tooth, we come back and back and back again to our fears, sitting to talk them over with the eagerness of a hungry man before a full and steaming plate.

Equally eager to embrace this suddenly vital and marketable artform, publishers rushed to feed the seemingly insatiable appetite for stories of the strange and the supernatural. Fear was no longer an aesthetic, but big business, and publishing was quick to make 'horror' a *kind* of book: a product one could tell, and sell, by its cover.

When Stephen King and James Herbert created their first novels, the word 'horror' did not describe a type of book; but by the early 1980s, readers were besieged by the word. For better – and, more often, for worse – 'horror' defined, and also dictated, a *kind* of fiction. Publishers eagerly branded their products – and their writers – as 'horror' through cover copy and publicity; some went so far as to use the word as an imprint. Magazines proclaimed their devotion to it. Entire shelves and sections in bookshops and libraries wore the name.

In this sudden quest for identity, for a way of labelling whatever impulse had given readers and film-goers the particular appetite for chaos that marked the fading 1970s, the coming 1990s, the moment was what mattered: for writers, notoriety and income; for booksellers and publishers, sales. Few considered the long-term consequences, and those who raised their voices were ignored, shouted down. The signifying fences of genre – brand-name writers, book cover art, even book titles, icons, styles – were erected to define, describe and confine.

A fiction whose fundamental impulse was the unsafe and the unexpected – the breaching of the taboo, the creation of physical and metaphysical unease – was being made safe for mass consumption as a fiction of the expected. Soon a 'horror' genre existed that was as recognizable as science fiction, the western, or the romance – and thus as capable of reproduction, marginalization and, indeed, denigration.

The business of publishing was also changing. Beset with economic woes and increased competition from other media, several publishing houses collapsed, while others were consumed in the frenzy for mergers and acquisitions. Publishers grew increasingly conservative, hedging their bets by focusing on two kinds of books: big bestsellers and small, rapid turnover books that, although written by different writers, followed established formulae (the medical thriller, vampire erotica, women in peril, small town terror) and could be packaged and sold repetitively, as ephemeral as monthly magazines.

By the middle of the decade, Stephen King had pushed his art – and himself – to the edge. His epic *IT* (1986) seemed a summation of his interest in what the marketplace called 'horror', and he turned his vision inward, writing a compelling triptych – *Misery* (1987), *The*

Dark Half (1988) and 'Secret Window, Secret Garden' (*Four Past Midnight*, 1990) – about bestselling writers haunted by their literary pasts; then, as a coda, he destroyed his trademark setting of Castle Rock in *Needful Things* (1991). Straub, silent for years after the bestselling *Floating Dragon* (1983), stepped apart from the crowd in a brilliant series of novellas and the psychological thriller *Koko* (1988), then broke away altogether in *Mystery* (1989) and *The Throat* (1993).

A new kind of horror writer was emerging in their wake: commodity brokers, not so much creators as duplicators who had read enough King to be capable of retelling *'Salem's Lot* in another setting but who, like their publishers, seemed interested in little else. The 'horror' novel had come to look, and read, like the literary equivalent of canned soup: there were different flavours, to be sure, but in the end, it was the same soup, made from familiar recipes, wearing identical labels, and assuredly safe for public consumption.

This impulse of 'horror' towards the expected is anathema: what once was popular existentialism was in danger of becoming popular mechanics. In a time when sex could kill, when America's space programme literally had exploded in its face, when entire industries – and communities – disappeared from the landscape of once-Great Britain, the need to put things right, if only in our entertainment, was understandable; but not since the 1950s had the literature of the imagination offered such an unmitigated Puritanism and desire for control. Most 'horror' novels of the eighties offered a message as conservative as their morality: Conform. Behave. Just say no.

'Horror' had become another palliative for the masses – a literature of happy endings, an incessantly didactic fiction with minor moral lessons, most of them reactionary and laced with bigotry. Just as MTV offered a soporific subjugation of rebellious rock-and-roll to the almighty dollar, the black-covered paperback had become a tidy commercial construct, a creature of form rather than substance, for the most part as hollow of content as the mindless marketplace was willing to accept.

Clive Barker emerged from this malaise like an avenging angel. His *Books of Blood* reshaped the ways that readers, writers and publishers perceived the short story – and, for a time, the literature of horror – while subverting the simplistic, ritualized conventions of genre, which rarely satisfied the philosophical and cultural needs of readers. His stories exercised an unbridled enthusiasm for the lush and the lurid, pushing at taboos of sex and violence, yet confirmed an unparalleled ambition and audacity. Soon touted by many, including Stephen King himself, as the 'future of horror', Barker in fact vindicated its honourable past: the dark fantastic.

The *Books of Blood* are framed in the manner of Ray Bradbury's *The Illustrated Man* (1951), their stories said to be etched into the skin of a charlatan whose psychic shenanigans have offended the dead. Any resemblance to Bradbury's gentle fantasies ends, however, with the series' first story, 'The Midnight Meat Train', a harrowing sojourn that depicts the New York subway as a rolling abattoir. Its content is what readers would come to recognize as quintessential Clive Barker: graphic, grotesque, and yet compellingly readable and breathtakingly original.

The stories offer an unusual diversity of narrative structures whose voices range from L Frank Baum to William S Burroughs. Their themes, although focused on supernatural and psychological horror, embrace espionage ('Twilight at the Towers'), *noir* ('Confessions of a (Pornographer's) Shroud'), homage ('New Murders in the Rue Morgue'), slapstick comedy ('The Yattering and Jack'), and the utterly fantastic ('In the Hills, the Cities'). He indulges none of the regionalisms perfected by HP Lovecraft, King and Campbell, setting his tales comfortably and convincingly in locales ranging from the gritty urban despair of Liverpool and the bright lights of Manhattan to the foreign, the wild and the exotic: South America ('How Spoilers Bleed'), Greece ('Babel's Children'), the Hebrides ('Scape-Goats').

Even his characters are different – in their occupations, ages and, most notably, ethnic and sexual diversity (the black long-distance runner of 'Hell's Event'; the bickering gay couple of 'In the Hills, the Cities'). If the details of his characterizations are often elusive, it is because he is uncomfortable with typecasting, in life and in art. As the doomed policeman Redman notes in 'Pig Blood Blues': 'Minds weren't pictures at an exhibition, all numbered, and hung in order of influence, one marked "Cunning", the next, "Impressionable". They were scrawls; they were sprawling splashes of graffiti, unpredictable, unconfinable.'

Although the plots of the stories are often conventional – or clever variations on traditional (or favourite) horror tales or films – the prose itself is remarkable in its elegance and intelligence. Unlike many of the fictions that surrounded them on the shelves, the *Books of Blood* were crafted, well-written, and so very classically English in their diction, echoing not contemporaries but Robert Aickman, Arthur Machen, even HG Wells. The contrast between Barker's graceful classicism and the intense, sometimes shocking, imagery was in itself a reason to take notice.

Indeed, the empowering element of these *Books of Blood* was the audacity of their imagery. Never before had horror (or any other) fiction been as consistently explicit in its sex and violence – and, indeed, in its linking of the two. Among the more memorable presences are the eponymous creatures of 'Rawhead Rex', a baby-eating monster of pure sexual appetite; and 'Son of Celluloid', a moviehouse cancer that spawns bloodthirsty replicas of classic film actors. At face value, the *Books of Blood* might seem just the thing to set the hearts of fundamentalists and censors aflutter; but Barker never panders. Instead, he seems intent on forging miracles from the mire and the mayhem. Here, as in other visionary moments, he is the literary equivalent of the special-effects geniuses who bring convincing and blood-splattered monstrosities to life on the cinema screen.

Not surprisingly, he attributes his interest in violence – and its exercise in the *Books of Blood* – to his experience on the stage and his passion for horror films: 'Because violence in the theatre has extraordinary power. My favourite playwright of violence is Webster; he's the grand master of the violent set-piece, in which there's a broad configuration of events, circumstances, relationships, which are leading inevitably to some dire conclusion. Brian De Palma's films are like that. The narrative falls apart in things like *Dressed to Kill*, but the films have poetry and incredible momentum. The extended sequence of pursuit, seduction, and finally death that begins in the art gallery and ends in the elevator stands as a whole piece, and it has a perverse grandeur, a baroque construction, which makes it interesting for itself. He's saying, *Forget the plot. Give your eyes to this. This is going to be worth watching.* And that's what interests me about the violence: it *is* interesting for itself.

'To some extent, I approach the violence in my stories as being set-pieces, so when there are murders, or people are undergoing transformations, readers know we're not going to avert our eyes. We're going to *look*.

'The kind of horror I like drags things into daylight and says, *Right. Let's have a really good look. Does it still scare you? Does it maybe do something different to you now that you can see it more plainly – something that isn't quite like being scared?*'[6]

Contrary to popular – and generic – notions, these stories were not written primarily to terrify, 'but to *excite*. I think of them as adrenalin stories – let's see how bad things can get and still want to go on and read, still want to turn the page to the next story. I very often write stories in high states of excitement. I cry a lot when I write stories. I laugh a lot when I write stories. I read everything aloud as I write – I play every part – so I seldom write with anybody else in the house, because I hate to be overheard in rehearsal. I'm often disturbed by what I write. Sometimes I can even disgust myself with a notion. But I'm not often frightened by the tales.'

What does frighten him? 'Absence. Nothing. Pascal said, *It is the absolute silence of empty space which makes me afraid*. Or words to that effect.

'The worst monster in the world is better than a blank space, to my mind. Better a candle in an otherwise total darkness, even if it's illuminating something with a grin from ear to ear with one hundred and ten fangs. Better the light – whatever it's illuminating – because you can deal with something that's there. So the images which disturb me tend to be images which come very, very close to flickering out entirely.'

In confronting and subverting the putative genre of horror – and forcing readers to look – he had, in one risky step, succeeded in redeeming the literature of the dark fantastic from the confines of mass marketing. In time, Clive Barker's ambitious debut would be seen as the icon of what could be called the anti-horror story: a fiction that demolished the very notion of 'horror' as a genre.

But first, it was time for celebration. On March 24, 1984, Clive and John Gregson held an informal book launch party at their flat on Hillfield Avenue in Crouch End: 'from Eight Until Late,' the invitation, written and illustrated by Clive, declared. 'Food, Books (and an Author) in Abundance!' The party was a great success, attended by many friends from London, including Barbara Boote and Nan du Sautoy of Sphere, and the former members of the Dog Company, who shared in the delight. 'It was truly a fantastic moment,' says Mary Roscoe, 'when we realized that the books had been published, and people wanted to read them! Being involved so closely, we all felt the same euphoria.'

Roy Barker, his wife Lynne and, best of all, Clive's parents had travelled from Liverpool to join in the festivities. Although Clive was the centre of attention, his mother soon shared the spotlight. 'There were lots of arty people, lots of men,' Roy recalls, 'and Joan was being worshipped: *Oh, you're the mum of Clive Barker!*' Joan had baked two large fruitcakes in the shape of a coffin, with a head and two hands made of marzipan, topped with red icing for blood. 'One of my fondest memories was going to Barker's publication parties,' Barbara Boote says. 'When his mother would come down with a cake she'd baked, with a hatchet through it and blood dripping off it ... Absolutely wonderful!'

When it was time to serve the cake, Clive was given the honour; he went at it with a huge kitchen knife.

'Other people cut their cakes,' Len Barker observes. 'He stabs them.'

11

FIRST BLOOD

CLIVE BARKER'S BOOKS OF BLOOD
VOLUMES ONE, TWO AND THREE (1984)

If therefore the light that is in thee be darkness, how great is that darkness!

— *The Gospel According to St Matthew 6:23*

Clive Barker gives notice of his ambition in the first story of the *Books of Blood*, a harrowing yet visionary excursion into the depths of urban violence called 'The Midnight Meat Train'.[1] Its protagonist is a bland everyman, Leon Kaufman, who once believed that 'New York was still a kind of promised land, where anything and everything was possible'. After three months in the urban jungle, he realizes that the city is not a 'Palace of Delights' but a lost cause: 'It bred death, not pleasure.' Its latest atrocity is an outbreak of subway slaughter, bodies hacked and disembowelled by a madman with the skill of a butcher.

The killer is Mahogany, observer of 'a great tradition ... like Jack the Ripper, like Gilles de Rais, a living embodiment of death, a wraith with a human face. He was a haunter of sleep, and an awakener of terrors'. For Mahogany, humanity is a herd, and he has been chosen to stalk us, 'selecting only the ripest from the passing parade, choosing only the healthy and the young to fall under his sanctified knife.'

Kaufman is destined to confront this predator on a late night subway express. Slumbering, he awakens to a car filled with corpses, and the ghastly sight invites him to indulge the zombiedom of the masses: 'Kaufman almost smiled at the perfection of its horror. He felt an offer of insanity tickling the base of his skull, tempting him into oblivion, promising a blank indifference to the world.'

When the butcher confronts him, Kaufman sees nothing fearsome, 'just another balding, overweight man of fifty'. He ignores his delirious rhetoric and his blade, and manages to slit Mahogany's throat. This bloody encounter would conclude most horror stories; but for Clive Barker, it is merely the beginning.

The train stops deep in the tunnel. Its doors open, and Kaufman is greeted by strange creatures: human, their flesh stained with disease and decay; some wear clothing made of flayed skin. 'We are the City fathers,' they tell him. 'And mothers, and daughters and sons. The builders, the lawmakers. We made this city . . . Before you were born, before anyone living was born . . .' They adjure Kaufman to take the butcher's place and bring them human meat: '[Y]ou must do it for us, and for those older than us. For those born before the city was thought of, when America was a timberland and desert.'[2]

In the darkness waits that elder being: the precursor of man, the 'original American', explicitly paternal ('the Father of Fathers') and beyond imagination.

Kaufman falls to his knees in horror and adoration: 'Every day of his life had been leading to this day, every moment quickening to this incalculable moment of holy terror.'

> It was a giant. Without head or limb. Without a feature that was analogous to human, without an organ that made sense, or senses. If it was like anything, it was like a shoal of fish. A thousand snouts all moving in unison, budding, blossoming and withering rhythmically. It was iridescent, like mother of pearl, but it was sometimes deeper than any colour Kaufman knew, or could put a name to.

That was all Kaufman could see, and it was more than he wanted to see.

The late Robert Bloch was known for his maxim: 'Horror is the taking off of masks.' 'The Midnight Meat Train', like many Barker stories, builds to that moment (his favourite in horror films and fiction) of 'unmasking' – when the veil is lifted, and reality and fantasy collide; when the petty assumptions of his characters, whose vision is impaired by the veneer of social or religious or political authority, succumb to a hidden and often unspeakable truth; when the traditional explanations – and, of course, traditional metaphysical defences – are tested. Blissfully embracing the usual dichotomies – good and evil, normal and different, man and beast – his characters learn that they, like us, live in a world of constant flux, defined by chaos, not order; and it is then that they awaken, transformed, recognizing that reality has all the certainty of a fantasy or, indeed, a dream.

The city fathers offer the head of Mahogany to the impossible 'Father of Fathers', and then feast on the train's payload. Their leader exhorts Kaufman – 'Serve . . . In silence' – and tears his tongue out. Then Kaufman, once the dreamer, awakens in a pristine, private station, and emerges to a new dawn – and a new vision of reality:

> The city would go about its business in ignorance: never knowing what it was built upon, or what it owed its life to. Without hesitation, Kaufman fell to his knees and kissed the dirty concrete with his bloody lips, silently swearing his eternal loyalty to its continuance.
>
> The Palace of Delights received the adoration without comment.

Like many traditional horror stories, 'The Midnight Meat Train' seeks the epiphany of the night journey, which I considered at length in *Stephen King: The Art of Darkness*. But when Kaufman emerges from the blood-soaked underworld, his journey brings something more than emotional or spiritual revelation. In this sense, Barker notes, his horror fiction differs dramatically from that of Stephen King: 'His stories are healing stories in a way that mine aren't. All horror heals; it opens some wounds and shows you how to close them again. But King heals to a great extent by dealing with the monsters as though they were alien. I heal by having characters realize that the monsters are part of themselves.' For Barker, 'the monsters and creatures, the dark side, need to be invited into the twilight so we can meet them. Horror fiction is a perpetual twilight where we can meet these things, *not* so we can send them back into the darkness saying, *I am cleansed and purged of you!* We are *not* purged of them, and it's not them or us. We should take them on board, they are part of ourselves.'[3]

In these confrontations, the lives of Barker's characters are fundamentally changed – sometimes into death – without hope of return to the myth of a status quo. All thought of the 'ordinary' as something to be desired is rejected. 'In a world in which we are sold a kind of blissful banality in which ordinariness is raised to the level of the heroic, actually being extraordinary, plunging one's hand into one's imagination and finding out its depths and heights, finding out the devils and angels that haunt it, is actually far more important.'

The mood shifts palpably to comic relief in 'The Yattering and Jack', the first of Barker's stories to be adapted for television, in George A Romero's brief-lived series 'Tales from the Darkside' (1987). The Yattering, a lower demon, is dispatched from Hell to secure the soul of one Jack J Polo, a gherkin-importer of no apparent consequence: 'This wasn't a Faust: a pact-maker, a soul-seller. This one wouldn't look twice at the chance of divine inspiration: he'd sniff, shrug and get on with his gherkin importing.' Forbidden from touching his intended victim, the demon's efforts escalate from practical jokes to murdering pets and finally, in a sublime moment, re-animating the Christmas turkey. When Jack, who seemed clueless, wins the war for his soul, his reward is mastery over the demon; but he can imagine nothing but the mundane, and asks it only to clean the house.

Perverse slapstick descends into blood-soaked irony in 'Pig Blood Blues', a bleak drama set in a juvenile prison that has echoes of Barker's difficult early years at Quarry Bank. Former policeman Neil Redman (colloquially, a 'pig') tries to save a sixteen-year-old from brutal bullying, only to learn that his wards worship a large and oddly beautiful sow, bearing it, like the 'Father of Fathers', offerings of human meat: 'She had a taste, since the first time, for food with a certain texture, a certain resonance. It wasn't food she would demand all the time, only when the need came on her. Not a great demand: once in a while, to gobble at the hand that fed her.'[4]

A boy has hanged himself as fodder for the sow, in a dire take on *Peter Pan*: 'To live forever . . . so he'd never be a man, and die.' Now the sow hungers for Redman: 'This is the state of the beast,' it urges, 'to eat and be eaten.'[5] Barker's swift return to the theme of anthropophagy, and its link with elder (indeed, primal) forces, underscores the directness with which he depicts violence and the taboo while grappling with the metaphysical. From their earliest pages, the *Books of Blood* demystify the body – and, when necessary, reduce it to meat – forcing the reader to admit to mortality and, indeed, to life in a food chain.

'Sex, Death and Starshine' returns to comedy with a satiric fable about the eternal struggle between art and commerce. Former child star Terence Calloway is a 'haggard cherub' whose face maps the 'excesses of sex, booze and ambition, the frustration of aspiring and just missing the main chance so many times'. He dreams of reviving his career with a production of *Twelfth Night* in northern England, 'trying to garner a reputation as a serious director; no gimmicks, no gossip; just art'.

Calloway's ambition is frustrated by 'the fatal flaw of this profession: actors' – and the material world of the eighties, whose suburban landscape 'didn't need theatres; it needed offices, hypermarkets, warehouses: it needed, to quote the councillors, growth through investment in new industry . . . No mere art could survive such pragmatism.'

Enter a mysterious patron, Lichfield, who offers Calloway a perfect Viola: his long-dead wife. (A 'lich' is a body, particularly a corpse.) On opening night, the dead rise from the local graveyard, an audience eager to witness a grand finale. When the theatre burns, Calloway joins the Lichfields, taking to the road as a touring company, intent on offering entertainment to the dead: 'In all his fifteen years of work in the theatre he had never found an audience so appreciative.'[6]

As this defiantly humorous dénouement suggests, for Clive Barker, conformity is the ultimate horror; only through the intrusion of chaos may we see our world clearly, know both its dangers and its possibilities. Otherwise, like the citizens of the breathtaking 'In the Hills, the Cities' who form into a giant and march off to battle, we are doomed.

This closing story of the first of the *Books of Blood* is one of Barker's finest fictions, and a remarkably prescient musing on the fate of Bosnia and Serbia.

While honeymooning in Yugoslavia, Mick realizes that his lover, Judd, is a political bigot: 'The arts were political. Sex was political. Religion, commerce, gardening, eating, drinking and farting – all political.' Judd, in turn, views Mick as a dreamer, and an intellectual lightweight: 'Mick was a queen; there was no other word for him ... His mind was no deeper than his looks; he was a well-groomed nobody.'

Their affair – and their mundane existence – are at an end. In the hills nearby, the twin cities of Popolac and Podujevo are deserted, their tens of thousands of inhabitants struggling to stand as one, forming into giants whose heads reach nearly to the clouds. Creatures of politics and history, they are locked into an 'insane consensus' that 'convulse[s] into one mind, one thought, one ambition': war.

When the giants face off in battle, Podujevo's flank weakens, unleashing 'a cancer of chaos through the body of the city ... Ten thousand mouths spoke a single scream for its vast mouth, a wordless, infinitely pitiable appeal to the sky. A howl of loss, a howl of anticipation, a howl of puzzlement. How, the scream demanded, could the day of days end like this, in a welter of falling bodies?'

The sociopolitical allegory is made clear as the citizens of the victorious Popolac swagger as one into the hills:

> They became, in the space of a few moments, the single-minded giant whose image they had so brilliantly recreated. The illusion of petty individuality was swept away in an irresistible tide of collective feeling – not a mob's passion, but a telepathic surge that dissolved the voices of thousands into one irresistible command.
>
> And the voice said: Go!
>
> The voice said: Take this horrible sight away, where I need never see it again.
>
> Popolac turned away into the hills, its legs taking strides half a mile long. Each man, woman and child in that seething tower was sightless. They saw only through the eyes of the city. They were thoughtless, but to think the city's thoughts. And they

believed themselves deathless, in their lumbering, relentless strength. Vast and mad and deathless.

Mick and Judd cannot comprehend the devastation; but as Popolac strides toward them, they look on in a rapture of religious intensity.[7] Judd, the pragmatist, is frozen by the sight, and is crushed by the giant's foot: 'Out like a light, a tiny, insignificant light . . .' But Mick, ever the dreamer, sees the passing foot as his only chance:

> Howling like a banshee, he ran towards the leg, longing to embrace the monster. He stumbled in the wreckage, and stood again, bloodied, to reach for the foot before it was lifted and he was left behind . . . He made one last lunge at the limb as it began to leave the ground, snatching a harness or a rope, or human hair, or flesh itself – anything to catch this passing miracle and be part of it. Better to go with it wherever it was going, serve it in its purpose, whatever that might be; better to die with it than live without it.

'Dread' introduces the second volume of the *Books of Blood*, with a profound critique of creators and consumers of horror – an unflinching invitation to consider the reason that we turn the pages of Clive Barker's fiction.[8] It is also a vengeful fable of Clive's frustrating years at the University of Liverpool.

Stephen Grace, a student whose surname bespeaks his innocence, receives an unexpected education at the hands of a maniacal mentor, Quaid. Like Barker, he studied Philosophy and English Literature. Dulled by the tedium of university life – 'I'm just completely lost' – he finds his master in a bar. Little is known about Quaid save his disdain for the reassuring lies taught in the ivied halls of academe: '*True* philosophy. It's a beast, Stephen . . . It's wild. It bites.' Any worthwhile philosophy, he insists, concerns 'the things we fear, because we don't understand them. It's the dark behind the door' – and it must be confronted: '[I]f we don't go out and find the beast . . . sooner or later the beast will come and find us.'

The world according to Quaid revolves around the inescapable axis of dread:

In Quaid's world there were no certainties. He had no secular gurus and certainly no religion. He seemed incapable of viewing any system, whether it was political or philosophical, without cynicism.

Though he seldom laughed out loud, Steve knew there was a bitter humour in his vision of the world. People were lambs and sheep, all looking for shepherds. Of course these shepherds were fictions, in Quaid's opinion. All that existed, in the darkness outside the sheep-fold, were the fears that fixed on the innocent mutton: waiting, patient as stone, for their moment.

Everything was to be doubted, but the fact that dread existed.

Quaid, who prefigures the manipulative (and equally mad) psychiatrist Decker of *Cabal* (1988) and *Nightbreed* (1990), finds in Grace the ideal collaborator – and prey. In a drunken gaffe, Grace discloses his deepest fear, instilled in childhood, when he was struck by a car and deafened; Quaid re-enacts the disabling experience, with an intent that seems murderous: 'Sartre had written that no man could ever know his own death. But to know the deaths of others, intimately – to watch the acrobatics that the mind would surely perform to avoid the bitter truth – that was a clue to death's nature, wasn't it? That might, in some small way, prepare a man for his own death. To live another's dread vicariously was the safest, cleverest way to touch the beast.'

Here Barker likens himself – and his readers – to the monster known as Quaid; for what else is he but a creator and observer of horror? Indeed, that is the question at the heart of 'Dread': What *else* is Quaid? As the story's climax reveals, he is quite mad, utterly incapable of making the vital distinction between the real and the imagined.

'Hell's Event', which follows, is mere funhouse entertainment with disconcerting shifts in point of view. Its plot hinges on an athletic contest between man and Satan (represented by a smarmy Member of Parliament) for the fate of the physical world. In its initial draft, Barker contemplated a professional wrestling match, but he settled on a gruelling foot race through the streets and squares of London.

The stridently feminist 'Jacqueline Ess: Her Will and Testament' is an intense amalgam of Luis Buñuel's *Belle de Jour* (1967) and Stephen King's *Carrie* (1974), in which a woman, unable to express her identity in the everyday world, achieves control through an elaborate fantasy existence, only to learn the shallow truth of power.

Trapped by marriage, Jacqueline Ess tries to take her life, but the razor's kiss summons the blood of feminine power. Her condescending physician offers excuses for her suicidal thoughts – women's problems, women's needs – and, gripped by a sudden revulsion, she thinks: 'Be a woman.' His body is ripped asunder in a bloody parody of the feminine – and a later victim is shredded until he 'looked, to her eyes, a little more like a sensitive man'.

Jacqueline Ess has returned from the shadow of death with a peculiar talent: her thoughts can transform. 'She'd gone through her life, it seemed, looking for a sign of herself, only able to define her nature by the look in others' eyes. Now she wanted an end to that.' The first step is vengeance on her faithless husband; the next is self-perfection. In exchange for her now-beautiful body, she seeks education in empowerment; but her lesson is 'never to regret her absence of instinctive compassion, but to judge with her intellect alone who deserved extinction and who might be numbered amongst the righteous'.

Dismayed by this truth – 'My God . . . this can't be power' – she withers into self-destruction, only to join, quite literally, the one man who loved her, melding their bodies into 'common waters made of thought and bone . . . Tangled in a wash of love they thought themselves extinguished, and were.'

This melancholy morality play offers a wicked commentary on sexual politics, and the misguided belief that power over others is the source of freedom – when, as Barker reminds us in a later story, 'Babel's Children', and the novel *The Damnation Game* (both 1985), power brings its own kind of slavery.

The mysteries of the flesh are explored further in 'The Skins of the Fathers' – a precursor of the novel *Cabal* (1988) and the motion picture *Nightbreed* (1990). A strange procession of monsters emerges from a desert in the American southwest, searching for their progeny Aaron – the 'exalted one', born of a local woman. His mother sees beauty in the menagerie, while others see only terror and sin: 'All the attributes of Lucifer were spread among the bodies of the fathers.'[9]

The townspeople, led by a xenophobic acolyte of law-and-order, combat the creatures in the name of Jesus Christ; but we learn that the monsters are not only the fathers of Aaron, but also the fathers of all mankind.[10]

'New Murders in the Rue Morgue', written over several days when Clive was snowbound in Paris, offers a homage and sequel to the fiction of Edgar Allan Poe.[11] Lewis Fox, a retired artist, is summoned to wintry Paris to help an old friend, Phillipe Laborteaux, who has been imprisoned for the murder of a nineteen-year-old girl, Natalie. He takes up the investigation and soon discovers the huge and heavily perfumed enigma who fancied Natalie. Speechless, it moves with small, mincing steps, 'the gait of an upright beast who'd been taught to walk, and now, without its master, was losing the trick of it . . . It was an ape'.

Inspired by Lewis's insistence that Poe's 'Murders in the Rue Morgue' was based in truth, Phillipe has trained an ape to pass as a man; but the experiment is doomed by the petty violence of the human condition: seduced by Natalie, the ape murdered her. 'Its days of innocence had gone: it could never be an unambitious beast again. Trapped in its new persona, it had no choice but to continue in the life its master had awoken its taste for.' Again Barker explores the nature of monstrosity and the myth of normality, investing his monsters with humanity and, in so doing, reminding humanity of its capacity for the monstrous – and celebrating, always celebrating, the liberation of the imagination from the flesh.

Volume Three of the *Books of Blood* presents its most cerebral stories, presaging more complex and developed fictions to come.[12] It is also the most thematically coherent of the first three books, its texts exploring the haunting power of the past, and the nature of identity and illusion.

Conventional horror fiction proceeds from the archetype of Pandora's Box: the tense conflict between pleasure and fear that is latent when we face the forbidden and the unknown. As the dazed cinema manager of 'Son of Celluloid', which opens Volume Three, puts it: '[W]hich was worse? To see, or not to see?' The *Books of Blood* are founded on the proposition that there are no taboos, no mysteries – and that the best fiction is anything but escapist; it is confrontational.

Clive Barker insists: We *must* see. He drags our terrors from the shadows and forces us to look upon them and despair – or laugh with relief.

Barker states his credo in matter-of-fact tones: 'Horror fiction without violence doesn't do a great deal for me. I think that death and wounding need to be in the air. You've got to get the reader on this ghost train ride, and there's got to be something vile at the end of it, or else why aren't you on the rollercoaster instead? And I like to be able to deliver the violence. There's never going to be any evasion. Whether it be sexual subject matter, whether it be violence, I'm going to show it as best I can.'

Show it he does in 'Son of Celluloid'; in the story's own words: 'This wasn't a look-behind-you thrill, there was no delicious anticipation, no pleasurable fright. It was real fear, bowel fear, unadorned and ugly as shit.' Indeed, it offers an ironic prophecy of Clive Barker's career in film: 'The cinema had become a slaughterhouse.'

Escaped convict Barberio, wounded by police and dying of stomach cancer, hides behind the silver screen of the Movie Palace. There, in a wash of light-borne images, he dies; but his cancer lives on, animating the emotional residue of film-goers – 'a ghost in the machine of cinema' – and taking the guises of John Wayne and Marilyn Monroe.

'I need to be looked at,' the conjured Marilyn tells us, 'or I die. It's the natural state of illusions.' Behind the fantasy lurks the appalling reality: 'An eye, a single vast eye, was filling the doorway . . . huge and wet and lazy, scanning the doll in front of it with the insolence of the One True God, the maker of celluloid Earth and celluloid Heaven.' It is a parasite, aching for its sustenance – the peculiar love that is given to goddesses and gods of the silver screen:

> That's why all those scenes were playing, and replaying, and playing again, in front of her. They were all moments when an audience was magically united with the screen, bleeding through its eyes, looking and looking and looking. She'd done it herself, often. Seen a film and felt it move her so deeply it was almost a physical pain when the end credits rolled and the illusion was broken, because she felt she'd left something of herself behind, a part of her inner being lost up there amongst her heroes and her heroines.

Maybe she had. Maybe the air carried the cargo of her desires and deposited them somewhere, intermingled with the cargo of other hearts, all gathering together in some niche, until–

Until this. This child of their collective passions: this Technicolor seducer; trite, crass and utterly bewitching.

When the overweight heroine sees the image of Disney's Dumbo, the great grey elephant whose name she had suffered as a child, she realizes the lie. She finds the rotted corpse of Barberio – 'I am a dreaming disease,' it tells her – and takes it into her embrace; in a literal enactment of the power of flesh over fantasy, she crushes it beneath her weight.[13]

This bittersweet fable of the cinema, able only to mime the past and not to create anew, is followed by 'Rawhead Rex', another one of Barker's inspired creations, and the first of his short stories to be adapted – far more bitter than sweet – as a motion picture; it is discussed at length in Chapter 15. Then comes 'Confessions of a (Pornographer's) Shroud', a tale of the ghostly vengeance enacted by Ronald Glass, a mild-mannered accountant who is framed by a gangster and then murdered. 'And that, to all intents and purposes, was the end of that. Except that it was the beginning.'

Glass is given life anew; his spirit passes into his funeral shroud 'like a morbid Adam raised out of linen'. The shroud invades the crime lord's private fortress (named, like Barker's communal home in Merseyside, the 'Ponderosa') and enacts a grisly revenge. In death, Glass finds the liberation and, indeed, joy that eluded him in life: 'He existed in mutiny against nature, that was his state; and for the first time in his life (and death) he felt an elation. To be unnatural: to be in defiance of system and sanity, was that so bad? He was shitty, bloody, dead and resurrected in a piece of stained cloth; he was a nonsense. *Yet he was.* No one could deny him being, as long as he had the will to be. The thought was delicious: like finding a new sense in a blind, deaf world.'

'Scape-Goats' twists the iconography of zombie films into an elegiac nightmare.[14] One of Barker's few first-person narratives, the story recounts the last day of four lost souls shipwrecked in the Hebrides. Echoing Joseph Conrad, the narrator tells us: 'I can think of no use for a place like this, except that you could say of it: I saw the heart of nothing, and survived.'

The island is a burial mound where the corpses of soldiers and sailors, washed up from ships torpedoed and sunk in the world wars, have been interred. The castaways find three sheep, and kill one – only to learn that the dead men 'had the rhythm of the sea in them, and they wouldn't lie down. So to placate them, these sheep were tethered in a pen, to be offered up to their wills ... [I]t wasn't food they wanted. It was the gesture of recognition – as simple as that.'

The castaways die, one by one, until finally Frankie, the narrator, drowns, entangled in the corpse of her hoped-for lover, Ray: 'Too late for love; the sunlight was already a memory. Was it that the world was going out – darkening towards the edges as I die – or that we were now so deep the sun couldn't penetrate so far? Panic and terror had left me – my heart seemed not to beat at all – my breath didn't come and go in anguished bursts as it had. A kind of peace was on me.'

The dire and pessimistic veneer of 'Scape-Goats' underscores Barker's insistent demand for making life worth living – and for celebrating its possibilities. His choice of a first-person narrative is canny, since it forces the reader to align with the indifferent Frankie, and hopefully to recognize that the craggy shoal on which she has foundered is an externalization of her worldview – and her story a dramatization of Barker's Pascalian dread, with darkness gradually absorbing all. There is no life in her but a futile hope for the attentions of Ray – who, alive or dead, feels nothing for her. There is little wonder that she should become one with the drowned dead, 'soothed by the rhythm of tiny waves and the absurd incomprehension of sheep'. Frankie and her friends are scapegoats for the sin of indifference.[15]

The powerful thematic threads of Volume Three weave into a climactic memento mori, 'Human Remains', which would later serve as an inspiration for Peter Atkins's script for Hellraiser III: Hell on Earth (1992). Gavin, a street hustler, is another creature of indifference, wearing 'a face that scarcely cared if you lived or died'; it is his 'trademark ... even part of his attraction'. Like the dreaming disease of 'Son of Celluloid', he needs a desirous gaze, a 'fix of attention'. He picks up an older man, Kenneth Reynolds, whose flat is laden with art and antiquities from Roman Britain; but Reynolds is hiding some-thing: a crudely-sculpted figure of a sleeping man.[16] 'Something about the statue fascinated him. Maybe its nakedness, and that second strip it was slowly performing underwater: the ultimate strip: off with the skin.' It is a strange golem that replicates what it desires – and its desire is Gavin: 'I am a thing without a proper name,' it tells him. 'I am a wound in the flank of the world. But I am also that perfect stranger you always prayed for as a child, to come and take you, call you beauty, lift you naked out of the street and through Heaven's window. Aren't I? Aren't I?' It knows his dreams: 'Because I am yourself . . . made perfectable.'

As the statue replicates Gavin's physical features, it also steals his emotions, his soul – and thus his loneliness and insubstantiality. When Gavin, certain of death, visits his father's grave, he finds his double there, its mimicry so perfect that it even has his toothache. Tears of mourning for his lost father cloud its eyes.

'Why is it all so painful?' it asks. 'Why is it loss that makes me human?' But Gavin can offer neither tears nor an answer, for he realizes the sad but simple truth: 'What did he know or care about the fine art of being human?'

There is little mystery about the popular and critical success of *Clive Barker's Books of Blood*. These three volumes introduced a bold and idiosyncratic vision, powered by provocative images and ideas – and several of the stories rank among the better tales of terror ever pub-lished. Barker's charismatic personality and boyish good looks made him a darling of the interview set; and, in North America, his British accent and quick wit would earn him media attention of the type afforded an invading pop star. The only real mystery is why his first American publisher, Berkley Books, then a division of GP Putnam, delayed the release of the *Books of Blood* for nearly two years, and then issued them only in paperback editions with garish, downmarket covers.

Ramsey Campbell's introduction to the *Books of Blood* was the first of many well-deserved accolades; but most early reviews focused on the graphic violence and sexuality of the stories, while others sought to impress readers with their 'discovery' of Clive Barker. The ever-escalating rhetoric used to describe the texts would, in time, soar to hyperbole – and reviewers and journalists on both sides of the Atlantic pretended with disappointing regularity that writers like Campbell and James Herbert, whose fiction had set the stage for Barker's break-through, did not exist.[17]

In October 1984, Barker's invasion of North America was given its most renowned boost by the best of all possible spokesmen: Stephen King. At the World Fantasy Convention in Ottawa, Canada, Stephen and Tabitha King, Peter Straub, and my wife and I circled a table at lunch. Straub presented King with the manuscript of a fine novella, 'Blue Rose', and the discussion turned to new and interesting writers.

Clive Barker's name came up instantly as Straub and I spoke enthusiastically about the *Books of Blood*, with loving descriptions of 'In the Hills, the Cities'. After lunch, King and Straub spoke on a panel, and when King was asked about new writers of horror fiction, he said: 'How many people have heard of Clive Barker?' Only a few people in the audience raised their hands, including Ginjer Buchanan, an editor with Berkley Books. King then offered a typically colloquial comment: 'Well, I haven't read this guy, but from what I understand it's like what Jann Wenner said – *I have seen the future of rock-and-roll, and his name is Bruce Springsteen.* Sounds like Clive Barker might be the future of horror.'

The North American rights to the *Books of Blood* had been licensed to Berkley by Nan du Sautoy: 'I remember spending years talking to people, saying simplistically, *This is the next Stephen King, believe me* – and people not believing me. It took a long while – until Stephen King's quote corroborated it – before people believed that he was something special. It was difficult trying to convince people that we had a really good author, because everybody likens everybody else to the new Stephen King, or the new this or that. People become immune to someone saying it from the heart, rather than just as hype.'

Berkley later sent the *Books of Blood* to King and asked if they could quote what he said at the convention – which was rendered, in its final incarnation, into the now-famous words:

'I have seen the future of horror, and its name is Clive Barker.'[18]

NOWHERE LAND

THE DAMNATION GAME (1985)

Now Faustus must thou needs be damned,
And canst thou not be saved.
What boots it then to think on God or heaven?
– CHRISTOPHER MARLOWE, *The Tragicall Historie of*
Doctor Faustus

Soon after his first meeting with Barbara Boote and Nan du Sautoy, Clive Barker realized how 'inappropriate it was to write short stories'. Given commercial publishing's disfavour for anthologies and story collections, it is rare for writers of any stature to see a book of stories in print, and virtually miraculous for a writer's first book to take this form; certainly it was a publishing first for a writer's initial three books, all story collections, to be issued simultaneously. Boote told Barker, in her typically soft-spoken but direct style: 'Now do something sensible and write a novel. Do yourself a favour and write something we can really sell.'

The prospect was daunting, but another new challenge that Clive embraced with characteristic enthusiasm: 'In a certain sense I was granted a little license to step back in time and do what people used to do in the forties – to publish short stories in *Weird Tales* or wherever, and to hone something about the way you think or what you believe or what you want to write about, and then actually get on to a novel.' When he started writing his first novel, the *Books of Blood* had been published, but the groundswell of excitement that would make him one of today's most visible writers was only beginning.

Since reading *Arabian Sands* (1949) by Sir Wilfred Thesiger, the first outsider to cross Rub' al Khali, the great south desert of Arabia known as the Empty Quarter, Clive had been fascinated by the idea of a journey into a landscape of nothingness, its mythology and meta-physics. He prepared an eight- or ten-page synopsis, which Vernon Conway offered to Sphere, of a novel in which an explorer discovers the ruins of Eden – and a lone angel – in the Empty Quarter. Return-ing home to England, the explorer unwittingly looses an apparently demonic, but in truth angelic, force. Sphere rejected the proposal – titled *Out of the Empty Quarter* – principally because it seemed like a fantasy novel. Readers of the *Books of Blood*, Boote and du Sautoy argued, would want and expect a horror novel.

'We weren't very keen on it,' Barbara Boote says. 'It was set in a desert, outside of Britain; it didn't seem to have a proper setting. It was more fantastical, and fantasy wasn't really what we were looking for. Horror is what we thought we should have, because his books of short stories are very much horror. We weren't going to say no to him, but we felt he could come up with another idea; and that's what we said to him: *Leave this on the back burner for a while, and come up with something else.*'

'What publishers don't like,' Nan du Sautoy notes, 'is somebody switching genres after they've been semi-established in one area.' Clive politely differed with the very idea that there was a distinction between 'fantasy' and 'horror'; it was the first of many battles to be joined over questions of genre and expectation, and one of the few in which he relented.[1] He soon offered Boote and du Sautoy a new proposal for *Mamoulian's Game*, a Faustian tale 'intended to be a very on-the-nose piece of horror'. After reviewing a detailed synopsis, Sphere contracted with Barker to write the book for an advance of £2,000. It was published in 1985 as *The Damnation Game*.[2]

Although this was Clive's first real attempt to write a novel, the transition seemed natural: 'I think of myself, despite the scale of my books, as being a rather economical writer. Even in *Imajica*; I feel like a short story writer even when I'm writing an 800-page book. It's dense with texture and ideas, and I'm trying always to press the largest amount of information into the smallest amount of space. And that comes with the experience of writing short stories first. It also comes from the experience of writing plays and seeing the live experience of the theatre scene, how readily people will become bored if you don't continue to stimulate them. So when I turned to the novel, it was a question of making sure that I kept the excitement that I have writing short stories alive in the larger form.'

But his work on the novel was soon complicated by the text – and competing demands on his time. Director George Pavlou called in November 1984 to tell him that their dream of collaborating on a horror film had been realized, and that Barker's script for *Underworld* was needed in a matter of weeks. Then Barker's agent, Vernon Conway, reported that *The Secret Life of Cartoons* was going into production with the West End as its goal, but that revisions of the play were required. And, as the *Books of Blood* garnered increasing acclaim and sales, Sphere urged Barker to prepare three more volumes – and to do so quickly in order to take advantage of an obvious window of opportunity. 'We were all editorially keen on Clive,' du Sautoy says. 'He wasn't somebody to whom we were going to say, *All right, we've given you a chance, and we're not going to follow it up.*'

Clive's discipline was extraordinary under circumstances that were nothing less than punishing. His father's work ethic echoed in him as he toiled seven days a week, with a daily goal of a set number of pages, often writing from morning long into the night. His personal life no longer existed; he was locked into creation at a pace that was both exhausting and exhilarating.

With so much work demanding his attention in so little time, it is not surprising that the first draft of *The Damnation Game* did not meet with Barbara Boote's desires; but she was one of an increasingly rare breed in commercial publishing: an editor who cared enough not to treat books simply as commodities to be plugged into slots in a publication schedule. She saw the tremendous potential of the novel

– and of Clive Barker – and she worked hard to bring out the best in him. 'He did masses of revisions,' she notes. 'His first draft was very much a first draft, a first novel type thing. And I think that was another reason why we wanted some more short stories. We didn't want too much of a gap. And we thought that the first novel wouldn't be ready in time . . . It was quite flawed, and he and I did quite a lot of work on it. We probably could have done a little bit more. He wasn't the easiest person to edit. Every comma we had a discussion about, which is fine, but I think it could have done with a little bit more of it. It could have been a better first novel.' She pauses, then adds with a smile: 'But he learned.'

> Hell is reimagined by each generation. Its terrain is surveyed for absurdities and remade in a fresher mould; its terrors are scrutinized and, if necessary, reinvented to suit the current climate of atrocity; its architecture is redesigned to appal the eye of the modern damned.

Despite their crimson glory, the *Books of Blood* were distinctive for a more subtle and subversive reason: their insistent metaphysics. The putative genre of 'horror' was decidedly Christian, schooled by the rigid, if not rigorous, thinking of Catholicism and fundamentalism. Given birth by two Catholic novels and films – *Rosemary's Baby* (1967, 1968) and *The Exorcist* (1971, 1973) – and embracing a rich history of crucifixes and holy water, the horror fiction that emerged in the 1970s was powered by the unease of a generation faced with the downfall of organized religion as a social, political, educational and moral force. Even fiction that rejected (and, on occasion, desecrated) the formalities of religion depicted the underlying struggle as Manichaean: good versus evil, light against darkness.

Along with its sensational imagery, Barker's early fiction was insistently subversive, seeking to explore and explode the mythologies of genre – and Western religion. Stories like 'Rawhead Rex' and 'The Skins of the Fathers' turn common religious precepts upside-down, summoning up awkward questions in the minds of those who read with something more than their eyes. Ironically, by turning the basic tenets of Judeo-Christian texts on their head, Barker has proved not only provocative but also among the more spiritual fictioneers of this generation.

When he turned to writing *The Damnation Game*, these metaphysical concerns were brought forward (and, in time, preoccupied his novels). He decided to retell a classic story: 'It is not that the old stories are necessarily the *best* stories; rather that the old stories are the *only* stories. There are no new tales, only new ways to tell.'[3]

The Damnation Game celebrates the timeless fable of Faust, which Barker has called '*the* best horror story': the ambitious man and his pact with hellish divinities; the pride, curiosity, or other appetite that is intrinsic to his nature; and the inevitable fall, succumbing to the very forces that he dared hope to control. With source material as diverse as folk tales and Goethe, Barker's direct inspiration came from his favourite rendition of the story, and the first that he encountered: Christopher Marlowe's feverish play *The Tragicall Historie of Doctor Faustus* (circa 1588).[4]

In Marlowe's version of the drama, Faustus, an ambitious scholar, sells his soul in pursuit of the magical arts. 'This is a man,' Barker notes, 'who has studied until study can reward him no longer. A man to whom science has become a cul-de-sac, philosophy a dead library, and who wants to drag the walls and the words down and see the world for himself.'[5] As the time of reckoning approaches, Faustus regrets the barter and seeks liberation from its terms. While Goethe spares his Faust, Marlowe allows no escape; in the final act, a bell tolls toward midnight as Faustus pleads for the mercy of God, but to no avail. A group of scholars enters to find 'Faustus' limbs/All torn asunder by the hand of death!' – and the Chorus intones its summation:

> *Faustus is gone: regard his hellish fall,*
> *Whose fiendful fortune may exhort the wise*
> *Only to wonder at unlawful things*
> *Whose deepness doth entice such forward wits*
> *To practise more than heavenly power permits.*

Although ostensibly an exhortation to standards of traditional Christian behaviour, the late RM Dawkins noted cogently that Marlowe's tragedy is 'the story of a Renaissance man who had to pay the medieval price for being one.'[6]

'At its centre,' Barker notes, 'is a notion essential to the horror genre and its relations: that of a trip taken into forbidden territory at the risk of insanity and death. With the gods in retreat, and the idea of purgatorial judgments less acceptable to the modern mind than new adventures after death as dust and spirit, all imaginative accounts of that journey become essential reading. In their diversity lies testament to the richness of our literature's heritage. In their experiencing, a sense of how the human perspective changes. And in their wisdom – who knows? – a guide to how we, adventurers in the forbidden magic of our genre, may behave when the last Act is upon us.'[7]

In *The Damnation Game* and its successors – 'The Last Illusion' (1985) and *The Hellbound Heart* (1986), and their motion picture adaptations, *Hellraiser* (1987) and *Lord of Illusions* (1995) – Barker consciously sought to reinvent the Faustian drama and to make sense of it for a contemporary audience. He reminds us of a painful truth: that, lost in the new religion of materialism, we, like Faust, are slaves of appetite and hubris who believe that something singular in our humanity will exempt us from the price that must be paid for our sins.

Written, like its inspiration, in five-act form, *The Damnation Game* opens in the ravaged landscape of 'Terra Incognito' – Warsaw in the final days of the Second World War, a Hell on Earth whose desolate splendour is the encampment of a carnival of carnage: sport with the severed heads of babies, traffic in human flesh, perverse pleasures untold. '[T]his was what the end of the world would be like': a place of moral, sexual, and spiritual abjection whose only resource is waste – and from which even death may offer no escape.

Two men meet in this purgatory: a nameless thief whose one indulgence is to gamble, and the legendary card-player Mamoulian, who never cheats but never loses. 'To him ... winning is beauty. It is like life itself.' Their encounter is presaged by a manic street performance of *Faust*: 'the pact with Mephisto, the debates, the conjuring tricks, and then, as the promised damnation approached, despair and terrors.' A game that will span decades – the Damnation Game – begins.

Fast-forward to the present and a prison cell at Wandsworth, England, where Marty Strauss, a gambler driven to theft to pay his debts, waits out his sentence for armed robbery. At his annual parole interview, Strauss is greeted by an outsider, William Toy, envoy of reclusive Joseph Whitehead – an aged imperialist patriarch (as his name implies) and owner of a vast pharmaceutical empire. Whitehead seeks a new bodyguard among prisoners eligible for parole. When Strauss is selected for the job, his warder muses: 'I wonder if you understand just what kind of freedom you've chosen–'

Strauss learns that there is no such thing as freedom; the world outside is simply a different kind of prison. Whitehead's Sanctuary is both refuge and madhouse, a cloistered estate in Oxford from which he never ventures. The industrialist is a self-made man whose uncanny instinct and willingness to risk everything on a single throw of the dice have brought him fame and fortune; but nothing can forestall the curse of age, harbinger of some inevitable but inexplicable damnation. Now he waits, prisoner of his prestige and power, surrounded by alarms, fences, guard dogs, eroding in the thrall of a long-forgotten fear:

> There was a time when he'd been a fox: thin and sharp; a night wanderer. But things had changed. Providence had been bountiful, dreams had come true; and the fox, always a shape-changer, had grown fat and easy. The world had changed too: it had become a geography of profit and loss. Distances had shrunk to the length of his command. He had forgotten, with time, his previous life.
>
> But of late he remembered it more and more.

As Whitehead recalls that prior existence, Marty ponders the provenance of his new master's wealth: '[W]as he also a thief? And if not that, what *was* his crime?' There were many crimes, but as Whitehead's fate encroaches, he rationalizes himself into an Everyman:

> But then, damn it, who would not have crimes to confess, when the time came? Who would not have acted out of greed, and envy; or grappled for station, and having gained it, been absolute

in their authority rather than relinquish it? He couldn't be held responsible for everything the Corporation had done. If, once in a decade, a medical preparation that deformed foetuses had slipped on to the market, was he to blame because there'd been profit made? That kind of moral accounting was for the writers of revenge fiction: it didn't belong in the real world, where most crimes went punished only with wealth and influence; where the worm seldom turned, and when it did was immediately crushed; where the best a man could hope was that having risen to his ambition's height by wit, stealth or violence there was some smidgen of pleasure in the view.

Locked inside the Sanctuary like a fairytale princess is Whitehead's daughter, Carys, a sad-eyed enigma whom Whitehead, ferociously possessive, has addicted to heroin in order to hold her close. Carys is psychic – a sensitive, able to feel what others think – and she welcomes the drug to numb her strange talent.

Inevitably Marty Strauss will become her knight-errant. The bodyguard is desperately alone – his wife and his outside life have deserted him, and servitude to Whitehead is his sole defining grace. He is one of Clive Barker's few true 'action heroes', a one-world but two-fisted man, solid and sombre, the working-class warrior whose dirty feet trod dirty places.[8] But when Marty, whose true prison is class, tells Carys, 'You could go *anywhere*', she confirms that the haunts of the rich are no different from those of the poor: 'That's as good as nowhere.'

Marty and Carys are prisoners of their society and their flesh; each lacks what, for Barker, is the singular means of transcendence – some kind of belief: 'Maybe that was part of the problem between him and the girl: they neither of them believed a damn thing. There was nothing to say, no issues to debate.' Carys, hostage to her father and the needle, has lost the will to believe in anything but the next fix, while Marty believes openly in accident, that messiah of the mechanistic: 'everything's chance'.

When a stranger breaches the defences of the Sanctuary to deliver a succinct message – 'Tell him that I was here' – Marty learns that the forces threatening Whitehead are magical. Whitehead was the thief who played cards with Mamoulian in Warsaw. It was a seduction; Mamoulian let him win, giving Whitehead money, power and industry in order to use him as a puppet. Now Mamoulian, who fancies himself the Last European, seeks to collect on their bargain.[9] At his side is a memorable villain: Anthony Breer, the Razor-Eater, a self-mutilating child-murderer whose suicide Mamoulian rewards with life anew.[10]

Mamoulian is a melancholy Mephistopheles, for whom trust – and its utter absence among his mendicants – has caused such heartbreak and pain that he yearns for the quietude of death:

> The cruelty of other people – their callous usage of him – never failed to wound him, and though he had extended his charitable hand to all manner of crippled psyches, such ingratitude was unforgiveable. Perhaps, he mused, when this end-game was all over and done with – when he'd collected his debts in blood, dread and night – then maybe he'd lose the terrible itch that tormented him day and night, that drove him on without hope of peace to new ambitions and new betrayals. Maybe when all this was over he would be able to lie down and die.

Despite his magic, Mamoulian lives in terror of the flesh: 'He loathed the body; its functions disgusted him. But he couldn't be free of it, or its appetites. That was a torment to him.' Whitehead, the greedy gambler, offered salvation; through him, Mamoulian could experience pleasures untold by proxy. Together the gambler and the thief accumulated wealth, power and women; but when Whitehead fell in love and married, he rebelled and cast out his mentor. 'The singularity of their mutual hatred had the purity of love.' When Mamoulian, weary of life, came to Whitehead to be killed, his vengeful partner denied him. Betrayed, Mamoulian murdered Whitehead's wife, and now he seeks to collect his due: 'Your death. Your soul, for want of a better word.'

Despite all appearances, the Last European is not the Devil: 'What I am is a mystery ... even to myself.' Guided by his eloquent, if nihilistic, syllogism – 'Nothing is essential' – Mamoulian's true face lurks somewhere deep beneath the skin: 'Half a hundred faces, each stranger than the one before, regressing towards some state that was older than Bethlehem.' Pale and sickly, terrified of sex – and indeed, all matters of the flesh – Mamoulian's decadence and air of lost aristocracy invoke a monstrous presence, a conjurer and illusionist full of bluff and bluster. His very proximity wipes everything clean.

He steals Carys and locks her in an empty house. 'It would take another Dante to describe its depths and heights: dead children, Razor-Eaters, addicts, mad-men and all. Surely the stars that hung at its zenith squirmed in their settings; in the earth beneath it, the magma curdled.' With Carys his captive, addled with drugs and intimidated by his conjurations, the Last European increases the torment, urging Whitehead on towards death.

When Marty learns the awful truth, he dreams of escape – to America, a fantasyland where his final destination echoes *The Wizard of Oz*: 'In Kansas, there would be a new story: a story that he could not know the end of. And wasn't that a working definition of freedom, unspoiled by European hand, European certainty?' But suddenly Whitehead is dead, a victim of heart failure; at the funeral, Mamoulian arrives with Carys on his arm. He has been denied his one desire: to goad Whitehead to come willingly into the void. Marty follows Mamoulian to Caliban Street, and rescues Carys; but not until he dares a look into Mamoulian's room. '*Welcome to Wonderland*,' he speaks aloud, but it is nothing like Kansas – or Oz: 'There was nothing to see, not even walls . . . *Nothing to be frightened of . . . Nothing here at all.*'

It is the emptiest of all possible worlds, an 'unbearable *zero*': nowhere land.

> [H]ere, meaning was dead. Future and past were dead. Love and life were dead. Even death was dead, because anything that excited emotion was unwelcome here. Only nothing: once and for all, nothing.
>
> 'Help me,' he said, like a lost child.
>
> Go to Hell, the room respectfully replied; and for the first time in his life, he knew exactly what that meant.[11]

To defeat the European, Marty realizes, they must know his secret life. 'There was no closing your eyes and turning your back on the

European. The only way to be free of him was to *know* him; to look at him for as long as courage allowed and see him in every ghastly particular.' Carys is the means, and her mind reaches out to Mamoulian and finds, at last, an answer: she falls into a moment out of time, October 1811, to find a prisoner-of-war named Mamoulian, a card-playing sergeant of the 3rd Fusiliers who is rescued from execution by an ageless monk: 'You were chosen.' Gifted with ancient wisdom, Mamoulian kills his tutor before realizing a sombre truth: 'I was just his tool. *He wanted to die.*'

> Don't you see how terrible it is to live when everything around you perishes? And the more the years pass the more the thought of death freezes your bowels, because the longer you avoid it the worse you imagine it to be? And you start to long – oh how you long – for someone to take pity on you, someone to embrace you and share your terrors. And, at the end, someone to go into the dark with you.

Mamoulian chose Whitehead as his assassin – by chance, as he was chosen by the monk. But Whitehead has cheated him, squandering his teachings for the life of the body, for appetite, and now Mamoulian will show him Hell:

> Marty could hear, in this litany, the voice of the puritan – a monk's voice, perhaps? – the rage of a creature who wanted a world purer than it was and lived in torment because it saw only filth and flesh sweating to make more flesh, more filth. What hope of sanity in such a place? Except to find a soul to share the torment, a lover to hate the world with.
>
> Whitehead had been such a partner. And now Mamoulian was being true to his lover's soul: wanting, at the end, to go into death with the only other creature he had ever trusted.

There is no Devil at their backs: 'Just old humanity, cheated of love, and ready to pull down the world on its head.' As Barker notes: 'The idea being that the worst thing in the world is not this idea of the Devil, which is a Catholic convenience, but the idea of a human being who is loveless and angry about it.' Indeed, *The Damnation Game* is *Faust* without Lucifer: 'Every man is his own Mephistopheles, don't you think?' Mamoulian tells Whitehead. 'If I hadn't come along you'd have made a bargain with some other power.'

Thus Barker's intent is made clear: to de-sanctify and humanize a story that classically has deeply religious implications. At issue is not the divine, but the metaphysics of petty magicians. If one rejects a first cause – the precondition of religious belief – then what happens to the rest of knowledge? This is the underlying question of *The Damnation Game*. If the heavens involve more than the tedium of mechanics, then Marty's stargazing, like Faustus's knowledge of astronomy, leads back to the fundamental question: who made the world? Denied the answer to that question, the trap of flesh – inevitable death – closes in on Whitehead and the European.

Whitehead, of course, has faked his death: 'Great men didn't just lie down and die off-stage. They bided their time through the middle acts – revered, mourned and vilified – before appearing to play some final scene or other.' The two men meet for a last game of cards, their story turned full circle, from wasteland to wasteland, the ruins of Warsaw to the burned-out husk of the abandoned and aptly named Pandemonium Hotel.[12] 'You never cared to make sense of it all?' Mamoulian asks; and Whitehead replies: 'Sense? There's no sense to be made. You told me that: the first lesson. *It's all chance.*'

The game turns from cards to combat, and both players are mortally wounded, with Breer killing his master, patiently chopping the body into ever-smaller pieces. When Marty returns to the hotel, 'an appalling possibility crept into his head and sat there, whispering obscenities'. The room is an abattoir in which the European's flesh crawls, sluglike: 'in a thousand senseless pieces, but *alive*'. Sickened but resolute, Marty grinds the pieces beneath his feet, squashing out their stolen life: 'All the power and wisdom of the European had come to this muck, and he – Marty Strauss – had been elected to play the God-game, and wipe it away. He had gained, at the last, a terrible authority.'

As the wasteland is committed to flame, Marty realizes the bitter truth of Mamoulian's homily: '*[N]othing* was the essence of his fear.' Even a Devil is preferable to absence; and yet the wordplay is obvious.

In fearing nothing, we should have nothing to fear – except, in Franklin Delano Roosevelt's famous dictum, fear itself.

Carys leads Marty from the killing ground, and he looks toward distant stars: 'There were no revelations to be had there. Just pinpricks of light in a plain heaven. But he saw for the first time how fine that was. That in a world too full of loss and rage, they be remote: the minimum of glory. As she led him across the lightless ground, time and again he could not prevent his gaze from straying skyward.'

Sphere's expectations for Clive Barker's first novel were as limited as its expectations for the *Books of Blood*; as Barbara Boote notes: 'When we first bought *The Damnation Game*, we weren't expecting to do very much again – hoping to do 20,000 copies in paperback.' Sphere purchased world volume rights to the book. Because it did not publish hardback, du Sautoy licensed the hardcover rights to editor Victoria Petrie-Hay at London's prestigious Weidenfeld & Nicolson: 'She then assumed she had discovered Clive.' Petrie-Hay saw *The Damnation Game* as another *Empire of the Sun* (1984) – a book by a putative genre author that could achieve mainstream critical acclaim and, perhaps, the prestigious Booker Prize, awarded annually to a British writer for achievement in the novel form. (Indeed, it was widely reported in the American press that *The Damnation Game* was nominated for the Booker Prize, but that was wishful thinking.)

Weidenfeld & Nicolson issued *The Damnation Game* in hardback in 1985; six months later, the Sphere paperback edition was published, backed with a £32,000 promotional budget. With a first printing in paperback of 90,000 copies, the novel had more commercial potential – and success – than the *Books of Blood*, but it was viewed by Sphere as a traditional 'middle' book. 'We saw it as a sort of low lead,' Boote recalls, 'and we put some advertising behind it, plus Clive doing PR. And we were hoping for film rights to be sold, of course.'

The Damnation Game did well in paperback, but like the *Books of Blood*, its initial success was critical rather than commercial. It was a profound debut novel, and remains the Clive Barker novel treasured by many fans and critics, particularly those who prefer conventional horror fiction. Only three years after its publication, British writer Adrian Cole selected *The Damnation Game* as his entry for *Horror:*

100 Best Books (1988). 'In *The Damnation Game*,' Cole wrote, '[Barker] is uncompromising and ruthless in his examination of the human condition, and the result is at once electrifying, horrifying and compelling ... Like Kubrick's *A Clockwork Orange*, *The Damnation Game* faces us with truths we may not wish to know. It is not a book to be taken lightly.'

Barker's own assessment, many years and novels later, is less enthusiastic: 'I thought it was a very direct novel. Now that I read it again, I think it's not so direct. It's rather disgusting, bleak, but it doesn't move as fast as I thought it did when I was writing it. I thought I was writing a real page-turner, and I don't think I was.

'It seems to work for me, in two particular places. I think it works very well in terms of invoking a certain grimy element of Britain. Obviously Ramsey [Campbell] has cornered the market on urban decay, but there are other things: those weird things that rich folks do – the sealed estates and the staying up all night and going to casinos, and the barely disguised decadence which hangs around certain of the excesses of the rich.

'I find the unhappiness of the rich very fascinating. I think that's actually a common feeling. It's why we watch "Lifestyles of the Rich and Famous", because we're hoping that they're all going to be terribly, terribly unhappy. So I liked the idea of the working-class guy, Marty Strauss, who's really seen everything – you know, the wrong side of the tracks since birth – being introduced into this world of the heroin-addicted daughter of the multi-millionaire who's terrified of his own shadow.

'The sense that the rich men of the world are often corrupt men – that interests me, too. It's very seldom clean money, if there is such a thing as clean money. I think if you trace any money back far enough, you get to slaves or terrible industrial stuff with dynamite or piracy or whatever; or more recently, to drugs.'

Some critics, particularly in the mainstream, were less receptive to its imagery; one reviewer called it 'spiritually bankrupt'. These responses did not trouble Barker; indeed, he gloried in them – 'What you can't do to most of the images in my books is ignore them' – and he found a special joy in his favourite review, which described the novel as '*Zombie Flesh Eaters* written by Graham Greene'.[13]

Working for the first time at novel length, Clive Barker created a memorable debut that, over the next few years, would find explication in a series of stories, novels and motion pictures that pursued his fascination with the tale of Faustus, the problem of evil, and the trap of the flesh.

Its Faustus, Whitehead, chooses Strauss as heir apparent; both men are imprisoned – not only by walls of stone, but also by a mechanistic worldview in which 'all is chance'. Whitehead's delusionary belief in materialism – and, thus, the illusion of control in a world of chaos – succumbs to the sordid reality of damnation. Like Faustus, Whitehead squanders his gifts in pursuit of worldly appetites, rather than seeking a transcendental truth, or simple happiness. The vindictive Mamoulian represents the prison of the flesh – his hatred for the weakness of the skin is the insistent reminder that all flesh must fail. Confronted by the inevitability of death, Whitehead follows the insatiable gluttony of his materialism to its bitter finale; while Marty, his perspective shifted skyward by the dreaming Carys, finds hope – and survives. In Barker's words:

'I think the dream of a new world is a hollow hope. I'm a lover of the idea of the Millennium because I think we have to totally reassess what our idea of culture is. Because clearly the values which we were breast-fed on, the whole idea that you could accrue and acquire, and the more you accrued and acquired, the happier you would be – the stuff that fuelled our parents' ambitions for themselves, and perhaps more particularly their ambitions for us – are phony. They don't work. They're not comforts. Two televisions will not get you through the night. Indeed, while we've been seeking these things to acquire, we've been distracted from any other conception of what cultural living or being should be about.

'We have lost, in that moment of distraction, our grip on the real things which can comfort us in moments of anxiety and duress. And I am talking, obviously, of spiritual values and the idea that the world can be made to make sense from the inside out. You start with the business of the soul; you start with the business of interior investigation. And then you say: *What does the world mean in terms of the internal life, the mythological life?* This is what I believe every writer working in the *fantastique* is scratching at, this itch to know.

Because over and over again, those fictions are about the eruption of higher meaning into a world without meaning, or relatively little meaning.'

13

THE NEW FLESH

The body politic, like the human body, begins to die from its birth,
and bears in itself the causes of its destruction.

— JEAN JACQUES ROUSSEAU, *Du Contrat Social*

In the autumn of 1985, Clive Barker was presented with the British
Fantasy Award and the World Fantasy Award, each honouring *Clive
Barker's Books of Blood* as the 'Best Collection' of 1984. Almost simultaneously, Sphere issued a set of three new *Books of Blood* in paperback;
but their initial print runs – 15,000 copies per book – underscore the
continued focus of his publishers on the genre market and the lack
of a commercial breakthrough. Sphere's limited success in licensing
the first *Books of Blood* and *The Damnation Game* in other territories
– particularly the United States, where Berkley/Ace paid advances of

$5,000 and $10,000, respectively, for North American rights – did mean that Barker, represented by a new agent, June Hall, received a more sizable advance of £15,000 for each new volume and that he retained world rights.

The fourth, fifth and sixth volumes of the *Books of Blood*, written for the most part while he drafted *The Damnation Game*, present stronger narrative structures and a decided maturation of style, with Barker relying more often on craft than sheer explicitness of imagery to convey his horrors. Indeed, Clive prefers the second series to the original, finding these stories richer, more confident, more steeped in paradox and metaphysics – and, on an intimate level, far more vicious.

The extremity of his aesthetics had not relented. In 'The Body Politic', human hands sever themselves from the wrists of their masters and crawl spider-like in bloody revolution. In 'The Age of Desire', a powerful aphrodisiac unleashes ghastly sexual urgings whose fulfillment can be found only in mating with death. Barker's desire for a 'celebration of perversity' is obvious; but despite their extremism, the second series of the *Books of Blood* exhibit an insistent conscience. '[T]aboo and perversity are not enough in themselves,' Barker contends. 'If we merely celebrate the urge to *appal* we may find ourselves defending mere sensationalism simply because it makes us nauseous. No, we must also have structure to our horrors and – given that any narrative worth its sweat has some underlying metaphysic – meaning too.'[1]

What the marketplace called 'horror' was a fiction that had, by 1985, lost its imagination, whose fundamental impulse was not subversive but reactionary; not expansionist but isolationist; not to explore but to exploit – to place unruly children and independent or sexually-active women in peril and thus to assert the right (or privilege) to rescue them ... or to watch them die. The dialogue between mind and heart, opened in the late 1970s in the fiction of Stephen King and Peter Straub, among others, had become one between mind and gut and, inevitably, the lower organs. Too often 'horror' had become the new pornography: a ritualized depiction of acts dissociated from emotion, so intent on sensation that its readers were rendered numb.

At its best moments, the dark fantastic is a visionary art whose palette is blood and tears, sweat and shit, and whose canvas is transcendent, without limits. It is an art that cannot be bridled by an expectation of propriety, an art that simply will not refuse to see. Although the imagery of Clive Barker's early fiction was touted and, inevitably, imitated, it was his sweeping assault on the philosophy of a 'horror' genre that truly distinguished his writing. The *Books of Blood* appeared at the very moment that the rigidly defined and ideologically simplistic notions of genre had stifled the fiction of fear, creating a downward spiral of cynical exploitation and repetition that would only dilute and finally extinguish the interest of readers.

From his earliest days in the theatre, placing seats on the stage and his performance on the floor, Clive had demonstrated both his awareness of convention and his urgent need to defy it whenever possible. The *Books of Blood* are filled with references to the essential traditions of horror, whether enacted in literary classics or low-budget zombie movies; and the self-consciousness of his plots – and their enthusiasm for the iconography of the violent and the monstrous – suggested to readers and reviewers (and even his publishers) that the stories were part of the newly established 'horror' genre, while inverting or exaggerating its premises and ultimately subverting the very idea of genre.

In the aftermath of the first *Books of Blood*, I proposed the term 'anti-horror' to distinguish the work of Clive Barker and other conscientious writers from the puerile pablum that the marketplace sought to define as 'horror'. Like any form of escapism, the 'horror' genre is a construct of the culture industry, a kind of collective wish fulfilment, offering imaginary (and, of course, happy) resolutions to the violent contradictions of everyday life. Its central fantasy is that we live in an ordered universe – which, of course, is a whimsical dream: our lives are neither calm nor orderly. In that dream, we are taught that goodness is found in sanity, conformity and the ordinary; that the social ideal is to be entertained by endless television sitcoms, to define our values by dollars and Deutsche marks, to mock the miraculous and to live in silent obedience. This is a fascist conceit, identifying chaos and diversity with evil and insisting that any ambiguity and, indeed, any ambition must be exorcised and destroyed – all in the name of order.

Anti-horror, as exemplified profoundly in the second series of the *Books of Blood*, is a knowing deconstruction of this impulse: a conscious subversion of formula that rejects the Manichaean simplicity of God and Devil, good and evil, pushing the reader into a realm of ambiguity, forcing us to confront the real world, outside and within – a place of possibilities, some dark and dangerous, others bright and beautiful, and all of them liberating. The intent of this fiction is not to horrify (although that effect is occasionally inevitable) but to force the reader to imagine.

Clive Barker writes from the firm belief that we live in a moribund society, one that is indifferent in its better moments, callous at its worst, and that desperately needs awakening from the banality that governs our lives through so many sources: television, politics, organized religion – and, indeed, genre. 'I think it's very important that people accept, embrace, celebrate the capacity for the monstrous in the world,' he says. 'That way, stories about fear may even teach one not to live in fear.'[2]

Like Stephen King, with whom he is inevitably compared, Barker is unashamed to confront the terrors of our daily lives and to do so in books that, at least initially, were issued as tawdry, down-market paperbacks; but while King, the avuncular storyteller, holds our hands as we face a darkening world, Barker thrusts us forward into the night. 'There is no delight the equal of dread' is the battle-cry of the *Books of Blood*, and this relentless enthusiasm propels the stories of its final three volumes.

'Why,' he asks aloud, 'do I put such a high value upon subversion?'

His answer is unequivocal: 'There are many reasons. The most pertinent here is my belief that fantastic fiction offers the writer exceptional possibilities in that direction and I strongly believe a piece of work (be it play, book, poem) should be judged by how enthusiastically it seizes the opportunity to do what it can do *uniquely*. The literature of the fantastic – and the movies and the paintings – can reproduce, at its best, the texture of experience more closely than any "naturalistic" work, because it can embrace the complexity of the world we live in.

'Which is to say: our minds. That's where we live, after all. And our minds are extraordinary melting-pots, in which sensory information

191

and the memory of same and intellectual ruminations and nightmares and dreams, simmer in an ever-richer stew. Where else but in works called (often pejoratively) *fantasies* can such a mixture of elements be placed side by side?

'And if we once embrace the vision offered in such works, if we once allow the metaphors a home in our psyches, the subversion is underway. We may for the first time see ourselves as a *totality* – valuing our appetite for the forbidden rather than suppressing it, comprehending that our taste for the strange, or the morbid, or the paradoxical is contrary to what we're brought up to believe, a sign of our good health. So I say – *subvert*. And never apologize.'[3]

'Whenever he woke, Charlie George's hands stood still.'[4]

From this opening line, complete with grammatical misdirection – a fussy schoolmarm would tell us that hands are incapable of standing and thus that Charlie George's hands 'were' still – 'The Body Politic' races from incipient madness to a surreal tour-de-force. This memorable inversion of 'In the Hills, the Cities' (in which humans join together to create giants) finds the parts of the human body in revolution against the whole – and introduces the fourth volume of *Clive Barker's Books of Blood* (1985), published in the United States as *The Inhuman Condition* (1986).

Fortyish Charlie George is losing control of his wits – or, quite possibly, his hands, which creep from beneath the sheets as he sleeps: 'This is a clandestine meeting, held purely between Charlie's hands. There they will stay, through the night, perched on his stomach, plotting against the body politic.'

The narrative shifts point of view from Charlie to his hands and back again, implying madness – what else would explain the secret life of hands? A psychiatrist, Jeudwine, strives for a scientific solution, yet concedes: 'perhaps attempting to be rational about the human mind was a contradiction in terms.'[5] Indeed, the hands have minds of their own; after strangling Charlie's wife, the right hand liberates the left with a meat cleaver:

> The sensation of freedom was exhilarating. Not to feel the imperative of the tyrant in its nerves; not to suffer the weight of his

ridiculous body, or be obliged to accede to his petty demands. Not to have to fetch and carry for him, to do the dirt for him; not to be obedient to his trivial will. It was like birth into another world; a more dangerous world, perhaps, but one so much richer in possibilities. It knew that the responsibility it now carried was awesome. It was the sole proof of life after the body: and somehow it must communicate that joyous fact to as many fellow slaves as it could. Very soon, the days of servitude would be over once and for all.

Tumbling towards its dénouement like a compressed version of an early James Herbert novel,[6] the story is an accumulation of violent ironies, concluding when Charlie George awakens in the hospital, acknowledging his insanity: 'perhaps it was just an illusion of servitude it had created these forty-odd years, a performance to lull him into a false sense of autocracy.'

An army of severed hands besieges the hospital, awaiting the parables and prophecies of their Messiah – Charlie's right hand. 'Seeing them gathered like this the metaphors collapsed. They were what they were: human hands. That was the horror.' Charlie climbs to the roof, followed by the hands and the knowledge of the trap of flesh: 'how good it would be to die and never worry again if his gums bled when he brushed his teeth, or his waistline swelled, or some beauty passed him on the street whose lips he wanted to kiss and never would.'

He leaps and inspires a holocaust of hands. 'They came in a rain after him, breaking on the concrete around his body, wave upon wave of them, throwing themselves to their deaths in pursuit of their Messiah.' But the revolution continues as another patient, whose legs were severed in an accident, awakens:

> And did his eyes envy their liberty, he wondered and was his tongue eager to be out of his mouth and away and was every part of him, in its subtle way, preparing to forsake him? He was an alliance only held together by the most tenuous of truces. Now, with the precedent set, how long before the next uprising? Minutes? Years?
>
> He waited, heart in mouth, for the fall of Empire.

'The Body Politic' works as a straight-ahead horror tale – and was adapted by Mick Garris in a made-for-television movie, *Quicksilver Highway* (1996) – but it is also an essential celebration of our rebellious flesh and the obsession with the body that has spawned pseudo-religious cults of health clubs and food fads, miracle cures and diet plans.

Flesh is a trap, Barker urges here and throughout his creative career; and magic – the power of the imagination – sets us free. 'The body does not need the mind,' he writes in the short story 'The Madonna':

> It has procedures aplenty – lungs to be filled and emptied, blood to be pumped and food profited from – none of which require the authority of thought. Only when one or more of these procedures falters does the mind become aware of the intricacy of the mechanism it inhabits. Coloqhoun's faint lasted only a few minutes, but when he came to he was aware of his body as he had seldom been before: as a trap. Its fragility was a trap; its shape, its size, its very gender was a trap. And there was no flying out of it; he was shackled to, or *in*, this wretchedness.

The liberation of mind from body is also at the heart of 'The Inhuman Condition', whose story, at first glance, is elementary: a quartet of hooligans shakes down a drunken derelict and the youngest – the vaguely sympathetic seventeen-year-old Karney – finds a knotted string among the feeble spoils. As each of its puzzlelike knots unravels, creatures emerge to exact vengeance. The story would find new incarnation as the short novel *The Hellbound Heart* (1986) and the motion picture *Hellraiser* (1987); its central themes inform the later novels of 'The Art'.

The knots fascinate Karney, who seeks some semblance of meaning in life: 'just to die a little less ignorant of mysteries than he'd been born.' When instinct rather than intellect is applied to the puzzle, the first knot is loosened and a 'muddied thing' swells from its midst, causing the death of one of his cronies.

The riddle takes on a 'fresh glamour': Karney, like Pandora, needs to know and the string is agreeable: 'It still required a human agent apparently – why else did it leap so readily into his hand? – but it was already close to solving its own riddle.' Another unravelling spawns another creature: '[T]he beast's anatomy defied his comprehension. There was something simian in its flayed, palpitating form, but sketchy, as if it had been born prematurely. Its mouth opened to speak another sound; its eyes, buried beneath the bleeding slab of a brow, were unreadable.' Karney asks – 'What are you?' – and the creature, its eyes strangely lucid, moans and points its finger at him.

When Karney unravels the final knot, it reveals 'a sickly infant, its limbs vestigial, its bald head vastly too big for its withered body, the flesh of which was pale to the point of translucence'. The first two creatures join the pallid child – 'an unholy family of reptile, ape and child' – and the secret of the cord is known:

'A new and perhaps insoluble puzzle was appearing from the pieces of the old, but, where *they* had been inchoate, this one would be finished and whole. What, though; *what?*' It is a holy trinity, solving the riddle of life: evolution.

Another kind of knot – the marital one – is untied in 'Revelations', in which the ghosts of the 1950s offer truths in the 1980s. Virginia Gyer, the fortyish wife of apocalyptic evangelist John Gyer, has been condemned by her marital vows to a loveless life made bearable only by drugs. Caught in a storm, the troubled couple finds sanctuary in a backroads Texas motel. There, thirty years before, another troubled couple, Sadie and Buck Durning, gave the motel its nickname of the 'Slaughterhouse of Love'. Sadie, who had learned of Buck's philandering, shot him dead. Tonight she and Buck return from the spirit world to celebrate the anniversary of the deed.

When Virginia realizes that she can speak with and see the dead, her revelation is far more powerful than the *Revelation of St. John the Divine* that her husband spouts by rote. But when she seeks vengeance on Buck's salacious ghost, she shoots her husband instead. In the aftermath, a bystander asks the inevitable question – Why? '[G]azing up at the moon and putting on the craziest smile she could muster,' Virginia offers the age-old reply: 'The Devil made me do it.'

The Devil's work is also that of man in 'Down, Satan!' – a short fable about a wealthy industrialist who, believing himself godless, conceives a unique solution: 'Suppose . . . I could contrive a meeting with Satan, the Archfiend. Seeing me *in extremis*, would not God be obliged to step in and deliver me back into the fold?' Gregorious constructs a Hell on Earth to tempt the Tempter, but despite the vilest of indulgences – butchered remains, corpses roasted in ovens – there is no sign of Satan. Locked away in an asylum, Gregorious dies; and Barker wonders aloud whether his strategy had succeeded: 'If, in giving up all hope of angels – fallen or otherwise – he had not become one himself . . . Or all that earth could bear of such phenomena.'

'The Age of Desire' opens with the vision of a burning man, 'the heat in his flesh licking him into ecstasies'. Inspector Carnegie, a paragon of order, is dispatched to investigate; his worldview is summarized as he passes a cinema decked with horror movie posters:

> What trivial images the populists conjured to stir some fear in their audiences. The walking dead; nature grown vast and rampant in a miniature world; blood-eaters, omens, firewalkers, thunderstorms and all the other foolishness the public cowered before. It was all so laughably trite: amongst that catalogue of penny dreadfuls there wasn't one that equalled the banality of human appetite, which horror (or the consequences of same) he saw every day of his working life.

A rogue experiment in sexual appetite – 'Project Blind Boy'[7] – has gone awry, transforming Jerome Tredgold, a paid guinea pig with a singular lack of comeliness, into a creature of unbridled passion. Listening to the radio, whose 'songs told one seamless and obsessive story: of love lost and found, only to be lost again', Tredgold realizes that we live in 'a world bewitched by desire'.[8] The 'burgeoning fire' of his desire creates a newfound passion to rape and kill without bothersome complexities: 'All moral consequence, all shame or remorse, was burned out by the fire that was even now licking his flesh to new enthusiasms.'

'Blind Boy' is a relentless aphrodisiac: 'Head was *nothing*; mind was *nothing*. His arms were simply made to bring love close, his legs to carry the demanding rod any place where it might find satisfaction. He pictured himself as a walking erection, the world gaping on every side: flesh, brick, steel, he didn't care: he would ravish it all.' The drug's inventor, Dr Welles, is a Puritan – and a madman, seeking

apocalypse: 'The world had seen so many Ages. The Age of Enlighten-
ment; of Reformation; of Reason. Now, at last, the Age of Desire. And
after this, an end to Ages; an end, perhaps, to everything. For the fires
that were being stoked now were fiercer than the innocent world
suspected. They were terrible fires, fires without end, which would
illuminate the world in one last, fierce light.'

'Love kills,' Welles notes succinctly, embracing his fate: 'Death was
here. And what was it, now he saw it clearly? Just another seduction,
another sweet darkness to be filled up and pleasured and made fertile.'

'Blind Boy' is an obvious metaphor for the descent of the sexual
revolution of the 1960s into the careless hedonism of the 1980s and
the damnation game played by a hunger for pleasure – a theme that
informed *The Hellbound Heart* (1986) and *Hellraiser* (1987). In particular, the spectre of AIDS haunts 'The Age of Desire' – Tredgold's
uncontrollable appetite renders him literally into a 'blind boy', incapable of seeing the consequences of his sexual acts: 'Not once did
it occur to his spinning, eroticized brain that this new kind of life
would, in time, demand a new kind of death.'

'I've always been interested in how we pursue pleasure,' Clive
comments, 'and how soon the pleasurable road turns into a cul-de-sac.
Then we have to turn around and look elsewhere. It's the law of
diminishing returns. It's: *Well, I've done this. What can I do next? I've
taken that drug. What's the next one available?* If hedonism doesn't
satisfy us – and plainly it *is* the law of diminishing returns – what
next?'[9]

The fifth volume of the *Books of Blood*, retitled for American consumption as *In the Flesh* (1987), offers equally fatal journeys into
the realms of the taboo; indeed, it opens with another instant classic,
'The Forbidden'.[10] Adapted by Bernard Rose as the motion picture
Candyman (1992), this story of urban legend given life is considered
at length in Chapter 25.

'In the Flesh', which links the claustrophobic imprisonment of *The
Damnation Game* with the dreamy fantasies of Barker's next major
novel, *Weaveworld* (1987), considers the fate of young Billy Tait, who
commits a serious crime in order to be sentenced to Pentonville Prison.
He seeks the grave of his grandfather, Edgar Tait, who murdered his
children so that the dark powers infecting his blood would not pass

to another generation. Before Edgar could find Billy's mother and complete the task, he was arrested, then executed at Pentonville: 'Hanged and buried, but not *lost*. Nobody's lost . . . Not ever.'

Billy senses the enigmatic power in his blood and aches to use it: 'To be *not* myself; to be smoke and shadow. To be something terrible . . .' As he conjures the shade of his grandfather, his cellmate, Cleve, dreams of a trek through an expanse of desert. 'I read somewhere,' Billy tells him: '*The dead have highways*. You ever hear that? Well . . . they have cities, too.' Cleve awakens to find a figure stitched from darkness – Billy's grandfather – and behind him, a strange city. He realizes his delicate mortality and the terrible loneliness of his place in the scheme of things:

> Sunlight was a showman. It threw its brightness down with such flamboyance, eager as any tinsel-merchant to dazzle and distract. But beneath the gleaming surface it illuminated was another state; one that sunlight – ever the crowd pleaser – conspired to conceal. It was vile and desperate, that condition. Most, blinded by sight, never even glimpsed it. But Cleve knew the state of sunlessness now; had even walked it, in dreams; and though he mourned the loss of his innocence, he knew he could never retrace his steps back into light's hall of mirrors.

The city is a purgatory for murderers; and Edgar Tait has manipulated his heir into taking his place there. The dream and its revelations imprison Cleve more securely than a building of brick and steel: '*People* brought the dream to him . . . They were *everywhere*, these embryonic killers, people wearing smart clothes and sunny expressions were striding the pavement and imagining, as they strode, the deaths of their employers and their spouses, of soap opera stars and incompetent tailors. The world had murder on its mind and he could no longer bear its thoughts.'

Imprisonment is an insistent theme in Barker's fiction, and he depicts not only literal prisons but also those of school and social class, family and marriage – and, of course, the flesh, as shown convincingly in 'The Madonna'. The seeker in this provocative drama is Jerry Coloqhoun, a desperate entrepreneur who plans to convert an indoor swimming hall into an entertainment complex. Lacking more legitimate backers, Coloqhoun turns to the mobster Garvey.[11]

The spiral design of the Pools is a vortex into the ocean of the feminine.[12] Three nymphs rise in naked splendour from the water, but one cradles an abomination that so horrifies Garvey that he smashes its tender flesh against the wall. He hears an utterly alien keening: 'All certainty trembled – masculinity, power; the twin imperatives of dread and reason – all turned their collars up and denied knowledge of him. He shook, afraid as only dreams made him afraid, while the cry went on and on.' Lost in the mazelike corridors, he comes upon the largest pool, where the three graces – and a dark shape churning the water – summon a greater mystery. Garvey awakens in a blur of paranoia and revulsion and commits suicide in the waters of the Thames: 'The prayer he offered up as the river closed over him was that death not be a woman.'

When Coloqhoun returns to the swimming hall, the nymphs lead him to its inner sanctum, where he is presented to a monstrous yet feminine prodigy: 'She is the Madonna. The Virgin Mother.' As he watches, the Madonna gives birth to a single-eyed 'something between a squid and a shorn lamb'. She requires no husband, no mate. None of her children is alike and those that survive go on their way: 'To the water. To the sea. Into dreams.'

After Coloqhoun makes uncertain love with one of the nymphs, he awakens to find his body unknitted and remade into that of a woman. Unlike Garvey, he succumbs to the enchantment and returns to the Pools, following the Madonna and her children into a whirlpool of draining water:

> There was light ahead. How far it lay, he couldn't calculate, but what did it matter? If he drowned before he reached that place and ended his journey dead, so what? Death was no more certain than the dream of masculinity he'd lived these years. Terms of description fit only to be turned up and over and inside out. The earth was bright, wasn't it and probably full of stars. He opened his mouth and shouted into the whirlpool, as the light grew and grew, an anthem in praise of paradox.

Coloqhoun concedes the thin veneer of sexual identity – that the 'dream of masculinity' is indeed a dream and that the imagination recognizes no distinctions as simple as masculine and feminine. We live in a world of paradox and ambiguity, Barker insists, and it is in paradox and ambiguity that we should rejoice. To deny that diversity may offer a kind of peace, but it is a false peace and one that empowers men like Garvey, who live – and die – in fealty to the false god of certainty.

'Babel's Children' is a natural bookend to 'The Forbidden'. More political satire than horror story, it takes its cue from two classics of sixties television: 'The Howling Man', a 'Twilight Zone' episode based on the eponymous short story by Charles Beaumont; and Patrick McGoohan's cult mini-series 'The Prisoner'.[13]

Fortyish Vanessa Jape takes a holiday alone in the Greek Islands, avoiding the tourist attractions in search of the uncharted path. Her very human need for the forbidden brings her to the odd and ominous sight of a man pursued by gun-toting nuns. '[C]ould she possibly turn her back on such a mystery?' Each of us could – and, in reality, probably would – turn our back; but in fiction, the realm of second chances, we can risk all to look into the shadows and see the dark. As often as we bray and challenge and doubt the characters who wander down the dark corridors, peer into the shuttered room, unhinge the locked closet, we read on and on and, like Vanessa Jape, we find strange truths.

'The trick of good farce,' an actor once told Vanessa, 'was that it be played with deadly seriousness.' Hidden in these hills is a silent, walled garrison that looks very much like a monastery. Inside are armed guards who care for five elderly men and women, a fey conclave of nationalities who sleep, eat and play games, racing frogs over a paved area that is etched with a map of the world.

The map, she learns, is a playing board. The world's leaders, fearful of nuclear annihilation, have created a new world order whose affairs are governed by an intellectual and moral élite. But the anonymous appointees became the 'world's domestics', while presidents and prime ministers, freed from the demands of power, pursued their preferred tasks of preening and preaching and profiteering. The committee's responsibilities became so excessive – and, in time, irrelevant – that its five surviving members, whose only desire is to escape, play mindless games to decide the fate of nations. 'When they became bored with sweet reason and the sound of their own voices, they gave up debate and took to flipping coins ... [a]nd racing frogs ... All *chance* ...'

A terrifying thought, perhaps, but 'is it any more terrifying than leaving the power in *their* hands?' Again, the true monsters are the artifices – those presidents and prime ministers – exposed here as carnival shills for the façade of order. 'Better the frogs,' Vanessa realizes; and she begins to play the games that decide the fate of the world.

Volume Five thus features four explorers of the infinite who find their rigid sense of reality overcome by dramatic revelation: Doubting Helen Buchanan of 'The Forbidden', the scholar who deigned herself capable of translating the writing on the wall, succumbs to the embrace of rumour and gossip; watchful Cleve Smith, a prisoner of pettiness, learns the murderous human heart; Jerry Coloqhoun succumbs to the power of the feminine; and Vanessa Jape, the explorer with a passion for the irresponsible, is overcome with responsibility. None finds salvation in the supposedly rational world or its symbols of order (academic thought, prison, architecture, politics), which prove unable to contain or control the chaos in which we live.

The sixth and final volume of the *Books of Blood* examines the last illusion: Death.[14] Its opening novella, 'The Life of Death', is a grim, ironic masterpiece of life in the modern plague years.

Elaine Rider is recovering from a hysterectomy precipitated by cancer: 'her life saved only by losing the capacity for further life.' She has lost her boyfriend and hope: 'she was no longer weighed down by some vague ambition for heaven ... There was nothing to come, nothing to aspire to, nothing to dream of.'

She witnesses the demolition of All Saints Church, a relic from the seventeenth century that has fallen prey to urban progress. Venturing inside, she meets a dour man named Kavanagh who studies the stones underfoot and shows her the curious inscription – '*Redeem the time*' – that labels a sealed crypt. She returns to the ruins in the night and enters the burial chamber, finding Death in all its brutal glory: it is a plague pit.[15]

Elaine returns to work and the world with renewed vitality: 'It was paradoxical, surely, that it was only now, when the surgeons had emptied her out, that she should feel so ripe, so resplendent.' When one of her co-workers collapses in a bloody convulsion and her dinner guests fall ill, she realizes that 'she had been nurturing a fatal child': she has brought the plague out of the crypt and into the world.[16]

Pursued by the authorities, she again meets Kavanagh and realizes his true identity: 'How, her whirling thoughts demanded, had she not recognized him sooner?; not realized at that first meeting, when he'd talked of the dead and their glamour, that he spoke as their Maker?' She welcomes his fatal embrace; but it is not the love – or death – that she (or the reader) expected. In an achingly profound irony, Kavanagh recites a madman's cant as he murders her. 'She realized now that he was not Death; not the clean-boned guardian she'd waited for. In her eagerness, she had given herself into the hands of a common killer, a street-corner Cain. She wanted to spit contempt on him, but her consciousness was slipping, the room, the lights, the face all throbbing to the drummer's beat. And then it all stopped.'

Plague is also central to 'How Spoilers Bleed', an indictment of imperialism that begins when three European despoilers enter a village in the Amazon Basin. Ringleader Locke, regretful Stumpf and mercenary Cherrick lay claim to the ancestral lands of an ancient, dying tribe, intent on exploiting its minerals and oil.[17] When Cherrick inadvertently shoots a child, he is cursed with words he only later understands: 'The man was speaking of the world and of exile from the world; of being broken always by what one seeks to possess.' His skin tears open at the slightest touch: 'The world was pressing on him – at least that was the sensation – pressing as though it wanted him out.' Soon his body is an open wound; but as he dies, Locke, ever the schemer, persuades Cherrick to cede him his share of the tribal land.

Stumpf, frightened and remorseful, gives his share to Locke and tries to escape; but he, too, begins to bleed. When the disbelieving Locke forces open the door to Stumpf's room, he brings sudden death to his comrade, who is torn apart by motes of dust carried on the wind. Locke returns to the village, anxious to make amends, but the huts are deserted. Other Europeans emerge from the brush, claiming the land for themselves. Locke looks down upon the carnage . . . and begins to bleed.

The imperialist critique of 'How Spoilers Bleed' and the revolutionary flesh of 'The Body Politic' collide during the Cold War in 'Twilight at the Towers', which prefigures the novel *Cabal* (1988) and the motion picture *Nightbreed* (1990).

Ballard, a British Secret Service operative, is assigned to meet a defecting KGB agent, Mironenko. Ballard is disaffected; despite years of duty, nothing in the world has changed. He has found his true home in Berlin: 'Its unease, its failed idealism and – perhaps most acutely of all – its terrible isolation, matched his. He and it, maintaining a presence in a wasteland of dead ambition.'

Mironenko, like Ballard, is world-weary, a man without faith or cause who rages against his masters. His despair has become physical; his head and hands are wracked with pain. 'His body, he had concluded, was in revolt against him. It was that thought which he had tried to explain to Ballard: that he was divided from himself and feared that he would soon be torn apart.'

Mironenko is a shapeshifter – a werewolf – and Ballard learns, in time, that he is the same, his monstrosity conditioned by politicians and warmongers to become an instrument of the state: 'It took years of suppression therapy, slowly burying the desire for transformation so that what we had left was a man with a beast's faculties. A wolf in sheep's clothing.' But Ballard is unwilling to serve his masters:

> He didn't want to be a beast like Mironenko. It wasn't freedom, was it, to be so terrible?; it was merely a different kind of tyranny. But then he didn't want to be the first of Cripps' heroic new order either. He belonged to nobody, he realized; not even himself. He was hopelessly lost. And yet hadn't Mironenko said at that first meeting that the man who did not believe himself lost, *was* lost? Perhaps better that – better to exist in the twilight between one state and another, to prosper as best as he could by doubt and ambiguity – than to suffer the certainties of the tower.

'[H]e felt a surge of grief for something he'd never had: the life of a monster.' The nameless creature that once was Ballard escapes into the night, to a building on the outskirts of Berlin, where his tribe awaits. These exiles perish less willingly than the tribesmen of 'How Spoilers Bleed'. It is twilight at the towers – those dark monoliths of west and east, order and reason. The ancient, primal forces linked with the planet – the tribesmen of 'How Spoilers Bleed', the shapeshifters of 'Twilight at the Towers' – struggle to exile the scientists, the spoilers, the would-be masters who ignore the animal and champion cold reason. 'There were other faiths, thought Ballard, beyond the one he'd once shared with the creature beneath him. Faiths whose devotions were made in heat and blood, whose dogmas were dreams. Where better to baptize himself into that new faith than here, in the blood of the enemy?'

The style shifts from espionage to that of hard-boiled mystery in 'The Last Illusion', which provides the blueprint for the motion picture *Lord of Illusions* (1995). Discussed at length in Chapter 27, the penultimate story of the *Books of Blood* introduces Barker's most prominent continuing character, private detective Harry M D'Amour.

'The Book of Blood (a postscript): On Jerusalem Street' concludes the *Books of Blood* by returning to their beginning and Simon McNeal, the phony medium who invented stories of the departed for his own profit until the dead, tired of his mockery, exacted their immaculate revenge – transforming his body into 'a living book, a book of blood, every inch of which was minutely engraved with their histories'.[18]

A paid assassin, Leon Wyburd, tracks McNeal down and kills him, stealing his skin for a mysterious collector; but Wyburd awakens in the night, deluged in blood: '*The stories go on . . . They bleed and bleed.*' He drowns in the red tide. Later, walking in that nether realm where the dead have highways, Wyburd meets another flayed man. As Wyburd tells him the story of his dying moments, he realizes, as Clive Barker had realized, the wonder of having reached the end: 'It was a great relief to tell the story.'

> Not because he wanted to be remembered, but because the telling relieved him of the tale. It no longer belonged to him, that life, that death. He had better business, as did they all. Roads to travel; splendours to drink down. He felt the landscape widen. Felt the air brightening.
>
> What the boy had said was true. The dead have highways.
> Only the living are lost.

This vignette closed not only the *Books of Blood* but also the first act of Clive Barker's literary career. Its haunting words were prophetic because now that these stories were told, Barker indeed 'had better business'. For his fiction and his creative ambition, there were new roads to travel. The landscape would widen and the air, on occasion, would brighten. Clive Barker was about to bring his visions to the cinema screen – and unleash a novel that would cast a gauntlet into the increasingly staid face of the fiction that publishing had defined as horror and fantasy.

14

INTO THE ABYSS

Sic, sic, iuvat ire sub umbras
(Thus, thus, it is joy to pass to the world below)
— VIRGIL, *Aeneid*

Somewhere, deep underground, there lives another breed – a distant kin of humanity whose distorted features, strange powers and love of the night have caused them to be known as monsters. One person ventures into their darkland and, when a lover follows, fertile secrets are unearthed.

This archetypal rendition of the night journey – the myth of Orpheus and Eurydice – would be presented in Clive Barker's third novel, *Cabal* (1988), and its motion picture adaptation, *Nightbreed* (1990). But first its dark descent was rehearsed in the *Books of Blood* stories 'The Skins of the Fathers' and 'Twilight at the Towers', then enacted in a small and, for the most part, forgotten motion picture: *Underworld* (1985).

Today, motion pictures are a vital element of Clive Barker's creative life. At this writing, more than ten films based upon his work have been produced; but in the early eighties, movies were, in his words, 'gold dust' – 'and of course you hear all the warnings, but you still go to camp down by Crystal Lake, don't you?' Like the doomed youths of *Friday the 13th* (1980), Barker greeted the ravenous monster known as the motion picture industry with wide-eyed innocence.

His naïveté was encouraged by a nervous idealism, his intense love of horror movies and his knowledge of horror's crucial role in film history. With the emergence of Hammer Films in the 1950s, there had been a strong tradition of modestly budgeted but well-made British horror movies.[1] Hammer single-handedly resurrected Frankenstein, Dracula and the Mummy from the rubbish bin of meeting Abbott and Costello, setting the stage for other small studios like Amicus and Tigon and Tyburn, whose essential product was horror.

Underworld seemed like a natural extension of this heritage; indeed, it was the first true British horror film of the 1980s. The project started in 1982 when Clive met George Pavlou, a graduate of the London International Film School, at a dinner party. Pavlou, a young director of television commercials, had worked as second unit director for British-based episodes of the American television series 'Hart to Hart'. His short films had been distributed by Rank, Twentieth Century-Fox and Paramount, and he was eager to direct his first feature. Terrified by William Friedkin's adaptation of *The Exorcist* – and echoing Barker's own response to viewing *Psycho* – Pavlou felt: 'Wouldn't it be great to manipulate an audience that way?' He wanted to make a horror film as 'my own way of trying to exorcise some evil spirits within myself – a lot of bad experiences as a kid'. At the dinner party, he told Clive: 'I want to make a movie and you're the only writer I know.'

There was an immediate friendship; Barker and Pavlou seemed a perfect creative match, with so many shared visual and textual references: the stylized violence and colour effects of the films of Dario Argento and Brian De Palma; the ethereal monstrosity of the films of Jean Cocteau and Georges Franju; the artwork of comic books and HR Giger, Moebius and Jean-Michel Nicollet; the hardboiled fiction of Raymond Chandler, David Goodis and Cornell Woolrich. Pavlou saw two of Barker's plays – a Dog Company performance of *Franken-stein in Love* and *Crazyface* at the Cockpit Youth Theatre – but it wasn't until Clive showed him some of his (then unpublished) short stories that Pavlou realized: 'This guy's really got something.'

He asked Clive to create an original story that would merge the conspiratorial complexities of Roman Polanski's *Chinatown* (1974) with the stylized imagery of Argento's *Suspiria* (1977) and *Inferno* (1980). Inspired by his intense claustrophobia, his love of *film noir* and his ceaseless passion for monsters and villains, Barker imagined a no-man's-land in which someone from above would meet something from below: a purgatory where dreams have gone out of control and lives are trapped between the rational and the irrational – a place where gangsters would meet mutants. True to form, he inverted the generic convention, taking the surface dwellers – humans who normally represent order, stability and 'good' – and exposing them as icons of moral depravity. The 'monsters' who dwell below and typically would represent chaos (and thus 'evil') were made sympathetic.

Pavlou initially planned to pursue the project as a controlled, small-scale production, 'shot on Super 16mm with a few mates, spending a year planning it, getting it right and with Clive as part of that team. I didn't want to do it with huge trucks lining the streets, teams of technicians who were very set in their ways, who were more concerned with their overtime payments and tea breaks than anything else. I wanted to do it with a small unit that worked as a family and to create something that was unique and interesting.'

But Barker's synopsis of *Underworld* – a dozen pages co-written with Pavlou – was 'magical . . . everyone who read them loved them'. Pavlou decided to pitch the synopsis to potential producers and financiers in London, which, in time, brought him to Green Man Productions, an independent production company owned by Kevin Attew and Don Hawkins. Using first-time directors, Green Man had earlier co-produced two eclectic low-budgeters, *After Darkness* and *Funeral Party* (which, despite their titles, were not horror films); but its forte was television commercials and music videos, including the critically acclaimed video album *Japan – Oil on Canvas*. Attew, a smooth-talking East Ender, and Hawkins, a soap opera actor, believed that, in *Underworld*, they had discovered the next big thing – and a natural extension of their expertise: a motion picture for the music video generation.

Green Man took the project to Limehouse Studios, a production facility in London's East End founded by Al Burgess. A former production accountant, Burgess had expanded into film and video development and production; Limehouse was then one of the two London studios where music videos could be created inexpensively. It took nearly a year, but to their credit, Green Man and Limehouse were able to finance and produce *Underworld* at a time when the British film industry was virtually non-existent.

In October 1984, George Pavlou received a call from Green Man, with the good news: 'We're in a go situation.' Then he was told that photography had to begin on January 5, 1985. Pavlou responded: 'It's impossible.' There was no script; months of preparation and pre-production would be necessary to make the film effectively. But the financing was contingent upon an immediate shoot; Green Man advised him: 'It has to be spent. Otherwise, there's no movie.' Only later, at the film's premiere at the London Film Festival, did Pavlou learn that the production was mounted with Irish tax shelter money, which dictated its timing.

Although *Underworld* garnered attention because it was, at the time, a rarity – a British-financed, British-crewed film made in England – the media denigrated it as 'horror'. When the film premiered late in 1985, it proved a disconcerting medley of minimal budget, rushed schedule, competing visions and creative compromise.

The film's initial budget was more than one million pounds, but that was soon reduced to £600,000. Although the producers later told Pavlou that the budget had 'crept up' to £800,000, he sighs with disbelief: 'I don't know how. I didn't even know where the money was coming from. They were telling me very little. These guys were very guarded.' The producers treated him as the 'arty director' and excluded him from conversations about the financial structure – although, as he freely admits: 'I was doing my first film and didn't give a toss where the money came from.'

Clive was busily writing *The Damnation Game*, but when Pavlou called, he turned from the novel-in-progress and attempted, with only minimal guidance, to write his first motion picture screenplay. In the meantime, Pavlou, struggling against impossible time pressures, began scouting locations and casting the film. Auditions were held without a script, since none existed; and Pavlou focused the prospective actors on characterization, to the point that some actors (certainly Miranda Richardson, who played Oriel) felt that the story centred on them – 'which was fortunate,' Pavlou notes, 'since they told their agents they wanted to be in it'.

A few weeks before Christmas, Barker presented Pavlou with a first draft screenplay that totalled about seventy pages. 'It was written like a play,' Pavlou says, and was not 'shootable' as a motion picture. The ideas were powerful, but it lacked a clear, structured narrative – 'which films are all about'.

Barker admits to his inexperience and innocence as a screenwriter: 'I had no sense whatsoever of the protocol, whether I had any rights in the process, none of that.' At his first meeting with the producers, he was told that budgetary constraints would preclude any major make-up, costuming or special effects and that sex and violence should be toned down. 'I was told to avoid the stuff which soared in the finest way in *Hellraiser*, which is the stuff about sex and monsters and really dark, weird shit. They just didn't want to have anything to do with it.' (Later, one of the producers, Don Hawkins, said that he thought Barker was essentially a pornographer.)

Although *Underworld* was conceived as a cross between Cocteau and Cronenberg – dreams as poetry, dreams as horror – Barker's vision had no pretensions; he wanted 'a *film noir* with monsters . . . something that was stylish, poetic and frightening, in which the morally deplorable characters had their act together in nice three-piece suits'.[2] In Hollywood shorthand, the movie (as its title cleverly implies) would be 'monsters versus mobsters'.[3]

Barker prepared a second draft, which was much better written than the typical shooting script, but its focus was transformation, relying, in Pavlou's view, 'too much on poetic suggestion rather than tight dramatic conflict'. After reviewing the second draft, Limehouse asked Barker for another rewrite, but then – without telling him – also hired a more experienced (although unfilmed) screenwriter, James Caplin, to prepare a new script adapted from Barker's earlier drafts.

'It was awful,' Pavlou says. Caplin's rendition was 'like *Rambo* – all action, no substance, no atmosphere – everything that Clive had intended was missing'. Caplin, who ultimately shared the screenplay credit, also revised the dialogue, indulging in clichéd gangsterisms.

Clive at age one, with the Union Jack and the family dog, Kemis. Liverpool, Coronation Day, June 3, 1953. *Courtesy of Joan Barker.*

ve at six months with his parents, ɔnard and Joan, and grandparents ɔert and Florence Barker. Liverpool, 53. *Courtesy of Joan Barker.*

vedale Road School photograph of Clive and his brother Roy. Liverpool, ca 1960. *Courtesy of Joan Barker.*

'I was a really bad Nazi.' Guernsey, Channel Islands, circa 1962. *Courtesy of Joan Barker.*

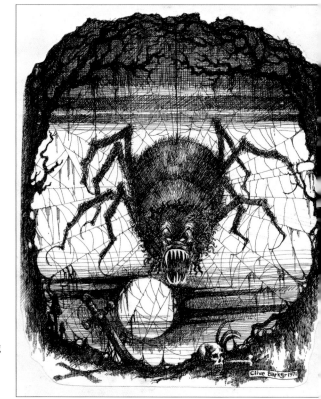

Intricate line drawing for The *Candle in the Cloud*, 1971. *Courtesy of Clive Barker.*

ft to right (top row) **Douglas Bradley, Jay Venn, Clive Barke**
ft to right (middle row) **Philip Rimmer, Mary Roscoe,**
*t to right (bottom row) **Julie Blake, Lynne Darnell,**
Oliver Parker.

tics on The Dog Company:

*"Their experience together shows in the style and
quality of their performances. These are young professionals totally dedicated to their art . . ."*
   Camden Journal.

*"I have nothing but respect for a company such as
this . . ."*
   Time Out.

" . . .inventive and exciting . . ."
   British Council Student Centre News.

" . . . a company who work together excellently . . ."
   Hampstead and Highgate Express.

*"Highly entertaining . . . The performers are really
pussycats . . ."*
   Performance Arts Magazine.

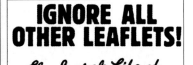

bove) The Dog Company. London,
ca 1981. *Courtesy of Clive Barker.* (Top right)
aft promotional poster for *Frankenstein in
ve.* London, 1982. *Courtesy of Clive Barker.*
ight) Promotional flier for the West End
oduction of *The Secret Life of Cartoons.*
ndon, 1986. *Courtesy of Douglas E Winter.*

April 15, 1985.

Ms. Ginjer Buchanan
The Berkley Publishing Group
200 Madison Avenue
New York, New York 10016

Dear Ginjer Buchanan,

It's easier, I find, to blurb a book (or series of them) when
you're not quite as excited and bowled over. I think Clive Barker
is so good that I am almost literally tongue-tied. Yes, I stick by
it: I have seen the future of the horror genre, and his name is
Clive Barker (the paraphrase actually comes from Jon Landau, who said
in 1970 that he had seen the future of rock 'n roll and his name was
Bruce Springsteen).

What Barker does in THE BOOKS OF BLOOD makes the rest of us
look like we've been asleep for the last ten years. Some of the
stories were so creepily awful that I literally could not read them
alone; others go up and over the edge and into a gruesome territory
that no one has really traversed since M.L. Lewis's The Monk.

Barker's scenes of glaring pulpy horror should cause instant
dismissal, but forty or fifty pages is enough to convince any reader
of sense and taste (funny word to use in connection with stories
like "The Midnight Meat-Train," but it's the right word) that this
is a tool, and not an end. The stories are compulsively readable and
lit here and there with furnace-gleams of wit.

He's an original. I hope there are folks at Berkley who understand
just how good he is, and how proud you should be of publishing him.
What he's doing will shortly make him an enormously saleable writer,
but what he's doing is also important and exciting.

And if you don't send me his novel, I'll have to send a few
vampires after you.

Regards,

Stephen King

Stephen King's letter to
Berkley Publishing praising
the *Books of Blood*, April 15,
1985. *Courtesy of Douglas E
Winter.*

Publicity photograph for *The
Damnation Game*. London, 1985.

Clive and his famous
progeny Pinhead.
London, circa 1987.

Frank (One) Hellraiser – one of
two visions of Frank's return
from the Outer Darkness for
Hellraiser, 1987. *Courtesy of Clive
Barker.*

On the set of *Nightbreed*.
London, 1989.

Illustration for *Weaveworld*,
1987. *Courtesy of Clive Barker.*

live with Norman Mailer. New York, 1987. *Photograph by Paul McMahon.*

Within 24 hours all the significant events in Mankind's history will be re-enacted in a mythological place; and they will all be for grabs. Up to some fines to protect the god from the evil.

Untitled illustration, date unknown.
Courtesy of Clive Barker.

Untitled illustration, date unknown.
Courtesy of Clive Barker.

Clive and Joan Barker in Clive's workroom at Wimpole Street. London, circa 1988. *Photograph by Leonard Barker.*

Untitled illustration, date unknown. *Courtesy of Clive Barker.*

In Hollywood, circa 1994. *Photograph by Marco Sacchi.*

An unhappy Pavlou turned back to Barker, but scheduling conflicts and limited studio time prevented the completion of another draft before the film went before the cameras. Principal photography began on January 5, as scheduled, but without a shooting script, as Pavlou and his actors worked from scenes and pages taken from all preceding drafts. During the five weeks of filming in London's Docklands and on locations in England and Ireland, both Barker and Caplin were asked to rewrite scenes – never a good sign – and the final product betrays its patchwork origins.

'I was begging the producers to tell Clive that they had another writer on board,' Pavlou says. 'It wasn't my place to tell him, because my loyalties were to the production – it's the animal that you're in charge of; you're the trainer, you've got to look after the animal, the beast. You can't afford to take loyalties; otherwise the whole thing can crumble. I didn't want to take that chance.'

Three weeks into photography, the producers finally told Barker about Caplin's script; and, in Pavlou's words, 'I was so happy to see him come on set, so we could sit down and sort it out. Because until then, every morning, before rehearsing a scene, I'd look at Clive's script, I'd look at the other guy's script and try and find ways of making the best out of those two possibilities – and maybe doing a little rewrite myself, to try to catch what Clive had intended, really, because that was my concern. I don't think he's ever realized that, but I was trying to be faithful to his vision, with the little money that they had given us, the little time they had given us to create it.'[4]

Hammer Film star and screen veteran Ingrid Pitt, who was cast as Madam Pepperdine, felt that *Underworld* had 'a rather fascinating principle' but laments: 'The script that I saw first was not the script that was eventually filmed. The film could have been tremendous if they'd had more money, but there was acrimony in the production team. We had to keep filming it and every morning in make-up one would get a new bit of writing. There were too many factions that didn't get together and make one film. What really matters is the power of the thought and the vision. If you have the right people with the right vision and power of persuasion, you can do this ... but if that is fractured, you don't come out with anything; it's all over the place and that's how I felt about *Underworld*.'

211

Touted as a 'high-fashion, fantasy-thriller', and set in near-future London, *Underworld*, with its neon *noir* visuals and integration of rock music, was compared with the work of Michael Mann, whose television series 'Miami Vice' was then at the height of its popularity; but Pavlou had never seen the show. Synthrock band Freur, known for the hit single 'Doot Doot', was recruited to provide an electronic soundtrack and several original songs; its members even changed the band's name to Underworld in the wake of the project.[5] In the wash of Freur's music, Pavlou and his director of photography, Sidney Macartney, offered up blue-lit, shadowed, smoky images of low-budget glamour: gauze-wrapped heroines, men in long overcoats, stylish automobiles, exotic weapons and even a jarring and wholly gratuitous dance number.

The film opens in violent mystery as masked invaders steal into a posh London brothel run by Madam Pepperdine (Ingrid Pitt). Their quarry is the quiescent young prostitute Nicole (Nicola Cowper), who waits for her next client dressed in virginal white, a curious vial of liquid in hand. The kidnapping is interrupted by Pepperdine's body-guard and, in the ensuing struggle, the mask of an attacker is ripped away to reveal the face of a monster. The guard is overcome and Nicole is spirited into the night.

Cut to daylight and the riverside retreat of Roy Bain (Larry Lamb), a retired, 'ever scrupulous' hood – the proverbial bad man with a heart of gold. A pair of thugs sent by gang lord Hugo Motherskille (Steven Berkoff) beckons the 'retired' Bain back into service with 'The Firm'.

Bain meets with Motherskille, a swaggering toff whose shady past now resides beneath a thin veneer of legitimacy: 'You are looking at an industrialist, Roy. Clean, straight, one hundred percent for the Party.' Claiming that favours are owed, he wants to find Nicole; and Bain, her former lover, is the man for the job: 'People never change, Roy. They may seem to, but deep down, deep down where it counts, they stay the same. You know the streets. You know the girl. You were fond of her once. Knowledge, talent and . . . motivation.'

Despite some visual presence, Lamb plays the role of Bain with an understatement verging on a sleepwalk. His womanhunt links two converging plotlines. Nicole is a sensual chameleon, adept at fulfilling the fantasies of her clients: 'Men who couldn't live with their dreams, but wanted to visit them . . . occasionally.' She is, of course, Bain's dream; and when he calls on Pepperdine and finds the vial of liquid in Nicole's room, he knows that the dream has become a nightmare.

The vial – and a web of silence and denial – lead Bain to Dr Savary (the ubiquitous Denholm Elliott), a rogue scientist whose experiments have produced a mindwarping drug known as 'White Man'. In a scenario that owes much to the early films of David Cronenberg, Savary has used humans as guinea pigs and White Man has changed them: 'This drug is euphoric . . . and powerfully hallucinogenic. A superb painkiller. Truly superb. People can do amazing feats of strength under its influence. Unfortunately, the side-effects are unpredictable. And when they're bad . . . they're terrible.' White Man makes dreams into flesh, deforming its initiates into dire parodies of men and women.[6]

Despite the dangers of White Man – whose name alone evokes the imperialist/evolutionary text of HG Wells's *The Island of Dr Moreau* (1896) – Savary continues his experiments, creating a bestiary of mutants that must live in hiding and in constant desire for the drug. Among the addicted is Nicole, for whom Savary, like Bain, has an overwhelming yet inexplicable passion: 'My addiction to Nicole is more painful, I promise you.'

Dr Savary, as his name suggests, is no seeker of scientific truth but a corrupt and cynical candyman who works only to develop tastier drugs for Motherskille to unleash on the streets. The puzzle parts thus fall into place: the criminal underworld, now walking in daylight as an amalgam of business and science and politics, is ranged against the literal underworld of outcasts and the dispossessed that its remorseless greed has created and now seeks to subdue.

Nicole has been taken to the underground habitat of the deformed and disfigured humans, hidden within a maze of sewers and abandoned railway tunnels. 'You are what you dream' reads a background graffito – and this is the fate of the mutants: their dreams have distorted their flesh. They adopt flamboyant, often self-descriptive names: Red Dog is canine and violent; Oriel (Miranda Richardson) is birdlike; Nygaard the researcher (Paul Bown) is hydrocephalic, wearing his brains on his face; and comedic relief is offered, inevitably, by Dudu ('but my friends call me Shit Face'). Unfortunately, the menagerie is realized with low-budget facial prosthetics and wigs; in some scenes, the mutants simply wear ski masks instead of make-up.

Despite her addiction to White Man, Nicole is physically unchanged. 'She seems to be immune,' observes Nygaard. 'The dreams don't take root in her.' The drug seems instead to preserve her, to keep her young and beautiful; and she represents salvation – 'the answer' – for the Underworlders. But Nygaard seeks a physical solution, not understanding Savary's crucial insight: 'She gives dreams away, doesn't she? You know, I sometimes wonder how real she could make those dreams . . . if she put her mind to it.'

Bain alone seems trapped between the two worlds: one of bright brutality, resolutely physical, a place of cause and effect; and the dark dreamworld, dirty and ugly and monstrous and yet holding the pure vision of his love. When Red Dog breaks into Savary's home to steal more of the drug, he runs amok, leaving a bloody trail back to the Underworld.

As Bain descends into the darkness, Nicole agrees to lure Dr Savary into the Underworld: 'Make him come where he can join his children.' Only her intervention saves Bain from the mutants; but he has been used by Motherskille – not to find Nicole, but to find the Underworld and thus lead the gangster's hitmen to a killing ground that will cover up the disaster of White Man: 'And now we can put the freaks out of their misery.'

Motherskille's heavies ambush and kill most of the Underworlders, finally gassing the remaining mutants before Bain, in turn, passes mortal judgment on the mobsters. At last there is only the bizarre love triangle: Nicole and Bain and Savary.

'You're my hope . . . my vindication,' Savary tells Nicole. Although physically unchanged, she has been transformed by White Man, given its power to make dreams real – his dreams. 'Show me your dreams,' she demands, taking the role of exterminating angel. As her eyes flare with superimposed colour, his flesh bloats and bubbles, distorts, tears away and finally bursts into flames.

Reunited over the corpse of the renegade scientist, Nicole and Bain kiss, but for the final time. She will not return to the world above: 'This is my home now.'

'This is just the beginning,' she tells him before disappearing into the Underworld. Bain walks, alone, into a new dawn.

Despite a rushed and troubled shoot, George Pavlou's problems only heightened in post-production. He found himself barred from entering the editing rooms: 'I was allowed to view the cut of a scene, but not to participate hands-on in the editing.' His version of the film – a 103-minute director's cut – was shown only once, at the London Film Festival in November 1985. A 93-minute version, shortened simply because the producers wanted a ninety-minute film, was released on film (and later, on video) in England and Europe.

Clive saw the finished film once – in the shortened version, on the day of its cinema release in England: 'I couldn't bear to look at it again.' The film received a brief theatrical run, with the producers unable to obtain major distribution. At the time, the name of Clive Barker lacked sufficient 'brand' recognition to encourage wider interest.

Charles Band's Empire Pictures acquired US distribution rights; but, in the belief that Americans would not appreciate the double entendre of the title, rechristened the film *Transmutations*. Ignoring the protests of Pavlou (and even the producers), Empire also cut the film to a 78-minute length. After a two-week regional release in the southern United States without promotional support, the picture disappeared from theatres. Pavlou was allowed to restore seven minutes of footage for a 1988 American video release by Vestron; but despite a package design intended to capitalize on Clive Barker's increasingly visible name, the video disappeared into B-movie obscurity.

Among the more intriguing elements of *Underworld* are those that are missing from its final incarnations. Budgetary restrictions thwarted some inspired visuals, notably Barker's original version of Dr Savary's climactic come-uppance. As initially conceived, the finale would have seen the scientist's face explode with hypodermic needles. (In discussing that imagery for this book, Clive suddenly looked perplexed, then smiled and told me: 'I haven't thought about this before, but that was the Pinhead thing right there' – referring, of course, to his most renowned character, created for the screen two years later in *Hellraiser*). Pavlou's crew prepared the effect, but at the last minute, the producers interfered, deciding that they didn't want to spend the money; instead, the crew was instructed to build an exploding head. 'It was all prepped,' Pavlou says. 'All we had to do was shoot it – spend two or three days shooting it. So they spent a week re-doing the effects and spent just as much money to get a naff effect – it's crazy.'

The ending, too, would have been different. As filmed, *Underworld* leaves Bain's fate unresolved, having him return to a world of bright sunshine even though he has been injected with White Man. As written by Barker, the finale would have found Bain returning home and, in a montage evoking Frank Capra's *Lost Horizon* (1937), visibly deteriorating as a result of his departure from the Underworld. 'He relinquishes all desire for life,' Barker recalls, 'and eventually he does return there, to the place where his life has meaning and Nicole, the strange girl he loves, is waiting for him.'[7]

Underworld is a well-intentioned but painfully compromised and frustrated film. Its made-for-TV expressionism pales before its inspirations, *Suspiria* and *Inferno*, and its shortcomings are most obvious in scenes whose ambition exceeds the budget. In retrospect, Barker believes that its stylishiness was miscalculated: '[I]t seemed to prettify. It was exactly the reverse of what I was doing in my fiction, which was to be sort of down and dirty and just realistic, in my lopsided version of realism . . . It didn't seem to have anything to do with me. What it needed was exactly the opposite of what George Pavlou gave it. What it needed was a completely down and dirty, unapologetically exploitative mind. It needed somebody who was going to say, *Oh, great, we're going to do a whole monster thing, we're going to do a whole mobster thing, and they're going to blow the fuck out of each other and it's going to be great fun!'*

He is careful to note that Pavlou is not to blame: 'I don't think the screenplay was good at all . . . I think there was a genuinely interesting idea in there, which, with enough gusto and energy and, perhaps, to be fair to George, enough money, could have worked as a film . . . He was very nice and well-intentioned but, I think, a fairly powerless man in this situation. It was his first feature. He was basically going to jump through hoops if they told him to.' Pavlou also suffered a personal tragedy during the production; and, on the morning that he and his crew were to film the climactic gun battle, they learned that their location manager had been shot dead in his flat.

Despite its many monsters, *Underworld* is not truly a horror film, but an adventure in the breaching of genre, which sought to push the traditional imagery of horror into the realm of the *fantastique*. Its impulses are those of anti-horror: not a single human, even Bain or Nicole, is portrayed in a sympathetic light; certainly none of them is innocent – and, in the end, the only remaining hope of innocence, the faux-virginal Nicole, proves capable of causing the most violent of deaths. In its neon *noir*, a gangster and a prostitute – the forces of chaos – are capable of representing all that is good, while the forces of authority and order are exposed as the very core of evil.

Its theme would prove quintessential for the evolving art of Clive Barker; but in the meantime, there was another motion picture already in progress. In the exhilarating aftermath of Green Man's decision to produce *Underworld*, Barker had agreed to sell options giving Green Man the right of first refusal on film adaptations of five stories from the *Books of Blood*: 'Human Remains', 'Confessions of a (Pornographer's) Shroud', 'Jacqueline Ess: Her Will and Testament', 'Sex, Death and Starshine' and 'Rawhead Rex'.

In November 1985, Green Man told George Pavlou that pre-production on *Rawhead Rex* would begin in January 1986, with principal photography to start in March. In January, he travelled to Ireland, where he would be required to shoot the film. 'It was misty, raining, you couldn't see out of the windows,' Pavlou says. 'You couldn't get out of the car and these guys were looking for locations! I should have known then that this was the time to say: *Enough is enough*. And just walk away. But I didn't.'

15

RAW CELLULOID

RAWHEAD REX (1986)

'[T]hat was what the flickering reminded him of, the flicker of celluloid through the gate of a projector, one image hot on the next, the illusion of life created from a perfect sequence of little deaths.'
— CLIVE BARKER, 'Son of Celluloid'

'Rawhead Rex' is one of the truly distinctive and definitive stories of the *Books of Blood*.[1] True to its title, it represents Clive Barker at his most visceral, ushering the reader into a rip-roaring funfair ride with ever-escalating doses of violence and transgression. At its heart rages one of Barker's more memorable creations, the eponymous child-devouring nightmare whose appetite for death and destruction is perversely sexual and without bound. Yet those who judge 'Rawhead Rex' only by its imagery, although certain to find entertainment (or fodder for reactionary criticism), will miss its insistent and subversive intent.

Set in Zeal, a bucolic village lost in London's suburban sprawl, 'Rawhead Rex' proceeds from a time-honoured horror story scenario: a local farmer, Thomas Garrow, discovers a strange boulder while clearing fallow land and rolls the stone away, unlocking an ancient mystery. 'Suddenly there was no sense in heaven or earth.' A beastly hand reaches from the foul depths beneath the stone and its fearsome owner, a thing called Rawhead, emerges. Garrow stands in hopeless silence: 'There was nothing in him but awe. Fear was for those who still had a chance of life: he had none.' Rawhead kills Garrow, then drives his corpse head-first into the upturned earth, 'the very grave his forefathers had intended to bury Rawhead in forever'.

As he – Rawhead Rex is insistently male – sets out to wreak vengeance for his entombment, Barker lovingly unveils each detail of the creature's monstrosity. Rawhead is a primal force as mythic and vivid as another monstrous monarch, Kong. Nine feet tall and the width of two men, his rows of needle-sharp teeth are set in a moon face with fiery eyes: 'They were for all the world like wounds, those eyes, as though somebody had gouged them in the flesh of Rawhead's face then set two candles to flicker in the holes.' With each new element of description, each new atrocity, it becomes obvious that Rawhead Rex is a living, breathing, all-consuming phallus; indeed, it was imagining such a creature that compelled Barker to write the story. Appetite incarnate, Rawhead hungers for the flesh of children and is quelled only by the smell of menstrual blood: 'It was taboo, that blood and he had never taken a woman poisoned by its presence.'

Barker quickly signals the ruthlessness of his creature and his fiction. A model nuclear family – the Nicholsons and their seven-year-old, Amelia – is introduced and threatened, but Rawhead's ravenous attention is diverted by a farm animal. While a traditionalist would have the family escape and become crucial players in the finale, Barker deftly turns the tables and makes them into meat. Amelia is eaten alive as her mother, unable to intervene, watches. It is a powerful and effective reminder: in Clive Barker's fiction, as in the real world, no one is safe – especially the innocent.

The principal human players in this blood-drenched drama are men of the cloth: the country vicar, Reverend Coot, and his daffy verger, Declan Ewan. At their humble outpost of St Peter's, the Anglican church at Zeal, Declan tells Coot of local legends of the Beast of the Wild Woods, the last of a primitive breed who once owned this land – a child-devourer whose burial by the villagers centuries before is depicted in a carving on the altar. Rawhead's return inspires curious expectancy in Declan, but something else, spontaneous and surprising, in Reverend Coot: 'an erection so powerful it was like discovering the joy of lust all over again.' When the creature visits the churchyard, Declan kneels in worship of his new lord and saviour. It is one of Barker's more notorious scenes:

> Declan's vestments were torn and dirtied, his thin chest bare. Moonlight caught his sternum, his ribs. His state and his position were unequivocal. This was adoration – pure and simple. Then Coot heard the splashing; he stepped closer and saw that the giant was directing a glistening rope of its urine onto Declan's upturned face. It splashed into his slackly opened mouth, it ran over his torso. The gleam of joy didn't leave Declan's eyes for a moment as he received this baptism, indeed he turned his head from side to side in his eagerness to be totally defiled.

Clearly this is not the first of Barker's transgressions (and certainly not the last – only pages later come details of an eviscerated child), but it is among his most profound, linking the religious with the repulsive, the sacred with the profane.

The Reverend is suitably disgusted, even though his religion consumes (if only symbolically) the flesh and blood of its saviour. How, Barker asks the reader, could this celebration of the body's waste differ? No warning about the perils of blind faith could be as profound: 'Had Declan guessed, when he eulogized about this monster, what power it would have over his imagination? Had he known all along that if the beast were to come sniffing for him he'd kneel in front of it, call it Lord (before Christ, before Civilization, he'd said), let it discharge its bladder on to him and smile?'

When the Reverend invokes the name of his Lord, Rawhead pursues him into the sanctuary of the chapel, his obscenities encouraging Coot to roll away the stone of his beliefs: 'Wouldn't it ask for worship, just like any God? And wouldn't its demands be plain and real? Not ambiguous, like those of the Lord he's served up 'til now.' In the vestry, Rawhead confronts the symbol of Christian power above the mantelpiece: 'The image woke no tremors of fear or remorse in him: it was a picture of a sexless martyr, doe-eyed and woe-begone. No challenge there. The true power, the only power that could defeat him, was apparently gone: lost beyond recall, its place usurped by a virgin shepherd.'

Rawhead literally crushes Reverend Coot, becoming Lord and King of Zeal. His voracious reign is celebrated in another powerful set-piece, as his wrath descends upon another family – the Miltons, Londoners in retreat from the hassle and hustle of urban life. With clever misdirection, Barker focuses his narrative on their young daughter, Debbie, then suddenly shifts point of view to their son, Ian, who is left behind in the car. We watch through Ian's eyes as Rawhead takes him in agonizing slow motion:

> He looked through the back window as it hauled his torso into the open air and in a dream he saw Daddy at the gate, his face looking so, so ridiculous. He was climbing the gate, coming to help, coming to save him but he was far too slow. Ian knew he was beyond salvation from the beginning, because he'd died this way in his sleep on a hundred occasions and Daddy never got there in time. The mouth was wider even than he'd dreamed it, a hole which he was being delivered into, head first. It smelt like the dustbins at the back of the school canteen, times a million. He was sick down its throat, as it bit the top of his head off.

Mastering fuel and flame, Rawhead sets the village of Zeal ablaze. As the inferno rages, the ravaged Coot directs Ian's father, Ronald Milton, to the altar of St Peter's. Hidden inside the wooden façade is a shaped stone, alive with primal energy: 'The stone was the statue of a woman, a Venus ... her belly swelling with children ... All this time, under the cloth and the cross, they'd bowed their heads to a goddess.'

When Milton raises this symbol of the archaic feminine, Rawhead is defeated: 'It was just a symbol of course, a sign of the power, not the power itself, but his mind made no distinction. To him the stone was the thing he feared most: the bleeding woman, her gaping hole eating seed and spitting children. It was life, that hole, that woman, it was endless fecundity. It terrified him.'

The villagers – Zealots, indeed – fall on Rawhead with primordial

221

fury. With his roasted eyes an echo of Oedipus, he succumbs: 'There would be no resurrection this time, no waiting in the earth for an age until their descendants forgot him. He'd be snuffed out absolutely and there would be nothingness.' Nothing save the final image of a limp and dying beast, its bladder emptied, urine draining into the earth.

Few of Barker's stories match the full-throttle momentum of 'Rawhead Rex', its garish mayhem, or its canny sense for creating suspense by misdirection. On the simple level of a ghost train ride, 'Rawhead Rex' delivers more excitement and sensation than a fistful of contemporary horror novels; and, despite its didactic finale, there is mythic power in the premise: the male impulse, loosed of the bounds of society (and its pants), yet brought down by the feminine in the fine tradition of *King Kong* (1933) and *Alien* (1979).

Although Barker typically casts his monsters as sympathetic creatures, Rawhead is a harbinger of the void: insatiable, wholly destructive and not a mere killer, but an eater of children – the anathema of life. The story tests the extremes, looking for the answers that follow. Certainly it challenges the suppression of the feminine, particularly in the realm of religion – a recurrent theme of Barker's fiction, as is that of the body politic (here, the danger of man's thinking with his penis instead of his head, a tale that must be told again and again, until one day when, perhaps, we will get it right).

Fear of the feminine – as idealized in the notion of an archaic 'Mother Goddess' – often finds its source in anxieties about the generative ability of women. From a male perspective – and certainly that of Rawhead – the power of procreation endangers the norm, just as menstrual blood threatens the relationship between the sexes. It is impure, contaminating, a polluting object and yet also a sign of fertility and differentiation.

Rawhead is the true Zealot; he enters the seemingly 'impure' city to cleanse it by consuming its children – thus denying procreation, the source of feminine power. In truth, Barker argues, the masculine impulse, once freed of the feminine, offers only devastation; without acceptance of – and integration into – a world that, by its nature, is impure and that glories in differentiation, Rawhead is reduced to nothing but a purveyor of waste.

*

'Rawhead Rex' reads like a blueprint for a classic horror film; indeed, the story owes a vague debt to Ridley Scott's *Alien* (1979), which itself borrowed freely from sources as diverse as AE Van Vogt's novel *The Voyage of the Space Beagle* (1939) and Edward L Cahn's low-budget *IT! The Terror from Beyond Space* (1958) – which, in turn, echo the primal monster tale, *Beowulf* (circa 600–1000 AD). But the motion picture *Rawhead Rex* (1986) was doomed from its first tentative steps toward celluloid.

After the trying experience of *Underworld*, Clive faced a dilemma. Green Man had exercised its option to produce *Rawhead Rex* and teamed with Dublin-based Paradise Productions to finance the film. George Pavlou was asked to direct; and, as Pavlou notes: 'This time, for me, it wasn't that dream project. It was business. There was supposedly Hollywood money involved; Empire was supposed to be putting money into it, plus other monies from other sources.' Green Man budgeted *Rawhead Rex* at three million dollars and pre-production was moved to EMI Elstree Studios, where *Star Wars* had been filmed. 'So it's bound to be a good production,' Pavlou thought. 'It's bound to give me proper preparation time.'

Barker was asked to write the script and he agreed, if only to attempt to influence the outcome of the project. Money – which he lacked – played an important role in the decision. 'I just want the film to be an all-out monster movie with lots of blood and cheap thrills,' he said at the time. 'I wrote the best script I could and I'm hoping for the best.'[2]

The best was not to come: from the outset, the adaptation was hurtling toward disaster. Green Man's partners even disagreed about whether to produce the film; Don Hawkins thought it was a mistake. With major backing from Irish tax shelter money, the law required that principal photography take place in Ireland, which inverted the atmosphere from the sunshine of an English summer to a bleak Irish winter. Only six weeks of pre-production work were possible and shooting commenced in March 1986.

After writing a draft and a half of the script, Barker was not even invited onto the set. Although producer Kevin Attew (who, in unblinking hype, described *Rawhead Rex* as both '*Jaws* on land' and 'the ultimate monster movie for adults') was quoted as saying that 'Clive was always a phone call away', no phone call was ever made. Changes in action and dialogue – many based upon budgetary concerns, others based on moral ones – were made without consulting him. His powerful story was effectively orphaned by the producers.

The success of any film adaptation of 'Rawhead Rex' would turn, inevitably, upon the creature. Other aspects of the story – setting, characters and even the essential plot – are mundane; audiences had seen much of it before. What audiences had not seen was this singular creature, its singular point of view and its singular antics when loosed upon the world. The story dances a fine line, weaving, like Ridley Scott in *Alien* or John Carpenter in his remake of *The Thing* (1982), a fifties plot with an eighties sensibility; but its triumph is in placing the reader inside the mind of the monster. And, despite Barker's growing reputation as a provocateur of graphic detail, 'Rawhead Rex' cleverly feeds us the monster's features in small bites – indeed, he never fully shows us Rawhead, leaving room for each reader's imagination to fill in the details and thus enhance its monstrosity.

Pavlou's film had no such sanctuary: it was show-and-tell time. By the mid-1980s, the special effects revolution was over, forever changing the way in which audiences would look at motion pictures. After the on-screen atrocities of *The Exorcist* (1973) and the amazements of *Star Wars* (1977), anything seemed possible; even the unimaginable could be shown on the screen, from the vaginal video slit of Max Renn's stomach in David Cronenberg's *Videodrome* (1983) to the likes of Jabba the Hutt.

The monsters, too, had changed. As if wary of the profundity of an era of special effects, the directors of the most effective horror films imagined two kinds of creatures: the zombie, a pale but violent reflection of man exemplified in the films of George A Romero and Lucio Fulci; and the alien, which Scott and Carpenter and Cronenberg brought to nervous life with the aid of such special effects and design talents as HR Giger, Carlo Rambaldi and Rob Bottin.

Set against these precedents, *Rawhead Rex* could succeed only through the kind of visual flair and exceptional creature effects that were an anathema to a limited budget and tight shooting schedule. Barker's script, like the story, placed the monster on view for long periods of time. 'He was going to be seen a lot,' Pavlou says, 'because we were making a different kind of movie, where we weren't hiding the monster. Because we were so sure that Rawhead was going to be so good that he had to be seen and felt.'

When, during the brief pre-production period, Barker and George Pavlou visited the creative effects crew, Clive provided them with sketches of Rawhead. The crew rejected them as 'anatomically impossible and expensive', but they proposed an alternative. 'It looked good on paper,' Pavlou recalls; but money problems arose – not for the first, or last, time. The effects technicians, led by Peter Litten, originally planned a twenty-piece prosthetic suit, which would have required seven hours to assemble; for the final film, they were forced to settle on a one-piece costume that took fifteen minutes to put on.

Pavlou was unhappy, but 'not because of the suit – it could have been any design. The issue was whether Clive was happy with how Rawhead looked, because he has his own vision of these things.' Matters became worse when Pavlou asked the producers to hire David Prowse to play Rawhead, given his size and experience in costumed roles (including the physical role of Darth Vader in the first *Star Wars* trilogy). The producers wouldn't pay for Prowse, but told Pavlou: 'There's a young deer farmer, a German guy who's nineteen years old, six foot eleven and we're talking the kind of money we can afford.' Pavlou was mortified: 'He didn't know what a film camera looked like, let alone how to perform in a suit. So we're talking *Plan 9 from Outer Space* here, right?'[3]

Filmed in seven weeks in County Wicklow, Ireland, under the working title 'Rawhead' – and with an ever-decreasing budget – the adaptation shifts the setting from suburban London to the Irish town of Rathmorne; and this is but the first of its changes. In a concession to the backing of Empire and the almighty American film market, the character of Ronald Milton, the grieved father who ended Rawhead's reign, was supplanted by Howard Hallenbeck, an American tourist played by TV mini-series stalwart David Dukes. Hallenbeck, a university professor, visits Ireland with his annoying family – wife Elaine (Kitty Piper) and two rambunctious children – in pursuit of a book about 'the persistence of sacred sites' from pre-Christian times. (In Barker's original screenplay, Hallenbeck was an advertising executive.) As soon as the Hallenbecks arrive at Rathmorne, the stone is rolled away and Rawhead emerges.

Pavlou's director of photography was John Metcalfe, whose cinematography had sustained the *Alien* imitator *Xtro* (1983). Gone is the subdued look of *Underworld* and in its place a rather straightforward, by-the-numbers rendition of a 1950s monster-on-the-loose melodrama. Though Pavlou is clearly capable of creating suspense – there are effective set-pieces lost in what is otherwise matinee fare – his efforts succumbed to the production's obvious weaknesses, the weather and withering finances. When he asked the producers to fly Clive to Ireland to assist him, he was told that there was no money. Planned shots from the monster's point of view were eliminated as the exterior shoot, already made difficult by the March weather, became almost impossible when Ireland suffered its worse storm in years. The camera crane was blown over by ferocious winds and each day the crew had to douse the foliage to remove snow. Then Pavlou was unable to proceed with planned night shoots. For the first few days, he was told that the crew had to wrap at midnight because of the threat of snow – 'but it had been snowing continually'. Limited to only four hours of night work, he was forced to shoot without adequate rehearsals. Three weeks into principal photography, Pavlou learned that he was working on a budget that was a lie; his financing was two million dollars, not the three million dollars budgeted and announced by his producers.

No one was protecting his interests, or, in turn, those of Clive Barker. 'The producers didn't understand the physical nature of a film,' Pavlou says. 'What it takes to create these kinds of effects. And I was still learning; I was naïve, among other things. I thought they had the money to back me up.'

With constant weather problems and changes in locations, the shoot became a war of physical endurance: eighteen hours a day, seven days a week, for seven weeks. 'Things happened so quickly that, to this day, I can't tell you why things happened.' There was no time to prepare creatively: 'It was crazy.' But, as Pavlou admits, 'I loved it. I'd do it again ... but differently. And if Clive had been there, things would have been different.'

Less than ten minutes into the film, Rawhead erupts from the earth in a full-length, daylight shot; we know, in that instant, that we are watching a very big man in a creature costume, a peculiar motley that looks something like Miss Piggy in shredded military fatigues. (In a promotional interview, effects technician Peter Litten described his creation as a cross between Neanderthal man, punk and gorilla – and, unfortunately, he was right). Less than twenty minutes into the film, we are offered a full close-up of Rawhead's face, and despite the best efforts of the screen magicians, the reality check is over; it is a clever, but nevertheless obvious, mask. By the half-hour mark, Rawhead has been offered to the viewer so repeatedly in close-up that all hope of horror is lost.[4]

Lost, too, is Rawhead's relentless and shocking violence. In sanitizing the story for the screen – Attew and Pavlou agreed early on 'to go for taste, suggestion and stylishness'[5] – the child-devourer is turned into a less discriminate killer whose supposed viciousness is often depicted by having it lift men by the throat and shake them. The gore, when it comes, is surprisingly sterile, as unreal as the creature. Severed heads look unerringly like props. In one dubious scene, a girl runs out of the woods clutching her lover's hand and we are expected to believe she doesn't realize that his body is missing, severed away by Rawhead.

Without proper visual accompaniment, the framework and subtext of Barker's narrative collapses. Rawhead lurks forever at the edge of the town, purpose and intent unknown, and the viewer soon wonders if he is watching an inferior precursor of *Predator* (1987). Barker's fiction was powered by its willingness to place the reader in the mind of Rawhead, to understand its cravings and its unbridled lust for vengeance; but in the film, the creature is a cypher, just another savage beast on the loose.[6]

Despite the presence of a church, the religious and metaphysical elements – and the symbolic struggle of masculine and feminine – are downplayed. An ineffectual Reverend Coot (Niall Tobin) is over-whelmed by the Verger Declan (now surnamed with the Irish O'Brien and played with scene-stealing abundance by Ronan Wilmot). Surprisingly, Declan's baptism in urine is shown – in a startling scene, albeit distant and by no means detailed.

'[T]his is Christ's house,' insists Reverend Coot; but Hallenbeck offers a retort that goes without answer: 'It wasn't always his, was it?' The windows of the church tell the story of Rawhead's ancient downfall, and when Hallenbeck, with the help of the dying Reverend, puts the puzzle parts together, he finds the stone image of a pregnant woman beneath the altar. But when he wields the stone against Rawhead, nothing happens; it is only when his wife arrives, stumbling from out of nowhere and into the finale like the cavalry in endless Westerns, that things are made right. Elaine raises the stone, rays of light emerge and the spectre of a woman in flowing robes – echoes of the finale of *Underworld* – appears to conquer the beast. 'A woman,' Hallenbeck says, in a kind of stupified wonder. 'It had to be a woman.'

Yet it is Hallenbeck who finally dispatches Rawhead with a blow, sending the monster's body crashing into the earth beneath a weight of stone. Swiftly erasing the fleeting suggestion of feminine power, Hallenbeck embraces his suddenly teary-eyed, fearful, shaking wife. Then he utters the most dreaded words ever to haunt the conclusion of a horror film: 'It's all over now . . . it's all over.' True to formula, it is *not* over. When a young boy visits the cemetery the next morning, up pops Rawhead for a final roar before the merciful fade to black.[7]

That fade also marked the end of Clive Barker's shortlived association with Green Man Productions. Green Man announced plans to produce 'Jacqueline Ess: Her Will and Testament' with George Pavlou directing; 'but by then,' Pavlou says, 'to be honest with you, I'd had quite enough'.[8] The Green Man partnership dissolved and its option on 'Jacqueline Ess' and three other stories – 'Human Remains', 'Confessions of a (Pornographer's) Shroud' and 'Sex, Death and Starshine' – lapsed without renewal. When, in the wake of Barker's ascension to stardom, former Green Man partner Kevin Attew proposed to adapt the four stories as films, the threat of a court action was necessary to stop him.

Clive Barker and George Pavlou survived the experience with the grace and optimism of professionals – and they remained friends, although their creative paths diverged. Pavlou's regrets are personal ones, founded in Barker's public criticism of the films: 'My disappointment is that he's disappointed. That saddens me. I see the faults in those films as well. With a little more experience on my part, it could have been a lot better. But at the end of the day, the results are the sum of the parts.'

Vestron UK, which distributed *Underworld* and *Rawhead Rex* on video, approached Pavlou to direct another horror film. 'By then, I was very disillusioned with the whole thing.' With the birth of his first child, he found more sane and secure work filming television commercials. Today he heads a successful advertising agency in London and pursues his interest in horror film with occasional low-budget projects. He was thrilled by Clive's later triumphs: 'I'm very happy for him – and I think he deserves it. Because he worked so hard for it. And anyone who works that hard deserves what they get.'

Barker, in turn, accepted the films as part of his continuing education – and as a kind of epiphany: 'It was a really rotten experience for me; but it was a *useful* rotten experience. [It] was enough to make me realize that it was not that difficult . . . that, fuck, if these guys can do it, anyone can do it.

'Not only did it give me a sense that the people who made movies were not so capable, that this was not some rarified world where there was some kind of code and if you didn't get it, you couldn't do it. That there were actually people who were flying around by the seat of their pants, with a lot of pretensions – movie people, you know, insecure intellectually, impressionistic fudges; so much fudging going on . . . I also realized that if I was going to do it, it was going to need to get done in some way with my fingers in the pie. And that was a useful lesson.'

As always, Barker learned his lesson well. Within a year, he would be standing on a soundstage at Cricklewood in North London, directing his first feature film, *Hellraiser* (1987). He invited George Pavlou to the set and Pavlou, intrigued by what he saw, asked for a copy of the script. 'The script was brilliant,' Pavlou says. Indeed, as he read through it that night, he said to his wife: 'That Clive's such a bastard . . . he's kept the best for himself!'

For the film life of Clive Barker, the best – and also the worst – was yet to come.

16

SECRET LIVES

THE SECRET LIFE OF CARTOONS (1986)

'The way I see it, if you can't make a living in two dimensions, try three.'

— CLIVE BARKER, *The Secret Life of Cartoons*

'You ain't gonna believe this!' The words, ironically descriptive of Clive Barker's swiftly-spiralling success, flared from a comic-strip balloon on posters and advertisements in London during the fall of 1986. Spoken by a trench-coated, cigar-smoking rabbit whose furry paw clutched at a comely brunette, they introduced the latest major play to debut in London's West End: *The Secret Life of Cartoons.*[1]

Clive Barker was returning to the stage – and not to the creaky boards of fringe theatre, but to the playwright's Mecca. *The Secret Life of Cartoons* was his least serious writing for the stage, but its commercial prospects had triggered the dissolution of the Dog Company in 1982. Barker's theatrical agent, Vernon Conway, later found enthusiastic producers who would bring his comedic creation to one of London's venerable playhouses.

The play opened at the Theatre Royal in Plymouth before moving to the West End and the famous Aldwych Theatre, where its London premiere took place on October 15, 1986. Built in 1905 as a companion to the Strand, the Aldwych has a distinguished and diverse history. In 1960, the Royal Shakespeare Company made the theatre its London base before moving into the Barbican Centre. Although more recent productions at the Aldwych have included plays by Tom Stoppard, the theatre will be known forever as the 'home of farce' since housing a series of classic Ben Travers productions in the 1920s and 1930s.

The Secret Life of Cartoons was produced and presented as the latest entry in this grand comic tradition. Tudor Davis directed from a script by Barker that had been revised and expanded significantly from the one-act version performed by the Dog Company. The cast was led by British television personalities, including Derek Griffiths (best known as a presenter on the children's programme 'Playschool'); Una Stubbs ('Give Us a Clue'); and Geoffrey Hughes (from the long-running 'Coronation Street').

That the play was written by Clive Barker had little publicity cachet: when the play entered production, his fame was still limited, with the transition from cult author to media darling yet to come. It was the actors, as well as the farcical quality of the play, that were its selling points. In promotional materials, Barker's name was often conspicuously absent and, even when shown, it was relegated to a type size smaller than that given to the supporting cast.[2]

The Secret Life of Cartoons drew its inspiration from the abiding passion shared by Barker, Doug Bradley and fellow members of the Dog Company for Warner Brothers cartoons. Written as a late-night companion to *Frankenstein in Love* at the 1982 Edinburgh Festival, the play brought a cartoon world into collision with domestic sitcoms from the golden age of American television. What might happen, Barker posited – years before the motion pictures *Who Framed Roger Rabbit?* (1988) and *Cool World* (1992) – if cartoon characters were to invade the mock reality of 'I Love Lucy' or 'The Dick Van Dyke Show'?[3]

On its serious and darker side – which would be lost on the stage of the Aldwych – *The Secret Life of Cartoons* also evoked the classic motion picture *Harvey* (1950), in which Jimmy Stewart played Elwood P Dowd, a kindly eccentric whose best friend is an invisible six-foot-tall rabbit. The film's other characters are concerned about Elwood's mental health, but as the film progresses, we realize that Elwood is not only sane, but more centred and sound than anyone around him. Like this sentimental fable, *The Secret Life of Cartoons* sought to reveal the tyranny of conformity – the folly of seeking normalcy (or even trying to define it) without imposing an order that denies the glory of individuality. 'How come,' Elwood wants to know, 'people become your friends and suddenly start bossing you around? Why are people like that?'

Set in Manhattan during the mid-1950s, *The Secret Life of Cartoons* is a two-act light comedy written in an uncharacteristically breezy style (as underscored by its opening stage direction: 'O.K., so here's the scene'). Like classic farce, it is an exercise in controlled anarchy, centred on sexual embarrassments and escapades, with a wildly varied cast of characters racing on and off stage in ever-more-rapid sequences, delivering lines filled with wordplay and puns and delivering snappy punchlines and retorts worthy of burlesque comedians. Its action is more readily transferred to the printed page than its humour, which depends heavily on stylized delivery, sight gags and physical comedy.

The play chronicles the breakdown and repair of the marriage of Lorraine and Dick Caplan. Set in a single room of a cramped and gloomy fifth-storey apartment, the couple's differences are obvious in the design: Lorraine's efforts at tasteful decoration have been undone by Dick's array of the garish – comic books and Marx Brothers film posters and cartoon memorabilia. Signs illustrated with cartoon characters mark the doorways to the kitchen, the bedroom and the hallway outside; beneath the picture window, an arrow points down with a warning: '50 foot drop'.

Lorraine, slightly tipsy, prepares a celebratory dinner for Dick's thirty-fourth birthday. As she refills her glass with vodka, the delica-tessen delivery boy, Arnold Fleischer, arrives with an armload of gro-ceries and an infatuation that fuels Lorraine's wishful fantasy of an affair. Arnold tells Lorraine the story of a hysterical customer who claims she saw a six-foot-tall rabbit behind the delicatessen.

Arnold exits and when Lorraine goes into the bedroom, a six-foot-tall Bugs Bunny – thinly disguised, for copyright reasons, as Roscoe Rabbit – sneaks into the apartment, dressed in parody of an American tourist: sunglasses, suitcase and shriekingly loud attire. 'He looks immaculate,' read Barker's stage directions, 'as he does in all the disguises he will adopt in the next hour and a half. Scarcely a hare out of place.'

The Rabbit is breathless, nervous, on the run from unidentified pursuers; but he falls in love at the first sight of Lorraine. He wisecracks with her in high style, then finally admits that he's looking for Dick: 'It's risky, but I couldn't leave without saying goodbye.' We soon learn that Dick is a cartoon animator and that Roscoe, his most popular creation, has come to life, broken his contract and fled the studio: 'My career in movies is over; and you know, I don't care. The way I see it, if you can't make a living in two dimensions, try three.'

Lorraine offers him a drink. 'I must say you're taking this very well,' the Rabbit tells her. 'A lot of people would think it unnatural, you know, me being here in the flesh.' Lorraine thinks that the Rabbit is a comedian in costume, sent by the studio to help celebrate Dick's birthday; and, as she tells him: 'I've got used to a little quiet insanity over the years.' Soon she discusses her lack of a sex life with the Rabbit. 'Who better?' he says. 'We didn't invent sex, but we are into researching it.' In the first of a running series of gags involving phone calls to the police – answered by a Sergeant Beethoven – the Rabbit snatches the phone from her and pleads for help.

Enter nosy neighbour Isolde Steinberg, a harridan in shower cap and dressing gown who tells Lorraine about 'this gigantic Duck dangling outside my bathroom window, looking at me lewdly'. When Lorraine goes to investigate, the red-moustached, shotgun-wielding Rabbit Hunter – an ersatz Yosemite Sam – hauls himself through the window and into the apartment: 'I'll get you for this, wabbit!' Dangling from his waist by a length of rope is Danny Duck, lisping and irritated in the best tradition of Daffy. Sent by the studio to 'get' the Rabbit, their plans are foiled repeatedly in ultraviolent yet harmless cartoon slapstick. The Rabbit asks a question posed repeatedly in Barker's work, whether comedic or tragic: 'Must we always be hounded just because we're ... different?' A confused Lorraine forces the Rabbit Hunter out of the window and the grateful and increasingly randy Rabbit kisses her.

At the height of the madness, Dick – a '[h]andsome, all-American lunatic' – arrives with a paper bag, which he opens to reveal a pistol and a bottle of pills. 'I came home for sanity,' he says, then enters into a long conversation with himself, alternately using the Rabbit's voice and his own as he contemplates suicide. He has lost his job at the studio because his drawings of the Rabbit have disappeared: 'Every sketch, every cel. Like he just upped and ran away.' The studio claimed that Dick destroyed the work after a creative dispute: 'They wanted more violence, less dubious remarks.'

The orders have come from the unseen enigma who runs the studio: the Mouse. 'Dick never knew,' the Rabbit tells Lorraine, 'none of the artists know. They just get their pay-cheques and don't ask questions. But take it from me, there is a Mouse in charge. A very unpleasant Mouse.'

While Dick showers, the Rabbit seduces Lorraine with kisses and sly words: 'Besides, I am Dick. A part of him anyway. It's not adultery. Not with your husband's magnum opus. Well is it?' When Dick discovers the Rabbit and Lorraine in the bedroom, he edges out onto the window ledge, wearing only a towel. The Rabbit Hunter and the Duck try to talk him back inside, but he slips and plummets, naked, to the street below.

Act Two opens later that evening as Police Sergeant Beethoven surveys the wreckage. Dick has survived the fall, landing on a pile of boxes outside the delicatessen; but the hysterical Isolde Steinberg is carted off to the hospital, imploring: 'Ask them about the Rabbit!'

Beethoven attempts an interrogation: 'This bunny could not, by any stretch of the imagination, be considered a pet. As I understand it we are talking about a biped, something over six foot tall, dressed, depending on which account you care to believe, in an Hawaiian style shirt, full evening dress or nothing at all. Tell me about the Rabbit. Please.' Instead the couple offer a fragmented summary of their failing marriage. Lorraine expected 'big things' of Dick, not the 'kid's stuff' of cartoons: 'She wanted me to be Rembrandt.' But Dick fell in love with animation:

> They're not funnies! They're animated films. They require a lot of dedication and hard work, twenty four paintings for every second of screen time, several thousand for a five minute film:

That's sweat, officer Beethoven, that's sweat and blood. And why? Because it makes America laugh.

Not just America, the world. It's a universal language: chases, sieges, tricks, disguises. These funnies, as you call them, will be remembered long after they've forgotten *Citizen Kane*.

Roscoe Rabbit is the ultimate expression of his creator's imagination: 'I gave everything I could to the Rabbit, you know? I gave him all my wittiest remarks, all my funniest routines. I even gave him my libido.' Now his creation has followed him home and his on-screen nemeses, the Rabbit Hunter and the Duck, have been sent in pursuit. 'They play by the same rules off screen, it seems. Chases, sieges, hair-breadth escapes . . . It's not a bad idea at that.' But then Dick realizes what it means for him: 'I don't think it's over . . . I don't think it'll ever be over. It's a perpetual chase, isn't it? No beginning, no end.'

The policeman takes Lorraine aside and encourages her to help him stop the rabbit-impersonator: 'Probably a Commie. Lots of Commies working undercover these days. This is the first one I've come across working as a furry animal, but they'll try anything. That's why we got out the order: shoot on sight . . . [Y]ou must understand how important it is we grind out these subversive elements.' As he makes a telephone call, we learn that he, too, is working for the ubiquitous Mouse.

After a brief and bitter argument, Lorraine leaves. Dick sulks in front of the television set until a cartoon vision of BB – a thinly disguised Betty Boop – steps out of the screen and into the apartment. 'All these years darling, I wanted you and wanted you,' she coos, 'but always known you were too far from me. Until now.' Everything, even the apartment, has fallen under the influence of the studio, melting into the world of cartoons: '[T]ake it from me, this place belongs to the Mouse . . . This business is run by cartoons.'

She shows Dick the fine print of his contract with the studio: 'If you break the rules . . . this place reverts to the studio. You don't have any control here any longer. Anything could happen . . .' At last she coaxes him into the bedroom. 'The Mouse doesn't want any ink shed. He just wants the Rabbit. You're not going to stop him, are you?' In the midst of the seduction, the Rabbit Hunter enters through the window yet again and offers the audience his opinion: '[T]here's no need for this constant obsession with sex. What happened to the good old days when the world was full of little furry things beating the stuffing out of each other? Chases and disguises, that's what I like to see ... Chases and disguises and scenes in which fluffy animals get blown to pieces.'

Lorraine and the Rabbit (now in full drag, 'a cross between Scarlett O'Hara and something from Tennessee Williams') return from their assignation in time for Lorraine to discover Dick's indiscretion. In a moment of calm in the eye of the farcical storm, Dick announces his surrender to conformity:

> You know what I'm going to do, Rabbit? I'm going to give up cartoons forever. I'm going to work in a proper profession, with a boss who doesn't think he's a mouse. I'm going to go into my office every morning and do something sensible with my life. I'm going to stop reading *Superman* comics and take *New Yorker*. I'm going to learn to understand the jokes. I'm going to be normal. Yeah. I am. And I won't miss you at all, Rabbit.

Then, at the climactic moment, the Mouse arrives: 'Enter, to a burst of razzmatazz music, the Mouse. He has a fur-collared coat and silk scarf draped around his padded shoulders. He wears dark glasses. A fat cigar, well-chewed, lolls in his mouth. At a short, sharp gesture from him the music stops dead.' He announces his candidacy for President – as a Republican – and reclaims the apartment, including its view: 'I own the skyline.'

Lorraine and Dick and the Rabbit are left with a desolate space – a bare lightbulb in the middle of an empty room. 'Five hours ago,' she tells the Rabbit, 'I had a marriage, an apartment, a reputation, sanity ... Then you arrived.' She tells Dick that she wants a divorce: 'I can't live with a man who was out-manoeuvred by a Mouse.' As he tries to reason with her, the Rabbit coaches and coaxes him: 'Tell her you love her.' When he finally tells her, she replies: 'Kiss me'; but in the darkness, the Rabbit slips into his place – 'You know what, you're sensational' – until Dick finally stumbles into her arms.

With the couple reunited, the Rabbit exclaims: 'Ah, forget it! I'm off to Rio.' And when they ask – 'What's in Rio?' – Barker offers a deranged and celebratory finale:

> An explosion of sound and light: which illuminate Dick and Lorraine embracing centre-stage, eyes closed as they kiss, too involved to notice the South American dancers, masked for Carnival, that are cavorting around, led by the Rabbit, dressed in his American tourist outfit, as he was at the beginning. The frenzy of dancing continues, as the Rabbit leads the celebration out of the window. Suddenly all the lights go out, except for one lingering pool on Dick and Lorraine's embrace. They open their eyes.
> LORRAINE: Did you hear something?
> DICK (as the Rabbit): Probably the earth moving.
> They smile and resume kissing as the pool of light fades to black out.

Clearly *The Secret Life of Cartoons* was intended as pure comic entertainment. Barker himself calls it 'a piece of feather-light nonsense',[4] although its text echoes themes central to his more characteristic works. In using archetypes of famous Warner Brothers and Walt Disney cartoon characters, he brings a mythology of chaos into our seemingly ordered world; but the play's genius is that this chaos, unlike that of conventional horror fiction and film, is an endearing one. Seen with utter objectivity, cartoon characters are monsters; it is only because of their two dimensions and playful antics that we fail to think of them in those terms. The play's genesis and performance as a companion to *Frankenstein in Love* was truly inspired: Roscoe Rabbit is an affectionate Frankenstein's monster – a shadow-self constructed from fragmented and repressed desires who haunts his creator out of love.[5]

Clearly Barker's infatuation with cartoon characters arises from their anarchical tendencies, their ambiguous but insistent sexuality and their outrageous and hyperdestructive behaviour, from which they always seem to bounce back – violence overcome. As *The Secret Life of Cartoons* confirms, their authority is life-transcending (and affirming), because cartoon characters know that, to win out, reality must and should be bent and altered. 'Cartoons are pure imagination,' the play tells us: 'no rules, no regulations. It comes from the heart.'

The West End production of *The Secret Life of Cartoons* closed after a short run, a victim of mixed and generally negative reviews. Writing in *The Times*, Irving Wardle, who was apparently bewildered by the thought of a writer of horror fiction penning a humorous play, lamented the absence of terror: 'Mr Barker has chosen to pursue the idea into comedy with dire and theatrically illiterate results.'[6] Yet writers of horror fiction have penned legendary comedies: Ira Levin, the author of *Rosemary's Baby* (1967), scripted the Broadway and film sensation *No Time for Sergeants* (1955, 1958); and William Peter Blatty created *The Exorcist* only after making his mark as the screenwriter of several Hollywood comedies, including *A Shot in the Dark* (1964). Clive Barker's own readers could attest to the genuinely humorous vignettes in the *Books of Blood*. The issue was not whether a writer of horror could also write for laughs, but whether *The Secret Life of Cartoons* was translated effectively to the stage.

Roy Barker, who was delighted to see his brother's name 'up in lights', was far more forgiving: 'I thought it was a scream.' But much of the negative criticism was fair; certainly the West End production did not meet with Clive's original intentions. 'All the subtext went to the wall,' Clive notes, 'and with it the reality that might have made metaphor of the nonsense. What remained were the nonsenses, with which critics have problems, as they are by definition not susceptible to analysis. (The nonsenses, that is. I'm certain a good number of critics would benefit from analysis.)'

Doug Bradley, who had played the Rabbit in the Dog Company performances of *The Secret Life of Cartoons*, was stunned by what he saw at the Aldwych: 'It was very different. It had become a light entertainment piece, which we were not doing at all. We were absolutely inhabiting the world of Warner Brothers cartoons . . . And that's what it was: an attempt to put a Warner Brothers cartoon on stage, to try to obey all the conventions of a Warner Brothers cartoon and to find a way to make that work with human beings. Roger Martin directed and he met it with exactly the same level of energy. If we could have taken *The Secret Life of Cartoons* into the West End, we could have made it work.'[7]

Nan du Sautoy and Barbara Boote of Sphere Books saw both productions of the play and share Bradley's view: 'It was a good combination,' du Sautoy notes, laughing with memories of the Dog Company performance: 'a sophisticated way of putting over reality versus fantasy. A complicated but charming and amusing play. Because it was done in a fringe theatre, it was also so much more immediate.'

The original play, as performed by the Dog Company, was only an hour long. In its transformation to a West End production, the script's length had to be doubled. Bradley comments: 'The decisions that were made about how to do that were, in my opinion, wrong. Basically when they reached the interval, they had done what we did. I remember thinking, *What are they going to do in the second half?* And it didn't really do *anything* in the second half, which is where, for me, it died. I thought a lot of the casting was wrong and the whole tone of the piece was . . . not right. It had become something quite safer. It was a bastardization of what we had done and I thought it was going to meet the fate that it did.'

Equally damning was a self-conscious, self-parodic staging, which tried too stridently to amuse the audience. A time-honoured maxim of the stage, repeated by a sometime actor in the *Books of Blood* story 'Babel's Children', holds that '[t]he trick of good farce was that it be played with deadly seriousness'.

The reviews also signalled the inevitable critical backlash to Clive Barker's sudden and sweeping success: the play took to the Aldwych stage during a wave of publicity surrounding his books and the announcement that he would direct his first motion picture, *Hellraiser*. Although popularity seems a peculiar reason to condemn talent, perhaps the play's Rabbit sums it up best: 'You give them a seat and a funny hat and suddenly they're critics.'[8]

In an interview published in October 1986, Clive announced that he was preparing another play for the London stage, while also working on a planned production of *The Secret Life of Cartoons* in the United States. He was considering stage adaptations of two *Books of Blood* stories: a comedy, 'The Yattering and Jack', and the dire 'Human Remains'. Events other than mixed reviews swiftly overtook his dreams of extended runs on the West End and Broadway.

After *The Damnation Game* was sold to Sphere, Clive had realized that Vernon Conway's forte was the theatre, not publishing, and that he needed an established literary agent to represent him in future negotiations with publishers. He retained June Hall, who was known for a hardball approach to agenting and contracts; she had, in Barbara Boote's words, 'a proper, pushy literary agency . . . She was very tough'.

Hall set about assuring that Clive Barker, rather than Sphere, controlled his publishing destiny. She negotiated far more substantial advances of £15,000 per book for the second three *Books of Blood* and she declined to license world rights to Sphere, limiting the transaction to United Kingdom rights – thus depriving Sphere of the financial benefits of sublicensing the books to the potentially more lucrative North American market and in foreign translations. Hall then approached several American publishers directly.

Clive was disappointed by the efforts of Berkley Books (then a division of GP Putnam and now an imprint of Penguin Putnam), which had acquired the North American rights to the original *Books of Blood* and *The Damnation Game*. In a remarkable miscalculation, Berkley ignored the surging publicity and delayed its publication of the books for an unconscionable amount of time. ('The whole thing was amazingly slow,' says Sphere's Nan du Sautoy.) Although the first three *Books of Blood* were released in England in March 1984, Berkley did not issue them in the United States until mid-1986; and *The Damnation Game*, published in England in 1985, did not appear in the United States until 1987. To make matters worse, Berkley treated the books as downmarket genre fiction, packaging the *Books of Blood* with garish blood-and-guts covers and scheduling *The Damnation Game* under its genre-oriented Ace hardcover and Charter paperback imprints.

Clearly it was time for a change. Barker's name and talent had come to the attention of Ann Patti at Simon & Schuster, a powerful New York editor who had discovered Virginia ('VC') Andrews and who sought a writer of literary and popular significance for Simon & Schuster's fledgling Poseidon Press imprint. Promising more money and a sympathetic, respectful treatment of his material, Patti wooed Barker away from Berkley and other suitors, acquiring the North American rights to the last three *Books of Blood* and the third novel to be published in the US, *Cabal*.

The result, however, was bibliographic confusion. Patti wanted to divorce her new acquisitions from the original *Books of Blood* in order to disabuse readers of the notion that reading the first books was necessary to the second ones – and, equally important, to get the texts into print without waiting for the dilatory Berkley to issue the first set. Barker agreed, with reluctance but a sense of inevitability, to Patti's proposal. The name 'Books of Blood' was dropped from the second three volumes in their American incarnations and the texts were reorganized and titled after their lead stories: *The Inhuman Condition, In the Flesh* and *Cabal* (which only added to the confusion, since it merged the new novel with certain stories from *Books of Blood Volume Six*). Simon & Schuster's reluctance to acknowledge the Berkley editions carried so far as a refusal to list the *Books of Blood* among Barker's works in the prefatory pages of the Poseidon releases. (Berkley was equally forthcoming; even today its paperback editions acknowledge no books by Clive Barker save those published under its logo.)

The benefits of the move to Simon & Schuster were immediate. The publication date of *The Inhuman Condition* was August 1, 1986, effectively simultaneous with Berkley's release of the first three *Books of Blood* (which were published in June through October of that year) – and a year before Berkley finally got around to publishing *The Damnation Game*. The Poseidon editions were handsome hardcovers whose artful dust jackets suggested the literary rather than the visceral; and, for the first time, major American newspapers and magazines reviewed Barker's books.[9]

There were other, deeper implications. The move from Berkley and its downmarket, generic typecasting presaged a change of publishers in London – and in the way that Clive Barker would allow others to view his fiction. He had already tasted publishing's preference for fulfilling expectations when Barbara Boote and Nan du Sautoy had rejected his proposal to write the fantastical *Out of the Empty Quarter* and urged him to write a horror novel instead. The hype that now surrounded him was increasingly threatening, as if with each new pronouncement of his mastery of 'horror' he was being defined, catalogued, pigeonholed.

Clive knew that 'horror' was a limiting and increasingly dubious term for his ambition. Ever diplomatic, he soon indicated a preference to be known as an 'imaginer' – and, later, as a 'fabulist' or writer of the *fantastique*. He would fondly paraphrase composer Michael Tippett's wish to create music that would make its audience believe it was breathing the air of another planet; and, with that wish in his heart, he began to write, as his second novel, the book that Sphere had denied him – a novel of remarkable ambition that, in time, would be called *Weaveworld*.

With his relentless work ethic, he spent much of 1985 and 1986 writing the novel, along with his motion picture scripts for George Pavlou and occasional short fiction. June Hall offered the completed manuscript to Sphere. Although Barbara Boote was disappointed with its leanings towards fantasy, she wanted to acquire the book. Sphere, she insists, saw Clive Barker in generic terms: 'We thought he was going to stay a horror writer – different from anyone else, but a horror writer.' The publisher also feared that Clive would abandon the writing life for film. 'I always thought he was at least as visual as verbal,' Nan du Sautoy notes. 'And film and theatre seemed to be his natural direction.' Boote agrees: 'Clearly that was the way he was going. In fact, I didn't think he'd carry on writing for as long as he has ... I thought books were a stage he was going through on his way to Hollywood. And I was wrong.'[10]

When Sphere declined to pay the substantial advance that June Hall deemed suitable, she took *Weaveworld* to several other London publishers and called for an auction. In the bidding, Sphere offered a £40,000 advance for the novel; but Eddie Bell, the publisher and chief executive officer at William Collins (which later merged with Harper & Row to become HarperCollins) weighed in with an offer intended to make a statement about his belief in Clive Barker and his desire to have him as a Collins author: a £250,000 advance on royalties for the rights to *Weaveworld* and a second, unnamed novel.

At the time, Barbara Boote felt that it was a 'completely mad amount ... and at that level, it was just out of the question for us. There was no justification. It was madly overpaying, which has never been our policy. And it must have been due to excitement in the States coming back, because we hadn't made that much [on the earlier books] to actually pay that ... We were very pleased for Clive, but we were really annoyed that we'd lost him.' Du Sautoy echoes her feelings: 'It was a shock – so much so quickly. But we always felt he was going to go somewhere. We knew that he was going to get to the top . . . but it seemed unnecessarily high. They clearly bought Clive in a big way, which we did, too – just not quite yet.'

The money offered by Collins was enticing, but, in Clive's mind, Eddie Bell and editor Andy McKillop 'persuaded me out of Sphere's hands and into those of Collins'.

Although Barbara Boote 'saw what was in the work first', her working relationship with Clive was not always a happy one. 'I was someone difficult to edit,' he says. 'I would be defending every damned thing. I was difficult. I was opinionated. I am just as opinionated now. But I was writing a kind of text which needed a different kind of editor . . . I was writing fiction with semi-colons, for fuck's sake, and it was surprisingly rare in horror fiction that people were writing beyond the one full sentence. We were quite civil about it, but we didn't always see eye to eye. The obvious example is that she did not want me to publish "In the Hills, the Cities". There were testy things like that.'

Boote had her own vision for Clive Barker; it concerned him that, after rejecting his proposal to write the book that would become *Weaveworld*, she did not really like the novel he then wrote for Sphere, *The Damnation Game*. 'She found it too European. She wanted a Stephen King book. She said, *Why have you given me a Fassbinder book*? Which I took as the greatest compliment, although it was not intended as such. It *is* a European book; it's a weird book. I like that book and I tried hard to marry up traditional elements with non-traditional elements: There's a zombie, but he doesn't realize it. There's a deal with the Devil, but there's no Devil. So I thought there were some strong things in the book, but my sense was she didn't like it; she didn't think it was commercial enough.

'Weidenfeld and Nicolson [the hardcover publisher of *The Damnation Game*] liked it immensely. They were the literary end of things. That was the distinction – and that was the problem. Sphere was, and remains, sort of cheap and cheerful.

'I had other ambitions; and *The Damnation Game* was perhaps an unhappy marriage of those ambitions. I thought the book had been able to marry the art, if you will, with the commercial end.

'Now I go off in a completely new direction; now I do *Weaveworld* and it's huge and it's a fantasy and it's precisely what she doesn't want me to do. Because she's grooming me to be Jim Herbert's replacement or Dean Koontz's replacement or whatever it was and I'm absolutely not up for that. Then Eddie Bell comes in and he *gets it*. He realizes that he's taking on somebody who's going to keep changing his mind, which has proved to be the case. But I've always changed my mind for reasons. And he's going to take a risk with me – and he realized instantly that I was someone who wanted to take the risks and I realized instantly that he was somebody who was going to take risks with me.

'He was a man of great style. We went to breakfast. Eddie and Andy and June Hall – and every fucking person of importance at Collins was there. They all said, *We will make this a number one bestseller – and, by the way, have some more champagne.*

'I just looked at June Hall. I had never been treated this way and it was, like: *Fuck*!

'Eddie Bell was offering a huge amount of money – and I liked him. I liked him immensely. He's a working-class man. I think of myself as a working-class man. I like that. He's a Glasgow man; I'm a Liverpool man. I felt that he was a direct-dealing guy; he wasn't going to bullshit. He was a man I was going to hug; he was a man who, even though there was an age difference of only three years, I was going to think of as my father in the publishing world. Which he proved to be: he protected me, he watched over me, he promoted the hell out of me, he allowed me to experiment.' And he would make good on his promise: *Weaveworld* would become a number one bestseller in hardback and paperback.

Although major publishers now embraced Clive eagerly, a different sentiment stirred in the minds of other writers who had found success in the realm of horror. Charles Grant, a writer of subdued, atmospheric fiction who had fostered the careers of an untold number of young writers, voiced concern about Barker's sudden popularity. In a controversial interview, Grant opined that 'what Clive needs is a good editor', and wondered aloud whether the pace and breadth of his creative endeavours would kill him – perhaps even literally: 'Ten years from now, people could be saying, *Clive Barker? Whatever happened to old Clive?* Now, he may go on to be a great film-maker. That's wonderful! Good for him. He may go on to be a great writer. Fantastic! But he's got to make his mind up, one way or another, what he wants to do'.[11] (Almost ten years later, with great grace and pride, Grant would present Barker with the Grandmaster Award at the 1995 World Horror Convention.)

Dean R Koontz, who, after labouring in virtual anonymity for a number of years, found bestsellerdom in a series of novels of terror and horror, offered harsh words of his own in an introduction to the anthology *Night Visions 6* (1988).[12] He declined to name Barker, lambasting a 'reasonably well-known writer' who had 'written and spoken often about what he sees as the "virtue" of pushing into new realms of perversity and repulsion'. With its accusations of 'intellectual McCarthyism' and 'moral and intellectual bankruptcy', the introduction had, as is often the case with such essays, far more to say about its author than it did about his intended victim.

Barker was genuinely surprised and dismayed by these diatribes and the apparent lack of camaraderie within the writing community. He had worked for years in a creative collective, with friends and collaborators who re-energized each other's art and who celebrated success. He had imagined that professional writers – particularly those devoted to the often-marginalized fiction of horror and fantasy – were similarly inclined and would welcome his success, if only as an indicator of the continued vitality of the literature they loved. But by the mid-1980s, the writing of horror fiction had taken on a certain self-obsession and, indeed, a desperation. Festering in the long shadow of Stephen King, too many writers seemed driven to bring down their peers (if not betters) and to subdue any effort to push against the safe notions of genre – of horror as entertainment – through metaphysical challenges, trangressive depictions of sexuality or violence, or, indeed, literary ambition.

From virtually the moment that King's breakthrough hardcover, *The Dead Zone* (1979), stormed up the *New York Times* bestseller list, prophecies of impending doom – the 'death of horror' – were voiced. It would take more than a decade before the putative genre of horror disintegrated; and by then, Clive Barker had transcended this fiction, although he would never entirely escape its name. For good reason: he was about to create one of this generation's most memorable horror films.

17

HELLBOUND

THE HELLBOUND HEART (1986)

For the imagination of man's heart is evil.
— The Book of Genesis 8:21

The romantic struggles enacted in *The Secret Life of Cartoons* found a far less farcical parallel in Clive's personal life. After nearly a decade together, Clive and John Gregson found their once-cosy domestic life – 'a very happy time', Clive laments – fractured irretrievably. As John looked on with increasing hostility, Clive lost himself in the competing demands of his newfound public life and the more private life of the imagination. He was working hard, and living hard; and John – a lapsed Catholic whose mother once told him that 'his homosexuality was a cross she had to bear' – felt increasingly uncomfortable with Clive's independence and celebrity, and at times, became abusive. Mary Roscoe watched with a sense of helplessness as the two men ended their relationship: 'Things as we knew them were changing. Everything was changing. Clive and John, who had been a kind of institution together for ten years, suddenly split up.'

The days of quiet pleasures in the flats at Crouch End were over.

'My memories of those places were security and stability,' Roscoe says. 'Now no one knew what was going to happen. The *Books of Blood* had seemed like a nice idea – they were going to make Clive a few thousand pounds – but now someone was making a film out of 'Rawhead Rex', and in this country, where no one makes films; and Clive knew that he had to get on this rollercoaster, because it was going ahead of him, whatever happened.'

Barker was consumed, physically and emotionally, by a whirlwind of creative effort: scripts, rewrites, new stories, a new novel – to the exclusion of having a personal life. 'Publishing was easier then. Making a movie for $900,000 was a very different prospect from making a movie in the present landscape. There was also that element of thinking: *How can I say no to this?*'

'Personal relationships have their place,' he said at the time, 'but everything is put aside for work. To me the idea of a wife and children is a millstone, getting between me and the things I want to do. My most intimate relationship is with my imagination. It always has been. My imagination is the one thing that I really like about myself. It is the longest one night stand I've ever had. And it has never let me down. Yet.'[1]

Indeed, his imagination produced, during that arduous time, a short novel that would inspire, in turn, his best-known creation – the motion picture *Hellraiser* (1987). It is, ironically, his least-known text: *The Hellbound Heart* (1986). This compact novel was first published in a sparsely-distributed small press anthology, *Night Visions 3* (1987),[2] whose mass market paperback edition was retitled *The Hellbound Heart* (1988).[3] By then, the novel had been superseded by its hugely popular film adaptation, and it was not published on its own until 1991.[4]

The Hellbound Heart is a crucial text, not simply because of its progeny, but also because it evidences a writer in transition. Clive Barker had conquered the so-called 'horror' genre; now he was setting out to transcend its confines. The novel, like its predecessor *The Damnation Game*, is Faustian – a story, in its own words, '[a]bout the condition of the damned; about love lost, and then found; about what despair and desire have in common'. Its lineage includes Barker's early film project *The Forbidden* and the short stories 'In the Flesh' and 'The Inhuman Condition'.

Dissolute hedonist Frank Cotton seeks, as always, a new sensation: 'Frank had talked of life lived in delirium; of an appetite for experience that conceded no moral imperative.' He is intent on solving a mysterious puzzle box called Lemarchand's Configuration, whose six black lacquered faces are said to chart 'the interface between the real and the realer still'. He found the box in Düsseldorf, kept by a man named Kircher: 'To solve the puzzle is to travel, he'd said; or something like that. The box, it seemed, was not just the map of the road, but the road itself.'[5]

Frank chances upon the solution, opening the box to a sudden sound of music, then finding new alignments that summon the distant, sombre ringing of a bell – an echo of the striking of midnight at the finale of Marlowe's *The Tragicall Historie of Doctor Faustus*. The final solution consummates the revelation of an unknown world:

> The doorway was even now opening to pleasures no more than a handful of humans had even known existed, much less *tasted* – pleasures which would redefine the parameters of sensation, which would release him from the dull round of desire, seduction and disappointment which had dogged him from late adolescence. He would be transformed by that knowledge, wouldn't he? No man could experience the profundity of such feeling and remain unchanged.

Frank glimpses the secret realm from which the bell tolls: 'A world of birds, was it? Vast blackbirds caught in perpetual tempest. That was all the sense he could make of the province from which – even now – the hierophants were coming: that it was in confusion, and full of brittle, broken things that rose and fell and filled the dark air with their fright.'[6]

From the far side of the Schism emerges a quartet of enigmatic hierophants known as the Cenobites: 'theologians of the Order of the Gash . . . Summoned from their experiments in the higher reaches of pleasure, to bring their ageless heads into a world of rain and failure.'[7] Their anatomies are 'catalogues of disfigurement'; but Barker's descriptions of these strange pilgrims are elusive and oblique, evoking dire possibilities in the minds of his readers:

Why then was he so distressed to place eyes upon them? Was it the scars that covered every inch of their bodies; the flesh cosmetically punctured and sliced and infibulated, then dusted down with ash? Was it the smell of vanilla they brought with them, the sweetness of which did little to disguise the stench beneath? Or was it that as the light grew, and he scanned them more closely, he saw nothing of joy, or even humanity, in their maimed faces: only desperation, and an appetite that made his bowels ache to be voided.

The Cenobites are acolytes of modern primitivism, their flesh riven and reinvented with surgeries that seem sadistic yet sensual. The first, its voice and appearance sexless, addresses Frank. 'When it spoke the hooks that transfixed the flaps on its eyes, and were wed, by an intricate system of chains passed through flesh and bone alike, to similar hooks through the lower lips, were teased by the motion, exposing the glistening meat beneath.' The second Cenobite – soon to find fame, and a place in the pantheon of monsters – is pierced with pins: 'Its voice ... was light and breathy – the voice of an excited girl. Every inch of its head had been tattooed with an intricate grid, and at every intersection of horizontal and vertical axes a jewelled pin driven through to the bone.'

Frank is disappointed by these dour and outré visitors. He had envisaged Lemarchand's Configuration as the gateway to a wonderland of sexual fantasies – oiled and willing women, virgin whores who would grant him unimaginable ecstasies: 'The world would be forgotten in their arms. He would be exalted by his lust, instead of despised for it.' When finally the Cenobites ask the time-honoured question – 'What do you want?' – his reply is a simple one: 'Pleasure.'

But the Cenobites are not Aladdin's djinn, set free from a bottle to grant wishes on command; and the pleasures they propose are far beyond Frank's comprehension: 'Your most treasured depravity is child's play beside the experiences we offer.' Frank, forgetful of the essence of a bargain – that a price must be paid – is assaulted with memories and sensations until '[i]t seemed there was no end to this, but madness. No hope but to be lost to hope'. With this thought, he passes from his torment, viewing the fourth Cenobite, sensual and deadly, and realizing belatedly: 'There was no pleasure in the air; or at least not as humankind understood it.'

A year later, twentysomething Rory Cotton and his wife, Julia, enter his grandmother's house on Lodovico Street in London.[8] Bequeathed to Rory and his older brother, Frank, the house has been vacant since Frank's sudden disappearance.

The marriage is teetering on an uncertain brink. Rory is madly in love with Julia, and dotes on her with puppyish adulation: 'Sometimes – particularly when doubt moved her as it did now – her beauty came close to frightening him.' But Julia is torn between practical Rory and memories of his sensual brother: 'Frank the smiling, seductive chameleon; Rory the solid citizen.'

As she oversees the unpacking, she hears the sound of bells, harkening to the day, four years before, that she had last stepped into church: to marry Rory. '[T]he thought of that day – or rather, of the promise it had failed to fulfil – soured the moment.' A week before the wedding, Julia had succumbed to Frank's 'beautiful desperation': 'Their coupling had had, in every regard but the matter of her acquiescence, all the aggression and the joylessness of rape.' Then Frank disappeared, leaving Julia with heated memories and a mounting abhorrence of the mild-mannered Rory, whose lovemaking is a 'boorish truth': 'She wanted nothing that he could offer her, except perhaps his absence.'[9]

Enter Rory's friend Kirsty, eager to help the couple with their move. Kirsty's 'dreamy, perpetually defeated manner' offends Julia. The women have little in common save Rory: 'Julia the sweet, the beautiful, the winner of glances and kisses, and Kirsty the girl with the pale handshake, whose eyes were only ever as bright as Julia's before or after tears.' Jealous of Julia – and attracted to Rory – Kirsty is, like each of them, haunted by a vague despair.

Julia is drawn obsessively to the damp upper room of the house, 'a dead woman's womb' that carries the feral child whom Julia will midwife. When Rory's hand is cut accidentally, his blood drips onto the floor of the room. Late that night, its wall unfolds to the sound of tinkling music, and a ragged thing reveals itself to Julia:

> It was human, she saw, or had been. But the body had been
> ripped apart and sewed back together again with most of its pieces

either missing or twisted and blackened as if in a furnace. There was an eye, gleaming at her, and the ladder of a spine, the vertebrae stripped of muscle; a few unrecognizable fragments of anatomy. That was it. That such a thing might live beggared reason – what little flesh it owned was hopelessly corrupted. Yet live it did.

It is Frank – or, rather, what is left of Frank after his sojourn on the far side of the Schism, that 'place of bells and troubled darkness'. His brother's wound provided lifeblood, and he has a singular need for more.

Julia eagerly suckles her resurrected lover.[10] While Rory is at work, she frequents bars, picking up lonely men, hurrying them home and into the damp upper room, where she sacrifices them to her intended. The blood delivers Frank from the netherworld: 'He was a travesty. Not just of humanity, of life.' When he emerges, more naked than any babe – bereft entirely of his skin – Julia wraps him in the swaddling of gauze. Together they plot the usurpation of the house.

For Frank, however, Julia is 'a trite, preening woman' whose conquest before her betrothal to Rory was an act of spite, not love: 'In a week or two he would have tired of her.' She was just another body, ripe for the taking – a celebration of the moment, and nothing more: 'Everywhere, in the wreckage around him, he found evidence to support the same bitter thesis: that he had encountered nothing in his life – no person, no state of mind or body – he wanted sufficiently to suffer even passing discomfort for ... If nothing was worth living for it followed, didn't it, that there was nothing worth dying for either.'

Then he had learned of Lemarchand's Configuration, 'this dream of a pleasure dome where those who had exhausted the trivial delights of the human condition might discover a fresh definition of joy.' In embracing its journey, Frank, like Icarus and Faustus before him, was a victim of hubris: '[H]is real error had been the naïve belief that *his* definition of pleasure significantly overlapped with that of the Cenobites.' On their side of the Schism, pleasure was pain, and vice versa: '[P]erhaps they'd meant it. Perhaps not. It was impossible to know with these minds; they were so hopelessly, flawlessly ambiguous.'

Freed from the incomparable suffering of his 'mistaken marriage' with the Cenobites, Frank seduces Julia with lies. She feels an excitement far beyond the sexual, one that is a queasy mixture of the Promethean and the motherly: 'She had *made* this man, or re-made him; used her wit and her cunning to give him substance. The thrill she felt, touching this too vulnerable body, was the thrill of ownership.'

Rory, concerned about Julia's erratic behaviour, asks Kirsty to look in on her. Kirsty arrives as Julia brings home the last of her victims, and believes that Julia has taken a lover – which, of course, she has. Frank gazes down on Kirsty from the upper window and finds her plain-faced innocence, so ripe for corruption, worthy of pursuit.

Kirsty slips inside the house: 'a fierce curiosity had seized her, a desire to know (to *see*) the mysteries the house held, and be done with them.' She finds Julia's prey, his body wasted by Frank's ministrations, and then Frank, bandaged from head to foot. His voice, so like Rory's, mesmerizes her. With a leering invitation – 'Come to Daddy' – he closes in on her, 'all pus and laughter, and – God help her – *desire*'.

Frank dismisses her shock and disbelief: agonies may not be dreamed away; but, in Sadean splendour, they are experiences to be endured and, perhaps, even enjoyed. 'She knew he was telling the truth; the kind of unsavoury truth that only monsters were at liberty to tell. He had no need to flatter or cajole; he had no philosophy to debate, or sermon to deliver. His awful nakedness was a kind of sophistication. Past the lies of faith, and into purer realms.'

Kirsty escapes from his violent clutches, taking the puzzle box with her, but faints on the street outside. She awakens in a hospital – where, to pass the time, she works at the lacquered curiosity until she breaks its secret code, summoning first music, then the tolling bell – and, at last, one of the Cenobites.

Although she has bested the Configuration by accident, Kirsty is damned, and must be taken to the other side. 'No tears, please,' the Cenobite tells her. 'It's a waste of good suffering.' She proposes an exchange: Frank Cotton for her life. The hierophant grants a vague approval: 'Deliver him alive to us then . . . make him confess himself. And maybe we won't tear your soul apart.'[11]

Kirsty returns to the house on Lodovico Street without fear, possessed by a far more ambiguous feeling:

She had opened a door – the same door Rory's brother had opened – and now she was walking with demons. And at the end of her travels, she would have her revenge. She would find the thing that had torn her and tormented her, and make him feel the powerlessness which she had suffered. She would watch him squirm. More: she would enjoy it. Pain had made a sadist of her.

She finds Julia and, of all people, Rory in a setting of demented domesticity. Rory has blood on his face, a drink in his hand, and a story to tell: Frank is dead. But then his lips betray him: '*Come to Daddy*.' It is Frank, wearing the flesh of his brother: 'Rory's corpse was upstairs, left to lie in Frank's shunned bandaging. The usurped skin was now wed to his brother's body, the marriage sealed with the letting of blood.' Kirsty tears the mask of borrowed flesh from his face. In the struggle, Frank's knife, poised to slit Kirsty's throat, plunges into Julia's side; he feeds on her corpse like a starved animal.

At last the unlikely Beauty and the Beast find themselves in the upper room. But as Frank speaks Rory's name, she is defiant: 'A skin was nothing. Pigs had skins; snakes had skins. They were knitted of dead cells, shed and grown and shed again. But a name? That was a spell, which summoned memories. She would not let Frank usurp it.' She realizes then that the Cenobites are waiting for Frank to name himself; and as he says the fateful words – 'That's right. I'm *Frank*' – the hierophants arrive in vengeful glory: 'They had their hooks in him, the flesh of his arms and legs, and curled through the meat of his face. Attached to the hooks, chains, which they held taut. There was a soft sound, as his resistance drew the barbs through his muscle. His mouth was dragged wide, his neck and chest ploughed open.'

Kirsty has earned her freedom from the Cenobites – and, perhaps, from her 'perpetually defeated manner' – but as Frank begins to scream, she dares one look back, witnessing his gruesome fate:

> He was *in extremis*; hooked through in a dozen or more places, fresh wounds gouged in him even as she watched. Spreadeagled beneath the solitary bulb, body hauled to the limits of its endurance and beyond, he gave vent to shrieks that would have won pity from her, had she not learned better.

Suddenly, his cries stopped. There was a pause. And then, in one last act of defiance, he cranked up his heavy head and stared at her, meeting her gaze with eyes from which all bafflement and all malice had fled. They glittered as they rested on her; pearls in offal.

In response, the chains were drawn an inch tighter, but the Cenobites gained no further cry from him. Instead he put his tongue out at Kirsty and flicked it back and forth across his teeth in a gesture of unrepentant lewdness.

Then he came unsewn.

Outside the silent house, a creature with a burning head, known only as the Engineer, jostles Kirsty – and passes the puzzle box, resealed, back into her hands. Thus Kirsty, her name so very Christlike, becomes the heir of Kircher – the new Keeper of the Key. On its lacquered surface are glimpses of ghosts – the faces of Julia and Frank – but Rory is nowhere to be seen:

> There were other puzzles, perhaps, that if solved gave access to the place where he lodged. A crossword maybe, whose solution would lift the latch of the paradise garden; or a jigsaw in the completion of which lay access to Wonderland.
>
> She would wait and watch, as she had always watched and waited, hoping that such a puzzle would one day come to her. But if it failed to show itself she would not grieve too deeply, for fear that the mending of broken hearts be a puzzle neither wit nor time had the skill to solve.

Despite its brevity, *The Hellbound Heart* is a complex novel that melds de Sade with grotesque and Gothic imagery in an insistently domestic drama. 'In the final confrontation of any great tale,' Barker would write in *Weaveworld*, 'dialogue was redundant. With nothing left to say, only action remained: a murder or a marriage.'

Three failed marriages are evoked: the conventional marriage of Julia and Rory; the Faustian pact between Frank and the Schism ('the mistaken marriage which the prisoner had made'); and the wedding of Rory's skin to Frank's body ('the marriage sealed with the letting of blood').

Julia wishes to be rid of Rory, whom she has married out of a misplaced sense of duty. '[S]he was lost. Married to a man she felt no love for, and unable to see a way out.' But Frank, the man whom she desires, has married pleasure and its pursuit in every form – until, at last, he finds its extreme in the Schism. He emerges with the desperate yearning for that which he despises: the ordinary life of Rory. Indeed, he wants to become Rory, to have all that Rory owns – the house, the body of Julia, the gentle love of Kirsty and, in the final act, Rory's very skin. At its most elemental level, his comeuppance is the revelation that possession is not enough.

Even love, it seems, is not enough – at least the love enacted by Frank and Julia, which is insistently sexual and certainly unsatisfied. The evil of appetite is a repeated theme in Barker's work, and in *The Hellbound Heart* he offers a searing condemnation of lust in the guise of love – and the pursuit of pleasure in fulfilment of a spiritual void. Frank's sin is not his self-indulgence, but his hollow – and thus hellbound – heart: 'he had encountered nothing in his life – no person, no state of mind or body – he wanted sufficiently to suffer even passing discomfort for.' Certainly this is a critique of those who equated gay liberation with sexual liberation – and, more generally, a generation's pursuit of pleasure without regard for its consequences. The tragedy of sexual appetite was coming home to Clive Barker: friends were dying, victims of the modern plague of HIV.

The play may once have been the thing, but now Clive Barker sought the experience of making motion pictures on his own terms. Distressed by the initial film adaptations of his work, *Underworld* and *Rawhead Rex*, he considered ways to take control of his on-screen destiny – and, if possible, to bring his visions to life on celluloid.

Clive insists that *The Hellbound Heart* was not conceived as a template for a film (indeed, it is an exorcism of his failed relationship with John Gregson); but as he wrote the short novel, he realized that it was ideal for low-budget film-making. Its cast of characters was small, and its claustrophobic atmospheres required a handful of settings, all of them mundane. Its visionary elements, although demanding critical maquillage, could be accomplished without major expense. 'I hadn't shot an inch of celluloid, and no one was going to throw a large-scale budget at me. I didn't *want* one. I mean, if I'm going to fuck up, I want to fuck up on a low budget!'

Wary of the complications of financing, and lacking contacts in the film industry, he considered adapting the novel to film in the way George Pavlou originally planned to create *Underworld*, shooting it on his own with a small cadre of friends, using 16mm or even Super 8 film, if necessary. He asked Pavlou if he would act as producer, and contacted his old friend Doug Bradley, who, after the dissolution of the Dog Company, had paired with Oliver Parker as the comedy team 'Romeo and Duplicate' – solely to qualify for Equity cards. With union status, Bradley and Parker were pursuing careers as actors in provincial repertory and London fringe theatre.

Then Clive was introduced to Christopher Figg, a young assistant director with an impressive pedigree, including *The Dresser* (1983) and *A Passage to India* (1984). Figg had ambitions as a producer, and he was interested in developing a horror film. Clive was insistent on directing, and Figg knew that, unless their project could be mounted on a small scale, the chances of finding financial backers for a first-time director were slight; indeed, they considered shooting the project as a showreel, in hopes of proving Barker's directorial talent to prospective financiers. Attentive to Figg's advice, Barker rewrote *The Hellbound Heart* as a screenplay, and they set off on a winding path that led, in time, to Hollywood. 'I talked about it and talked about it,' Barker says, 'and eventually, several people said yes. So it was a relatively bloodless experience, so to speak.' After a deal involving Virgin Films fell through, New World Pictures (founded by exploitation legend Roger Corman) committed to a budget of $4.2 million.

Principal photography began in early 1987 as Clive Barker – suddenly a motion picture director – took control of a sizable budget and a crew of specialists without himself having any professional experience in film-making or its techniques. 'When I started out, I didn't know the difference between a ten-millimetre lens and a thirty-five millimetre lens. If you'd shown me a plate of spaghetti and said that it was a lens, I might have believed you.'

Rushes were flown each day by Concorde from the set in London to New World's screening rooms in Hollywood, and Barker found himself accountable for his work with an unaccustomed, and some-what uncomfortable, immediacy:

'A book speaks for itself. But a movie is perpetually in progress. Everything you do in a given day – your screw-ups, your occasional moments of triumph, are visible the next day. And when your producer asks you what happened or why you did such and such, you've got to have answers. You're spending a lot of money, even when it's a modestly-budgeted picture. These people aren't philanthropists – they've given me money for my idea, and that is an act of faith, and I owe them a lot for it. I owe them a successful picture, but I also owe them explanations. And that took time to learn, too.

'I'm glad that you only have to do one first picture.'

18

RAISING HELL

HELLRAISER (1987)
HELLBOUND: HELLRAISER II (1988)
HELLRAISER III: HELL ON EARTH (1992)

Pain is such a little thing...
— HG WELLS, *The Island of Dr Moreau*

'What's your pleasure...?'

The cinema, in a dreary sixties building near Piccadilly Circus, seemed an unlikely place for the raising of Hell. Inside, the audience for the press screening, ten or so disconsolate survivors of another rainy afternoon in London, looked like a gathering of lost souls. One of them, a prominent newspaper critic, slumped into her seat and promptly fell asleep, perhaps even before the words flashed onto the screen: *Clive Barker's Hellraiser*.

After writing stage plays, short stories, novels and screenplays, the next logical step for this prodigious talent was to direct his own motion picture. With the swiftness that marked his volcanic entry into the popular culture, Clive Barker brought *Hellraiser* to the screen less than a year from its conception – in time for the American release of his first novel, *The Damnation Game*, and the publication, in Great Britain and the United States, of his breakthrough novel, *Weaveworld* (1987).

The press preview on that wet afternoon was an inauspicious introduction to an instant classic of contemporary horror film. Unlike most other entries in the scream cinema of the eighties and nineties, *Hellraiser* (1987) proved successful in both commercial and critical terms – even that sleeping scribe managed to write a positive review – and established Clive Barker as a name to be reckoned with in the entertainment industry. The opening credits gave notice of his intent; although it was his first film as a director, he received a proprietary credit: this was no mere *Hellraiser*, but *Clive Barker's Hellraiser*.

True to that title, the film was insular, intimate and certainly more akin to a personal canvas than a mass-marketed film.[1] Chris Figg worked hard to assemble a team that, as Barker puts it, would be 'sympathetic to my ignorance and not try to exploit it'. A crucial collaborator was the director of photography, Robin Vidgeon, whose credits included working as a cameraman for Steven Spielberg on *Raiders of the Lost Ark* (1981) and *Indiana Jones and the Temple of Doom* (1984). With inspiration from Italian horror films, and particularly those of Dario Argento, Vidgeon's stylish photography was attuned to Barker's demanding aesthetic: 'What we tried to do was make the picture more beautiful as the images became more unpleasant.'

'The major anxiety,' Clive recalls, 'was that there would be some extraordinary effects shot set up – all those people waiting – and that Barker couldn't make up his mind about how he wanted to photograph it.' Each night, for his own protection, he drew storyboards of every shot. 'As the weeks went on, I began to understand how the shots that I had in my head could be created on the screen. I was also sharing the vocabulary, so that, halfway through the shoot, instead of drawing the thing on a piece of paper, I could say, *Robin, I suggest that we get an eighty-five on this and we do it from here, pull out a tracking board there* and so on and so forth.'

His education concerned not only technical details, but also the politics of the film industry. Clive's choice of soundtrack musicians, the industrial/electronic band Coil, was considered unacceptable by New World, but he was delighted by the excellent (although more conventional) score by Christopher Young.[2] He was also required to accept the standard Hollywood contractual requirement to deliver a film that would earn an R rating from the Motion Picture Association of America. The MPAA and the British Board of Film Classification, in turn, insisted on cuts in *Hellraiser* before allowing it to qualify for an R rating in the US and an 18 rating in the UK. 'We lost twenty seconds of screen time,' Clive notes. 'We lost no scenes, but seconds within scenes where they said, *This is simply too intense.*' (Former Dog Company member Julie Blake was then working for the BBFC as a Senior Examiner, responsible for reviewing and categorizing motion pictures; she 'declared an interest', excusing herself from the review of *Hellraiser*.)

For Clive, the most exciting aspect of *Hellraiser* was the opportunity to use special effects to bring the fantastic creatures of his imagination to life. 'Having worked in the theatre, it wasn't too strange to see my characters given life on film. What was different was seeing the various beasts and special effects – theatre hasn't often lent itself to that kind of material – and that was a revelation.'

To create these visions, Barker and Figg enlisted the services of make-up effects artist Bob Keen, whose work had first appeared in *Return of the Jedi* (1983), *The Dark Crystal* (1983) and *The Neverending Story* (1984). Keen had formed Image Animation in 1987 to provide expert special effects for projects like *Hellraiser*: 'Bob Keen and the special effects crew did a really tremendous job,' Barker notes. 'They never said to me, *No, you can't do that. No, we will not attempt that. No, that's too gross. No, that's too weird.* And I'm pleased that they were courageous enough to go to the limits on the picture. There's some really grisly stuff, but there's also stuff that's very bizarre. Now there's a healthy tradition of grisly horror effects, but they really had to do some clever thinking to achieve some of the stuff I was asking for – because it was weird.'

A favourite among Barker's creatures was the most elaborate construction: the Engineer. Although described as a fire-headed man in *The Hellbound Heart*, Clive wanted something more extravagant on film: 'I spent many evenings with the special effects team, exchanging drawings. We wanted to create something that didn't resemble anyone else's beast. And it was an absolute delight, a wonder, to be something of a midwife – and to see this thing appear before one's eyes and, you know, be beastly.'

Clive concedes that he is 'really childlike' when it comes to the subject of monsters: 'I'll go a long way to see a good monster. I love Jabba the Hutt. When I learned that Bob Keen had helped produce Jabba, I knew this was a marriage made in heaven.' It was a childhood dream come true, inspired by his love of Ray Harryhausen's extraordinary special effects films – the likes of *The 7th Voyage of Sinbad* (1958) and *Jason and the Argonauts* (1963).

Despite its multi-million dollar financing, *Hellraiser* was, by industry standards, truly a low-budget production. It was shot in Cricklewood in North London, using an actual location for the house and two uninsulated soundstages built in the 1930s for silent films and rarely used since. A pub stood behind the stages, and every time a truck arrived to unload kegs of beer, shooting had to halt because of the noise. But it didn't matter; Clive Barker was recreating a world on film – a world of his imagination – and nothing would get in his way: 'The recreation of worlds which can only be the product of the mind that made them – that are so singular that they are simply and absolutely themselves – that is something I want to continue to do, on both the screen and the page ... It's just the best thing that one can do with one's time.'[3]

His debut as director was assured, indeed visionary, troubled only when his ambition exceeded his budget – and when New World insisted that, despite the film's English setting, most of the minor players' voices should be post-dubbed in 'American'. Evocatively filmed by Vidgeon, *Hellraiser* succeeds because of Barker's persistent imagination, Bob Keen's special effects and a capable cast led by Andrew Robinson and Clare Higgins.

In creating *Hellraiser*, Barker worked from the belief that groundbreaking horror films – particularly those from major studios – involve advances in tone. (An example is *The Exorcist* (1973), when the possessed Regan's urination on the carpet is more heard than seen.) He often calls *Hellraiser* an Anglo-American film that is French in tone; certainly it is an inversion of Cocteau's *La Belle et la Bête*

('The Beauty and the Beast') (1946), and a more immediate precedent is Andrzej Zulawski's delirious *Possession* (1981). Certainly the visual style of *Hellraiser* melds Cocteau and Zulawski with the furious violence of the horror films of Dario Argento and Lucio Fulci, with eye-widening set-pieces whose visual elegance, if not beauty, co-exist with garish blood-letting. But Barker's advance in tone is as straightforward as it is subversive: *Hellraiser* brought mundane domesticity, the stuff of television soap opera, into collision with the photographic artistry of Joel-Peter Witkin and the tattoo-and-piercing subculture of modern primitivism; and thus swept sado-masochist imagery into the mainstream without the fetishistic commonalities of leather-clad dominatrices and drones of master and servant. Its foreboding tone and imagery disturb and confound the viewer, largely through its Gothic sensibilities, in which puzzles and doorways and walls (and even worlds) open onto other realms, dire and delicious places beyond good and evil, pleasure and pain.[4]

Like its source text, *Hellraiser* is a perverse love story that tests the limits of desire. Sean Chapman plays dissolute pleasure-seeker Frank Cotton, who, when asked his life's unanswerable question – 'What's your pleasure, Mr Cotton?' – receives a curious puzzle box, now known as the Lament Configuration: 'Take it . . . it's yours. It always was.'

When Frank solves the riddle of the box, we witness a bloodbath: shiny steel hooks emerge and tear through his flesh, decorating the room with chains and body parts. Four strange creatures, wounded caricatures of humanity swathed in leather, emerge from the shadows and assemble the broken pieces of Frank's face. They are the Cenobites: 'Explorers in the further reaches of experience.' These Sadean pilgrims from Hell are hieratic wonders of living and dead flesh, outfitted like futurist punk archbishops – and their manner and intent, although threatening, is resolutely ambiguous.

The Lead Cenobite is a pinheaded wonder played with sacerdotal elegance by Doug Bradley. When Barker offered his former schoolmate and Dog Company companion the part, Bradley was not entirely pleased: 'I was very, very unsure about doing this. Because I'm thinking: *This is a chance to do a movie – that's great. But I'm going to be buried in latex, so nobody will even know it's me, so what use is this to me*? I would have been even more reluctant if it hadn't been for the fact that it was a chance to work with Clive again. And I had been a fan of horror films since I was a teenager. And I'd be getting to play the monster! So that excited me enough to make me want to say yes. But even then, if I had had the choice of playing Pinhead or playing one of the male leads, I would have made a sensible actor's decision to play one of the male leads – and that would have been a very wrong decision. But it wasn't a decision I had.'

Once inside the complex make-up, which took hours to apply, Bradley 'understood the character fully, in ways difficult to articulate'. The Lead Cenobite is an earnest and eloquent being whose mingling of grace and the grotesque had not been seen since Boris Karloff played Frankenstein's monster. Although Barker would compare the Lead Cenobite with the murderously genteel Dracula interpreted by Christopher Lee, it is Bradley's deliberate pacing and dignity, coupled with his extraordinary make-up, that sets Pinhead apart from any other monster of post-war cinema.

The true power of this creature, however, is his way with words; the Lead Cenobite offers finely wrought phrases and dark humour. In recent years, movie monsters have been silent juggernauts of destruction like the eponymous creatures of *Alien* (1979) and *Predator* (1987), or cyphers like Michael Myers of the *Halloween* films or Jason Voorhees of the *Friday the 13th* series. In the worst case, they offered psychopathic rants or sophomoric puns, like Freddy Krueger of *Nightmare on Elm Street* fame. None spoke to the condition of *being* a monster. Barker imagined Frank and his Cenobite nemesis as capable of speaking to their dilemma in elegant terms: 'Evil is never abstract. It is always concrete, always particular and always vested in individuals. To deny the creatures as individuals the right to speak, to actually state their case, is perverse – because I *want* to hear the Devil speak. I think that's a British attitude. I like the idea that a point of view can be made by the dark side.'[5]

The Lead Cenobite and his fellow Hierophants of Hell are extraordinary creatures. To some, their echoes of modern primitivism, a subculture of physical transformation through tattooing, piercing, and other forms of body-play, might suggest self-abuse or mortification; but to others, they are creatures of elemental individuation, if not self-enhancement. In an esoteric sense, Barker invites us to join in their pursuit: the search for a new flesh. Although seemingly monstrous, the Cenobites are impartial jurists who preside over the fate of the true monsters: Julia and Frank.

The plot is that of *The Hellbound Heart*: Larry Cotton (Andrew Robinson) and his second wife, Julia (Clare Higgins), arrive at the house where brother Frank's ritual went awry. The casting of Andrew Robinson is particularly inspired. Known by film-goers for his portrayal of the psychopathic Scorpio killer in Don Siegel's *Dirty Harry* (1971), his turn here as a bastion of domesticity is unnerving. Accompanying the couple is Kirsty, reinvented as Larry's daughter from a prior marriage; Ashley Laurence is insistent in the role, not a drab loser but a lovely heroine, intent on preserving her father's innocence – and her own.

In an exquisite set-piece, Barker juxtaposes flashbacks of Julia's dalliance with Frank with shots of Larry hefting that most domestic of symbols, a bed, into the house (one of the movers is played by Dog Company veteran Oliver Parker); at the moment at which Julia and Frank consummate their passion, a nail plunges into Larry's hand, spilling his blood onto the floor, the seed of new life for Frank.

Frank's return from the Outer Darkness is a triumph for Bob Keen and his Image Animation team. 'The blood brought me this far,' Frank tells Julia: 'I need more.' Julia seduces strangers, bringing them to his hiding place in the upper room, where she dispatches them with a hammer. With each murder, it is Julia who becomes the monster, her features icy, a porcelain goddess of death. At last Frank needs only new skin, and the choice is obvious: brother Larry.

Frank is a creature of appetite whose rape/seduction of Julia asserts a domineering male sexuality that quiet, sensitive Larry lacks. Frank's sexual violence spawns, in turn, Julia's appetite for seduction and murder. Only through the destruction of other men – all of whom seem weak – can she gain equality with Frank, and win him back. 'We belong to each other now,' Frank tells her, 'for better or worse . . . like love. Only real.' And in the finale, Frank literally supplants Larry in the domestic hierarchy, wearing his skin and offering to Kirsty, with sincere perversion, the words 'Come to Daddy'.

In *Carrie*, a novel (1974) and film (1976) that deeply affected Barker, the bloodstained virgin forced her peers, especially the testosterone-driven boys, to accept the irrational feminine. In *Hellraiser*, Julia is the bloodstained bride, birthing the return of male oppression. The Lament Configuration, as the key to the Outer Darkness, opens doors to the pleasures of Heaven or Hell: 'I thought I'd gone to the limits,' Frank explains. 'I hadn't. The Cenobites gave me an experience beyond limits. Pain and pleasure, indivisible.' Thus *Faust* is transformed into a Sadean fairy tale, with Julia the wicked stepmother. 'Some things have to be endured. Take it from me. And that's what makes the pleasures so sweet.'

Kirsty steals the puzzle box; awakening in a hospital, she solves its furtive riddle, summoning a magnificent creature – the Engineer – and finally the Cenobites: 'Explorers in the further reaches of experience. Demons to some, angels to others.' Her crying is meaningless – 'No tears, please. It's a waste of good suffering' – but she enters her own pact with the darkness, offering Frank in her place.

When Kirsty returns to the house, she confronts Frank and Julia, the monsters who have replaced her parents, and finally tears the skin of her father's face to reveal the horror beneath, prompting Andrew Robinson's brilliant ad lib: 'Well, so much for the cat-and-mouse shit.' Frank accidentally stabs Julia, and finishes the deed with a perfunctory apology: 'Nothing personal, baby.' Then he pursues the younger flesh of Kirsty, but when he traps her in the upper room, again his lips betray him: 'Frank's here . . . Your dear old Uncle Frank.'

His true identity revealed, the gates of Hell are opened and the Cenobites emerge with their instruments of torture, setting upon Frank with experiments unimagined even by the Inquisition – yet he licks his lips in twisted pleasure. 'Jesus wept,' he tells us, and laughs as his body is torn apart.

The Cenobites, joined by the extravagant atrocity known as the Engineer, take up the pursuit of Kirsty. 'We have such sights to show you,' the Cenobites promise; but her response is unequivocal: 'Go to Hell.' Rearranging the puzzle box, she sends them back into the darkness where, like all nightmares, they belong.

Finally Kirsty staggers into the night as the house, like its many predecessors – from Frankenstein's castle to the House of Usher – burns and collapses. She tosses the box into the flames, but a shambling man plucks it away, transforming into a skeletal dragon that takes flight into the night sky.

Until this final scene of destruction and liberation, the camera's brief forays into the outside world are forced and narrowing perspectives, urging the psychology of the labyrinth. The settings echo the claustrophobic horror films of Argento and Mario Bava. By running against the grain of then-popular 'stalk and slash' psychokiller films, *Hellraiser* resurrected the Gothic and embraced the supernatural without apology. Its unsettling ideas – godlike monsters, sado-masochism, lust for a dead-skinned man – were presented in a cleverly accessible and acceptable style.

Although Clive Barker was known for the explicitness of his imagery, a crucial aesthetic of *Hellraiser* is its unwillingness to explain. Once the audience accepts, as it must, the magic of the Lament Configuration, then all that follows has the logical insistence of a nightmare: a world in which walls give way to the halls of Hell; a priesthood of pain that emerges from the shadows to offer wisdom; and physical monstrosities that ultimately prove less horrifying than the machinations of the human mind. And the mundane domesticity of the central drama serves as a powerful anchor for what, in other hands, would seem wild leaps into the unknown.

Directing for the screen was unlike anything Clive had experienced on the stage, although, as noted, there was some improvisation in *Hellraiser*. He gloried in the role of director: 'Writing is quite a solitary experience. But it gives you absolute and complete power. Whatever your pen desires to create is created. Nobody questions it, nobody challenges it, nobody tries to better it. Nobody puts pressure on you to weaken or dilute it. However, you do this in splendid isolation. In movies, you are dealing with other people's talents. You're trying to make a marriage of minds where the actor and the special effects person understand what you're talking about, and you, in turn, understand what they're talking about. And if they have objections, you should be ready to listen, because actors act for a living – Andy Robinson . . . has been an actor for a long while. He knows his craft. And there were many times when Andy's insight – and the insight of the other actors, and of Bob Keen and the special effects people – improved what I had written.

'I don't know whether Hitchcock actually said that actors are cattle; but if he did say that, he was wrong. Good actors can give you insights that, if you sat refining your screenplay for a thousand years, you would never have discovered.

'Now, having come from the absolute authority of the page, it is, frankly, a slap across the face to remember that there are other people out there who have valid opinions and observations. There were many occasions in the picture where the actors' ideas were much more responsive to the characters they were playing than my ideas. The person I'm *not* going to be happy to work with is the person who simply listens to everything you say and then does it.'

Hellraiser recouped its production costs within its first three days of release, and today, more than a decade after its premiere, remains a staple of video sales and rentals; indeed, it was one of the first DVDs released in England. 'It was the most gentle and creative introduction to film-making imaginable,' Barker says. 'There were no raised voices, no histrionics. There was just a sense that we all knew what kind of picture we wanted to make, how it should look, and we were all there trying to create the same thing.

'It was a wonderful ten weeks. So much so that I felt distinct withdrawal symptoms when it was all done. And . . . a very considerable hunger for the next one.'

The opportunity would come again – and soon. With *Hellraiser*, Clive Barker's imagination had lit the fuse of a multimedia explosion. His creations were about to take on a life of their own in comic books, trading cards, action figures, models, Hallowe'en masks, T-shirts, jig-saw puzzles, phone cards, jewellery, tattoos – and, perhaps inevitably, a series of motion pictures.

In the final scene of *Hellraiser*, the Lament Configuration survives, to be offered at a distant marketplace with the question: 'What's your pleasure, sir?'

Our pleasure was an immediate sequel. *Hellraiser* was far more than a critical and commercial success; it became a phenomenon, and created an icon of popular culture in the enigmatic character of Pinhead. Although Barker has planned several serial projects, he had no such ambitions for *Hellraiser*. 'Toward the end of filming, there inevitably began the rumours that you always hear, that the producers loved what they were seeing – and so there were rumours about sequels. In retrospect, obviously if *Hellraiser* worked, there was going to be a sequel – as light follows day, and especially in the horror climate of the time. I mean, you had the *Halloween* franchise, the *Friday the 13th* franchise, the *Nightmare on Elm Street* franchise. If New World got their hands on a successful horror film, with the potential for a series, which *Hellraiser* obviously had, it was going to happen.'

Barker wanted Julia to continue on as the series villain; but filmgoers, fans and the publicity machine had embraced the enigmatic and more traditionally monstrous Pinhead. The popularity of the Black Pope of Hell came as something of a surprise to Barker and Doug Bradley. Although the Lead Cenobite (as he was called throughout production and, indeed, in the film's credits) served as the central image for promotional posters, he spent only five of the film's ninety-four minutes on screen. But film-goers, anxious for a new kind of monster, were thrilled by Pinhead, and New World Pictures was eager to fulfil their expectations in the way it knew best: a sequel.

Barker had moved on to other projects, including a new novel and pre-production on another motion picture, *Nightbreed*. Although he participated as executive producer and co-writer of the screen story, the reins of *Hellbound: Hellraiser II* (1988) were passed to director Tony Randel, who worked from a script by Barker's long-time friend and former Dog Company member, Pete Atkins.

Since returning to Liverpool in 1980, Pete had stayed in touch with Clive – his 'long distance best friend' – and the two occasionally traded short story manuscripts. In 1987, Atkins sent Clive a novella, 'The Vampires of Summer', which later served as the template for Atkins's first novel, *Morningstar* (1992). Barker, then in post-production of *Hellraiser*, called and asked Atkins if he had ever written a screenplay. 'No,' Pete told him. Clive said: 'If a producer ever asked you the same question, would you lie?' Pete replied: 'Yeah, of course, are you insane?' Clive gave Chris Figg a copy of 'The Vampires of Summer' and recommended Pete as the screenwriter for *Hellbound*. Figg called and, as Atkins freely admits: 'I lied.'

The success of *Hellraiser* was obvious to those who also participated in the sequel. 'We had moved up in the world,' Doug Bradley notes with characteristic humour: 'I mean, I had a dressing room.' Principal photography had shifted from the creaky boards of Cricklewood to the legendary stages of Pinewood Studios, home to the Gotham City of Tim Burton's *Batman* (1989).

Although visually rewarding and textually intriguing, *Hellbound: Hellraiser II* is uneven, embracing the rich imagery of its predecessor but disintegrating into confusion in its final act. Despite the best intentions, something was lost; indeed, Barker himself was not satisfied with the outcome.

The story begins only hours after the conclusion of *Hellraiser*, as Kirsty awakens in the Channard Institute, a psychiatric hospital.[6] In the night she is visited by a skinless apparition who paints the wall with its blood: 'I AM IN HELL. HELP ME.'

Dr Channard (Kenneth Cranham) is a searcher whose maxim is quintessential Clive Barker: 'We have to see. We have to know.' But like so many of Barker's psychiatrists, Channard is the sickness, not the cure. 'The mind is a labyrinth,' he tells his associates before blithely drilling a hole in a patient's skull. 'A puzzle. And while the paths of the brain are plainly visible, its ways deceptively apparent, its destinations are unknown, its secrets still secrets. And, if we are honest, it is the lure of the labyrinth that draws us to our chosen fields, to unlock those secrets.'

The secrets he seeks are those of the Lament Configuration, and the key is offered by Kirsty and another patient, blonde and innocent Tiffany (Imogen Boorman).[7] At Channard's home, he sacrifices one of his patients, summoning Julia back from the Outer Darkness. He offers her more blood – and the restoration of her flesh – in exchange for her knowledge of the distant, ambiguous realm of the Cenobites: 'The suffering . . . the sweet suffering.'

So far, so good: Randel and Atkins tap the menace and momentum of *Hellraiser* and move their story forward with stylish assurance. Robin Vidgeon's photography sustains the Gothic ambience of the original.[8] The set design is labyrinthine, offering in the Channard Institute a neo-Gothic cathedral whose sub-basement is a true bedlam. Clare Higgins's Julia is feral, while Ashley Laurence's Kirsty has a desperate resourcefulness; *Hellbound* proffers all the makings of a taut masterpiece, then literally goes to Hell.

Kirsty and a helpful intern, Kyle (William Hope), enter Channard's estate – conveniently unlocked and unguarded – and find three puzzle boxes; but Kyle announces: 'We're not going to do anything until I check the house.' His idiot waltz is met by Julia. 'Come to mother,' she says, and drains the life from him. 'I'm no longer just the wicked stepmother,' she tells Kirsty. 'I'm the Evil Queen.'[9]

Through Tiffany's puzzle-solving skills, Channard opens the box. 'It's what I've always wanted. I have to see. I have to know.' The Cenobites enter, but do not take Tiffany. 'It is not hands that call us,' Pinhead pronounces. 'It is desire.' The action shifts to an epic yet ineffectual Hell – first a dark carnival, and then a complex labyrinth presided over by a rotating monolith. 'Oh my God,' Channard says; but Julia corrects him: 'No, this is *mine*. The god that sent me back, the god I serve in this world and yours. The god of flesh, hunger and desire. *My* god . . . Leviathan . . . Lord of the labyrinth!'

Too late Channard realizes the double cross. 'Why do you think I was allowed to go back?' Julia says. 'For you? No, it wanted souls. And I brought you!' He is ravaged, then reborn as a Cenobite. 'And to think I hesitated,' he announces with hungry glee, seconds before an overtly phallic drill penetrates his skull, rendering him into an unfortunate out-take from Elm Street, wisecracking relentlessly ('The doctor is in!') as he kills.

Lost in its own labyrinth of too many ideas and too little time and money, the storyline succumbs to special effects: Julia tears Frank's heart out, killing him – but he is already dead (and we are, after all, in Hell); then Julia is hoovered down a drainlike passage and stripped of her skin. At last the Cenobites, little more than bit players in this instalment, confront our heroines; Kirsty bargains for escape by disclosing their essential humanity. With this epiphany, Channard enters and dispatches Pinhead and company with further *bon mots* and discouraging ease.

Although capable of defeating the Cenobites, Channard cannot overcome Kirsty or Tiffany, and succumbs to their innocence. His pursuit of Tiffany is thwarted when Julia reappears and kisses him. The distraction is enough: Tiffany reworks the puzzle, and the labyrinth is undone. Channard's head is ripped from his body, and Kirsty, who was wearing Julia's skin, saves Tiffany.

In the boxed-up remains of Channard's home, the bloody mattress – and the promise of further sequels – remains. A twirling pillar of souls in torment rises from the mattress, patterned with images of the labyrinth: Pinhead, Channard and finally the face of Jesus Christ, who asks: 'What is your pleasure, sir?'[10]

Hellraiser III: Hell on Earth (1992) responded by accepting its inevitability as the third entry in a series; certainly it is the first of the films constructed in conventional (and, thus, commercial) terms. By the conservative estimate of its screenwriter, Pete Atkins, its story was the sixth to bear the name *Hell on Earth*; in 1989, Chris Figg had sold New World on a idea conceived by Barker and Atkins, and Atkins began drafting a screenplay. In the midst of pre-production, however, New World collapsed; in time, the rights to the *Hellraiser* franchise were acquired by Trans Atlantic Entertainment, which approached Tony Randel to direct the new film. Randel and Atkins devised a new story, but after further corporate machinations, Trans Atlantic decided that Anthony Hickox – whose previous films included *Waxwork* (1988) – would take the helm.

Pinhead was now the central element of the series; by the 1990s, he was not only an inductee into the *Fangoria* Hall of Fame, but the patron saint of piercing. He was also a far cry from the standard fare of creature features – an intellectual being, enigmatic, aloof and, most important, ambiguous. With *Hellraiser III: Hell on Earth*, all that would change. The atmosphere, plot and, most importantly, characterizations of the prior films were supplanted in a manoeuvre as telling as the replacement of Christopher Young's orchestrations with heavy metal. To resurrect Pinhead, the creators posit that his 'death' in the closing act of *Hellbound* severed his hellacious essence from his human core, World War One-era British army officer Elliott Spencer (also played by Bradley). Freed of his humanity, Pinhead is reborn as an evangelic evildoer as ferocious – and familiar – as other contemporary screen monsters. It is Pinhead's 'Coming to America', arguably as distant from Clive Barker as *Abbott & Costello Meet Frankenstein* was from James Whale.

Hell on Earth also shrinks from the Gothic complexity of the original and the cosmic excess of Tony Randel's sequel to a commonplace scenario: *Invaders from Mars* (or, in this case, Hell). The forbidden desires that lurked beneath the uncomfortable imagery of the earlier films are reduced to a hankering for kinky sex. The gore is less plentiful, and less disturbing, as Hickox opts for humour and lame irony. It is a smaller, more conventional and safer film than its predecessors, less interested in its ideas than in ticket sales.

Atkins's story has real promise: in a nameless American city, bad-boy nightclub owner JP Monroe (Kevin Bernhardt) purchases the Pillar of Souls – now an ornate sculpture – in a curious art gallery. Installed in his bedroom, the Pillar serves as an altar before which his bondage sexcapades are offered, awakening the interests of one quite pinheaded parishioner. 'There is no Good, Monroe. There is no Evil. There is only the flesh and the patterns to which we submit it.'

Enter Joey Summerskill (Terry Farrell), a fledgling TV reporter and Kirsty's heiress as the Teflon tigress against whom all Hell is powerless. After witnessing a hellraising chainpull in a hospital emergency room, she enlists punkette drifter Terri (Paula Marshall) in an investigation that leads to the art gallery, a blurry video of Kirsty and, at last, to the spirit of Elliott Spencer, who warns of the dangers of Pinhead Unbound.[11]

After the requisite infusion of blood frees Pinhead from the pillar, he wreaks minor terror, wasting JP's club and a few storefronts and automobiles; but budgetary constraints dissipate the promised 'Hell on Earth', save in the visions of World War One and Vietnam interpolated throughout the drama, a reminder of man's own monstrosity that makes Pinhead's antics pale by comparison. 'There was absolutely authorial intent to have as one of the subtexts of the picture the fact that Hell on Earth has always existed in the man-made form of war,' Atkins notes. 'It is World War One, after all, that creates Pinhead out of Elliott Spencer. In other words, Hell on Earth produces Pinhead, not vice versa.'

Pinhead's reincarnation, so welcome to enthusiasts of the series, proves miscalculated. Doug Bradley is incomparable in the role (and carries much of the movie); but the once-sedate philosopher of fear – and giver of 'an experience beyond limits, pain and pleasure indivisible' – has become a mugging caricature. Bradley offers some sublime moments – notably an inspired travesty of Holy Communion – but a Pinhead freed from the rules of Clive Barker's game is no longer

Pinhead; instead we have the familiar glib malevolence of Freddy Krueger: A Nightmare on Hell Street.[12]

The results are not particularly terrifying or disturbing; but they are intensely commercial: a demystification of the *Hellraiser* canon and a reordering of its impulses into a didactic understandable to the mass audience of film-goers – good and evil, black and white, pleasure and pain. 'One of the great nights of chagrin for me,' Clive says, 'was when we tested *Hellraiser III* and the audience, to a man, preferred it to the first and second movies – and liked it because it was funnier and faster and there were more explosions and there were more special effects.'

Hell on Earth was a financial success at a time when the horror film was waning. Anthony Hickox and Pete Atkins prepared for a fourth instalment, but the franchise succumbed again to corporate machinations, finally winding its way to Miramax Films, the once-maverick distributor that, after a string of successes with foreign and independent releases, became a new major studio in the Hollywood of the 1990s. In 1995, Miramax green-lighted another sequel, with Barker involved as executive producer. Pete Atkins was teamed with first-time director Kevin Yagher, the special effects genius who created the 'Crypt Keeper' for HBO's 'Tales from the Crypt' series and who provided make-up and effects for several *Nightmare on Elm Street* films, John Woo's *Face/Off* (1997) and Tim Burton's *Sleepy Hollow* (1999), which he also scripted.

In a deft tactic to return Pinhead to his more priestly incarnation, Atkins prepared an ambitious script whose action spanned centuries, and which would serve as both prequel and sequel to the earlier films. He envisioned three interwoven stories set in eighteenth-century France, contemporary America and the distant future – where the scientist Dr Merchant, a descendant of Le Marchand, the original designer of the puzzle box, beckons Pinhead to a space station, intent on closing the gates of Hell forever through a reversal of the Lament Configuration. *Hellraiser: Bloodline* collapsed during production, however, with the producers demanding radical changes and additional photography. Kevin Yagher refused to allow his name to be used on the film, opting for the director's credit to be given to Alan Smithee, the official pseudonym of the Directors Guild. Pete Atkins, in turn, believed that the series had reached its finale in creative and commercial terms.

Miramax had a different perspective. In 2000, the studio produced yet another sequel, *Hellraiser V: Inferno*. Directed by Scott Derrickson from a screenplay by Derrickson and Paul Harris Boardman, the film's connection to its original creators was remote, with Doug Bradley the sole element of continuity. In his third and final day of shooting on the film, Bradley celebrated his one-hundredth day in the complex make-up of Pinhead. The character had taught him, through 'media fostered assumptions, something of the lesson of Karloff – of being typecast, tending to mean being cast as the bad guy'; but Pinhead also offered him the pleasure of appearing in feature films, music videos, MTV programmes, and becoming a living icon of popular culture. Although sometimes disappointed by the later *Hellraiser* films – 'there have been some situations in which I haven't felt entirely at home, haven't felt the character was entirely at home' – he sees the future of Hell in practical terms: 'I guess we'll know when people have had enough.'[13]

With transcendent irony, *Hellraiser* – and particularly its sequels – identified Clive Barker in the public mind with a repetitive and fallacious marketing category of 'horror' at the very moment he was expanding his horizons as a writer and film-maker. Indeed, his next novel, *Weaveworld* (1987), released at almost the same time as *Hellraiser*, sought to shift his dialogue with readers away from the expected – and the horrific – and into the realm of the fantastic.

19

FILIGREE AND SHADOW

WEAVEWORLD (1987)

But still the hands of memory weave
The blissful dreams of long ago.
– GEORGE COOPER, 'Sweet Genevieve'

From its opening sentence – 'Nothing ever begins' – *Weaveworld* steps boldly across the boundary of genre, giving notice that Clive Barker is not a writer of horror fiction, but a master storyteller.[1] A fiction whose very subject is fiction, *Weaveworld* is the natural successor to 'The Forbidden' and 'The Life of Death', stories in which Barker explored the crucial meaning of stories – particularly those of the dark fantastic – in our lives. It is also his first published novel to adopt the style of epic fantasy; and one of his few truly autobiographical works.

In ordinary usage, 'fantasy' is understood as a projection of the desires of the mind (if not the body) onto reality; from President Jimmy Carter's famous admission to 'lust in the heart' to more explicitly sexual invocations, the pejorative is implicit in the word. By the mid-1980s, 'fantasy' also suggested another safely-defined marketing category of fiction and film. Where once storytellers could work with the free play of imagination, there was a tendency to associate fantasy with such droll signifiers as dragons and wizards, unicorns and elves, and increasingly familiar mythologies: barbaric sword-and-sorcery, Arthurian and Celtic lore. Generic fantasy fiction offered the literary equivalence of Renaissance festivals – a neo-Luddite wish, if not belief, that a pre-industrial existence offered a better (and, perhaps, more spiritual and significant) way of life. Certainly these fictions brought simplistic childhood notions – the bifurcation of good and evil, white magic and black magic – into adulthood, while insisting that their stories were mere entertainments so divorced from our reality as to exclude meaningful resonance. Where once CS Lewis and Charles Williams understood the power of fantasy as an extended metaphor, the bookshelves had been filled with novels whose essence was 'escape' – and which distanced their imaginary worlds from the mundane (and difficult and frightening) machinations of reality.

Clive Barker was intent on reclaiming this time-honoured literature from the clutches of commercial constructs – and on redeeming its power through a narrative that was a story about stories: a fantasy about fantasy.

'There is no first moment,' he writes in *Weaveworld*, 'no single word or place from which this or any other story springs.'

> The threads can always be traced back to some earlier tale, and to the tales that preceded that; though as the narrator's voice recedes the connections will seem to grow more tenuous, for each age will want the tale told as if it were of its own making.
>
> Thus the pagan will be sanctified, the tragic become laughable; great lovers will stoop to sentiment, and demons dwindle to clockwork toys.
>
> Nothing is fixed. In and out the shuttle goes, fact and fiction, mind and matter woven into patterns that may have only this in common: that hidden among them is a filigree that will with time become a world.

This stylistic strategy – introductory narration (an authorial intrusion equivalent to a motion picture voice-over); omniscient point of view; panoramic canvas; and reliance on a lengthy, episodic narrative

– urges the repositioning of Barker's art. A genre is many things, especially a marketing category, but it is foremost a category of discourse – a set of rules that defines (or is defined by) audience expectations. Thus readers and publishers expect 'horror' novels or 'crime' novels or 'romance' novels or, indeed, Clive Barker novels – like jokes – to be told in a particular style and structure; and Barker, quite obviously, disagrees.

With its credo stated, *Weaveworld* invokes a plot device as familiar as Alice's looking-glass: The discovery of a world – people, places, things – hidden inside a carpet. From this premise explodes a complex fantasia that would challenge all conceptions of Clive Barker as 'the future of horror' and, indeed, a writer of horror fiction.

Calhoun Mooney meanders through the twenty-sixth year of a mediocre life, employed at a Liverpool insurance office and awaiting marriage. As his last name suggests, he is a dreamer. After his mother's death, he has returned home to tend to a despondent father and his racing pigeons. One of the birds enacts Cal's subconscious desire for escape: '[T]ired of the pecking order of the loft and the predictability of each day – the bird had wanted out; wanted up and away. A day of high life; of food that had to be chased a little, and tasted all the better for that; of the companionship of wild things.' Cal pursues the fleeing pigeon to an abandoned house, whose furniture is being plundered to pay off its hospitalized tenant's bills. As he climbs to snatch the bird from its perch, he loses his footing and plummets earthward, where the removal crew has unfurled a carpet. Reality winks out of existence, the elaborate weave of the carpet shifting, the restless knots untying, the colours merging: 'Implausible as it seemed, the carpet was coming to life.'

> A landscape – or rather a confusion of landscapes thrown together in fabulous disarray – was emerging from the warp and the weft. Was that not a mountain he could see below him, pressing its head up through a cloud of colour?; and was that not a river?; and could he not hear its roar as it fell in white water torrents into a shadowed gorge?
>
> There was a *world* below him.[2]

The miracle of unravelling thread was first presented in Barker's seminal story 'The Inhuman Condition' as a symbol of evolution; here it becomes the very act of creation. The mysterious weave offers Cal the possibility of transcendence – and Wonderland: 'To be there, in that world, would be to live a perpetual adventure.'

> [H]e'd seen something wonderful, and he knew in his bones that his life would never be the same again. How could it? He'd climbed the sky and looked down on the secret place that he'd been waiting since childhood to find.
>
> Everything he'd ever wanted had been in that land; he knew it. Everything his education had taught him to disbelieve – all miracles, all mystery, all blue shadow and sweet-breathed spirits. All the pigeon knew, all the wind knew, all the human world had once grasped and now forgotten, all of it was waiting in that place.

Yet Cal knows instinctively that such a place is not the idyllic dreamscape offered up in storybooks and fables: 'They were too perfect, those childhood kingdoms; all honey and summer . . . The true Wonderland was not like that, he knew. It was as much shadow as sunlight, and its mysteries could only be unveiled when your wits were about used up and your mind close to cracking.'[3] For Cal the choice is easy: 'The glories he saw in his mind's eye had to be preserved from the foulness that embraced him, from its makers and masters, and in such a struggle his life was not so hard to forfeit . . . he'd *search*, search until he found the place he'd seen, and not care that in doing so he was inviting delirium. He'd find his dream and hold onto it and never let it go.'

Cal's struggle is joined by Suzanna Parrish, a twenty-four-year-old London potter whose life of 'calm good order' is spoiled when she is summoned to Liverpool by her dying grandmother, Mimi Laschenski, the owner of the abandoned house – 'She *was* different. She could give her dreams away with a touch.' Mimi is the last custodian of Weaveworld – the carpet, created by a magical race known as the Seerkind to conceal vestiges of their idyllic world, the Fugue, from humanity and the evil destroyer known as the Scourge. She gifts Suzanna with a vision of Weaveworld and a book of fairy tales with an enigmatic epigraph: *'That which is imagined need never be lost.'*

> The stories were familiar, of course: she'd encountered them, in one form or another, a hundred times. She'd seen them re-interpreted as Hollywood cartoons, as erotic fables, as the subject of learned theses and feminist critiques. But their bewitchment remained undiluted by commerce or academe. Sitting there, the child in her wanted to hear these stories told again, though she knew every twist and turn, and had the end in mind before the first line was spoken. That didn't matter, of course. Indeed their inevitability was part of their power. Some tales could never be told too often.[4]

The carpet is sought by dark and otherworldly intruders led by the consummate salesman Shadwell, a 'bear in a Savile Row suit'. *To sell is to own*: 'That was the most important lesson Shadwell had learned as a salesman. If what you possessed was desired ardently enough by another person, then you as good as possessed that person too.' He wears 'the expression of a man looking for converts' and a jacket whose seductive lining shines bright with the most treasured desire of the beholder: 'Tell me what you'd like and it's yours . . . Free, gratis, and without charge. You tell me what you see in there, and the next minute it's in your hands . . .'[5]

Shadwell is the stalking horse for his inhuman consort, Immacolata the Incantatrix: 'the eternal virgin, whose celibacy gave her access to powers lovers were denied'. With features 'as blank as a dead child's', the Incantatrix is a paradox of incandescent beauty and fury. She wields a peculiarly feminine magic, the menstruum, 'that stream of bright darkness which was the blood of her subtle body . . . an etheric solution in which it was said the wielder could dissolve all experience, and make it again in the image of her desire'. Her companions are the wraiths of the sisters she killed in the womb: the wretched oracle Beldam, also known as the Hag, 'her body like phlegm on a wall'; and Magdalene, the blind and unholy Mother Pus, whose bloated stomach births vile children known as by-blows.[6]

For years Shadwell and Immacolata have stalked our world – the 'Kingdom of the Cuckoos' – in search of the Fugue. For Shadwell, the carpet is the ultimate commodity, but Immacolata seeks vengeance; her desire to rule the Seerkind had been thwarted, and she was exiled from the Fugue.[7] They steal the carpet, leaving only a torn fragment behind.

Cal and Suzanna find an attraction far beyond the physical, and become companions in a mystery greater than love or life: 'He'd known her only a night and a day, but she awoke in him the same contradictions – unease and profound contentment; a sense that she was both familiar and unknown – that his first glimpse of the Fugue had aroused . . . they belonged together in this enterprise: she the child of the Fugue, he the innocent trespasser. Against the brief pleasure of making love to her he set the grander adventure, and he knew – despite the dissension from his cock – that he had the better of the deal.' As they sleep, the fragment of carpet unknots into five personages in antiquated clothing, left at the carpet's border because they were riff-raff, the shame of the breed.

Here the novel shifts from the dialect of horror into fantasy, as the Seerkind begin their tale with these ominous words: 'We weren't always lost . . . Once we lived in a garden.' There are four Roots of the Seerkind: Ye-me, the weavers; the musical Aia; the dancing Lo; and Babu of the breath. Each had special skills: 'Powers you'd call miraculous.' They thought nothing of these raptures until the sprawl of humanity touched them: 'Then we realized that your kind like to make laws. Like to decree what's what, and whether it's good or not. And the world, being a loving thing, and not wishing to disappoint you or distress you, indulges you. Behaves as though your doctrines are in some way absolute.'

Humanity reacted to the Seerkind with fear and loathing – and desire: 'The skills we had . . . you Cuckoos called *magic*. Some of them wanted it for themselves. Some were afraid of it. But few loved us for it. Cities were small then, you must understand. It was difficult to hide in them. So we retreated. Into the forests and the hills, where we thought we'd be safe.' Then the Scourge appeared, an inhuman creature with a single ambition: to eliminate all magic from the world. The Seerkind were trapped: 'On one side, Humankind, growing more ambitious for territory by the day, 'til we had scarcely a place left to hide; and on the other, the *Scourge*, as we called it, whose sole intention seemed to be genocide. We knew it could only be a matter of time before we were extinct.'

The carpet was created, a perfect hiding place for the Fugue – 'What's more easily overlooked than the thing you're standing on?' – secreting the Seerkind and their chosen places: houses and fields, a forest, lakes, city squares and streets assembled into a township known as Nonesuch, awaiting the day they would awaken to a forgetful, or more forgiving, world.

But humanity does not forgive or forget; its paragon of order, Police Inspector James Hobart, cannot countenance the irrational (and thus, the magical). 'It was the Law and how to keep it that obsessed him . . . Not for him the niceties of the sociologist or civic planner. His sacred task was to preserve the peace, and his methods – which his apologists described as uncompromising – found sympathy with his civic masters.' Hobart, the eternal rationalist, is convinced that the destruction is man-made, and finds in Suzanna a worthy scapegoat, insisting that her book of fairy tales is evidence; that it means something, a code or cypher – and he is right.

When Shadwell proposes the Sale of Sales – an auction of the carpet to wealthy bidders who hunger for the miraculous – Cal and Suzanna intervene, and in the confusion that follows, a knife cuts into the centre of the carpet. 'Instantly, a shock-wave ran through every inch of warp and weft, as if the knife-point had severed a strand upon which the integrity of the whole depended. And with that strand cut, the Weave was loosed . . . It was the end of the world, and the beginning of *worlds*.'[8]

The miracles of the Fugue are endless: it is a flux of reinvented images, a surrealist Wonderland in which incomplete fragments of our reality – corners of rooms, the half-span of a bridge – have been 'torn from their context like pages from a book'. Cal witnesses the fabled orchard of Lemuel Lo, with its intoxicating fruit; twins who merge their bodies and exchange genders; the dreamy delights of Venus Mountain, where psychedelic images dance in tranquil majesty; and finally a strange man at the edge of a place known as the Gyre.

Shadwell, disguised by Immacolata, offers himself as the messiah of the Seerkind, then turns on them with a vengeance. When the Seerkind are defeated in battle, Cal and Suzanna follow Shadwell into the living heart of Wonderland: 'Always, worlds within worlds . . . In the Kingdom of the Cuckoo, the Weave; in the Weave, the Fugue; in the Fugue, the world of Mimi's book, and now this: the Gyre.' It is a realm of pure creation – and thus, destruction. Shadwell wounds Cal, then enters its sanctum, the Temple of the Loom.

For Shadwell, the Loom offers 'a fabulous fecundity which brought with it the promise of heroic decay' – and godhood; but inside he sees nothing but corpses. There is no Loom, Immacolata tells him, but the Loom is there: 'Did you really expect to find a *thing*? Another object to be possessed? Is that your Godhood, Shadwell? Possession?' Enraged, he kills the Incantatrix, a final profanity that summons nothingness: the end of the Fugue. Wonderland is no more.

This climactic confrontation would constitute the finale of most novels, but for Barker it is merely the anacrusis. 'Magic might be bestowed upon the physical,' Barker tell us in the aftermath, 'but it didn't *reside* there. It resided in the word, which was mind spoken, and in motion, which was mind made manifest; in the system of the Weave and the evocations of the melody: all *mind* . . . It was like love. Or rather love was its highest form: mind shaping mind, visions pirouetting on the threads between lovers.' Then begins the concluding act – 'Out of the Empty Quarter' – derived from the synopsis offered to Sphere as his first novel.

Only a hundred of the Seerkind have survived. Cal and Suzanna live apart: 'They'd seen Hell and Heaven together. After that, surely everything else was bathos . . . [W]hat they shared now was perhaps the highest aspiration of all lovers: between them they held a world.' Meanwhile, Shadwell and the disgraced Hobart venture into the Rub' al Khali: the Empty Quarter, that barren wasteland in the Arabian Peninsula, two hundred and fifty thousand square miles of uninhabitable desert immortalized by Sir Wilfred Thesiger. 'Before the explorers, the *Rub' al Khali* had been a blank space on the map of the world. After them, it remained so.' Visitors to the heart of this darkness, like those who dared Joseph Conrad's Congo, return irrevocably changed.[9]

In this 'connoisseur's nowhere' Shadwell seeks the Scourge,

summoned by its wail of grief to consummate destruction of the Seerkind and the magic and chaos they represent. 'Until he stepped into the presence of that creature – until he learned the source of its cleanliness – he could not be cleansed himself. That he longed for above all things.'

They find a wall, fifty feet high, that encloses only sand; but as they sleep, the dunes form into an illusion: 'What had at first sight seemed a miracle of fecundity was a mockery . . . Scentless, colourless, lifeless: a dead garden.' Inside waits the awesome, hundred-eyed creature known as the Scourge:

> [T]he thing, despite its solidity, defied fixing. Were those wheels that moved at its heart, tied with lines of liquid fire to a hundred other geometries which informed the air it occupied? Did innumerable wings beat at its perimeters, and light burn in its bowels, as though it had swallowed stars?
>
> Nothing was certain. In one breath, it seemed to be enclosed in a matrix of darting light, like scaffolding struck by lightning; in the next, the pattern became flame confetti which swarmed at its extremities before it was snatched away. One moment, ether; the next, juggernaut.

In speaking the name of the Seerkind, Shadwell awakens lost memories in the creature, which reveals itself as the mightiest of all angels, Uriel: 'The archangel of salvation; called by some the flame of God.'[10] Its sanctuary is not a garden, but *the* Garden – Eden – where Uriel was left to stand guard: '*There were others here,*' the Seraph said, '*that called this place Eden. But I never knew it by that name . . . This was a place of making . . . For ever and ever. Where things came to be . . . To find a form, and enter the world.*' Humanity was raised from the earth in hundreds of places; in Eden were higher spirits – and the Seerkind were their offspring who, growing curious, left the Garden for our world.[11]

Driven insane by loneliness, Uriel is enticed from the Garden by Shadwell, plotting vengeance – a holocaust of cleansing fire – upon the Seerkind and, indeed, all living things. The action shifts from a wasteland of heat to one of cold: a blizzard descends upon England, painting the world in the white darkness of the void. Tormented by prophetic nightmares, Cal seeks out a Fortean collector of anomalous phenomena – precursor of Grillo of *Everville* (1994) – to help him locate the remaining Seerkind; he finds, among the collector's relics, Shadwell's wish-fulfilling jacket.

As Uriel approaches the Seerkind's final hiding place, it possesses Shadwell's body, restoring its fiery purpose; the snow is set aflame, and the Seerkind are revealed. But Cal dons the jacket of illusions and shows its lining to Uriel-in-Shadwell. The Salesman sees nothing, but the Angel looks and desires so powerfully that the jacket is unthreaded. As it takes its dream, it bursts the skin of Shadwell: 'The vision stood revealed: as bright as Uriel, and as vast, as well it had to be, for the image the raptures had made was *another* Uriel, the Seraph's equal in every way.' The Angel's most profound desire was 'simply, to see its own true face, and seeing it know how it had been before loneliness had corrupted it'. Its sanity restored, the Angel gazes skyward, to the stars: 'There were heavens it had business in, where the age it had wasted here was but a day, and its grief, *all* grief, an unknown state.' It ascends in triumph.

Cal, touched by the vast loneliness of the Angel, is lost in a wasteland of the mind, until at last he remembers seeing a strange old man in a house bordering the Gyre – and recognizes that man as himself. With this knowledge, he knows that he will live, one day, in that world – and that the Fugue is not lost. With the book of fairy tales, Cal and Suzanna reawaken the magic of the Loom, their memories restoring the Fugue, fulfilling the storybook's prophecy: '*That which is imagined need never be lost.*'

The final pages of *Weaveworld* exalt the triumph of memory: the ways in which we collectively sustain something we knew as children, that belief in possibilities – an optimism that too often retreats in adulthood, finding its only solace in the imagination. Like Jacqueline Ess, Suzanna learns the true source of power: 'Most of her life she'd associated power with politics or money, but her secret self had learned better. Imagination was true power: it worked transformations wealth and influence never could.' With this knowledge, there are no frontiers, no limits – not even those of the flesh:

There was time for all their miracles now. For ghosts and transformations; for passion and ambiguity; for noonday visions and midnight glory. Time in abundance.

For nothing ever begins.

And this story, having no beginning, will have no end.

Despite its glorious ambition, *Weaveworld* received a curiously mixed reception on the two sides of the Atlantic Ocean. In the United Kingdom, once Collins 'acquired' Clive in 1986, Eddie Bell sent its marketing and publicity machine into overdrive almost a year before the novel was published – 'it being Eddie's conviction,' notes Jane Johnson, now Clive's editor at HarperCollins, 'that if the trade read Clive's work they would be as bowled over by it as he was himself.' Collins mounted one of the largest promotional campaigns in publishing history, with heavy advertising and a nationwide tour that included several crucial television appearances; the publisher even commissioned the Royal College of Art to create a handwoven 'Weaveworld' carpet and Linda McCartney to photograph Clive for the dust jacket. Perhaps more crucially, Collins issued the novel without generic packaging or any reference to 'horror'; indeed, the cover of *Weaveworld* described the book as 'an epic adventure of the imagination'.

British reviewers raved, and the reading public responded: the novel went straight to number one on the hardback bestseller lists, and sold more than 250,000 copies in its first year in paperback. 'Publication of *Weaveworld* was a phenomenon in the UK,' notes Jane Johnson, 'a very different experience to the reaction in the US. *Weaveworld* is what made Clive a household name.'

At Sphere, Barbara Boote felt that other forces were at play: 'Harper-Collins made *Weaveworld* work dramatically, partly because they pulled every kind of favour and bribe to get the books into the shops. They gave extra discounts and things at a time when nobody else did that sort of thing, and we were all thinking, *That's just not what you do.* But they got a huge number back; so the gross sale was brilliant, but the net sale was not so good. In terms of Clive's profile, it was brilliant; everybody had heard of Clive Barker. So as a career move, it was terribly helpful. As a moneymaking exercise for HarperCollins, it would have been pretty dicey – but help for the future.'

Jane Johnson demurs: 'The Collins edition netted a vast quantity, and the returns were not huge at all. It sold on and on, in both hardback and then a year later in paperback – both editions going to number one: an extraordinary achievement.' *Weaveworld* remains, to this day, Barker's bestselling book in England (with sales exceeding 500,000 copies in the paperback edition) and a favourite of many of his devoted readers. Moreover, available information indicates that Barker's net sales – the number of copies sold versus the number of copies published – have been consistently higher than the norm.

In the United States, however, Simon & Schuster declined to break Barker's link with horror – repeating the Stephen King 'future of horror' quote on the novel's dust jacket – and did not promote the book effectively. Many reviewers seemed genuinely puzzled that Barker would not revisit the familiar territory of terror explored in earlier books. *Kirkus Reviews* hailed the novel – prematurely and incorrectly – as 'the most ambitious and visionary horror novel of the decade'. Writing in the *Washington Post Book World*, EF Bleiler allowed that 'Barker's conversations are well-handled, but the writing otherwise is pedestrian and often clichéd'. In his sudden arc of success, it seemed forgotten that Clive Barker was growing up in public as a novelist.

Weaveworld has its flaws, which would recur, on occasion, in later novels: its narrative sprawls, moving forward more by impulse and instinct than by storytelling structure; and characterizations tend to proceed from manner, not motive. But for some, the novel's unforgivable and seemingly inexplicable conceit was its departure from the generic expectations of horror. While some reviewers and journalists acknowledged, often grudgingly, that Barker had ventured into new terrain, others steadfastly refused the evidence and repeated the by-now familiar 'future of horror' cant; for example, in reviewing *Weaveworld*, the *Philadelphia Inquirer* termed Barker 'the undisputed prince of creepy crawly'.

Lost in the American reviews, bad and good, were the thematic concerns of the book, and the emerging conscience – and career – of a writer. As underscored by its scene of frozen clocks, *Weaveworld* and its author struggled with an apocalyptic idea: the clash of time and eternity. In seeking godhood, Shadwell would arrogate unto himself a false hope of life eternal, while Cal and Suzanna refuse to deny their mortality, holding instead a hope for the future – a hope that the eternal, being a fixed place, would deny them.

The novel's title, we must understand, holds a double meaning: the 'weaveworld' is not simply the magical carpet, but also the larger, integrated world posited by Barker's finale: a world in which the physical and the imagined are interwoven and accepted. This fantasy of the reconciliation of the life of the body and the life of the mind would become integral to Barker's later work, reaching an apotheosis in *Imajica* (1991). It is an indictment of the materialistic perspective that rejects, if not impugns, the fantastic, and it is summed up in a single sentence: 'After tonight there would be only one world, to live in and to dream; and Wonderland would never be more than a step away, a thought away.'

Weaveworld thus explores the possibility of Wonderland as an extended metaphor for the imagination – it is '[n]ot a dream at all, but an awakening' – a theme Barker would return to time and again in his novels, particularly in *Imajica* and the trilogy of 'The Art'. Thus *Weaveworld* was only the first of several complex – and, for some, difficult – fantasies from his pen; and, characteristically, it subverted the form. Just as horror had been defined in generic terms, the 'fantasy' novel of this generation was a construct over which JRR Tolkien and Arthurian legend held particular sway: a place of escape and idyll, inhabited by elves and magicians and happy endings. Barker's Wonderland offers no mindless escape, but mindful exploration. '[H]e'd brought new wisdom from the high places. He knew now that things forgotten might be recalled; things lost, found again ... That was all that mattered in the world: to search and find.'

At heart, *Weaveworld* is a fantasy about why we want and need fantasy. It is horror only in the rarest and best sense of the word, and strives for a unique fusion (indeed, blurring) of fantasy and horror into a fiction of the dark fantastic.[12] In these pages, Barker also supplants a long tradition of novels in which characters move freely between a world of 'reality' and another of 'fantasy' – which includes many of his favourite books of childhood, such as *Peter Pan* and, of course, the novels of ER Eddison.

'I have never liked the division between horror fiction and fantasy fiction and science fiction,' he explains. 'There is a *fantastique* genre

– Stephen King's fiction is *fantastique*, in the classic and proper sense. In the sense that it explores something which is unlikely, to say the least – something which is an imagined thing. One day, in a more enlightened age, Marquez and Borges and King and Machen – and probably Dickens – will all be studied on the same syllabus, because they are all authors who reinvent the world.

'Now in one sense, all authors reinvent the world; but some of us do it with more enthusiasm than others, with more desire to see the world shaped to our particular longings and anxieties.

'I do not consider myself a horror writer, any more than I consider myself a fantasy writer or science fiction writer. I am a writer who works in my imagination. The only difference in the world of literature, it seems to me, is between the guy who writes out of a perceived reality and the guy who creates one for himself.'

Just as Freud had rejected the notion that dreams and nightmares were different things (both being the product of sleep), Barker – though by no means a Freudian – elaborately erased the notion that horror and fantasy were different things (both being products of the imagination). Nevertheless, reviewers, readers and even publishers were unable, or unwilling, to accept a Clive Barker without boundaries, and without some convenient hook on which to hang his creative endeavour. His American publisher, Simon & Schuster, insisted upon releasing the paperback edition of *Weaveworld* with a cover that sported the face of an almost comically crazed man. It was an irony predicted in the novel itself, when Shadwell contemplates the problem of 'selling' Immacolata in terms applicable to Barker's own fiction: 'For one, she was paradoxical, and the buying public had little taste for that. They wanted their merchandise shorn of ambiguity; made simple and safe.'[13]

With its sentimental landscapes, its reinvention of childhood fantasies as the stuff of adult fiction, and its dedication to David J Dodds, *Weaveworld* is a text whose insistent theme is the coming of age. In its pages, Clive Barker offered a solemn farewell to Liverpool, and the protective shelter of genre, finding new confidence in himself and his relationships.

In their final difficult days, Clive and John Gregson went to lunch with one of John's friends, who brought along David Dodds, a quiet and unassuming nurse who worked with AIDS patients. 'And here,' Clive says, 'was this incredibly handsome, gentle, funny, civilized and charming soul. And we got on incredibly well. My feelings ran deep for him very quickly – and that was reciprocated.'

John was gregarious, an ebullient man who would tell spiralling humorous stories: 'He could giggle like no one else,' says Mary Roscoe. But David was subdued and shy; his sense of humour was strong, but expressed with quiet calm. With a powerfully positive personality, David offered an anchor of reality and friendship that Clive needed. His understanding and instinctive caring seemed to mesh well with Clive's chaotic life and personality – although, when they met, David knew nothing about Clive Barker. 'The day I met him,' Clive notes, 'we were in a newsagents, and I said, *This is what I do*. I opened up a copy of *Penthouse*, and there was a piece about the shooting of *Underworld*.'

In time, David would become Clive's personal assistant; but first, the men became lovers and best friends. 'John and I fell apart because he could not bear the idea that he would lose control over me. When I started to become successful, he started to lose control; and the only way he knew to assert it was to be physically abusive. And I was not good at fighting back.

'Then, when I met David Dodds, it was like meeting a gentleman after having been with a fuck. When I met David, I couldn't believe that I had been dragged so low that my self-esteem would allow me to be treated the way I had allowed myself – and the phrase is *allowed myself* – to be treated. There were a few terrible weeks where John knew I was going to leave, and his fury knew no bounds; and then it was over, and it was gone.

'It was unbelievable. It was like a new me.'

In the late summer of 1987, Clive gave John Gregson the flat he had purchased 'in some small return for the support he had certainly given me while I was working on the *Books of Blood*'. Clive and David moved into an elegant Georgian house at 36 Wimpole Street in London, with large, high-ceilinged rooms that exuded warmth and comfort. Its living room was presided over by two large canvases, and objects from Clive's childhood (including an angel he created in art classes at Quarry Bank) stood next to props from *Hellraiser*. Upstairs was his bedroom and his study, which looked out on Wimpole Street – a sedate view – and on the next floor, David's bedroom and guest rooms.

There, Clive and David celebrated the paperback publication of *Weaveworld* with a launch party, which produced the inevitable journalistic commentary on the earnings of bestselling writers and the irony of good taste mingling with the stuff of horror.[14] On Sunday evenings, Clive gathered the former members of the Dog Company in a luxurious sitting room and they would drink champagne and eat and talk into the morning hours. Although some friends found his newfound wealth difficult to accept, Mary Roscoe observes: 'No one would say Clive hadn't earned it. I've never known anyone who worked so hard. Clive is a workaholic . . . Every waking moment, he is working. He knows how to play as well. Certainly he knows how to relax, or at least appear to relax; on a Sunday night, when he would invite us all around, he would sit there with a cigar and a big bottle of champagne, and tell jokes like the rest of us. But come nine o'clock in the morning, he would be at his desk, writing, whereas I would have a hangover and be stumbling around my flat thinking, *Why did I drink so much last night?* Clive would be working, and by midday he would have rung me with another draft of another story. So I thought he had earned every penny of it, and deserved it.'

Clive's most sublime reward for writing *Weaveworld* came on a quiet afternoon, not long after the novel's release, as he walked the halls of his new publisher, Collins. As he passed one of the offices, he noticed an older gentleman sitting alone, reading; suddenly he recognized him. It was Sir Wilfred Thesiger – adventurer, author of *Arabian Sands* and the inspiration for this mighty novel that had, in turn, made Clive Barker a mighty force to be reckoned with in our culture.

20

A BREED APART

CABAL (1988)

Flesh could not keep its glamour, nor eyes their sheen. They would go to nothing soon.
  But monsters were forever.

— CLIVE BARKER, *Cabal*

The story of the lost breed – the nightbreed – haunts Clive Barker's fiction and film. With the very first sentence of the *Books of Blood* – 'The dead have highways' – we were offered the possibility of a shadow life that intersected with our rigid notions of 'reality'. True to this vision, Barker takes his readers and viewers repeatedly, almost obsessively, to the place where worlds of light and dark, day and night, coincide (and sometimes collide), asking us to consider whether the mundane and the fantastic may be reconciled.

In early stories like 'Twilight at the Towers' and 'The Skins of the Fathers', Barker hinted at an evolving lore of mythic outsiders. His script for the motion picture *Underworld* was his first extended effort to give life to a parallel breed. The Underworlders were social outcasts, fringe dwellers, men and women warped by the effects of a renegade drug – a stark commentary on social and scientific ills. When Barker returned to the theme in *Weaveworld*, he offered the Seerkind, faded memories of the inhabitants of fairy tales who represented the dwindling, but not yet extinct, hope of holy magic in a secular, rationalist world. The Underworlders and the Seerkind were essentially human, essentially benign. The inhabitants of *Cabal* (1988)[1] are not.

Cabal is, indeed, a hymn to the monstrous. Its central and subsidiary themes are quintessential Clive Barker: the conflicts between body and mind, the rational and the imaginary; and the conflicts between the different, the disenfranchised, and the inflexible forces of law and order, caste and class. Its 'monsters' – the mythic Nightbreed – are a celebration of the imagination, gifted with skins and skills that are the stuff of dreams, yet evoke humanity's relentless xenophobia: the desire to reject and oppress those who, for such mundane reasons as skin colour or sexual preference, are considered 'wrong' or 'evil'.[2]

Although originally published as a novel in the United Kingdom, *Cabal* was issued in the United States as part of an eponymous fiction collection that also included most of the sixth, and last, volume of the *Books of Blood*.[3] As Barker admits, he wrote *Cabal* as 'a kind of filler': after *Weaveworld*, he had intended to produce a new collection of short stories, but he found more satisfaction in a longer narrative. 'I like the 30,000 to 40,000 word length. It's actually a nice length for me . . . it allows me to feel I'm doing more than a short story, but I don't have to make some vast commitment of time.'

Cabal is the most spare and experimental of Barker's novels, and thus, for some readers, the least satisfactory. In its pages, he dispenses for the most part with traditional narrative techniques – sequential plotting, character development, climactic revelation, resolution – in favour of cinematic conceits such as jump-cuts and montage. Not surprisingly, the novel – whose subtitle, in the British edition, is 'The Nightbreed' – was the blueprint for his motion picture *Nightbreed* (1990).

Barker did not write *Cabal* as the template for a film. He had conceived a series of short novels (and, perhaps, intertwining stories) that would explore the mythology of a lost breed – and that would resurrect his vision for *Underworld*. Clearly *Cabal* (and, later, *Nightbreed*) sought to exorcise that cinematic misadventure and to redeem the fundamental power of its narrative; throughout the novel, Barker refers to the home of the Nightbreed as 'the Underworld'.[4]

Cabal is thus a seminal novel of anti-horror. It lacks a conventional plot, adopting instead the schema of an excavation, the stripping away of layer after layer of falsehood to reveal a hidden truth: a truth of role reversal. In its pages, we find that the supposed monsters are the sympathetic characters (and heroes), while their enemies, humans symbolic of science, religion and authority, are conformists so steadfast in their distaste for difference that they seem little more than soulless, devouring zombies.

The principal players in this drama, Aaron Boone and his girlfriend Lori, are virtually cyphers; certainly they are the most opaque of the leading characters who inhabit Barker's novels. We learn little about their lives. Their ages (apparently young), their jobs (Lori works in 'an office'), their origins and even their desires – save for each other – are effectively unknown. So intent is Barker upon casting Boone and Lori as Everyman and Everywoman that even their looks are hidden; we know only that Boone's face is 'his glory' while Lori's face is 'sweet'.[5]

By downplaying conventional characterizations, Barker takes an immense risk. His intent is clear: to transfer the emotional schema that we identify as 'human' (compassion, maternal urges, love) to the so-called 'monsters', and thus to shift the perspective of the reader: 'The workings of the world seem a little more preposterous through the eyes of monsters.'[6]

Boone, a young Canadian battling mental illness, has been under the care of psychiatrist Dr Philip Decker for five years. 'Decker was a rock; he was Reason, he was Calm.' He is, in other words, everything that is suspect in the nightmare worlds of Clive Barker. With cold calculation, Decker concludes his latest session of therapy by dealing Boone a gruesome tarot consisting of photographs of crime scenes: 'There were eleven photographs in all. Every one was different – rooms large and small, victims naked and dressed. But each also the same: all pictures of a madness performed, taken with the actor already departed.'[7] The faces in the photos have been unmade with cuts – eyes dug out, lips slit off, noses in ribbons, all victims of the serial violence of the elusive 'Calgary Killer'.

Although the photographs are meaningless to him, Boone confesses the crimes to Decker – 'I'm a monster' – but the psychiatrist, intent on understanding Boone's illness, declines to contact the police. He offers Boone medication, and Boone wanders into the night, his one cherished thought of Lori, the lover whom he has spurned. He attempts suicide but awakens in a hospital, wounded but alive. There he hears 'a name that would with time make a new man of him. At its call he'd go like the monster he was, by night, and meet with the miraculous.' The name is Midian – a legendary city of refuge where his sins, real or imagined, would be forgiven. '[W]hile his avowals of eternal love had proved hollow in a matter of weeks, Midian made promises – midnight, like his own, deepest midnight – that even death could not break.'

According to the Old Testament, Midian was a nomadic tribe which lived to the east of Israel. After playing a key role in the spiritual development of the Israelites, the Midianites were slaughtered in fulfilment of the word of God. According to Clive Barker, it is the place where another tribe of nomads dwells – and their fate proves the same as their Biblical progenitors.[8]

Journeying north into the Canadian wilderness, Boone finds a ghost town and its cemetery, walled and massive, another crossroads of the dead. '[H]ere were magnificent tombs, avenue upon avenue of them, built in all manner of styles from the classical to the baroque, and marked ... with motifs from warring theologies.'

It is Midian, home of the Nightbreed, the hidden remnants of the world's monsters. Below is their hermitage, a place where even the most gruesome creature might find peace. The inhabitants, although nightmarish, offer Boone a transforming truth. The reptilian man-thing known as Peloquin rejects him: 'You're not Nightbreed ... You're meat. That's what you are. Meat for the beast.' He bites at Boone's flesh, and as Boone escapes he feels a sudden thrill, a 'sensitivity that was almost erotic' – and he realizes that he is innocent of any crime.

It is Decker, not Boone, who is the Calgary Killer: 'Who would have doubted, seeing the bloodied man and the clean, which was the lunatic and which his healer? But appearances deceived. It was only the monster, the child of Midian, who actually altered its flesh to parade its true self. The rest hid behind their calm, and plotted the deaths of children.' Boone, the sacrificial lamb upon the psychiatrist's altar of rationality, is hunted down and shot to death by the police; but his body, like that of Christ, disappears from beneath its shroud.

The point of view shifts to Boone's lost love, Lori. She can do nothing but follow in Boone's path, trying desperately to understand why he committed such violent crimes – and why she loves him still: 'Ghosts could be laid with laughter; misery was made of sterner stuff.' Wandering on her widow's pilgrimage, she asks an eternal question about the dead: 'How can he be so . . . *irretrievable*? There should be some way we could *reach*, don't you think, some way to reach and touch them . . . Otherwise, it's all nonsense, isn't it? It's all sadistic nonsense.'

Drawn to the necropolis, she flirts with the idea of a shadow breed: 'Here was a place sacred to the dead, who were *not* the living ceased, but almost another species, requiring rites and prayers that belonged uniquely to them.' Her search unveils new mysteries – the epic size of the graveyard, the curiosity of the many nationalities and animals buried there, and at last some*thing*, hiding beneath a tree, a catlike creature caught and wounded by the sunlight. When she brings the animal into the shadowed entry of a mausoleum, its skin changes, morphing into that of a human child.

Inside, Lori is greeted by two of the Breed – the child's mother, Rachel, and the patriarch of Midian, Lylesburg. She cannot bring herself to follow them below, yet when she turns to leave, '[t]he shadows seemed unwilling to relinquish her . . . She felt them weave themselves into her blouse and hook themselves on her eyelashes, a thousand tiny holds on her, slowing her retreat.' She has touched the power of darkness, glimpsed the possibilities of night; and when she emerges from the fertile embrace of the shadows into the world outside, she is greeted by 'the brutality of light and sky' – a vista 'plainly devoid of deities'.

Like most of her kin, Lori first perceives Midian and its occupants as evil: 'demons – things of rot and wickedness', living in the depths of 'a miasma so profound it could have rotted the faith of a saint'. But that night she meets the true incarnation of evil:

[R]unning at her was a sewing-box doll: zipper for mouth, buttons for eyes, all sewn on white linen and tied around the monster's face so tightly his saliva darkened a patch around his mouth. She was denied the face but not the teeth. He held them above his head, gleaming knives, their blades fine as grass-stalks, sweeping down to stab out her eyes.

It is Decker: 'He was the New Death; tomorrow's face today . . . the human fiend made myth.' Behind his 'façade of civilized concern', as palpable as his button-eyed mask, lurks the vicious killer who used Boone, so susceptible to manipulation and medication, as a scapegoat. For Decker, murder is done for the purest of reasons: 'For the fun of it, of course. For the pleasure. We used to talk a lot about *why*, Boone and me. Digging deep, you know; trying to understand. But when it really comes down to it, I do it because I like it.'

Lori faces a choice – the police or Midian – and the night has offered an epiphany:

> Yesterday she would have chosen to go to the law. She would have trusted that its procedures would make all these mysteries come clear; that they would believe her stories, and bring Decker to justice. But yesterday she'd thought beasts were beasts, and children, children; she'd thought that only the dead lived in the earth, and that they were peaceful there. She'd thought that doctors healed; and that when the madman's mask was raised she would say: 'But of course, that's a madman's face.'
>
> All wrong; all so wrong. Yesterday's assumptions were gone to the wind. Anything might be true.
>
> *Boone might be alive.*

At Midian, Lori and her pursuer find Boone, resurrected, a messiah of the darkness whose flesh is now fantasy. Though his heart has stopped, he lives: Peloquin's bite has sent the balm of the Nightbreed into his veins, transforming him into a powerful shapeshifter who hungers for blood. 'I'm not behind this face,' Boone tells the disbelieving Decker. 'I *am* this face . . . You drove me into the hands of monsters, Decker. And I became one. Not your kind of monster. Not the soulless kind.'[9]

Boone takes Lori to the true Midian: not the empty town, not even the necropolis, but a network of tunnels and chambers burrowing deep underground. 'After a dozen corridors she no longer knew horror from fascination.' Its denizens – werewolves, vampires, demons, shapeshifters – are, like Boone, the mingling of archetypal monsters and a new mythology. 'They didn't belong to Hell; nor yet to Heaven. They were what the species he'd once belonged to could not bear to be. The *un*-people; the *anti*-tribe; humanity's sack unpicked and sewn together again with the moon inside.'

At last Lori enters the final chamber, the abode of the sacred and profane. 'She wanted to flee the place with a passion – wanted to forsake it and forget it; and yet it *summoned*. It was not Boone's presence that called her, but the pull of the holy, or the unholy, or the two in one; and it wouldn't be resisted.' There lives Baphomet, the architect of Midian, the most powerful and most vulnerable of its occupants – a body hacked limb from limb, god and goddess in one sundered body, suspended in an icy pillar of flame. In witnessing its awful glory, Lori can do nothing but scream:

> No story or movie screen, no desolation, no bliss had prepared her for the maker of Midian. Sacred it must be, as anything so extreme must be sacred. A thing beyond things. Beyond love or hatred, or *their* sum; beyond the beautiful or the monstrous, or their sum. Beyond, finally, her mind's ability to comprehend or catalogue. In the instant she looked away from it she had already blanked every fraction of the sight from conscious memory and locked it where no torment or entreaty would ever make her look again.[10]

Because Boone, in saving Lori, has violated Lylesburg's insistent maxim – *'what's below remains below'* – the reunited lovers are banished from Midian. Alone in the precarious outside world, Lori accepts Boone for 'as much and as little as he was. Man. Monster. Dead. Alive.' To survive, he must forgive himself and live with himself, not with what other people would make of him. He must also realize that, like each of us, 'Boone the man and Boone the monster could not be divided'.

In this sudden crisis of reality, Lori understands the strange ways of the world, the trap of the flesh, the inevitability of death, and the liberating power of the imagination:

> Against that the monsters of Midian – transforming, re-arranging, ambassadors of tomorrow's flesh and reminders of yesterday's – seemed full of possibilities. Weren't there, amongst these creatures, faculties she envied? The power to fly; to be transformed; to know the condition of beasts; to defy death?
>
> All that she'd coveted or envied in others of her species now seemed valueless. Dreams of the perfected anatomy – the soap opera face, the centrefold body – had distracted her with promises of true happiness. Empty promises. Flesh could not keep its glamour, nor eyes their sheen. They would go to nothing soon.
>
> But monsters were forever. Part of her forbidden self. Her dark, transforming midnight self. She longed to be numbered amongst them.[11]

'Maybe the monsters *were* forever. But so were their persecutors.' Around Decker gather the figures of patriarchal authority, forming the unholy triumvirate that haunts Clive Barker's fiction. Joining the psychiatrist, that pillar of rationality, is the pillar of the law, Sheriff Irwin Eigerman, a man for whom 'bright ideas and excretion were inextricably linked', and whose compulsion for good behaviour abhors any deviance, particularly the sexual: '[Z]ombies belonged in the late movie, as sodomy did on a lavatory wall. They had no place in the real world.' Eigerman summons, in turn, the local priest – Father Ashbery – the pillar of the church, for whom there is One True Religion, One True God, One True Order.

'They stole such authority for themselves, these people. Made themselves arbiters of good and bad, natural and unnatural, justifying their cruelty with spurious laws.' Each pursues their common bogeymen – those who differ – with relentless, machinelike fervour: 'Who then were the *real* dead? The silent-hearted, who still knew pain, or their glassy-eyed tormentors?' The answer need not be voiced, because it is clear that these hitmen of homogeneity are the real dead, as lifeless as zombies.

Decker's passion for destruction is born not simply of hatred, but also of an undoubted envy. With a band of locals gathered as vigilantes

– that mindless horde, ever eager to storm the castles of Dr Frankenstein and Count Dracula – Decker and Eigerman plot the destruction
of Midian and its monsters: 'They *were* freaks . . . Things in defiance
of nature, to be poked from under their stones and soaked in gasoline.'
True to this desire, gasoline is poured down the gullets of the tombs
and mausoleums and ignited, and many of the Nightbreed die in a
holocaust of its holy fire and sunlight.

In the midst of the inferno, Boone confronts Decker: 'This wasn't
a patient's revenge on his corrupted healer; this was a beast and a
butcher, tooth to knife.' Unmasked, undone, Decker is helpless, defeated and finally torn to shreds by the bloodthirsty Boone. 'He was
no longer innocent. With this slaughter he became the killer Decker
had persuaded him he was. In murdering the prophet he made the
prophecy true.'

With their refuge destroyed, the Nightbreed erase all signs of Midian
and prepare to move along: 'What was below could remain below no
longer.' They have a new leader – their messiah, baptized in the icy
flame of Baphomet: 'He was no longer Boone. He was Cabal.' His body,
an 'alliance of many', once human, now beast, touched by the hand of
a new god (or, perhaps, the oldest one), is given the power of heat and
blood and making children: 'But he would be frail too, or frailer. Not
just because he bled, but because he was charged with purpose.'

As the Nightbreed scatter into the darkness, Cabal is charged with
the task of rebuilding what he has destroyed: to heal Baphomet and
make its broken parts whole. Lori's love for Boone is so strong that
she drives Decker's blade into her stomach, a mortal wound that forces
Boone to save her – by biting her and making her part of the Breed,
to live with him forever in the welcome arms of the night.

Cabal is a parable of redemption and forgiveness – of self and of
others. It is a plea for the celebration of diversity and the demolition
of conformity. 'A working definition of evil,' Barker observes, 'is the
eradication of anything and everything that is different from you.'

The creatures of Midian are monstrous not only because of their
looks, but also because they do not behave according to society's rules;
in the most basic sense, they are an expression of gay culture, ethnic
culture, teen culture – any and every manifestation of difference from

the conventional constructs of 'normality' and 'morality' enforced by law and religion and social structure – and, indeed, by generic horror fiction and film.

Cabal reads like an engaging manifesto, urging the overthrow of the fascist impulses that praise, demand, celebrate conformity – and that, particularly in our popular entertainment, not only divide 'good' from 'evil', but also establish clear-cut signifiers of that distinction: day and night, white and black. ('The night, which had always been a place of promise, belonged too much to the Breed, who had taken its name for themselves. And why not? All darkness was one darkness in the end. Of heart or heavens; one darkness.') Our role, whether as creators or simply as human beings, is to invoke or at least accept diversity and ambiguity, rather than stifle it.

Midian, like other Clive Barker wonderlands, represents his longing for the place beyond – the Never-Never Land that is not a physical retreat, or escape, but a condition: a place beyond space and time – 'Eden, if you will' – the home toward which we instinctively and imaginatively strive.

As *Cabal* was being written, Clive himself was striving – and being summoned – toward another place, one arguably the opposite of Eden: Hollywood. With the heady success of *Hellraiser*, the moment seemed ripe for his singular vision to find expression in motion pictures and television. Only two practical hurdles remained: his relative inexperience in the machinations of the industry and his geographical distance from Los Angeles.

The apparent solution was presented by American writer and director Mick Garris, who, like Clive, was represented by Hollywood super-agency Creative Artists Agency. In 1988, CAA arranged for them to meet during one of Clive's visits to Los Angeles. Their mutual passion for horror film, coupled with Garris's more traditional grounding in the ways of Hollywood – and his residence there – seemed a firm foundation for an effective working partnership.

Garris had recently completed work as story editor, writer and director on Steven Spielberg's 'Amazing Stories' television series (1985–86); he had scripted **batteries not included* (1987) and then written and directed his first feature film, *Critters 2* (1988). Although each man would attain considerable success on his own, their collaborative efforts were, for the most part, frustrated by the whims of producers – and present an intriguing question of what might have been.

Their initial efforts focused on 'Spirit City USA', a series that Barker was developing for ABC Television. Garris scripted a one-hour pilot episode based on a story idea by Barker; it was intended that Clive would direct the pilot episode, and that Barker and Garris would share the writing and 'created by' credits.

'Spirit City USA' was based vaguely on the *Books of Blood* story 'The Last Illusion', which Barker later adapted as the motion picture *Lord of Illusions* (1995). It was, in Garris's words, 'scary with a sense of humour'. The series would have opened on the first anniversary of the death of a famous Houdini-like magician who had perished during his greatest escape trick. His friends and mentor gather in the basement of Hollywood's Magic Castle, hopeful of his promised return from the dead. The promise seems unfulfilled, and the mourners drink to his memory and depart. At last, when only his mentor remains, the floor cracks open and the magician appears; but before the portal to Purgatory is closed, one hundred spirits escape from the nether side. Each week's episode would have involved the magician's pursuit of the escaped spirits while he attempts to resolve the central mystery: his death was not accidental, but murder. Not a ghost but a living dead man, he must solve this crime in order to move on to a higher plane or perhaps even remain on earth, where he finds romance with his mentor's daughter.

'It had a very light heart to it,' Garris notes, 'in addition to the darkness.' The effective combination of anthological elements with an ensemble of continuing characters piqued the interest of producers through the 1990s – until, in 1998, Warner Brothers produced the short-lived Fox Television Network series *Brimstone*, which indulged a suspiciously similar premise. Peter Horton played Ezekiel Stone, a police officer who, when he dies in the line of duty, is condemned to Hell for the murder of his wife's rapist. When 113 souls escape from Satan's playground, the Devil offers Stone a second chance at life by acting as his bounty hunter and returning the souls to perdition.

Barker, pleased with Garris's work on 'Spirit City USA', decided in

1989 that Garris should script a planned full-throttle adaptation of the *Books of Blood* novella 'In the Flesh' as a feature film, which Barker planned to direct for Warner Brothers. Clive's pitch to the studio was blunt and direct: 'It's *Alien* in a prison.' He planned to deliver a ferocious film, and certainly not a punch-line horror movie: 'Very dark, very grim, very creepy,' Garris says. 'There was not much humour, other than the audaciousness of Clive's situations.'

When a looming conflict with the motion picture adaptation of *Cabal* made it unlikely that Barker could direct *In the Flesh*, Garris was asked to take over as director. A second draft screenplay was completed in November 1989, but the project simply frittered away in the hands of the studio: 'Like everything that doesn't go beyond the development stage,' Garris notes. 'Which is almost everything. The norm is that they don't get made.'

In the wake of this second stillborn project came the one motion picture developed by the collaboration that was, after nearly a decade, produced – but without any echo of their names, although it indulges Barker's puzzle box imagery: *The Mummy* (1999).

In 1989, Jim Jacks, an executive at Universal Studios (who later formed a production partnership for the movie with Sean Daniel) met with Barker and Garris to consider *The Egyptian Project*, an outline written by Clive for a film he proposed to direct from a script by Garris. 'It was great . . . and bizarre,' Garris says. 'I thought: *I cannot imagine a major studio making this movie.*' But the premise, with its Egyptian setting and imagery, seemed to fulfil Universal's plans to remake its classic *The Mummy* (1932), and the studio gave Garris the go-ahead to write the script. 'It's very twisted, very sexual, very creepy – not at all a studio picture; and not at all like the script for the movie that was finally made. The closest relative would have been *Chariots of the Gods*; but it's a very twisted sexual story, too, with ambisexuality at the heart of it. Not gay sexuality or bisexuality, but multisexuality. It's really a kick. All of it being guided by wanting to make a really scary movie, and not fill it with wisecracks. To this day, the studio has never given me notes on that first draft. They never even said, *No, we're not going to pursue this* . . . It just went away.'

Barker and Garris moved on to individual projects, with Garris scripting *The Fly II* (1989) and directing episodes of the television series 'Freddy's Nightmares' and 'Tales from the Crypt.' Universal asked George A Romero – and later, Joe Dante – to direct a more traditional remake of *The Mummy*; and Romero, John Sayles and Alan Ormsby wrote scripts. In 1994, Romero returned to the project and wrote three new drafts; Universal was excited about the film again, but parted ways with Romero and, in 1995, asked Garris to rewrite and direct the film. After several additional scripts, the project passed from his hands and through a series of other writers and directors until *The Mummy* was finally produced and released in 1999 with one of the more convoluted screenwriting credits in recent memory.[12]

In the meantime, Mick Garris had his first major success as a director in a project based on an original script by Stephen King: *Sleepwalkers* (1992). He decided to cast Clive as one of several cameo players: 'Clive can act, and he'd never done a movie; I thought it would be really cool for him to appear in a Stephen King story.' Thus Clive Barker's first feature film role as an actor found him playing a forensic examiner, 'starring' with King and Tobe Hooper (the director of *The Texas Chainsaw Massacre*, among other films) in a complex steadicam tracking shot.

After almost a decade, the creative collaboration between Barker and Garris found fruition in *Quicksilver Highway* (1997), a motion picture written and directed by Garris as the pilot for a potential Fox Television Network series. The film paired adaptations of Stephen King's short story 'Chattery Teeth' and Barker's *Books of Blood* classic 'The Body Politic' within a 'wraparound' scenario written by Garris and starring Christopher Lloyd. Garris's satiric rendition of 'The Body Politic' featured another cameo appearance by Barker, in the role of a physician. The tradition continued when Garris, as supervising producer of the ABC Television series 'The Others' (2000), again cast Clive in a cameo role in the episode 'Don't Dream It's Over'.

21

GOD'S MONKEY

THE GREAT AND SECRET SHOW (1989)

We will now discuss in a little more detail the Struggle for Existence.
— CHARLES DARWIN, *The Origin of the Species*

'Men once. Spirits now. Enemies forever.'[1]

Emboldened by the successes of the novel *Weaveworld* and the motion picture *Hellraiser*, Clive Barker repaired to the loft at Wimpole Street to chart his most ambitious project to date: an epic trilogy of novels known as 'The Art'. Not content to rest on laurels that he knew were temporary, Barker sought a narrative structure that would expand perceptions of his fiction and breach the boundaries of genre that seemed to confront him at every turn. The inspiration came foremost from his uneasy admiration for the 'trilogy of all trilogies', JRR Tolkien's *The Lord of the Rings* (1954–55), and his disappointment with the contemporary fantasists who laboured beneath its long shadow.

As a youth, Clive had preferred the dour, labyrinthine fantasies of ER Eddison, and particularly the Icelandic scholar's masterful first novel, *The Worm Ouroboros* (1922). When reading the lighter, more popular novels of Tolkien, he was enchanted by their insistent other-worldliness, but also by their girth. The epic length of *The Lord of the Rings* was a challenge as he pondered the creation of an alternate reality – separate from, but somehow linked to, our own – and how the saga of that otherworld should be told. Although the influences of Eddison and Tolkien resound in several of his novels, Tolkien's thrall has been tempered by what he found lacking in *The Lord of the Rings* – and what he has sought to provide in his modern variations.

'I once had a very pretentious friend who was a music fanatic,' Clive says. 'And when I went through my Wagner phase – and I was a huge Wagner fan, and to some extent, I still am – he said, *You'll grow beyond it to get to Mozart*. And I remember resenting that power-fully, because it implied that there was some hierarchy where the most refined spirit would understand Mozart only once they had been through the crasser composers – once they'd passed through Verdi and Puccini.

'I remember a similar thing being said about *The Lord of the Rings* by Ingastina Eubank, the person who taught me Shakespeare at univer-sity: that one day I would get beyond this, and I would get to the human drama. I was seventeen, eighteen, whatever, and I remember Ingastina, who wrote a lot on Shakespeare – she's a very bright lady – saying, *Why do you deal with these fantastical worlds?* Of course, if I'd had my wits about me, I'd have said, *Everything in Shakespeare is fantasy*. The only thing which isn't fantasy is its observations about human nature; and if any art is any good, then that's going to be there – it's going to be in *Reservoir Dogs*, it's going to be in *Peter Pan*, it's going to be there.'

Where Barker diverged most clearly from Tolkien was in an insist-ence that novels of fantasy should offer some literal connection to our reality. When early critics sought to find allegory in *The Lord of the Rings*, comparing its epic struggle between good and evil with the Second World War, Tolkien steadfastly denied that his fantasies had even metaphorical implications. Most contemporary fantastists likewise urge an escapist separation from realism and reality. Barker challenges the urgency of fantasy toward abstraction, recognizing that even the most realistic of fiction may transform into fantasy, if only through the passage of time:

'What's interesting about *Reservoir Dogs* is that it's of this moment, it's here and it's now. In forty years time, it will no longer be the here-and-now, it will be another thing; and if it's being seen, as well it might be, by people in forty years time, it will be as remote from their experience as *The Lord of the Rings*. When you read the *Newgate Calendar* – it's the *Reservoir Dogs* of its time – it's an account of the criminal underworld doing its thing and how they worked and how they were punished and so on. It reads now as some fabulously elaborate fantasy, because the vocabulary has changed; because what people were doing to one another has changed; because the punishments seem incredibly elaborate and arbitrary. What is realism will really only last you ten years, and then it becomes something else.'[2]

'The Art' was also, in a very real sense, Barker's creative journey to America. Its opening volume, *The Great and Secret Show* (1989), was the first of his novels to be set in the United States, and it seemed to underscore his growing belief that a move to America was inevitable to further his career in film and fiction.

The Great and Secret Show intentionally indulges what, by the late 1980s, was the salient template of contemporary horror fiction: the small town isolated and besieged by dark forces. Made classic by Stephen King in *'Salem's Lot* (1975) and nurtured to elegance in Peter Straub's *Ghost Story* (1979), this plot structure had become a staple (and, indeed, a cliché) of the putative genre when Barker took it, and with typical aplomb, shook at its very roots.[3]

Randolph Jaffe, 'a balding nobody with ambitions never spoken and rage not expressed', takes centre stage for the novel's opening act. At nearly thirty-eight years of age, Jaffe is a certified loser, slipsliding from job to job in hometown Omaha, Nebraska, until becoming a bottom-grade postal worker. Assigned to sort out the dead letters, Jaffe soon realizes that, as lord of lost mail, he sits at some spiritual crossroads of America. Within each torn envelope he glimpses the nation's secret life, and soon realizes the inevitable: 'the world was not as it seemed.'

Struck down by this sudden wisdom like Saul on the road to Damascus, Jaffe is converted to a faith he does not entirely comprehend:

> It was not about love. At least not as the sentimentalists knew it. Nor about death, as a literalist would have understood the term. It was – in no particular order – something to do with fishes, and the sea (sometimes the Sea of Seas); and three ways to swim there; and dreams (a lot about dreams); and an island which Plato had called Atlantis, but had known all along was some other place. It was about the end of the World, which was in turn about its beginning. And it was about Art.
>
> Or rather, *the* Art.

Although there are a myriad of ways to describe this strange something known as the Art, 'the exceptional mystery is that there was no Artist'.

Jaffe also discovers an enigmatic medallion, not unlike a crucifix: a cross of wood on which a human figure, *not* Christ, is suspended. In order to cloak his newfound wisdom, Jaffe murders his supervisor and sets the post office aflame; then he wanders the country, consumed by the need to learn more:

> There'd been much talk in the letters about *crossroads*, and for a long time he'd taken the image literally, thinking that in Omaha he was probably *at* that crossroads, and that knowledge of the Art would come to him there. But once out of the city, and away, he saw the error of such literalism. When the writers had spoken of crossroads they hadn't meant one highway intersecting with another. They'd meant places where states of being crossed, where the human system met the alien, and both moved on, changed. In the flow and flurry of such places there was hope of finding revelation.[4]

Like a mythical seeker of wisdom, lost in the wilderness, Jaffe finds a shaman in the desert outside Los Alamos, New Mexico: it is Kissoon, the last guardian of the Art, who dwells in a Loop – a place out of place, a time out of time.[5] Kissoon tells Jaffe of a mythic dream-sea known as Quiddity: '*Between this world, called the Cosm – also called the Clay, also called the Helter Incendo – between this world and the Metacosm, also called the Alibi, also called the Exordium and the Lonely Place, is a sea called Quiddity . . .*' Somewhere in that great sea is the island of Ephemeris – and on the island is the Great and Secret Show, which is seen three times: 'At birth, at death, and for one night when we sleep beside the love of our lives.'[6]

One of the dream-sea's shores is our reality, whose perimeters are sleep and death. On the far shore is the vast and complex Metacosm, dominated by an enigmatic species called the Iad Uroboros – named for the serpent that devours its own tail, symbolism immortalized by Eddison's *The Worm Ouroboros*. The Iad has dire appetites: 'For *purity*. For *singularity*. For *madness*.' They are a force of profound horror: 'The deepest terrors, the foulest imaginings that haunt human heads are the echoes of *their* echoes.'

Kissoon was a member of the Shoal, a tiny sect of seventeen 'who had one dogma, the Art, one heaven, Quiddity, and one purpose, to keep both *pure*'.[7] Guardians against invasion of the dream-sea by either species, man or Iad, all of the Shoal but Kissoon have been murdered.

When Kissoon rebuffs Jaffe at the seeming gates of Eden, the former postman finds an unlikely ally in Richard Wesley Fletcher. A visionary scientist of being and becoming – '*Alchemy, biology and metaphysics in one discipline*' – Fletcher was renowned for his evolutionary studies, but was disgraced by an addiction to mescaline. 'Like Jaffe, he believed heaven could be stolen.'[8]

With Jaffe's backing, Fletcher engineers the Nuncio, a miraculous synthesis of the evolutionary impulse whose first use advances an ape into a boy. Although Fletcher soon realizes his folly, he falls victim to the substance even as Jaffe embraces it. Rarefied by the Nuncio, they evolve into higher beings, demiurges of good and evil, yin and yang, locked in an eternal struggle. But as Salman Rushdie asked in *The Satanic Verses* (1988): Can good be evil, and evil good? Their warring incarnations plummet to earth in the small southern California town of Palomo Grove.

There, four teenaged virgins emerge from a swim in a pond of rainwater with insatiable sexual drives that cloak a more fervent desire:

for fertility. One of the girls, barren, goes insane; and although four children are conjured, one is killed by its mother, while the three survivors wait eighteen years to learn their destiny: Jo-Beth and Tommy-Ray McGuire, identical twins spawned by Jaffe's seed; and Howard Katz, sired by Fletcher.

After this mighty opening act, the plot escalates with a galvanizing of forces in the isolated town. Former television comedian Buddy Vance loses his way on a morning jog and stumbles into a crack in the earth, there to face the fallen angels that once were Jaffe and Fletcher: 'The forms emerging from the darkness a short distance from where he lay seemed in one moment to resemble men like himself, and in the next unalloyed energies, wrapped around each other like champions in a war of snakes, sent from their tribe to strangle the life from each other . . . Men once. Spirits now. Enemies forever.'[9]

The thing now called the Jaff feeds on Vance, summoning his terata – a prodigy born of his private fears and given primitive life, without face or mind but 'legs by the scrabbling dozen'. Riding the terata to the surface, the Jaff raises an army from the secret fears within the townspeople. It is a perfect recruiting station. Built on a faultline by greedy real estate magnates, Palomo Grove is the place where the American imagination, withered by comfort and complacency, has come to die: a planned community that had 'every facility but the facility to feel'. While mysteries walk and the earth cracks open to spit out wonders, the inhabitants of Palomo Grove sit watching game shows on TV.

Fletcher follows, with his allies, the hallucinogenia, born of a more rare element: rich and pungent imaginings. The terata and the hallucinogenia – pure projections of our subconscious lives – are the demons and the angels of this narrative. 'Fletcher thought of air and sky,' Jaffe laments, 'and I thought of power and bone. He made dreams from peoples' heads, I made stuff from their guts and sweat.' Each seeks to use these allies to reclaim his children.

Enter Nathan Grillo, a disgraced investigative journalist – his professional career frittered away in search of the hidden agenda, the life beneath the life – who has hit bottom as muckraker for a suburban newspaper: 'He was a reporter; a conduit between the known world and the unknown.'

It was his belief that nothing, but nothing, could stay secret, however powerful the forces with interests vested in silence. Conspirators might conspire and thugs attempt to gag but the truth, or an approximation of same, would show itself sooner or later, very often in the unlikeliest form. It was seldom hard facts that revealed the life behind the life. It was rumour, graffiti, strip cartoons and love songs. It was what people gabbled about in their cups, or between fucks, or read on a toilet wall.

The art of the underground ... rising to change the world.

The world is indeed changed. Vance's estate in the hills overlooking Palomo Grove – a cathedral of carnival, decorated with gaudy sideshow panels, 'the True Art of America' – becomes Jaffe's sanctuary. He desires to steal the dreams of America – not everyday dreams, but dreams of what it means to be born, and fall in love, and die: 'A dream that explains what *being* is for.' 'He'd be a thief in Heaven, and therefore King of Heaven, given that he'd be the only presence there qualified to steal the throne. He would own the dreamlife of the world; be all things to all men, and never be judged.'

Jaffe forfeits his reason in pursuit of godhood, and then he forfeits his life. Taking the guise of Buddy Vance, he holds a gathering at the gaudy mansion; for what darker creatures might he summon than those from the heart of Hollywood? 'He would find fears in these addicted, bewildered, inflated souls of a kind he'd never have found in the mere bourgeois.' As the guests – tinseltown's movers and shakers, studio executives, movie stars, agents – gather at the manse, he greets them, raising terata from their sordid souls.

The weakened Fletcher literally flames out, but not before passing his secrets to Tesla Bombeck, a feckless screenwriter. His act of self-immolation burns his hallucinogenia-producing soul into a hundred or so of the townspeople, who dream their personal divinities into existence; but humanity's gods prove a sad lot: the shallow and the superficial 'beautiful people', characters from television soap operas and game shows, models from billboards and magazines.

The novel's midsection, like that of *Weaveworld*, wanders, fraught with circumlocution, marshalling its complex impulses as it transforms itself, erasing the siege mentality of the small town horror novel by sallying forth to exotic territories. Tesla is dispatched by Fletcher's dying revelations to gather the remnants of the Nuncio and destroy it; but her mission is interrupted by Tommy-Ray, who wounds her and tastes the Nuncio. He is resurrected as the Death-Boy, cleansed of fear and flesh. There is no choice for Tesla: death or the Nuncio. Its kiss takes her straightaway into the dream wilderness of New Mexico, and the hut of the devious Kissoon in that place called Trinity: a movie set, a deserted sham, waiting for destruction. 'She was in a different place, but place was just another kind of being, and all states could, if the means were found, speak with every other state. Ape with man, man with moon. It was nothing to do with technologies. It was about the indivisibility of the world.'

Strengthened with the black soul of Hollywood, his spirit annealed for this moment of moments, the Jaff reaches for that place beyond our world, clutching at solid wall, '[p]ulling the substance of reality towards him as though it were made of sun-softened candy'.

> It was as if the whole room were projected on a cinema screen and the Jaff had simply snatched hold of the fabric, dragging it towards him. The projected image, which moments before had seemed so life-like, was revealed for the sham it was.
> *It's a movie*, Grillo thought. *The whole fucking world's a movie.*
> And the Art was the calling of that bluff. A snatching away of the sheet, the shroud, the screen.

What plays behind the silver screen of the world? At this moment Howie and his dream-army arrive; the battle that follows is purely physical, the stuff of men and dogs, two tribes tearing at each other, the didactic essential: 'Fletcher's love of light against the Jaff's passion for darkness.' But it is too late: the hole in the fabric of reality has been torn, and the Jaff is literally devoured by the abject terror of what he has seen waiting on the other side, while the three children – Howie, Jo-Beth, Tommy-Ray – and many others are taken, in terror or in ecstasy, through the psychedelic whirlpool and into Wonderland. 'Quiddity was the essential sea; the first, the fathomless.' Its waters make changes in its swimmers, as their bodies are reshaped in the image of their souls, rage and love and lust made solid. Ephemeris, the fabled island at its centre, resembles a vast, floating cathedral, the subconscious inspiration for the architectures of Gothic splendour. 'This was the place in which all his species that knew of glory got their glimpses. A constant place; a place of comfort, where the body was forgotten (except for trespassers like himself) and the dreaming soul knew flight, and mystery.'

It is indeed a holy place – a New Eden, but an Eden imperilled. As Death-Boy Tommy-Ray, floating in despair in the dream-sea, watches the placid sky darken, a simple knowledge consumes him: 'That there was an evil coming he had never known the likes of; that no one had ever known the likes of . . . It was called the *Iad*, this night, and the chill it brought had no equal on any planet in the system; even those so far from the sun they could bear no life. None owned a darkness this deep, this murderous.'

The Iad Uroboros are never seen, only their encroaching veil of darkness; but it is enough to offer a singular knowledge: 'Whatever the Iad were, they brought pain: relentless, unendurable. A holocaust in which every property of death would be explored and celebrated but the virtue of cessation, which would be postponed until the Cosm was a single human sob for release.'

There is still hope. 'Miracles happen,' Jo-Beth tells Howie, but he demurs: 'No they don't . . . They're made.' Pursuing an essential maxim of horror – that all good secrets are in our past, below us in an archaeological and an evolutionary sense – Tesla and Grillo descend into the crack in the earth to find what remains of the Jaff. Tesla bargains with the lunatic: her life for the meaning of the medallion. It is a crucifix, with evolution on one axis, from a single cell to Godhood, and on the other axis the Cosm and the Metacosm – what we know and what we don't know. In the middle is a figure with its arms outstretched, palms open – not Jesus, not flesh and blood at the crossroads, but a symbol of Quiddity: the mind. 'The figure was floating, in Quiddity, arms spread out as he, she, or it dreamed in the dream-sea. And somehow that dreaming was the place where everything originated: the first cause.'[10]

They emerge from the depths to find the Grove collapsing around them, the schism from Vance's house sending shockwaves through the earth, finally reducing the town to a grave of ashes: 'Its worse sin had been hypocrisy – going on its blithe, sunny way wilfully concealing its secret self.'[11]

In the aftermath comes the revelation of the true Trinity – not Father, Son and Holy Ghost, but Trinity, New Mexico, where the first atomic bomb was detonated on July 16, 1945: 'The Three-in-One reduced to a single place – a single event, indeed. This was the Trinity that superseded all others. In the imagination of the twentieth century the mushroom cloud loomed larger than God.' And it is the prison for Kissoon, who is revealed as the murderer of the Shoal.

Tesla, anointed by the Nuncio, is a female saviour: 'She didn't need to deny the confusions and contradictions to be powerful; she needed to embrace them.' Empowered by the drug and the sudden will to live, she swallows the scene and moves it to another stage, the wasteland of Trinity, into the light of the Loop's perpetual dawn, and with it the schism between our reality and that far shore.

> [M]ind was in matter, always. That was the revelation of Quiddity. The sea was the crossroads, and from it all possibilities sprang. Before everything, Quiddity. Before life, the dream of life. Before the thing solid, the solid thing dreamt. And mind, dreaming or awake, knew justice, which was therefore as natural as matter, its absence in any exchange deserving of more than a fatalistic shrug. It merited a howl of outrage; and a passionate pursuit of *why*. If she wished to live beyond the impending holocaust it was to shout that shout. To find out what crime her species had committed against the universal mind that it should now be tottering on execution. That was worth living to know.

As time in the Loop is unfettered, the beginning of Man's Last Madness, the nuclear explosion, and the promise of evolution – woman, man and ape in one bruised body – find the Iad undone, sealed in a moment of lost time.

'Without dreams,' this complex novel contends, 'life was nothing.' Clive Barker has sometimes called himself a 'Jungian horror writer' – and in a powerful sense, *The Great and Secret Show* was Barker's rendition of Jung's famous dream of walking the streets of Liverpool to discover 'the pool of life'. The pool's name, Barker suggests here, is Quiddity: the dream-sea in which we are transformed by our very thoughts and emotions.

The novel is, of course, a paean to the imagination, and to the power latent in the commonality of the pool of images available to human thought and experience. The rituals of religion and society and even entertainment seem directed at seeking stasis in that pool – in wanting still water; while Barker is insistent on stirring the sea.

Late in the pages of *The Great and Secret Show*, investigative reporter Nathan Grillo observes that 'the vocabulary was impoverished when it came to evil'. But the vocabulary of the novel is anything but impoverished; Barker deconstructs the template of *'Salem's Lot* and its endless imitations into a fiction of astounding (and sometimes confounding) complexity. From its opening pages, Barker removes the blinkers of genre: first ridding his text of icons (King's vampires, for example) and supplanting the familiar with unique beings whose supernatural existence also includes a theological argument. The text is alive with ambiguity, erasing the conventional vocabulary of God and Devil (although, as always, Barker reserves a special place for religious authoritarians who voice their beatitude when confronted with the strange, the different: 'There's not a clean soul among them! *Kill 'em all!*').

Most notable, perhaps, is the way in which *The Great and Secret Show* strives to rid Barker's readers of the notion, made popular by the *Books of Blood* and *Hellraiser*, that his art is intent on the explicit, the violent, the bloody, to the exclusion of more complex concerns. The early pages of *The Great and Secret Show* repeat the word 'subtle' – an unconscious mantra, perhaps, but also an indicator of a talent intent on moving ever forward. His refusal to skew his fiction to audience expectation earned critical respect – and the respect of his friends. As Doug Bradley notes: 'He could have very easily kept on churning out the *Books of Blood* for the next twenty or thirty years and made himself a millionaire. He could write five hundred *Books of Blood* – it's not an issue. So I respect him for, as always, not taking the easy route. He puts himself out on a limb. He puts himself in a position of danger of losing the audience that made him a bestselling author in the first place.' As the commercial response to *The Great and Secret Show* demonstrated, however, taking that risk actually brought him a larger audience.

The novel proved Barker's most successful book in America to date; its hardcover edition ascended onto the *New York Times* bestseller list on February 11, 1990, and it was the first of his books to sell over one million copies. Simon & Schuster's confused packaging and marketing of the US edition of *Weaveworld* were supplanted by the canny and sympathetic efforts of Eddie Bell at HarperCollins. *The Great and Secret Show* was the first Clive Barker novel to be published by HarperCollins in the United States. Taking the fiction at face value and without a generic spin, the publisher allowed Barker to transcend categories – and, indeed, to become a publishing category unto himself. The reviews were overwhelmingly positive; and although many reviewers applied the catchphrase 'magic realism', likening the text to the writings of Jorge Luis Borges and Gabriel García Márquez, the more accurate descriptive was, quite simply, dark fantasy – which Barker, unlike Tolkien and his many emulators, had elected to enact on a canvas that included reality.

'What I am striving toward constantly,' Barker notes, 'is a fantastical metaphor for the complexity of how we experience the world. Fantasy at its best allows us both external and internal impressions. We can move from the psychological to the physical to the surreal to the realistic, but the fantastic, like magic realism – I think one's a different way to describe the other – allows us a more total way to describe how we move in our lives, how we get through our lives, than "realistic" fiction. Because we live in our imaginations at least as much as we live in the "real" world. In other words, I would say fantastic fiction is a more truthful rendition or replication of the living experience. Because the living experience is also the dreaming experience, is also the fantasizing experience. And what I'm trying to represent on the page is not what it's like to get up in the morning and brush your teeth, but what it's like to get up in the morning and then dream of Never-Never Land for two minutes and then go take a crap. And what's missing in "realistic" fiction is the visit to Never-Never Land.'[12]

With *The Great and Secret Show*, Barker had secured, at last, critical respectability – and commercial success – on both sides of the Atlantic. Only five years earlier, the unknown playwright had licensed the world rights to the first three *Books of Blood* to Sphere for the sum of £1,000 per book. In January 1989, after Clive delivered the manuscript of *The Great and Secret Show* to William Collins, the publisher agreed to pay an 'unprecedented' advance of almost two million pounds for the UK rights to his next four novels.[13] Underscoring the publisher's belief in the power of Clive Barker's imagination, the agreement was based on a sheet of paper that simply listed four titles: *Cabal* Parts II and III, and the second and third books of 'The Art'. Over the next decade, only one of those novels would be completed. Having written of Hollywood and its Great and Secret Show, Clive Barker was about to become its victim.

22

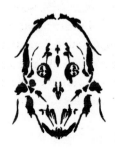

THE BASTARD CHILD

NIGHTBREED (1990)

Ah, the great brotherhood. It made Calloway want to spit, the familiar claims of sentiment. When he thought of the number of so-called allies that had cheerfully stabbed him in the back; and in return the playwrights whose work he'd smilingly slanged, the actors he'd crushed with a casual quip. Brotherhood be damned, it was dog eat dog, same as any over-subscribed profession.

— CLIVE BARKER, 'Sex, Death and Starshine'

'Movies change; and change; and change.'[1] These words, written by Clive Barker midway through the filming of the motion picture *Nightbreed* (1990), proved disturbingly prescient. The intended successor of *Hellraiser*, and Barker's first major-budget film, *Nightbreed* suffered from constant change at the hands of fate and financiers. Barker also suffered; his career in film-making nearly ended as swiftly as it had begun.

The closing years of the twentieth century were a time of new icons in horror cinema. The traditional monsters, defined in the Universal films of the 1930s and refined by Hammer in the 1950s and 1960s, were challenged by a series of masked cyphers with human names: Michael Myers, Jason Voorhees, Freddy Krueger. The elder statesmen – Frankenstein's monster, vampires, werewolves – were shunted aside in the 1980s (and then essayed in remarkably tame extravaganzas from 'mainstream' directors like Kenneth Branagh, Francis Ford Coppola and Mike Nichols) in favour of the natural born – or bred – killer, who found his ultimate expression in Dr Hannibal Lecter of *Manhunter* (1984) and *The Silence of the Lambs* (1989).

Upon winning a Best Actress Oscar for her encounter with Dr Lecter, Jodie Foster pronounced that *The Silence of the Lambs* was not a 'horror' film – and perhaps, for all the wrong reasons, she was right. With its ever-increasing emphasis on special effects, the generic horror film of the 1980s had too often reduced the actor to a marginal role as a dimensionless but blood-ripe tally in the body count. Lost in the thrall of ever-escalating special effects (now taken from the eye of the camera and imposed by computer graphics), directors and audiences alike had forgotten the essential humanity of horror: that it is an emotion, not an image or an event. A generation of film-makers and film-goers was experiencing a 'horror' film that was more concerned with seeing than with feeling, and whose frame of reference was not human experience but prior films. As homage followed sequel followed remake, a circle was closing – the once-dangerous serpent that offered the forbidden fruit of horror was eating its own tail.

Despite a parallel rise in the popularity of horror fiction, these films rarely adapted contemporary novels and stories (except in the case of the ubiquitous Stephen King); and indeed, they often told no story at all. Situational horror was the vogue, and the situation obsessively shown and reshown was a vision of humanity trapped and besieged by an insanity seeded somewhere in the past – a rather convenient analogy for crime, disease, terrorism, a perceived loss of control. As always, the horror film was showing us dire truths that we preferred not to acknowledge: David Cronenberg warned us of HIV just as surely as George A Romero warned us of Waco. And each director offered bitter prophecies of the state of the horror film as we slouched toward the Millennium: the television that created life in its own image, the zombies who were us.

After an initial success, usually with an independent low-budget feature, many directors of successful horror films were swallowed up by the genre or the broader motion picture establishment, usually via a sequel, a remake or a Stephen King adaptation. The truth was as inevitable as it was bitter: horror film is an outlaw artform whose power is usually diminished by success within the industry – which, like any other business, is concerned with safe, marketable commodities defined by dollar signs and not aesthetics. Only a handful of directors seem to have escaped the phenomenon relatively unscathed; even Cronenberg, Romero and Dario Argento, who fought to remain independent, have suffered by making movies that were inadequately budgeted and ineptly distributed.

Clive Barker sought to transcend this problematic environment with *Nightbreed*, 'a small epic of the *fantastique*' based upon his short novel *Cabal*. This cinematic night journey would redeem his 'magical' concept for *Underworld*, leading viewers into a dark underground to 'confront buried mysteries' of self and society:

> Those mysteries bite. Several of the Breed have an appetite for human meat. Some are more bestial than human; others have a touch of the Devil in them, and are proud of the fact. To set foot in their domain is to risk death at their hands. But it is also a chance to see the lives of Naturals like ourselves from another perspective. The workings of the world seem a little more preposterous through the eyes of monsters.[2]

After his fitful start as screenwriter for George Pavlou's wounded adaptations, and his triumph as writer and director of *Hellraiser*, Barker understood that motion pictures were more often about commerce than art. Although his innocence had been lost in the making of *Underworld* and *Rawhead Rex*, his experience on *Hellraiser* had been so positive, and the film so well-received, that he and producer Chris Figg pressed on to *Nightbreed* – and a budget several times that of *Hellraiser* – with a confidence and, perhaps, cockiness that would unravel into chaos as the film neared completion.

Until *Nightbreed*, Barker's singular disappointment with the motion picture industry was its eagerness to censor, and to kowtow to edits and ratings demanded by his contracts, the British Board of Film

Classification and the Motion Picture Association of America.[3] But his wars over snipped seconds of celluloid would soon seem like minor skirmishes; in *Nightbreed*, his creative vision was corrupted and, indeed, lost – not to censors, but to his own backers.

At its conception, the film seemed unique and unstoppable, a provocative vehicle for bringing monsters to life in a vivid and convincing way – and not as a horror film but a fantasia. Even before writing *Cabal*, Barker had described the story to Bob Keen and Geoff Portass of Image Animation, who had supervised the special effects for *Hellraiser* and *Hellbound: Hellraiser II*; he met again with them in the summer of 1988, and together they began sketching out the designs of creatures that would fulfil the alternate mythology of the novel. When the book was complete, Barker and Chris Figg took the project to Joe Roth at Morgan Creek, the American production company that had financed David Cronenberg's *Dead Ringers* (1988); on the strength of the text, and *Hellraiser*, Morgan Creek agreed to finance *Nightbreed* with an $11 million budget.

Although *Nightbreed* is set entirely in Canada, only one week of location shooting was conducted there. Principal photography took place on five soundstages at London's Pinewood Studios, with Robin Vidgeon again serving as cinematographer. By then, Barker dreamed of creating 'the *Star Wars* of monster movies', and considerable expense was lavished on realization of the creatures, which was accomplished almost entirely through make-up, prosthetics and other in-camera effects.

Casting the creatures was a pleasant and sometimes familiar task. Clive called upon Doug Bradley for the role of Lylesburg, the Nightbreed's law-giver; fellow Dog Company alumni Oliver Parker for the rebellious Peloquin; and two other former Cenobites (Nicholas Vince, who played Kinski, and Simon Bamford, who played Ohnaka). Bradley wasn't entirely happy with his part, which seemed like a 'watered down' version of Pinhead; but the project struck him as something quite strong: 'I was convinced we were making an outstanding movie. What we were shooting was a very faithful adaptation of *Cabal*. It was clear to me that we were *not* making a horror film. We were making a dark fantasy, a fantasy-romance about the love between a girl and a dead man. And that's not the movie that people saw.'

In an inspired casting choice, Barker persuaded legendary director David Cronenberg to play psychotic psychiatrist Philip Decker, who manipulates the night's hero, Boone, into believing he is a serial killer. Boone, played by hunky Craig Sheffer, escapes from custody in search of the mythical refuge of monsters known as Midian. Pursued by his girlfriend, Lori (Anne Bobby) – and, in time, by Decker – Boone finds refuge and revelation beneath an isolated Canadian cemetery. He discovers the fabulous Nightbreed, creatures of myth and legend, and learns that he is indeed a monster, but not a murderer: he is a shape-shifting prophecy, Cabal, the reluctant saviour of the Breed. But his arrival also signals the destruction of Midian; and Decker, eager to make Boone his scapegoat, finds willing accomplices in the local authorities – led by Sheriff William Eigerman (Charles Haid) and Reverend Ashberry (Malcolm Smith) – who set upon the Nightbreed with xenophobic fervour.[4]

The story was intended to juxtapose the excesses of conventional monster movies with the fantasia of Midian, following the journey of apparently doomed lovers, Boone and Lori, into and out of a fractured Wonderland. Its finale would offer a telling concatenation of monsters: the ancient, indeed mythic, creatures known as the Nightbreed; the late twentieth century's monster, the serial killer Decker; and the insistently human monsters, the paragons of law and order named Eigerman and Ashberry. The subversive flair seemed obvious: for once the monsters were the 'good guys', and the forces of the rational and conventional were exposed as 'evil'. As Barker notes: 'I liked the idea of the secret breed; I liked the idea of the guy who was going there for the wrong reasons, who thought he was guilty and wasn't. But most particularly, I liked the idea, thematically, of the old monsters against the new monsters.' The theme had been honoured consistently in his fiction; but well into the filming of *Nightbreed*, it seemed suddenly repulsive to the money men.

The turning point is, to quote Doug Bradley, a 'thorny subject' for all concerned. Bradley noted, early on, that the 'atmosphere had changed'. Tension on the set was apparent, and increasing daily. The ambitions of Barker and his creative team far surpassed their budget, and Morgan Creek was troubled by the spiralling expenses. Twenty-five sets were constructed at Pinewood; and Image Animation's special effects crew, which originally numbered a sizable thirty members, expanded to fifty-one people during the busiest phases, while the number of creatures to be shown on camera increased from fifty to nearly two hundred. The original budget of $11 million had been exceeded and, according to some sources, the final budget totalled well over $20 million.[5]

Seven weeks into filming, Bradley arrived on the set one morning and was told that producer Chris Figg 'had been sacked' – although, in fact, Figg had resigned in a dispute with Morgan Creek over the budget, nobly taking the fall for the financial excesses so that Barker could complete the shoot. The cast and crew were confused and concerned, but the worst was yet to come.

Morgan Creek had entered into a distribution agreement with Twentieth Century-Fox, which apparently had expected a big-budget version of *Hellraiser*. When Fox executives viewed Barker's cut of *Nightbreed*, the reaction was swift and cynical. In Doug Bradley's view: 'The bad guys, as far as I'm concerned, were Twentieth Century-Fox. They couldn't get the fact that the monsters were the good guys. And also, I think, it was the first point at which being the "future of horror" jumped back smack in Barker's face. It was: *We're giving these millions of dollars to you, the "future of horror", the director of* Hellraiser, *and you're telling us that this is* not *a horror film?*'

Fox decided to add three weeks to the production schedule, ostensibly for an 'enhancement shoot' with three new monsters, but in fact to force creative revisions that indulged its commercial perception of the film. Several new scenes were lensed, including an expository sequence with screen veteran John Agar and a coda obviously intended as the set-up for a sequel. Several actors, including Doug Bradley, were overdubbed with the voices of others (Bradley laughs in derision: 'Some fuckwit producer obviously fell out of bed one day and thought, *Hey, Lylesburg . . . he's German!*') Then Barker and his editor, Richard Marden, flew to Hollywood to meet again with studio representatives, only to learn that their revision of *Nightbreed* – which incorporated the new scenes but also, at Fox's demand, had been shortened from the two and a half hours of the original director's cut to two hours – should be subjected to further radical surgery. Fox demanded that the film be pared to ninety minutes, with the plot focused on Decker the serial killer, not the Nightbreed. Marden told Morgan Creek: 'I don't want to be a part of this – send me back to England.'

The final cut was assigned to the editor of *The Terminator* (1984), Mark Goldblatt, and a young assistant, Alan Baumgarten. The result, in Baumgarten's words, was that 'the film essentially was done by committee – the producers put a lot of heat and pressure on Clive and he was cornered'. Baumgarten is one of the few people who has seen the original two and a half hour director's cut: 'I remember liking it very much – feeling that it was a little long in places, but that it really worked.' As a result, performing the radical edits required by Fox 'was a tough job'.

The tragedy continued even after the film was re-edited; as Barker puts it: 'We were banned; there were seventeen scenes that the MPAA [Motion Picture Association of America] said had to go out. And this was a movie where we felt we would have no troubles at all ... The level of my own naïveté constantly startles me. Thematically the movie just got up people's noses. There were people who said – and they actually said this to me – *You can't make the monsters the good guys. You can't do it. And we're going to be hard on this movie because the monsters are the good guys.* It never even occurred to me. I mean, truly, I was that naïve. It never occurred to me that people would not see the liberal message which was contained here. But they didn't, and the MPAA came after it and so there was a lot of that stuff taken out.

'I mean, it got hit from all sides. When I look at horror movies as a genre, I see that it is completely out of step. There's very little out there that you can loosely call a horror movie whose heart is in the same place. That's both a huge weakness and finally its strength. I think it will be an interesting curiosity for a long time to come because of that. Because it contains that sort of fondness for the monstrous.'

The final outrage came one week before the film's release, when Twentieth Century-Fox disclosed its promotional campaign, which pitched *Nightbreed* as a 'slasher' film. Compromised, corrupted, eviscerated and then misrepresented, *Nightbreed* was released to lukewarm reviews and quickly disappeared from cinemas. Although its imagery is occasionally extraordinary, its narrative is the confused aftermath of a battle between creator and studio – which neither, of course, won.

'What is worse,' Barker says, 'is that I actually said to the prime players at Fox, *You fucked this* – and they said, *Yes, we did.*'

'I think he was stung very badly,' says David Dodds. 'I knew it was pretty bad because he came back home totally drained and very on-edge, saying that he probably wouldn't make another film for a long time. I think it changed his perception of the Hollywood life. I wouldn't necessarily say he became harder. He became more business-minded.'

The experience changed Clive's perspective on film-making – and his life. Only weeks after the film's release, he sat with me in a Manhattan bar, haggard and sad, and talked at length about the jeremiad of *Nightbreed*:

'I laboured for a year to put this movie on the screen. In my painting and my writing, I am in complete control of what I do. In movies, I am giving myself over to people over whom I have no power whatsoever. When I started making movies, with *Hellraiser*, I did it to get power over the product. I had seen people like Steve King and Ray Bradbury have wonderful books turned into really terrible movies and I wanted to stop that for myself. Now I'm more secure in the fact that the books will last. I'm going to have to live with other people making them into movies, and get on with what I want to do.

'I like making movies. I like working with other people. But I don't like it enough to let it make me lose sleep. And there are horrible things associated with the making of movies. Dealing with monstrous egos, dealing with people who actually have a hold over you.

'I've spent a year with some key players in the system, whose intellects and imaginations – how should we put this? – left room for improvement. And I'm not a masochist. I don't want to go back into their company.

'I'm glad that *Citizen Kane* exists, but I wish that, once Welles realized that the system was not going to accommodate his excesses any further, he'd turned to books. Because there was a genius frittered away in the politics. And it ain't going to happen to me.'

Despite the agonies of *Nightbreed*, even then he had no doubt that he would direct again. 'It's too much fun not to. But the cinema of the *fantastique* is primarily about spectacle. In books you can concern yourself with character and narrative thrust and so on, but in a horror or fantasy movie, character development means fuck all. What is Fay

Wray's character development – that she ends up regretting that she killed the gorilla? Cinema is about Fay Wray in King Kong's hands. It's about the head sprouting legs and walking away in John Carpenter's *The Thing*. It's about dreaming with your eyes open.

'I enjoy creating these kinds of images. But do the philosophical aspects of my books have a cinematic equivalent? No way. I can throw away the whole meaning of a movie in a paragraph or a sentence of a book.

'Cinema is great fun, but I have to view it as an indulgence. Because it *is* an indulgence. As an art form, it's the equivalent of potent graffiti.'

The filming of *Nightbreed* was, perhaps, the most trying time of Clive's professional life. In pursuit of his vision, he had lost control – not merely over his own creation, but over himself. He was drinking more, smoking cigars at a near-addictive pace, not taking care of himself – 'burning himself up,' says Mary Roscoe. To make matters worse, he fell off a stage in an accident and tore a ligament in his groin, which required surgery.

'I was not in great shape,' he says, looking back from the safe distance of years. 'But I felt like I'd lost it. I felt like I had lost the battle.

'It was the worst creative time in my life. I felt like there was so much I could have achieved and so many things which were getting between me doing that – some of them were my own making, some of them not. And I was painfully ignorant of the way that the politics of this business work; I mean, I was just a complete naif, and that was about being there in London as opposed to being here in Los Angeles – and, you know, coming over here once in a while and putting on the dog and pony show, and then you get on the plane and you go away and you're out of their minds. You are an insignificant player.

'I'm not saying I'm a significantly significant player now, but I am certainly more than I was then, because I'm here now, because I have deals, because I do all the politicking. You cannot make movies without being a personality, until maybe you've made an awful lot of movies and they've been hugely successful and then maybe you can return to a kind of controlled anonymity like George Lucas . . . I don't work in a genre that can be massively lucrative; I mean, it can never be lucrative at the level of *Home Alone*, because there just isn't that scale of audiences for this kind of material – there never has been. So what you have to say, and what I'm quite willing to say, is that I'll make these movies for a relatively modest amount of money, and I'll protect them as best I can and then I'll move on.

'And what *Nightbreed* taught me to do is to just get on – fuck, move on. You can lick your wounds and you can blame everybody in sight, but at the end of the day – I still believe that if I could one day get out of the vaults all the fucking stuff that should be in *Nightbreed* but isn't, and have the half-million dollars that it would take to reinstate it and give people the two-and-a-half-hour *Nightbreed*, it could be a really splendid movie; but it isn't there. And what is there is broken-backed as a consequence, but even in its broken-backed state, I don't think it's a bad picture. I think there's some very interesting, nice things going on in the picture, and they come out of the fact that the movie is what it is, which is a sort of *cri de coeur* on behalf of the monster. There's still a great paucity of sophistication in my technique as a maker of films, but even in its bastardized form, it's a reasonably deeply-felt picture.

'I am making an argument, if you will; it's a dialectic of a movie – on the one hand, the rationalist who is actually a secret child murderer, and on the other, the monsters who have enjoyed generations of burning and persecution. It's a movie which clearly played into a whole bunch of personal myths about my audience and about me. And a lot of black people like the movie, a lot of gay people like the movie, a lot of the people in black who read Neil Gaiman's *Sandman* like the movie – because the movie is on the side of the people who get kicked in the guts.

'Now that I look back on it, I'm surprised that anybody allowed me to make the movie, because it's got financial screw-up written all over it. The only way I could have gotten away with it is if I had been very sentimental about it. In that case, it wouldn't even have been a monster movie. *Edward Scissorhands* does the same thing in a way, but it's a fable, you know, and he's very sad.

'I wanted to have my cake and eat it. I wanted the monsters to have some of the monstrousness, which I think is a necessary part of capturing people's imaginations. I don't like Edward Scissorhands; I want to slap him and say, *Oh, for God's sake, just get an operation* – because he annoys me. But I like Peloquin. He's got a kind of fierce, unapologetic quality: *I am who I am, so take it or leave it.* And there wasn't enough of that in the final movie. I was served by a couple of really nice performances and a lovely score from Danny Elfman and some nice visuals. So it's not by any means a satisfying picture, but I have a fondness for it. It seems weird to say, but its heart was in the right place.'

So was the heart of Clive Barker: in the midst of all the pressure and the pain, there were moments when he found the time to escape the role of writer, director and burgeoning celebrity, and indulge the simple pleasures of friendship. While principal photography was underway at Pinewood Studios, former Dog Company member Mary Roscoe was acting in a far less heady locale: a pub theatre in Leicester Square, playing a prostitute in a fringe adaptation of Dostoevski. The play had foundered, and one evening, there was only one person in attendance. All she could see at first were his white Reebok trainers. Then: 'I suddenly realized that those trainers were Clive's – and that he was the only one in the audience.'

There were other, more complicated pleasures. While in Los Angeles during the film's pre-production, Clive met actor Malcolm Smith at a dinner party.

Born in North Carolina in 1960, Smith graduated from Boston University in 1982, where he held a scholarship in the acting program. After performing for several years in television commercials and theatre in New York City, he moved to Los Angeles in 1986 in search of motion picture roles.

Clive was smitten by Malcolm's striking good looks and enthusiastic charm. Soon Malcolm was cast as Ashberry, the twisted minister in *Nightbreed*, and the two men pursued a cloistered, long-distance romance for almost two-and-a-half years. They started talking about living together as Clive pondered the continuing call of Hollywood. 'Ultimately,' Malcolm says, 'we both took a deep breath, and he moved here.'

Mary Roscoe wasn't surprised: 'Clive has always had a deep fear or dislike of heterosexual behaviour, settling down with one person. He's always needed a partner, but he's always wanted freedom to express himself through other relationships, especially friendships.' His best friend, David Dodds, remained at his side, and would move to America and continue in his role as personal assistant. Clive, in turn, would lose himself in his work, turning from the disastrous outcome of *Nightbreed* to his longest and most difficult novel, *Imajica*.

23

AND DEATH SHALL HAVE
NO DOMINION

IMAJICA (1991)

*The greatest event in the history of the Earth, now taking place,
may indeed be the gradual discovery, by those with eyes to see, not
merely of Some Thing but Some One at the peak created by the
convergence of the evolving Universe upon itself . . .*

    There is only one Evil: Disunity.

      − PIERRE TEILHARD DE CHARDIN, *The Future of Man*

True to its title, Clive Barker's *Imajica* (1991) is an invocation of magic
and the imagination, an epic novel whose eerie and erotic enchantment
resists the convenient labels by which fiction is marketed today.[1] In
its 800-plus pages – his longest novel to date – Barker again slips the
bonds of genre, mingling realism and the *fantastique* with the abandon
of a consummate dreamer. Although staggering in its weight and
complexity (later paperback editions were split into two volumes),

329

Imajica perfects Barker's vision of transforming the dialogue of horror and fantasy, the mysterious and the mundane, into a singular pursuit of (im)possibilities.

The novel opens with deceptive simplicity, in the machinations of television soap opera: Charles Estabrook, a bathroom fixtures tycoon, decides in a fit of passion and pique to kill his estranged wife, Judith Odell. He hires a mysterious assassin, Pie'oh'pah, to perform the deed; but Judith is spared through the intervention of a former lover, John Furie Zacharias, otherwise known as Gentle – a dissolute, womanizing artist whose forté is forgery. What results is one of the more peculiar and perilous love triangles in contemporary literature.

As we have come to expect of Barker's fiction, no one – indeed, no world – is who or what it seems. The attempted murder is the first salvo in a conflict beyond space and time. Our reality is only one of five Dominions, the In Ovo, sundered by a tragic mystery from the greater universe: Imajica.

Judith is born not of flesh, but magic: she is a simulacrum, a twin created in centuries past to satisfy the urges of competing lovers; and as a willing hostage to desire and destiny, she becomes the Helen of Troy of this surreal manifesto. 'Here was the woman for the love of whom this whole sorry catalogue of death and desolation had been started, and in her company he felt himself renewed, as though the sight of her reminded his cells of the self he'd been before his fall.'

The hitman Pie'oh'pah – 'Nobody and nothing' – is another outsider; he is a 'mystif', an androgynous shapeshifter who assumes the form most pleasing to its beholder. Its genitalia are less sexual than an evocation of the purity of dreams:

> It was neither phallic nor vaginal, but a third genital form entirely, fluttering at its groin like an agitated dove and with every flutter reconfiguring its glistening heart, so that Gentle, mesmerized, found a fresh echo in each motion. His own flesh was mirrored there, unfolding as it passed between Dominions. So was the sky above Patashoqua and the sea beyond the shuttered window, turning its solid back to living water. And breath, blown into a closed fist; and the power breaking from it: all there, all there.

Gentle is seemingly immortal; greedy for sensation, he has 'been loved and lionized: for his charm, for his profile, for his mystery . . . For two centuries he'd never had to ask the questions that vexed every other soul at some midnight or other.' The questions, of course, are imperative to the human condition: 'Who am I? What was I made for, and what will I be when I die?' Now he suffers for his state: 'I want to be one man with one life. I want to know where I begin and where I end, instead of going on and on . . . I'm afraid there'll be no end to it . . . [a]nd then I'm going to be lost. I want to be this man, or that man, but not every man. If I'm everyone I'm no one, and nothing.'[2]

When Pie'oh'pah takes Judith's form and seduces him, the artist is repulsed, then obsessed, finding revelation and redemption in the shapeshifter's arms. Gentle is the Son of God, the most recent in a succession of would-be saviours (Jesus Christ among them) whose ministry is the literal healing of the Imajica: the splintered realm of the imagination, in waking and sleep, worship and dreams, and ultimately in death.[3] He has lived nineteen lives since his birth, his unconscious programmed by Pie 'to ease him out of one life and into another in a fog of self-ignorance that only lifted when the deed was done, and he awoke in a strange city, with a name filched from a telephone book or a conversation. He'd left pain behind him, of course, wherever he'd gone . . .'[4]

In the prologue of the *Books of Blood*, Barker wrote of a phenomenology of Five Worlds. The Imajica is that realm, its five Dominions separated not by space or time, but by the frailty of human spirit and imagination. Once in every two hundred years comes a moment when the Fifth Dominion, the Earth of our waking hours, may be reconciled with its lost continents, and the Imajica made whole; but, with every two hundred years, there has been failure.

The date of reconciliation is approaching, but Gentle's calling as a messiah is challenged at every turn – ridicule, repression, reprisal and revolution, the stormclouds of millennial chaos brewing – and finally brings him face-to-face with his father, God Himself. Hapexamendios is the deity of the Old Testament and fundamentalist fervour – vengeful, proprietary and singularly male. In ages past He has stamped out all competition, particularly the worship of goddesses: 'He was One, and simple. They were many, and diverse ... Hapexamendios came into the Dominions with a seductive idea: that wherever you went, whatever misfortune attended you, you needed only one name on your lips, one prayer, one altar, and you'd be in His care.'

As in 'Rawhead Rex' and other Barker fictions, the reigning masculine must confront the problematic feminine – and, confirming the analysis of Julia Kristeva, 'confesses through its very relentlessness against the other, the feminine, that it is threatened by an asymmetrical, irrational, wily, uncontrollable power.'[5]

At the heart of *Imajica* is an intensely subversive inquiry into the figure of Jesus Christ that confronts Judeo-Christian mythology and its penchant for sexism and suffering, blind faith and obedience, and apocalyptic inevitability. It is a collision of Testaments, Old versus New: the God of repression and retribution is confronted, and at last overthrown, by the God of love.

From his earliest plays and stories, Barker has repeatedly exercised his distaste for the hypocrisy and hate-mongering instincts of organized religion – fundamentalism and Catholicism in particular – but he finds the story of Jesus, and its depiction in the artwork of William Blake, Gerard Manley Hopkins and so many others, intensely moving and powerful. In *Imajica* he sought to interrogate the failure of contemporary fantasies to embrace the central figure of Western mythology. He intended to 'snatch this most complex and contradictory mystery from the clammy hands of the men who have claimed it for their own in recent years, especially here in America. The Falwells and the Robertsons, who, mouthing piety and sowing hatred, use the Bible to justify their plots against our self-discovery. Jesus does not belong to them. And it pains me that many imaginative people are so persuaded by these claims to possession that they turn their backs on the body of Western mysticism instead of *reclaiming* Christ for themselves.'[6]

This mammoth text poses a singular question: 'Why should she care what Lord it was ... as long as He came?' Barker asserts that we should care greatly, and that is the novel's insistent message: that if God indeed made us in His image, then we should strive, in turn, to make Him in ours. To do that, in Gentle's words: 'We have to be whole ... We have to be ... reconciled ... with everything we ever were before we can go on ... before we can get home [to the] place before the cradle. Heaven.' And with that reconciliation, that knowledge of ourself, comes a powerful truth:

'He can't hurt me any more.'
'Who can't?' Clem asked.
'My enemy,' Gentle replied, turning his face into the sunlight.
'Myself.'

Imajica thus offers a uniquely contemporary – and Christian – fable that dispenses with the cant of organized religion as well as the medieval mindset that typifies traditional fantasy novels. There are no dragons or gryphons here, but the modern monstrosities of censorship and homelessness and AIDS. Barker indulges neither the sword-and-sinew heroics of JRR Tolkien nor the cloying metaphors of CS Lewis and Charles Williams. Instead *Imajica* offers an existential-romantic quest, a speculation on the nature of woman and man, Goddess and God, Jesus and Christ, reality and dream. Its most apparent influence is the all-but-forgotten wonderwork, read in Clive's childhood at Tiree, of British fantasist ER Eddison.

'If we were Gods,' asked Eddison in his novels of the Machiavellian paradise called Zimiamvia, 'able to make worlds and unmake 'em as we list, what world would we have?' This is the central dilemma of *Imajica*: the nature and means of creation (and, thus, salvation). Worlds within worlds, stories within stories, characters within characters, phantasms within phantasms, this is a majestic maze of myth-making, a fiction that questions all assumptions of its reality – and our own. In these pages, Barker proves more than a dreamer extraordinaire. Taking his rightful place among the very best writers of the dark fantastic, he offers a fiction of (im)possibilities as the truest mirror of our lives, one that shines back brightly the depths and heights of the human spirit as well as the surfaces of the skin.

Central to his critique is the fundamentalist conception of God as a being obsessed with repression and control – and the inconsistency of this idea with the God of creation. The notion of an authoritarian God, Barker posits, is the source of stagnation, alienation, segregation, decay and inevitable self-destruction. Hapexamendios is not omnipotent: he could not truly defeat, but merely entrap, the goddesses; and he is imperfect, 'as if he'd forgotten what it was like to be whole'.

> His head was enormous, the shards of a thousand skulls claimed from the buildings to construct it, but so mismatched that the mind it was meant to shield was visible between the pieces, pulsing and flickering. One of His arms was vast, yet ended in a hand scarcely larger than Gentle's, while the other was wizened, but finished with fingers that had three dozen joints. His torso was another mass of misalliances, His innards cavorting in a cage of half a thousand ribs, His huge heart beating against a breastbone too weak to contain it and already fractured. And below, at His groin, the strangest deformation: a sex He'd failed to conjure into a single organ, but which hung in rags, raw and useless.

Like the angel Uriel of *Weaveworld*, this God plans a holocaust of fire to pass final judgment on Imajica, destroying the goddesses and all living things – a cleansing that will give him a world he will possess alone. He destroys Gentle's mother with a 'single blinding flame'; but since Imajica, once completed, is a circle, the flame returns to him: 'Behind Him, now the fire. As it came Gentle thought he saw his mother's face in the blaze, shaped from ashes, her eyes and mouth wide as she returned to meet the God who'd raped, rejected, and finally murdered her. A glimpse, no more, and then the fire was upon its maker, its judgment was absolute . . .'

God is dead. The corruption latent in Hapexamendios's paternal power-mongering is revealed in a vision of the First Dominion, 'decayed from horizon to horizon. Everywhere rot, and more rot: suppurating lakes of it, and festering hills.' With the death of this impostor – and 'the centuries-old encrustation of power plays and rituals' enacted by popes and pastors – a new world is born: a world of the reconciled.

> It was not, it seemed, an earth at all, but another sky, and in it was a sky so majestic that to his eyes all the bodies in the heavens of the Imajica – all stars, all moons, all noonday suns – could

not in their sum have touched its glory. Here was the door that his Father's city had been built to seal, the door through which his mother's name in fable had been whispered. It had been closed for millennia, but now it stood open, and through it a music of voices was rising, going on its way to every wandering spirit in the Imajica and calling them home to rapture.

Order, Barker concludes, is an intrinsically sterile state, a façade constructed by those with power to maintain their power – and to cloak the decaying and corrupt consciousness that seeks only to control. When its artifice is exposed, the seeming decay and corruption may be seen in a new light as the fertile chaos of creation. The restored Imajica is thus a new and hopeful realm, governed not by the restoration of order, but by the restoration of possibilities.

Barker, like his reluctant messiah Gentle, is driven by 'his painter's hunger to see'; and *Imajica* is foremost a novel about the artist's desperate quest to understand and reconcile the world around him with the disparate worlds of his imagination – his hopes, his fears, his dreams – and the mythology of a saviour: 'All these mysteries were, she knew, part of a single system if she could only grasp it: one form becoming another, and another, and another, in a glorious tapestry of transformations, the sum of which was Being itself.' Along the way, Barker's by-now-familiar obsessions are enacted: reality unfolding like a puzzle box; unholy scavengers lurking in the shadows and the cracks in the wall; damnation as redemption; desire as the measure of life and of death; and good and evil, gods and devils, as interchangeable conceits.

To the uninitiated, it might seem curious that a writer who so swiftly had become an icon of our popular culture would abandon the source of his celebrity – horror – and move on to uncharted regions; but once again, Barker had proved that his ambition was boundless. Indeed, it is from ambition that *Imajica* suffers, overlong and weighed down with enough descriptive baggage for several epics.

This is a grandiose novel: a book that demands patience and perseverance of its readers, and delivers great and secret things in return. As Gentle realizes in the closing act, knowledge is not dispensed simply.

The journey to reconciliation and self-realization may take years – perhaps even a lifetime:

> He doubted there'd be an instant of revelation ... It would most likely be slow, the work of years. Rumours at first, that bridges wreathed in fogs could be found by those eager enough to look. Then the rumours becoming certainties, and the bridges becoming causeways, and the fogs great clouds, until, in a generation or two, children were born who knew without being taught that the species had five Dominions to explore and would one day discover its own Godhood in its wanderings. But the time it took to reach that blessed day was unimportant. The moment the first bridge, however small, was forged, the Imajica was whole; and at that moment every soul in the Dominion, from cradle to deathbed, would be healed in some tiny part and take their next breath lighter for the fact.

Imajica is occasionally compared with Stephen King's metaphysical epic *The Stand* (1977), in which humanity, decimated by disease, struggles with supernatural forces while reinventing the sociopolitical pact. Although vastly different texts, each novel is weighty (and, indeed, the longest book by each writer) and illuminates Biblical themes in fantastical contexts. Although *The Stand* is highly popular, it is among Barker's least favourite Stephen King novels: 'I generally don't like post-apocalyptic fiction. I like my apocalypses to contain giant insects.'[7]

Imajica is a novel born in the true meaning of apocalypse – revelation – and it continues Barker's interrogation of the power that imaginary landscapes hold over him: 'I have an abiding interest in the notion of parallel dimensions, and the influence they may exercise over the lives we live in this world. I don't doubt that the reality we occupy is but one of many; that a lateral step would deliver us into a place quite other. Perhaps our lives are also going on in these other dimensions, changed in vast or subtle ways. Or perhaps these other places will be unrecognizable to us: they'll be realms of spirit, or wonderlands, or hells. Perhaps all of the above. *Imajica* is an attempt to create a narrative which explores these possibilities.'[8]

The breathtaking magnitude of his narrative, however, is clearly linked to the frustrating, wounded aftermath of the many months he devoted to the 'bastard child' known as *Nightbreed*. Turning back to the written word, where no one could interfere with his ambition, Barker lost himself – intentionally, at first – in a novel whose length and complexity soon seemed overwhelming; the book was eighteen months in the writing, with the final three months spent working fifteen hours a day:

'I must tell you that the deeper I got into writing *Imajica*, the more certain I became that completing it was beyond me. I have never come closer to giving up as I came on this book, never doubted more deeply my skills as a storyteller, was never more lost, never more afraid. But nor was I ever more obsessed. I became so thoroughly immersed in the narrative that for a period of several weeks toward the end of the final draft a kind of benign insanity settled upon me. I woke from dreams of the Dominions only to write about them until I crept back to bed to dream them again. My ordinary life – what little I had – came to seem banal; and featureless by contrast with what was happening to me – I should say Gentle, but I *mean* me – as we made our journey toward revelation.'[9]

In identifying his undoubted presence in his principal character, Barker underscores the critical role of this text in his creative career. At the novel's opening, Gentle is a forger of paintings – a sly metaphor for a writer of genre fiction whose focus is the repetition of the plots and themes of his predecessors; but Gentle's epiphany, perfected in the finale, is that his only hope of salvation awaits in his own imagination – the reconciled Dominions – and not in the imagination or authority of others.

In Clive's original conception, Gentle would find the courage to create his own artwork, and begin with a painting of Imajica. But as he was completing the book, he happened to read my review of *The Great and Secret Show* for the *Washington Times*, which described him as 'a mapmaker of the mind, charting the farthest reaches of the imagination'.[10] He saw, in those words, the true calling of his protagonist. Thus Gentle determines, in the closing pages, to devote his remaining years to the making of a map:

[U]nlike the paintings he'd forged, maps weren't cursed by the notion of a definitive original. They grew in the copying, as their inaccuracies were corrected, their empty spaces filled, their legends redevised. And even when all the corrections had been made, to the finest detail, they could still never be cursed with the word finished, because their subject continued to change ... By their very nature, maps were always works in progress, and Gentle – his resolve strengthened by thinking of them that way – decided after many months of delay to turn his hand to making one.

The map Gentle creates is, of course, a rendition of himself: 'he'd fashioned a self-portrait. Like its maker, the map was flawed but, he hoped, redeemable: a rudimentary thing that might see finer versions in the fullness of time; be made and remade and made again, perhaps forever.'

With its compendium of locations around London that Clive had known and loved, *Imajica* was the last book he would write in England. As he penned the final pages, the house on Wimpole Street had been sold, 'its contents boxed up and sent on to Los Angeles, so that all I had that I took comfort in had gone from around me. It was in some ways a perfect way to finish the novel; like Gentle, I was embarking on another kind of life, and in so doing leaving the country in which I had spent almost forty years ... the book became my farewell to England.'[11]

Although his ambition in motion pictures had been tempered by the harsh experience of *Nightbreed*, the move to the United States was inevitable. Only through a physical presence in Hollywood did he feel it was possible to achieve some semblance of control over his next film project.

But there was a second reason: Malcolm Smith lived there. Clive is more romantically driven than he might even acknowledge to his closest friends. The romance of the cinema and the romance with Malcolm became inextricably entwined, and he followed his heart, making the decision to move in the summer of 1991. By May of that year, Clive, Malcolm and David Dodds were living together in a rental house in Beverly Hills, awaiting the renovation of their new home farther up the hill, which Clive had purchased from actor Robert Culp: a lovely Spanish mansion that once belonged to another British pilgrim to the city of sunshine and celluloid, Ronald Colman. Although some friends would suggest, with a hint of jealousy, that Clive had drifted into Hollywood debauchery, his living arrangements suggesting he had taken both a wife and a mistress, the personal dynamic was far more chaste and complex; its essence was that of an intimate family. David was Clive's best friend, while Malcolm was Clive's lover; all three men worked together and, for a time, the relationship was secure and satisfying for each of them.

With the migration to Hollywood came an inevitable note of resentment from some friends, fans and critics in England. Although Clive ostensibly had ventured to the United States to make movies, for the first several years he focused his attention on writing and painting while developing several potential film projects.

Pete Atkins, who later moved to Hollywood to pursue his own screenwriting career, felt that the resentment signified a difference in cultural attitudes: 'The British don't like success or celebrate success; they pretend they do, but they'd rather turn on people. There's a weird nay-saying element to the English psyche. Clive moved to California because he's someone who believes in possibilities. Of course, there's a big downside, because everyone talks bullshit here. It's a choice. But I think he'd rather be living in a place where 99% of it is bullshit, but people encourage and believe and applaud, than a place where they try to contain things.'

Although Clive had departed England, his next endeavour – an illustrated novel – would return him to his childhood. *The Thief of Always* (1992) brought a new legitimacy to Barker's literary journey and another new audience: the world of art. It also brought him a new editor and advocate, Jane Johnson.

Johnson joined HarperCollins UK in 1991, when the small independent house she worked for – Unwin Hyman (previously Allen & Unwin, and the publisher of JRR Tolkien) – was acquired by the larger corporation. An accomplished editor and writer (her own novels – *The Wild Road* (1997), *The Golden Cat* (1999), *The Knot Garden* (2000) and *Nonesuch* (2001), all from Random House – were published pseudonymously), Johnson had read Barker's fiction avidly and met him at several British Fantasy Conventions in the mid-1980s. Clive's original editor at Collins, Andy McKillop, was leaving for Arrow, Random

House UK's mass market imprint (where he now serves as Publisher) 'just as *Imajica* was about to be published in hardback in November 1991,' Johnson notes, 'leaving Clive "orphaned".'

When Clive returned to England on a promotional tour for *Imajica*, he visited the HarperCollins offices in Hammersmith to sign stock. 'He walked past my office and I called out a greeting,' Johnson recalls. 'Clive stopped in mid-stride – we hadn't seen one another for two years – and we chatted away gleefully for several minutes, much to the surprise of the Managing Director, Jonathan Lloyd. Clive then requested that I be invited to his publication dinner. The next day I received a call from Jonathan.'

In a memo to HarperCollins CEO Eddie Bell on November 6, 1991, Jonathan Lloyd wrote: 'Clive had arranged for Jane Johnson to attend his publication dinner and it was obvious that the chemistry between Clive and Jane was excellent. He called me this morning and asked that she be his editor and she of course is thrilled.' Johnson notes: 'I was: as a newcomer to the company, quite a lowly editor at that point. I was Senior Editor, which in publishing terms (publishing scatters grand-sounding titles to its staff rather like the Brazilian Army, as a sop to status) meant very little other than that I ran around fixing problems and doing the donkeywork – with responsibility for publishing Tolkien, science fiction and fantasy, and reporting to Malcolm Edwards, far more senior and experienced than I. I felt extremely honoured that Clive – a "blue-chip" author, a big bestseller with considerable cachet in the publishing community – should have made the very personal and unprecedented step of approaching the MD and making such a request. And, of course, Clive being Clive, no one would gainsay him.

'For me it was wonderful on two counts: firstly, I adored Clive's work, and had done so all the way from the *Books of Blood*, and I loved Clive, too – we'd always shared a huge enthusiasm for works of the *fantastique*; but also it made everyone at HarperCollins sit up a little and take a longer, harder look at me. In a big house it's easy to overlook editors (who beaver quietly away making the big machine run); and although I had a reputation for acquiring interesting works – Kim Stanley Robinson's *Mars* trilogy, for example, and commissioning Alan Lee to create our huge illustrated *Lord of the Rings* –

I was both a newcomer and an outsider, an acquired editor who did "that weird genre stuff". It helped lift the whole profile of the fantastic in-house, too.'

By March 1992, Jonathan Lloyd had appointed Johnson to act as Clive Barker's primary editor worldwide, editing not only for the United Kingdom but also for HarperCollins US – 'and that has, since then, always been the case. Eddie Bell acquired and I did the editorial work and steered the marketing and sales drive'.

Her first responsibility was to oversee the paperback edition of *Imajica*, which was published in August 1992; 'and it was a great thrill to take it straight onto the bestseller lists: we sold over 200,000 copies in the first month alone. But even before then, Clive had been talking about a plethora of different projects – a phenomenon that amazed me at the time. My only experience had been with authors who focused on one book at a time – but here was a man who not only had in-numerable movie projects underway, but who was generating new ideas and concepts for books, on almost a weekly basis! It was exhilarat-ing – something of a fairground ride – and sometimes hard to keep up. Clive has an amazingly fertile imagination, and a powerful generative, creative urge: the ideas keep coming and changing shape. It's a chal-lenge to an editor and to a publishing house to step up to the mark and accommodate so many projects, all of which are very different from one another.'

Indeed, the first new work Clive offered to Jane Johnson was surpris-ingly different – and dangerous. 'Almost as soon as *Imajica* was put to bed and Clive was technically supposed to be working on his next big novel (the follow-up to *The Great and Secret Show*, eventually to be *Everville*), he suddenly proposed the idea for an illustrated children's book, known at this early stage as *Harvey*. He talked about it with me and I thought the idea was wonderful, but risky, given Clive's repu-tation – originally as the "future of horror", then as a very adult dark fantasy writer. Who knew how the trade, or the audience, would react to the thought of the author of the *Books of Blood* and the creator of *Hellraiser* producing a children's book? Eddie Bell, our CEO, felt the same way: excited at the idea of the book – such a brilliant fable, with a universal appeal – but anxious that our blue-chip bestseller might be about to get us all shot!'

In the end, Bell devised a creative deal whose terms signalled the unusual nature of the project while protecting the interests of Harper-Collins: he agreed to license world English language rights in the book for the sum of a gold sovereign – 'which, in the final deal, turned into a rather more prosaic dollar'. As Clive tells it: 'When I went to him with *The Thief of Always*, I said, *Eddie, I don't know about this, I don't have a clue. He said, I love this book. I'll buy it for a dollar, and you can have, obviously, much larger royalties in the end.* I shook his hand, and we did it, and we both made shitloads of money.'

In May 1992, the typescript arrived on Jane Johnson's desk, and her first true editing work with Clive Barker commenced. 'Its new title was *The Thief of Always*. I read the first sentence – *The great grey beast February had eaten Harvey Swick alive* – and I knew I was reading a future classic.'

24

THE SERPENT'S TAIL

THE THIEF OF ALWAYS: A FABLE (1992)

We two kept house, the Past and I,
The Past and I . . .
— THOMAS HARDY, 'The Ghost of the Past'

After the epic journeys of writing *Imajica* and moving to California, it was little wonder that Clive Barker turned next to the shortest novel of his career. It was also no surprise – save, perhaps, to those still naïve enough to believe that the *Books of Blood* or the *Hellraiser* films defined him – that it was a children's book, embellished with his own illustrations: *The Thief of Always: A Fable* (1992).[1]

Barker's fledgling attempt at a novel, *The Candle in the Cloud*, written in 1971 before he began studies at the University of Liverpool, was a fantasy for young adults, as was his story cycle *The Adventures of Mr Maximillian Bacchus and His Travelling Circus* (circa 1974–75). Later in the 1970s, he and his friends had written several stories for children, although none of them was published or is known to survive. Only one complete short story from his youth has been found: 'The Wood on the Hill', a handwritten manuscript dating from earlier years (circa 1966), when he attended Quarry Bank Grammar School.

'The Wood on the Hill' was inspired by a favourite story, Edgar Allan Poe's 'The Masque of the Red Death', and by Clive's sadness about the loss of his first tree. Its complete text, which underscores Clive's remarkable storytelling skills – even as a young teenager – is published here for the first time in the Appendix.

On Oakdale Road, the back of the Barkers' terraced house was paved concrete, about a hundred square feet in size. When the family moved to their new home on Rangemore Road, young Clive was delighted with its back garden, green with grass and a tree. 'This sounds hopelessly melancholy, in a way, but the having of a tree was a big deal to me. We were moving to this place where there was green, and we had a tree.' His parents decided, for reasons now forgotten, that the tree had to be removed. 'So the tree comes down, and I am *furious* at this! And that sparked this idea of the story of a woman who plots against nature, and who is, in turn, plotted against.'

'Once upon a time,' the story tells us, 'there grew a wood, dark and old, on a hill'[2] – the setting is based on Liverpool's Woolton Woods. In a great white house nearby dwells a beautiful, but vain and wicked, Duchess who claims ownership of all the land. She has many friends among the aristocracy ('which means,' the story explains in an aside, 'they had lots of money and weren't quite sure what to do with it'), and they are 'the most hateful people you could imagine. They were either very fat because they ate too much, or very thin because they would not eat at all, in case they marred their beauty.'

One autumn afternoon, the Duchess discovers the wood on the hill, and decides to hold a Hallowe'en ball there. Ignoring her frightened servant Michael, who warns that the wood is haunted, she orders woodcutters to clear trees and erect a bonfire for the grand affair.

As night falls on the final day of October, the Duchess dons her ornate silver mask; but when she and her guests gather on the hill, the innate beauty of the wood is gone: 'It seemed, somehow, darker.' The bonfire roars and champagne is quaffed. 'Beneath their Hallowe'en masks, fat faces dissolved into rolls of hysterics, disdainful faces sneered, military faces looked grim.' Revellers despoil the wood, cutting initials into an old oak and casting branches onto the bonfire while the Duchess laughs.

The orchestra is silenced as a distant church bell tolls to midnight, when the guests will remove their masks; but at the twelfth toll, '[b]lack, hideous creatures with eyes of fire and wings of death' emerge from the shadows. The wind summons 'the dragons of the north, bringing them back to wreak a terrible vengeance' – and the trees come to life, their branches and roots clutching at the panicked party-goers. As a General tries to calm the throng, a great claw strikes him, tearing his mask away: 'And the Duchess saw that he really did have a skull instead of a face.'

The Duchess flees, never to be seen again. When the villagers venture back into the wood, they find the smouldering bonfire, and a 'mask of silver leaves, torn by huge talons, not of our world'. Freed from their cruel mistress and the aristocrats, the villagers frolic in the wood, planting new trees to replace the ones that were cut down. Michael, the former servant, becomes the wood's guardian, telling tales of dragons that some people think are mad. 'Old Michael knows the woods, and the woods know him. For Michael talks to the trees, especially a very beautiful silver birch that appeared, quite inexplicably, in the middle of that dark clearing. A shining silver tree, which Michael tends with great care, even in the deep winter.'

The appeal of writing for a young audience continued into Barker's years as a playwright; and, indeed, three of his later plays – *Crazyface*, *Subtle Bodies* and *Colossus* – were written specifically for London's Cockpit Youth Theatre.

In the aftermath of the publication of the *Books of Blood*, Clive repeatedly expressed his desire to write a children's book, if only to fulfil his mother's fondest wish: that he might create a story like those she had invented for him as a child. Indeed, in 1988, Clive announced that he was working with illustrator Jane Ray on a children's book 'about the creator deciding that the world should be boxed up and put away. Everything. And about a girl and her iguana who manage to escape this fate with hilarious results. It's a very strange little book, actually'.[3] The project was never completed.

Then, in 1990, while battling the massive manuscript of *Imajica*, he conceived of the perfect premise for a short novel that he would dedicate to his mother: *The Thief of Always*.

There was another reason, however, why Clive chose to create this mingling of illustrations and text at this particular time. *The Thief of*

Always is another gentle renunciation of his identification with 'horror' – which, despite an ever expansive series of novels culminating in the undeniable fantasia of *Imajica*, would not fade away. It was also an effort to make explicit something that many of his readers had yet to realize. By writing in a different form and for a younger audience – and by directly invoking the words 'A Fable' – Clive wished to remind the recalcitrant literalists among his readers that his aspirations exceeded entertainment, and that he was fiercely interested in the meaning of his stories.

In interviews, Barker began describing himself as a 'fabulist' – noting, with a mischievous grin, that the word, in its common dictionary definition, had two meanings: a creator of fables and a liar.

The Thief of Always is a deliberate and darkly sentimental inversion of Clive's beloved childhood companion, JM Barrie's *Peter Pan*; it also reprises the confrontation between Cal Mooney and Shadwell the Salesman in *Weaveworld*.[4] It is striking not only for the evocative cover illustration and forty-three black-and-white drawings that Barker created specifically for the book, but also for its focus on youthful characters. In his earlier published fiction, children played secondary roles at best, coming to the forefront of his plots in nominal ways (as bystanders and victims) save in 'The Skins of the Fathers' (1984). Indeed, in *The Thief of Always*, Barker offers his first (and, to date, only) child protagonist.

Harvey Swick is ten years old, an only child growing up in the archetypally middle American town of Millsap.[5] Suffering from post-Christmas doldrums, Harvey feels eaten by the great grey beast of February, wondering whether he will survive until spring. 'Don't sit wishing the days away,' his mother warns him. 'Life's too short.'

'I don't know what I want,' Harvey laments. 'I just know I'll die if I don't have some fun.' As if these words were an incantation, a visitor flies in through his bedroom window. It is not Peter Pan, but Rictus, a smooth-talking, fast-walking carnival shill whose grin is 'wide enough to shame a shark'. He offers Harvey a vacation: 'I know a place where the days are always sunny . . . and the nights are full of wonders.'

The temptation is too great. Like a Pied Piper of pandemonium, Rictus leads Harvey from the safety of home through a grey maze of streets to a stone wall that towers out of sight into fog. 'It *looks* like a wall,' Harvey realizes, 'but it's *not* a wall.' It is the barrier of reality, breached only by those who will believe in what waits beyond: the Holiday House, where every child's wish, when spoken, comes true. Harvey steps through the wall and into Wonderland:

> The House was more wonderful inside than out. Even on the short journey to the kitchen Harvey glimpsed enough to know that this was a place built for games, chases and adventures. It was a maze in which no two doors were alike. It was a treasure-house where some notorious pirate had hidden his blood-stained booty. It was a resting place for carpets flown by *djinns*, and boxes sealed before the Flood, where the eggs of beasts that the earth had lost were wrapped and waiting for the sun's heat to hatch them.

Harvey meets and befriends two other children: jolly, bespectacled Wendell, forever lost in frolic and foodstuffs; and freckled, melancholy Lulu, for whom the delights of the House have somehow paled. There have been other children, but no one knows what happened to them. 'Back home, I s'pose,' says Wendell. 'Kids come and go, you know?' The threesome enact the roles of id, ego and superego in the confrontation between youth and the price of wonder.

At the Holiday House, each day is a cycle of seasons: morning offers the first day of spring, while afternoon is hot with summer; evening brings shadowed autumn, a full moon and Hallowe'en, while the night is chilly winter, warmed by a Thanksgiving feast and then the delights of Christmas. 'It was a day of holidays, the third as fine as the second, and the fourth as fine as the third, and very soon Harvey began to forget that there was a dull world out beyond the wall, where the great beast February was still sleeping its tedious sleep.' His doubts are set aside in the pleasure of the moment: 'What did it matter, anyway, he thought, whether this was a real place or a dream? It *felt* real, and that was all that mattered.'

The matron of Holiday House is the ancient Mrs Griffin – '[s]he had a face like a rolled-up ball of cobwebs' – a comforting cook and confidante forever surrounded by her rhyme-christened cats: Blue-Cat,

Clue-Cat and Stew-Cat. But when Harvey contemplates the perfection of the House, Mrs Griffin proves suddenly sad. 'Nothing's perfect,' she tells him. 'Because time passes ... And the beetle and the worm find their way into everything sooner or later.'

The House is indeed less than perfect, confirming Cal Mooney's observation in *Weaveworld*: 'They were too perfect, those childhood kingdoms; all honey and summer ... The true Wonderland was not like that, he knew. It was as much shadow as sunlight, and its mysteries could only be unveiled when your wits were about used up and your mind close to cracking.' While the children gorge themselves on the delights of Mrs Griffin's kitchen, they witness the gruesome, accidental death of Clue-Cat. Later Harvey discovers a gloomy lake hidden behind the thick and thorny bushes to one side of the House: 'This was a place where dead things belonged.' The increasingly listless Lulu is drawn to the water, in whose depths wait ever-circling fish:

> They were almost as large as he was, their grey scales stained and encrusted, their bulbous eyes turned up toward the surface like the eyes of prisoners in a watery pit.
>
> They were watching him, he was certain of that, and their scrutiny made him shudder. Were they hungry, he wondered, and praying to their fishy gods that he'd slip on the stones and tumble in? Or were they wishing he'd come with a rod and a line, so that they could be hauled from the depths and put out of their misery?
>
> What a life, he thought. No sun to warm them; no flowers to sniff at or games to play. Just the deep, dark waters to circle in; and circle, and circle, and circle.

That all is not right in Wonderland becomes obvious when Harvey meets Rictus's siblings, the grim guardians of the House: brother Jive, a nervous clown whose 'tics, jigs and jitterings ... had wasted him away until he barely cast a shadow'; Marr, a sluggish oaf whose touch can reshape flesh; and Carna the tooth-stealing devourer, a nightmarish reincarnation of the winged monkeys of *The Wizard of Oz*.[6] Their employer is the mysterious Mr Hood, the builder of the House, who wants only special children like Harvey as his guests.

Because each day, its seasons and its spectacles, is like the last, Lulu has no Christmas wish: 'I've been here so long I've got everything I ever wanted.' Harvey's first wish is for the impossible, 'to see just how much magic the House possessed': a painted wooden ark, lost long ago, that his father once built for him. He opens the package that waits beneath the Christmas tree to find the ark and its steerage of paired animals; it is not a reproduction, but exact to the point of a remembered imperfection. But what has been lost cannot be so easily regained: on his seventh day at the House, he plays at the lake, and the ark and its passengers sink into its dreary depths.[7]

Later, as a Hallowe'en prank, Marr transforms Harvey into a vampire so that he can frighten Wendell. He is intoxicated by the fulfilment of his dreams of flight, and by the feeling of power – the same feeling that Clive had felt in childhood, when viewing *Psycho* for the second time and knowing what was to come: 'He liked the feeling of the wind beneath him, and the cold moon on his back. He liked the sharpness of his eyes, and the strength of his claws. But most of all he liked the fear he was causing; liked the look on Wendell's upturned face, and the sound of panic in his chest.' But he rejects Jive's imprecation to bite Wendell and taste his blood.[8]

Harvey is shaken by the experience. Happiness and fun, he realizes, have a weighty cost. Lulu's time in the House is at an end, and she is devolving into one of its minions: 'She wasn't human any longer. She was becoming – or had already become – a sister to the strange fish that circled in these dark waters, cold-blooded and silver-skinned.' Harvey's thoughts turn to escape.

At first the boys find no route through the misty wall, but with the help of Blue-Cat, they stumble back onto the streets of Millsap. Hungry Carna pursues them, but falters, wounded by the white light of reality. As it crawls back through the wall and into the shadowland beyond, Harvey realizes: 'There was a lesson here, if he could only remember it. Evil, however powerful it seemed, could be undone by its own appetite.'

In Millsap he feels 'different, *marked* by this adventure'; and when he returns home, he learns another, more painful lesson. His parents are old and frail; thirty-one years have passed.

The moment he'd set eyes on his mother – so changed, so sorrow-ful – it was instantly clear what a terrible trick Hood's house had played upon them all. For every day he'd spent there a year had gone by here in the real world. Every morning while he'd played in the spring warmth, months had passed. In the afternoon, while he'd lazed in the summer sun, the same. And those haunted twilights, which had seemed so brief, had been another span of months, as had the Christmas nights, full of snow and presents. They'd all slipped by so easily, and though *he* had only aged a month, his mom and dad had lived in sadness for thirty-one years, thinking that their little boy had gone forever.

That had almost been the case. If he'd remained in the House of Illusions, distracted by its petty pleasures, a whole lifetime would have gone by here in the real world, and his soul would have become Hood's property. He would have joined the fish circling in the lake; and circling; and circling.

'Was there some way to undo the damage that had been done? To take back the stolen years, and live them here, with the people who loved him, and whom he loved dearly in return?' Harvey has no choice but to return to the House of Illusions. He and Wendell find the way back too easily, and although Wendell is swiftly seduced by its delights, Harvey has a purpose: he is the redeemer, the usurper . . . the messiah.

He descends the fifty-two steps to the cellar of the House, where he frees Mrs Griffin from a crude coffin. She was the first child to enter Holiday House, her damnation as its matron caused by her wish for eternal life. Now she has only one desire: 'To die . . . To slip out of this skin, and go to the stars.'

'Hood isn't Death,' she tells Harvey. 'Death is a natural thing. Hood isn't . . . There's such a terrible emptiness inside him. He wants to fill it with souls, but it's a pit. A bottomless pit–'. He is, indeed, a thief of always: 'he took all those years away to feed himself . . . Blood was life, and life was what Hood fed upon. He was a vampire, sure enough. Maybe a king among vampires.'

Harvey defeats the keepers of the House, showing them the illusions of which they are made: Marr, who reshaped others into their dreams, is revealed to have a dream of nothing, and dissolves into stale mud and spittle; Jive's single taste of the House's food reminds him of his birthright of dust, and he disintegrates. Then Harvey ascends to the top of the house, there to confront Hood in the dirty, cobwebbed attic: 'Who but a master of illusions would live in a place so bereft of them?' And at last, Hood is revealed in all his glory: he *is* the House.

> His face was spread over the entire roof, his features horribly distorted. His eyes were dark pits gouged into the timbers; his nose was flared and flattened grotesquely, like the nose of an enormous bat; his mouth was a lipless slit that was surely ten feet wide, from which issued a voice that was like the creaking of doors and the howling of chimneys and the rattling of windows.

Harvey has one strength; like Hood, he is a thief: 'What you stole I can steal back.' Hood sends Carna against him: 'If he *was* a Thief of Always, as Hood had said, perhaps it was time to prove it. Not with dust, nor with stolen conjurations, but with the power in his own bones.' Harvey gently touches the wounded beast, giving it the death it desires. Then he secures Hood's promise to give him anything he asks – if he, in turn, agrees to stay. Harvey wishes for the ark, again restored, but this time with perfect little animals of flesh and blood; for a flourish of flowers, no two of them alike; for banquets of outlandish fare. Each wish drains the House of its magic, until finally Harvey asks for a moment of always, in which all seasons exist at once, and the wish conjures an awesome sight:

> In their place came a juggernaut: a thunderhead the size of a mountain, which loomed over the House like a shadow thrown against Heaven.
>
> It had more than lightning at its dark heart. It had the light rains that came at early morning to coax forth the seeds of another spring; it had the drooping fogs of autumn, and the spiralling snows that brought so many midnight Christmases to the House.

The warring seasons dissipate the power of the Vampire King, and the House collapses. The souls of the children taken by the evil edifice emerge from its ruins, floating lights that stream toward the lake. Mrs

Griffin joins them, with 'another life to go to, where every soul shone'. But Lulu rises from the lake, restored to human form, and with her, a procession of laughing children, all of them freed. The lake, once their prison, spirals down into the earth – a flood in which Harvey plays the role of Noah.

Rictus shambles toward them, clutching a token of Hood's magic; but the Vampire King rises, destroying his servant and confronting his usurper:

> Here, at last, was the evil that had built the Holiday House, shaped more or less as a man. He was not made of flesh, blood and bone, however. He had used the magic Rictus had unwillingly provided to create another body.
>
> In the high times of his evil, Hood had been the House. Now, it was the other way around. The House, what was left of it, had become Mr Hood.[9]

In his final incarnation, Hood is one of Barker's eternal bogeymen, a raggedy-man: 'Hood's pursuit had thrown his coat of rags into disarray, and there was something between its folds, he saw, darker than any night sky or lightless cellar. What was it? The essence of his magic, guarding his loveless heart?'

Harvey tears the coat aside: 'There was no great enchantment at his heart. In fact, there was no heart at all. There was only a void – neither cold nor hot, living nor dead – made not of mystery but of nothingness. The illusionist's illusion.' Hood struggles to conceal that void and fails, tumbling into the vortex of the vanishing lake. 'Reduced to a living litter of flotsam and jetsam, he was drawn into the white waters at the whirlpool's heart, and shrieking with rage, went where all evil must go at last: into nothingness.'

The battle over, the survivors gather at the wall to say their farewells, then disappear into the mist, delivered back to the times from which they had stepped so many seasons before. Returning home, Harvey finds his parents restored to youth: 'Here was his prize, staring down at him: his mother and father, looking just the way they had before Rictus had come for him. The stolen years were back where they belonged, in *his* possession . . . "I'm a good thief," he said.'

His parents do not believe his story, so the next day he takes them to the place where the Holiday House had stood. It is just a hill; but another visitor, an older man, tells him: 'Maybe the earth has its own magic – good magic, I mean – and it's buried Hood's memory forever.' It is Lulu's husband, sent in her place. 'She remembers you the way you are – young, that is – and she'd like you to remember her the same way.'

Thus *The Thief of Always* again inverts *Peter Pan*, which, in many ways, concludes as a tragedy. Peter, despite his adventures, must suffer eternally because he has refused adulthood; he will never know adult emotions – love, pain, loss. 'It stands for me,' Barker says, 'at the crux of the problem of fantasy, because a great deal of fantasy is adolescent, reductionist, misinformed about the human condition, and masturbatory. I don't mean that in a sexual sense; I mean it's unproductive, sterile. *Peter Pan* is about two visions of the fantastic. Peter Pan's vision is: *I want to be a boy forever and forever and, therefore, be at the window looking in.* Wendy decides to come back and produce children and dream of the Neverland and die.

'The beautiful pain of that story is at the basis of what I want to do in fantasy. I want to examine how we deal with that problem. How we deal with the problem that, if we embrace Neverland too strongly, we are forever sucking our thumbs, but if we die without knowing Neverland, we've lost our power to dream . . . If you merely write to escape, you are not interpreting the world, and true fantasy is a way of interpreting the world. I'm trying my damnedest to write a fantasy about the way the world was, is, and could be, which is just about what the Bible tries to do.'[10]

It is significant that *The Thief of Always* was written and published as Clive reached his fortieth birthday. Mrs Griffin's reminder to Harvey is a stark one: 'I want you to take what joy you can from being here. Use the hours well, because there'll be fewer than you think.' The novel was written at a time of reassessment, and it seemed that Clive's distance from home, in miles and in years, had taught him the importance of his parents – if only in providing him with a childhood that he could return to so fondly in his dreams and imagination. In the blur of time that marked the first decade of his career as a writer and film-maker, Clive had lost himself in a kind of Holiday House whose glimmering delights proved sometimes deceptive and always consuming; caught up in the momentum and the madness, he had lost precious years with his family.

'Being the parent of a Clive wasn't easy,' Len and Joan say, almost in unison. 'It's been different,' Len says, 'let's put it that way.' There were days, months, years of confusion and concern – before and after his success. In *The Thief of Always*, he acknowledged the lesson of those years, and offered a solemn vow: 'Time would be precious from now on.' This is not a lament of wasted youth, but an acknowledgment that those years may be reclaimed: confronted, used by the writer, the artist, to become a 'good thief' – healing wounds and repaying the price of dreams. 'He'd fill every moment with the seasons he'd found in his heart: hopes like birds on a spring branch; happiness like a warm summer sun; magic like the rising mists of autumn. And best of all, love; love enough for a thousand Christmases.'

Although licensed to HarperCollins for only one dollar, *The Thief of Always* was published in substantial first printings on both sides of the Atlantic, with 100,000 hardback copies issued in the United States. To quote its text: 'There has to be some sane explanation.' To which Harvey Swick replies: 'There *is* . . . It was magic.'

If *The Thief of Always* marked a reconciliation of the man and the child inside Clive Barker, it also brought Clive's private passion since childhood – his artwork – directly into the public eye. His cover art and line illustrations for *The Thief of Always* were integral to the text, assured and professional. With a surge of confidence and a sense of the confessional, Clive then took his artwork out of the studio and into the heady realm of exhibitions, with his first opening at the Bess Cutler Gallery in Manhattan.

Although to some it seemed that 1993 was the year of Clive Barker the artist, nearly his entire life had been devoted to sketches and paintings; from his earliest years, Joan Barker recalls, Clive drew incessantly, 'almost like a nervous tic. He couldn't stop doing it.' At school, he carried a sketch pad everywhere, creating images at a prolific rate, and his friends recount endless stories of how he would use anything available – from ruled notebooks to restaurant napkins – for obsessive bouts of drawing.

Obviously Clive's imagination and storytelling style are rooted strongly in the visual, and even before *The Thief of Always*, he would illustrate his narratives, often creating elaborate character sketches and storyboards to accompany the writing of stories and novels. To this day, he writes everything – stories, novels, motion picture scripts, even his faxes – by hand, often sketching along the way. (He feels – perhaps ironically for a writer whose manuscripts have totalled over a thousand pages – that handwriting leads to economy, and that each word must count because of the labour of writing it down.)

Even as a youth, Clive took his artwork seriously; indeed, he had hoped to attend the Liverpool College of Arts. Although drawing and painting gave him pleasure, they were never a hobby; Pete Atkins recalls a conversation with Clive, soon after they met, in which they both realized they didn't have hobbies. 'If you really like something,' Atkins notes, summarizing their shared philosophy, 'it can't be a hobby. It has to be an obsession – it has to be something that you *do*.'

Clive's first dedicated artistic endeavours were the adolescent comic books he created for himself and his brother Roy, patterned after Jack Kirby's legendary Marvel Comics. One day, a teacher at Quarry Bank – Mr Whitehead, who taught woodwork ('which I was terrible at,' Clive notes) – asked to see the comics. 'They were very sexual,' Clive says. 'At the age of thirteen or fourteen, I had taken comic book sexuality one step further. There were bare breasts and, although I'm sure there wasn't full frontal nudity, the violence was just flabbergasting.' Whitehead's reaction was surprising; he didn't scold Clive, or denigrate the pages: 'He became a fan. It was quite interesting. Norman Russell validated my literary life. But Whitehead, and then Alan Plent, validated my artistic life.'

Encouraged and mentored by Plent and Rodney Warbrick, his Quarry Bank art instructors, Clive spent hours elaborating his considerable skills; but he remains effectively self-taught, learning through inspiration and hard work rather than through conventional instruction. 'The thing with Plent and Warbrick was that they were old-fashioned painters, and I wasn't – although I've latterly become one.'

After graduation from Quarry Bank, and his acquiescence in his parents' wish that he attend the University of Liverpool rather than art school, Clive occasionally sold illustrations – typically to magazines of gay erotica – but he did not seriously pursue the commercial or the critical potential of his artistic talents. More than a decade later, however, his successes in publishing brought minor opportunities – and those talents, which he never believed he could use publicly with any serious effect, garnered increasing interest in the marketplace.

The original British editions of *Clive Barker's Books of Blood* featured covers illustrated with distorted photographic images. 'We thought that put across the originality of them, and that worked quite well,' Barbara Boote of Sphere says; but another option was soon presented. 'Clive offered to do the covers himself, and we'd seen that he was a good artist.' Sphere decided to reissue the books with new cover art by Clive – which also adorned the Weidenfeld & Nicolson hardcover editions – just after *The Damnation Game* was published in 1985: 'To give them a fresher look,' Boote notes, 'and also another selling point – a cover by Clive.'

In 1986, Sphere's Abacus imprint released Richard Miller's picaresque fantasy *Snail*, which was adorned with an original colour cover by Clive Barker. Over the next several years, his artwork appeared sporadically in magazines and books, typically as a cover or stand-alone illustration for a work of horror or fantasy – and for little or no financial reward.

Then his artistic passions were kindled by a familiar source: those sometimes guilty pleasures of Clive's youth, comic books. Save for his nostalgic paean *The Secret Life of Cartoons* and the comedic short story 'The Yattering and Jack', Barker's mature narratives seemed distant from the realm of Looney Tunes and superheroes; but by the mid-1980s, the world of comic books had changed, with more mature storylines and imagery – and, indeed, an increasingly popular hybrid of text and art known as the graphic novel.

In 1988, Clive met an enthusiastic fan, Steve Niles, at an American Film Institute screening of *Hellraiser*. Niles, a member of the Washington DC, proto-punk band Gray Matter, saw the creative and commercial possibilities of adapting Barker's short fiction as an adult-oriented series of graphic novels. Clive agreed to license several of his stories, including 'Rawhead Rex', and Niles formed a small imprint, Arcane Comix, intent on issuing a line of books anchored by Barker's creations.

The project was underfinanced, however, and Arcane folded before bringing any of Barker's stories into print. Niles took his adaptations-in-progress to Eclipse Comics, which produced, under the editorship of Fred Burke, graphic novel versions of ten *Books of Blood* stories in a five-volume series, *Tapping the Vein* (1989–92). Clive was sufficiently pleased that he licensed the rights to additional *Books of Blood* stories, several of which Eclipse issued in single-book adaptations, including *Son of Celluloid* (1991, adapted by Steve Niles; artwork by Les Edwards), and *Dread* (1992, adapted by Fred Burke; artwork by Dan Brereton).

Although focused on the *Books of Blood* era – and thus the more grotesque elements of Barker's fiction – the Arcane/Eclipse publications involved production values that were rare in the comics field, with hardcover and trade paperback editions; the series was available in bookstores as well as traditional comic stores and established a sub-genre of its own. Barker and Niles then collaborated on a two-part graphic novel for Fantaco, *Night of the Living Dead: London* (1993). Intended as an official comic book sequel to George A Romero's classic horror film *Night of the Living Dead*, the story was conceived by Barker, written by Niles, and illustrated in a neo-expressionist style by Carlos Kastro.

More conventional comic book adaptations came with three series released by Epic Comics – at the time, the more 'serious' side of Marvel Comics and, indeed, the most prestigious imprint in the business. Named after, and loosely derived from, the novel *Weaveworld* and the motion pictures *Hellraiser* and *Nightbreed*, the books sought to revisit and extend the mythologies created by Barker.

Hellraiser, a quarterly whose first issue appeared in 1989, drew upon a talented array of writers (including Peter Atkins, Neil Gaiman, Mark McLaurin, Philip Nutman, Del Stone Jr and Nicholas Vince, who played 'Chatterer' in the original film) and artists (including John Bolton, Bill Koeb, Dave McKean and Bernie Wrightson). Perhaps the most successful, and certainly the longest-running, of all Clive Barker-related comics, *Hellraiser* spawned several special editions (including a 'best of' collection selected by Clive) before reaching its final issue in 1993. It was supplemented in 1991 by a highly imaginative series, *Clive Barker's Book of the Damned*, which assembled artifacts of the *Hellraiser* mythology – faux journals, letters, pictures, advertisements, excerpts from books – in epistolary form. Because of its insistent originality and visual splendour, *Book of the Damned* remains a creative zenith of the comic adaptations.

Epic also introduced *Clive Barker's Nightbreed* in 1990, with DG ('Daniel') Chichester acting as consulting editor. The initial four issues adapted the screenplay of the film; with issue five, the comic essayed a new storyline written by Chichester and others that concluded with its twenty-fifth issue in 1993. Along the way, *Nightbreed* included a four-issue confrontation with Rawhead Rex; Epic also published the two-book 'crossover' *Jihad*, which merged the ongoing storylines of the *Hellraiser* and *Nightbreed* comics. Finally, beginning in December 1991, Epic issued a three-volume adaptation of *Weaveworld*. Written by Erik Saltzgaber, the books were a faithful adaptation in conventional comic style, and proved once again that depiction is often an anathema to the fantastic.

Inevitably, this furious wave of other artists who rendered Clive's words into pictures – sometimes inspired, sometimes mundane, sometimes amateurish, but always emphasizing the visual qualities of his prose – excited his imagination and helped him reconsider the place of his own artistic talent in his worklife. He flirted briefly with the notion of creating original characters and stories for the comic book medium, and, working with DG Chichester and Erik Saltzgaber, developed *Primal* for Dark Horse Comics. Premiering in 1992 as a graphic novel subtitled 'From the Cradle to the Grave', its moody atmospheres could not compete with more traditional fare, and the planned series lasted only two issues.

By then, the conclusion was obvious: Clive's artwork, which he had considered essentially a private exploration for almost three decades, was on a level superior to almost everything that had been offered in interpretation of his prose. If his words were to be interpreted again, then his own hand should provide the illustrations. 'Clearly I had to legitimize that side of myself,' he notes, 'by having those images go into a book – and feeling like they weren't laughed at, of course.' The spectacularly successful result, *The Thief of Always*, not only confirmed the legitimacy of his talents, but thrilled his avid readers – and served as the entrée into another level of art: the heady realm of gallery exhibitions.

In January 1993, Clive appeared as a special guest at the *Fangoria* 'Weekend of Horrors' convention in Manhattan, where he displayed images from *The Thief of Always*. Bess Cutler, whose SoHo gallery championed contemporary artists, inquired about his paintings in plain-spoken terms: 'Well, we'd love to exhibit them.' The invitation was appealing, and not only to his ego; the opportunity to exhibit his artwork in an established gallery was a rebuttal to the culture of compromise he had experienced in Hollywood. With each new canvas – which, when displayed, would provide a direct communiqué between artist and beholder – Clive could strike a blow against the stranglehold of mass-marketed cinema and television on the public imagination, vindicating his belief in the words of Salvador Dalí, who wrote, as early as 1932: 'Contrary to current opinion, the cinema is infinitely poorer and more limited for the expression of the true functioning of thought than writing, painting, sculpture and architecture.'[11]

With remarkable speed, his first one-man exhibition – 'Clive Barker, Paintings and Drawings 1973–1993' – opened on March 19, 1993, at the Bess Cutler Gallery. 'By which time I'd put two or three or maybe four pieces on canvas,' Clive says. 'But I'd also dug up a lot of older stuff. I was appalled to find that I'd been the worst custodian of my own work imaginable! Many of my drawings were in really poor shape. I've always been pretty casual about it, because the image-making has been either a form of note-taking – *oh, that's an image which I'll one day use*, and that's the best way of setting it down – or they've been entertainments for my own relaxation.'

Although the exhibition included several illustrations from *The Thief of Always*, his cover art for the British editions of the *Books of Blood*, and designs and studies for limited edition books, plays and film projects – along with a hundred ink, pen, pencil, charcoal and mixed-media drawings created over the years for his private pleasure – its centrepiece was an instalment of several large new oil paintings, including 'Axis (Primal Goddess)' and three works that were auctioned at Sotheby's on June 26, 1993.

The Bess Cutler Gallery was overwhelmed during the two months of the exhibition, which was extended twice. The commercial and critical response was so strong that a second exhibition opened at the gallery in October 1993. Barker responded, in turn, with more inventive and substantial pieces, including two remarkable oils, 'The Arsonist' and 'Blue Study'. But despite the warm reception to his work, he approached this new experience with caution: 'I'm deeply suspicious, and remain deeply suspicious, of the art world. I think it's a phony world. It's a world where a very small number of critics and collectors are in cahoots to support their own nonsensical bigotries. Apparently the director of MOMA – we can't really attribute it to him, because it may be apocryphal, although I don't think it is – said: *The only way HR Giger gets into this museum is if he pays for a ticket.*

'Now that's indicative of an attitude. Giger, however you view his work, is clearly an artist who has a very particular, singular and persuasive vision. One who believes completely in his vision. One who is very aware that his vision is more than surface. It's about things – quite what those things are, we could argue about forever.

'The problem that *fantastique* painting has vis-à-vis modernism is that modernism is essentially about ways to see. Cubism is about the way the eye interprets. The *isms,* by and large, have been about the artist's way of seeing, in terms of interpreting reality. What the fantastic artist often does – and Giger is a prime example – is say: *I'm not terribly interested in seeing apples. I'm not interested in interpreting the way to see an apple. I'm interested in the fruit you haven't even seen before – and I'm going to represent it as realistically as possible.* So it's a form of realism about magical things, and that takes that kind of painting out of the mainstream of twentieth century art, which has been increasingly self-conscious; it has been increasingly about the process of the artist, and about the artist, to the point that, in conceptual art, very often the canvas – if there is a canvas – is blank and what sits beside the blank canvas is writing, describing why the canvas is blank. So then it becomes about me and the art, rather than the thing you see.[12]

'I love making images. But why spend a good portion of my working life putting these images onto canvas, onto paper, if all they're going to do is be sucked into this system? Or probably – more likely, actually – rejected by that system and therefore have no life at all.

'What Bess offered me was the energy and enthusiasm to find my audience with this material.' Which happened far more quickly than Clive or Bess Cutler imagined. In the nine months after the March

1993 opening, in three exhibitions and several convention appearances, the Cutler Gallery sold nearly two hundred pieces of his artwork at prices ranging from $400 for drawings to $20,000 for major oil paintings, plus thousands of posters and T-shirts.

The endeavour was not particularly profitable for Barker: 'If I was to do a calculation, just in monetary terms, it's a ridiculous way to spend my time. It's the kind of thing that would have my accountant beating his head against the wall, saying, *Clive, stop this!* But it is deeply satisfying, and as long as the audience is there, it's something I want to continue to do. Clearly, it's something I've always enjoyed, and I've done it for the better part of twenty years, just giving drawings away over and over again.'

By 1995, his art was exhibited at the historic Laguna Art Museum, yet he also displayed more trangressive works in showings at countercultural venues such as the Luz de Jesus in Los Angeles. The distinction that the world of art might draw between the two galleries was meaningless to him; the important thing was that the public had intimate access to his images. He proffers one of his favourite volumes, a *Book of Hours*, as an inspiration for his art – and his attitude about art – opening it to an illuminated painting of medieval French country life invaded by three haloed angels. 'I get a great thrill from that. It's what art does best – reminds me that we're living in a world which is full of metaphor, in which our dream lives are, any minute, about to break into our "real" lives. Sleep is just a little way away; death is just a little way away; change is just a little way away. It's no use cleaving to the status quo – the status quo is a lie, because look, there are angels sitting in the corner, and one of them has a werewolf on its knee.

'That's not far from the basic notion of horror stories, in which the metaphor and reality are compressed into thirty pages. I think it's important that you get as many real things rubbing shoulders with the *fantastique* as possible. You should always be pressing the audience's acceptance level and saying, *Look, you thought you understood? Okay, now here comes another beast, another angel, another problem. Work this one out.*'

FORBIDDEN CANDY

'THE FORBIDDEN' (1985)
CANDYMAN (1992)

> *'What's blood for, if not for shedding?'*
> — CLIVE BARKER, 'The Forbidden'

'Like a flawless tragedy, the elegance of which structure is lost upon those suffering in it, the perfect geometry of the Spector Street Estate was visible only from the air.'[1] These words, ripe with the godlike power of the dramatist, invite the reader into the archetypal Clive Barker story, 'The Forbidden', lead novelette of the fifth *Books of Blood* (1985) and Ur-text for the motion picture *Candyman* (1992). As written by Barker and translated for the screen by Bernard Rose, 'The Forbidden' enacts a perfect geometry of its own: shrewd and subtle fiction rendered expertly into a conscientious yet commercial film.

As its very title announces, 'The Forbidden' is an excursion into the taboo; but unlike the graphic set-pieces for which the *Books of Blood* are known, the story dwells less on the imagery of the proscribed and profane than on its allure – the compelling question of why we approach the lid of Pandora's Box, so certain of the terrors that wait inside, yet so eager to have it open. It is one of the more self-conscious, and perhaps the most self-reflective, of Barker's early stories.

The plot is vintage Barker, following his favoured pattern of the night-quest; but for once, the quarry is not the dark fantastic, but the dark reality of the contemporary urban netherworld: the ghetto. Helen Buchanan, a self-assured graduate student, journeys from her ivory tower at an unnamed British university to the Spector Street Estate – an urban redevelopment project despoiled by its denizens, who have been caged there by poverty and social caste. There she intends to study the traffic of art and language spray-painted on the walls, fuel for a heady thesis, 'Graffiti: The Semiotics of Urban Despair'.

For Helen, the estate is aptly named, a necropolis 'with little to seduce the eye or stimulate the imagination'; but like other ruins, this Gothic maze of ravaged flats and maisonettes buries secrets ancient and accursed. Although others have studied the writing on the wall, Helen believes that her scientific rigour will reveal something beyond 'the usual clamour of love letters and threats', a Rosetta Stone that will interpret the graffiti, make its meaning whole. This is the first of her conceits – that logic can make sense of art and unreason – and one that, for her, like other Barker characters, proves worse than fatal.

While busily photographing epithets and slogans, Helen meets Anne-Marie Latimer, who, cradling her baby son, Kerry, plays tour guide to the ghetto, spinning tales of poverty, squalour, an infestation of insects and, at last, murder. Her story's grisly splendour grows in the telling: in a nearby maisonette, an old man was cut to ribbons, his eyes taken, and the corpse left to rot. The deed, she contends, was performed by a man with a hook for a hand.

That night, Helen's husband, Trevor – a vacuous, womanizing lecturer at the university – dismisses the story, as he does Helen, with relish. Its telling holds neither purpose nor power for him; he seems incapable of wonder or fear, and for that, Helen cannot forgive him: 'She despaired of ever seeing a haunted look in his dull eyes; and what worth was a man who could not be haunted?' The epitome of Barker's 'wise apes', Trevor is so assured in his sterile, book-bred knowledge that he is blind, 'lost in a wasteland of stale rhetoric and hollow commitment'.

Trevor's very lack of belief – indeed, of the ability to believe – spurs Helen onward, and she returns to the estate, hoping to confirm the lurid tale. At a burned-out, abandoned maisonette – the murder site, perhaps – she finds a nightmarish portrait spray-painted on a wall, the doorway forming the mouth of a howling, hungry man. It is, for Helen, a crucible, the stuff of illumination and transformation. 'That such an image might be stumbled upon in surroundings so drab, so conspicuously lacking in mystery, was akin to finding an icon on a rubbish heap: a gleaming symbol of transcendence from a world of toil and decay into some darker but more tremendous realm.' Then she notices the phrase scrawled beneath the boarded windows: '*Sweets to the sweet.*' She does not realize – not yet – that it is a caption, underscoring the terrifying yet tempting treacle of the portrait: the bittersweet taste of the forbidden – the apple offered to Eve, the single bite of which measured the fate of Eden.

Helen learns nothing further about an old man's death, but passers-by eagerly relate another story of violence: a retarded boy attacked with a razor in the public lavatories, castrated and left for dead. When she revisits the stories at a dinner party, Trevor's chill arrogance is supplanted by the heated barbs of another academic, Purcell, who dismisses them as 'urban legends': contemporary fairytales of improbable and ironic events, told as true and usually attributed to a 'friend of a friend'.[2] The issue turns quickly from the tale to the telling, as Barker recites a simple, but too often unspoken, truth about the human urge (if not need) for the tale of terror.

'Why tell these horrible stories if they're not true?' asks Trevor's assistant, Bernadette; and Purcell's glib answer – that their subject is taboo – is insufficient. Bernadette proposes that the most forbidden of subjects, death, though explored constantly in the news, is never quite close enough: 'Maybe . . . death has to be *near*; we have to *know* it's just around the corner.' Only in these 'horrible stories' – the stuff of fiction – may the veil of reality be lifted, and the true face of death made known.

Helen returns to the estate, determined to verify or discredit the tales. Needy children seek a 'penny for the Guy' – a ritual of oncoming

Guy Fawkes Day, and a sly reminder, unheeded by Helen, of the way in which even fact, with time, may be rendered irrevocably into myth.[3] Anne-Marie greets Helen with frightened discomfort and denies telling her anything; it is the anxiety of expectancy – of an imminent arrival. Helen is again the outsider, a pariah in this realm of the vital, everyday existence she had deigned herself competent to study. She throws off the guise of researcher and visits the abandoned maisonette, to look a final time on the raging face painted there, '[n]ot as an anthropologist among an alien tribe, but as a confessed ghost train rider: for the thrill of it'.

The maisonette has been sealed, its door locked, its broken windows boarded over; yet something is inside – a dog, perhaps – whining, imprisoned, scrabbling to escape. As Helen departs, she sees policemen and an ambulance circling Anne-Marie's flat. Someone has killed baby Kerry, slitting his innocent throat. Sickened, Helen staggers away from the eager and ever-growing crowd, rebelling against the very emotions that had drawn her, only moments before, to seek the face of the howling man:

> There would be nothing to see, she knew, and even if there had been she had no desire to look. These people . . . were exhibiting an appetite she was disgusted by. She was not one of them; would never *be* one of them. She wanted to slap every eager face into sense; wanted to say: 'It's pain and grief you're going to spy on. Why? Why?' But she had no courage left. Revulsion had drained her of all but the energy to wander away, leaving the crowd to its sport.

At home that night, Trevor urges her to forget the incident: 'You were just passing through.' But Trevor, predictably self-absorbed, is wrong: 'Nobody ever just *passed through*; experience always left its mark. Sometimes it merely scratched; on occasion it took off limbs. She did not know the extent of her present wounding, but she knew it was more profound than she yet understood, and it made her afraid.' Unlike the self-proclaimed intellectuals of her cloistered scholastic set, Helen has faced the unknown, actually seen through to the other side; it is no longer the stuff of books, certainly not of a thesis, but part of her life – and now she feels herself drawn, like a moth to a flame, into its enigma.

With the morning news, Helen realizes that Kerry had been murdered before dawn, his corpse lying but a few feet away when she talked with Anne-Marie. She hurries to the police, who deny knowing about other murders on the estate. When confronted with the inevitable question – why, then, would these stories be told? – a detective recounts the endless false confessions he has heard. 'Maybe,' Helen tells him, 'if they didn't tell you the stories . . . they'd actually go out and do it.' Then she reflects:

> And the stories *she'd* been told, were they confessions of uncommitted crimes, accounts of the worst imaginable, imagined to keep fiction from becoming fact? The thought chased its own tail: these terrible stories still needed a *first cause*, a well-spring from which they leaped . . . Were these inventions common currency, as Purcell had claimed? Was there a place, however small, reserved in every heart for the monstrous?

Helen returns to Spector Street for Kerry's burial and a final truth. Death has brought the estate to life: the atmosphere is less one of sorrow than of celebration. It is Bonfire Night, when Guy Fawkes's effigy will be sacrificed to the flames. As the funeral cortège passes, Anne-Marie shows no grief; she seems oddly elevated by the proceedings, resplendent in her fabled fifteen minutes of fame.

As the crowd disperses, onlookers heading home or to further proceedings at the crematorium – or the bonfire – Helen ventures again to the abandoned maisonette, thoughts of saving the trapped dog offered as excuses for her true desire: another vision of the portrait inside. Now the door is unlocked, the dog escaped or dead, and she enters to look upon the horrific holy of holies. Before the painting waits an obscene tithe, a heap of squalid bedding adorned with brightly-wrapped chocolates and caramels – and bloodied razor blades.

A buzzing, a flight of bees, surrounds Helen, and the shadow of a man steps between her and the world outside, bringing the sweet smell of candyfloss with him. As she makes her excuses, searching desperately for an exit line, the intruder begins his seduction:

'I came for you,' he said.

She repeated the four words in her head. *I came for you.* If they were meant as a threat, they certainly weren't spoken as one.

'I don't . . . know you,' she said.

'No,' the man murmured. 'But you doubted me.'

'Doubted?'

'You weren't content with the stories, with what they wrote on the walls. So I was obliged to come.'

The drowsiness slowed her mind to a crawl, but she grasped the essentials of what the man was saying. That he was legend, and she, in disbelieving him, had obliged him to show his hand.

And there is but a single hand to show her; the other is missing – in its place, a hook. He is a creature of whispers and storybook fears, the stuff of old wives' tales and bedtime cautions: the Candyman.

She knew him, without doubt. She had known him all along, in that place kept for terrors. It was the man on the wall. His portrait painter had not been a fantasist: the picture that howled over her was matched in each extraordinary particular by the man she now set eyes upon. He was bright to the point of gaudiness: his flesh a waxy yellow, his thin lips pale blue, his wild eyes glittering as if their irises were set with rubies. His jacket was a patchwork, his trousers the same. He looked, she thought, almost ridiculous, with his blood-stained motley, and the hint of rouge on his jaundiced cheeks. But people were facile. They needed these shows and shams to keep their interest. Miracles; murders; demons driven out and stones rolled from tombs. The cheap glamour did not taint the sense beneath. It was only, in the natural history of the mind, the bright feathers that drew the species to mate with its secret self.[4]

Dour but penetrating thoughts: the Candyman is what brought Helen to the wall – *sweets to the sweet* – and what brought the crowd to Anne-Marie's flat as baby Kerry's corpse was removed. He is the maimed, the monstrous, the macabre, the marvellous – the sideshow huckster in life's carnival of the forbidden: the motorway accident, the shocking news footage, the porno film, the horror story.

As Helen tries to flee, she flings the blanket from the bedding at him, and unveils the naked, ravaged body of Kerry – not taken for burial, but left as an offering to the Candyman. This final revelation overwhelms her. She begs for mercy, but he asks only if she believes in him. When she says that she does, he asks, without pause: 'Then why do you want to live?'

Why, indeed? The Candyman's condition, like that of Guy Fawkes, is a blessed one: to exist only as rumour – to live in people's dreams, rituals, religions, but not to *be*. 'The sweetness he offered was life without living: was to be dead, but remembered everywhere, immortal in gossip and graffiti.' His seduction is not easily resisted. 'Be my victim,' he croons. 'Your death would be a parable to frighten children with. Lovers would use it as an excuse to cling closer together.' Still she will not give into him, granting him only a kiss – and with this dulcet taste of the forbidden, she fades into the mercy of unconsciousness.

She awakens to witness Anne-Marie carrying the baby's corpse toward the bonfire. Helen follows, entering the pyramid of piled timber and discarded furniture, the altar of a reality whose meaning has been elevated by time and telling to the lofty height of myth. The Candyman is there, waiting for her. The pyre is lit, and as the heat claims her, she falls, resigned to her fate, into his embrace. There is only one consolation: 'Perhaps they would remember her . . . Perhaps she might become, in time, a story with which to frighten children.'

And in her final moments, she sees Trevor, moving among the celebrants, questioning them, seeking her, and she wills him to look past the flames, to see her burning brightly against the night: 'Not so that he could save her from death – she was long past hope of that – but because she pitied him in his bewilderment and wanted to give him, though he would not have thanked her for it, something to be haunted by. That, and a story to tell.'

In this sublime story about stories, Clive Barker thus rejects the timeworn, and so very safe, notion of horror fiction as the essence of escapism, reminding us of the truths – sometimes hollow, often divine – that burn at the heart of the fiction of fear. Indeed, with typical élan, Barker uses 'The Forbidden' to subvert his own readership, to question their very presence in his world, to remind them of their seduction at his hands, to ask them to consider that elusive 'first cause' for the tale of terror, a book of blood. Is there a place, however small, reserved in every heart for the monstrous? And if so, should it be denied, should we be made its victim – or should we accept its wisdom and burn brightly with the knowledge of how and why it holds us in its sway? Among the least touted, yet most profound, of the stories that make up the *Books of Blood*, it is little wonder that 'The Forbidden' should be adapted as a motion picture.

With its breathtaking overture, the music of Philip Glass accompanying a gyrosphere camera's glimpse into the less-than-perfect geometry of downtown Chicago, *Candyman* gives prompt notice that it is no ordinary horror film.[5] Its opening credits fade into a swarm of bees, and a deep male voice, vibrant with menace, utters that most memorable line of 'The Forbidden': 'What's blood for, if not for shedding?' A woman's scream pierces the Chicago skyline, and as bees rise in millions to weave dark storm clouds over the city, the voice pronounces: 'I came for you.'[6]

Written for the screen and directed by Bernard Rose, *Candyman* is a calculated trumping of the increasingly infantile sub-genre of man/monster films (*ie*, the *Friday the 13th* series), singlehandedly reinventing these films for an adult audience and prefiguring the highly successful and self-conscious *Scream* series.

Rose, a graduate of the National Film and Television School, whose career blossomed in music videos – directing two early staples of MTV, 'Relax' for Frankie Goes To Hollywood and 'Red, Red Wine' for UB40 – made his feature film debut with *Body Contact* (1987), and then directed the memorable *Paperhouse* (1989), which deftly manipulated horror film conventions into nightmarish psychological drama, and the harrowingly violent but unfortunately titled *Chicago Joe and the Showgirl* (1990), a criminal romance based upon the 'Cleft Chin Murder' case that scandalized World War Two England.

It was during the filming of *Chicago Joe* at London's Pinewood Studios that Rose first met Clive Barker, who was then completing work on *Nightbreed*. The two directors had lunch together. 'I didn't know his work, actually, at the time I met him,' Rose notes (and, indeed, to this day, he has never seen *Hellraiser*). 'But about six months later, I picked up one of the *Books of Blood* and read it – when I read the story "The Forbidden", I immediately called Clive and asked him if I could have the rights to it.'

The story seemed perfect for adaptation as a motion picture. 'I really liked the story,' Rose says. 'I liked a number of the stories, actually, but I thought that one was a really good film, because it had an incredibly simple but powerful premise: the idea that, if the people stop believing in the gods, then there is a moment of time that the gods have before they disappear from currency where they can some-how exist independently of the people, and strike back, as it were. The movie didn't really turn out that way, although the idea is at its heart.' Rose, in turn, was the perfect writer/director to bring Barker's words to life on the screen: 'I've always liked the horror genre. I'm not one of these people who ever thought that I was "slumming" when making a horror film.'

As executive producer of *Candyman*, Clive Barker's role was limited once Rose was given the helm as director: Rose wrote the screenplay and exercised fundamental creative control over the outcome, includ-ing significant additions and embellishments to the plot that made the film his own. 'And Clive was very supportive of all that. He was great; we had a very good relationship during the entire time of making that picture. And then the film made money as well. I remember it as one of those times when everything pretty much came out good. It doesn't always happen in the movie business, you know.'

The result was indeed compelling cinema that succeeds on its own terms rather than on those of Barker's novelette. It is powered by Rose's dream-driven style and rich sense of allegory, and the atmospheric cinematography of Anthony B Richmond – and marred only slightly by an inevitable surrender to the imagery of horror.

The very change of title omens the shift of focus from myth to monster, but Rose's adaptation, unlike most recent attempts to trans-late the prose of horror into pictures, is blessedly intelligent. Barker's principal characters survive essentially intact, although bestowed with different surnames and more detailed domestic, histories. Virginia Madsen plays Helen Lyle, an attractive, hard-driven, white middle-class graduate student at the University of Illinois-Chicago. With a black co-researcher, Bernadette (Kasi Lemmons), Helen is preparing a thesis on contemporary urban folklore, tape-recording undergraduate accounts of 'the scariest story I've ever heard'. In the film's first narrative sequence, a student recounts a stereotypical campfire tale of a babysitter's encounter with a hook-handed killer known as the Candyman. 'If you look into the mirror and say his name five times,' she tells Helen, 'he'll appear behind you, breathing down your neck.'

The dare echoes the Faustian quandary that pervades Barker's darkest fiction; it is also a concession, perhaps, to the popcorn-chewing masses, for whom the damning power of human doubt and disbelief – the cornerstone of 'The Forbidden' – may have been too diffuse an explanation for the Candyman's existence. With this overt act of invocation, Rose ratchets up the suspense, but also reduces the Candyman from a creature of myth to a bogeyman who waits in the shadows for those foolish enough to summon him.[7]

Helen's research continues despite her insufferable, self-indulgent lech of a husband, Trevor (Xander Berkeley). She learns that a serial killer is at large in the Cabrini Green public housing project, using construction vents between walls to invade his victims' apartments through bathroom mirror receptacles; hence, it would seem, the lore of the looking-glass. It is here that the film's transposition of locale from England to America is truly inspired: Cabrini Green is one of America's most desperate ghettoes, a dream of urban renewal turned into a nightmare of violence. (Even the location shooting for *Candyman* was fraught with peril, with the producers literally buying peace with local gangs to allow safe access to Cabrini Green.)

'It's just one of those awful things,' Rose says, 'but . . . if you shoot a film set in a working-class estate in Liverpool, then basically every single character in your movie is going to be talking in an incomprehensible accent – and that is a really serious problem if you want to market the film outside the UK. You could set it in a tower block in London, but if you can't do it in Liverpool, then why not move it to America? And then, of course, once you move it to America, you get the whole race, as opposed to class, issue.

'When I went to Chicago, I said to the film commission, *Take me to the worst place in Chicago.* And they said, without pausing: *Oh, you mean Cabrini Green!* I thought that this was definitely an arena of pure terror – and white people have an irrational fear of what goes on in those places. The truth is that 99% of the time, people are just carrying on with their lives in a very mundane fashion. The terror and the dread that people feel about those kinds of housing projects is largely irrational. It's not even racism – it happens in England with class, with poor people in the block, which is how the story is written. It's the terror of poverty, which is, for some reason, one of the oldest fears – and I'd never seen that done in a horror movie before.'[8]

On a laughing dare with Bernadette, Helen recites the Candyman's name five times while looking into a mirror – and her descent into Hell begins. First is the literal descent, as the impulse to visit Cabrini Green – 'an entire community . . . attributing the daily horrors of their lives to a mythical figure' – is irresistible. Braving the gang-infested project, Helen and Bernadette find the abandoned apartment where the murderer struck, and a curious slogan – '*Sweets to the sweet*' – spray-painted across the outer hallway. Helen's curiosity leads her to a portal presided over by the portrait of a howling man; beneath it is an offering of wrapped candy and razorblades. One of the residents, Anne-Marie McCoy (Vanessa Williams), tells them about the fearsome killer known as the Candyman.

At dinner that night, Helen's excitement is derailed when the condescending Professor Purcell (Michael Culkin) notes his paper on the Candyman, written a decade before, which reveals the historical backstory that Bernard Rose developed to explain the origins of the monster. According to a legend dating to the late 1800s, a renowned black portrait artist, hired to capture the virginal beauty of a wealthy white man's daughter, fell in love with her. The father, infuriated, enacted a grisly vengeance, hiring hooligans who sawed off the artist's painting hand, then smeared honeycomb over his body, leaving him to be stung to death by bees. His body was burned and the ashes scattered over Cabrini Green, which he supposedly has haunted ever since.

Helen is not dissuaded. She returns alone to the project to photograph the howling face, and meets a lonely boy named Jake (DeJuan Guy). When she asks about the Candyman, he takes her to a public restroom where, the story goes, a retarded youth was castrated. Inside the grim lavatory are more spray-painted words and a toilet full of bees. A quartet of gangbangers saunters in, their leader wielding a dockworker's hook. 'I hear you're looking for the Candyman, bitch,' he says. 'Well, you found him.' He beats her and leaves her for dead.

When Helen identifies her assailant in a police line-up, he is charged with assault – and the murders that have plagued Cabrini Green. 'Candyman isn't real,' she tells the still-frightened Jake. 'He's just a story, you know . . . like Dracula or Frankenstein.' But the story soon comes to life. In a deserted parking garage, distracted by her photographs of the surreal portrait from Cabrini Green, Helen is greeted by an ominous shadow whose mesmerizing voice, fraught with heavy breathing, calls to her: 'Helen . . . I came for you.'

Out of a backlit obscurity steps a dominating figure cloaked in a mélange of nineteenth-century motley and 1970s pimpwear. 'Do I know you?' Helen asks, her eyes dreamy, stung with flashbulb images of the howling man. 'No,' he answers, although of course she knows him: it is the Candyman – not the gang lord who took his name, but the fantasy and folklore made real. '[Y]ou doubted me . . . You are not content with the stories, so I was obliged to come.' He shows Helen the hook he wears in place of a hand, and implores her to become his victim.

Tony Todd embraces the role of the Candyman with fierce nobility. With his imposing frame and princely features, he is perhaps the most seductive monster (other than a vampire) to appear in years. His Candyman is also implacable, a recurring nightmare who invades Helen's fragile world again and again until all of its lies are revealed. Rose's script remains true to the words the Candyman spoke in 'The Forbidden', and eschews the insipid schoolyard wit mouthed by the likes of Freddy Krueger, which so corrupted *Hellraiser III: Hell on Earth*.

The Candyman's arrival trips what was a linear plot into the realm of delirium: 'I am the writing on the wall, the whisper in the classroom. Without these things, I am nothing. So now I must shed innocent blood . . . Come with me.' Helen swoons, then awakens, covered with blood, to screams; she has been transported to Anne-Marie's apartment, where she sees the severed head of the German Shepherd and a meat cleaver, which she plucks from the gore-stained floor. Suddenly Anne-Marie attacks her, demanding the return of her baby; as they grapple, Helen wounds Anne-Marie, and police officers burst into the apartment to find Helen wielding the blade over her.

After a night in jail, the police release Helen into the custody of Trevor: an unrealistic but convenient turn of events. The Candyman invades her home with a threat: either baby Anthony or Helen must die. His preference is made clear: 'Your death will be a tale to frighten children, to make lovers cling closer in their rapture. Come with me, and be immortal.'

Bernadette interrupts the seduction and pays a brutal price; the Candyman disembowels her, leaving damning evidence – another bloody knife – in Helen's hand. This time the authorities secure Helen in a psychiatric hospital. Her only visitor is her loving tormentor, who invades her padded cell to whisper much more than sweet nothings – the conduit to the heart of Barker's novelette: 'I am rumour. It is a blessed condition, believe me. To be whispered about at street corners, to live in other people's dreams, but not to have to be.'

A month later, Helen awakens from ceaseless sedation to learn that she has been charged with murder. Her story, when told to a consulting psychiatrist, confirms her apparent madness – until the Candyman arrives to eviscerate him. 'You're mine now,' he tells Helen, and frees her to stagger home, where she finds what should have been obvious all along: a female student has moved in with Trevor, and the lovebirds are busily remodelling the apartment to remove every trace of Helen.

'It's over,' Helen tells Trevor – and herself. There is nowhere left for her now but Cabrini Green, where she becomes a bloody Alice, passing through the looking-glass into the ravaged Wonderland of the Candyman. The gutted apartment opens magically into a cathedral of crimson glory on whose walls are painted the legendary stations of his cross: each brutal act of the torment engineered by the vengeful father of his long-lost love. At last Helen finds his sleeping body, laid out on a bier. She cuts at him with a hook, which merely awakens him.

She asks for the child in exchange for her own life, and it is an offer he cannot refuse, the betrothal that he has desired for so very long: 'Our names will be written on a thousand walls . . . Our crimes told and retold by our faithful believers. We shall die together before their very eyes, and give them something to be haunted by.'[9]

With the sting of his kiss, the Candyman and his hostage are gone. On the wall are new words – '*It was always you, Helen*' – and a portrait of his dead love, who looks just like her. She hears the baby's cry – from the Green, where broken boards and boxes have been stacked for a bonfire.[10] As Helen hurries into the night, struggling through the maze of detritus toward the child, the occupants of the project gather, dousing the kindling with fuel, believing that the Candyman is somewhere inside. As the bonfire is ignited and flames rise around her, she fights to rescue Anthony, but the Candyman appears – even he has betrayed her. But she thrusts a flaming shaft into his heart and makes her way through the inferno, giving up her own life to save the child. Burned, bereft of hair and flesh, she places the baby at the feet of Anne-Marie, and the Candyman, defeated, explodes into a wash of flames and angry bees; only then does Helen collapse and die.

In a Hollywood world, however, there can be few truly unhappy endings. The rescue of the baby (who had perished cruelly in 'The Forbidden') is insufficient. Vengeance, that stalwart of silver screen finales, must be enacted. Helen is buried, her internment witnessed by a handful of mourners – Trevor, his lover and Purcell; but as the casket is lowered into the earth, the residents of Cabrini Green, led by Anne-Marie, march across the rolling hills of the cemetery to pay their respects and to offer a symbol of her sacrifice. Little Jake tosses a scorched hook – the last remnant of the Candyman – onto Helen's coffin.

That night, as Trevor lingers in the bathroom, lamenting Helen's death, his paramour beckons to him from the kitchen, where she worries a steak with a knife. In time he faces the mirror and begins to sob, calling Helen's name . . . five times. Like the Candyman, Helen appears, hook in hand, to gut Trevor, leaving his bloody corpse for his new girlfriend, incriminating knife in hand, to discover.

Rose's insistent use of mirror imagery is, at first glance, an unnecessary intrusion upon Barker's text, but it proves a canny strategy. The mirror offers not only a mechanism for summoning the Candyman, but also a visual symbol of the ironic parallels lurking within 'The Forbidden'. By invoking the inescapable racial tension of his setting, Rose pushes Barker's suggestions of caste conflict into a virtual supertext. White and black, positive and negative, life and art: mirrors, all of them, some shining darkness, others light. Thus *Candyman* is a constantly unfolding riddle of doubling: Helen's posh condominium is a duplicate of Cabrini Green, its intended use as public housing abandoned when city planners realized that the surrounding geography would not confine its dark-skinned dwellers; Anne-Marie's baby is the one Helen wishes for, and that her barren life with Trevor cannot provide; and, in the finale, Helen is reborn as the new Candyman.

In creating what he describes as a 'modern Gothic', Rose sought to emphasize 'the romantic horror of death', heightening the sexual tension between Helen and the Candyman. In the novelette, Helen's desire is for that delight which Clive Barker holds as paramount: dread. His story makes literal the power of storytelling to give life and meaning to our deepest fears. Although the opening act of *Candyman* adopts this impulse – which is, after all, the motivation for Helen's initial visit to Cabrini Green – slowly but surely Rose's rendition succumbs to another strategy. Helen is haunted by the Candyman not because of her disbelief, but because she is his long-lost love reincarnate. Thus is desire inverted: while in 'The Forbidden', it is Helen whose passion ignites the flames of her destruction and deification, in *Candyman*, the lust is a more familiar one: the monster's libido.[11]

'In the story,' Rose notes, 'the whole back story of Helen is very sketchy. Clive mentions, at certain odd times, that Trevor has returned, in a bad mood, from one of his many girlfriends. The thing about a movie is that those psychological things must be played out explicitly; because when someone is living with a husband who's cheating on her, that will become the dominant force in their lives. Something literary can allude to that, and expect readers to fill in the gaps; but in a movie, you can't have missing scenes – people would say, *Wait a minute, she'd have to have the fight with him, and then she'd have to have this* ... So there's that odd soap-operatic quality as a subplot that isn't the kind of thing you normally see in a horror film. And my idea was that, therefore, this is really why she had this yearning for some impossible *Liebestod* – a love/death experience with a mythical figure.'

Although clearly the best motion picture made to date from the *Books of Blood*, *Candyman* must explain what 'The Forbidden' chose to leave unexplained, defusing Barker's vague mythology and making it known, palatable and, inevitably, safe. Rose notes: 'For me, certainly, the second half of the film doesn't work as well as the first; because the moment you start making all the unknowable things concrete, which you have to do in order to photograph them, there's always the element of disappointment. Because film is so literal; you can only basically deal in objects. Even if they're computer-generated objects, they're still objects, and have to somehow be represented. And all horror films fall apart at the point when you bring on the villain – for that reason.

'One of the reasons *The Exorcist* is so well-sustained is that Friedkin doesn't ever really bring the villain on; he just shows the villain's effect on this little girl. You never actually see it, but it's still very scary. It's an old problem with movies; and from my point of view, although I like individual parts of the second half of the movie, I think the second half is not as good as the first.'

Audiences and critics disagreed. Despite Rose's reservations, *Candyman* is a superior horror film: mature and elegant, yet fierce and frightening. Its success demanded the inevitable: a sequel and, indeed, a prospective series that might replicate the *Friday the 13th* and *Nightmare on Elm Street* money machines. When the idea of a sequel was presented to Bernard Rose, however, he offered a unique solution: to forget the character of the Candyman and return instead to the source material, transforming another *Books of Blood* gem, 'The Midnight Meat Train', into *Candyman II*.

'One of the things I believed from the very beginning,' Rose says, 'was that if you made a sequel to that film, with the same guy running around with the same hook, then the film would be boring from the first frame – because you know who you're going to see, you know what he's going to do ... and I could give a shit. But that's always what happens with horror movie sequels. You know what the guy looks like, and what he does ... so now he's going to do it again.

'So I thought, well, rather than doing a sequel which is a remake, it would be far better to go to a different place. And then, of course, the bogeyman that the people would conjure from their wanting so badly to believe in a bogeyman would look and feel and sound different, because it would come from *their* culture – it would be particular to *them*.'

Rose wrote a provocative script, setting the sequel in London's infamous Whitechapel district. 'The bogeyman who is conjured, basically, by a bunch of East End policemen who work on a beat with prostitutes, is Jack the Ripper – because, in an odd sort of way, they needed him to come back.' The film was conceived on a tripartite level, seguing back and forth between historical Jack the Ripper sequences in the 1890s and present-day sequences on the same streets, then concluding with the central characters 'riding on a tube train full of meat' – its final act adapting 'The Midnight Meat Train'.

'We should have made it, actually,' Rose says. 'I think it would have been a good movie.' But the producers, Propaganda Films, disagreed vehemently: 'They *hated* it. They wanted to make a film with the Candyman. I thought they were going to end up remaking the first one, which is essentially what they did – and it was pretty bad, I thought.'

Clive believed, in turn, that 'The Midnight Meat Train' would work better as a film on its own, without implicating the mythology of *Candyman*. In early 1993, with Barker's encouragement, Rose began work on a separate motion picture adaptation, leaving the *Candyman* sequel to other hands; but he soon abandoned the project, and instead wrote and directed a rumination on the life of Ludwig Van Beethoven, *Immortal Beloved* (1994), starring Gary Oldman; and a moving adaptation of *Anna Karenina* (1997) with Sophie Marceau.

The working relationship between Barker and Rose did not end, however: 'He has an imagination that matches mine perfectly,' Clive says. In early 1997, Universal Pictures announced that the two creators would be reunited for a motion picture adaptation of *The Thief of Always*. Kennedy-Marshall Company at Paramount had originally optioned the supernatural fable for an animated feature film, but when the rights reverted, Universal optioned the book for a live action version to be written and directed by Rose that would also include digital effects and puppetry – co-produced, appropriately, by Lisa Henson, the daughter of the late 'Muppets' creator Jim Henson.

As of this writing, *The Thief of Always* remains in development based on a revised version of Rose's screenplay; but Rose declined to continue as director after the producers decided to work entirely in digital animation. 'That takes four years,' Rose says. 'I don't have what it takes to hang around for four years. The film I was going to make was live action, very little digital – just some effects. I wanted to use more live effects, actually. My problem with the story, as an animated film of any kind, is that if you have somebody entering a fantasy world, then they have to come from somewhere that's real – otherwise you can't tell the difference.'

Rose then turned to new technology, shooting *ivansxtc* (2000), an updated version of Tolstoy's 'The Death of Ivan Ilyich' set in a Hollywood talent agency, in high-definition digital format. 'It's signalling my exit from Hollywood. I've had enough, basically. I don't think it's about them; it's about the new things. I think that technology has reached a point where you don't need to ask anyone's permission to make a film. So therefore anyone can and should make a film, in the same way that they would write a novel. That doesn't mean that everyone is going to write a novel, obviously; and it doesn't mean that all novels that are written are going to be published. But it puts the means to make a film within the scope of anybody who wants to pick it up – and because the technology is changing, the nature of the films will change.'

Hollywood, however, seemed reluctant to change. After Rose's departure from the *Candyman* sequel, Propaganda pursued the vehicle it desired: a resurrection of the hook-handed monster in the hope of a new horror film franchise. The results – *Candyman: Farewell to the Flesh* (1995) and *Candyman: Day of the Dead* (1999) – would confirm an observation made in the very story on which the original *Candyman* was based: '[M]onsters were seldom very terrible once hauled into the plain light of day. As long as this man were known only by his deeds he held untold power over the imagination; but the human truth beneath the terrors would, she knew, be bitterly disappointing.'

26

FINDING A RELIGION

EVERVILLE (1994)

[I]t is easier to sail many thousand miles through cold and storm and cannibals, in a government ship, with five hundred men and boys to assist one, than it is to explore the private sea, the Atlantic and the Pacific of one's being alone.

— HENRY DAVID THOREAU, *Walden*

In the rigorous pursuit of definition, a time-honoured device for critiquing and marketing the dark fantastic has been a simplistic division between 'supernatural horror' (the stuff of Bram Stoker's *Dracula* (1897)) and 'psychological horror' (exemplified by Robert Bloch's *Psycho* (1959)). As suggested by the maturing fiction of Clive Barker and the parallel pursuits of Thomas Harris, there is no meaningful distinction. If literature is a mirror, however warped, of our existence, then there is no useful purpose (save for marketing and mindless criticism-by-numbers) for dividing up sides this way.

Consider: the 'real' world is a supernatural one. Even if written by an atheist, a fiction must acknowledge that reality is filled with people who believe, principally through religion, in the existence of the

380

supernatural. Our reality is also not entirely explicable; it is haunted by mysteries that lack scientific solutions. Thus the 'real' world includes, at the very least, the *possibility* of the supernatural, if not the supernatural itself; and any 'psychological' fiction set in that world is thus implicitly supernatural – just as any conscientious 'supernatural' fiction, including *Dracula*, is insistently psychological, for what is horror but an emotion, a point of view, a state of mind?

In championing 'realism', critical perspectives often propose a limited (and limiting) art defined by the very absence of the prospect of the supernatural. These interpretations are modes of exclusion, founded upon an urge to ignore or avoid (or, indeed, repress) the inexplicable elements of reality that make the reader or reviewer uncomfortable.

Ironically, a discerning look at most 'supernatural' horror stories reveals intensely 'psychological' fictions that have as little to do with the supernatural as 'hard' science fiction. The typical vampire is a logic-bound construct who exists (and desists) by explicable and rational – not supernatural – rules. Burial soil, crucifixes, garlic at the window, the aversion to sunlight, the need for blood: all hallmarks of a natural (if not necessarily human) being; the murderous necrophiliac Ed Gein, an icon of 'psychological' horror, is far more difficult to comprehend. The traditional werewolf is a better example: a hirsute Mr Hyde, the overtly physical manifestation of the beast within, is not at all different from a run-of-the-mill psychotic killer. That you may need silver bullets instead of hollow points to drop him is irrelevant. We may as well argue that an alligator is supernatural – the only difference being that some of us have seen alligators. In other words, vampires and werewolves are imaginary monsters, but not imaginary theosophies, ways of explaining, in direct terms, the dilemma of our existence. When presented with a creature – whether werewolf or alligator – the question is not whether the creature does exist or could exist. The question is: what does the creature represent? Or better yet, the one so rarely asked: what does the creature believe?

Which leads us, in turn, to the more important question: what do we believe? We think of our most universal notion of the supernatural – 'religion' – as another box to be ticked on the census form, right after male or female, single or married, Caucasian or African-American or Native American or Asian or Other. What will it be . . . Baptist, Catholic, Adventist, Buddhist, Atheist? In other words, we are taught to think of religion in organized terms, as a rigid system of beliefs that can be packaged and marketed as 'Lutheran' as neatly as a kind of fiction can be packaged and marketed as 'horror'. This is a kind of thinking that leads to quick denials, and to more dividing lines: pro-this, anti-that, religious right, godless left.

The Bible is the bestselling book of Western civilization, and whatever we might think of it (or the many lies built around it), there is no doubt that it is a fascinating document – and one that cannot easily be neglected, since its words rule our lives. Whether we like it or not, the Bible is the moral dialectic upon which Western culture was founded, has evolved, and is regulated.

One of the curiosities of fundamentalist creeds – those that purport to read the Bible literally or, at the least, directly – is that their ministers work less often from the Bible than from their own embellishments of its text. The Bible itself is fiction, of course. Even if we hold to its truth – the truth of its words, the truth of its God – we must consider its writers, who, after all, were only human. Whether inspired by grace or special wisdom, they saw the world through their own eyes and used their own words to commit 'truth' to the page – just as, centuries later, translators would use their own words (many of them inaccurate) to convey that 'truth' to new readers. More important, the Bible *uses* fiction; and there, you see, is the rub.

The problem confronting fundamentalists – the supposed Biblical literalists – is that Jesus Christ, the hero of the very book in which they find their literal 'truths', speaks in parables. He tells stories. He knew the power of fiction, and used fiction to instruct and elevate those who would listen to him. And the very act of storytelling by the man whom many believe was God incarnate is rather convincing proof that the God of the Bible indeed works in mysterious ways: that he will, when appropriate, offer stories rather than literal truth to explain the human condition (and thus, perhaps, a creation story to explain evolution and its responsibilities).

The ministers have hijacked the Bible, and the time is long overdue for the people to take it back. Clive Barker is doing just that.

*

His first books were titled in blood, and he was knighted the 'future of horror', but Clive Barker was not typecast so easily. After *The Damnation Game*, an accomplished first novel that was unmistakably the stuff of horror, he surprised and confounded and delighted readers by penning a series of books that broke ranks with expectation and genre. In *Weaveworld*, he gave notice that horror fiction was merely the beachhead in his invasion of the realm of the *fantastique*. By the time of his monumental *Imajica*, reviewers and copywriters were scrambling for a new label; but by then, Clive Barker was a genre unto himself.

Everville is the second book of a trilogy-in-progress known as 'The Art'.[1] Although their literary antecedents include ER Eddison's Zimi-amvian novels and Tolkien's *The Lord of the Rings* – to which they inevitably have been compared – the books of 'The Art' are written without the affectations of latter-day faerie. Their more crucial inspiration is medieval dream-vision literature – William Langland's *Piers Plowman* (circa 1360), the works of the unknown 'Pearl poet' (circa 1400) and John Bunyan's *The Pilgrim's Progress* (1678); but Barker's decidedly contemporary fiction speaks in every critical passage to reality.

The opening novel of 'The Art', *The Great and Secret Show*, offered a hallucinatory battle royal between men and demigods centred on the discovery of an unChristian cross and an evolutionary drug known as the Nuncio. Set firmly in, and then subverting, the *'Salem's Lot* template of eighties horror fiction – the small town isolated and besieged by evil – *The Great and Secret Show* eschewed the generic ploy of a monster-threatened reality and proposed instead an interpen-etration of realities, a setting in which characters might dream with their eyes open. Barker cleverly poised one dream of America – the false dream of Hollywood, played out on ever-flickering screens – against the true dream of self-knowledge, the hope for an existence that transcended flesh.

In *Everville*, Barker deconstructs another American dream – the dream of the West, of pioneers and *lebensraum*. (It is no small irony that Hollywood, at the westward limit of the continent, should become the dream machine of America, the means by which we have sought to conquer the remainder of the globe.) His story does not pick up on the trail of *The Great and Secret Show*, but nearly one hundred and fifty years before the events of that novel, on the Oregon Trail.[2]

The time is October 1848; the place is Wyoming. A lost and ragged band of pioneers, many of them immigrants, staggers through a violent snowstorm, the final test of an ill-fated trek that left Independence, Missouri, in search of a promised land but has found only spiritual reckoning and death. The pioneers' focus is singleminded: 'Now more than ever we must have faith in the dream of the West.' That faith is inflexible: 'they would testify to the end of their lives that for all the sorrows of this life, no man should turn from God, for God was hope, and Everlasting.' But the pioneers' dream of Eden is lost in grey mountains – ice, snow and death. One child has survived: Maeve O'Connell, a sickly twelve-year-old whose daft father dares to imagine the glorious, shining city that he will build when their travails are complete – a paradise on the far side of the Rocky Mountains called Everville.[3]

Caught in a snowstorm, their ranks thinned by relentless adversity, the pioneers hear the clarion of trumpets as an angelic creature approaches. The pioneers defend their Christian virtue by wounding the creature, then killing Maeve's father. Maeve drinks the honeyed blood of this thing named Coker Ammiano – a half-breed, child of a trespasser and a dream – who leads her up the hillside to a congregation of the otherworldly. A marriage ceremony is defiled when she speaks, and in the violent aftermath, she sees a crack in reality – and on the other side, the dream-sea, Quiddity. As the crack closes, Coker lets the rift shear his wings from his torso. Maeve tends his wounds, and tells him of the shining dream of Everville.

At Independence, Maeve's father had met Owen Buddenbaum, a prissy student of the occult who seeks the parallel reality known as the Metacosm – the home of Quiddity, which is visited but three times by humans: at birth, at death and upon consummating true love. Buddenbaum's name – Thomas Mann's Buddenbrooks by way of L Frank Baum – evokes his transplanted European sensibilities, the decadence and old money of *The Damnation Game*, and a hint of the diabolical: 'His business was the epic, after all.' But the stakes of his game are beyond damnation; he plays for redemption and that secret wisdom known as the Art. Buddenbaum gives Maeve's father a strange cross and tells him: '*Dreams are doorways . . . If we but have the courage to step over the threshold.*' After her father's death, Maeve finds the cross – twin to the medallion of *The Great and Secret Show* – among his possessions, and a note that reads: '*Bury this at the crossroads, where Everville begins.*'

Fast forward to the end of the twentieth century and the Oregon town founded by the surviving pioneers. Everville has become, with enough time and revisionist history, as American as apple pie and assassination. It is a setting that, like Palomo Grove of *The Great and Secret Show*, seems consciously Kinglike: a small town in bucolic retreat, laced with petty intrigue – unsolved crimes, infidelity, oldtime religion. This Norman Rockwell façade is peopled by those who came after the settlers, the builders of suburbs and founders of committees: 'men and women who had lost all sense of the tender, terrible holiness of things.' The town's secrets are locked securely inside the walls of the Everville Historical Society, which prefers the official history: 'It was highly selective of course, but then so were many history lessons. There was no place in this celebration of the Evervillian spirit for the darker side; for images of destitution, or suicide, or worse. No room, either, for any individual who didn't fit the official version of how things had come to be.'

There is no mention of Maeve O'Connell, her father or the true genesis of Everville in this hallowed fabrication. Maeve fulfilled her father's dream, and Buddenbaum's desire, by burying the cross and then singlehandedly creating the town of Everville through feminine wile: she built a whorehouse at the crossroads. Men – and, in time, the town – followed; but then, for the usual reasons – '[t]oo much righteousness and too little passion'– the brothel was burned. Maeve was exiled; later, she and her family were hanged, and the ashes of deception were spread.[4]

Each year, Everville celebrates its fable with a festival; but on this anniversary, time folds backward and, as truths both physical and spiritual are revealed, a different kind of celebration occurs. What Buddenbaum set in motion those many years ago – a dance of being and becoming – reaches its grand (and occasionally gory) finale.

The dance card features a muckraking lawyer with the unlikely name of Erwin Toothaker, who uncovers the truth in the faded ink of a confession; his pursuit of the mystery leads him into the arms of a mysterious robed wanderer – and death: 'He started to sob, as much in rage at [his life's] desertion as in fear, and he went on sobbing as the substance of him was sucked away and sucked away, until there was not enough of him left even to sob.' Toothaker becomes a phantom, alive yet unseen and unheard, wearing a cast-off jacket whose pockets are filled with mementos of his life. Joining the spirits of the city fathers who haunt the town, he confronts the despair of a ghostly existence: 'What was the use of living in hope of life after death if all it amounted to was this absurd, empty round?'

His despair is echoed in the experience of star-crossed lovers: an overweight doctor's receptionist, Phoebe Cobb, and her unlikely paramour, a black painter, Joe Flicker. Phoebe's marriage, and her life, have reached a dead-end. The faces of terminal patients look back at her as if from a mirror:

> There was always such emptiness towards the end; such bitter looks on their faces, as though they'd been cheated of something and they couldn't quite figure out what. Even the church-goers, the ones she'd see in front of the tree in the square at Christmas singing hallelujahs, had that look. God wanted them in his bosom, but they didn't want to go; not until they'd made sense of things here.
>
> But suppose there was no sense to be made? That was what she had come to believe more and more: that things happened, and there was no real reason why. You weren't being tested, you weren't being rewarded, you were just *being*. And so was everybody and everything else, including tumours and bad hearts: all just being.
>
> She'd found the simplicity of this strangely comforting, and she'd made her own little religion of it.

Then Joe Flicker entered her life, offering, as his last name suggests, a flicker of love and hope – the dream of an existence beyond that of simply being. When Phoebe's brutal, vindictive husband interrupts their lovemaking, Phoebe fights back and accidentally causes his death. Joe, a wounded fugitive, ventures up the mountain overlooking

Everville and finds the crack in the world, escaping into the fabled Metacosm, where he explores the wonders of Quiddity. He eats of the dream-sea's fishes, drinks of its water and finally sets sail on a harrowing voyage with a peculiar Noah and a crew of zombie slaves. His fear brings revelation:

> It was a long time since he'd begun a sentence with *Our Father*, but the words came back readily enough, and their familiarity was comforting. Perhaps, he thought, there was even a remote chance that the words were being heard. That notion – which would have seemed naïve the day before – did not seem so idiotic now. He'd crossed a threshold into another state of being; a state that was just like another room in a house the size of the cosmos: literally a step away. If there was one such door to be entered, why not many? And why should one not be a door that led into Heaven?
>
> All his adult life, he'd asked why. Why God? Why meaning? Why love? Now he realized his error. The question was not *why*, it was *why not*?

Why not? The question resounds throughout *Everville*. Metaphysical issues have always haunted Clive Barker's fiction, but in *Imajica* and *Everville* he confronts them with a courage unprecedented in contemporary horror and fantasy. This is the stuff of CS Lewis and Charles Williams – though by no means as orthodox, and exercised without the polemic of William Peter Blatty or Russell Kirk. It is the fruition of Barker's longtime enthusiasm for William Blake – a visionary, illuminated fiction for a fading millennium – and places him firmly in the ranks of more mainstream post-war metaphysical writers like William Golding, John Fowles and Iris Murdoch.

Why not? Joe Flicker's perilous voyage is paralleled in the night journeys of the novel's other lead characters, but its imagery is the most explicit. He sails Thoreau's 'private sea' – 'the Atlantic and the Pacific of one's being alone' – without knowing, but in time learning, that its waters are public, the realm of humanity's relentless wishing, hoping, dreaming.

The unlikely – and unwilling – heroine of the epic is Tesla Bombeck, the failed screenwriter of *The Great and Secret Show* who, touched by the Nuncio, rose like any good messiah from the dead but who does not know, or care, why. Her allies are Nathan Grillo, the putative lead of the first novel, who now slumps, withered and dying, before a computer database devoted to the weird; and demon-haunted New York private eye Harry D'Amour.[5]

Tesla is cynical, hard-bitten and tenacious – a pistol-packing sceptic with a taste for lost causes. 'You know,' Tesla says. 'I have a very good soul in my head … The pity of it is, it isn't mine.' The personality of Raul, the ape evolved to a man through the workings of the Nuncio, still lives inside her, wondering: *'Would it be so bad … To have a messiah.'* She refuses to believe in saviours or love or hope or inevitability, and resolutely denies her power. Her definition of life? 'One big fucking joke.' Over the past five years she has travelled by motorcycle across the mainland states, finding only a bitter truth: 'All I know is, you're alone in the end. Always.' The one-time screenwriter has nothing but beginnings – 'always setting off on an unknown highway or opening a conversation with a stranger – and never getting to the second act. If the painful farce of her life to date was going to have any resolution, then she was going to have to move the story on.'

Nathan Grillo has encamped in Omaha, the crossroads of America, to become a clearing-house for information about the events in Palomo Grove and, soon enough, baffling events of all kinds – 'putting the pieces together, one by one, until he had the whole story.' Like Tesla, he searches for connections, explanations, somewhere in the chaotic rumour-mill of America. His ever-expanding database, an electronic bulletin board called the Reef, fills a network of computers. Faced with nationwide sightings of martyred John Wesley Fletcher, a nascent Elvis or Bigfoot, Grillo muses: 'I used to think it mattered whether or not things were real. I'm not so sure any more … Maybe the messiahs we *imagine* are more important than the real thing.' In his forty-third year, he has succumbed to multiple sclerosis: 'a mystery as profound as anything in the Reef, and a good deal more palpable.' Death is coming for him, and soon.

Harry D'Amour, a cameo player in *The Great and Secret Show*, moves to centre stage in *Everville*, just as he would do in the motion picture *Lord of Illusions* (1995). As always, the Devil is on D'Amour's mind. The devout detective is Barker's Jacob, wrestling not with flesh and blood, but with spiritual wickedness in high places – demons, within and without. 'The demons find you, because you need them,' a psychic tells D'Amour. 'You need them for the world to make sense to you.'

Through D'Amour, Barker confronts the essential argument of Blatty's *The Exorcist* (1971): that the existence of demons confirms the existence of angels – that, if there is a Devil, there must be a God: 'It's one of those useless subjects.' But D'Amour embraces Blatty's view of the singleminded purpose of spiritual evil: his demons, like those that torment Father Damien Karras, are relentlessly excremental 'because that's what they want the world to be: Shit'. They would make us despair of our humanity, of the possibility that the human condition is joyful – and possibly divine. Sadly, no one is willing to listen to such thoughts:

> At the beginning of his career – when his investigations as a private detective had first led him into the company of the inhuman – he had entertained the delusion that he might with time help turn the tide against these forces by alerting the populace to their presence. He soon learned his error. People didn't want to know. They had drawn the parameters of belief so as to exclude such horrors, and would not, *could* not, tolerate or comprehend anybody who sought to move the fences.

Death, demons, dismay: Barker's haunted investigators move through a world of sorrows – not the candyfloss realm of generic horror or fantasy fiction, where order can and will be restored, but the shrouded uncertainty that we know as life. We should understand by now that answers to the real questions are never easy, but we choose too often to embrace the bright light of escape – sunshine and television and the fiction of happy endings. As a mysterious wise man (who looks suspiciously like Jesus) tells Tesla: 'You wanted connections, and they're there to be found. But you have to look in the terrible places, Tesla. The places where death comes to take love away, where we lose each other and lose ourselves; that's where the connections begin. It takes a brave soul to look there and not despair.'

As Tesla, Grillo and D'Amour search out those terrible places, Phoebe Cobb pursues her lost love, Joe Flicker, through the phantasmagoria of the Metacosm, experiencing its wild wonders: the ceaseless gaze of the golden-eyed fish known as the Zehrapushu; a man of dust and rock called King Texas; the miraculous b'Kether Sabbat, an inverted, populated pyramid that would dwarf Manhattan; and the curious city of Liverpool, constructed by the dreaming of an ancient crone named Maeve O'Connell. The eternal orphan and outcast lives on; and inevitably, she must return to Everville – for something is summoning her home.

The end times are approaching. 'The fact was, *something* would happen. If not tonight, tomorrow night. If not tomorrow night, the night after. The world was losing its wits.' Their harbinger is the treacherous Kissoon: a member of the Shoal, a group of sorcerers who strived to preserve the secrets of Quiddity. Kissoon murdered his compatriots so that he could control the enigmatic power known as the Art. He took their bodies to Trinity – the site of the first nuclear bomb test – but was trapped there, creating a loop in time, holding the moment before the nuclear blast at bay – until at last the moment would not hold.[6]

The danger at large is beyond the physical and even the spiritual: 'Demons were simple. They believed in prayer and the potency of holy water. Thus they fled from both. But men – what did men believe?' Like Phoebe before she found love, most men believe only in being – a polite way of saying that they believe only in self, and thus, in time, in nothing. And to believe in nothing is to give that most horrible of things – nothing – life.

From beyond Quiddity comes the living nothing called the Iad Uroboros – a tsunami of fleas and mountains, mountains and fleas – 'Not *it*. Them. It's a nation. A people. Not remotely like us, but a people nevertheless, who've always harboured a hunger to be in your world.' When Flicker asks why, the reply is simple: 'Does appetite need reasons?'

The Iad swarms over the Metacosm and into our world, undoing everything in its path. For D'Amour, the Iad and the Anti-Christ are the same thing: 'It's all the Devil by another name.' But the Iad defies such simplistic notions as good and evil. Perhaps we dreamed it into being; perhaps it is the darkness in the collective soul of our species: 'Uroboros, the self-devouring serpent, encircling the earth while it ate its own tail. An image of power as a self-sufficient engine: implacable, incomprehensible, inviolate.' The Iad is the ultimate cancer, the HIV of the human spirit: '[W]hat she saw put her in mind of a disease – a terrible, implacable, devouring disease. It had no face. It had no malice. It had no guilt. Perhaps it didn't even have a mind. It came because it could; because nothing stopped it.'

While a traditional horror or fantasy novel would concern itself with the answer to this juggernaut – how it might be stopped, put back in the box – *Everville* is concerned with a much greater, more vital mystery: the mystery of life in its shadow.

The annual festival begins with a pageant, telling the story – that shameless fable – of the founding of Everville. It ends in chaos – but a gloriously inventive, life-affirming chaos – as countless other stories, the secret histories and the secret fantasies, are told. Seth Lundy, a seventeen-year-old who hears the sound of hammers 'knocking on the sky from Heaven's side' becomes Buddenbaum's ward and lover. Though other travellers to the shores of Quiddity have returned in melancholy, Buddenbaum is possessed with ambition. He arranges sights for seemingly-divine creatures known as the Jai-Wai, vigilant witnesses to death, destruction and tragedy whose appetite is never satisfied: 'They're just like people, only more *evolved* ... I'm an ape to them. We're *all* apes to them.' He creates experiences for them – makes them feel, which grows strange gems of flesh and sorrow. Tiring of the same old slaughters, Buddenbaum has arranged the apocalyptic events at Everville, desiring another Palomo Grove, people driven to madness and mayhem by their own nightmares.

Buddenbaum's patient puppetry has engineered a gateway to the Art: 'He would be free of every frailty, including love; free to live out of time, out of place, out of every particular. He would be unmade, the way divinities were unmade, because divinities were without beginning and without end: a rare and wonderful condition.' The long-buried medallion at the crossroads has accrued the power to change the world. With the possibilities in place – human, animal, the dreaming and the divine – everything dissolves at the crossroads: 'Flesh and spirit, past and future, it all turns into *mind*.' But the Art is not Buddenbaum's to possess. It is Tesla who falls into its everlasting embrace and who, at the moment of death, sees the singular truth, buried for so long in our consciousness:

> And there it was, shining in the dirt: the cross of crosses, the sign of signs. In the long, slow moments of her dying fall, she remembered with a kind of yearning how she'd solved the puzzles of that cross; seen the four journeys that were etched upon it. One to the dream world, one to the real; one to the bestial, one to the divine. And there at the heart of these journeys – where they crossed, where they divided, where they finished and began – the human mystery. It was not about flesh, that mystery: It was not about hanging broken from a cross or the triumph of the spirit over suffering. It was about the living dream of mind, that made body and spirit and all they took joy in.

Buddenbaum's invocation – *'Dreams are doorways . . . If we but have the courage to step over the threshold'* – proves true. 'Maybe the door's *supposed* to be open,' D'Amour is told. 'Maybe we have to start looking at what's in our dreams, only with our eyes open.' Dreams are the signs that the promise of the Art – the promise of that higher being, or higher state of being – was not a hollow promise; that the human mind could know the past, present and future as one eternal moment.[7] Each person is a vessel for the infinite: for the possible. 'We were born to *rise*. To see more. To know more. Maybe to know *everything* one day.'[8]

Tesla does not die; she rises, resurrected in the Art, and with her comes the beginning of the end: 'It's time for us all to put our lives in order, Harry, whether we're dead, living, or something else entirely. It's time to make our peace with things, so we're ready for whatever happens next.'[9]

'Every art but one was a game of delusions.' The essential art – *the Art* – is the living dream of mind: the imagination, always creating, showing, telling. For there is indeed one True Religion: '[I]t's the stories that matter, however they're told . . . And every life, however short, however meaningless it seems, is a leaf . . . [o]n the story tree.'

'Stories don't die,' insists Barker's finale. 'They change . . . Your seeing all this enriches it, evolves it. Nothing's ever lost.' The lives on the story tree – of the novel, and of our reality – are thus precious, in their diversity and their transience: 'Even the ugliest, the least of the infant's scrawls, would nourish somebody. Nothing would be wasted; nothing lost.'

Everville is a vast celebration of story – and of life in the constant shadow of death (and the darker shadow beyond). It speaks to the only kind of fiction that matters: the fantasies of reality, the stories whose telling informs and uplifts the human condition. In this narrative, and particularly in its voice, Barker's literary maturity and subtlety are manifest; this is the work of a more accomplished, flexible and authoritative novelist.

It is also a book of beginnings, from a writer who, like his own Tesla Bombeck, is a connoisseur of stories and journeys, always beginning and rarely ending. (Tesla's need to 'move the story on' is wryly self-conscious.) While *The Great and Secret Show* walks paths familiar to readers of horror and fantasy, *Everville* wanders deeper into the dark forest. Although it may be read on its own, clearly the two books are best read in sequence.

Working with unbridled enthusiasm and ambition, Clive Barker created a unique middle book that is much more than a bridge to some grand finale, spinning out new, and sometimes supervening, stories while embellishing not so much the action but the ideas of the first book. The narrative veers, circles, collapses, moving forward less through plot than the insistence of its imagery. The casual reader may find the sheer profusion of characters, plots and images overwhelming – or hypnotic, as Barker's psychotropic prose engages and eludes, focuses and blurs, offers illusions and delusions, truths and lies. With its epic sprawl and constant spiralling, *Everville* is not for the lazy, but it is profoundly rewarding – and, in its closing pages, deeply moving.

'Stories help you make connections,' Barker says. 'That's what you hope stories will do: help you connect dot A with dot B, even though dot A and dot B may be in completely different places on the map. And one of the things stories do amazingly well is bridge continents in a sentence. They're here, they're there, they put these things together the way thought does; the way the mind does. Our minds can connect up, apparently arbitrarily, something which happened to us when we were six with something which is happening to us right now. And what we want to be are continuums. But what we are is chopped liver.'

When Tesla ventures into Grillo's home, she finds the computer file he had written to her, knowing that he would soon be dead. He had tried to write an autobiography, but his words seemed mere clichés. When he tried instead to describe what happened in Palomo Grove, the result was the same.

> I couldn't let the truth go. I wanted to describe things just the way they'd happened (no, that's not right; the way I remembered them happening), so I killed what I was doing trying to be precise, instead of letting it fly, letting it sing. Letting it be ragged and contradictory, like stories have to be.
>
> What really happened in Palomo Grove doesn't matter any more. What matters is the stories people tell about it . . .
>
> I know if I could just let . . . every damn thing I ever felt or saw be part of the same story and called that story me, instead of always looking for something separate from the things I've felt or seen, it wouldn't matter that I was going to die soon, because I'd be part of what was going on and on. Connecting and connecting.
>
> The way I see it now, the story doesn't give a shit if you're real or not, alive or not. All the story wants is to be told. And I guess, in the end, that's what I want too.

The promise of the word, Barker tells us, is clear. Just as each story has a life, each life is a story. Each life, each person, is a vessel for the infinite, the possible; and as each story is told, retold, heard, seen, it is touched, changed, given new life – eternal life: 'Stories don't die . . . They change . . . Your seeing all this enriches it, evolves it. Nothing's ever lost.'

In the beginning was the word, and the word was: *Once.*
As in *Once upon a time . . .*[10]

27

LOVE AND THE DEVIL

'THE LAST OF ILLUSION' (1985)
LORD OF ILLUSIONS (1995)

Flesh is a trap and magic sets us free.
— CLIVE BARKER, *Lord of Illusions*

With his ferocious directorial debut in *Hellraiser* (1987), Clive Barker moved his visions from the printed page to the screen with astonishing ease. By creating an instant classic of low-budget film-making, Barker spawned a series of sequels and a growing legion of enthusiasts who wondered what might happen if this polymath were given the backing of a major studio. No one was more disappointed in his second film, the challenging but compromised *Nightbreed* (1990), than Barker himself. His self-styled 'bastard child' suffered from the heavy-handed interference of Twentieth Century-Fox executives, as well as a marketing campaign that pitched the anti-horror epic as a slasher film. The toll was such that it would lead him to wonder aloud whether he would ever direct for a major studio again.

As his career on the stage, in publishing, in film and in art made clear, however, there was no stopping the imagination or the ambition of Clive Barker. Since as early as 1985, he had worked to adapt his *Books of Blood* story 'The Last Illusion' into a motion picture.[1] The story introduced Barker's continuing character Harry M D'Amour, a New York private detective whose cases lead inexorably into darkness. With its uncertain identities and climactic siege, 'The Last Illusion' echoes the zombie films beloved by Barker; but he wanted to make the film because he saw great things in D'Amour, particularly something lacking in contemporary horror film: a continuing character on the side of good.[2] In his quest to develop a series of Harry D'Amour films, Barker also penned an original script, *The Great Unknown*, in the late 1980s.

It would take nearly ten years, but early in 1994, the newly-reincarnated United Artists gave Barker the green light to direct *Lord of Illusions* – a modestly-budgeted adaptation of 'The Last Illusion'. By then, Barker's script was more an embellishment than an adaptation of the story, using its characters and premise as the basis for a more complex and vivid drama. Because the studio was anxious to position itself in the marketplace with product, the film was rushed into production on a gruelling schedule, with nearly three months of principal photography commencing on July 26, 1994, for a fixed release date of February 17, 1995. With more than one hundred opticals, over a hundred make-up effects, and the first fully digital gore effect, the film was an editing and post-production nightmare that was further complicated when composer Christopher Young decided belatedly that he could not finish a score within the time allotted. Fortunately, the bright talents of Simon Boswell were available, and he produced a moving symphonic accompaniment.

Conscious of his deadline, and of prior encounters with the industry's censors, the Motion Picture Association of America and the British Board of Film Classification, Barker crafted his use of violence to optimize the R rating that he was obligated by contract to deliver. The MPAA branded the film NC-17 after its initial viewing and marked eleven scenes for editing because of violence. The majority of the edits were accepted readily, since they were stalking horses, intentionally inserted by Barker to draw the attention of the censors. A unique strategy allowed him to avoid cuts in a vision of a blood-drenched demon: 'That short scene was troublesome to the MPAA. We presented it to them in full colour, and they basically wanted us to cut it back severely. We ended up leaving it at the length we presented it to them, but tuning out some of the colour.' Another scene, in which a character is literally pincushioned with blades, simply could not be changed. Barker took the unusual step of writing a letter to the MPAA that explained his intentions, and he preserved the scene. Given the imminent release date, a handful of more difficult cuts were accepted, although begrudgingly, in order to obtain the R rating. 'Only a few frames,' Barker says, 'but for some reason or other, they see the removal of a few frames as being enough to keep the American soul from being corrupted.'

The MPAA proved a relatively easy hurdle; it was the studio, and test audiences, that caused the deepest cuts in *Lord of Illusions*. As February 17, 1995, approached, it became apparent that United Artists would either have to use Barker's 121-minute cut of the film or postpone the release. As might be expected, the studio opted for delay, arguing that the director's cut was too long. The first test screening of *Lord of Illusions*, targeted at shopping mall theatre demographics, added to the confusion: the focus group of twenty viewers rated the director's version excellent (except for the love scene, which did not play well at any of the screenings), but the general audience responded with only average scores. The principal criticism concerned narrative and character development; from the perspective of the youthful audience, promptly embraced by United Artists, there was too much talk interfering with the action and effects.

UA instructed Barker to eliminate twenty minutes from the film. He and his editor, Alan Baumgarten – whom he had met during the agonizing final cut of *Nightbreed* – returned to the editing bay and made a series of difficult choices that eliminated twelve-plus minutes – mostly entire scenes – to produce the theatrical version, whose running time was 108 minutes. One of the few benefits of the delay was that Barker had time to add new optical effects in the fiery finale.

United Artists tentatively targeted a May release date, but Barker resisted scheduling the film against the so-called summer 'blockbusters'. *Lord of Illusions* was an $11 million film, and although it had the look of a more expensive production, the acting fees alone for two of that summer's films – Kevin Costner in *Waterworld* and Sylvester Stallone in *Assassins* – exceeded Barker's total budget. The result was another postponement; *Lord of Illusions* finally made its première on August 25, 1995.

The film opened well, with more than $5 million in box office receipts on its first weekend, but stalled in the face of heavy competition and mixed reviews – many of which focused on the absence of the narrative that, unbeknownst to critics, padded the cutting room floor. Nevertheless, the theatrical run earned back Barker's budget and beyond; and because of the growing cachet of unrated and director's cuts in the home video market, he would have the satisfaction, denied with *Nightbreed*, of having viewers witness the version of *Lord of Illusions* that he intended them to see. (In a groundbreaking achievement, Barker personally persuaded Blockbuster Video to stock the director's version of the film despite its unrated content.)[3]

Although widely available on videotape in both the R-rated theatrical and unrated director's versions, the only meaningful way to experience *Lord of Illusions* is via the MGM/UA 'Deluxe Letter-Box Edition' on laser disc and DVD of the 'Unrated Director's Cut'. The package features an entertaining and illuminating commentary by Barker, and a bounty of supplemental material: the original cinema 'teaser', the original cinema trailer, a 'making of' documentary, a selection of scenes that were not used in the theatrical or director's versions of the film, a storyboard-to-film comparison, a gallery of still photos and a gallery of the conceptual artwork for the film's promotional posters. It is one of the more exceptional catalogues of creativity to emerge in recent memory.

Lord of Illusions has its foundation in 'The Last Illusion', which introduces Harry M D'Amour, the house detective of Clive Barker's universe. The short story pursues a traditional, if peculiar, mystery – the death of famed stage illusionist Swann – into more exotic realms: the battle for Swann's body and soul. The story proceeds from Barker's love of film *noir*; it is, in precise terms, Raymond Chandler with magic and monsters.

D'Amour is a down-at-the-heels private eye who works out of an office in midtown Manhattan that is an unabashed homage to forties *noir*: a third-floor rat-trap, cramped and chaotic, littered with furred coffee cups and alimony demands, and, by the close of 'The Last Illusion', the remains of hungry demons. 'He'd had a dirty life: spying on adulteries for vengeful spouses; dredging gutters for lost children; keeping company with scum because it rose to the top, and the rest just drowned.' He is Catholic – a devout believer who has some small reputation as a diviner of the occult. He drinks hard, hates crowds, and carries a .38 pistol that he is quite willing to use: 'He had always been a bad shot when given more than a moment to take aim, but *in extremis*, when instinct governed rational thought, he was not half bad.' D'Amour hates the sight of blood, even when it is not his own. Lurking within him is a grief that, when stoked, ignites into flames of disgust, anger and violence.

D'Amour's pursuit of the unknown is not a chosen profession; he finds the anticipation of evil crucifying. He is driven by his most conspicuous failure – an Easter bloodbath on Wyckoff Street and his first encounter with infernal wings: 'once touched by such malignancy . . . there could be no casual disposal of it.' Thus the dogged persistence that singularly defines Harry D'Amour: 'He had to follow it to its source, however repugnant that thought was, and make with it whatever bargains the strength of his hand allowed.' The task is neverending: 'In Harry's experience it was only the good who needed sleep; iniquity and its practitioners were awake every eager moment, planning fresh felonies.'

Swann, the 'Magus of Manhattan', is a David Copperfield-like impresario whose stage shows defy the imagination. As he seduces a backstage guest, he tells her: 'Take it from me; seeing is not believing.' In a moment he is dead, felled by a sword that plunges from one of his mechanical illusions. His widow, Dorothea, receives a letter from him, instructing her to have his body cremated: '*My sweet darling, I'm afraid. Not of bad dreams, or of what might happen to me in this life, but of what my enemies may try to do once I'm dead.*'

Dorothea hires D'Amour to guard the magician's corpse, and Swann's former assistant, Valentin, tells him of a conspiracy to murder Swann: 'Dead; yes. Past saving? No.' A wiser man would go on with his life – but not D'Amour:

He was none the wiser now than he'd been at the outset, except that he'd learned again the lesson he'd been taught at Wyckoff Street: that when dealing with the Gulfs it was wiser never to believe your eyes . . . Not a complicated lesson, but it seemed he had forgotten it, like a fool, and it had taken two deaths to teach it him afresh. Maybe it would be simpler to have the rule tattooed on the back of his hand, so that he couldn't check the time without being reminded: *Never believe your eyes.*

Thirty-two years earlier, Swann made a bargain with the mysterious Gulfs, agreeing to serve as their ambassador if they gave him magic: 'The ability to perform miracles. To transform matter. To bewitch souls. Even to drive out God.' The bargain is archetypally Faustian: 'Nothing the Prince of Lies offers to humankind is of the least value . . . or it wouldn't be offered. Swann didn't know that when he first made his Covenant. But he soon learned. Miracles are useless. Magic is a distraction from the real concerns. It's rhetoric. Melodrama.'

When Swann realized he had sold his soul for frivolity, he plotted revenge: 'By taking Hell's name in vain. By using the magic which it boasted of as a trivial entertainment, degrading the power of the Gulfs by passing off their wonder-working as mere illusion. It was, you see, an act of heroic perversity. Every time a trick of Swann's was explained away as sleight-of-hand, the Gulfs squirmed.'

Swann was marked for death, and worse; now the forces of Hell are closing in to consummate his fate. Valentin prays that, if they destroy Swann's physical remains, the consequences of his covenant will be averted. D'Amour and Valentin secure the magician's body in D'Amour's office, but when Dorothea arrives, she reveals that Valentin is inhuman: he was Swann's original tempter, a demon who came to love his prey – while she, in desperation, has given herself over to damnation.

A host of demons is loosed upon them, their rapacious assault preceded by a cacophony of unearthly music. In his dying act, Valentin sets the fire that gives Swann freedom: the illusionist stands, raising his flaming hands to the demons, then embracing the greatest of the monsters, the Raparee, giving it his fire. 'Disbelief was for cowards; and doubt a fashion that crippled the spine. He was content to watch

– not knowing if Swann lived or died, if birds, fire, corridor or if he himself – Harry D'Amour – were real or illusory.'

The demon horde flees as Swann lays down to rest, the fire consuming him. Finally there is only D'Amour, left with a slender ray of hope: 'Things came and went away; that was a kind of magic. And in between?; pursuits and conjuring; horrors, guises. The occasional joy . . . That there was room for joy; ah! that was magic too.' The last illusion, he understands, is death.[4]

D'Amour returned in 'Lost Souls' (1985), originally published in a Christmas issue of *Time Out*.[5] This dark fantasy (subtitled 'A Christmas Horror Story') finds the detective in a continued pursuit of demons – in this case, Cha'Chat, a thing of clustered eyes and cropped fur. We meet his blind psychic friend Norma Paine ('I'm a telephonist, Harry; I just make the connections. I don't pretend to understand the metaphysics'), who dispatches him to a derelict Manhattan market, where a merchant, seeking to atone for a squalid life, offers free food to all for the holidays; but when customers die in an ensuing rampage, he commits suicide.

D'Amour finds and wounds the demon, but he learns of a darker secret. In a hotel near Times Square waits Darrieux Marchetti, also called the Cankerist, a member of a secret order of theological assassins. Marchetti has murdered a woman and his true prey, her baby: the tiny body of a messiah. 'Be thankful,' he tells D'Amour: 'Your world isn't ready for revelation.' But it is, for D'Amour, another lesson: 'Each moment was its own master . . . and he would have to take whatever comfort he could find in the knowledge that between this chilly hour and dawn there were innumerable such moments – blind, maybe, and wild and hungry – but all at least eager to be born.'

D'Amour returned to the world of Clive Barker unexpectedly, and as a minor player, in *The Great and Secret Show* (1989), where he is older and certainly wiser. In the closing pages of the novel, Jim Hotchkiss, a resident of the besieged California town of Palomo Grove, seeks his missing wife. Believing that she may have returned to her native New York, Hotchkiss contacts a PI with an odd reputation: 'He specializes – I guess – in supernatural stuff.' Enter Harry D'Amour.

Hotchkiss receives a telephone call from the detective, but the subject is not Hotchkiss's wife. Instead, D'Amour warns about the doom descending upon Palomo Grove, if not the world: the Iad Uroboros are crossing the dream-sea, Quiddity, intent on breaching our reality. The warning connects D'Amour with failed screenwriter Tesla Bombeck, commencing a friendship and a crusade that will last for years. He offers his sombre truth – 'I've met demons, and they never look the way you think they're going to look' – and, after urging Tesla to pray, exits as quickly as he came.

Everville (1994) was the first novel in which D'Amour took centre stage. Almost a decade has passed since the events in 'The Last Illusion', and D'Amour – described vaguely in earlier texts – is fleshed out for the reader: 'a well-made fellow in his late thirties, with three days' growth of beard and the eyes of an insomniac.' He has a long nose, strong jaw, wide brow, with grey hair and frown-lines well in evidence. '[H]is stare was troubled, the smile on his lips tentative to say the least.' The Devil is on D'Amour's mind; he is hounded by a constant feeling of dread.

D'Amour has fought his war against darkness alone and in secrecy: 'At the beginning of his career . . . he had entertained the delusion that he might with time help turn the tide against these forces by alerting the populous to their presence. He soon learned his error. People didn't want to know.' His weapons now exceed mere guns, and his armour includes nearly a dozen tattoos – talismans and sigils to hold the Devil at bay.

In D'Amour's chosen battleground, New York City, 'he had niches and hiding places; he had people who owed him, people who feared him. He even had a couple of friends.' One of them is addict-turned-painter Ted Dusseldorf; another is blind medium Norma Paine; and, years ago, there was Father Hess, who died that Easter Sunday on Wyckoff Street, while the victorious demon spoke a riddle to D'Amour: 'I am you and you are love and that's what makes the world go round.'

Now Dusseldorf has information for D'Amour about an occult ceremony that exiles from Quiddity will hold in a deserted tenement. When the two investigate, the ritual is interrupted by the violent prophet Kissoon, who butchers the celebrants – and, like Father Hess before him, Ted Dusseldorf. This doubling event summons D'Amour into the greater mystery – the Art – and to the town known as Everville. It is a journey that leads not to an end, but to the beginning: the house on Wyckoff Street and the demon that still waits there for Harry D'Amour. Indeed, as Norma warns him: 'The demons find you, because you need them ... You need them for the world to make sense to you.'

Lord of Illusions weaves Barker's evolving mythology of Harry D'Amour with his Faustian obsessions in a dark inversion of the Parable of the Prodigal Son. The result is a metaphysical thriller that is also a remarkable self-critique of the art and artifice of film-making.

'There are two worlds of magic,' we are told in an authorial introduction (which was added to the theatrical release in an effort to remedy the cuts in the narrative). 'One is the glittering domain of the illusionist. The other is a secret place, where magic is a terrifying reality. Here, men have the power of demons. And Death itself is an illusion.' Even the less astute members of the audience must realize, if only instinctually, that the 'glittering domain of the illusionist' is best known to them as the very screen that they watch.

The full-throttle opening, with cars speeding across an empty desert toward a dire destination, portends – and then delivers – violence. It is 1982, and a quartet of renegades led by Philip Swann (Kevin J O'Connor) invade the Mojave Desert hideaway of apocalyptic cult leader Nix (Daniel Von Bargen). The compound's murky, desolate rooms are adorned with imagery of dread and despair patterned after Barker's own artwork.

Nix is an unnerving presence – benevolent, fatherly, yet dishevelled and obviously crazed; as his name implies, he is the harbinger of the void. We see him juggle flame for his childlike acolytes. 'And the fire said to me: Nix, Nix, you're my instrument. From now on, you'll be called the Puritan ... You will find a few good men and women, and together, together you will cleanse the world.'

Nix holds a twelve-year-old girl hostage as lure for the prodigal Swann, Nix's favourite 'son' and Lucifer, who somehow fell (or fled) from grace. When Swann and his companions enter the vile sanctuary, weapons in hand, Nix taunts Swann: 'I knew you'd come. I have so much power to give you, Swann. All you have to do is *beg*.' After levitating, Nix thrusts his fingers beneath the skin of Swann's temples and into his skull. 'How would you like to see the world the way it really is? You must see flesh with a god's eyes.' Swann, touched by the hand of this great pretender, looks at his friends and sees morphing abominations, the primeval muck of the grave: 'Do you want to be like that, Swann? Mud, shit?' Nix offers Swann a ripe invitation: 'Come here . . . share the power.'

But the girl, freed from her bonds, takes up Swann's fallen pistol and shoots Nix. Swann, shaking off the visions, applies a diabolical mask whose screws tighten into Nix's head, completing the kill; but not before the Puritan voices a convincing prophecy: 'This isn't over, Swann.'[6]

Fast forward to 'Thirteen Years Later'[7] and rainswept Manhattan, where Harry D'Amour (played convincingly by Scott Bakula) sits with a beer and a pistol, pondering the events headlined in the *New York Post*: 'PRIVATE EYE IN BROOKLYN EXORCISM DRAMA.'[8] The tableaux is mythic *noir*: the troubled detective, alone in a shadowy, ramshackle office that represents the chaotic world he struggles, but fails, to make right. An old friend, Loomis (Wayne Grace), arrives with a cosy West Coast assignment to take the enigmatic Brooklyn débâcle off Harry's mind: 'You'll like LA. It has great women, great weather.' Cut to a referential (and reverential) shot of a bright boulevard of palm trees, and D'Amour finds himself in the City of Angels.

His holiday goes quickly to Hell when he discovers a fortune-teller pincushioned with the blades of Nix's devoted 'other son', Butterfield (the delectably evil Barry Del Sherman). The victim is Caspar Quaid (Joseph Latimore), one of Swann's compatriots in the raid on the compound, and his dying words echo Nix's prophecy: 'There's something terrible coming home . . . soon.'[9]

Swann is now a showy impresario with a glamorous stage show and lifestyle. At his lavish estate, the fearful and fragile Swann worries over Quaid's death. 'I think they killed him,' he tells his striking wife, Dorothea (Famke Janssen, the very image of a forties *noir* heroine). Dorothea asks Swann's oily assistant, Valentin (Joel Swetow), to find the detective who discovered Quaid's murder and, that night, D'Amour accompanies her to Swann's performance at the Pantages Theater, a spectacle of frenzied dancers and high-tech set dressing that holds his audience – just as Nix held his congregation – in thrall. But Swann's new illusion – an escape from bondage beneath an array of rotating swords – ends in tragedy when he is skewered by the falling blades.[10]

D'Amour seeks clues to the mysterious 'accident' at the Magic Castle, where he meets Vinovich (the ever-delightful Vincent Schiavelli), an egotistical debunker who claims that Swann was tainted with evil, his illusions fake miracles that, like those of the Bible, could be replicated with ease. Through Vinovich, Barker underscores his metaphysical argument: '[W]e walk a narrow path between . . . divinity and trickery.' Intent on denying the otherness of humanity, Vinovich (like Nix) puts forward a purely mechanistic world view, arrogating unto himself, as the ultimate rationalist, the ability to make others believe, through his trickery, that he may be divine.

D'Amour tracks another of Swann's companions, Jennifer Desiderio (Sheila Tousey), to a local sanitarium. 'We have to agree on what's real and what's not,' her doctor tells him, echoing Vinovich: 'That's what holds us together.' Jennifer fears Nix – 'He's coming back . . . He's digging his way out' – and she throws herself in front of a passing car to escape his coming vengeance.

With the aid of a young magician, Billy Who (Lorin Stewart), D'Amour loots documents about Swann and Nix from the Magic Castle. Emboldened by his discoveries – 'Maybe they're not tricks' – D'Amour returns to Swann's estate to find Dorothea standing watch over Swann's coffin. 'This is the way he wanted it,' she tells him, 'no autopsy, no embalming. Nobody meddling with his body . . . Flesh is a trap. That's what he used to say. Flesh is a trap and magic sets us free.'

Confronted with D'Amour's evidence, she admits to the reality of Nix and his magic: 'He could levitate without a wire. And he could get into people's heads, make them see things. Terrible things.' Dorothea was the twelve-year-old saved by Swann, the girl who shot Nix; and Swann's stage show was the real thing – magic, not illusions.

In this awkward moment, their sexual attraction is suddenly palpable; D'Amour kisses Dorothea, and in their passionate lovemaking, Swann is reborn. The house is invaded by an unfolding origami puzzle, a creature of flame that pursues D'Amour until he breaks open the coffin and tears the corpse's face away. It is a dummy: 'Looks like you're not a widow after all.'

Swann, as his names suggests, has taken a dive in order to elude Nix and shift attention from Dorothea. His experience with Nix enacted the Faustian pact: 'I was going to discover the secrets of the universe. That's why I liked Nix. He promised me all these explanations.' But Nix's only revelation was his despairing view of the true state of man: 'Shit.' D'Amour persuades Swann to emerge from hiding with the seductive promise of resurrection: 'If Nix is back from the dead, then he is some kind of a god, and he'll find you wherever the fuck you go; but if he's just another phony messiah, then you can stage the greatest comeback in history.'

Meanwhile, Butterfield kidnaps Dorothea and bullies Valentin into revealing Nix's burial place. He unearths the body and brings it to the desert hideaway. As Nix's mendicants shear the hair from their heads, then crawl on broken glass, Butterfield unleashes the Puritan from the mask that imprisons him. The resurrected Nix is monstrous, tattooed with scars and wounds into a postmodern primitive. He wants only Swann.[11]

Ungrateful and unforgiving, Nix scorns Butterfield and summons his flock: 'Children? Will you suffer to come unto me?' He offers them the eternal wisdom of the grave: death. With a stamp of his foot, the ground breaks, opening a hole in the earth over which Nix levitates, clutching Dorothea. As a similar hole opens sphincter-like in his forehead, dark clouds roll overhead – the image of the maggot-cloud that haunts Barker's art – and Nix announces: 'I have to give something back, so I'm giving you.' The rainfall dissolves the desert earth, sucking his worshippers into its embrace: 'You're not worthy, none of you. Only Swann is worthy!'

Swann gathers what is left of his courage and confronts Nix to settle their 'unfinished business': pupil versus tutor, son versus father, lover versus lover. Nix reveals his imagined destiny: 'I should have been honest with you from the start. I wasn't born to show people the error of their ways. I was born to murder the world.' With a dire warning – 'No one can save you now but me' – he urges Swann to join him: 'You know I'll kill you when we're done … But until then, it'll be just the two of us, the way it always was.' When Swann's feelings for Dorothea intervene, Nix crushes him with a series of psychic blows – and a disparaging aside: 'She's just flesh …'

Finally D'Amour confronts the white-robed Nix: Love against nothing. 'You've got Swann's disease,' the Puritan tells him. 'You think that a little courage, a little love, that it'll all be all right.' Nix applies his fingers to D'Amour's temple, offering him a vision of a dark and dying world. When D'Amour sees Dorothea as ravaged flesh, she urges 'It's not real' and kisses him, the first step in his redemption, which is made complete as she takes up his fallen pistol and the circle turns. Again she is the avenger; she shoots Nix and the visions cease – although he rises for one last illusion.

'What the fuck are you?' Dorothea cries, and Nix, as always, has an answer: 'A man who wanted to be a god, then changed his mind. I'm going to be rot and shit from now on . . . I'm going to show the world what's waiting at the end, and I'm going to make it despair.'

Swann levitates D'Amour, who, in a glorious Oedipal inversion, gouges out Nix's eyes. The Puritan plummets into the pit, toward a glowing magma that is death or Hell – or both. Swann dies in Dorothea's arms, and as D'Amour peers into the abyss, Nix rises again – his Swann song – to strip his pupil's body of its flesh before succumbing to the flames. Over a concluding montage, we hear Nix's voice – 'You must see flesh with a god's eyes' – and then the comforting words of Dorothea: 'Flesh is a trap. That's what he used to say. Flesh is a trap and magic sets us free.'

Lord of Illusions is clearly Clive Barker's most accomplished work for the screen; whether it is his best work is a matter of debate. Certainly it is a brave film whose power only grows with repeated viewings. Playing by Hollywood's rules, Barker created a mature horror movie of the rarest breed – one that speaks to, and maintains, moral ambiguity – while also pursuing intellectual argument.

As in earlier works of film and fiction, Barker takes insistent risks. He succeeds in the use of bright sunlight and earth tones, and in some remarkably innovative set-pieces; but as he concedes, his effort to mingle California *noir* with horror, hamstrung in the theatrical release, proved troublesome for audiences and reviewers: '*Lord of Illusions* made them a little uncomfortable by mingling very extreme imaginative stuff with a real guy in a real city. In a *Friday the 13th* or *Nightmare on Elm Street* picture, the whole thing is encased in a little bubble. I was trying to say, *Well, my imagination runs all the way from walking the street to William Nix, so let's see what happens if we put these two things in the same movie.* And for audiences, I think that was problematical.'

Although the film's text is Faustian, its subtext is undeniably sexual – and subversive. At first glance, Dorothea seems insistently objectified, and certainly for the male leads, she acts as a kind of exquisite trophy – first in bondage to Nix, later in her sleek emergence from Swann's swimming pool, and then as D'Amour's sexual conquest. But in a film whose essential drama is male conflict, it is Dorothea who proves the usurper and the victor.

A pistol, that traditional symbol of phallic power, is held by both Swann and D'Amour when we first see them; but the guns are knocked repeatedly from their hands, mock castrations that render them help-less before the cleansing flame of the Puritan. It is Dorothea who proves impervious to Nix's trickery and lies, and who assumes the role of exterminating angel, wielding the gun to kill Nix in the opening act and again to bring about his downfall in the finale.

Swann's sexuality is, at best, ambiguous; Dorothea tells D'Amour in their first meeting: 'We don't share our lives like a lot of people do.' Certainly their bond is not physical: 'I didn't marry him for love.' Her romantic tryst with D'Amour, although jarring, is as inevitable as the detective's last name. Only through the mediation of the decidedly heterosexual Harry is Swann 'reborn'.

Nix's desire for Swann, in turn, transcends the fatherly: 'You shouldn't have taken him away from me,' he tells Dorothea. 'We were going to be together. When I finished with the world, we were going to keep each other company . . . in the dark.' And the presence of the leering Butterfield, with his foppish attire and overtly sexual bullying, suggests the true threat of his Lord.

By defying what some might expect of a gay film-maker – the film's central relationships are intensely masculine but not homosexual – Barker makes clear that the desire expressed by Nix is less erotic than enslaving. The Puritan is the envoy of patriarchal power: the bringer of an extinguishing light, rationality burned to its brightest degree. Swann was his apprentice, his son, his vessel – but he took his father's magic and corrupted it further, turning it to mere commerce. Their relationship is a journey toward some terrible knowledge, and Barker's messianic overtones give their combat an unresolved mythic urgency.

With his background in theatre, Barker understands the ideological role of place, and his films have used settings insistently to externalize the personalities and conflicts of his characters. The world of *Lord of Illusions* is, indeed, the world of the stage: its three male leads inhabit stylized, mythic landscapes that are mirrors of their inner selves. Nix is never seen outside his desert sanctuary, a wasted landscape as vacant as his soul; Swann has erected the false glamour of his mansion and stage show to mark (and mask) the superficiality of his spirit; and D'Amour is a Chandlerian everyman, street-smart and sexy, but wounded – and, as the demonic flashbacks suggest, haunted by something beyond the combat of Nix and Swann. (Particularly in the theatrical release, D'Amour's character seems incomplete and requires viewers to rely on generic typing; there is no clear reason for his dogged pursuit of the mystery save some vague sense of responsibility, a calling to a higher cause of putting things to right.)[12]

The notion of the 'world as a stage' has a long tradition, dating back at least to the Renaissance, when stagecraft was a crucial element of statecraft. In *Lord of Illusions*, Barker clearly wrestles with the role of stagecraft in godhood and religion. His magicians are posed Christlike, from Nix's perch in the compound to Swann's image hovering over Hollywood Boulevard, and later over his secular flock at the Pantages Theater; each offers his own deluded message of salvation; and, of course, each is 'resurrected'.

It is the illusion, not true magic – the message – that enthralls the audience; and like Nix, Swann holds his devotees in contempt: 'It's important to distract them from their banality for a few minutes.' By using his gift as a trivial entertainment – passing off wonder as mere illusion – Swann has degraded Nix's religiosity, turning its deluded ambition into the basest desire for distraction. When D'Amour confronts Swann – 'What a waste. You can do shit that most of us can only dream about, and you go around pretending it's just some trick' – Swann replies dourly: 'Illusionists get Las Vegas contracts, D'Amour. Magicians get burned.'

There is no doubting the implicit argument that Barker offers about the dilemma of the artist, and particularly the film-maker – who is, after all, a kind of god, capable of creation, evolution and destruction within the confines of his or her medium. Particularly in films of fantasy and horror, the strength of artistic vision is defined by its capacity for illusion rather than its intellect. It is a remarkable self-critique for a film so driven by special effects; and it is cruelly ironic that this very message should have been deleted in favour of those effects in the film's theatrical release.

With *Lord of Illusions*, Clive Barker had freed himself of the demon known as *Nightbreed*. As for Harry D'Amour, we will no doubt see more of him – and his demons: 'Every time I finish one of these damn investigations,' he tell us, 'I end up thinking, maybe that didn't happen. Until the next time.'

28

EXTINCTION

SACRAMENT (1996)

sac·ra·ment \'sak-re-ment\ n [ME *sacrement, sacrament,* fr. OF &
LL; OF, fr. LL *sacramentum,* fr. L, oath of allegiance, obligation,
fr. *sacrare,* to consecrate] 1: a formal religious act that is sacred
as a sign or symbol of a spiritual reality; *esp*: one believed to have
been instituted or recognized by Jesus Christ 2 *cap*: the eucharistic
elements; *specif*: BLESSED SACRAMENT

'This will not come again ... Nor this, nor this ...'[1]
'From very early on in my life,' Clive Barker says, 'I had an intense
sense of nostalgia. At the age of eight, I was nostalgic. I know that
sounds pathetic and silly, but it's true. I was. I had a very clear sense
that things were *passing*. I would get to the end of the summer, and
I would have a very strong sense of time passing – and that this will
not come again. Now I still have it, but past the age of forty, I feel
like I've earned it.

'There was something very powerful about that. There remains
something incredibly powerful to me about the idea of the unrepeatable experience. A human being is an unrepeatable experience. You

411

felt that about your dog. She would not come again. She was who she was: very particular, very specific, very extraordinary.'

Clive spoke those words in 1995; he was gripped with an acute melancholy. His cousin Mark had just died from complications resulting from AIDS, and he had decided to write a novel that spoke to his feelings of loss, and to Mark's individuality – and the 'unrepeatable experience' of Mark and other gay men whose lives had been cut short by the plague. 'Gay men don't repeat their species. Gay men are born to extinction. They're not propagating, they're not increasing their tribe, by definition. And one of the reasons it felt exactly right to me that the hero of this book should be gay is because the book is about things that don't continue – and it seems doubly powerful and doubly moving, right now, that this tribe that doesn't propagate is being so catastrophically destroyed.'

Will Rabjohns, the protagonist of *Sacrament* (1996), is a controversial photographer of endangered and dying species. 'For most of his adult life he'd made photographs of the untamed world, reporting to the human tribe the tragedies that occurred in contested territories. They were seldom human tragedies. It was the populace of the other world that withered and perished daily. And as he witnessed the steady erosion of the wilderness, the hunger in him grew to leap the fences and be part of it, before it was gone.'[2]

That hunger is born of a hollow ambition that has driven Will since his youth: 'He was not . . . designed for happiness. It was too much like contentment, and contentment was too much like sleep.' The novel's opening act brings him to Hudson Bay, where images of polar bears wallowing in garbage will provide a mournful conclusion to what may be his final book of photographs. In his forty-first year of life, he is lost to melancholy, the onset of middle age and a dire sense of things winding down. In a world that seems defined by death, his success is meaningless, and the purpose of his photographs, and of his life, is unclear. 'The less alive you were, the better chance you had at living. There was probably a lesson in that somewhere, though it was a bitter one.'

When a bear is wounded, a misguided sense of responsibility leads Will into its violent embrace. *This is death*, he thinks: 'This is what you've photographed so many times. The dolphin drowning in the net, pitifully quiescent; the monkey twitching among its dead fellows, looking at him with a gaze Will could not stand to meet, except through his camera. They were all the same in this moment, he and the monkey, he and the bear. All ephemeral things, running out of time.'

It is not death, but epiphany. Ravaged and comatose, Will's body heals while his mind returns to the thirteenth year of his youth in England. The second son of Eleanor and Hugo Rabjohns – a philosopher and domestic tyrant whose later scholarship echoes Julia Kristeva – Will grew up in the shadow of his brother, Nathaniel (who, like Barker's own brother, Roy, seemed more truly his father's son); but when Nathaniel died in an accident, Eleanor withdrew into polite madness and Hugo moved the family from Manchester to the Yorkshire village of Burnt Yarley.[3]

There, in a ruined maze known as the Courthouse – a madman's throne of judgment for those who would abuse animals – Will meets the man and woman whom he will learn to love and hate more strongly than his parents: 'Jacob Steep, with his soot-and-gold eyes and black beard and pale poet's hands' and glorious Rosa McGee, 'who had the gold of Steep's eyes in her hair and the black of his beard in her gaze, but who was as fleshy and passionate as he was sweatless and unmoved.'

This curious, unearthly pair join with Will in the most crucial of the triadic structures through which his life has been defined: Will and his parents, Will and his childhood friends, Will and his photographic team, Will and his lovers – a series of incomplete men and women united and transformed by the enigma that is his life. Steep is the 'Killer of Last Things', stalking the planet with knife in hand to put an end to each dying species. Once he had believed that, by recording each act of extinction in a journal, he could earn God's forgiveness; but now, like the elder Will, whose photographs no longer seem sufficient, Steep doubts the purpose of his life; soon he argues that, without purpose, there is no God – and no bounds to violence: 'We're alone, with the power to do whatever we want.' His consort, Mrs McGee, mingles desires both carnal and fatal, played out through her 'rosaries' – strange ropes that cavort like viperous extensions of her flesh. Their odd coupling has spanned three centuries, and Rosa's womb has carried eighty-seven children, all of whom died at birth.

Steep's ennui is leavened by the young and inquisitive Will, who offers the prospect of a new companion. Steep offers his apt pupil a simple but lasting lesson: 'Living and dying we feed the fire.' His secret knowledge of the darkness, and the need to hold it at bay, seems profound and seductive: 'For an instant ... Will saw himself at Jacob's side, walking in a city street, and Steep was shining out of every pore, and people were weeping with gratitude that he came to light their darkness.'

Steep's tutelage is swift and certain: Will learns to feed the fire – to kill – by casting a moth into a flame. When, wielding Steep's thirsty blade, he butchers two birds, Steep asks him to imagine that they were the last of their species: *'This will not come again ... Nor this, nor this ...'* Such an act, Will realizes, could change the world.[4]

When Will and Steep touch, the spilled blood summons a vision of Steep's past. In 1730, elsewhere in the bucolic English countryside, Steep was sent to confront the visionary artist Thomas Simeon, whose talents had succumbed first to debauchery and then to the patronage of a mysterious mystic and satyric sermonizer named Gerard Rukenau. Simeon had been brought to Rukenau's retreat in the Hebrides to chronicle, in paintings, the construction of an arcane cathedral known as the Domus Mundi (literally, the 'House of the World'). When Simeon left, Steep was dispatched to bring him home; but the painter committed suicide, poisoning himself with his pigments, rather than return to Rukenau. Before his death, he offered Steep the petal of a flower, and the meaning of the true sacrament:

> I have the Holy of Holies here, the Ark of the Covenant, the Sangraal, the Great Mystery itself, right here on the tip of my little finger ... If I could paint this perfection ... put it on a sheet of paper so that it showed its true glory, every painting in every chapel in Rome, every illumination of every Book of Hours, every picture I ever made for every one of Rukenau's damned invocations would be ... superfluous.

Steep blamed Rukenau for the painter's death and rejected his teachings: 'You gave him your genius; he paid you in lunacy. That makes him a thief, at very least. I won't serve him after this. And I will never forgive him.' The rage of his apostasy translated into the zealous assault upon creation that became his life's work: 'If the world were a simpler place, we would not be lost in it . . . We wouldn't be greedy for novelty. We wouldn't always want something new, always something new! We'd live the way Thomas wanted to live, in awe of the mysteries of a petal.' His passion for simplicity – and, in time, for absence – finds Steep, like the misguided forces of morality in *Weaveworld* and *Imajica*, seeking to cleanse the world and create a New Eden without error or imperfection – the ideal place to find God, to understand the purpose of his existence.

Steep's memories, like his lessons, taint Will, transforming a lost child into a lost man who desperately chronicles the last of things: 'He *shaped* you, Will. He sowed the hopes and the disappointments, he sowed the guilt and the yearning.'[5] When, as an adult, Will looks upon one of Simeon's paintings, he recognizes the horrifying relationship to his own photographs: 'They were the before and after scenes, bookends to the holocaust text that lay between. And the author of that text? Steep, of course. Simeon had painted the moment before Steep appeared: all life in terror at Steep's imminence. Will had caught the moment after: all life *in extremis*, the fertile acre become a field of desolation.'[6]

When Will awakens from his coma, little has changed since his mauling by the bear – or, indeed, since his youth. 'They were in a world of endings, of early and unexpected goodbyes, not so unlike the time from which he'd woken.' He is living in the midst of death – of animals, to be sure, but also of friends, and especially his best friend and former lover Patrick, now dying of AIDS.

The past, once remembered, pursues Will with feral intensity. Lord Fox, an avatar of his guilt, haunts Will, forcing him to look upon the ravaged world with the unfettered eyes of his childhood: 'God wants you to see,' Lord Fox tells him. 'Don't ask me why. That's between you and God. I'm just the go-between.' The creature confronts Will with a conundrum, proposing that 'the passing of things, of days and beasts and men he'd loved, was just a cruel illusion and memory, a clue to its unmasking'. This revelation only amplifies Will's painful knowledge that he, like Steep, is a pretender: pretending to find purpose in life, pretending to be human.[7]

Gay and without family or children, Will is a race of one, and Steep and McGee, awakened from their dire labours by Will's memories, plot his extinction. They return to Burnt Yarley and assault the now-aged Hugo Rabjohns; but Will, who can no longer grieve, offers the perilous pair their only hope: knowledge and healing. When he touches his nemesis again, the vision he sees is both frightening and enlightening:

> This is what Steep saw when he looked at living things. Not their beauty, not their particularity, just their smothering, deafening fecundity. Flesh begetting flesh, din begetting din. It wasn't hard to fathom, because he'd thought it himself, in his darkest times. Seen the human tide advancing on species he'd loved – beasts too wild or too wise to compromise with the invader – and wished for a plague to wither every human womb. Heard the din and longed for a gentle death to silence every throat. Sometime not even gentle. He understood. Oh Lord, he understood.

When Will tells Steep that God moves each of them, 'the words, though he'd never thought he'd hear them from his own tongue, were true.'

> God *was* in him now. Always had been. Steep had the rage of some Judgmental Father in his eye, but the divinity Will had in him was no less a Lord, though He talked through the mouth of a fox and loved life more than Will had supposed life could be loved. A Lord who'd come before him in innumerable shapes over the years. Some pitiful, to be sure, some triumphant. A blind polar bear on a garbage heap; two children in painted masks; Patrick sleeping; Patrick smiling; Patrick speaking love. Camellias on a windowsill and the skies of Africa. His Lord was there, everywhere, inviting him to see the soul of things.

Will's journey home to Burnt Yarley and his childhood is but an arc of another and greater circle. He pursues Steep north to the most fertile of the Inner Hebrides, tiny Tiree – 'the granary of the islands' – where Clive Barker spent so many memorable days in his youth. There, hidden in an icy outcrop of rock, is the legendary 'House of the World,' the Domus Mundi; but its interior is a grey darkness, lit with pale flames that disclose walls and floors made of filth and clogged with rotting trash, a sad mirror of the dying psyche of the world.

High atop an elaborate web of knotted rope and filthy woodwork waits the throne of Gerard Rukenau. Despite his serpentine looks, the mystic is no satanic majesty, just a man whose arrogance and pride have engineered his own prison and Hell. A step outside of the Domus Mundi would forfeit its gift of immortality; embittered and lonely, Rukenau has covered its glory with dirt and excrement, rigging the elaborate ropework to assure that he never has to set foot upon the House of the World again.

Rukenau was the bastard child of a church-builder. Abandoned by his father, he determined to build a cathedral that God so desired to visit that all of his father's churches would be left empty. He studied architecture and magic, learned the sacred geometries, and finally enlisted the aid of the Nilotic, an angel who could construct a temple so profound that 'a priest might see the Creator's labours at a single glance'. But a glance was not enough for Rukenau; he needed an artist's vision – the vision of a Thomas Simeon – to comprehend the Nilotic's efforts.

When the outcast Steep, who had failed to return Simeon to the Domus Mundi, re-enters its halls, he greets his former master with the killing blade; but Rosa follows, scouring the filth from the walls and exposing the glories hidden beneath: a vast temple of life whose essence is 'the throb and shimmer of living things', the 'glorious . . . *madness*' that is also the glory of creation.

As Rukenau dies, he offers a final revelation: Steep and Rosa are one. They are the angel known as the Nilotic, divided by his necromancy. Each half, male and female, has adapted to the world of humanity through their experience of gender, embracing the most superficial impulses of man and woman: to terminate and to procreate. 'Living in the world with stolen names, learning the cruel assumptions of their gender from what they saw about them, unable to live apart, although it was a torment to be so close to the other, yet never close enough.' Now, in the House of the World, a mere touch reunites them, Rosa's bleeding brightness merging with Steep, marrying him, becoming whole . . . becoming one.

The Nilotic moves into the heart of the House, intent on undoing it, and Will follows. 'The deeper they ventured the more it seemed he was treading not among the echoes of the world, but in the world itself, his soul a thread of bliss passing into its mysteries . . . He did not grieve, knowing his life was a day long, or an hour. He did not wonder who made him. He did not wish to be other. He did not pray. He did not hope. He only was, and was, and was, and that was the joy of it.'

The journey takes him home again, to Burnt Yarley, where he walks the cold slopes of his youth, the forgotten places and faces that live inside him still, seeing them with sublime wisdom: 'The creators of the world had not retreated to the heights. They were everywhere. They were stones, they were trees, they were shafts of light and burgeoning seeds. They were broken things, they were dying things, and they were all that sprang up from things dying and broken. And where they were, he was too. Fox and God and the creature between.' Finally his footsteps lead to the place where the birds had fallen and, in time, to San Francisco and Patrick's house, where Will fulfils his promise to attend his friend's final moments. But when Patrick goes gently into the night, Will feels an unaccustomed discomfort. For the first time in his life, the man who watched and chronicled the dying of so many breeds feels like a voyeur. 'Maybe it would be better just to go, he thought; leave the living to their grief, and the dead to their ease. He belonged in neither tribe, it seemed, and that unfixedness, which had been a pleasure to him as he went through the world, was now no pleasure at all. It only made him lonely.'

At last, it seems, Will Rabjohns is awake, and alive. He is no longer content to stand idly by, watching, waiting, for death to come. 'The season of visions was at an end, at least for now, and its inciter had departed, leaving Will to take his wisdom back to the tribe. To tell what he'd seen and felt in the heart of the Domus Mundi. To celebrate what he knew, and turn it to its healing purpose.' There is only one place for him: 'his only true and certain home, the world.'

It is a lesson for both the artist and the man. The act of creation, like that of existence, must be defined on our own terms, not those of others – certainly not those of parents or teachers, critics or readers, and certainly not those of politics, whether social or sexual – and, ultimately, in terms of sacrament. Creating and existing, Clive Barker reminds us, are acts as sacred as those of communion, signifying or at least striving to signify a spiritual reality; if not, they are as purposeless and as vile as murder.

Sacrament is arguably the best of Clive Barker's novels, and one of the most directly and profoundly autobiographical of his fictions. It is his first novel with an openly gay protagonist (which, even in these 'enlightened' times, caused some concern at HarperCollins US, which felt it hindered its commercial prospects); and it is one of a handful of contemporary novels in which the sexuality of the protagonist, whether gay or straight, is absolutely essential to its plot. There is, however, no sense of polemic. Just as the novel cannot be read as a paean to animal rights, its take on gay lifestyles is by no means a gentle or encouraging one. In the very real world of *Sacrament*, gay and straight relationships are equally difficult and troubled; Barker argues convincingly against gender roles and stereotypes, as well as warning of the dangers of defining oneself through them.

The plot is a characteristic puzzle box of secret histories whose telling and retelling are the key to revelation. In these pages Barker revisits themes – notably, the urge for unity and transformation – that have been crucial to earlier works. It is no accident that *Sacrament* echoes another autobiographical novel, *Weaveworld*, at essential moments, but here Barker strips away the veneer of fantasy (which plays but a minor role in the narrative), finding the courage to create a metaphoric Wonderland that cannot be ignored or dismissed as the stuff of escapism. For Clive Barker the fantasist, *Sacrament* is remarkable in its retreat from the elaborate otherworldly mythologies of *Imajica* and the novels of 'The Art' in favour of a subdued unreality whose most chimerical qualities are Biblical in character. It is equally remarkable in its refusal to concede that unreality, to suggest that its tropes have anything but direct and vital meaning for the reader – and the writer.

Will Rabjohn's profession as a photographer of dying species is an elegant and inspired metaphor for the writer, the film-maker, the artist of the dark fantastic – in other words, for Clive Barker himself. The truth is underscored in a telling aside about reviews: 'The critical response to both the books and exhibitions had often been antagonistic. Few reviewers had questioned Will's skills – he had the temperament, the vision, and the technical grasp to be a great photographer. But why, they complained, did he have to be so relentlessly grim? Why did he have to seek out images that evoked despair and death when there was so much beauty in the natural world?'

Why? Because darkness, Barker counsels, is very much in the eye of the beholder. The bloodthirsty scourge known as Jacob Steep is only the most recent of the light-bearing zealots who burn their way through the pages of his fiction. Steep fears the dark, and wants more than anything to hold it at bay; but Will Rabjohns, like Clive Barker, wants to know the dark, to embrace its mysteries, to rid us of the fear of the unknown and all that is done in its name. *Sacrament* is a testament to the explorers of that darkness, and a challenge to those who would write in its name.

At one juncture, Will offers a brief riposte, discussing a New Age spiritualist who comforts Patrick: 'Oh, there's light in my pictures . . . light aplenty. It just wasn't the kind of illumination [she] would want to meditate upon.' Before entering the Domus Mundi, Will considered his photographs as a kind of bleak magic, one that, like his childhood killing of the birds, might work change in the world, but through negation and despair; it is, in a sense, the bleak magic of the *Books of Blood* or *The Damnation Game*. But the light Will offers after entering the House of the World shines brightly: '*Take pleasure not because it's fleeting, but because it exists at all.*' The light is one that his photographs, like Clive Barker's own work in so many media, cannot capture, but which the artist, with wisdom and conscience, can suggest and indeed exalt: 'This presence of all things, seen and unseen, around and about, remember. There will be days in your life when you'll need to have this feeling again, to know that all that's gone from the world hasn't really gone at all; it's just not in sight.'

During the writing of *Sacrament*, Clive also began to wrestle with the public perception of his own sexuality. Like his avatar Will Rabjohns, he felt that he was 'a bundle of contradictions . . . a lot of gay men are. They want something other than what they were taught to want, and it . . . *muddies* them somehow.'

After meeting Bill Scobie in his teenaged years – his first awareness of an openly gay man – Clive had believed, for a long time, that sexual preferences should be displayed personally and privately, not socially. He made no secret of his sexual orientation, and his fiction offered obvious clues from as early as the *Books of Blood*. In the initial draft of 'In the Hills, the Cities', he had portrayed his bickering couple as heterosexual; but Pete Atkins noted its homosexual undercurrent, which Clive then made explicit – only to have his editor at Sphere, Barbara Boote, urge: 'Don't publish it.'

Clive was always open, but never insistent, about his sexual preferences. His tastes had an element of the voyeuristic: he loved to see sexual expression, whatever its form; but for many years, he cloaked his own expression with a reserve and a belief in privacy. As Mary Roscoe says: 'I didn't know he was gay for a long, long time; and I'm an actor – you meet gay people all the time, there's nothing unusual about it. And yet I never knew he was gay for about four or five months. I remember thinking: *You look so straight, the sort of boy my mum would think, "He'd be a nice boy to marry."* There's a kind of college boy image, but inside there's this extraordinary, almost demonic lust for the perverse, the subversive. I think he plays with that all the time, in everything he does, with the outside and the inside art; they're usually at odds in some way.'

In *Sacrament*, he gathered the strength to offer insight, without monsters and metaphors, into his existence as part of a lost and isolated breed – the reality behind his visions of the Nightbreed: 'Men whose mothers and fathers – however loving, however liberal – would never understand them the way they understood their straight children, because these gay sons were genetic cul-de-sacs. Men who would be obliged to make their own families: out of friends, out of lovers, out of divas. Men who were self-invented, for better or worse, makers of styles and mythologies that they constantly cast off with the impatience of souls who would never find a description that quite fitted. If there was a sadness in this there was also a kind of unholy glee.'

In the novel's final pages, he finds, in the sadness and the glee – and the 'unrepeatable experience' of gay men – a redemptive power:

421

'We're not going anywhere, because we don't come from anywhere. We're spontaneous events. We just appear in the middle of families. And we'll keep appearing. Even if the plague killed every homosexual on the planet, it wouldn't be extinction, because there's queer babies being born every minute. It's like magic . . . You know, that's exactly what it is. It's magic.'

'One of the more intriguing aspects of horror fiction and film,' Barker notes, 'is the way in which it has been used to normalize sexual conduct . . . While for the moralist – and especially the censor – sex is something that you do or see, an act or event with a set duration that has at its centre the notion of performance, Hollywood has adopted this principle, making sex scenes virtual set-pieces that define film more generically than their broader content, as has its self-regulatory MPAA, which purports to rate films on the basis of content analysis.

'In fact, sex is something much more expansive – from the mere physical intimacy or touching of lovers to a way of thinking and of fantasizing. A child has no discernment in exploring sexual possibilities, but simply seeks the pleasure, while the process of adulthood is one in which these possibilities are repressed, contained, and an "acceptable" view of sex is adopted. True horror fiction – like homosexuality – is taboo for, among other things, its willingness to indulge or accept erotic possibilities.'

While writing *Sacrament*, Clive decided to arrange for a series of interviews with leading gay magazines, including *The Advocate*, *Out* and *Ten Percent*, in order to confirm his sexuality. In a moment of uncomfortable objectification, *Ten Percent* presented a cover story describing him as 'Devil Doll' and his interview as a 'coming out'. In fact, the interviews were not about coming out, but speaking out:

'This is as true now as it was thirty years ago when we did *The Holly and the Ivy*: things grow in you, they grow in you and they have to speak out. And they grow in you because an excitement grows in you and you have to speak it. I don't mean this in a mystical way, or anything like that, it's just that I can remember standing in my bedroom and having an idea. I can remember having ideas. It's the best feeling, there is no feeling in the world like having an idea. That's so stupid, it's almost like a Monty Python routine: *Duh, I had an idea.*

'When something comes to you, when something speaks to you, it trails consequences. It gives you purpose. You become its object. You are now in service of it. It's bigger than you are, it's more important than you are. It wants to be in the world. It's a life-form. It's an explanation; it's a justification. It gets you up in the morning. It makes you want to be alive. And it helps you understand why you are.'

Sacrament opens with the following credo:

> I am a man, and men are animals who tell stories. This is a gift from God, who spoke our species into being but left the end of our story untold. That mystery is troubling to us. How could it be otherwise? Without the final part, we think, how are we to make sense of all that went before, which is to say, our lives. So we make stories of our own, in fevered and envious imitation of our maker, hoping that we'll tell, by chance, what God left untold, and in finishing our tale, come to understand why we were born.

'Now that,' Clive says, 'is the high-fallutin' version of what I'm talking about. That my film-making and my picture-making, my word-making, is all in service of knowing why I was born. Until I know that, I'm very happy with feeling the energy that comes from being in service of it.'

29

ANCIENT OF DAYS

'ANIMAL LIFE' (1994)
'CHILIAD: A MEDITATION' (1997)

> *For the movements of a man's life are in spirals: we go back whence*
> *we came, ever returning on our former traces, only upon a higher*
> *level, on the next upward coil of the spiral, so that it is a going back*
> *and a going forward ever and both at once.*
>
> — GEORGE MACDONALD, *England's Antiphon*

'It's all the same story . . . It's about being born, and being afraid of dying, and how love saves us.'[1]

In 1994, Clive Barker returned to the short story form, writing 'Animal Life', the first entry in a six-author Summer Fiction Series for *USA Today Weekend*.[2] Although his career in books had commenced with the devastating short stories of *Clive Barker's Books of Blood*, which were quickly followed by three more volumes of short fiction, he had penned only a handful of stories in the decade since his debut: 'Lost Souls', a story of Harry D'Amour for the 1985 Christmas issue of *Time Out*; the subtle and darkly sentimental novelette 'Coming to

Grief' for my anthology *Prime Evil* (1988); a vignette set in the mythic dream-sea Quiddity, 'On Amen's Shore', for the small press publication *Demons and Deviants* (1993); and 'Pidgin and Theresa', a surrealist wonder set in his former neighbourhood of Crouch End, for *The Time Out Book of London Short Stories* (1993).

Each fiction was dramatically different in tone and setting; but each, like his earlier short stories, kept its distance from the personal life of Clive Barker. Only 'Coming to Grief', a homage to Ray Bradbury and Ramsey Campbell that offered a moving portrayal of a woman who returns to Liverpool to confront her mother's death – and her child-hood fears – seemed to implicate autobiography.

That was not the case with 'Animal Life', which was based directly upon Clive's experiences in the devastating Los Angeles earthquake of January 1994 – and in the far more personally devastating shake-up of his once-happy home. This brief fable of an Angelino's confron-tation with catastrophe marked a fundamental change in Barker's emotional existence and his approach to the written word.

Ralph, a swimming pool contractor, barely survives the infamous earthquake, but witnesses a wonder: his dog and sole companion, Duffy, sitting at the kitchen table, eating ice cream – and talking. Spooked by the temblors, Duffy had escaped the house, following a pack of coyotes into a stand of trees, where animals of all kinds congregated around a crack in the ground. Smoke rose from the hole; after breathing it, the animals could speak. A strange woman – an earth goddess, perhaps – emerged from the depths: 'She was huge, maybe 300 pounds, and beautiful. Every kind of blood in her, every kind of feeling in her face, all at once. Rage and love and rapture . . .' She asked the animals a dire question: 'I need to know whether I should shake this city to pieces.'

When Ralph asks the outcome of their vote, an aftershock strikes; the house collapses, burying everything that he owns save Duffy, who again runs away. Ralph sets out in search of him: 'If he could just find his dog, it would be a sign that his life was not beyond reclamation. He would rebuild it, with stronger foundations.' He passes scenes of destruction, some of them strangely welcome, and finally comes upon a place concealed by trees. There he recognizes the awesome and irresistible possibilities of the unknown:

The grove was deserted. But there was everywhere evidence that an extraordinary congregation had gathered here. Hoof marks and paw marks in the churned dirt, feathers and fur flitting about, splashes and pellets and mounds of excrement spread all around.

And in the middle of the grove, a crack in the earth. Tentatively, he approached it. There was no smoke. The ground was still and cold. Whatever miracle had been here – if any – it had passed.

Out of the trees bounds Duffy; but when Ralph tries to tell the dog that he believes his story, Duffy only barks and runs in circles. Ralph follows the dog back to the ruined house. Uplifted by Duffy's joyful mood, he begins planning the new house that will be built over the ruins. 'He would not, however, waste his heart loving it, he decided, in case the vote had gone badly and the animal running ahead of him was pretending simple doghood to keep his master from despair.'

This brief meditation on the frailty of humanity's alliance with nature – and inversion of the early play *Dog* (1978) – also offered a glimpse into the emotional earthquake that shook Clive's personal life and brought his household (but not his house) to ruin. As he laboured endless hours on the motion picture *Lord of Illusions* and the novel *Sacrament*, his six-year relationship with Malcolm Smith disintegrated. In time, he would find himself alone with his beloved dog Lola, although even her simple pleasures could not keep him from despair.

Ironically, the attraction originally shared by Clive and Malcolm proved central to their break-up. Malcolm's good looks and gregarious personality gave him power as an actor, on and off the stage; and his personal ambition was robust. Initially, he had accepted the semi-secrecy of their romance, wary of wagging tongues that might claim nepotism in Clive's casting of Malcolm in the role of Ashberry for *Nightbreed*. After Clive's move to California, however, the lovers were far more open about their relationship, attending premieres and other social events as a couple; yet Malcolm soon felt uneasy about being perceived, in the public eye, as Clive's partner. He did not want to stand in Clive's shadow, but to secure his own identity as an actor and writer; yet his success seemed increasingly entwined with the world of Clive Barker as their relationship extended into a host of new business projects. Salient among these endeavours was a series of original comic books published by Marvel Comics.

Early in 1993, Marvel, cognizant that its series based on the motion pictures *Hellraiser* and *Nightbreed* would soon reach an end, invited Barker to originate a cast of new, cutting-edge superheroes for comics to be issued under its fledgling Razorline imprint, which was directed to a more mature demographic.

The appeal to Clive's imagination was intense – after all, Marvel Comics were a vital inspiration of his youth – but he knew that he could pursue the project only if his personal participation could be kept to a minimum. Malcolm, whom he trusted implicitly, seemed the ideal choice to represent his interests. Clive developed character concepts for four eponymous series – *Ectokid*, *Hokum & Hex*, *Hyperkind* and *SaintSinner* – which were billed as 'Super Heroes from the Mind of Clive Barker'. Malcolm took on the role of 'consultant' for the intended 'Barkerverse', acting as the liaison between Barker and Marvel's creative team, exerting editorial influence when needed and even writing several of the stories.

The comic books proved the most ephemeral of Clive's contributions to the popular culture, and tested the limits of his ability to control quality and content. From the beginning, however, his desire was to act merely as a point-man: to create the characters and let others control their creative existence. 'I think my job here,' Clive noted at the time, 'is hopefully to create some mythologies that writers and artists will, in years to come, find intriguing and bring their own things to. I want to be democratic about this: I'm the pump primer here. My attitude is much as it is with the *Hellraiser* sequels – that I will watch over this stuff, and give support, encouragement and ideas when requested. But my initial gift, if you like, is the gift of an idea that I hope will be rich enough to encourage diverse hands and imaginations to play with.'

The four titles shared the same setting: a comic book version of our reality that is revealed to be part of a cycle of ten worlds known as the Decamundi. Three titles made their debut in September 1993: *Ectokid*, the adventures of Dex Mungo, half-human and half-ghost, who haunts our world and the realm of the Ectosphere, a perilous purgatory between here and the hereafter; *Hokum & Hex*, which features a failed stand-up comic, Trip Monroe, who obtains magical powers and becomes the last line of defence against an extra-dimensional villain, Felon Bane ('in other words, earth's last, best hope . . . is a joke'); and *Hyperkind*, whose pages are steeped in the traditions of the 'Golden Age' of comics, proposing that the powers of the Paxis, a 1940s alliance of superheroes similar to the Justice League of America, are resurrected in four children of Hollywood Boulevard – a jock, a rich girl, a drug addict and a street urchin – who must confront an ancient evil (and the destroyer of the Paxis), Paragon John. The most radical of the 'Barkerverse' comics in style and artwork, however, was the delirious *SaintSinner*, which first appeared in October 1993. It chronicles young Philip Fetter's possession by two competing entities – an angel and a demon; he becomes their personal battleground, while evolving into something more, or less, than human.

In December 1993, Marvel introduced, under its more conventional Epic imprint, two new series based on the *Hellraiser* films. The first was perhaps inevitable: *Pinhead*, a comic championing the anti-heroic Pope of the Other Darkness that was produced without Barker's creative input or supervision. Written by DG Chichester and Erik Saltzgaber, its first issue did not even mention Barker's name, although subsequent issues provided a proprietary credit. Despite its best intentions, *Pinhead* succeeded only in rendering its mighty character into a cartoon – and reached its nadir in *Law in Hell*, a two-book confrontation between Pinhead and the anti-hero of another Marvel series, *Marshall Law*.

Clive Barker's The Harrowers: Raiders of the Abyss, whose first issue was adorned with a glow-in-the-dark cover, was said to be 'ripped from the pages of *Hellraiser*' (an oxymoron, since *Hellraiser* was a motion picture). Written by Malcolm Smith and McNally Sagal, the comic introduced a motley crew of humans who are selected in a preternatural lottery by the goddess Morté Mammé to do battle with Leviathan, the ruler of Hell. The series, intended to reinvent the mythology of *Hellraiser* in more conventional comic book style, ultimately 'crossed over' into the pages of *Pinhead*.

The comics of the 'Barkerverse' were greeted with a lukewarm response, and the several series fell victim to their inconsistent quality and poor timing – the comic book market was glutted with new product. Conceived in part as nostalgic evocations of the comics Clive had adored in his youth, the characters and their stories may have seemed tame to a new generation of readers who had grown up with the *Books of Blood* and *Hellraiser*. Although three additional 'Barkerverse' titles – *Wraitheart*, *Mode Extreme* and *Schizoid* – were announced in a planned relaunch that would move the content closer to the Marvel Universe, none of the new books reached the stands. After less than a year in print, the existing titles were cancelled in the spring of 1994.

In the meantime, *Ectokid* had drawn the avid attention of network television as a potential Saturday morning children's cartoon series – and of Virgin Interactive, which was seeking successors to its best-selling computer game *The Seventh Guest*. Clive and Malcolm pitched the premise of *Ectokid* to Virgin as a CD-ROM adventure game known as *Ectosphere*.

In another creative departure, *Ectosphere* and its dimension-transcending hero, Dex Mungo, took Barker's creative vision into the realm of pseudo-science fiction. A scientific researcher discovers that, at death, particles in the brain accelerate and disappear: this is our consciousness, speeding into another dimension – the Ectosphere. With the backing of the US government, the researcher develops the Aurat, a machine that simulates death, allowing living beings to send their consciousness into the Ectosphere and return – thus enacting, scientifically, the myth of Orpheus.

The researcher learns, however, that something on the other side, in the Ectosphere, desires to enter our reality – with ill intent. Mortally wounded by government agents when he tries to destroy the Aurat, he is placed in the machine by his wife; when he dies, she uses the Aurat to return his consciousness to our reality so that he can disable the machine by erasing its essential algorithm. His wife is pregnant, however, and the proximity of the fetus to these perturbations gives their son, Dex, the power to accelerate his consciousness and move, by force of will, into the Ectosphere.

Although the game was abandoned by Virgin after years of costly development, Clive and Malcolm also pitched the concept to Aaron Spelling Productions, which, in 1995, acquired the rights to produce *Ectosphere* as a motion picture. Mark Kruger, who co-wrote the screenplay of *Candyman: Farewell to the Flesh* (1995), prepared at least two draft scripts with input from Clive and Malcolm; a later script was written by Fred Vicarel and the film remained in development until 1999, when it too was abandoned.

The collaboration seemed a new pinnacle of their relationship; but in fact, it marked the end of everything they had shared. 'We worked together quite well,' Clive says. 'He had a good imagination and good storytelling abilities, and he was a good actor.' But romance had blinded Clive.

'It is the great error of my life, in terms of relationships. John Gregson was not an error. John was a growing, whilst Malcolm was an error. He represented a lot of things I now know I should have gone nowhere near. Actors, for one thing, who bring with them their own baggage – particularly if they're in a relationship with a producer and a director. It's dumb; just don't go there, you know?'

Clive was intrigued by the efficacy of new technologies and the potential of computer games and the internet as fertile outlets for his creativity, but unlike Malcolm, he was rarely interested in the lifestyle of hardware and material things.

Until coming to the United States, Clive had never had the time or inclination to learn to drive an automobile; and he admits to occasional problems with electric can-openers. To this day he refuses to use a computer or even a typewriter to write, preferring the intimacy of the pen. He also had learned the truth of the maxim that money did not buy happiness; but Malcolm's measure of success was different.

In pursuing careers in acting and writing – two difficult and uncertain professions – Malcolm had found opportunities in Hollywood, but by the mid-nineties almost all of them were rooted in his relationship with Clive. The tie of the personal to the professional weighed on him. Finances, which were sometimes stretched thin in those early years in Beverly Hills, were another source of tension. Increasingly Malcolm expressed a need to 'prove' his independence; and that discontent soon led, perhaps inevitably, to an emotional rift that could not be healed. As with many relationships, the intensity of their mutual attraction and their shared interests had obscured vital differences in how each man viewed the world and the significance of their life together in it.

Clive was heartbroken. 'I realized, really: *Jesus Christ, where are we?* He didn't know what he wanted, and I don't know whether he does now – I hope he does now.' The distance between them became palpable when Malcolm turned to regimes of 'smart drugs' and homeo-pathy, 'which struck me as being one of the more bizarre forms of health study,' Clive says. 'I could not share his passion for this; I thought it was nonsense. I thought we were in crystal territory, and I said so. And that was the beginning of the end.'

By 1996, their relationship, like their creative collaborations, had reached a dead end. In an anguished and difficult endgame, Malcolm left Clive – and California – to pursue his new-found calling. 'He went off to Portland to study homeopathy. We never speak, and I have no desire to speak to him. I wish him well, because there was a big heart in there somewhere.

'The interesting thing is that you're entirely responsible for these things. There's no blame attached to any of this. I volunteered for this relationship. I feel very deeply for Malcolm, and I wish him well still. I think it's important to wish people well. He didn't murder anybody; our relationship failed.'

But with the failure of the relationship came a deep and abiding sense of despair – and bouts of a dark and ominous loneliness. Clive was struggling with a terrible, undiagnosed depression, including the pall of anhedonia: the inability to experience even the simplest pleasures of things. He turned his gaze homeward, to his mother and father, seeking their advice and comfort. 'Clive thinks more clearly now,' Joan Barker says. 'As life goes by, if Clive has a problem, he calls – he talks at length with Len. It's different from when he was twenty. He comes back to his parents. He's asked for our advice, which he doesn't always take; but when Malcolm left, he was on the phone, straightaway.'

His parents and his brother, Roy, were troubled: 'Now that Clive is far away, I do worry for him,' Roy says, 'in that he has got the fame, he's got the money, but does he have any true friends? Really,

really true friends? People that, if the whole thing turned upside-down tomorrow, would still be there? His family always will be here . . . and my concern for him is that his family, our two children, they don't know him well enough. He's Uncle Clive and he's a famous writer and he's just written a book. And it doesn't anger me, it just saddens me. Because he can't switch off. And I know it's the same with my parents.'

With Clive so far away, there was only one assurance for his family: David Dodds, who had stood by him through the highs and the lows – the lover who had become the best of friends. 'As long as Dave's around,' Roy says, 'Clive will be okay. Dave is the one person I know who, if it all went belly-up tomorrow, would still be there.'

Although time, and his long conversations with his father and mother, would heal the wounds of failed romance, Clive's despair would not relent. He consulted his doctor and was referred to a psychiatrist, who, in turn, prescribed a course of anti-depressants; but medication did not resolve his emotional agony. Then, in one of his many telephone calls home, his parents disclosed more distressing news: Len Barker had been diagnosed with leukemia.

A few months later, I received a long letter from Clive, written from a house on Kauai – a retreat that he had discovered in the Hawaiian Islands. He had survived the crippling disease of depression through the only course available to him: creation. He was spending hour upon hour in his studio, painting with a relentless passion that was unlike anything he had experienced with his work in fiction or film; and he was writing, but with a new sense of purpose, and a new sense of self-revelation. His letter spoke of a bliss unlike any he had felt in years.

> There's a tropical rainstorm, and the geckos are taking refuge under the eaves, where doubtless they'll find a fine meal of spiders. I'm in bliss. So very far from Europe, yet here I'm reminded of being a child back in Liverpool more than I ever am in LA or New York or even London: of dreaming of this balmy faraway. And now, on the radio, the *In Paradisum* from the Fauré *Requiem*. I can't believe the synchronicity of it. The music rises and the rain beats down even harder, as if applauding . . .

Attached to the letter was the revised manuscript of a short novel, 'Chiliad: A Meditation', which he had promised to write for me – and which he had drafted when he was last on Kauai, trying to escape from his depression: 'my head so fogged by despair I wanted to throw myself in the sea just to wash it clean. And if the tide had taken me I wouldn't have much cared.'[3] I turned the pages of the manuscript with nervous wonder, for this was a story told in the first person, not by some invented narrator, but by Clive Barker: his voice, his emotion, his pain, his passion. It was a meditation, indeed – on himself, and on the end of days.

'Chiliad' had been conceived as the result of a structural challenge I presented to Clive while creating the anthology *Revelations* (published in the United Kingdom as *Millennium*) (1997).[4] The book was intended as an 'anthology/novel' that would mark the end of a century and the beginning of a new millennium with a sequence of ten short novels, each one set in a different decade of the twentieth century. When the ten decades were completed, Clive accepted the daunting task of creating a two-part novella that would 'wrap around' the other stories, beginning in the distant past and concluding at the millennium – while remaining a fiction that could be read on its own terms.

The result was 'Chiliad' – its title another term for the passage of a thousand years – whose two sections, 'Men and Sin' and 'A Moment at the River's Heart', provide the opening and closing acts of *Revelations*. The first paragraphs of 'Men and Sin' introduce its narrator, a witness to the flowing waters of the imagination: 'In my mind, the river flows both ways.' It is Clive Barker, offering himself to readers with a directness and honesty that he would not have imagined only a few years before.

Until writing *Sacrament*, Clive seemed to define himself as an 'external' writer, fulfilling the Shakespearean model of a quiet and intensely philosophical observer of his imagination who, through fiction, created external landscapes, often abstract and fantastic, which he then embellished with histories, characters, ideas and, of course, stories. There were few immediate connections between his fiction and his life; instead his limited forays into autobiography were anecdotal, as in *Weaveworld*, or more typically thematic, expressions of urgings and sense memories rather than concrete incidents from his life.

Perhaps the most obvious, and consistent, of these themes was that of an escape from the mundane into the miraculous, which enacted his youthful yearning to fulfil the fantasies of *Peter Pan* and escape the banalities of life in Liverpool. ('Not that Len and Joan aren't wonderful parents,' Pete Atkins comments. 'They are. But they probably didn't seem that wonderful to him at eighteen – to be cruel. They lived in a very nice house in a very nice neighbourhood in a suburb of Liverpool, but in his heart and his imagination – and also specifically in his sexual imagination – Clive was very much a changeling, an outsider who didn't want that, who wanted something bigger and better. It's a very boyish, almost a pre-pubescent impulse; not that Clive thought that he was royalty, but he thought he should have had a more exciting life.')

Clive's reluctance to indulge the autobiographical was also consistent with his personal reserve and his shyness; and grounded in the way he guards memories of life's precious moments: 'You happen to fall in love to Gladys Knight & the Pips. So forever, whenever Gladys Knight & the Pips plays, it's a sense memory: you can taste the person, it's like they're here. Well, it's the same with a view out of the window, or a smell: the world will transform around you. I have incredibly powerful feelings from my childhood, but I use them sparingly – in part because I'm afraid of spoiling them by repetition: you go back and you go back and, eventually, they don't mean anything to you any more. And part of it is that some writers have gone too often to the well, and it's become a literary device rather than something that they feel: they're writing about their own writing, rather than writing about the feeling. I worry about that; I'm genuinely concerned about that happening, so I try to be very sparing about it.'

'Chiliad' was anything but sparing; its pages are a confessional of lost love and deep depression. 'In my forty-fourth year,' Clive Barker – becoming his own story – tells us: 'a malaise crept upon me, and took me in its jaws.' It is a powerfully felt, and powerfully descriptive, summation of the disease, whose singular darkness is often the very inability to express its symptoms.

Emerging from his ruminations on himself, his agony and his art is another, more linear story set around the turn of the first millennium in the English village of Tress. A rough-hewn local named Shank finds his mate, Agnes, face-down and dead in the mud of the riverbank. Heartbroken, Shank 'becomes death-in-life'; he tracks down and butchers three suspicious hillmen, not knowing they are innocent of the crime. Entangled in the last of his victims, Shank drowns in the dark waters of the river. 'His bones go into the mud; and the sun never shines on him again.'

The river flows on – 'Nothing of significance will change here for almost a thousand years' – until 1940, when a crippled Luftwaffe bomber jettisons its payload of destruction, originally intended for London, and demolishes the church at Tress. After the war, an artist is commissioned to design four stained-glass windows for a new sanctuary, but he completes only three of the designs:

> They are glorious; the triumphs of his career. One depicts John the Baptist, standing in a river, with a congregation of happy acolytes waiting to be blessed. A second shows Christopher, bearing the child Jesus on his shoulders across another river, this one wilder than that in which John stands. The third is of Christ the Redeemer, walking on the waters, while fish leap around His wounded feet . . .
>
> The fourth window was reputed to depict the Second Coming, when the river would flow back against itself; and the sun, moon, and stars all shine at the same hour, and Christ, and the frightened soul who carried him, and the shaman who baptized him, would come together in glory to forgive the sinners and share with them the secret of bliss. But the artist dies of a heart attack before he finishes his great work, and the fourth window instead is made of plain glass, through which the congregation sees only sky.

The concluding section, 'A Moment by the River's Heart', returns us to our narrator, and his disturbing dreams and dark depression. On the threshold of a new millennium, a thousand years after the deaths of Agnes and Shank, another troubled man wanders the riverside near the reconstructed church. 'The man's name is Devlin Coombs, and he was until yesterday a married man of forty-one, happily unrenowned. He worked at a small insurance firm in the city . . . Tuesdays and Thursdays he attended night school studying ceramics ... He will make no more pots; nor will he make love to Mary Elizabeth, for last night, his beloved wife's body was washed up by the river.'

Devlin can only mourn her loss, 'and wonder, while he mourned, how she had come to such an end ... All he could know now – the only mystery he could solve – was the identity of the man who had taken her life.'

The police pursue the crime with stolid and scientific sensibilities, while Devlin's quest indulges the fantastic. Through a chain of circumstances – or destiny – he contacts a psychic, and on New Year's Eve, she provides him with a strange flame that will illuminate his journey into the past.

Transported in a momentous shift of light, Devlin finds himself at the river's edge, hidden by the calm of the flame. It is the day of Mary Elizabeth's death, and he watches, enthralled, as she walks along the riverbank – and meets a young man there. Devlin's horrified eyes take in the truth: they are lovers, and this place is their rendezvous; and the murderer, coming from between the trees in righteous anger, is Devlin himself, the deed repressed by his shredded sanity. 'And all he can do is watch. All he wants to do is watch. He can't stop this scene being played out; it's already history. He came here only to discover the guilty party, and there he is, in all his vengeful glory, wielding the knife with such speed the lovers don't have time to run.'

Using the strange power of the flame, he interrogates his other, the Devlin who stabbed his wife and her lover to death; but his journey to understanding has only begun. To comprehend this act of violence – and his capacity for murder – he is taken farther back in time, to his childhood and the moment when his sister and her lover caught him peeping at their own sexual dalliance; but this explanation is insufficient, and Devlin is carried back and back again in time, the flame lighting the path to an inevitable revelation.

> You know what happens next. The parable is perfectly transparent. But I have to tell you; I have to believe that my meaning resides not in the gross motion of the tale, but in the tics of syntax and cadence. If not, every story may be boiled down to a few charmless sentences; a sequence of causalities; this and this

and this; then marriage, or death. There has to be more than the telling of stories, just as there must be more to our lives.

In his regression into his past – and the past of all humanity – Devlin witnesses the crimes, petty and prime, of generation upon generation, 'mind within mind, harm within harm'. At last he finds himself at the riverbank on the eve of the first millennium, in the aftermath of the death of Shank's woman, Agnes. Seeing her corpse restores him to a 'terrible sanity', and he confronts the narrator, who imagines a conversation in which Devlin pleas for redemption. The narrator is unmoved: 'The man acts as though he has a measure of self-determination; as though he can step away from me and still live, somehow. It's impossible, of course. I conjured him in service of my story; he can have no existence beyond my dream of him; he can take no journey that I do not first imagine.' But then, he realizes, he is about to be proved wrong: Devlin can step away from his creator, and take on a life of his own – 'and the thought exhilarates me'.

The narrator can only follow his creation, who leads him to a weeping man, a blade clutched in his hand; it is Agnes's killer – the local priest. When he sees Devlin, awash in the enigmatic flame, he mistakes him for his Saviour. As he embraces the flame, Devlin burns into nothingness; and the priest, transfigured by his hope and faith, however misguided, lies down to die in the open field.

Observing this encounter, the narrator finds his own revelation: the meaning of his agony, perhaps, but certainly the meaning of his art. 'Perhaps on reflection it's not loneliness I feel. Perhaps it's envy, that they found one another, and redeemed their souls with faith and flame and were so comforted by what they believed they could die a wretched death and count themselves blessed.'

His story completed, the narrator places his notebook where it might one day be found and read. Then he wades into the waters of the river to meet his fate – as unknown and incomplete as the four windows of the church, and fulfilling in its very absence of finality, and thus its evocation of possibility:

I cannot tell you if John of the Desert, dressed in his coat of goatskins, awaits me there, his hands spilling baptismal water; or if Christopher the Giant will come to set me on his shoulders, calling me Chylde; or if Christ may come, trout leaping at His heavy hem, eager to strew their rainbows before His pierced feet.

Or if I will be only carried away, looking through the plain glass of my eyes, hoping to see before I drown sun, moon, and stars hanging in the same firmament.

Born of despair, 'Chiliad: A Meditation' is a moving threnody on loss – of time and loved ones – and the intense loneliness of the artist and writer in his search for meaning: the connections of his work to the world and to himself. It is one of Clive's favourites among his own fiction: 'Because there is so much going on and so much ambiguity at the same time; and the presence of the first person narrator, providing this interweaving of the past and the present, and the windows and the river, comes closer than most of what I've attempted to avant-garde fiction. It plays with much more complex ideas about what words can do – and it's probably one of my least-read pieces. A piece of which I'm proud as hell; and its ambiguity is part of what I'm proud of – it has many meanings and perhaps different meanings depending on where you are in your life at a given time.'[5]

Its narrator's search for connections included, whether consciously or not, a search for love – and love in the higher sense, one that surpassed the physical and that might overcome the bleak certainty of isolation, the sense of an inescapable 'aloneness', that fuelled Clive's depression. While his doctor and his family offered the conventional explanations for his illness – his failed relationship with Malcolm, the stress of constant work, the crisis of reaching middle-age – Clive began to consider the ways in which his depression and despair were a part of his very being as an artist:

'I go through cycles of feeling psychically vulnerable. Sometimes I feel as though everything I've done is me attempting to square up to the terrible fact of being born, with the handbook on how to live life being such a small volume. You can't get up in the morning and say, *Okay, I'm going to be an artist*, and not face up to the profoundest questions you are capable of going after, even though you're going to fail over and over again.

'Quite early on in my life, I pictured this spider's-web fine wire hanging over a bottomless void, and us all poised on it – and the curiosity to me, frankly, is why people don't talk about this more. I don't understand how our culture can be so empty metaphysically. How so many people seem to go through their lives without pondering the issue of what we're here for and what it means to be born.

'When you've ticked off the things which were markers in your life – what you've wanted to achieve – and you've achieved them, there are less distractions. You can kid yourself less that the void is not there. The fact that you're walking around in a $3 million house in the middle of the night does not help you deal with it; the only thing which will still help is going and writing stuff down – that will absolutely help. To try to make stories, to try to make paintings, and to share them; they remain lifelines. It's the only part of self-description in which I can imagine myself, as I grow older, healing the hurt.

'This hurt was not visited upon me by my mother or my father or by anything psychological; it was simply waking up with my eyes open and thinking, *What is this business of being alive?* And what function do stories – particularly stories which have been told many times in some form or another, like fairy tales and folk tales – have in helping us heal ourselves, and be better with one another?

'I can write three or four lines of poetry or three or four lines of prose and feel a happiness which no deal that an agent could make for me could ever come near approaching. And the older I get, the narrower the number of possibilities about how to stay sane become. I fear that – I fear that a lot.'

True to this perception of self-description as self-help, Clive retreated into his art, writing 'Chiliad: A Meditation' and painting, always painting, seeking connections and a renewed sense of purpose. He plotted a new novel, and began work on a series of canvases that, although originally painted as individual pieces, soon suggested an anxious pattern that would become known as *The Book of Hours* – and later, *The Abarat Quartet*. Then, in a moment of sublime synchronicity, came the final connection.

On the afternoon of Easter Sunday, 1996, Clive set down his paintbrushes and decided to try to lose himself for a while among the people of Los Angeles. He drove his Lexus down from his house in the hills, heading for a club in Hollywood called The Faultline.

Driving to the same club, but from another direction, was photographer David Armstrong. Born on July 28, 1966, in Chicago, Illinois, David was the youngest of five children. Raised by his aunt in the aftermath of a difficult divorce, he had been brought to Los Angeles in 1971 by his mother, an aspiring actress known as 'the Lady'. David then experienced a 'strange childhood', shuttled between Los Angeles and Seattle as his mother shifted her pursuits: 'She liked religion and men.' Although born Catholic, the Lady cycled through Protestantism, Jehovah's Witnesses, the Black Muslims: 'The last I heard, she was a two-hundred-and-fifty-pound Mormon.'

Often left alone at home, David escaped his confusing reality through reading and artwork; he also found himself attracted to men, but lived in harsh denial of those feelings. He studied painting and graphic arts at the Cornish Art Institute in Seattle; and, following his graduation in 1986, moved to Los Angeles – where, at the age of twenty-one, he married his sister's best friend, who was ten years his senior. 'I had to prove to myself that I wasn't gay, that I was *normal*.' He began work as one of four employees of Fetish Group, a clothing company that soon employed more than three hundred people.

David continued to wrestle with his sexual feelings – 'I was just trying to fit into the society, and I was so miserable' – and decided that the solution was to father a child. His daughter, Nicole, was born on July 5, 1988. She was so beautiful that friends and strangers encouraged David and his wife to audition Nicole as a child model; and ultimately, at the age of four, she starred in a widely televised Sears commercial for 'Treasure Trolls'. Her agent advised David, however, that she needed head shots; when he learned that the photographs would cost $900, he decided to shoot the pictures himself. 'I had no clue about how to use a camera,' he admits; but the response was so positive that he founded his own business as a head shot and fashion photographer.

In the mid-1990s, he quit his job with Fetish Group – and his marriage. 'One day I woke up and realized that I was miserable, and that I was making my other half miserable, because the whole thing was a lie.' Because he truly loved his wife, he felt that their marriage should end. He devoted himself to photography, turning occasionally to experimental projects. 'I did quite well on my own as a photographer; but it felt like I had turned a hobby into work, so I wasn't getting the pleasure doing the commercial shoots. I had to do something creative – artistic things, funky things – for pleasure.'

Then came that fateful Easter Sunday. David had been invited to meet friends at The Faultline. Driving down Melrose, he spotted an empty parking space near the club. 'So I turned around, put my signal on, and started to back into the space ... and this jerk in a Lexus sedan just comes in and steals my parking space!' David drove around the block and found another space. As he walked toward the club, he decided to confront the driver of the other car. 'I see the guy – I don't see his face, he's digging around in his car – and I went up to him and said, *Excuse me, you stole my parking space ... you saw me waiting there*, and he turns around and I said: *But that's okay!* Because ... oh, he was cute!'

It was Clive, smoking a cigar and wearing paint-mottled khakis and Doc Martens boots. 'I would never have expected this guy to be affected by finding a dying baby dolphin and holding it in his arms, and crying for days over that experience.' Indeed, David would never have expected this man to be Clive Barker. (An avid reader of Anne Rice and Stephen King, David had never read a Clive Barker book, but his daughter had persuaded him to see the *Hellraiser* films.)

Inside the club the men began to talk – first about David's friends (who never arrived), and then Clive's artwork and David's photography and his daughter. After nearly two hours, David said: 'By the way, what's your name?' When Clive answered, David didn't believe him. 'Clive Barker isn't gay,' he thought, 'and he's not cute, either.'

Finally, David checked his watch and told Clive he had to leave – he had an Easter ham baking at home. Clive laughed and said: 'I've never heard that one before.' David replied, 'If you don't believe me, why don't you come over?' Clive agreed – 'and the rest is history,' David says. 'I'd never believed in love at first sight, but that was it for me. I knew that I was in love with this guy.

'When I first started to date men, I thought it was something wrong, and something dirty, and Clive made me proud to be a gay man, and a gay artist. He made me proud of who I was. And it was a big weight off my shoulders to just be who I am, and not to think that I was going to burn in Hell, or that someone was not going to like me, for being gay.

'I used to think it was a bad thing; but when I met Clive, it was just right.'

30

REDEMPTION

GALILEE (1998)

And he said unto them, I must preach the kingdom of God to other cities also; for therefor am I sent.
And he preached in the synagogues of Galilee.
                              – The Gospel According to St Luke 5:43–44

'*What must I do in the time remaining? Only everything.*'[1]

The conundrum faced by Edmund Maddox Barbarossa, the narrator of *Galilee* (1998), is that of Clive Barker's creative existence. In less than two decades, he has written more than ten novels and fifty short stories; he has written and directed three motion pictures (while scripting or producing seven others, and generating the *Hellraiser* and *Candyman* film franchises). His art and photography have been exhibited and reprinted around the globe; and his interviews and critical and social commentary have appeared in media of remarkable variety.

With *Galilee*, Barker's ever-expansive aesthetic and stylistic pursuits find an ideal structure, producing his most controlled and widely appealing novel to date. It is the first of his novels to be written in the first person, embracing and perfecting the experimental structure of 'Chiliad: A Meditation' (1997), in which he inserted himself directly into his story. Although the ostensible narrator of *Galilee* is Eddie Barbarossa, better known as Maddox, this wheelchair-bound dreamer (who never leaves his stepmother's estate, save through the telling of tales) is a thinly-veiled avatar of the author, offering Barker's most autobiographical and revelatory text.[2]

An apocalyptic prophecy rouses Maddox from years of self-pity and procrastination to begin penning a long-promised history of his family; but it is a Clive Barker history, in which fact and fantasy meet and mingle with equal significance: 'The time has come to tell everything I know. Failing that, everything I can detect or surmise. Failing that, everything I can invent. If I do my job properly it won't even matter to you which is which.'

The truth, Barker reminds us, is often best told through fable. '[T]here are so many matters that I'm going to trust to my instinct on,' Maddox advises, 'matters that cannot be strictly *verified*. Matters of the spirit, matters of the bedroom, matters of the grave. These are the truly important elements. The rest is just geography and dates.'

His family is a living fiction; the Barbarossas are myths, if not divinities, 'hiding away from a world which no longer wants or needs us'. Its founders are two souls as ancient as heaven: Nicodemus Barbarossa, a long-absent and apparently dead father who, like many of Barker's male deities, is a priapic legend whose singular urge is to fornicate; and his lover and the 'mother of mothers', Cesaria Yaos, 'an eternal force . . . born out of the primal fire of the world'. Their lifespans and talents transcend those of humanity, conjuring miracles and madness, taking life in an instant and, quite possibly, giving it. The extraordinary pair have spawned, together or by illicit tryst, four ungrateful children, each evoking a classical deity, yet finding nothing in the modern world but pain.

Christ was born in a stable; Nicodemus perished in one. Cesaria mourns, awaiting his rumoured return, in the family mansion. Known as L'Enfant – another lost child, rotting with a malaise that is spiritual as well as physical – this replica of Thomas Jefferson's Monticello was built at the turn of the eighteenth century in a North Carolina swamp. Like the best of Gothic castles, L'Enfant is a place where the past is present, and the present past – where time heals no wounds, but merely preserves them. '[I]n a place such as this rage and love and sorrow do not remain invisible. They exist here as they existed at the beginning of the world, as those primal forces from which we lesser things take our purpose and our shape.' It is also, inevitably, a microcosm of the world outside, a secret hidden within the greater secret that is America: 'L'Enfant's roots lie too close to the roots of democracy's tree for the two not to be intertwined.'

Maimed in the same mysterious accident that killed his father, Maddox's disability is insistently symbolic; for nearly one hundred and fifty years he has lived within the comfortable confines of his imagination, hidden with his stepmother, waiting for the miraculous while everything around them has 'dwindled into pettiness and domesticity'. When he finally finds the nerve to enter the dome room of L'Enfant, its skittering shadows part to offer visions of an elder wisdom (which is that revealed in the Domus Mundi at the finale of *Sacrament*): 'It takes something profound to transform us; to open our eyes to our own glorious *diversity*.' Maddox realizes that he is standing – that he can walk again – in a moment that echoes Barker's resolution of the puzzle that had haunted his own storytelling:

> For now I had the answer to the question: what lay at the centre of all the threads of my story? It was myself. I wasn't an abstracted recanter of these lives and loves. I was – I *am* – the story itself; its source, its voice, its music. Perhaps to you that doesn't seem like much of a revelation. But for me, it changes everything. It makes me see, with brutal clarity, the person I once was. It makes me understand for the first time who I am now. And it makes me shake with anticipation of what I must become.

In embracing a more personal role and responsibility as an author, Barker pronounces, through Maddox, the refined goal of his writing:

> And in my heart I realize I want most to *romance* you; to share with you a vision of the world that puts order where there has been discordance and chaos. Nothing happens carelessly. We're not brought into the world without reason, even though we may

never understand that reason. An infant that lives an hour, that dies before it can ever lay eyes on those who made it, even that soul did not live without purpose: this is my sudden certainty. And it is my duty to sweat until I convince you of the same.

With this manifesto, Barker steps away from the bleak and chaotic impulses of many of his early horrific texts, while reminding his readers that even the most violent and grotesque of his fictions is fraught with a concern for meaning (and, often, metaphysics). *Galilee* does not reject his abiding impulse for horror – indeed, there are several fine moments of *frisson* in the novel – but it does invite readers to evolve with him to a level of storytelling that is transcendent: 'All I want now is the time to enchant you.'

Enchant us he does. *Galilee* is an epic supernatural romance, blending the visionary fantasies of ER Eddison and Mervyn Peake with the contemporary Gothic of Daphne Du Maurier and William Faulkner; but its prime literary antecedents are *Alf Laylah* ('A Thousand Nights'/ 'The Arabian Nights') (circa 850) and William Beckford's eccentric fantasia *Vathek* (1782). Its narrative elements are disparate: confessional, historical, folk tale, fairy tale, fantasia, romance and 'that most populist of idioms, the rags-to-riches story'. In these pages the grotesque and the domestic are harmonized, as Barker pursues his relentless (and increasingly Biblical) vision of a world interpenetrated with the supernatural, where reality and fantasy are not opposites, but one.

The novel is anchored by its namesake: 'adored boy-child, lover of innumerable women (and a goodly number of men), shipwright, sailor, cowboy, stevedore, pool player and pimp; coward, deceiver and innocent. My Galilee.' A black man whose beauty is without equal, this firstborn of gods chose his own name at the age of six, prefiguring a life spent at sea, tossed by time and tide from port to port but never back to home. This latter-day Dionysus is 'an order of nature unto himself, and the rest of us have to take what little comfort we can from the fact of his unhappiness'.

As these descriptions suggest, the tale of this demigod is complex, told in a series of epistles about the people whose lives he has entered and touched like an ocean breeze, 'visible only by its effect'. It is nearly two hundred pages into the narrative before that 'cluster of contradictions' known as Galilee moves onto the stage, and even then he appears only as an illusion.

Maddox procrastinates and prevaricates, circling on his subject with a mingling of pleasure and peril, and it is through Maddox that Barker marshalls that most startling resource of his storytelling skills – his love of beginnings – to create a novel of awesome power that resounds with personal redemption.

Its central characters are not truly Galilee, but his biographer, Maddox, and Rachel Pallenberg, whose destiny is to become Galilee's true love. Rachel, who resembles silent film actress Louise Brooks, is wooed from the life of a midwestern commoner into marriage to one of America's most eligible bachelors, Mitchell Geary. She becomes an American Diana, the latest trophy-bride of a Kennedy-like dynasty ruled by the patriarchal fist of aged Cadmus Geary.

The Geary family was founded on, and is guided by, a relentless materialism that surpasses the familiar maxim of business before pleasure; for the Gearys, it is: 'Business before anything.' When Rachel literally fails in her appointed labour, suffering a miscarriage and finally the news that she cannot bear children, her marriage collapses. She returns to her home town, where memories of the 'drab affair' of a society gala surely echo Clive Barker's own dismay with the fleeting glamour of Hollywood and celebrity; but the visit also demolishes any sentimental thoughts of home – and any hope of safety. Rachel realizes that there is darkness at the heart of the Geary family. 'Something else moved these people, and it wasn't money. Nor was it love; nor did she think it was power. Until she knew what it was she would not be safe, of that she was certain.'

Rachel's departure is the first of the signs, offered by an astrologer, of the fall of the House of Geary: 'Crime had mounted upon crime over the generations, sin mounted on sin, and God help them all – every Geary, and child of a Geary, and wife and mistress and servant of a Geary – it was time for the sinners to come to judgment.'

The second sign involves a man from the sea, the elusive Galilee, who is drawn by fate – and the higher power known as love – to Rachel: 'The romance approaches, as inevitably as the apocalypse . . . because, of course, they are one and the same.' Rachel repairs to a place familiar to Clive Barker: a house on the Hawaiian island of Kauai, a magical Eden where she meets, at last, the shadow known as Galilee. But there is no seduction; at least not one that is physical. Galilee offers her a fable, and then disappears. He has built this island home, and here he has visited and seduced each of the Geary women – whose family is his mortal enemy.

Within forty-eight hours, the Geary dynasty is in ruin: murder and destruction spiralling out of a hidden past and into the present, with but a single certainty: 'In the end, everything comes back to Galilee.'[3] The link between the Gearys and the Barbarossas – and their 'elaborate edifices of influence and power and ambition' – is hidden within another story, this one told by a long-dead narrator: Captain Charles Holt. His journal, written in the final days of the American Civil War, tells of his desertion from the decimated ranks of the Confederate Army to return to Charleston, South Carolina, where he finds his house turned into an abattoir – and a man named Galilee.

'One by one, all the secrets are coming out, like stars at twilight.' Thus Rachel learns that her lover and awakener is more than human. 'The paradox is this: that the darker it gets, the more of these secrets we can see. Eventually, they're arrayed in all their glory; and it's the very things we hid from sight, the things we're most ashamed of, that we use to steer our course.'

In the aftermath of the war, a wounded Galilee revealed to Holt – and thus humanity – the path to L'Enfant, triggering unspeakable violence that has echoed down the decades: 'Blood begets blood; cruelty begets cruelty.' The man who saved Galilee's life on that savage day demanded a favour in return – and took the name of Geary, founding a financial empire. 'The roots of the family into which she'd married were deep in blood and filth; was it any wonder the dynasty that sprung from this beginning was in every way shameful and hollow?'

In this engrossing epic of two families – one spiritual, the other material – entwined by fate and fancy, Barker explores the perils of the magnificent alongside those of the mundane, deftly eschewing, as he has throughout his career, the use of the fantastic as nostalgic escapism. His demigods are as troubled as his demimondes. By investing the Gearys with the dream of materialism that is America, Galilee perfects his own dream of escape; but he learns, too quickly, that even gods have no freedom – particularly from their worshippers. His dalliance with the first Geary's wife leads to a pact in which he must comfort the Geary women with passion even as he comforts the Geary men with power and wealth.

It is an ironic trap. The absence of love is Galilee's singular fear (and, indeed, that of all gods): 'Not just the loneliness and the sleepless nights, but the horror of being out in the fierce, hard light that burned over him, set there by his own divinity.' The love he brings to the Geary women is nothing but a physical labour – until he meets, and is haunted by, Rachel. 'It was she who'd reminded him of his capacity for feeling, letting these unwelcome things have access to his heart. It was she who'd reminded him of his humanity, and of all that he'd done in defiance of his better self.'

Lover, fool, tempter, exile – literally and symbolically at sea – Galilee is, in the final act, the prodigal; and his return home is mythic: 'There were more visions and fevers and acts of delirium at work that night than had been unleashed on this continent since the arrival of the Pilgrims.' It is time, at last, for forgiveness, as Galilee brings new life – and Rachel – to L'Enfant, which will become their home.

When, in the closing pages of the novel, Galilee reads what Maddox has written, he says: 'Quite a story. Is any of it true?' In this glib rejoinder, Barker offers another revelation crucial to his maturation as a novelist. The truth of *Galilee* has less to do with its characters or their adventures than with its recognition of the importance of the storyteller – his voice and his conscience – in the telling of tales. In this wisdom is a redemption, one that is not merely personal to Clive Barker but also paramount to readers of the dark fantastic, who work their way, again and again, through novels and stories without point or purpose until coming upon the likes of *Galilee*.

In Barker's own words, it is a redemption that is fundamental to our art, and our humanity; thus Maddox concludes:

> I've come to see that as nothing can be made that isn't flawed, the challenge is twofold: first, not to berate oneself for what is, after all, inevitable; and second, to see in our failed perfection a different thing; a truer thing, perhaps, because it contains both our ambition and the spoiling of that ambition; the exhaustion

of order, and the discovery – in the midst of despair – that the beast dogging the heels of beauty has a beauty all its own.

Arising from the depths of his depression, Clive Barker had written his most elegant, intimate and sensual novel – and a text in which the recovery from his illness and his nascent relationship with David Armstrong were inescapably central.

'This is what I see,' read the pages of *Galilee*: 'a man who has just confessed his guilt, and will make amends, in time. A man who loves telling stories, and will find a way to understand what he's telling, in time. And a man who is capable of love, and who will find somebody to love again – oh please God yes; in time, in time.'

By the time the manuscript of the novel was complete, its epic romance was paralleled by the secure and fulfilling love that Clive had found in his own life – with his own Galilee, David Armstrong.

'It was very obvious, very quickly, that this person was changing my life at an incredible rate,' Clive notes, 'and that he was doing it by the sheer force of who he was. And here I was, telling this story about a person who seems to have her life all set up, and then it turns into a different thing because of the presence of this man.

'I was feeling all of these things I had never felt before. And I knew they were the stuff of romance, in a very obvious way. Nothing ironic about it.

'I think my books can be divided up into the ironic and the unironic. By irony, I mean sort of having my tongue in my cheek when I'm writing – almost all the short stories have that quality. They're playing, you know. *Weaveworld* is a very unironic book, straight from the heart: this is my dream world. *Galilee* is the same.

'I was being profoundly changed by this person. Joyfully, excitedly changed. And that is the stuff of romance: to be changed by someone, and to learn you *can* be changed. And I wanted to express that without having to in any way put quotation marks around it. Because there are no quotation marks around my relationship with David. It is the *realest* relationship I've ever had, in the sense of being charged with a feeling, constantly, constantly, constantly. There is no middle ground. There is no moment when you are with David when you are not with David. That's just who he is. And he woke me up – he slapped me

Joan Barker and her sons near the Hanoi Light. Guernsey, Channel Islands, circa 1964. *Photograph by Leonard Barker.*

Ken and Joan Barker. Tiree, circa 1995. *Photograph by Clive Barker.*

Len Barker and his sons at Calderstones Park. Liverpool, circa 1965. *Photograph by Joan Barker.*

Clive's Report Book, Quarry Bank Grammar School. Liverpool, Easter, 1965. *Courtesy of Clive Barker.*

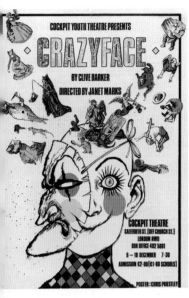

Poster for the Cockpit Youth Theatre production of *Crazyface*, designed by Chris Priestley. London, 1982. *Courtesy of Douglas E Winter*.

Invitation to the publication party for *Clive Barker's Books of Blood*. London, 1984. *Courtesy of Clive Barker*.

Clive and David Dodds. London, circa 1986. *Photograph by Bill Gross*.

Stephen King and Clive on the set of *Sleepwalkers*. Los Angeles, 1992.

Clive becomes Pinhead.
London, circa 1988.

Clive and his
breakthrough novel,
Weaveworld. London,
1987.

Clive with his mural for the New York Club. Manhattan, 1993. *Photograph by Cheryl Bentzen-Green.*

Untitled illustration, date unknown.
Courtesy of Clive Barker.

Clive with his painting
John Mischief. Beverly
Hills, California, circa
1998. *Photograph by
David Armstrong.*

From The *Abarat Quartet:
On Babilonium. Courtesy
of Clive Barker.*

From *The Abarat Quartet: Kaspar Wolfswinkel. Courtesy of Clive Barker.*

Clive reading to Nicole Armstrong.
Beverly Hills, California, 1999.
Photograph by David Armstrong.

A different Dog Company. Beverly Hills, California, 1998.
Photograph by David Armstrong.

Clive and David Armstrong. San Diego Sea World, 1999.

and he woke me up and he said, *Be with me. Don't be some other place, be with me. You're with me,* be *with me.*

'And I had lost focus on that – on being there; I had lost focus because perhaps I had become too in love with the idea of being the abstracted artist. Perhaps I was tired. Perhaps I was all those things. Certainly "Chiliad" came from a despairing place that was pre-David. And now comes this guy who just shakes me up and says, *You are still alive. Check it out.* And that is challenging. It's challenging particularly to somebody like me, because I was slightly on the way to losing myself in the middle period of my career.'

After their chance meeting on an Easter Sunday, the two men became constant companions; David soon moved in with Clive, but only after each understood that the decision had consequences. 'This was a package deal,' David says. 'I told Clive, *I have baggage: I have a daughter, a dog and a best friend who doesn't go away.* And Clive said the same thing: *I have a best friend – David Dodds – and I have dogs.*' The symmetry was remarkable; but for Clive, Nicole Armstrong brought an added blessing to their relationship: the pleasures of a child.

David Armstrong did not know that *Galilee* was being written about him until the day came when Clive asked him to read a section of the manuscript. It was a thinly-veiled version of a story David had told Clive about an incident from his infancy, when he had 'escaped' from his parents. Soon the novel seemed to echo, with increasing insistence, their life experiences – particularly in the romance between Galilee and Rachel Pallenberg, and also, it seemed, in its happy ending.

Late in 1997, David asked Clive to 'make an honest man out of me'. On November 29, 1997, they held a private wedding ceremony after a dinner with a few family members and friends. 'We exchanged vows – just Clive, myself and God.' That California declines to recognize same-sex unions was immaterial: 'We did it before God, and that's all that matters,' David says. 'We recognize it, and our friends, and whoever we meet on the street. We're married.'

The first of many difficult hurdles of perception to clear was an explanation of their relationship, and their marriage, to Nicole. She was eight when she first met Clive; David told her that Clive was his roommate and that they worked together. 'I wanted her to see that it wasn't about two gay guys. I wanted her to see the love between two people.' In 1998, when she was ten, David tried to discuss the marriage, but he didn't need to say much; Nicole went to Clive and said: 'First of all, welcome to the family. And the second thing, I'm happy for both of you.' Clive was teary-eyed, but as she left the room, she turned and asked him: 'Is now a good time to ask for an iguana?'

The marriage was a more difficult proposition to present to their parents. When the promotional tour for *Galilee* brought Clive and David to Chicago, Clive said: 'Isn't it time for me to meet your dad?' When David's father and stepmother, Prentis and Willie B Armstrong, met them, Willie B took David aside and said, 'I know what you came out here to tell us, and your dad and I may not like it, but we just want you to be happy. Your daddy knows, and we want you to be happy, and you don't have to say anything.' David was profoundly relieved; but that night, when they went out to dinner, Clive turned to Prentis and said: 'So, shall we get down to business? Your son and I have been married for two years, and I love him. What do you think about that?'

David was mortified. After a long pause, his father looked up and said, 'Well, as long as you two love one another, that's all that matters. As long as you two are good to one another.' Clive turned to David and said, 'Did you hear that? What do you think about that?' David could only reply: 'This is really good soup. I like this soup.'

Clive's parents, in turn, met David when they visited California. 'They were really nice,' David says. 'His mom – I love this woman to death. It was like getting a new mom and dad. At first, I was really nervous, but they turned out to be such wonderful people. It was kind of an honour to be embraced by them like that.'

Becoming a stepfather was another learning experience – for Clive and for Nicole. One night, David said: 'Why don't you go tuck her in, and tell her a bedtime story?' A circle of sorts seemed to turn, from the nights years before when Clive's mother would offer him bedtime tales; but after Clive was gone for twenty minutes, David heard Nicole scream: 'Dad!!!' He entered her bedroom just as Clive was saying, 'Good night, little girl … bye bye.' She was crying, and said to David: 'He told me about the shark people who come out when little girls with curly black hair aren't asleep by eleven o'clock, and they come and they *eat* them and then they take them into the sea and they become a shark person!'

'I said, *Clive, you can't tell her those stories.* But it worked like a charm. At night she started asking, *What time is it?*

'Now,' David says with a smile, 'they get along so well that they scheme against me.'

31

OF GODS AND MONSTERS

CANDYMAN: FAREWELL TO THE FLESH (1995)
GODS AND MONSTERS (1998)

Friend?
— JAMES WHALE'S *Frankenstein*

By the mid-1990s, Clive Barker's dream of making a home and a name in Hollywood, the city of dreams, had come true. Reversing the difficult aftermath of *Nightbreed*, he had become a minor mogul, with film projects constantly in development and new offers to write, direct, and produce feature films and television projects arriving with each new month.

Ironically, the most critically acclaimed of the motion pictures to carry his name is the only one not based on his creations: *Gods and Monsters* (1998), written and directed by Bill Condon. Although *Hellraiser* remains the most popular (and, for its distributors, the most profitable) of his films, *Gods and Monsters* – for which Clive Barker acted as executive producer and 'patron saint' – achieved lavish critical acclaim, as well as three Academy Award nominations and numerous other honours. Equally ironic, perhaps, is the fact that the film had its genesis in one of the least regarded of Barker's film projects, *Candyman: Farewell to the Flesh* (1995).

When Bernard Rose's proposal to essay a sequel to *Candyman* that mingled the lore of Jack the Ripper with 'The Midnight Meat Train' – and thus supplanted the first film's hook-handed killer – was rejected by Propaganda Films, the producers commissioned a far more conventional script intended to fulfil their vision of a film franchise. Written by Rand Ravich, who later wrote and directed *The Astronaut's Wife* (1999), and revised by Mark Kruger, *Candyman II* resurrected the Candyman from the beyond while shifting the setting of his murderous antics from Chicago to New Orleans.[1]

After more than two years in development, with a finished script and a date for principal photography looming, Bill Condon was hired to direct *Candyman II*, soon known as *Candyman: Farewell to the Flesh*. Condon, a graduate of Columbia University, had co-written the cult movies *Strange Behavior* (released in the UK as *Dead Kids*) (1981) and *Strange Invaders* (1983) before making his directorial debut – in the same year and with the same studio as Clive Barker – with *Sister, Sister* (1987). Set in Louisiana and starring Jennifer Jason Leigh and Eric Stoltz, the bayou Gothic was a commercial failure. 'So I sort of went to movie jail,' Condon says, 'which in this case was making a lot of cable movies. Actually I had a great time. It was my Roger Corman period – I made five films in two years, each one shot for two million dollars in eighteen to twenty days – and there wasn't much interference, believe it or not.' Created for broadcast on the USA Network and later released on videocassette, the films included *Murder 101* (1991) with Pierce Brosnan, which received the Mystery Writers of America's Edgar Award; and *White Lie* (1991) with Gregory Hines.

When Condon's agent, Adam Krentzman of Creative Artists Agency – who also represented Barker – mentioned that a *Candyman* sequel was in development, Condon made a 'real push to get in there and meet on it'. After meeting Condon, Barker, in turn, 'really pushed' for him to direct the film; he had enjoyed *White Lie* – which, like *Sister, Sister* and the *Candyman* sequel – was set in the American South; but Condon also shared many of Barker's passions: 'I have a real love of film and film history, as does Clive; but also, obviously, of horror films. And once we got that discussion going, that probably had a bit to do with it. I also had more concerns about the script than some other people.'

After its lengthy period in development, *Farewell to the Flesh* was rushed to the screen; Condon's selection as director came only ten weeks before principal photography started in the summer of 1994, with a targeted theatrical release in February 1995. 'Of all the things I've been involved with,' Condon notes, 'this is the one in which I had the least creative input. It was developed by an awful lot of people with a lot of agendas. At one point they were even considering taking the Candyman out of any relationship to a black neighbourhood or black culture, because the original film hadn't done well in Japan, and overseas there were countries where movies that were "too black" don't do well. It was that sort of thing. So much of the approach was how to build a franchise, and maybe not be so true to what was interesting and unique about the story and that first movie.'

The centrepiece of *Farewell to the Flesh* is the historical mystery that Bernard Rose added to 'The Forbidden' in creating *Candyman*: the genesis of the hook-handed supernatural killer as Daniel Robitaille, the artistic son of a slave whose romance with a daughter of white wealth was met with a cruel death. The closing moments of *Candyman*, in which Virginia Madsen's Helen Lyle returns for vengeance, wielding the Candyman's hook, are forgotten. Just as in the *Hellraiser* sequels, the intended continuing character, Julia, was deposed by the more traditionally monstrous Pinhead, *Farewell to the Flesh* exalts the more traditionally monstrous Candyman (again played by Tony Todd). It is Mardi Gras in present-day New Orleans, and Annie Tarrant (Kelly Rowan), a schoolteacher who is almost Helen Lyle's double, is haunted by the news that her brother, Ethan (William O'Leary), has been accused of a gruesome murder whose handiwork – not unlike that of the Candyman – had been unleashed on their father years before.

As the dire image of the Candyman appears in the drawings of one of Annie's troubled students, her efforts to dispel the myth – by repeating the Candyman's name five times while facing a mirror – bring him fully to life. 'Be my victim,' he entreats her, but she escapes, only to learn that her family hides the secret of the Candyman. Her grandmother was Robitaille's fabled lover, and somewhere there is a mirror that captured the artist's soul at the moment of his death. By breaking the mirror, the Candyman's soul will be released and his monstrosity destroyed.

The film suffers, like the *Hellraiser* sequels, from the script's impulse to explain: to reduce the mythic to the mundane, codifying a formula for the life (and death) of the Candyman. Its setting, Condon notes, also weakened its dramatic impact. 'Once I started making the film, there was some frustration about how it developed. In retrospect, you see these things more clearly, but it seemed to me that the genius of the first movie is that it reinvented the haunted house in a contemporary way. What is the scariest place that we don't want to step into? And that's Cabrini Green. Whereas the second movie found itself on more familiar territory, with a great big rundown plantation house.'

The result is a film with interesting visuals, notably in Condon's use of mirror imagery, but that, hamstrung by story and setting, could not begin to match the original. 'Clive was just amazingly supportive and respectful,' Condon notes. 'We had a wonderful relationship making it; but the place where, for me, it really switched over into something that was deeper and became a real friendship was when the movie opened – and was universally ignored or reviled. I think you can't get much lower on the cultural totem pole than a sequel to a horror movie.

'What was extraordinary is that – it's a familiar story but it's so true, and it's part of why I identified with James Whale – when you have a failure, suddenly everything *stops*. Your phone doesn't ring for days. People are either too embarrassed or just truly have moved on. But Clive was amazingly supportive during that time; we had endless phone calls, about everything. You only get a few moments when you can test someone's character, and usually it's in moments like that – and I'll never forget that he was there during that period.'[2]

After production on *Farewell to the Flesh* was completed, but before its release, Barker and Condon discussed other potential projects – but not another sequel. Indeed, neither of them had any role, save inspirational, in the direct-to-video disappointment *Candyman: Day of the Dead* (1999). Written by Al Septien and its director, Turi Meyer – and 'based on characters created by Clive Barker' (who otherwise declined to have his name on the film) – the enterprise seemed doomed from its conception. It is, of all things, a low-budget remake of *Farewell to the Flesh*, with the setting shifted from New Orleans at Mardi Gras to Los Angeles during a celebration of Los Dias de Los Muertos. Pouty and puffy 'Baywatch' babe Donna D'Errico plays Caroline McKeever, the great-great-granddaughter and last living descendant of murdered artist-turned-Candyman Daniel Robitaille (Tony Todd). Intent on vanquishing the myth of the Candyman, she arranges for a gallery showing of Robitaille's paintings but, inevitably, must speak the Candyman's name five times in front of a mirror. The rest is a history that inhabits a reality seen only in horror movies: a chain of ever more unbelievable events that slouches toward a finale in which Caroline defeats the hook-handed nemesis by burning his artwork.

Instead of another sequel – or, indeed, another horror film – Bill Condon, with Clive Barker's eager encouragement and assistance, pursued the sublime. In the spring of 1995, as *Candyman: Farewell to the Flesh* opened on its brief theatrical run, Dutton published Christopher Bram's fifth novel, *Father of Frankenstein*, an engaging speculation on the mysterious final days of director James Whale, who was found dead in his swimming pool, an apparent suicide, in 1957. Whale, an Englishman who survived the trenches of World War One to find fleeting fame as the director of *Frankenstein* (1932) and *Bride of Frankenstein* (1935) – as well as *The Old Dark House* (1932), *The Invisible Man* (1933) and *Show Boat* (1936) – had struggled against a Hollywood studio system that frowned upon his creative iconoclasm and his open homosexuality.

Although *Booklist* opined that 'Whale's tiny fandom and those who keep track of Bram as one of the best gay novelists constitute this minor performance's natural readership,' one reader of *Father of Frankenstein* – Bill Condon – had a quite different perspective. He read the novel just after *Farewell to the Flesh* was released – and after months of trying to find new work. Through a mutual friend, he talked with Christopher Bram, who went to see *Farewell to the Flesh*; Bram liked the film and agreed to let Condon personally option *Father of Frankenstein*. There was no studio backing – only the financial assistance of Gregg Fienberg, the producer of *Farewell to the Flesh*. (When Bram was writing the novel, *Ed Wood* was being made by Tim Burton, 'so it was another *Ed Wood*, and that was a good thing,' says Condon; but by the time the book was finished and circulated to prominent producers and studios, *Ed Wood* had opened and hadn't done well, 'so it was another *Ed Wood*, and that was a bad thing.')

'When you're in that place where you become frustrated by what you've been able to do,' Condon notes, 'and your most interesting scripts are the ones that weren't made, just to be getting back into that feature director world is important. And you always have that fantasy, which is ridiculous, that: *Oh, well, those nightmare movies helped those other directors.* James Cameron did it; but of course that works out so rarely. It really felt to me that I didn't care about anything any more but the fact that, on *Farewell to the Flesh*, I met people at Propaganda, which made small movies; and I met Clive and I met Gregg. So I had an image of how I could get the movie made. That's all I cared about. I'd saved a little money. I didn't take any other work. And I made this vow to myself that I was going to work until we got this movie made – and if I couldn't, then it would just be over. I wouldn't do it any more. I don't know if I would have stuck to that, but that's how it felt: this incredible need to finally do something that completely reflected what I wanted to do.'

With that decision made, and the book optioned, Condon called Clive – 'not knowing, because I don't think he'd ever done it before, that he would have any interest in becoming a part of something that wasn't based on his own material'. Only a few weeks earlier, Dutton had sent Barker an advance copy of *Father of Frankenstein*, inviting him to provide a promotional quotation; he responded enthusiastically because of his admiration for the text and the films of James Whale. (As Condon notes, there were certainly parallels between the lives of Whale and Barker. A year later, when he screened a rough cut of *Gods and Monsters* at Clive's house, 'I told him: *You know, if you're not careful, you might end up like that.* He threw something at me.')

Condon asked if Clive would become involved in the project; and Clive, whose enthusiasm for Condon's work had not waned from the day that he urged his hiring as director of *Farewell to the Flesh*, said: 'I will just do whatever I can do to make sure that the picture gets made.' In Condon's words: 'He immediately said *yes*. So it was this wonderful thing, you know.' As executive producer, Clive became what Condon would call 'the patron saint of *Gods and Monsters*'.

The process of bringing the text to celluloid, and then to motion picture screens, was long and arduous. Over the next six months, Condon wrote the screenplay – for which he would win an Academy Award – but when his agents sent the script to 'all the obvious places' in Hollywood, every studio and producer turned it down. Through another agent at CAA, Condon arranged for the script to be sent to Ian McKellen, the accomplished (and knighted) British stage actor who had co-written and starred in Richard Loncraine's *Richard III* (1995), among many other films. Condon had written the script with McKellen in mind for the role of James Whale, and in time, the actor was persuaded to read it.

In March 1996, McKellen travelled to Los Angeles for the Academy Awards ceremony; Barker and Condon seized the moment, inviting him to Clive's house in Beverly Hills – and 'slowly and somewhat painfully bringing him around to the idea of playing the role,' Clive says. 'He thought the movie was too depressing and that it sent out a bad image of gay life.' McKellen's initial hesitancy was indeed political: Whale was openly gay in the Hollywood of the 1930s, and very successful and unapologetic – and thus, in a sense, a hero. 'Why not tell that story?' McKellen asked. 'Why tell the story of him in decline?' Condon responded: 'And of course the answer is that it's much richer dramatically – and it happened, too.' Barker told McKellen: 'Although it is not a movie of mirth and merriment, nevertheless it is an incredibly sympathetic portrait of a man in pain – and the kind of role he was never going to see again. It's a wonderful role, and he dominates the movie.' McKellen left the meeting 'somewhat convinced', Condon says – 'guarded but enjoying the discussion'.

The following day, Condon met McKellen at the Four Seasons Hotel, where he was staying, and confronted his second objection: the veteran actor, then entering his late fifties, had decided to work more often in Hollywood. 'Having agreed to do *Apt Pupil*, playing a seventy-seven-year-old ex-Nazi, then frail, old James Whale with a shock of white hair would mean that people's first introduction to him would be as a succession of old men. He thought that everyone would be convinced that he was at death's door.' Condon's rejoinder was inspired: 'I showed him pictures of James Whale on the set of *Bride of Frankenstein*, and reminded him that he also would be playing him at that point in his life, when he was in his forties. He looked at the pictures, and he said that Whale was *dishy*. I think something turned for him at that point.'

Duly persuaded, McKellen began to accompany Condon and Barker to meetings with potential financial backers. 'It was really hard finding that money,' Clive notes. 'It was absurdly hard to find $3.1 million to make a movie that then won all these awards.'

Initial financing was secured from Regent, which pre-sold United Kingdom rights to the BBC. Despite its relatively limited budget, the film was constantly at risk. 'These independent movies are so hard to pull together,' Condon says. 'The thing that finally happens is that you've got to have something that just forces them to pull the trigger. In our case, Ian McKellen had committed to an eighteen-month season at the National Theatre, so if we didn't start on a certain date, that was it – the movie with Ian McKellen wouldn't happen. And I didn't want to make it with anyone else. So that forced everybody's hand, including Regent's – and, as a new company, they were forced to go before they had all their money in place, so at the last minute, we went to Showtime and made a million dollar pre-sale of the cable rights.'

The other casting decisions were also Condon's, and all were inspired, particularly Lynn Redgrave as the Teutonic housemaid Hannah, and Brendan Fraser as Whale's gardener and unlikely confidant, Clayton Boone. 'This was Bill's picture,' says Clive, who worked wholly in the background, providing critical moral and material support. 'When we first met Ian McKellen,' Condon says, 'we got to do it at Clive's wonderful house, and not at my little hut in Silverlake, so that we seemed more together than we actually were – that's a little thing. A big thing was that, when we were in pre-production and the money wasn't all there, Clive was willing to float the production for a while, actually putting up cash to help us keep going. Besides making not a dime on the movie, he did share in the cost of shooting the movie in widescreen. To do that and still be able to make a video that will work on most television sets, you have to use a process called Super 35, which involves a special optical step at the end that costs around $35,000 – and Gregg and Clive and I paid for that out of our own pockets. So this movie *cost* him money.'

When completed, *Gods and Monsters* was met with indifference in its January 1998 debut at the presumed Mecca of American independent film-making, the Sundance Festival. The film defied the perceived expectations of movie-goers – it was not a horror film, but about a director of horror films; its cast was older; its themes were neither light nor 'edgy' in a youth-oriented sense, but dark and, of course, involved homosexuality – and the attending distributors believed that it lacked commercial potential. 'Basically there were many companies who said that it was too much trouble,' Condon says. 'That, even at its best, it would not appeal on a breakout level.' The companies that ultimately bid on the film – including Lion's Gate Films, which secured the distribution rights – were all new, and had not even existed a year before. Condon then took the film on 'a sort of Willie Loman tour domestically, from small town to small town, showing it at festivals, trying to get it written about. What you don't realize, unless you make movies, is that the period of writing and development, pre-production and production, is nothing compared to what you go through in the distribution phase, in terms of the difficulty, frustration and sometimes just time. From Sundance in January to the film's release in November and then even on to the Oscars the next April was a non-stop, daily, full-time job.'

Finally, after a strong reception at the New York Film Festival in September 1998, Condon's hard work paid off, and the critical response and word of mouth snowballed. When *Gods and Monsters* was released theatrically by Lion's Gate in November 1998, it quickly recouped its cost and became the most critically acclaimed motion picture of the year.

Among its many honours was to be named Best Picture of 1998 by the National Board of Review (and later by the Independent Spirit Awards). Clive flew to Manhattan to present Condon with the Award; while he was there, the Academy of Motion Picture Arts and Sciences announced its Oscar nominations of Ian McKellen for Best Actor, Lynn Redgrave for Best Supporting Actress, and Bill Condon for Best Screenplay Adaptation. The response was 'pure elation', Condon says, 'and that sense of hearing from people, the constant wonderful connection you make with people in your life, a stream of phone calls that goes on for weeks . . . really, really exciting.'

From the beginning, Condon felt that 'the thing that brought *Gods and Monsters* true greatness – not to downplay anybody else's contribution, but the thing that touched it with genius was Ian McKellen. That performance, I felt, was just a major achievement. And part of the work in that year was doing as much as possible to keep the focus on him, and to help make sure that that nomination happened. He hadn't been nominated for *Richard III*. It felt like a really satisfying sense of accomplishing something, that he had been nominated. And even the night of the Oscars was quite bittersweet for all of us because of that.'

Although Condon won the Oscar for Best Screenplay Adaptation at the 71st Academy Awards, the Best Actor Award was not presented to Ian McKellen for his portrayal of James Whale, but to Roberto Benigni for his role in *Life Is Beautiful*. McKellen did receive Best Actor accolades from many other sources, including the National Board of Review, Broadcast Film Critics Association, Independent Spirit Awards and the Los Angeles Film Critics Association. Lynn Redgrave won the Golden Globe, Independent Spirit and London Film Critics Awards for Best Supporting Actress; and Condon's screenplay also won the Golden Satellite Award. The DVD edition of the movie, which includes a running audio commentary by Condon and *The World of Gods and Monsters: A Journey with James Whale*, an excellent documentary written by David J Skal and narrated by Clive Barker, was named DVD of the Year by amazon.com.

Life changed for Bill Condon in the aftermath of *Gods and Monsters*, but it was the sense of accomplishment that mattered – and the knowledge that, working with Clive Barker, Gregg Fienberg, Ian McKellen and so many others, he had prevailed by creating a motion picture that truly could be called his own. 'I'd always felt that, with anything I'd done before, there should have been a subtitle running under it, saying, *You should have seen what this might have been*. There's always a certain amount of compromise involved with anything. And just to have the confidence of having done something that you've felt completely proud of does change you on the inside.'

Hollywood, however, remains unchanged. 'It's easier, but not easy,' he says, particularly when your creative pursuits differ from the expectations of the mainstream – and indulge the stuff of horror and the fantastic. Both Barker and Condon wanted to continue their association, and in March 1999, Barker's production company, Seraphim Films, announced the development of *Love and Taboo*, an anthology of twenty short films with gay and lesbian themes; Barker and Condon would each write and direct an instalment, with Barker directing a 'wraparound' story, and the remaining segments would be contributed by independent film-makers. Over a hundred proposals have been received to date, but as of this writing, the project had found no studio interest.

Condon also commenced work on a project that has been anticipated for years: an anthology film based on the *Books of Blood*. This kind of film had been rumoured, pitched and, in the early years, optioned by the producers of *Underworld* and *Rawhead Rex*; but Condon's notion of how to present the anthology seems the most transgressive and true to the aesthetics of the original texts.

'If there's any model,' he notes, 'it is the original *Hellraiser*. It's to make a movie that is just as taboo and upsetting as that film.' Intent on working with a very small budget, Barker and Condon matched three talented young film-makers to three *Books of Blood* stories, while also 'bringing the gay context up to the surface'. Indeed, a script written by Condon described the production as a 'gay, art-house hard-core horror movie'. He laughs. 'So that might appeal to an audience of one – or, as I suspect, there are a lot of people who might be attracted to that.'

Implicit in the project – since abandoned – was the knowledge that many stories in the *Books of Blood* could be adapted as motion pictures – and that, at least in the realm of horror movies, sequels are often more marketable than original ideas. 'We thought of it not only as an opportunity for young directors to make their first feature film, but also ... what would be interesting next time would be to work with three women. Women have so rarely filmed horror, so to see three women's take on some of these stories would be great.'

In the years that have intervened on the long journey of the *Books of Blood* from text to film, Clive Barker's perspective on the stories – and himself – had changed in dramatic ways. Not only have his once-proprietary instincts, which had caused him to threaten litigation against the original option-holder of some of the stories, effectively vanished, allowing him freely to encourage others to make what they would of the stories as films; but also, like the narrator of his confessional 'Chiliad', he had found more than contentment in the idea of his creations surviving, and thriving, without him: 'the thought exhilarates me.'

32

STORIES OF OUR OWN

THE ESSENTIAL CLIVE BARKER (1999)
COLDHEART CANYON (2001)

I am a man, and men are animals who tell stories. This is a gift
from God, who spoke our species into being but left the end of
our story untold. That mystery is troubling to us. How could it be
otherwise? Without the final part, we think, how are we to make
sense of all that went before, which is to say, our lives. So we make
stories of our own, in fevered and envious imitation of our maker,
hoping that we'll tell, by chance, what God left untold, and in
finishing our tale, come to understand why we were born.

— CLIVE BARKER, *Sacrament*

Years ago, in a moment of quiet introspection, Clive Barker told me
of a fond wish: that his creations might somehow take on a life of
their own and wander out into the world – leaving him in solitude,
and anonymity. 'I would like one day to wander, in my last hour,' he
said, 'through the collective unconsciousness, the culture of which I
was a part, and find little places where I was. And none of these things

would have *This was made by Clive Barker* at the bottom ... because that, finally, isn't the point.'

Soon afterward, he found himself celebrating Hallowe'en on West Hollywood's Santa Monica Boulevard. Among the partying throng was someone costumed as his most famous creation: Pinhead from the *Hellraiser* films. Giddy with drink, Clive decided to introduce himself. 'I created you,' he told the reveller, who replied: 'Fuck off.'

It was his wish come true, and also a fine metaphor for the Frankensteinian relationship between creator and creation that has evolved in the *Hellraiser* series, with each new entry moving ever distant from Barker's original conception. A few years earlier, the spurious Pinhead's response would not have seemed so rude or uninformed. With his ever-spiralling success, Clive Barker has become that figment of the popular imagination known as a celebrity, with its share of pleasures – and perils.

In the motion picture *Lord of Illusions* (1995), Barker's *noir* heroine with an Oz-like name, Dorothea, laments: 'Sometimes people get lost – even good people. Too much money, too much fame.' Her words echo the sentiments of His Satanic Majesty in the play *The History of the Devil* (1980): 'Do you know how difficult it is not to believe what people say about you? Not to become your own publicity?'

During the two dazzling but difficult decades that brought Clive Barker from starving playwright to bestselling novelist, exhibited artist and Hollywood player, there were temptations and indulgences, but he did not lose himself in fame. Indeed, as *The Thief of Always* (1992), *Sacrament* (1996) and *Galilee* (1998) suggest, perhaps in making a public journey from innocence to experience, he found himself. That career was celebrated in *The Essential Clive Barker* (1999), a unique mosaic of his writing that he selected and assembled personally for readers and fans, old and new.[1]

Obviously the events of the past twenty years have changed Clive Barker. 'Inevitably,' notes Doug Bradley, his long-time friend and collaborator (and the actor who portrayed Pinhead on film). 'He was successful, where he had not been so successful before. He was earning large amounts of money, where he had not been doing that before. He had a lot of people beating a path to his door. He had a lot of people wanting a piece of his action, who had not been there before.

And he had power that he had not had before. You can't throw all those things at someone at once and expect him to remain the same person. Fundamentally, he didn't change at all – and that's been true right the way through. Granted, he used to be broke and lived in a flat up the road from me, and now he's a millionaire and lives in Beverly Hills. That redefines people in obvious ways; but fundamentally, when I pick up the phone and talk to him, it's no different at all.'

When, early in the 1990s, Clive returned home to Liverpool and visited Quarry Bank Grammar School for a television documentary, he arranged to meet his former teacher and mentor, Norman Russell, outside the Headmaster's study. Russell was talking with a group of fellow masters; in his words: 'This figure in jeans was there waiting for the Sirs to finish speaking, and it was Clive – a man of great distinction and wealth and so on – but still waiting for Sir to finish talking. It was incredible. A lesser person couldn't do that. He seems to have bypassed all the nonsense that can go with success. It doesn't seem to have touched him at all. He could have been quite insufferable if he wanted to be; but he's very kind to me.'

That patience and kindness have extended to an ever-growing legion of readers and fans. Moved by the public's embrace of his *Books of Blood*, Clive decided to respond individually to each fan letter – a task that soon proved impossible. 'Clive knows that he affects so many people,' says Mary Roscoe, 'and he wants that to be a genuine relationship. He cares about the individuals, as far as it is possible; though there are too many of them now. But in the beginning, when there were several thousand rather than several million, I would take down, in shorthand, individual letters to Japanese fans, Americans, somebody from Bradford, somebody from Birmingham, you name it. We sat down together and wrote individual letters. And that was interesting, because I started to realize the effect that these books were having on people.' In time, the evolution of new technologies allowed Clive to resume personal interaction with fans – first in the pages of *Lost Souls*, the magazine of an authorized fan club operated by Cheryl Bentzen-Green and Stephen Dressler, and then in an official website, *Lost Souls* (www.clivebarker.com).[2]

But fame also brought perils. On October 8, 1988, while touring the United States to promote *Cabal*, Clive made an appearance at the Forbidden Planet bookstore in Greenwich Village. Lines snaked out of the store and around the block; some people waited for hours to spend a few moments with Clive and have him sign their books. During the session, he was approached by a man some described as a 'punk', but whom Clive recalls as a 'perfectly normal-looking guy, who sounded quite articulate and self-possessed'. The man suddenly slashed a razor blade along the veins of his arm, offering the wound to Clive; nonplussed, Clive signed the book, then put his hand in the blood and pressed his wet palm into the book. The man was shown out of the store.

More often, the perils of fame were more insidious: those of celebrity. 'The public sees him as the creator of *Hellraiser*, the *Books of Blood*, all these crazy, weird things,' laments David Armstrong, 'but they don't know the real Clive, who's a soft, gentle soul – a guy who wears Gap clothing, just an everyday, normal person. We don't live in a Gothic mansion with coffins in the basement; he loves flowers, he loves animals. People don't see the sensitive side of him. Sometimes, in public appearances, he'll try to explain it, but no one gets to see how gentle he really is, and how gentle his eyes are . . . and that's the first thing that attracted me to him, his eyes – warm, gentle – and that's why I couldn't believe he was Clive Barker.'

Clive is also intensely, and self-consciously, shy: 'A lot of my life has been taken up with overcoming a fundamental shyness about being in the world,' he says. 'I'm useless out there. I've never said a truthful thing at a party in my life. I'm not very good in those circumstances, unlike here [at home]: the comfort of a world which I have in some measure shaped. You know how uncomfortable I am at the conventions and engagements; and as I've grown older I've become more and more uncomfortable. I used to despise myself for it, because I know the people want to talk, and they're nice folks and all; it's just I'm not very good at it. Or if I'm good at it, it's because I put on another self, a showy self which doesn't feel like a true person. I am not naturally born to that, so I sort of create this little fellow who goes out and does that for me. And it works fine, but I've always said that the most interesting things about me are contained inside the work I'm making.'[3]

His work, in turn, has been haunted by the problem of genre and expectation; and the history of his evolution – particularly as a writer – has been marked by defiance of the comfortable pigeonholes that the marketplace and the media have adopted in an attempt to define him.

'There are few people who are role models for me. Of course there's Blake; but few modern people. I think George Lucas falls into that category, as someone who is invisible most of the time, which I like. Lucas had a huge effect on our culture, providing us with names for ballistic missiles and that sort of cultural backchaff; but he appears only once in a while on TV, doesn't he? I love that; I think it's great. He isn't a celebrity, and I think I've gotten past that point now.

'There were two expectations of me. The first was that I would be the next Stephen King. The second was that I would be a more iconoclastic individual publicly than I particularly wanted to be. That was fed by a couple of very successful appearances, purely by chance, on 'Politically Incorrect' and other talk shows, where I got to say some outrageous things because the camera was on me and the adrenalin was flowing. And open invitations thereafter to just do that; offers to go and do stuff on Comedy Central and this and that. And you look at that and say, *Why the fuck would I want to do that?* Not because they're not nice people – because they are nice people – and not because you don't actually get a chance to say some things, because you do; but because, in a very short time, you're the faggot who goes on 'Politically Incorrect' and makes outrageous comments. And the chance of anybody ever getting to my artwork with the clear, open heart that I want them to have is reduced. They're going to have to get past *me*; instead of a conduit, I've become somebody who blocks their way.'

Fame brought remarkable opportunities, not merely to pursue the ephemeral antics of celebrity, but also to advocate his creative vision in interviews and television appearances – and to explore new avenues for his creative powers. He was asked to write, and possibly direct, the motion picture *Alien³* (1992), but he declined for the simple reason that it was the third entry in a series based on someone else's aesthetic and universe. He later turned down an offer to make his big-budget directorial debut on the Arnold Schwarzenegger vehicle *End of Days* (1999). ('There would have been something entertaining about doing a Schwarzenegger picture,' he notes, 'but in the end you have to make choices. You get one life and you have to choose between the things you're going to put your time into and the things you're not. I don't regret that choice, particularly having seen the movie.') While he felt perfectly comfortable in rejecting these and other high-paying, high-visibility offers, he is also content in contemplating a six-month hiatus to fashion a theatrical work that would be 'so avant-garde that no one would want to see it' or to propose writing an unabashedly pornographic collection of illustrated short stories, *The Scarlet Gospels*, which his longtime publisher, HarperCollins, declined to print.

As these propositions suggest, Clive Barker works without concern for critics or the machinations of the culture industry, recognizing that, once he has committed his vision to the page or celluloid or canvas, the assessments of others are beyond his control; he decided, years ago, not to expend emotion on anything but the next creation. 'It's much more important,' he says, 'that somebody sees that what I'm doing is not like anybody else's than that they like it. Being liked as an artist is lower on my list of priorities than I would sometimes prefer it to be.' It is idealism, perhaps – this belief that talent, if exercised, will win out; but Clive lived on welfare and his wits for ten years, and he has never forgotten what it meant to labour in the shadows for so long and then, at last, succeed.

'If you believe in yourself,' he insists, 'you must do it.' His inspiration is convincing in its simplicity, and he is its living example: dreams can become realities if you commit yourself to the task, intent on your own vision, and not that of other artists or a genre or the presumed expectations of the marketplace.

In a worthy summation of a twenty-year career as a professional writer – for the stage, books and the screen – *The Essential Clive Barker* presents excerpts from Barker's writing that are organized around thirteen themes. None of the selections is new; instead, Barker surveys choice elements of his writing, with an eye for passages that offer particular insight into his creative vision and the ways in which his stories and plays and novels intersect.

'Private Legends', the lengthy essay that introduces *The Essential Clive Barker*, is alone worth the price of admission: a fine mingling of autobiography, creative manifesto and insights about the art and craft of prose, it is indeed essential to an understanding of Barker's varied and prolific creations. As this introduction notes: 'I don't expect anybody to pick this book up, begin on page one, and dutifully read on to the end ... I think one of the pleasures of a collection like this is that it encourages a nomadic spirit. You wander here and there, guided only by some vague instinct.' Nomads will find a rich selection of prose in these pages, and even devoted readers may be surprised by the diversity of themes that Barker has selected as essential to his vision.

Although the opening sections are devoted to the *sine qua non* of the *fantastique* – 'Doorways' and 'Journeys' – and other themes, such as 'Bestiary' and 'Terrors' and 'Making and Unmaking', are inevitable in cataloguing his aesthetics, two sections of *The Essential* deserve special note. In 'Old Humanity', Barker collects three worthy interludes from his early fiction – the novels *The Damnation Game* and *Weaveworld*, and the novelette 'The Forbidden' – that explore his fascination with the haunting of the modern by the ancient, particularly in our telling of stories, and the invention and evolution of myths and legends. In 'Memory', he examines the power of nostalgia in his art, and the epic struggle between remembering and forgetting that he has confronted in life and literature. As he notes here, and so eloquently: 'The man who is remembering must take the responsibility for what he remembers.'

Gathered in these pages are stories, vignettes, set-pieces, mood-pieces, dreams, visions, nightmares, indulgences, insights: like the magical carpet of *Weaveworld*, a tapestry that is rich with fantasy, horror and humanity. *The Essential Clive Barker* is a writer's reflection on the state of his art, and a perfect guide for readers who find the creative twists and turns of Barker's career either daunting or difficult, at times, to understand. It is also a fine bedside companion – best read, as he intended, in spare moments, paged through almost at random like a Bible or a book of poetry.

The diversity of content showcased in *The Essential Clive Barker* also underscores the aesthetic of evolution and re-invention that is the singular hallmark of Barker's creative life: from plays and musicals and pantomimes to short stories and novels and films to comic books and children's books, artwork and photography and animation, and even theme parks – a flux whose only constant is change.

When Clive chose to look back on his *Books of Blood*, more than a decade after their original publication, his reaction was instructive: 'I look at these pieces and I don't think the man who wrote them is alive in me any more.'

> We are all our own graveyards I believe; we squat amongst the tombs of the people we were. If we're healthy, every day is a celebration, a Day of the Dead, in which we give thanks for the lives that we lived; and if we are neurotic we brood and mourn and wish that the past was still present.
>
> Reading these stories over, I feel a little of both. Some of the simple energies that made these words flow through my pen – that made the phrases felicitous and the ideas sing – have gone. I lost their maker a long time ago.[4]

Although these words may have shocked and disappointed some readers, they were no surprise to Clive's friends and collaborators. As Doug Bradley notes: 'Clive has always held horror near to his heart, never strayed far from it; but I knew, at the same time that Stephen King was saying that Clive was the "future of horror", Clive was saying, in his head, *The hell I am!*'[5]

The Essential Clive Barker revisits the pleasures and perils of his identification with horror: 'I have, to be honest, an ambiguous response to that reputation. It has been all too often an easy peg for lazy journalists to hang a headline on; and for a certain order of reviewers, more interested in turning a phrase than exercising their intellects, it has been a stick to beat me with. But then if it hadn't been that it would have been something else; we all make rods for our own backs. I still enjoy crafting horror movies. It's a genre, which, for all its inanities, can still stir people up, which is always pleasing. It's such a primal form – it deals in the meat and bone of our existence – yet the moral issues it raises can be surprisingly complex: that's an attractive package.

'As to writing horror, I think I'm done, barring a few pieces I still have in the works, designed to finish mythologies that still need closure.

Of course I'll still go after a *frisson* if I see that the narrative offers me one; I just can't imagine devoting an entire novel to the business of scaring the reader. Sometimes, in fact, there's more potency in a darkness that creeps out of nowhere, its presence unsuspected, than in a fiction that announces from the first word that it intends to scare.'

Curious words, it might seem, for a writer who announced his glee for the stuff of shock some fifteen years ago, when the *Books of Blood* rocked the staid foundations of horror – and yet understandable ones for a writer who found his ambitions suddenly cloistered by his own success and spent years writing himself into creative freedom.

The problems of expectation and celebrity are essayed by Barker in his latest novel, *Coldheart Canyon* (2001), its title an evocation of the duality of its setting: Hollywood.[6] In its pages, the city of celluloid dreams is rendered into a wasteland that is physical as well as spiritual.

It is night in Coldheart Canyon, and the wind comes off the desert.

The Santa Anas, they call these winds. They blow off the Mojave, bringing malaise, and the threat of fire. Some say they are named after Saint Anne, the mother of Mary, others that they are named after one General Santa Ana, of the Mexican cavalry, a great creator of dusts; others still that the name is derived from *santantata*, which means Devil Wind.

Whatever the truth of the matter, this much is certain: the Santa Anas are always baking hot, and often so heavily laden with perfume it's as though they've picked up the scent of every blossom they've shaken on their way here. Every wild lilac and wild rose, every white sage and rank jimsomweed, every heliotrope and creosote bush: gathered them all up in their hot embrace and borne them into the hidden channel of Coldheart Canyon.

There's no lack of blossoms here, of course. Indeed, the Canyon is almost uncannily verdant. Some of the plants were brought in from the world outside by these same burning winds, these Santa Anas; others were dropped in the feces of the wild animals who wander through – the deer and coyote and raccoon; some spread from the gardens of the dream palace that lays solitary claim to this corner of Hollywood. Alien blooms, this last kind – orchids and lotus flowers – nurtured by gardeners who have long since left off their pruning and their watering, and departed, allowing the bowers which they once treasured to run riot.

But for some reason there is always a certain bitterness in the blooms here. Even the hungry deer, driven from their traditional trails these days by the presence of sightseers who have come to Tinseltown, do not linger in the Canyon for very long. Though the animals venture along the ridge and down the steep slopes of the Canyon, and curiosity, especially amongst the younger animals, often leads them over the rotted fences and toppled walls into the secret enclaves of the gardens, they seldom choose to stay there for very long.

Perhaps it isn't just that the leaves and petals are bitter. Perhaps there are too many whisperings in the air around the ruined gazebos, and the animals are unnerved by what they hear. Perhaps there are too many invisible presences brushing against their trembling flanks as they explore the clotted pathways. Perhaps, as they graze the overgrown lawns, they look up and mistake a statue for a pale fragment of life, and are startled by their error, and take flight.

Perhaps, sometimes, they are not mistaken.

Coldheart Canyon was conceived as a short book, to be written in the manner of *The Hellbound Heart* and *Cabal* while Clive completed his years of work on the illustrations for *The Abarat Quartet*. 'Partly because I've put so much creative effort into the painting that it's just used a lot of me up, and I couldn't face the idea of doing another big book. Those things are completely life-consuming; and the paintings have been the life-consuming part of my existence of late.

'I wanted to do something that was smaller, but at the same time I wanted its smallness to be justified; so I wanted a small subject. And what's really smaller than Hollywood?' But the novel grew and grew: 'I found that, once I was writing about Hollywood, it was too fucking depressing unless I started to write with an element of fantasy. Once the fantasy started flowing, I started to have fun with the Hollywood parts. In a way, they played off one another. Some of the most pleasurable parts were when I was letting the anger out – all the hard, nasty, cynical feelings I have about this town – and describing some of the lunacies that I've seen.

'The Hollywood of *Coldheart Canyon* is the Hollywood of producer deals, actors who are out of control, egos which are out of control – all of the things, in other words, that wait down the line when I've done the next movie deal.

'I've been blessed, by and large, in my little life as a director, with very pleasurable people to work with. I've seldom had much ego to deal with. I'm not a shouter, and when people realize that I like to treat people with dignity and I like to be treated with dignity in turn, most people respond really well. I think those things begin at the top; and if you're at the top, if you're a producer or director and you say, *Okay, look, this is not going to be one of those places where people can be in tears every two minutes, or yelling and screaming and slamming Winnebago doors*, then very quickly people get the message.

'I will cry because people die. I will not cry because movies are hard to make. It's just not something that's worth crying over. It isn't. There are priorities for tears, I think.'

Central to the story of *Coldheart Canyon* is the problem of fame, and the strange synergy between fame and fortune – whether financial or, more significantly, artistic – that Barker has witnessed in Hollywood: 'It's about what dreams you have as an artist, and how very seldom you see those dreams truly realized.

'I'm using actors, as opposed to writers, as the core of the narrative, although there are some fun asides on the horrors of writing in this town, which just seem to get worse.' He notes a recent episode involving New Line Cinema, which paid him handsomely for an original script called *American Horror*: 'It cost them fucking $400,000 to get it into their hands, and it took them *three months* to read it! It's just unbelievable. So there are horrors; but I've been trying to write about Hollywood in terms of a metaphor for the world – of how the world just consumes, uses up, your highest hopes for yourself.'

Actors also represent the highest form of the idolatry known as celebrity, which is at the heart of the novel. 'Celebrities,' Clive notes, 'are people who are something other than the thing that they do. So: an actor who is also a celebrity is *not* a celebrity because he is an actor. An actor who is also a celebrity is a celebrity because of a marriage that he made, or a drug bust. If he was just a plain old actor, he would not be a celebrity – he'd be Robert Duvall.'

The issue of celebrity is central to his dissatisfaction with Hollywood – and, increasingly, with publishing. 'The interesting thing, I think, for writers right now is that they want to turn us into quantities: *they* being the publishers and booksellers in the broadest sense. The only way you'll be interesting, and therefore be worthy of *People* magazine or expressing thoughts which they think are important, is by being something *other* than a writer.

'So a writer needs to be a celebrity, needs to be something else as well; and those magazines, *US* and *People*, which sell vast numbers and whose reviews are important to the sale of your books and my books are really only interested if they can characterize you as something *other* than a writer, because . . . what is a writer? He sits home and writes – how boring.

'Now there are things other than being a writer that they don't want to know about, like being homosexual. That's really one step in the other direction, away from celebrity. Unless you're Harvey Fierstein, you can't really do that. But you *can* be a professional wacko.

'I cannot count the number of times over the past many years that people have said, *Where's the nearest cemetery?* So I can be photographed there, of course. Not hundreds of times – that's an exaggeration – but many, many dozens of times, without any reference to the content of the book I've just written. Because a reasonably sane-looking, once-young man in a cemetery has a story attached to him, perhaps.' He shakes his head, laughing with wonder and despair. 'Actually, that was the first picture that ever appeared of me in *People* magazine.'

With *Coldheart Canyon*, as in his other recent fictions, Clive Barker seems more tuned to himself, more aware of the importance of his presence within the stories he chooses to tell. 'I feel wiser the more I write,' he says. 'And I felt, even when I was making something like [his Quarry Bank magazine] *Humphri*, that I was exploring myself and that I was explaining myself to myself, the way that any imaginative writer does. You feel emptied out by what you've made, but you also feel as though the journey to get there has made you, if it's any good, richer and stronger and more knowing and more self-knowing. The telling of stories is a particularly easy metaphor because it's the ultimate procedure: it's causality, it's connectedness, it's making sense where there apparently is not sense. It's saying: *This is connected with this is connected with this is connected with this . . .* and before you know it, you've got a story. And you are like God, because you can put *The End* on. And God puts *The End* on, but we don't, in our own lives; we just have to wait it out.

'Making art is very empowering, I think. It empowers you because you start to feel very special – because, as Norman [Russell] rightly observed to Pobjoy about *Humphri*, only one person can make that thing, and that's you. It may not be a very good thing, but hey, it's mine. And that's a huge amount of what's going on here. I did find the making of images and the making of books and stories – and later on, movies – very empowering. I still find it very empowering; and a part of me feels self-disgust about that. I feel schizophrenic. There's a part of me that loves the razzamatazz of it all: *Oh, there's five hundred people waiting outside the bookstore? Bring them on in*! And there's another part of me, and it's just as strong, which would love to be completely invisible. It actually despises the other part.

'That's one of the reasons why Blake is so important to me. I believe in art and artists most when they follow their own instincts, wherever their instincts lead and however ill-equipped they are for the journey. Melville called *Moby Dick* his homemade quilt of a book. When I look at my creative life to date, I think of most of my stuff, including my movies, as homemade quilts. They might be $11 million homemade quilts, but that's essentially what they are – they're made with whatever I had at the time. I don't think of myself as very slick. I would sometimes like to be more slick. I think of myself as somebody who just makes things with whatever's right to hand, and then I'm going to move on and make another thing, with whatever different things are to hand.

'It goes even as far as this: I think my complete reluctance to have anything but a pen is a reluctance to ever be a modern writer. I really think that part of me is saying, *No, it's going to stay amateur*. It's never going to be a profession, any more than painting is going to be a profession or movie-making is going to be a profession – it's not what I'm going to do. Which often strikes me as bizarre: fifteen books on, and it's not my profession. Pathetic, isn't it? But it's definitely the way my head works.

'I'm living this artificial life in my middle period right now, which I'm aware is something gloriously phoney, which is LA, which is Mickey Mouse Town – you know, *What are the grosses for the weekend?*, all of that crap. And I'm enjoying it on this very simple level. I'm having fun with it as this sort of game; but just being in a simpler place is something that I definitely feel awaits me in five, ten years time. Because the things I really love to do, to paint and to write, are things I can do anywhere. Books fit very nicely into this contemplative life. Books and sky and sea go together in my imagination. Movies don't. Movies are this artificial thing, this brittle thing. There's nothing brittle about books. There's a magic about books which is to do with their solitariness.' Thus, as he has written: 'A book is one place you can never take a friend . . . You must go absolutely alone, and deal with each revelation as it appears. In that sense, perhaps reading best approaches the condition of living; it is ultimately, perhaps triumphantly, a solitary experience.'[7]

It is also, he recognizes, a regenerative experience. Without children of his own, his stories, his art, his endless creations – and the examples they offer for others – inevitably take on a role that is parental, in the best sense of the word. 'I have to tell what I know,' he wrote in the novel *Galilee*. 'That's why I'm here; I have to tell people all that I've seen and felt, so that my pain is never repeated. So that those who come after me are like my children, because I helped shape them, and make them strong.'

In exercising the solitary magic of books, Clive Barker's success, critical and commercial, has traced an unusual pattern: his earliest works were targeted at a niche audience – and, indeed, a disreputable genre – which he then transcended through the sheer weight of an ever-expansive literary ambition. His books shifted through different publishers on both sides of the Atlantic before finding an open-minded and enthusiastic home at HarperCollins. 'Not a single book of Clive's has ever been published under any genre imprint by HarperCollins in the UK,' notes his editor, Jane Johnson. 'He's always been published as general fiction, never as horror or fantasy or sf. We have always seen him as a mainstream author, and ensured that perception has carried out into the way we market and sell his work to the book trade and the public. I think Barker fans know his work will challenge them as it always has: they buy into his imagination, they enter his world, and that's how we like to sell him. Our shoutline on the marketing material for *Everville*, the first of the big novels I edited, was *Open Your Mind* – inferring: *and let Clive in*!'

In a publishing industry that has rapidly consolidated into the control of a handful of international conglomerates – Clive's original publisher, Sphere, was acquired by Penguin UK (part of the Thomson Group) and then by Macdonald (owned by Robert Maxwell), which was merged with the Warner Publishing Group into Little Brown UK – accountancy has replaced literary merit as the defining principle of too many imprints. Decisions are based increasingly on past sales figures, a game of numbers in which few major houses might have patience with Clive Barker, given the extraordinary commercial appeal of writers like Stephen King, Dean R Koontz and Anne Rice, with whom he is often compared. Jane Johnson comments: 'Although King is a special case, especially with more recent works, these guys have generated a book a year, centred in a very specific area of the market. This is how you grow an author to huge sales – by repeating the message again and again, and by giving the readership what they want, rather than taking them by surprise, as Clive often does. It's the very fact that Clive takes risks and is so Protean that makes him such a fascinating author to work with: but also it's a big challenge for a publisher.

'In purely commercial terms, what any publisher would have liked from Clive would have been one big novel a year – a *Weaveworld*, a *Great and Secret Show*, an *Imajica*. That the publication of the big books has been punctuated by a number of less traditional projects – *Hellbound Heart, Cabal, Thief of Always*, the two volumes of plays – has meant fancy footwork for his publishers; but (to extend that metaphor horribly) it keeps us on our toes. His sales are strong, but they aren't blockbusting like those of King and Rice and Koontz, purely because he refuses to be trammelled by commercial restraints.'

Barker's unconventional ambitions have provoked several unusual publishing transactions – and commercially risky projects. His illustrated novel for young adults, *The Thief of Always*, was licensed by HarperCollins for a single dollar because of the perceived potential for disaster in a marketplace that might not accept a children's book written by a horror maven. Two collections of his stage plays, *Incarnations* (1995) and *Forms of Heaven* (1996), were later issued in hardback despite the likelihood of limited audience appeal. 'It was a difficult publishing decision,' Johnson says, 'but my decision was for completism, rather than pure hard-headed commercialism. The compromise, in the UK, has been to keep the two volumes in hardback, instead of carrying them to paperback, since paperback is the ongoing lifeblood of any work, and that's the figure that keeps showing up on sales computers.' Even *The Essential Clive Barker* posed concerns in a marketplace where short story collections and anthologies (let alone a mosaic of excerpts from previously published works) are an anathema; Clive agreed to license that book for a minimal advance for the simplest of reasons: 'Because I wanted to see that book.'

With Eddie Bell's departure from HarperCollins in 2000, Clive's increasing discomfort with the industry was manifest. 'I kept changing direction, and he didn't mind. And he never said don't – ever.'

That was not the case with his earlier publishers, such as Sphere, which rejected his proposal to write the novel that became *Weaveworld* and urged him to write to generic expectation rather than pursue his personal vision. That spectre of mainstream publishing's ceaseless desire for safety – and self-censorship in deference to an imagined audience – was presented again late in the 1990s, when Clive wrote a new introduction for a special 'collector's edition' of the *Books of Blood* (1998), whose publishing rights remain in the control of Sphere (now part of Little Brown) in the United Kingdom and Berkley (now part of Penguin Putnam) in the United States.

His manuscript mentioned an elaborate Hallowe'en costume devised and worn on the streets of Hollywood by his lover, David Armstrong, which reconfigured David into 'an amalgam of sexual excess and demonic elegance' that 'might have stepped out of one of the stories in this collection'. Clive's effusive description of the costume included the following two sentences: 'He'd put on several leather accoutrements and had endowed himself with a grotesquely large dildo, which swung before two water-filled black balloons. From the top of

481

the cleft of his otherwise naked butt hung a tail that would not have shamed a stallion.'

The response from Little Brown was disheartening: 'Barbara Boote said, *Don't* – because she would not have me reference dildos in the introduction to the book. I said, *This is the introduction to a series of books which are notorious for the excessiveness of their violence and the graphicness of their sexuality, and you're telling me I can make no reference to David's Hallowe'en costume, in which he'd gone out as a demon with a huge plastic dick?* And I lost the battle; they would not do it.

'I told the story to Susan Allison [at Berkley], and we laughed . . . *How stupid.* And then, about three weeks later, she came back and said she needed to do the same thing.' (The sentences were removed entirely from the British edition, while the American version retains only the phrase 'He'd put on several leather accoutrements.')

This minor skirmish was merely the prelude to a more difficult episode: the decision by HarperCollins to decline to publish a new and intentionally transgressive collection of short stories, *The Scarlet Gospels*. 'It was to be a small, intense, deeply sexual book,' Clive says. 'Unapologetic.' The stories, which he would illustrate, were intended as experiments in erotica and pornography based upon Biblical themes: 'Unapologetically erotic and comprehensively erotic. I wanted every conceivable element of the human erotic urge: gay, straight and then some.' With a hundred illustrations – paintings, manipulated photographs, drawings – and forty fictional vignettes, *The Scarlet Gospels* included such wonders as 'Jehovah's Bitch', which, written in Barker's most experimental style, considered the fate of a man whose sexual dalliance with God's mistress triggers the vengeance of the Almighty.

'My love for the pornographic – or a Lucio Fulci film or a piece of frozen sculpture or something else that is roughly done – is me trying to build a relationship of trust with an aesthetic which is not my natural aesthetic. My natural aesthetic is to be piss-elegant, over-thinking, over-polished. *Imajica* is a book where I gave into all those instincts, and I love that book as a consequence. But this love of the more crude – it's part of the energy of these things, these gouged things, these argumentative things.'

Clive pitched the collection to HarperCollins personnel while he was showing them photo transparencies of images from a children's book in progress, then called *The Book of Hours* – and now known as *The Abarat Quartet*. 'They really went nuts; they loved it. Then I cleared all that stuff out, and I put out the *Scarlet Gospels* stuff. I showed them fifteen pictures, some images that I would build the stories around. They all backed off to the edges of the room. They were appalled. It was fascinating. You would think that something radioactive had just been put on the table. There are very stark things there. I'm very proud of them.'

'I saw *The Scarlet Gospels* as a very commercial prospect,' notes Jane Johnson, Clive's editor at HarperCollins. 'And, at that time, a much easier "sell" to the book trade (with its taboo qualities, shrinkwrapped packaging and "Adults Only" stickering appealing immensely to the core of Clive's readership) than *The Abarat Quartet*, since Clive was far better known for the visceral nature of his fiction than for his appeal to the children's market. But the discussion was always about strategy and what was in Clive's best interests . . .' Johnson hoped that both projects – the increasingly momentous *Abarat Quartet* and *The Scarlet Gospels* – could be published with the kind of timing that would not send 'mixed messages' to booksellers and readers.

The night after Clive presented *The Scarlet Gospels*, Eddie Bell called him, and in one of their last official conversations, advised Clive that he'd had 'a stream of people coming into this office' with prophecies of imminent disaster – particularly because of the negative publicity that might attach to the children's books. As Clive recalls: 'This was not simply my deciding, along with HarperCollins, that the timing had to be changed. Eddie was advising me to take the project off the table, which I did. I always respected his instincts, as you know.'

Thus, although he had offered *The Scarlet Gospels* to HarperCollins for an advance of one dollar, the book was shelved, perhaps permanently.[8] 'When publishers think about books,' Clive says, 'they don't think of them now as art – as something that comes from the heart of the creator, an expression of who a creator is . . . They think about bottom level. Which is, to my mind, sort of like raising cows and just thinking about hamburger – nothing about the living animal, just about the dullest, most bland reduction of the thing at the end of it all.

'When Eddie Bell and I had our conversation about *The Scarlet Gospels*, Eddie was trapped in a political world, where his instincts as a friend of the creator – and not just me, but many creators – were hopelessly compromised.

'What Eddie brought was this team effort. We would sit up nights at the American Club. We designed covers together. We wrote copy, drunk, together. There was just this sense, that I miss so much, that these were people who really enjoyed doing something together. It was publishing the way publishing no longer is, and publishing never again will be, I fear. The only thing he kept going after me for, which I never delivered to him: he wanted one last big horror novel from me – and I think I will still deliver that. I have one in me, I think – one fucking huge, balls-to-the-wall horror novel – and I think I will deliver that.

'A lot of the magic has gone out of publishing for me. And I see Eddie's removal as being indicative of a failure of the system. A system that does not have room for a maverick like Eddie Bell, that cannot embrace and use the limitless skills and imagination of an Eddie Bell, is doomed. It will end up like movies – we will end up with publishers who are like some half-assed movie company which can only produce poor, poor echoes of its own worst product.

'I mourn the reduction of the quality of the debate between writer and publisher, and writer and agent, and publisher and agent. I think it's become crass. And if that sounds hypocritical, given the fact that I've made a shitload of money in publishing, it should be contexted by the fact that I've done a lot of deals which were completely off the main track in terms of structure – that were not about taking a million and a half up front. *The Thief of Always* is an example; *The Essential* is another example.'

The issue presented by *The Scarlet Gospels* was the one that Clive has faced repeatedly in his multifaceted career: the collision of his ambition with commerce. The project seemed, to many at Harper-Collins, an invitation to commercial suicide – not merely for the collection, but for Barker's publishing career. Unlike *The Thief of Always*, a book of undoubted market potential that, because of its author's reputation for dark and adult themes, posed a risk of not fulfilling that potential, *The Scarlet Gospels* seemed, with its unabashed pornography and implications of blasphemy, likely to stir market senti-ment against its 'blue-chip' writer.

Although Clive was dismayed, his editor, Jane Johnson, worked through the difficult impasse with characteristic optimism. 'I think Clive is – and I don't say this lightly – a genius. He has the most extraordinarily powerful imagination of any writer – indeed, any artist – I've encountered in my almost twenty years in the industry. It is a wayward imagination – but that's what makes it so extraordinary: it doesn't run down the same old tramlines as so many authors' imaginations do, but ranges freely and widely out over every area of human experience – life, death, love, worship, wonder, pain, pleasure, transcendence, mutability, the search for meaning amidst chaos and, of course, all the glorious taboos surrounding gender and sexual experience. Big, big subjects.

'Nothing is forbidden to him; or, through his work, to us. I think, in many ways, he is the most ambitious writer since the metaphysical writers of early English literature: his roots lie with *Piers Plowman*, Chaucer, Bunyan, Donne and Blake. It infuriates me that the *literati* will not acknowledge this extension of our literary heritage. It's partly because Clive has been so successful, and the British, especially, love to stamp down visible success – somehow it's just not cricket for a young unknown Liverpudlian writer (wrong background entirely – *didn't go to the right university, my dear*) to storm the bestseller lists, and then go on to Hollywood. It's a snobbery I've encountered all my years in the industry while working with the *fantastique*: people love to put it down as shallow and childish, and somehow of the wrong class – just look at the outrage generated when Tolkien's *Lord of the Rings* was voted, in the biggest poll ever conducted in the UK, "Book of the Century" – just because their own imaginations have lost elasticity.'

In this instance, his publisher had lost elasticity – but not faith. Crucial to its decision was a consideration of the potential negative impact of *The Scarlet Gospels* on the far more expansive and crucial series of illustrated books that Clive had been developing for nearly four years. Known originally as *The Book of Hours*, this once very private pursuit would prove the most spiritually (and commercially) rewarding, and possibly the most culturally pervasive, of Clive Barker's adventures in the dark fantastic: *The Abarat Quartet*.

FOR EVER MORE

THE ABARAT QUARTET (2002 and beyond)

[T]he end is ever at the beginning and the beginning at the end for ever more.

— ER EDDISON, *The Worm Ouroboros*

At three minutes past five on the morning of August 20, 1999, as I was writing the final draft of this book, Len Barker died at a hospital in Liverpool. It was the end of his three-and-a-half year battle with leukemia. His family was with him: Joan, his wife of more than fifty years; his sons, Clive and Roy; and his new son, David Armstrong.

In the depths of this loss, Clive felt an uplifting sense of something gained. 'The generosity of spirit that is in Armstrong – in the deepest sense, the spirit – and the gusto and the appetite for life are an education. Watching him with my family when Dad passed away. Watching him with Dad, who had been difficult on a couple occasions with me about David. Watching my father – so close to death that he had no more than a handful of words – say, *Welcome, David*. And say to the nurse who's looking at this black face amongst all these white faces, *This is David, he's part of the fun*. And to have David as part of that charmed circle, I hope, around Dad in his final minutes, is the kind of experience that changes the way you view somebody forever. As though David wasn't so deep in my heart already, he went even deeper for those moments, because that was a hard, hard thing to do – and it was hard for Dad, too. He was there in those last minutes, realizing that David and Clive were here at his bedside, and that he had an extra son today.'

When Clive rose from his father's bedside, dawn was breaking, its light pouring through the windows – a long night had ended. 'There were noisy seagulls swooping on the wind outside. My father loved the sea. I mentioned to my brother that maybe he was with them now.'

After the funeral service, as mourners left the church, they witnessed an extraordinary sight: 'There's my brother and his wife and their kids, and there's David and myself, hand in hand – and I thought, *That's an education for these people.* Because these are not people who are familiar with the idea that a black person of any sex could be with a white person of any sex; or particularly that a black man and a white man should be standing, hand in hand, receiving people at the end of a funeral.

'I think it's good to teach, and I felt like it was saying something, just by being there – we were saying something to people who do have racist hearts. Because Liverpool has that shit deep in it, and has always had that shit deep in it. There's always been a contempt for blacks spoken – I'm sorry, out of my parent's mouths, and those of their contemporaries – and fear and so much else that is negative. Maybe they think a different way now about blacks, about gay men and women. Maybe they think a different way about interracial relationships. Maybe they think a different way about their prejudices, which are deep in their hearts – and their fears, which are deep in their hearts.

'I was so proud of my mother, for being David's mother. It's humbling, because these are hard things for David and they're hard things for my mother – and suddenly it didn't matter anymore, all these things, all these prejudices were seen in a heartbeat for what they were, just stupid things that didn't mean anything.

'David loved my Dad because he sees my Dad in me – and there's a lot of him in me. It was great. It was the most painful thing, and it was the most wonderful thing.

'Whatever happens, all the bad shit in your life, I think you have to work a little to pull the good shit out. But this time I didn't have to do any pulling: there it was. It was right there in front of me. This terrible loss was something wonderful.'[1]

Consumed by grief, Clive returned to his home in Beverly Hills and found himself standing in the midst of the nearly two hundred and fifty canvases of new artwork he had created in the years dating back to his deepest hours of depression – ironically, the very time that his father's illness had been diagnosed. A handful of disparate paintings, created solely as an escape, soon seemed charged with meaning, as he discovered connection after connection – and a story, which he called *The Book of Hours*. Twenty-five colour oil paintings would provide the central panels of this illustrated novel, to be written, like *The Thief of Always*, as a children's book that also spoke to adults. Each painting would depict an island that was also an hour of time, and one of twenty-five chapters of a fantastic adventure; but as canvas after canvas poured out of him with an intensity he had never before experienced, Clive realized that his story could not be contained in a single book.

Over the next three and a half years, working entirely for himself – without a contract from his publisher, without any assurance that his creations would hold interest to anyone, save perhaps as individual paintings to be exhibited or sold – he generated this vast collection of canvases, all of them depicting the landscapes and inhabitants of the twenty-five islands, a mystical archipelago known as the Abarat. He envisioned an epic of epics, *The Abarat Quartet*: four novels illustrated with four hundred oil paintings and illustrations.

'Because all the paintings preceded the text, I have, in a way that I've never done before, allowed the imagistic life of the material to lead the way. What I've discovered, which is very important to me in terms of my faith in the idea of the collective unconscious, amongst other things: I was quietly, sort of invisibly, telling the story to myself; and when I stepped back from it and started to put all this stuff together without having any conscious knowledge of what it was, there was a story there. There were connections there. There were all kinds of connections I hadn't seen.

'I can't emphasize strongly enough how this whole experience has changed an idea about process for me. I haven't figured out how it impacts the rest of my writing career. These paintings would not exist had I not run out of patience with a certain kind of writing that I was doing. I'm excited, because whatever happens to these things in the books, and in Hollywood, is an irrelevance to their presence here. It's exciting to see these things appear in front of me – and to have that wonderful feeling of personal irrelevance, which is at the heart of all great creation: *I don't know how this came about. It has nothing to do with me.* It's much easier to do that for me when painting than it is when writing. That might be because painting, drawing, preceded writing, as it does with all children. You make these sort of marks, and there is a sense in which I still just make a mark: I'm mark-making.'

The magnitude of the task of painting so many large, varied and detailed oils on canvas is difficult to convey in words: far from the simplicity suggested by the idea of 'mark-making', the physical labour alone is arduous and time-intensive. Writing, which for more than twenty years took primacy in Clive's long working days, became sec- ondary to painting as his traditional work schedule – writing every morning and, often, late into the afternoon and evening – collapsed in service of the art. Although, by early in 2000, he had perfected two hundred and fifty finished canvases, many of them four by five feet and larger, he had also painted and discarded more than a hundred others. 'I would say I lose one to every two achieved, roughly, which I don't think is terrible odds. The only time it really, really hurts me is when I have been at it and at it and at it, and I just can't crack it.'

Some of the paintings – simpler and smaller pieces – were completed in relatively brief periods of time; but the more sizable pieces, and those with a wealth of colour and detail, could take weeks, if not months, of applied effort. A particular hurdle was the immense triptych that offers a geographic overview of the Abarat. 'I painted that triptych twice. I painted it once as a triptych of three canvases, each four feet by five feet, and spent about three weeks on it – and realized that I could not get sufficient detail into it at that size. So I destroyed those canvases. And I had three new canvases specially constructed that were two and a half times the size, and had a scaffold built, and then spent a month making it a different way. And it's hard, it's very, very hard . . .

'When I'm after something, and I don't really know what that thing is and the exploration is there, it's not a formal thing, it's a feeling: *What am I getting at here*? And an interesting thing about a painting is that it contains all its drafts. Unlike a book, where each draft is thrown away, as it were, to contain the next, a painting, especially an oil painting, will contain them all.

'The drafts are all here,' he says, moving to an intense and complex oil that represents one of the twenty-five island-hours of the Abarat. The canvas depicts a woman struggling with an image of death, and eventually may be called 'Five O'Clock in the Morning': 'Because my father died at five – and because most people who die in hospitals die between four and five, when the arc of the body is lowest – I want to make the island where the struggle with death happens the hour when Dad died.

'Here are the first mountains,' Clive says, indicating an area of darkened sky, and what is hidden within the finished work. 'They were probably blue and green, because I put all this on top of them. Obviously this was once a much brighter piece; I was looking for a more optimistic thing than it ended up being. So the layers and the levels are all there, inside the painting. I find that interesting, because the method of scraping and scratching and gouging that I use is constantly revealing the levels which I thought were failures, but turn out to be a necessary part of the solution – so that if you scratch the yellow away, you'll pull out the purple, the blue – and there's something about the *handmadeness* of it. There's something about the way you tussle and the way the thing can only be made, in a way, through a series of failures.

'Whatever the process is, it's just so painless. Even when it doesn't work – and you leave it or you throw it away, trash it – usually you take something from it that you can build on. Part of it is because the business of making a painting has something of a pleasure element, which isn't there for me in writing. And I'll go back and I'll tussle with it again and again, and eventually I'll crack it. It might take me years, but eventually I'll crack it. There are pictures here which took me years. In the version you see here, there are three or four trashed versions. I don't feel the same way about writing. There are things in my bottom drawer that are never going to see the light of day. I will destroy them before that happens – they're just not good; but in paintings, there's a lot of things where I think: *Well, I haven't cracked it yet, but I'll come back to that. I'll make it work.'*[2]

More profoundly than any of his novels and films, the paintings consumed Clive; and *The Abarat Quartet*, like his relationship with David Armstrong, marked a turning point in his life and his career. The writer of the *Books of Blood* and the director of *Hellraiser* was gone; in his place was a talent for whom each act of creation was an unmitigated exploration and expression of self. The insistently external constructs of his earlier fiction, however entertaining and edifying, had been set aside in service of an increasing urge (and, perhaps, need) to essay the internal – the dreams and desires and emotions and agonies that were Clive Barker – however difficult and painful the task might prove.

The day after he returned from his father's funeral, Clive painted 'The Grieving Man', a stark image of a seated man covering his eyes. 'I painted it without making a stroke on the canvas or even knowing what I was going to paint until I'd painted it. It took me maybe fifteen minutes to paint it. And it makes my eyes prick to look at it, because I can feel absolutely what I was feeling the moment I was painting it. There aren't many pictures in these rooms which have the same degree of connection with something so violently felt; but, in a way that is simply not true of the *Books of Blood*, all of these pictures touch some place in me – more truthful and more intimately *me* – than those exercises in wilful violence and shock. Which I had a thoroughly good time with, and I'm tired as hell of.

'You've known me many years now, and the person who lots of people projected as the writer of those things was being projected by the writer – and that was why they were appearing on the page. The closer I have gotten to these paintings, the closer I get to the thing which doesn't have a proper name – that just operates because it's there in front of you – the closer I have felt to something which is uniquely *mine*.'[3]

The delicious ambiguities of his artwork – and the way in which the paintings speak for themselves – seem strikingly to fulfil his desire to be rendered anonymous and, indeed, irrelevant. 'When I've finished the four hundred and something paintings I'm doing for this project, I'm going to hire a huge warehouse and I'm going to hang all of the paintings in the darkness, all nicely lit. I'm going to hire a cherrypicker and we're going to take a picture – and I'm going to be this tiny little thing among them. And what it will be about is this: *You know, you can't really see his face – but that's not what's really important. What's important is that this little guy, whoever the fuck he is – he's sort of slightly irrelevant in this picture – poured all this stuff out of him. Isn't that cool?*'

Clive decided that he would offer *The Abarat Quartet* to his publisher, HarperCollins, on the basis of the artwork-in-progress and an oral summation of the story. He then initiated a unique dialogue with the major motion picture studios, which he recounted on a sunny afternoon while waiting for Jeffrey Katzenberg, one of Hollywood's legendary players – the former head of Walt Disney Studios and currently partner, with Steven Spielberg and David Geffen, in DreamWorks SKG – to visit his home, view the paintings and hear him tell the story of Abarat. The visit was one of many by studio executives who pondered the potential incarnations of the paintings – not simply as a series of theatrical films but also as interactive games, animations, theme park rides and merchandise.

'It's a much more complicated question than it first appears, but you know why: because people are sold things in this town very simply – the thirty-second pitch. Which I will indulge in freely if I can, because there is value in the thirty-second pitch. I took *American Horror* to New Line, and I said, *This is* Age of Innocence *meets* Aliens. An unlikely pairing – but they got it, you know. I sold that movie in two minutes. So there can be value in that, but there are also times when that simply doesn't make any sense.

'I have refused to talk with anybody from any studio unless they were here in the room with the paintings. Which has been quite an interesting situation, because I'm actually saying to these guys, *Look, if you want to send up your third in command, then I'll talk to him –* and then we have the second in command, and eventually Jeffrey Katzenberg – as per this afternoon.'

Every major Hollywood studio came to view the paintings. 'I'm daily an odd mixture of Barnum and CS Lewis,' Clive says. 'We've had a parade of the movers and the shakers through this house because of the presence of these paintings – which is astonishing. The fact that they're paintings, and that people don't talk a lot about painting in this town, is useful. When the word got out that there were so many of them, there was a sense of: *Oh, okay, this is really something I should see, at least to say that I've seen it.* And it has sometimes been extraordinary. We've had grown men behave like children, going from room to room with their mouths open wide; and I feel as though I've seen these pictures, which have used up such a huge amount of my energies, validated. In just the sheer pleasure they give people.

'People in this town are very cynical. They've seen everything – that's the feeling. Their sense of wonder has taken a major wounding over the years. I say: *Look, this is four books, it's four hundred paintings. It's, so far, three and a half years of my life. Think of it this way – that you're buying Dorothy's adventures on the road; that you're buying Oz. It's a world.* And they do get that, because traditionally, in very success-ful fantasy material – *The Wizard of Oz*, the *Star Wars* pictures, the *Planet of the Apes* movies – you're buying a *world*. You're not even buying one narrative; you're buying many interlocking narratives.

'So they get the general principle. They also see the toys and the theme parks and all of that stuff – and they see something else, which they never, ever see, which is that it's already been designed. And that is quite a thing to see, because when you go in with the two-minute pitch, all the work is still to be done. A two-minute pitch gives you only the bones of bones; but you come in here, and there is colour and form and characters. I could sit you down in this room and you would create your own stories very quickly out of this stuff, which would be every bit as interesting as the stories I'm going to tell, because images just *do* that.

'There is also real joy in being returned to a handmade quality. A lot of images in movies now are so slick, polished, and so – to my mind – often dead as a consequence. This *Toy Story* look, in which everything has the same textural value: nothing's wrong with anything, it's just that nothing catches your spirit in the way that something more handmade, like *Pinocchio* or *Fantasia*, does. And the hand-madeness, the markedness of the paintings – the fact that they're gouged and scored, that the canvases show the evidence of the war which has gone on between my intentions and my work, the marks of my pleading to get them to do something, to say something – is refreshing to these people. Because they see – *we* see – a lot of images that are very polished. Cinema is so much about polish now, and it's so easy to polish things, to digitally fix things.'

At the heart of the epic story that integrates the paintings is a sixteen-year-old Minnesotan, Candy Quackenbush, who crosses the boundary between our reality and the parallel dimension of the Abarat. In the archipelago of island-hours she meets Finnegan, a man whose bloodlines mingle the Abarat's opposing populations. He leads a band of rebels against the Lord of Midnight, Christopher Carrion, who seeks to conquer the twenty-five islands and then make our reality part of his empire.

Clive leads us, as he guided the parade of visiting studio executives, through his gallery, revealing salient characters and settings – and the depth and diversity of imagery that has been so many years in the making. The wondrous inhabitants of Abarat include monsters and pirates and chubby birds, 'and a little Tolkien here, and the girl who's in love with a pizza slice, and this thing, which I think was at Wood-stock.' Then: a delirious portrait of a glowering man. His skull houses a glass-paned fishtank whose waters he inhales; it is Christopher Carrion. 'Christopher's grandmother sewed up his lips because he uttered bad words when he was a young man, and she didn't approve. He recycles his own nightmares into this soup, which he sort of marinates and inhales. If you stand back from this picture, you'll see the nightmares in its textures – there's one, there's one and there's another – and it's really, really hard to do that with words.

'This is the villain; this is the bad guy; and this picture *pours* ambigu-ity. There are all kinds of things this picture says to you besides straight villainy. Or, to take a more naked example' – he gestures to another canvas – 'here is a strange mixture of paganism and the skull of a dragon turned into a church. This place exists for a period of a sentence in the book, but I liked the idea so much, I thought, *What a great fucking thing this will be to see*. This dragon was killed by Finnegan; its body lies where it fell and rotted, the bones forming a road up to the church where Finnegan was about to be married when the dragon appeared and killed his bride-to-be. Finnegan dispatched the dragon, and its body and the church fell into decay.

'Candy Quackenbush comes to this church, and even though she thinks she's never been in this world before, says: *I've been here. I was almost married here.* So the book is very unlike *Oz*, which is about a stranger in a strange land. This is about somebody who we slowly realize is not a stranger here, but actually *belongs* here; and that's a bit like Alice falling down the rabbit hole and knowing exactly where she is. It's the inversion of what, classically, these stories are about. And the romantic arc of the book is the most important arc I can think of, which is how lovers who were separated can be reunited.'

On April 15, 2000, Clive's dream was realized when his hoped-for suitor, Walt Disney Studios, announced that it had entered into a wide-ranging agreement to transform the novels of *The Abarat Quartet* into a major franchise. 'On this project,' reported Michael Mendenhall, the studio's President of Marketing and Synergy, 'Clive clearly has a creative direction that's very in line with our studio.' The result was, without doubt, his most lucrative contract to date and the largest literary/film rights deal of the year: Disney agreed to pay some $4 million in advance for theatrical, theme park, television, gaming and merchandising rights to his literary properties, to be followed by another $4 million when the first motion picture goes into production. The heads of Disney's various divisions had visited Clive's house to view the artwork five times, but it had taken twenty-six pitches to secure the final agreement.

'Disney and Abarat are the next four years of my life,' Clive said at the time the deal was announced; but the reality was that *The Abarat Quartet* was only the latest pinnacle in a life that has been, and will be, devoted to a single constant: creation. Even as he returned to work on his next canvases, Clive was drafting the novel *Coldheart Canyon*, which would be published before the first novel of Abarat; and his ongoing film and television projects suggested a minor media empire.

In 1999, MGM/United Artists approached Clive to devise three feature films based on the stories of Edgar Allan Poe. His vision for the first of 'The Poe Projects' would have merged Poe's seminal detection fiction, 'The Murders in the Rue Morgue', with the *Books of Blood* sequel, 'New Murders in the Rue Morgue'; he also proposed an examination of Poe's real-life relationship with editor Rufus Griswold. Meanwhile, Fox Television Network commissioned Clive to develop and produce several made-for-television movies, including the intriguingly titled *Hoop Hell* and *Silo*. His own production company, Seraphim Films, began development of the novel *Galilee* as a potential television series, and a feature film adaptation of Barker's most successful stage play, *History of the Devil: The Movie*.

But too often Hollywood is a place of beginnings, with few happy endings. Again and again, Clive found himself in meetings, pondering propositions that, more often than not, led nowhere – save to more meetings and more propositions. Even *American Horror*, which he wrote and planned to direct for New Line Cinema, fell victim to the celluloid cycle renowned as 'development hell'.

The frustrations of Hollywood, where nine out of every ten projects fade into oblivion – while the tenth merely suffers – powered the vengeful prose of the novel *Coldheart Canyon*; but with typical persistence, Clive continues to wrestle with the corporate conundrums of his adopted home. Film and television projects inspire his imagination, although he seems increasingly inclined to limit his participation, acting more often as producer than as screenwriter and director. In addition to the epic potential of *The Abarat Quartet*, current projects include a dark psychological thriller, *Bloody Mary*, a feature film based on the eponymous urban legend; and *Saint Sinner*, a made-for-television movie for the Sci Fi Channel. A motion picture adaptation of *The Damnation Game* is in its initial stages with Phoenix Pictures and Warner Brothers; *The Thief of Always*, based on a script by Bernard Rose as revised by Matthew Jacobs, remains actively in development with Barker as executive producer; and the long-awaited adaptation of *Weaveworld* as a six-hour television mini-series, based on a script by Michael Marshall Smith as revised by Peter Lenkov, is still pending at Showtime.[4]

Clive's imaginative exercises in Tinseltown were not limited to film and television. In 1998, he was offered a truly pleasurable diversion: the opportunity to create a Halloween maze for the Universal Studios Hollywood theme park. *Clive Barker's Freakz*, which opened for the month of October 1998, resembled a mad mingling of performance art and theatre, with thirty-five actors loosed in a labyrinth of more than a dozen rooms with differing gloulish themes; it was succeeded, in 1999, by a new maze called *Clive Barker's Hell*.

Although he is a self-confessed 'technophobe', Clive is enamoured of the possibilities of storytelling in videogames, the internet and other new media. (If it wasn't already obvious, his words confirm a singular truth about his life: 'I'm a storyteller. I've moved from theatre to books to movies to paintings. I'm always interested in finding new ways to tell stories.') Early in the 1990s, a computer game was derived from the motion picture *Nightbreed*, but without his direct participation; his own first tentative step into the realm of electronic gaming, *Ecto-sphere*, was ultimately abandoned by Virgin Interactive after years in development. In 2001, however, Electronic Arts/DreamWorks Inter-active released *Clive Barker's Undying*, a highly successful computer role-playing game that Clive guided personally throughout the design process. Set in Ireland during the 1920s, *Undying* is a first-person, and quite novelistic, interactive 'shooter' that puts players in the role of Patrick Galloway, a mage who, while wielding weapons in his left hand and magic spells in his right, is dispatched on an arcane quest to unravel the mysteries of the cursed Covenant family.

Clive also conceived a next generation internet entertainment com-plex to be known as *Primordium*. This enterprise, which erupted from his subconscious in the midst of his many wearying meetings with studio representatives about *The Abarat Quartet*, truly exemplifies his relentless urge to create.

'The way my mind works is bizarrely free of intellectual effort,' he says. 'I found this word, primordium, which I loved. I was going to use the title for *American Horror*, but it didn't apply. Then I thought, *Damn, you know . . . this is a website*. What do I like describing most? I like describing alien cities. So I wanted an alien city – a website that would be a repository, an archive, of everything I have created.'

He approached Joe Roth, a former executive at Twentieth Century-Fox and Disney, and suddenly found himself embroiled in another complex project – one that ultimately would founder, but whose pur-suit typifies the boundless ambition, and the quest for the new, that drives – and sometimes haunts – Clive Barker. 'One part of me is saying, *This is foolishness*. But another part is saying, *To be continually engaged, to be continually excited about getting up in the morning, I need to feel like I'm pushing onto new ground . . . and this is new ground.*

'My best hope for another thirty years of creation is to continue to surprise myself. If I can continue to find forms and shapes and stories and ideas and challenges that have not been in my head, that I allow to grow organically, as the paintings have – or that come very quickly, like *Primordium* – then I think I've probably got another thirty years of creation in me.

'The seeds of that are in all those relationships years ago at school, with Phil Rimmer and Doug Bradley and Pete Atkins and all of these incredibly smart, curious people. Because somewhere in my head and somewhere in my heart is the idea that it's all possible; and it's never gone away.

'I like Cocteau's art; but what I like most is the *idea* of Jean Cocteau. That's what's important to me: the idea of a man who can do all these things, and who does them without, as it were, looking over his shoulder – and just moves on and moves on and moves on. When I look back over my shoulder, I don't like the work, so it's onward, onward, it'll be better next time. But also there's the sense that there's still this thing I can't do, which is the man changing into the fox – this magic thing that I can't do. Which I'm willing to accept, intellectually; I just never *feel* it.

'Is this a common thing? A pining, now, as an artist? Is this what all artists go through, all the time, which is worry that what they've done is just worthless crap, because it can't ever work on them the way it works on other people?

'I come to the house and sit with the paintings for a while, trying to assess their effect. Because the hardest thing for the artist is to know what they've done: *What have I done? What have I wrought? What effect does this really have?* Because you did it, you don't know.

'I've seen people come in here, and I've seen eyes fill with tears, and I've seen people dance with happiness, and I've seen grown men sit on the floor . . . but I don't know why. I feel as though some deep anxiety in me would be comforted if I could understand why. I get glimpses of it, but only glimpses; and most of the time, it's despair. Deep despair. I don't like to emphasize it too much, but I have an incredibly low opinion of what I've done – partly because of the transcendent things that people have done to me. Artists. Which, intellectually, I know I'm doing to other people sometimes; but I've never done to myself. It's just the nature of the art – I can't do it. So I sit and I try to see these things with new eyes.

'At some deep place in myself, there's a deep aching hole that's not going to get filled. The theatre work that I saw over the years – Kabuki, Lindsay Kemp, *Fantasia* – these things haunt me as things which I'm aspiring to . . . and sometimes I wish I'd seen less. Sometimes I wish I could narrow my focus on the things which moved me, because I wouldn't be aspiring to move people in the same way in so many other areas. Because I'm never going to paint *The Raft of the* Medusa; it's a painting that has broken my heart for twenty-five years.

'It's one of the reasons that music is so wonderful for me, because I have no aspirations there – or talent. Whenever I do have some talent, or desire to achieve, it's an agony, all the time.

'It's also one of the reasons I have every book I can find on Günter Grass, and every book I can find on Cocteau and Blake, because there's a sense in which I fear that I will be judged as a jack of all trades and master of none. If you judge Blake as a painter, he's not a great painter. If you judge him as a poet, I'm not even sure he's that great a poet. If you judge him as an artist, he is extraordinary. I think the same is true with Cocteau. When you step back from seventy-one years and think of what he did . . .

'The only way to judge Cocteau is to judge the man in his entirety. You need to see his capacity, the way he strove to make sense of his imagination by locking together disparate parts of it. This intercon-nectedness of media – it's my wanting to feel as though I can be judged not as an author, not as a painter, not as a film-maker, but as an imaginer. And I feel very vulnerable until such time as somebody grasps, as you have, the wholeness of it.

'History has taken its toll on me. There were so many smarter ways to have managed the career that I have. What I had ten years ago was a literary career. The way I chose, I don't regret at all, but it put pressures on me; and sometimes it makes me sad, because I don't have as many books in me as I thought I did. Maybe I'll find a new energy; but I've done twenty books, including some big ones, and I wanted there to be two more *Imajica*s in me – two more big things – and I'm going to have to struggle for one, I think. It's hard; and it all relates back to this thing about being fascinated, at an early age, with all these areas, and being the self-made guy, not in a business sense, but self-educated in these areas, unguided, untaught to a great degree. It has a lot of strengths, but actually a lot of weaknesses, too, because you do trip over yourself, over and over again – and everything seems like an adventure.

'You saw how this grew. Almost everything has been an accident. Not driven by some overweaning vision: I stumbled into all this stuff. This is the model for the chaos of something growing organically out of a passion which then will not be unseated. I get so tired that I sit and cry, but then if I don't let it out, it makes me crazy.

'I'm looking at delivering *Coldheart Canyon* and the *Abarat* books, and I've turned in the screenplay of *American Horror*, and I have so many paintings to finish. And I'm as close to out of my depth as I've ever been – not creatively, but in terms of how much energy there is in me, how many hours there are in a day. Everyone comes up here and says, *Well, when do you sleep*? It used to be a joke, and now I begin to see that it's a legitimate question.'

In this relentless, often exhausting, passion to create – and to challenge his powers of creation – Clive Barker insists on the transforming power of the imagination, and the need to charge every moment of his life with meaning and significance: 'to feel the sense of connectedness and wholeness and love that you have at the best moments of your life, at the epiphanous moments.' In his art, whether delightful or defiant, a singular drama – the drama of his life – is rehearsed: the opening of doors into new territories, which are more fertile than the territories left behind, moving forward, ever forward, in search of that place where things mean more.

As his alter ego Will Rabjohns senses in the novel *Sacrament*, staring into a boundless distance to the dream of a perfect island that is Tiree, Clive's childhood Eden:

> Forty some years on the planet, and the chill smell of sharp salt still moved him, bringing back childhood dreams of the faraway. He had long ago made these dreams a reality, of course, seen more of the world than most. But the promise of sea and horizon still caught at his heart, and tonight, with the last of the light sinking west, he knew why. They were the masks of something far more profound, those dreams of perfect islands where perfect love might be found . . . What lay across those waters, far from the comfort of this little harbor, was not just an island; it was

the possibility that his spirit's voyage would find completion, where he would come to know, perhaps, why God had seeded him with yearning.

The roots of that yearning, says Clive Barker, are clear; and can be found 'in this kid who, with a bunch of other kids, said: *'We can do it all. We can have it all.'*

APPENDIX

'THE WOOD ON THE HILL'

A CHILDREN'S STORY BY CLIVE BARKER
(CIRCA 1966)

Once upon a time in a land far from here, there grew a wood. This wood was dark and very old for it could remember the times before there were any people on earth, when the sky was always filled with fire, and there lived great birds, more terrible than I have words to tell. It could remember the years when the dragons lived in the valley, until the Great Winter came and they were all driven away by the snow. It was only a small wood then, and a little frightened by the world . . .

But, by the time I write my story, the wood had grown up, and the people had come to the valley and built cottages where once the dragons had roamed and stomped. It was content, watching the slow passing of the years. The warm summers filled with laughter, the ripe autumns, the cold winters, the springs when the snow melted and hope came again into the world. It watched the children who played in its branches grow to be strong men and graceful women, and, in their turn, have children of their own. He watched the brook grow to a stream, and thus to a rushing river. The years passed peacefully, and each day was a joy greater than the last, for the world was still waking.

Now not all that far from the wood stood a large white house with marble pillars, surrounded by tall yew trees and great gardens, all neatly set out with paths of pink gravel and fountains with cupids in the middle. This house belonged to a Duchess who owned all the land around her house, for she was very rich. It said, on a piece of paper which she always kept locked safely away in a box somewhere, that every leaf, every blade of grass, every flower, bird, animal and tree belonged to her. This pleased the Duchess greatly, because I am afraid she was not a very nice person. In fact, at times her manners were absolutely frightful, and she had a very quick temper. When she flew into a rage, which she did quite often, she would scream at the servants (she had thirty-one) until the windows rattled and the china tinkled. And sometimes, if she was particularly vexed, she would kick the furniture or the footman (whichever were nearby at the time). As if that were not bad enough, she was also exceedingly vain. Sometimes she would spend hours sitting in front of the mirror and looking at herself. I must admit that she was indeed very beautiful, but that did not make her vanity any the less dreadful.

Having told you how horrible the Duchess was at times, you might think that she has no friends. But you would be quite wrong. In fact she has lots of friends, all members of the aristocracy (which means they had lots of money and weren't quite sure what to do with it). The Duchess' friends, however, were the most hateful people you could imagine. They were either very fat because they ate too much, or very thin because they would not eat at all, in case they marred their beauty. Beauty! I may truly say that the Duchess' friends were quite the most ugly people in all the world.

Four times a year at Christmas, on her birthday in April, on Midsummer Night and at Hallowe'en, the Duchess would throw a party, and invite all her friends. Her parties were always wildly successful and were great social occasions. Why they were so successful I cannot possibly imagine, for if you or I were to have gone to one I am sure we would have hated it. All the guests ever did was stand around, talking about the war and the trouble they were having with their servants, and how awful everybody else looked and how boring everybody else's conversation was. I fancy the Duchess knew in her heart how hateful all the guests were, but still she threw her parties, because it was all she had to do.

Now one day, in late September, when the leaves were just beginning to fall in the wood, the Duchess was out riding on the hills. It was a fine, clear afternoon, and she was thinking about what colour she ought to have her new pet dove dyed. You see, she hated it being so white, because she thought it might make her look less beautiful.

The Duchess was so deep in thought, that she rode further from the house than she had ever ridden before, and the servants were just about to pluck up enough courage to tell her, when, quite suddenly, they found themselves at the foot of the hill whereon grew the wood that I told you about. The Duchess had never seen the wood before, and, calling to her servants to help her dismount, she demanded that she be taken to it. At this the servants muttered to each other under their breath, but they feared the Duchess too much to disobey. So Michael, the oldest one, bowing low, said:

'As Your Grace commands,' and led the way up the hill. The other servants followed some way behind, but finding the Duchess too concerned with the wood to notice their tarrying, they halted half-way up and stood, watching in silence.

The evening was drawing on now, and the wood stood quiet and beautiful, a thousand shades of gold and red. When Michael and the Duchess reached the top of the hill they found that the wind was quite strong, murmuring through the trees and blowing dead leaves about. The Duchess stood for a moment on the edge of the wood, thinking. Then suddenly, she turned to Michael:

'This wood!' she cried, shattering the stillness, 'I shall hold my next party here. It will be a Hallowe'en party, such as none have ever seen before, and I shall invite everybody.'

Michael was silent.

'What is it – you miserable old owl?' the Duchess cried. 'Is it not a brilliant idea? Everybody else throws their parties in their Grand Halls – oh but not I! No indeed! I shall throw my party here – in the wood on the hill. It will be the greatest celebration the crowd has ever seen!'

'But your Grace–' stammered poor old Michael, suddenly frightened, not by the Duchess, but by something much more terrible, ' – you can't!'

'Can't?' cried the Duchess.

'Can't??' screamed the Duchess.

'Can't???' exploded the Duchess.

'Why can't I?'

'Well . . .' the old man halted, 'well . . . because . . .'

'What?'

'It's haunted, m'am.'

'Haunted?' the Duchess said quietly, her anger suddenly gone.

'Haunted?' repeated the Duchess slowly, and looked at the wood through her spectacles, as if she were looking for the ghosts.

'Really?' she said after a moment. 'Haunted, eh? How quaint!' (Which was a very silly thing to say, but then again, as I have explained, she was a very silly Duchess.)

'How quaint!' she said again, 'ha! I do . . . er . . . so love . . . er . . . these peasant superstitions.'

Michael shook his head sadly. But the Duchess wasn't looking. She was far too busy talking to herself and making plans.

'It will be the social event of the decade,' she said excitedly. 'Everybody who is anybody will be there. And it's all so original. Nobody has ever had a ball in the middle of a wood before. I shall be the toast of society for absolutely ages. Oh, why am I so clever? It just isn't fair on the rest of the world!'

She turned to Michael.

'Find the best woodcutters in the country, do you understand?'

'Woodcutters, Your Grace?'

'Yes fool. I want a large clearing cut in the middle of the wood . . .'

'What?' cried Michael, his eyes wild with anger and fear, 'you're planning to chop down part of the wood?'

'Of course, replied the Duchess, 'I'm not going to have my guests dangling from the branches like apes!'

'But you can't! You mustn't. The wood isn't yours.'

'Isn't mine?' the Duchess laughed. 'Of course it's mine. I own all this.'

'Yes,' said Michael slowly, 'you own it all as far as lawyers and pieces of parchment are concerned . . . But –'

'But what?'

'Oh, Your Grace, the wood isn't – yours. I mean, it is yours legally – but there are others . . .'

'Who?' snapped he Duchess.

'Just others,' the old man replied, avoiding the Duchess' eyes, his hands shaking with fear.

'You're speaking nonsense, you old bat. You're mad.'

'Very well then, Your Grace, I am mad. But still –'

'Still nothing. You will do as I say or I'll have you hanged for your silly ramblings.'

Michael had no choice but to nod meekly. Well, he thought to himself, what more can I do? It is foolish to meddle with such things, but I can do nothing. What happens now is not my fault.

Then the sun slipped behind the horizon, and darkness fell. Suddenly, the beautiful trees became strangely menacing in the half-light, looming grey and huge above the Duchess and the bowed figure of Michael. The night was upon them, and they were far from home.

'Come –,' said the Duchess hurriedly, for she was a little unnerved by this strange transformation. 'Let us return.'

As they walked down the hill Michael smiled a little to himself. Not a happy smile, you understand, but a resigned smile of one who knows what is about to happen, and who also knows that he may do nothing about it.

Even if the Duchess was vain, she was certainly no coward, and once she had an idea in her head she flatly refused to let it go. So, although she still had a few lingering doubts about the woods, she was nevertheless resolved to throw her party there. She had long since convinced herself that there was nothing to fear. Well, nothing a bonfire and an orchestra would not cure. Thus, the preparations began.

Invitations were sent to all the neighbouring lands, with:

THE DUCHESS

REQUESTS THE PLEASURE OF YOUR COMPANY

AT A GRAND HALLOWE'EN BALL

IN THE WOOD ON THE HILL

ON OCTOBER 31ST

R.S.V.P.

written on them in the finest copper-plate.

Meanwhile, in the woods, the clearing was being made, the bonfire piled up, the tables set out, the entertainers rehearsed and a thousand and one other arrangements made. All kinds of people, each with his or her separate task, and each believing that their job was the most important, and that they were working the hardest.

Hallowe'en grew nearer. In the house the Duchess was busy picking off names on her guest list and ordering wine and food. One morning, about a week before Hallowe'en, the old sorcerer who had been ordered to make the fireworks arrived with his creations, arms full of brightly-coloured squibs and rockets and ripraps and Catherinewheels and Roman candles and dragon-flames and snow-flowers and some that even he had not got a name for, because he didn't know what they would do. When he heard where the Duchess was planning to hold her party, however, he became most upset.

'The woods?' he exclaimed in alarm, dropping the fireworks everywhere, 'but that is forbidden!'

'By whom?' the Duchess demanded angrily. 'Who forbids it?'

'They do. Those who own it. It is most foolish to hold your party there. It will be a failure!'

At this the Duchess flew into a rage. How dare this tatty old magician suggest one of her parties might be a failure! The arrogance of the fellow!

'Old man!' she screamed, 'I suggest you take that remark back. I have but to snap my fingers and you will die.'

'Oh,' said the sorcerer, undisturbed by the Duchess' tantrums.

'Cower in fear, idiot! I threaten you with a death so horrible that men will talk of it a hundred years hence! I repeat myself – take that remark back!'

'Shan't,' said the sorcerer, and yawned.

'Why you – Guards! Guards! Seize him!'

'I think not,' the sorcerer said calmly, and disappeared in a puff of smoke. By the time the guards arrived, therefore, the room was empty save for the Duchess, still quivering with anger and a few dead leaves that the sorcerer had left on the carpet where he had worked. But long after he had gone the Duchess could hear his soft laughing, and in the end she ordered the room to be locked up and never to be entered again.

Well after that, as you might have guessed, the Duchess began to doubt the cleverness of her plan, and regret her decision. But by that time it was far too late. All the guests had been invited. The wine, the food ordered. The masks and fireworks made. There was nothing she could do.

On the morning of October 31st the Duchess woke after a terrible nightmare in which she had been chased by something she could not see, through a forest in which the trees were as big as mountains, or else she was the size of a butterfly, one of the two. And in the dream she had met all of her friends, the ones I told you about, only they had become monstrously misshapen and horrid. First she had met Lady Boswell-Humphries, who had apparently swapped bodies with a pig because that way, she said, she could eat more. Beside her, sitting on a toadstool, was the Admiral's wife, whose head was slowly turning into a gramophone, her nose becoming the huge black horn. Further along she came upon the Archbishop, dangling from a convolvulus, and trying, so he explained, to fly. She saw the Marquis' wife too, who had become a spider during the night and was busy drinking the blood of the peasants that had become trapped in her dark web. But worst of all was the General, whom the Duchess discovered in the blackest part of that terrifying forest, trampling on beautiful white flowers and muttering 'tut-tut, terrible waste,' to himself as he did so. His head was bowed so the Duchess could not see his face until he looked up at her. But when he did the Duchess collapsed to the cold ground in a dead faint, for she saw with horror that he no longer had a face, but had instead, a grinning skull with no eyes, white in the darkness of that forest.

At that moment, the Duchess had woken from her nightmare, to find that the sun was streaming through her window and there were birds singing in the yew tree outside. The day could not have been nicer. Dismissing her nasty dream as the result of something that had disagreed with her, and making a mental note to sack the cook, she got dressed and went downstairs.

She was too excited for any breakfast, or lunch, or tea, and spent the morning making a few final adjustments to her hair and then, in the afternoon, having a long, warm bath and getting dressed. She had a beautiful gown, which had been made by a hundred seamstresses especially for the occasion. It was the colour of a silver birch, and was stitched with thread of gold. As evening approached, and the shadows lengthened, she boarded her golden coach and, with her servants riding close behind, was driven to the woods.

By the time she reached the hill the sun had almost set. The wood looked rather as it had that first day, five months ago, when she and Michael had climbed the windy hill. But now, she thought to herself, there was something different about it. It seemed, somehow, darker. She shivered for a moment, though the evening was not cold. Then, putting on her mask, which was a beautiful, intricate design of silver leaves, she made her way between the trees to the clearing, ready to receive her first guests.

Over five hundred guests had been invited to that party, and every single one of them came. Thus, by 10 o'clock the clearing was filled with people, all talking or drinking or eating or dancing or laughing or trying to do all those things at the same time. The noise was dreadful. What with the fireworks, the guests and the orchestra playing, the party must have been heard miles away.

Outside the wood, in the white moonlight, the footmen and servants and coach-drivers sat and listened to the assorted sounds of laughter and merry-making, and looked up occasionally from their card-games to catch a glimpse of the bonfire or the fireworks between the trees. The horses all seemed strangely uneasy. They shuffled and neighed and some whimpered in the way horses do. But the coach-drivers merely went on playing cards and envying their masters.

About 11:30 p.m. Mrs Fortesque fainted, probably the heat her escort said, but really because she had drunk too much. She had to be attended to by her friends and then taken home long before the party was due to finish. For long years afterwards Mrs Fortesque would talk of that night and how divine providence had seen fit to save her alone.

The party continued. The laughter became more hysterical, the music louder and more insistent. Logs were heaped on the bonfire. It crackled and roared. Case after case of champagne was opened and emptied, tray after tray of food prepared and devoured. Beneath their

Hallowe'en masks, fat faces dissolved into rolls of hysteria, disdainful faces sneered, military faces looked grim. Each played his or her part better than ever before. And above their heads, unknown to the guests, the trees were whispering to each other softly, whispering in a language as old as the world itself. Whispering of a vengeance planned.

Someone carved his initials in the trunk of an old oak. He will die, said the whisperer. Another man threw a living branch on to the blazing bonfire and smiled as it burned. He too, said the whisperer. And in the midst of her guests the Duchess laughed beneath her mask of silver leaves, and forgot all that had been told her. And the whisperers hated her the most – for she had begun it all, caused these murders, these desecrations. For her there could be no death too terrible.

The Duchess had arranged that at the stroke of midnight all lights should be extinguished (except for the bonfire of course) and that everybody should take off their masks and reveal who they were (everybody knew really, but it was still fun). So, as midnight grew near, the Duchess told the orchestra to stop playing, which they did. As soon as they stopped, of course, the talking stopped too, and all the guests turned to look at her.

'My Lords, Ladies and Gentlemen,' she began (a solitary cheer from the Admiral, who had had a little too much to drink). 'It is almost midnight' (another cheer from the Admiral; this time halted abruptly by the Admiral's wife pushing a gooseberry tart inside his mouth). 'If we are silent,' the Duchess continued, 'we shall be able to hear the striking of the church in the valley. Then, on the twelfth stroke, let us all make merry until the dawn!'

The clearing was silent except for the bonfire's cracklings. No one moved. The Admiral had fallen asleep, gooseberry tart smeared round his mouth. Then, far, far away, the bell chimed.

One . . .

Two . . .

. . . The Duchess thought something moved in the trees . . .

Three . . .

Four . . .

. . . Dark forms shifting and gathering . . .

Five . . .

Six . . .

... The sorcerer was right ...
Seven ...
Eight ...
... The woods were alive ...
Nine ...
Ten ...
... And seeking vengeance ... !
Eleven ...
 ... Twelve!

On the twelfth stroke, the woods attacked!

From out of the shadows appeared creatures forgotten since the world was young. Black, hideous creatures with eyes of fire and wings of death. Screeching, flapping monstrosities defying description.

The Duchess screamed. A great wind sprang up. The torches were blown out. In the flickering light of the bonfire the guests fled, scattered by huge claws. The wind whistled, colder than ever before, bringing back on its shrieking darknesses the dragons from the north, bringing them back to wreak a terrible vengeance ...

The tables were overturned. Screaming people ran everywhere, but there was no escape. The trees were alive! Branches became arms which tightened about men's throats, roots seemed to wrench themselves from the earth to halt the guests' hysterical flight.

For a single, terrible moment, the Duchess caught sight of the General, silhouetted against the blazing fire, crying out.

'No! Don't panic. For goodness sake don't –' Then a great claw struck him, ripping his mask off. And the Duchess saw that he really did have a skull instead of a face. Then, in madness, she fled from that place of horror. It was almost as if the wood wanted to let her go, for though she feared that at any moment a flapping monstrosity would descend from the trees upon her, none did. Thus half-weeping and half-laughing in madness, she fled from the wood into the moonlight and ran until the tormented screams were faint on the cold night wind ...

The Duchess was never seen again. And when the villagers ventured into the wood they found only the smouldering bonfire, nothing more. No – that's not quite true. They found one other thing. A mask of silver leaves, torn by huge talons, not of our world.

Some say that the Duchess still lives, an old woman now, quite mad since that unholy night. Others say that she ran away to Ireland with an officer in the Hussars, but some people would say that.

But in the valley, the villagers know, for they are free now of their masters and run in the woods as of old, and dance and sing of endless summers to come. They do not fear the woods. For they planted young trees where the old ones were cut down, thus destroying the last remains of that grim celebration, so that none should ever know of it again.

Old Michael still lives to this day, in a cottage built for him on the edge of the woods, and he is the woods' guardian. Only he remembers truly the events of that night, only he knows the fate of his proud mistress, the Duchess. Some say that what he saw turned his mind, and that now he is quite mad. But they are the unbelievers. The villagers know Old Michael is not mad, they know he speaks the truth. The dragons he mutters about are not figments of his imagination, nor are the whisperers in the trees. Old Michael knows the woods, and the woods know him. For Michael talks to the trees, especially a very beautiful silver birch that appeared, quite inexplicably, in the middle of that dark clearing. A shining silver tree, which Michael tends with great care, even in the deep winter.

And the woods will never be dark again, for each day is a joy greater than the last, and the world is at peace.

The End

NOTES

Unless otherwise noted, all conversational quotations are taken from interviews conducted by the author, as supplemented by select quotations from material contributed by Peter Atkins, Alan Jones, Stephen Jones, Angus MacKenzie and Philip Nutman.

Foreword
How can Gauguin and Goya . . . Clive Barker, 'Foreword', *Clive Barker's Nightbreed: The Making of the Film.* London: Fontana/Collins, 1990.
What did it matter . . . Clive Barker, 'In the Flesh', *Clive Barker's Books of Blood Volume Five.* London: Sphere, 1985.

Chapter 1: The Pool of Life
1. Carl G Jung, *Memories, Dreams, Reflections.* Ed. Aniela Jaffé. New York: Pantheon, 1973 (revised edition), pp197–99. Carl Gustav Jung (1875–1961), a student of Sigmund Freud, ultimately rejected Freud's teachings and developed the theory of the 'collective unconscious', stressing the importance of archetype and symbolism in psychoanalysis and art. His texts include *Psychology of the Unconscious* (1916) and *The Undiscovered Self* (1957). Beat poet Allen Ginsberg, echoing Jung, declared at the height of Beatlemania that Liverpool was 'the centre of all human consciousness'.
2. Len and Joan Barker did not believe in middle names, and each of their sons has only one given name.

Chapter 2: Oakdale Road
1. Penny Lane became so famous that, in Clive's words, 'the sign was always being nicked by Beatles' fans'. Today the street's name is simply painted on a wall near its intersection with Oakdale Road.

2. Riverside and oceanside settings would play a crucial role in Clive's fiction, perhaps most notably in the novels of 'The Art' and the deeply personal 'Chiliad: A Meditation' (1997) and *Galilee* (1998).

3. Young Clive owned several copies of *Peter Pan*, with two favourites: 'I had a copy illustrated by Mabel Lucie Atwell – actually that was *Peter Pan in Kensington Gardens* – the illustrations of which are, in retrospect, kind of sickly. I had an Arthur Rackham illustrated version, which was more to my taste – that was also *Peter Pan in Kensington Gardens*, a beautiful edition with beautiful illustrations.'

4. 'I didn't see *Peter Pan* on stage,' Clive notes, 'until the first time the Royal Shakespeare Company did it, and they did it with a man playing Peter Pan. The RSC actually did it three Christmases running, and they did it brilliantly. They took the play, the novel and Barrie's letters – and they took the stage instructions from the play, believe it or not, and folded it all into a three-hour entertainment which had JM Barrie as a character, wandering around, our guide to Never-Never Land, commenting on the characters. He was a very sad man, you know. His life was filled with all manner of undertow and strangeness, and that comes through in this adaptation.'

5. 'There was something about the authorial voice. The authorial voice in *Treasure Island* is Jim – Stevenson *is* Jim. Lewis Carroll's authorial voice is very chilly and detached. CS Lewis is far too cosy. Baum is American cosy, very avuncular, not very stylish; he never rises to poetry. Barrie's voice was *very* particular . . .

   'One of the things that readers buy is a voice. When they buy Anne [Rice], they buy Anne's voice – and Anne's voice is very lush, very sensual, very personal, very female. I think of her as writing very female books. I get into sticky territory explaining what I mean by that, but they move from emotion to emotion very freely – and they're primarily about emotion. What she's concerned with is getting to another place where somebody feels excessively about something. And they seem soft to me, in that sense. They seem like they're made of some chiffon and the innards of oysters; it's all sort of moist and wavy.

   'Steve King's voice is incredibly strong and very, very specific; and it's slightly louder than everybody else's in the bar. And he's definitely in a bar. And it's very appealing, isn't it? He wants to keep you interested – and he'll do just about anything to keep you interested.'

6. 'The fact that I had no way to interpret the event doesn't mean it went away. Indeed its power to impose itself upon my imagination may have been made all the stronger because I lacked those skills. It became, as it were, a private legend, an image drawn on the rock of my skull, from which all manner of other tales and pictures would in time be derived.' The image of a winged man – sometimes flying, sometimes falling – would recur throughout his plays, fiction, art and film.

7. The 'Civil War News' card set, totalling 88 cards, was released by Topps in 1961. The original designs for each card were sketched in pencil by Bob Powell,

and then rendered into full colour paintings by Norm Saunders, who had worked as a pulp magazine cover artist in the 1930s and 1940s. Powell and Saunders teamed up in 1962 for the more famous 'Mars Attacks' trading card set.

8. 'Movie posters contain so much of what I like,' Clive says. 'They're lurid, they're accessible, they can be great fun. They can be witty. I love hook lines – you know, *Just when you thought it was safe to go back into the* . . .

'When [Dario Argento's] *Suspiria* came out over here, one of the reviews said, *This horror movie is the way that you always imagined horror movies to be before you could get in.* I had to be first at the box office to see this movie. Because invariably, your imaginings are much better.'

9. Clive Barker, 'The Specialty of the House Introduction', *Dark Voices: The Best from The Pan Book of Horror Stories.* Ed. Stephen Jones and Clarence Paget. London: Pan, 1990.

10. Cilla Black (whose real name was Priscilla White) was a secretary at Len Barker's workplace, British Insulated Callender's Cables, before becoming Liverpool's first international pop star of the 1960s.

11. Clive Barker, 'The Painter, The Creature and The Father of Lies: An Introduction', *Incarnations: Three Plays.* London: HarperCollins, 1995.

12. *Ibid.*

Chapter 3: In a Lonely Place

1. 'The whole idea of the island – to the modern child, it's probably Disneyland, the Magic Kingdom, the place which contains every adventure you ever wanted to have. Never-Never Land is the Edwardian vision of that: there are Indians, there are crocodiles, there are secret caves, there's Skull Island, there's the pirates, and there's also an underground cave in which the lost boys live, so everything you ever needed and wanted in an adventure is there. It's a full-service magic island.'

2. 'When I came to write *Weaveworld* and I wanted Cal to arrive at a place that seemed as near as damned perfection, the only thing I wanted to write about was an orchard. So Lemuel Lo gets his orchard, and Cal spends his first night in the Weaveworld in an orchard. And that is plainly autobiographical, because it's associated powerfully with my feeling that *happiness is an orchard* – and it's not just any orchard, it's a particular orchard. But I don't think you need to know these things; the book doesn't ask to be decoded that way.

'When fantasists write idylls of various kinds – it's very clear that Tolkien, when he's writing about the Shire, is writing lovingly about his neighbourhood – they're writing about a way of life, they're writing about something which they love and want to see preserved.

'I think this is more true of things you evoke that are pleasant than unpleasant – that I'm accessing my childhood constantly for things which are signs of something idyllic. Another case in point: the penultimate sections of *Sacrament* are set in the Hebrides, in Tiree, and part of that is because I know the place and I can describe it with some accuracy and ease, but part of it is that it's just a pleasure to tread there. If I'm going to spend three weeks of this writing process in any place, why don't I spend it in one place I know and like?'

3. *Macchair* is a Gaelic word indicating the area of common ground located between the ocean and the body of the island owned by crofters.

4. Years later, Clive would recognize this urge – the desire to become lost – in his creative life: 'there is at the heart of the pleasure I take in making images and stories a desire to be lost in the imagined world awhile; to wander mapless in a place that doesn't work by the rules of the waking world.' Clive Barker, 'Laughter, Love, and Chocolate: An Introduction', *Forms of Heaven: Three Plays*. London: HarperCollins, 1996.

5. Clive Barker, 'Private Legends: An Introduction', *The Essential Clive Barker*. London: HarperCollins, 1999.

6. 'True Love' earned Grace Kelly her first and only gold record; it was Bing Crosby's twenty-first. Recorded for the motion picture *High Society* (1956) on January 22, 1956, with the Johnny Green MGM Orchestra, the 45 rpm single hit the charts in October of that year, where it remained for twenty-two weeks, reaching as high as number three. 'A Woman in Love' was composed by Frank Loesser for the musical *Guys and Dolls* (1955), with its most well-known performance by Frank Sinatra for the film.

Chapter Four: Quarry Bank

1. In the British school system of the 1960s, students attended grammar school in five consecutive forms, each one year in length. At the conclusion of the fifth form, students would take O Level examinations, which determined whether they could proceed to the sixth form, which was divided into two years: the lower sixth and the upper sixth. In the upper sixth form, students would take A Level examinations, which determined whether and where they could attend university.

   In Clive's fourth form, Bruce Prince, who supervised and directed several school plays, was his English instructor.

2. Clive's writing was also artistic in its appearance, Russell says: 'all in nice round writing, never a mistake made, or crossed anything out – nothing. The interesting thing was he used to space his words well on the paper: it was nice to look at, as well.'

3. Neither Melville nor Chandler was taught at Quarry Bank. 'I was brought up in the English grammar school,' Clive notes, 'and in the English grammar school of the sixties, American Literature was a contradiction in terms.'

4. As Russell recalls: 'He was only a little chap, again about thirteen, and he would stand up there in the presence, and there was no nervousness, he could space himself on the school stage, and then he would hold the whole audience of parents and pupils in rapture by the total of an incredible, long speech. I can't remember the details, but just watching and listening to him being so articulate, and then taking him aside the next day and saying, *Look, I'm going to teach you how to breathe*, because he needed to take control of his breathing

to be able to speak at greater length, and be more fluent – and you could do this with him because he believed you, and when you told him something, he learned it.'

5. Morrison Hall was demolished in 1980; its site is now buried beneath a supermarket car park.

Chapter 5: The Company of Dreamers

1. Although Quarry Bank teachers were called 'Sir' and 'Miss', Norman Russell decided to drop the requirement and use Christian names. 'Unheard of in those days, and quite dangerous in some ways to cross that divide between the front of the class and the class. But we were a team, exploring together; we'd stagger out of those classes sometimes in a state of euphoria. Every one of them got three grade As at A-Level, including English – they all got an A, the lot of them, because they were so good. They came together, they cohered; they used to strike sparks off each other. You could say anything – you could say, *King Lear was a silly old man, staggering through a storm*, and just sit back and let them get on with it: *No, he wasn't . . . Yes, he was . . . Ah, but . . .* It was just like a play, watching them. You threw an idea and let them thrash it out. Whereas most classes wait politely for you to say, *What does this mean? Well, it means this and this*, and they end up sharing your view.'

2. Quarry Bank's vaguely defined 'liberal studies' curriculum had been established because students were having increasing difficulty with the A-Level examination on 'general studies', which had no formal preparation or instruction. 'If you wanted to teach liberal studies,' Clarke recalls, 'you told Pobjoy, who slotted you into the timetable, and you could tell the kids whatever you liked. Nobody ever really checked up on you.' In her course 'Mechanical Art', which was attended by Clive as well as Doug Bradley and Lynne Darnell, 'we didn't do anything for two terms except sit around gabbing and collecting old bicycles . . . We never actually produced any mechanical art, but we produced a lot of good ideas.'

3. 'The danger here,' Norman Russell observes, 'is that you say, *Oh good, everybody is doing what I want, so that I am happy, and I don't really care whether they're happy or not*. And that is probably the blasphemy against the Holy Ghost mentioned in the Bible: to say that I am so perfect, I am so right, I am so genetically predisposed to act in this way that I must be right, and everybody else who does differently, then they're wrong, which means they're damned, the lot – that's the blasphemy against the Holy Ghost.'

4. 'You can go too far with this,' Clive says, 'but whenever I go to Ireland, I remember that I have Irish blood in me, and there is this melancholy side to the Irish. There's a lot of Guinness and tears spilled on a Saturday night, you know. And I sit with my Irish friends, and we talk, and I feel, in the rhythm of their conversation and in their ease with poetry and with the fantastic, something that I completely understand – about how they will spin a yarn of ghosts and Guinness; it's just part of who they are.'

5. Scobie also notes: 'I think he was a creature of his time: a world in which

there was good rock music and good classical music, there was some jolly good literature coming out, some quite good poetry. Clive reacted well to a world that he didn't have at school, at university – where these things mattered, where modern literature and modern music could be talked about, without saying, *Oh rubbish, Picasso's faking, he's making a fool out of you.* You could actually have arguments about it with other people who actually read these books and listened to this music and could talk to you about it, so you weren't reading or listening in a vacuum.'

6. Clive Barker, 'Ramsey Campbell: An Appreciation', *1986 World Fantasy Convention Program Book*, 31 October – 2 November, 1986.

Chapter 6: Hydra Rising

1. 'One of the things I am proud of,' Clarke says. 'It was I who took it upon myself to say to Clive: *Don't go to art college, go to university.* I'm still glad that I did, although some might say that he would have been better if he'd gone to art college. But what I wish I had said was: *Go to Oxbridge.* He should have gone to King's at Cambridge ... He's done very well without it, but I think it would have saved him a lot of time and energy. He would have found his home there.'

   Speaking today, Pete Atkins feels that, by attending university, Clive unintentionally took the path that brought him fame as a writer. 'It's like Mimi Smith said to John Lennon: *The guitar's all right as a hobby, John, but you'll never make a living from it.* And Clive heard the same thing. *How many people make a living as an artist? You can't go to art school, it's ridiculous, get a degree.* In one sense he was derailed slightly. If he had gone to art school, would the writing have been something he kept up as a hobby – and would now be emerging, in the same way that now the art is emerging?'

2. 'Academe nauseates me and always has,' Clive notes. 'So I went there not caring – which is the best way to endure those kinds of things ... I hate the vivisection of literature, which is a necessary part of analysis, and I hated the idea that they took this stuff apart and they talked about the bits they understood and avoided the bits they didn't. They talked about Poe, but they didn't talk about the fact that he was in love with his fourteen-year-old sister; they talked about Whitman, but they didn't mention that he was gay.'

Chapter 7: London Calling

1. One memorable rehearsal took place as they walked along a deserted stretch of railway where someone, it was said, had hanged himself; the corpse of the suicide would appear in the short story 'Pig Blood Blues' (1984).

2. Unpublished. All quotations in the text are taken from a undated script 'in draft' provided by Clive Barker. Copyright © 2001 by Clive Barker.

3. A chapter of *The Damnation Game* called 'The Fat Man Dances' is derived from Bradley's antics as Sugarman. Because Bradley would turn Sugarman into a song-and-dance man in rehearsals, Clive wanted to write a spin-off play with that name. 'There's hardly a wasted idea,' Bradley notes. 'And it

    goes back to his eclecticism: there is hardly a moment that isn't presenting itself to Clive as potentially something very powerful.'

4. Clive's own feelings about Lamede may have been summarized in the short story 'Sex, Death and Starshine' (1984): 'Bookkeeping was his forte, and he'd used it to stay as close to the stage as he could, hating his own lack of art as much as he resented that skill in others.'

5. *The History of the Devil* was later published in *Incarnations: Three Plays*. London: HarperCollins, 1995. All quotations are taken from the first edition.

6. When Clive was preparing a promotional poster for *History of the Devil*, he showed Mary Roscoe a collection of the photographs of Joel-Peter Witkin. 'I remember Clive being drawn to a picture of a young black man whose left arm was a stump, and Clive saying it was one of the most sexy and beautiful and poetic images. And I was so shocked. I guess I had a fear of disability like most people do, yet Clive seemed able to look at things; he's never been frightened of anything. I don't mean that he would rush out and want to see someone run over by a car, just to look at it – although maybe he would, but not because he's perverse, but because I think he has no fear. The human form is of so much interest to him, in all of its extraordinary ways, whether damaged or perfect, whatever, it's all wonderful to him, magical.' He painted the young man, with angelic wings on his back; but the final poster featured a drawing of Doug Bradley as a horned, bearded devil, nude and covered with blood. Roscoe laughs: 'So when I came to type the *Books of Blood*, somewhere I knew Clive was just going to peel off layers of skin and reveal people who were filled with worms.'

7. 'In choosing this style,' Barker writes in the production notes, 'I was to some extent making a virtue of a necessity – the company for which the play was written had no money for sets or costumes – but the consequence of the choice was liberation. The play is full of extravagant scenes that I would never have dared make a part of the tale if we'd been attempting a realistic staging. A sky-ride on the Devil's back, the destruction of a Greek city, a descent from heaven – these are hopelessly expensive effects for a playwright to put into a text unless they're to be evoked with some stylized physical business and a few lines from a commentating actor. The audience then has the pleasure of co-creating the illusion with the performers; enriching the experience for both sides of the equation.'

8. The barren site is of the Devil's choosing: 'He wanted to be tried here, in this filth: in this air. Why? Bit of a puzzle, isn't it? What happens to a thing that's lived five thousand years: What's beyond the wisdom of Methuselah? Decadence: a slow descent back into the mud. I think the law looks a little insubstantial out here: I think it looks like . . . words.'

9. It was this event, and not Kyle's legal skills, that was the reason for his selection as the Devil's advocate: 'That's why you chose me, isn't it? Because I was the son of the son of a man who'd served you, and you believe in history, in what's in the blood, in the great, squalid tradition.'

10. Judge Popper instructs the invisible jurors in similar terms: 'If you want a

little guidance, for what it's worth, let me say this: He's a mixed bag. So are we all. Even the best of us. I don't think we can doubt that he's done harm. Perhaps terrible harm. But he's also been cheated and betrayed. The question is: does he deserve paradise? Do any of us, come to that? (*A long beat. He ruminates, plainly troubled.*) It's curious ... watching him these couple of days, hearing the stories ... to find a fallen angel so like ourselves. I don't find that very comforting, personally. I would have liked a little less humanity in him. But the similarity's no reason to punish him ... Is it?'

Chapter 8: Dog Days

1. *Paradise Street* was later published in *Forms of Heaven: Three Plays*. London: HarperCollins, 1996. All quotations are taken from the first edition.

2. 'For me,' Roscoe says, 'everything since has been a bit of an anticlimax; because if you start at that point, meeting that kind of intense creativity, it's very rare. And for it to be my first job, I thought it was all going to be like that. After I got out in the flow of professional work, I realized that there were very few people who had minds like Clive and the rest of them, who were interested truly in the art of making a play exciting, really probing the imagination, and at the same time getting bums on seats. We really wanted people to see it. We were not into being obscure and pretentious and élitist in any way; it was commercial all the time: *People must come and see this and love it.*'

   A few years later, Clive asked Mary to assist in typing the manuscripts of the *Books of Blood* and his early novels. 'I went off to my theatres with my typewriter and my script. I was doing *Diary of Anne Frank* during the day and typing *Weaveworld* in the evening.'

3. There is also a fine invocation of the bread-baking at the Dog Company's rehearsal space at the Earth Exchange. 'Art's hot bread,' Ben Jonson pronounces. 'It's necessary. It's not like religion. Religion's a plum: it stops mouths. And it's not truth, that's meat – It's for cannibals. But art's bread. Warm, fresh. Made with our hands, see?'

4. *Frankenstein in Love* was published in *Incarnations: Three Plays*. London: HarperCollins, 1995. All quotations are taken from the first edition.

5. Clive Barker, 'Production Notes' and 'The Painter, The Creature and The Father of Lies: An Introduction', *Incarnations: Three Plays*.

6. The Biblical reference to the earthly father of Jesus is obvious; but there is also a genealogical element to the name: Mary Shelley's doctor was named Victor, while James Whale's was named Henry.

7. She offers to reveal the atrocities to the audience by lifting the shroud that covers the impaled head: 'But no. You don't want to see the appalling sight beneath this cloth. Do you? You're not sick, like some I could mention. The author for one.'

8. Barker's stage descriptions of the monsters are particularly vivid: '*THEY ARE DRESSED IN A PATHETIC PARODY OF CIVILIZED CLOTHING. A SUIT, MAYBE A TIE EVEN, CAN BE GLIMPSED, SHITTY AND BLOODY, MINGLED WITH GANGRENED BANDAGES AND RAGS. PHYSICALLY,*

THEY FORM A CONTRAST. FOLLEZOU HAS THE FACE OF A CADAVER, WELL-PUTRIFIED. HIS FLESH IS DARK GREEN, GREY AND BROWN, WITH LIVID SORES WHERE HIS WOUNDS FESTER. MATTOS RESEMBLES A GROTESQUE FOETUS, HIS CRANIUM UNNATURALLY LARGE, PALE PINK AND ALMOST BALD.' Ibid., p180.

9. Nearby, the stage directions tell us, is a bucket marked 'Soiled Dressings'.

10. 'Bring me rot. Puerile, smiling rot. Attend me with gangrene, and spoil, and every wormy, fecal thing you can unhouse. Pollute me. Revolt me. Do your worst. Please. The blushing bride must find her blushes somewhere. Let mine be sores.'

11. In her introduction to the third edition of *Frankenstein* (1831), Shelley – unlike her fictional doctor, who rejected his creation – concluded: 'I bid my hideous progeny go forth and prosper. I have an affection for it.'

12. 'I was very clear about that,' Bradley recalls, 'and I was happy with that. It sounds like an odd thing to say – I wasn't really happy, but I was pragmatically happy, because it was very obvious that that is what had to happen. What had to be. And also, I was wanting to say to Clive, *Cut the apron strings. We're in your way. Go and do whatever.*'

Chapter 9: The Play's the Thing

1. *Crazyface* was later published in *Forms of Heaven: Three Plays*. London: Harper-Collins, 1996. All quotations are taken from the first edition.

2. Tyl Eulenspiegel, a fourteenth century peasant trickster who may be fact or fiction, has been immortalized in numerous fictions, an epic poem by Gerhart Hauptmann and a symphony by Richard Strauss.

3. *Subtle Bodies* was published in *Forms of Heaven: Three Plays*. London: Harper-Collins, 1996. All quotations are taken from the first edition.

4. Clive Barker, 'Laughter, Love and Chocolate: An Introduction', *Forms of Heaven: Three Plays*.

5. It is here that the words 'Come to Daddy', which would feature prominently in the motion picture *Hellraiser*, appear for the first time in Barker's work.

6. Barker uses nameless characters called 'Dream Technicians' to 'stage-manage' the scenes that follow. Unseen by the cast but obvious to the audience, they use lights and props to choreograph the imagery of the sinking ship and its disappearance into the ocean, the life-boat, and the departure of drowned passengers.

7. Clive Barker, 'Production Notes', *Forms of Heaven: Three Plays*.

8. *Colossus* was later published in *Incarnations: Three Plays*. London: Harper-Collins, 1995. All quotations are taken from the first edition.

9. Goya's artwork features throughout the play in direct representations, references and allusions – as to Saragossa, whose siege is a subject of *Lo desastres de la guerra*. Several characters are historical subjects of Goya portraits, and the honesty of his renderings is a matter of dialogue: 'That was his problem: too many likenesses. Some of his portraits were so true they were slanderous.' Thus the French matron Madame Delvaux complains of his portrait of the

queen: 'He had no business painting her the way she was. His job was to improve on what nature had done to her, not report it.'

Goya's influence on Clive Barker's artwork and writing is substantial. The short story 'In the Hills, the Cities' was inspired by Goya's *El coloso, o El pánico* and Barker certainly shares Goya's unflinching willingness to record what he 'sees' imaginatively.

10. *See generally* Fred Licht, *Goya in Perspective*. Englewood Cliffs, NJ: Prentice Hall, 1973.

11. Here Goya describes his famous oil *El coloso, o El pánico* ('The Colossus, or The Panic'), which depicts an immense figure seated on a gentle slope, looking back toward the sky, beneath which lie, in the middle distance, tiny villages whose inhabitants are in a state of panic.

12. This tableaux echoes Goya's *Disparate de Miedo* ('Folly of Fear'), in which soldiers face a phantom who, on closer inspection, is a manmade artifice. One of Barker's soldiers, Gregorio, reacts by voicing the words that would become famous, in quite a different context, at the climax of *Hellraiser*: 'Jesus wept'.

Chapter 10: After the Danse

1. Kirby McCauley, ed., *Dark Forces*. New York: Viking, 1980; London: Macdonald, 1980.

2. *Eg*, Charles L Grant's *Shadows* (1979–1988); *Night Visions* (1984-present); and JN Williamson's *Masques* (1984–89); Dennis Etchison's *The Cutting Edge* (1987); and my own *Prime Evil* (1988). There were more single-author collections published in the space of ten years than in the previous fifty, with major works from Ramsey Campbell, Etchison, Grant, Stephen King, David J Schow and Karl Edward Wagner, as well as the rare charms of M John Harrison's *The Ice Monkey* (1983) and Thomas Ligotti's *Songs of a Dead Dreamer* (1990).

3. Stephen King was then published in the United Kingdom by Macdonald and New English Library.

4. This previously unpublished letter is printed with the permission of its author. Copyright © 2001 by Ramsey Campbell.

5. The year 1981 alone saw the publication of King's *Cujo*, Campbell's *The Nameless*, Jack Cady's *The Well*, Russell Hoban's *Riddley Walker*, Jack Ketchum's *Off Season*, Whitley Strieber's *The Hunger*, F Paul Wilson's *The Keep* and the magnificent *Red Dragon* by Thomas Harris.

6. His perspective is exemplified by his reaction to reading *Heart of Darkness* at university: 'It's a wonderful story, but when Kurtz eventually says, *The horror, the horror*, I remember saying to my tutor, *Well, what is it? What's going on here?* And she said, *Well it represents all kinds of things. It represents man's angst* ... *you know.* I said, *Look, cut the metaphysics – what's he been up to? What is really going on here?*' And she said, *It's important, isn't it, that these things remain vague, unfixed.* And I said, *Why? What merit is there in not telling all that you know? Does Joe Conrad know something that we don't? And if so, why isn't he telling us?*

'Now everything that I know about *my* stories, I put on the page. So when something appalling happens, everything I can conceive of about the scene goes down in print. I want it to be imagined, in the reader's mind, as completely as I can imagine it. For me, the joy of horror fiction is pushing the boundaries of the imagination and saying, *Let's confront the reader with something totally off the wall. How about two cities made of people?*

'Basically I have an image in my mind, and I'm trying to make the pictures work. Those sorts of images, if they're to work, have to be imagined by me in great detail. I assist that by doing drawings along the way. I always know what these things look alike. That's important to me. It's no use, for me, saying, *And then the city lumbered over the hill, and it was made up of seventeen thousand people.* How? What were they doing? What did it really look like?'

Chapter 11: First Blood

1. Clive Barker, *Clive Barker's Books of Blood Volume One*. London: Sphere, 1984. All quotations are taken from the first edition.
2. 'Kaufman thought of the city he'd loved. Were these really its ancients, its philosophers, its creators? He had to believe it. Perhaps there were people on the surface – bureaucrats, politicians, authorities of every kind who knew this horrible secret and whose lives were dedicated to preserving these abominations, feeding them, as savages feed lamb to their gods. There was a horrible familiarity about this ritual. It rang a bell – not in Kaufman's mind, but in his deeper, older self.'
3. Quoted in Matt Roush, 'Barker vs. the King', *USA Today*, August 22, 1986; and Neil Gaiman, 'Clive Barker', *Penthouse*, May 1985.
4. Barker depicts the sow with a wry mingling of sensuality and stark terror: 'A glamorous animal in her gross way, with her curling blonde lashes and the delicate down on her shiny snout that coarsened to bristles around her lolling ears, and the oily, fetching look in her dark brown eyes ... The sow was beautiful, from her snuffling snout to the delicate corkscrew of her tail, a seductress on trotters ...

'Didn't she speak, when angered, in that possessed voice, bending her fat, porky mouth to talk with a stolen tongue? Wouldn't she stand on her back trotters sometimes, pink and imperial, and demand that the smallest boys be sent into her shadow to suckle her, naked like her farrow? And wouldn't she beat her vicious heels upon the ground, until the food they brought for her was cut into *petit* pieces and delivered into her maw between trembling finger and thumb?'
5. As Redman views this bizarre scene, Barker deftly shows how myths are made: 'Suddenly the pig took on a different aspect. In his imagination he saw her reaching up to sniff at the feet of Henessey's twitching body, sensing the death coming over it, salivating at the thought of its flesh. He saw her licking the dew that oozed from its skin as it rotted, lapping at it, nibbling daintily at first, then devouring it. It wasn't difficult to understand how the boys could have made a mythology of that atrocity: inventing hymns to it, attending upon

the pig like a god. The candles, the reverence, the intended sacrifice of Lacey: it was evidence of sickness, but it was no more strange than a thousand other customs of faith.'

6. 'They looked, to all intents and purposes, like living men and women. But then wasn't that the trick of their craft? To imitate life so well the illusion was indistinguishable from the real thing? And their new public, awaiting them in mortuaries, churchyards and chapels of rest, would appreciate that skill more than most. Who better to applaud the sham of passion and pain they would perform than the dead, who had experienced such feelings, and thrown them off at last?

   'The dead. They needed entertainment no less than the living; and they were a sorely neglected market.'

7. 'Neither dread nor horror touched them now, just an awe that rooted them to the spot. They knew this was a sight they could never hope to see again; this was the apex – after this there was only common experience. Better to stay then, though every step brought death nearer, better to stay and see the sight while it was still there to be seen. And if it killed them, this monster, then at least they would have glimpsed a miracle, known this terrible majesty for a brief moment. It seemed a fair exchange.'

8. Clive Barker, *Clive Barker's Books of Blood Volume Two*. London: Sphere, 1984. All quotations are taken from the first edition.

9. Barker describes the creatures with a surreal fervour that is reminiscent of HP Lovecraft: 'Pyramidal heads on rose coloured, classically proportioned torsos, that umbrellaed into shifting skirts of lace flesh. A headless silver beauty whose six mother of pearl arms sprouted in a circle from around its purring, pulsating mouth. A creature like a ripple on a fast-running stream, constant but moving, giving out a sweet and even tone. Creatures too fantastic to be real, too real to be disbelieved; angels of the hearth and threshold. One had a head, moving back and forth on a gossamer neck, like some preposterous weather-vane, blue as the early night sky and shot with a dozen eyes like so many suns. Another father, with a body like a fan, opening and closing in his excitement, his orange flesh flushing deeper as the boy's voice was heard again.'

10. 'The creatures who were his fathers were also men's fathers: and the marriage of semen in Lucy's body was the same mix that made the first males. Women had always existed: they had lived, a species to themselves, with the demons. But they had wanted playmates: and together they had made men.

    'What an error, what a cataclysmic miscalculation. Within mere eons, the worst rooted out the best; the women were made slaves, the demons killed or driven underground, leaving only a few pockets of survivors to tempt again that first experiment, and make men, like Aaron, who would be wiser to their histories.'

11. Edgar Allan Poe's 'The Murders in the Rue Morgue' first appeared in the April 1841 issue of *Graham's Magazine*. In its text, Poe created the classic template of the detective story: an eccentric amateur criminologist, a dedicated assistant, an apparently insoluble crime, the wrongly accused person, the

locked room, and the surprising solution. C Auguste Dupin was the first modern fictional detective, and Poe's groundbreaking work left other writers, in the words of Sir Arthur Conan Doyle, the creator of Sherlock Holmes, 'with no fresh ground they can confidently call their own'.

12. Clive Barker, *Clive Barker's Books of Blood Volume Three*. London: Sphere, 1984. All quotations are taken from the first edition.

13. In 1985, Barker visited Hollywood, where he met with several motion picture producers, pitching them stories from the *Books of Blood*, including 'Dread' and 'Son of Celluloid'. The latter story provoked adverse reactions when he described it as 'a story about a cancer that does impersonations of movie stars'.

14. One of Clive's favourite films, Lucio Fulci's delirious *Zombi 2* ('Zombie'/ 'Zombie Flesheaters') (1979), is centred on the travails of two couples trapped on an island populated by zombies. The imagery of zombie soldiers living underwater was explored in Ken Wiederhorn's *Shock Waves* ('Death Corps') (1977) and Jean Rollin's *Le Lac des Morts-Vivants* ('Zombie Lake') (1979).

15. The word 'scapegoat' derives from the Biblical ceremony for Yom Kippur, in which the sins of the people would be placed symbolically on a goat, which was then sent into the wilderness. See *Leviticus* 16:8. Although Clive Barker's fiction rarely intersects directly with that of Stephen King, 'Scape-Goats' is a fine bookend to King's 'The Raft' (*Gallery*, November 1982; reprinted in *Skeleton Crew*, 1985), in which four students, stranded on a wooden float in a remote lake, succumb to assimilation by a carnivorous patch in the water. For King, the raft symbolized the youths' unconscious resistance to adulthood, while for Barker, the island is truly one of lost souls.

16. 'It was a statue, carved in the shape of a sleeping figure, only its head, instead of being tucked up tight, was cranked round to stare up out of the blur of sediment towards the surface. Its eyes were painted open, two crude blobs on a roughly carved face; its mouth was a slash, its ears ridiculous handles on its bald head. It was naked: its anatomy no better realized than its features: the work of an apprentice sculptor.'

17. Clive Barker's debut was so effective that some people speculated that the *Books of Blood* were the pseudonymous works of an established writer who sought to test the limits of the form. Thus, despite vast stylistic differences, Ramsey Campbell was approached by someone who was convinced that he was Clive Barker.

18. Writing several years later, Stephen King would offer a more detailed and insightful assessment of Clive's fiction:

> [A]lthough the stories in the *Books of Blood* are fantasies, Barker also tells the truth, and tells it with complete ecstatic savagery that is not grace in its hacking urgent falling-downstairs progress but becomes grace by the force of his personality and vision. He does not breathe grace into these stories; he beats it into them ... [H]e is observant, witty, satiric, and possessed of a clear moral vision – which is only to say he finds the truth

inside the lies . . . Barker's tales, both surreal and naturalistic at the same time, represent horror fiction at its best. Which is also its worst: nasty, insane, brutal, breathtaking, allegorical, assymetrical, deeply revolting and deeply challenging.

Stephen King, 'Introduction; You Are Here Because You Want the Real Thing', *Clive Barker's Shadows in Eden*. Ed. Stephen Jones. Lancaster, PA: Underwood-Miller, 1991.

Chapter 12: Nowhere Land

1. 'This was back in '85,' Clive notes, 'and while those walls are not rubble by any means, there are certainly substantial holes between the genre now, and you can pass to and fro without so much editorial questioning. I like to think I'm to some extent responsible for voicing the opinion that these things are interconnected and perhaps even interdependent.

   'Even relatively benign fantasies – CS Lewis, Tolkien – have large horrific elements in them; and horror, by and large, has some fantastical conceit wrapped up somewhere, unless you're talking about the psycho-on-the-loose kind of horror. The Red Death does come to Prince Prospero's castle. The dead do rise. Those are fantastical conceits, and I have tried to voice the opinion that these generic divisions are artificial and actually stultifying – convenient for publishers and inconvenient for readers and writers.

   'I was not in a place at that time to voice that opinion; I don't think anyone could have formulated it. So I simply backed down.'
2. Clive Barker, *The Damnation Game*. London: Weidenfeld & Nicolson, 1985. The novel was not published in the United States until 1987, when Putnam/Ace released its hardcover edition. All quotations are taken from the first edition.
3. Clive Barker, 'The Tragical History of Dr Faustus', *Horror: 100 Best Books*. Ed. Stephen Jones and Kim Newman. London: Xanadu, 1988.
4. The earliest printed edition of the play is *The Tragicall History of D Faustus*, which was published in 1604, eleven years after Marlowe was stabbed to death in a tavern quarrel. A different text, *The Tragicall History of the Life and Death of Doctor Faustus*, was published in 1611. Most modern editions are based upon the latter text but include passages from the 1604 edition that were censored from the 1611 version as blasphemous.
5. Clive Barker, 'The Tragical History of Dr Faustus'.
6. Quoted in the 'Introduction' to the Sylvan Barnet edition, *Doctor Faustus*. New York: Signet, 1969.
7. Clive Barker, 'The Tragical History of Dr Faustus'.
8. Indeed, the rough-and-ready, yet curiously fragile, Strauss is a wounded everyman who echoes the heroes of the novels of James Herbert. Barker's decision to use such a protagonist seems a clear concession to Sphere's insistence that his first novel fulfil audience preconceptions of horror.
9. 'After the war, when they started rebuilding Europe, he used to say there were no *real* Europeans left – they'd all been wiped out by one holocaust or another

– and he was the last of the line . . . Was that what made him European? To want to have his story told once more, passed down the line to another eager listener who would, in his time, disregard its lesson and repeat his own suffering? Ah, how he loved tradition.'

10. There is black comedy in the depiction of Breer as a zombie who does not realize his nature; but there is also exquisite tragedy: 'You cut up a thing that's alive and beautiful to find out how it's alive and why it's beautiful and before you know it, it's neither of those things, and you're standing there with blood on your faces and tears in your sight and only the terrible ache of guilt to show for it.'

11. Hell, as Carys senses – and Barker stresses constantly in his fiction – is a void: 'It was a legendary Nowhere, beside which every other dark was blindingly bright, every other despair she had endured a mere flirtation with the pit, not the pit itself.' Here, in the antithesis of creation, is the true meaning of damnation: 'He had felt, perhaps for the first time in his life, that his soul – a notion he had hitherto rejected as Christian flim-flam – had been threatened. What he meant by the word he wasn't certain; not, he suspected, what the Pope meant. But some part of him more essential than limb or life had almost been eclipsed, and Mamoulian had been responsible.'

12. 'In an earlier age Pandemonium – the first city of Hell – stood on a laval mountain while lightning tore the clouds above it and beacons burned on its walls to summon the fallen angels. Now, such spectacle belongs to Hollywood. Hell stands transposed. No lightning, no pits of fire.

'In a wasteland a few hundred yards from a motorway fly-over it finds a new incarnation: shabby, degenerate, forsaken. But here, where fumes thicken the atmosphere, minor terrors take on a new brutality. Heaven, by night, would have all the configurations of Hell. No less the Orpheus – hereafter called Pandemonium – Hotel.'

13. *Zombie Flesh Eaters*, known in the United States as *Zombie*, is the British title for *Zombi 2* (1980), Lucio Fulci's deliriously violent, unauthorized sequel to George A Romero's *Dawn of the Dead* (1979).

Chapter 13: The New Flesh

1. Clive Barker, 'Introduction', *Night Visions 4*. Arlington Heights, IL: Dark Harvest, 1986. The horror story, he argues, offers 'the truth of our condition in a way that is palatable, and honest, even in its fictional excesses. After all, we are born into a state of anxiety. *Born*, note; not made. Just as we are surely sexual from our first breath (because physical), so we are afraid (because vulnerable). It makes sense therefore that stories which dramatize our confrontation as spirits with the brutal business of physicality, and – at their best – seek to discover a pattern in our defeats and triumphs, should be of enduring interest.

'Stories of the body: the doomed machine in which we awaken, prone to the frailties of age and corruptions of disease. Stories of the mind: a system striving for reason and balance while the ape and the lizard we were – and, in our coils, still *are* – sink through its darker places. Stories of God and the Devil: the actors we have cast to play our moralities out. Stories heroic or absurd; epic or elegiac: but all, in their different ways, touching upon the fears that we live with day by day.'

2. Clive Barker, 'Stephen King: Surviving the Ride', *Fantasy Review*, no. 87, January, 1986.

3. He is not surprised, however, by the contempt with which the fiction of horror is often treated: 'The function these stories serve is too *raw*. It requires an admission of vulnerability in the experience; a willingness to confess to night-mares, in a culture that increasingly parades banality as feeling, and indiffer-ence as proof of sophistication ... We spend our working days making traps; stories that will corner the reader into confronting, in fictional form, experi-ences most of humanity spends its time assiduously avoiding.' Clive Barker, 'Introduction', *Night Visions 4*.

4. Clive Barker, *Clive Barker's Books of Blood Volume Four*. London: Sphere, 1985. All quotations are taken from the first edition. When Volume Four was published in the United States, it was retitled *The Inhuman Condition* (New York: Poseidon, 1986), and the order of the stories was rearranged 'to shift the tone of the book'.

5. It is nevertheless a unique case for the Freudian Jeudwine: 'Hands as symbols of paternal power, he said, were not common. Usually the penis predominated in his patients' dreams, he explained, to which Charlie had replied that hands had always seemed far more important than private parts. After all, they could change the world, couldn't they?'

6. Barker acknowledges Herbert's *The Rats* (1974) and *Lair* (1979) with references to stories of migrant rat-packs that devour anything in their path, and even offers a nod to the killer crustacean novels of Guy N Smith by describing the army of hands 'massed liked crabs'.

7. The 'Blind Boy' is Cupid, from Shakespeare's *A Midsummer Night's Dream* (circa 1596): 'Love looks not with the eyes but with the mind . . .'

8. Desire is inescapable: 'On advertising hoardings and cinema billboards, in shop-windows, on television screens: everywhere, the body as merchandise. Where flesh was not being used to market artifacts of steel and stone, those artifacts were taking on its properties. Automobiles passed him by with every voluptuous attribute but breath: their sinuous body-work gleamed, their interiors invited, plushly; the buildings beleaguered him with sexual puns. Spires; passageways; shadowed plazas with white-water fountains. Beneath the raptures of the shallow – the thousand trivial distractions he encountered in every street and square – he sensed the ripe life of the body informing every particular.'

9. Quoted in Brandon Jüdell, 'Devil Doll', *10 Percent*, April 1995.

10. Clive Barker, *Clive Barker's Books of Blood Volume Five*. London: Sphere, 1985. All quotations are taken from the first edition. When the fifth volume of the *Books of Blood* was retitled *In the Flesh* for publication in the United States (New York: Poseidon, 1987), the order of its stories was rearranged so that the title novelette would precede 'The Forbidden'.

11. 'Garvey liked the Pools with its adjuncts, the uniformity of the design, the banality of the decorations. Unlike many, he found institutions reassuring: hospitals, schools, even prisons. They smacked of social order; they soothed that part of him fearful of chaos. Better a world too organized than one not organized enough.'

12. From the bottom of one pool stares the design of a bright fish-eye, later brought to life in the novel *Everville* (1994).

13. 'Babel's Children' is a fine example of an idea that Clive had written down and saved, awaiting its time. The central premise – about a group of oldtimers who rule the world by giving their judgments to the apparent leaders – took on life when a friend told him about her visit to a Greek island.

14. Clive Barker, *Clive Barker's Books of Blood Volume Six*. London: Sphere, 1985. All quotations are taken from the first edition. The sixth volume of the *Books of Blood* was not published in the United States until 1988, when most of its stories were included in *Cabal* (New York: Poseidon, 1988), which also featured the first American publication of the novel of the same name.

15. 'The crypt was a charnel-house. Bodies had been thrown in heaps on every side; entire families pressed into niches that were designed to hold a single casket, dozens more left where hasty and careless hands had tossed them. The scene – though absolutely still – was rife with panic. It was there in the faces that stared from the piles of dead: mouths wide in silent protest, sockets in which eyes had withered gaping in shock at such treatment. It was there too in the way the system of burial had degenerated from the ordered arrangement of caskets at the far end of the crypt to the haphazard piling of crudely made coffins, their wood unplanned, their lids unmarked but for a scrawled cross, and thence – finally – to this hurried heaping of unhoused carcasses, all concern for dignity, perhaps even for the rites of passage, forgotten in the rising hysteria.'

16. 'The removal men had opened the door and found Death waiting on the other side, eager for daylight. She was its agent, and it – in its wisdom – had granted her immunity; had given her strength and a dreamy rapture; had taken her fear away. She, in return, had spread its word, and there was no undoing those labours; not now. All the dozens, maybe hundreds, of people whom she'd contaminated in the last few days would have gone back to their families and friends, to the work place and their places of recreation, and spread the word yet further. They would have passed its fatal promise to their children as they tucked them into bed, and to their mates in the act of love. Priests had no doubt given it with Communion; shopkeepers with change of a five-pound note.'

This essential element of 'The Life of Death' was evoked in Michele Soavi's motion picture *La Chiesa* ('The Church') (1991).

17. Civilization has decimated the once-great tribe to a scattered few: 'The forest in which they had prospered for generations was being levelled and burned; eight-lane highways were speeding through their hunting grounds. All they held sacred – the wilderness and their place in its system – was being trampled and trespassed: they were exiles in their own land. But still they declined to

pay homage to their new masters, despite the rifles they brought. Only death would convince them . . .'

18. In keeping with Poseidon's misguided effort to ignore the existence of the original three *Books of Blood*, the American edition of Volume Six, retitled *Cabal*, deleted 'The Book of Blood (a postscript): On Jerusalem Street', which obviously was intended to conclude the story cycle.

Chapter 14: Into the Abyss

I am indebted to George Pavlou for his informative interview – the only one he has given on the subject of *Underworld* – and for providing me with scripts and other production materials. I also wish to thank Philip Nutman, whose set report, 'Gangsters vs. Mutants', offers a contemporaneous account of the film's production; and Stephen Jones, who provided additional background information.

1. A brief but useful history of Hammer Films is presented in *The House of Horror*. Ed. Allen Eyles, Robert Adkinson and Nicholas Fry. London: Lorrimer, 1973; revised 1981.

2. Quoted in Philip Nutman, 'Gangsters vs. Mutants', *Fangoria*, no. 50, January 1986.

3. During principal photography, Barker summarized his hopes for the film: 'The thing about *fantastique* fiction is that it makes flesh of metaphor. I hope with *Underworld* to embody that: here are people whose dreams are made flesh and are suffering for it. But we, the audience, desperately want them to survive because they teach us about ourselves – our dreams and hopes. Unfortunately, this subtext has been pared down due to the budget.' *Ibid.*

4. Although Barker would state in interviews that only seven lines of his dialogue survived, this was clearly an exaggeration intended to distance him from the final film. *Eg*, Clive Barker and Dennis Etchison, 'A Little Bit of Hamlet', *Clive Barker's Shadows in Eden*. Ed. Stephen Jones. Lancaster, PA: Underwood-Miller, 1991.

5. Although the end credits of the motion picture mention a soundtrack album by Freur on CBS Records, none was released. Vocalist/guitarist Karl Hyde and keyboardist Richard Smith have since found greater success as Underworld, and their music was featured in the motion picture *Trainspotting* (1996).

6. In David Cronenberg's *The Brood* (1979), a mad psychotherapist encourages his patients to offer up 'the shape of rage', developing boils, welts and other physical manifestations of their emotional pain – until one patient's rage gives birth to a bevy of inhuman children who exact murderous revenge against her loved ones. In *Scanners* (1981), an experimental medication taken during pregnancy creates a 'breed' of telepathic and telekinetic 'scanners' whom a scientist seeks to find and control.

7. Quoted in Philip Nutman, 'Gangsters vs. Mutants'.

Chapter 15: Raw Celluloid

I am again indebted to George Pavlou for agreeing to an interview – the only one he has given on the subject of *Rawhead Rex* – and for access to scripts and production materials; and to Alan Jones, who wrote the only comprehensive set report on the filming of *Rawhead Rex*.

1. Clive Barker, *Clive Barker's Books of Blood Volume Three*. London: Sphere, 1984. All quotations from 'Rawhead Rex' are taken from the first edition.
2. Quoted in Alan Jones, 'Blood and Cheap Thrills', *Cinefantastique*, vol. 17 no. 2, March 1987.
3. The inexperienced Heinrich von Schellendorf caused several memorable incidents during the shooting of the film, including a battle scene in which, on the first take, he refused to throw a stuntman. When Pavlou called for cut, and asked what happened, von Buneau announced that he was 'afraid he would hurt him'.
4. Pavlou comments: 'Why do we see the monster too much? Well, if you've written whole scenes around the monster, and describing the monster's feelings and the monster's thoughts, you're not left with much of a scene, are you? And that was one of the basic problems with *Rawhead Rex*: Clive had spent too much time focusing on the creature. So you had to film the creature . . .

   'It would have been helpful if the producers had flown him out to Ireland, as you would with a scriptwriter on a film of that scale – and for me, someone who I really felt was part of our team. I knew I was dealing with someone who had a very special kind of vision. If he was there, and available, he could have seen those problems, and perhaps have rewritten the scene differently. But that didn't happen. And I certainly didn't have the time to sit down and start rewriting his script.'
5. Kevin Attew, quoted in Alan Jones, 'Blood and Cheap Thrills'.
6. An example of a low budget film that cleverly places the viewer into the mind of its creature is Sam Fuller's *White Dog* (1982).
7. A more ambitious visual adaptation of 'Rawhead Rex' was planned in comic book form by Stephen R Bissette and Rick Veitch. A comic book adaptation by other hands finally appeared in 1993 from Eclipse Comics.
8. Pavlou also realized that he was being used as a pawn, with Green Man announcing 'that I was going to direct another episode in the Clive Barker series', while its true intent was to sell the rights to Barker's stories to other potential producers.

Chapter 16: Secret Lives

1. Unpublished. All quotations in the text are taken from a 1983 script 'in draft' provided by Clive Barker. Copyright © 2001 by Clive Barker.
2. Given the nature of the play, one wonders whether Clive Barker's name would have been featured even if he then had the notoriety that he would soon achieve. That same year, the producers of *Stand By Me*, the motion picture adaptation of Stephen King's short novel 'The Body', assiduously avoided invoking King's name lest the film be identified with the pejorative 'horror'.
3. Barker's script identifies another source – said to be a true story, although it is apocryphal:

   > In the early sixties Mel Blanc, the voice of Warner Brothers' most popular characters – Bugs, Porky Pig, Daffy Duck, etc. – was in an automobile

accident. A triple fracture of his skull resulted, and a coma so profound nothing stirred him. Every day his doctor asked Blanc, 'Hey, how are you Mel?': no joy. His wife and son, constantly in attendance, also failed to wake him.

Then the doctor tried another question: 'Hey *Bugs Bunny*, how are you?' Out of his coma Blanc replied, *in the rabbit's voice*: 'Just fine Doc. How are you?' The coma lifted and Blanc made a complete recovery.

4. Clive Barker, 'Laughter, Love and Chocolate: An Introduction', *Forms of Heaven: Three Plays*. London: HarperCollins, 1996.
5. Stories of the splintered psyche are a grand tradition in horror fiction and film, from Mary Shelley's masterwork to Robert Louis Stevenson's *The Strange Case of Dr Jekyll and Mr Hyde* (1886), and, more recently, Stephen King's *The Dark Half* (1988) and Peter Straub's *Mr X* (1999). Clive Barker explored these themes in his play *Frankenstein in Love* and in several stories of the *Books of Blood*.
6. Irving Wardle, 'A Disgraceful Cartoon Comedy', *London Times*, 16 October 1986.
7. Bradley clearly enjoyed the role of the Rabbit: 'It was so much fun, partly because we used the convention of Bugs being a constant shape-changer, so I did a little bit of Groucho Marx, and Vivien Leigh in *Gone with the Wind*, you know, you want to become somebody else, become somebody else, and everyone believes you become that person because it's as easy as that in the cartoons.'
8. 'Just who the fuck does this guy think he is?' says Doug Bradley, mimicking the critical backlash with the sublime skill of a talented actor. '*He's a best selling horror writer, he's directing a feature film, and he wants a comedy in the West End*? So I think there was an element of: *Fuck he will.*'
9. At the request of editor Michael Dirda, I was privileged to write the first review of Clive Barker's fiction for the *Washington Post*. *See* Douglas E Winter, 'Clive Barker: Britain's New Master of Horror', *Washington Post Book World*, 24 August 1986.
10. To give Barbara Boote her due, she was not entirely wrong. Clive's ambition in film-making was strong at the time, although it would be tempered by a crushing confrontation with Hollywood's culture of compromise.
11. Quoted in Stanley Wiater, 'Charles L Grant', *Fangoria*, no. 65, July 1987.
12. Dean R Koontz, 'Introduction', *Night Visions 6*. Arlington Heights, IL: Dark Harvest, 1988.

Chapter 17: Hellbound

1. Quoted in Robin Eggar, 'L'Enfant Horrible', *Sunday Express Colour Supplement*, London, 1 February 1987.
2. Arlington Heights, IL: Dark Harvest, 1986. Each volume of the *Night Visions* series presented original fiction by three different writers, introduced by another writer or critic. *Night Visions 3* was introduced by George RR Martin

and included, along with *The Hellbound Heart*, short stories by Ramsey Campbell and Lisa Tuttle. Barker later wrote the introduction for *Night Visions 4*.

3. New York: Berkley, 1988. *Night Visions 3* was published in the United Kingdom
under the title *Night Visions*. London: Gollancz, 1987.

4. London: Fontana, 1991; New York: HarperPaperbacks, 1991. The novel's original rendition in *Night Visions 3* was marred by typographic errors; for example,
part of the second sentence, which should read 'the riddle was this – that
though he'd been told', was garbled into 'the nodle was this – man though
he'd been told'. As a result, all quotations in the text are taken from the
corrected, and definitive, Fontana paperback edition, *The Hellbound Heart*.

5. The Lemarchand Configuration is later described as 'a means to break the
surface of the real'. It is not coincidence that Frank should find the puzzle
box in Germany, which is, after all, the homeland of Doctor Faustus. 'Kircher'
is German for 'churchman'.

6. The restless flight of blackbirds is crucial imagery in Barker's experimental
film *The Forbidden*; it does not appear in *Hellraiser*.

7. In traditional parlance, a 'cenobite' is a member of a religious organization
who lives in a monastic community.

8. In a novel that is unerringly vague in its other geographic descriptions, Barker's
placement of the principal action in a house on 'Lodovico Street' is noteworthy.
It was the 'Ludovico Technique' that was applied to recondition the ultraviolent droog of Anthony Burgess's meditation on free will, *A Clockwork Orange*
(1962). Is the fate of a clockwork orange – mechanized beneath the skin –
preferable to having the ability to choose? This is an essential theme explored
in *The Hellbound Heart*.

9. The tolling of the bell also causes her to think of churchgoers – 'Were they not
coming tonight? Was the hook not sufficiently baited with promises of paradise?'
It summons a far different kind of supplicant – one whose hooks are literal.

10. 'She thought of Frank's embraces; of his roughness, his hardness; of the
insistence he had brought to bear upon her. What would she not give to have
such insistence again? Perhaps it was possible. And if it were – if she could
give him the sustenance he needed – would he not be grateful? Would he not
be her pet; docile or brutal at her least whim? The thought took sleep away.
Took sanity and sorrow with it. She had been in love all this time, she realized,
and mourning for him. If it took blood to restore him to her, then blood she
would supply, and not think twice of the consequences.'

11. From this dialogue emerged the memorable promotional line for *Hellraiser*:
'He'll tear your soul apart.'

Chapter 18: Raising Hell

1. Consider, for example, the other horror films released in 1987, which, more
often than not, were sequels: New World, the distributor of *Hellraiser*, also
released *Creepshow 2* and *House 2*; other fare included *Nightmare on Elm Street
III: Dream Warriors*.

2. Coil's music for *Hellraiser* was released by the band on its compact disc

Hellraiser Themes ('The Unreleased Themes for *Hellraiser*'), which included a fine endorsement by Barker: 'The only group I've heard on disc whose records I've taken off because they made my bowels churn.'

3. 'One of my great disappointments,' Barker says, 'is that movies that have attempted this sort of thing – *Labyrinth* and *The Dark Crystal*, for example – turned out so bland and commonplace. I would love to see one of the major studios invest in an adult film that recreated the world of your dreams in prosthetics and so on, with the same kind of detail that was lavished on *Blade Runner*. That is one of my favourite movies, because it invents the world from word one. You step into the world of *Blade Runner* and it is only itself.'

4. During production, Clive offered me this archly understated sketch of the plot: 'It's a movie about a guy who does a deal with dark forces in order to achieve the ultimate in physical pleasure. The deal goes horribly wrong, and he gets pulled – literally – into pieces. His spirit then haunts the upper room of the house in which this happens. A short while later, his brother and the brother's wife come to the house. The wife had a short but intense affair with the deceased. When she discovers, quite by accident, that his spirit is haunting the upper room – and that feeding blood to him will bring him back from wherever the hell he's been – she begins to seduce men, bring them back to the house and murder them. With the result that she gets her lover back; but unfortunately, when he comes back, so do the creatures that claimed him in the first place – with, as they say in TV magazines, hilarious results.'

5. Quoted in Phil Edwards, 'Hair-Raiser', *Crimson Celluloid*, no. 1, 1988.

6. Kirsty's boyfriend, Steve, has been 'sent home', banished and conveniently forgotten for the remainder of the series.

7. In an uncomfortable echo of *Nightmare on Elm Street III: Dream Warriors* (1987), Tiffany is a mute madonna who does nothing but solve puzzles. Her lips are sealed against some awful childhood crime, in which Channard is soon revealed as the culprit.

8. In one scene, lightning flashes across a print by Escher, directly quoting Dario Argento's classic *Suspiria* (1977).

9. Julia wears her own skin despite the fact that the original *Hellraiser* and its source, *The Hellbound Heart*, insist that Frank could not regain his own skin, but had to seek the flesh of another person.

10. Toward the end of making *Hellbound*, Doug Bradley was resting in his dressing room, lying flat on his back (since he could not sit while in full costume and make-up). Clive entered and started discussing the finale of *Hellbound*, in which the Cenobites, including Pinhead, were killed. The conversation centred on the metaphysical and mythological consequences of the splitting of Pinhead's humanity and monstrosity – and how he might be resurrected in a third film.

A few minutes after Clive left, Bradley realized: 'That wasn't a conversation about how we resurrect Pinhead – that was Clive telling me that, if there was a *Hellraiser III*, he didn't want me there, to be in it. And if *Hellraiser III* had gone ahead straightaway, if New World hadn't collapsed and there hadn't been all that long period of political upheaval and fall-out, he might very well have done that – tried to go without Pinhead. It would have been like making a *Nightmare on Elm Street* film without Freddy Krueger. But that's Clive. That's the way his mind works.'

11. 'I was an explorer of forbidden pleasures,' Spencer intones. 'Opening the box was my final act of exploration, of discovery. I found the monster within the box. And it found the monster within me.'

12. There are rare moments of power in this Pinhead Unbound, as witness the following monologue, finely crafted by Peter Atkins and pronounced by Doug Bradley: 'It's unbearable, isn't it? The suffering of strangers. The agony of friends. There's a secret song at the centre of the world, Joey, and its sound is like razors through flesh. Come, you can hear its faint echoes now. I'm here to turn up the volume. Here to press the stinking face of humanity in the dark blood of its secret heart.'

13. The *Hellraiser* phenomenon has spawned a spurious pseudo-sequel, *Hellgate* (1989), and the obviously derivative '*Hellraiser* in space', *Event Horizon* (1997).

Chapter 19: Filigree and Shadow

1. Clive Barker, *Weaveworld*. London: Collins, 1987. All quotations are taken from the first edition.

2. Barker chooses this moment to confirm the symbolic link of Cal and the escaped pigeon: 'And he was suddenly a bird, a wingless bird hovering for a breathless instant on a balmy, sweet-scented wind, sole witness to the miracle sleeping below.'

3. Brewing at the heart of the weave is an image that haunts Barker's fiction: 'And at the centre of this burgeoning province, perhaps the most awesome sight of all: a mass of slate-coloured cloud, the innards of which were in perpetual, spiralling motion.'

4. Barker's reverie on the power of fairy tales is impressive: '[T]he stories moved her. She couldn't deny it. And they moved her in a way only *true* things could. It wasn't sentiment that brought tears to her eyes. The stories weren't sentimental. They were tough, even cruel. No, what made her weep was being reminded of an inner life she'd been so familiar with as a child; a life that was both an escape from, and a revenge upon, the pains and frustrations of childhood; a life that was neither mawkish nor unknowing; a life of mind-places – haunted, soaring – that she'd chosen to forget when she'd took up the cause of adulthood.

'More than that; in this reunion with the tales that had given her a myth-ology, she found images that might help her fathom her present confusion.

'The outlandishness of the story she'd entered, coming back to Liverpool, had thrown her assumptions into chaos. But here, in the pages of the book, she found a state of being in which nothing was fixed: where magic ruled, bringing transformations and miracles. She'd walked there once, and far from feeling lost, could have passed for one of its inhabitants. If she could recapture that insolent indifference to reason, and let it lead her through the maze ahead, she might comprehend the forces she knew were waiting to be unleashed around her.'

5. A character very much like Shadwell is central to Stephen King's novel *Needful Things* (1991), and Barker reprises him as Mr Hood, the Vampire King, in *The Thief of Always: A Fable*. London: HarperCollins (1992).

6. In the wraith-sisters, Barker indulges the imagery of horror and, indeed, repulsion. Magdalene's body is 'a column of grey gas, laced with strands of bloody tissue, and from this flux fragments of finished anatomy emerged: a seeping breast, a belly swollen as if by a pregnancy months beyond its term, a smeared face in which the eyes were sewn-up slits'. As for the vile by-blows: 'No perversion of anatomy had been overlooked amongst them: bodies turned inside out to parade the bowel and stomach; organs whose function seemed simply to seep and wheeze lining the belly of one like teats, and mounted like a coxcomb on another's head.'

7. 'Unable to mellow her nature, and so pass unseen amongst the Cuckoos, her history became a round of blood-lettings, pursuits, and further blood-lettings. Though she was still known and worshipped by a cognoscenti, who called her by a dozen different names – the Black Madonna, the Lady of Sorrows, Mater Maleficorium – she became nevertheless a victim of her own strange purity. Madness beckoned; the only refuge from the banality of the Kingdom she was exiled in.'

8. 'Everywhere the eye went there were new and extraordinary displays. At first the explosion of forms was too chaotic to be made sense of, but no sooner was the air awash with colour than the strands began to shape finer details, distinguishing plant from stone, and stone from wood, and wood from flesh. One surging thread exploded against the roof in a shower of motes, each of which, upon contact with the humus of the decaying Weave, threw out tiny shoots. Another was laying zig-zag paths of blue-grey mist across the room; a third and a fourth were intertwining, and fire-flies were leaping from their marriage, sketching in their motion bird and beast, which their companions clothed with light.

   'In seconds the Fugue had filled the room, its growth so fast that [the] house could not contain it. Boards were uprooted as the strands sought new territories; the rafters were thrown aside. Nor were bricks and mortar any better defence against the threads. What they couldn't coax, they bullied; what they couldn't bully, they simply overturned.'

9. 'Nobody could set his eyes on such a void and return to hearth and home without having lost a part of himself to the wilderness forever. Many, having endured the void once, went back, and back again, as if daring the desert to claim them; not content until it did. And those unhappy few who died at home, died with their eyes not on the loving faces at their bedside, nor on the cherry tree in blossom outside the window, but on that waste that called them as only the Abyss can call, promising the soul the balm of nothingness.'

10. Uriel, whose name means 'God is Light' (or, more ominously, 'Fire of God'), is one of the Archangels of rabbinical teachings, and is typically depicted in

a Promethean stance – his open hand holding a flame that is a perilous gift to humanity. In Milton's *Paradise Lost*, he is called the 'Regent of the Sun' and 'sharpest-sighted spirit of all in heaven'. In non-canon lore, Uriel was the dark angel who wrestled with Jacob at Peniel; the destroyer of the hosts of Sennacherib; and the messenger sent by God to warn Noah of the impending Deluge. Legend, like *Weaveworld*, also places Uriel at the gates of the lost Eden, intent on reminding humanity to love God by wielding a fiery sword.

11. In a series of remarkable digressions, the Angel's tale is subverted, as Barker reminds us that *Genesis* is the first book of a history whose truth depends upon the strength of our imagination and belief. Shadwell adopts the tale as literal truth; but Suzanna – the practical artist – ponders the dilemma: 'I never believed in Eden . . . Not the way the Bible tells it. Original sin and all that crap. But maybe the story's got an echo somewhere in it . . . Of the way things really were. A place of miracles, where magic was made.' Immacolata contends, in turn, that the Scourge 'believes itself an angel. So, for better or worse, it is.'

12. Its notable predecessors in this pursuit included Stephen King's *The Stand* (1979) and Peter Straub's *Floating Dragon* (1985).

13. As Nan du Sautoy, former Rights Director at Sphere, recalls, the fantasy elements of *Weaveworld* were the fundamental concern that caused Sphere to decline to make a considerable financial offer for the book: 'We were surprised at the quality of it, but it was a matter of trying to break him out of the horror market, and that's always tricky. He wanted to be put on the general fiction shelves. The danger of that is that booksellers won't put books on both shelves – it's one or the other. If you're on the horror shelves, you're noticed by your fans, but if you're in general fiction, you can get passed over, so therefore you end up selling fewer. So it's always a bit tricky. We knew he had the potential to expand, but that it was going to be difficult to break him out of the horror genre. And then *Weaveworld*, being a fantasy, that's still shelved in the same area.'

14. *Eg*, Juliet Warman, 'Little House of Horrors: Master of Gore Lives It Up on Blood Money', *Today*, 3 September 1988.

Chapter 20: A Breed Apart

1. Clive Barker, *Cabal*. London: Fontana, 1988. All quotations are taken from the first edition. (The curious may note that the epigraphs of *Cabal* are all inventions, and one of Barker's great delights in writing the book.)

2. The irony, Barker has noted, is that 'we seek out this kind of material because we seek out a confrontation with the bizarre, the mysterious, the transformational. I therefore find it paradoxical that stories of this nature usually present the bizarre and the mutated as repugnant. I don't think we live in fear of the monster. We anticipate it, salivate at the thought'. Quoted in Philip Nutman, 'Bring on the Monsters!', *Fangoria*, no. 87, October 1989.

3. Clive Barker, *Cabal*. New York: Poseidon, 1988. The American edition collected the novel and four stories from *Clive Barker's Books of Blood Volume*

Six, London: Sphere, 1985 ('The Life of Death', 'How Spoilers Bleed', 'Twilight at the Towers' and 'The Last Illusion'). The final story in Volume Six, 'The Book of Blood (a postscript): On Jerusalem Street', is a vignette designed to provide closure to the six volumes; it was deleted as part of Poseidon's strategy to ignore the existence of the initial *Books of Blood* published in the United States by Berkley. Because of numerous typographic errors, including the excising of text, in the Poseidon edition, the British editions of *Cabal* are the preferred versions.

4. At its most fundamental level, *Cabal* also revisits and re-enacts the myth-making of *Weaveworld*, inverting its novelistic structure to produce a fantasy written in a horrific mode.

5. 'It wasn't that the sum of her features was unattractive . . . No, the trouble was she didn't look the way she felt. It was a *sweet* face, and she wasn't sweet; didn't want to *be* sweet, or *thought of* as sweet.'

6. Clive Barker, 'Foreword', *Clive Barker's Nightbreed: The Making of the Film*. London: Fontana/Collins, 1990.

7. This passage was abridged in the American edition, without Clive's permission, to read: 'There were eleven photographs in all. Every one was different, but also the same: all pictures of a madness performed, taken with the actor already departed.'

8. No archaeological remains have been attributed to Midian, and the only information about the tribe (other than elliptical references in Assyrian texts) is contained in the Bible. There, Midian is named as a son of Abraham's third wife, Ketorah (*Genesis* 25:2; I *Chronicles* 1:32). Through their eponymous ancestor, the Midianites trace their origin to the father of the Hebrews, but lived their nomadic existence in a separate territory, east of Israel in the Syro-Arabian Desert (*Genesis* 25:6; *Judges*, 6:3, 33; 7:12).

The Midianites first appear in the Bible as caravan leaders and traders who sold Joseph into Egypt 'for twenty shekels of silver' (*Genesis* 37:28,36). Later, Moses encountered them in an area of the Sinai peninsula that had become known as the 'land of Midian', and he married a daughter of Jethro, a Midianite priest (*Exodus* 2:15–21). It is believed that Moses received his revelation of Yahweh while living in Midian; and because of the influential role played by Jethro, there has been speculation that Israel may have adapted the worship of Yahweh from the Midianites (*Exodus* 3:1–2).

However, when the Israelites later met with Midianites in the territory of Moab (*Genesis* 36:35), the Israelites were seduced into pagan worship. The idolatry caused God to command Moses to carry out a war of vindication against Midian (*Numbers* 31:1–12; *Joshua* 13:21). Its cities and camps were razed and pillaged, and its women (other than virgins) and male children were put to death.

Later, the Midianites invaded central Palestine but were slaughtered by Gideon, and their kings captured and executed in what is known and celebrated as 'the day of Midian' (*Isaiah* 9:4, 10:26; *Psalms* 83:9). After this defeat, the tribe of Midian disappeared from recorded history. *See generally The Oxford*

Companion to the Bible. Ed. Bruce M. Metzger and Michael D Coogan. New York/Oxford: Oxford University Press, 1993.

9. 'So many masks. Was she the only one who had no secret life; no other self in marrow or mind? If not, then perhaps she had no place in this game of *appearances*; perhaps Boone and Decker were the true lovers here, swapping blows and faces but *necessary* to each other.'

10. Just as no movie screen could have prepared Lori for the sight of Baphomet, no movie screen has shown this vision of the maker of Midian – in *Nightbreed*, Baphomet is depicted as a huge broken statue.

   Historically, Baphomet is an incarnation or companion of Satan, a devilish parody of a goat with a pentagram between its horns and a caduceus between its legs. Admired by defrocked French priest Eliphas Lévi, and allegedly worshipped by the legendary Knights Templar, Baphomet is considered by some as a corruption of 'Mahomet' (or Mohammed) who, as the founder of Islam, was parodied and literally demonized on the medieval stage. *See* Sean Kelly and Rosemary Rogers, *Who in Hell: A Guide to the Whole Damned Bunch.* New York: Villard, 1996.

11. Thus Lori must contemplate the unimaginable – love with the resurrected Boone, an act of necrophilia and bestiality: 'She could never *kiss* the beast. So why did the thought of it make her heart pound?'

12. The final credits acknowledge Nina Wilcox Putnam and Richard Schayer, who wrote the story on which the 1932 film was based, and John L Balderston, who authored the 1932 screenplay, but also give screen story credit to Lloyd Fonvielle, Kevin Jarre and the director of the 1999 film, Stephen Sommers, while giving Sommers the ultimate screenplay credit.

Chapter 21: God's Monkey

1. Clive Barker, *The Great and Secret Show.* London: HarperCollins, 1989. All quotations are taken from the first edition.

2. 'When Bunyan writes *A Pilgrim's Progress*, it isn't reality as he was living it, because he was living in prison when he was writing it, for God's sake; but it has the *force* of reality because it has the force of his imagination behind it. And because his imagination is this incredible and self-consistent thing, which is about human nature but in a context that's been fantasticated, created by him, it has an incredible pertinence still.

   'One of the things that contemporary fantasy writers do too often is that they wish too much to be realists. And in caring to be realists or naturalists, they actually shoot themselves in the foot; because the very thing that is going to liberate their art into universal application is not "reality" – it's like you've got this wonderful helium-filled balloon, and just to make it prettier, you hang weights on it. Sure it looks pretty, but does it fly?

   'This is how I feel about Steve King: that Steve's desire to be instantly accessible – his desire to say, *You recognize the situation instantly, don't you folks?* – is incredibly dangerous to his power in the years to come. When I wrote an introduction to *'Salem's Lot*, I made the point by comparing what

Steve does with Poe. When Prince Prospero closes his castle against the Red Death, we don't even know what country he's in. But because we know who he is, and we know who his guests are, and we know what he's locking out – poverty and sorrow and grief – we can see that human divide, which is a universal divide, and it doesn't matter what country he's in. It's a five-page story, and if two of those pages had described what kind of after-shave he put on before he went down to the party, and what kind of cigarettes he lit up, the story would sit there right now just refusing to fly.

'The way I write, I sort of say, *Well, I'm going to give you enough to know that this is contemporary, because clearly this isn't set in a distant future* – but I'm not going to spend a whole heap of time talking about smoking, drinking, McDonald's, boom boom boom.'

3. The variants on *'Salem's Lot* defy cataloguing, but almost every horror writer of note, including Charles L Grant, Robert R McCammon and Michael McDowell (and many lesser talents) created one novel in the 1980s that used its weighty template.

4. Here, Barker again invokes a mythology that has evolved consistently from the earliest pages of his *Books of Blood*: 'The dead have highways' – and it is the intersections of those highways with those of the living that form the network of journeys that comprises his personal mythology.

5. A shaman, in Barker's view, is no mere medicine-man or witch-doctor, but a 'mind-healer' who 'gets inside the collective psyche and explains it'.

6. Humans are offered three visits to the dream-sea – in innocence, in love and in extremis: 'That's all we ever get. Three dips in the dream-sea. Any less, and we'd be insane. Any more . . . and we wouldn't be human.'

7. The Shoal was 'the secret behind all other secrets. Entire religions were seeded and nurtured to distract attention from it, to direct spiritual seekers *away* from the Shoal, the Art and what the Art opened onto.' Thus: 'Heaven's only one of many stories, told on the shores of Ephemeris.' It is there that humanity 'mingled briefly with absolutes; saw sights and heard stories that would keep them from insanity in the face of being alive. There, briefly, was pattern and purpose; there was a glimpse of continuity; there was the Show, the Great and Secret Show, which rhyme and ritual were created to be keepsakes of.'

8. Fletcher is clearly inspired by, and modelled loosely on, maverick 'ethnopharmacologist' Terence McKenna, who championed psychedelia as a source of spiritual transformation and evolution. *Eg*, Terence McKenna, *The Archaic Revival*. New York: HarperSanFrancisco, 1991.

9. The Nuncio coaxes forth the natural propensities of those it influences: the Jaff wears the face of a monstrous infant – a bearded fetus with vast eyes and tiny mouth – because his swollen evil seeks a condition of flesh that is tantamount to divinity. He is so consumed by dreams of power that his spirit atrophies. Fletcher, in turn, is a bewildered saint – a force for transcendence.

10. The revelation parallels that of Barker's short story 'The Inhuman Condition' (1985), in which a puzzle of knotted string cloaks the secret of evolution.

11. In this sequence, Barker offers a homage to one of his favourite films, George

Franju's *Les Yeux sans Visage* ('Eyes Without a Face'/'The Horror Chamber of Dr Faustus') (1959), as a character frees animals from their cages.

12. 'What we call naturalistic fiction is recent in the history of writing,' Barker observes. 'Almost every Shakespeare play, including the histories, has some supernatural element – ghosts, omens, witches – because, in that world view, and I think it's a richer and truer worldview, the strange, the fantastical, the imaginative impinges upon and intersects with the real, the naturalistic, the workaday. And that, for me, is how my life is. Not that I'm being followed around by ghosts; but I'm living on a day to day basis, and of course it's special to me because that's my business; but even if I were selling shoes, I would still be having sexual fantasies on a Friday about what we're going to do on Saturday night – and if I hated my boss, I might very well think about burying an axe in his head, which is a fantasy. I might be thinking about what it might be like when I go on vacation. Or I might be thinking about my childhood, or what I dreamt last night, or a book that I'm reading. So even in the most imaginatively impoverished of lives, there is still this largely unrecognized flow, intersection, interweaving of the imaginative and the work-day. The pragmatist in us and the dreamer in us are actually one and the same person; they're two sides of the same coin. It amazes me that, when I talk to interviewers, I talk to the press, how dumb they are about that, how they don't see that's a part of who everybody is. Isn't that a core part of their question: *Where do you get your ideas from*? That question implies that other people don't get ideas!'

13. 'Londoner's Diary', *Evening Standard*, 23 January 1989.

Chapter 22: The Bastard Child

1. Clive Barker, 'Foreword', *Clive Barker's Nightbreed: The Making of the Film*. London: Fontana/Collins, 1990.

2. *Ibid.*

3. Clive Barker, 'To See or Not To See', *Splatter: A Cautionary Tale*. By Douglas E Winter. Round Top, NY: Footsteps, 1987.

4. While preparing for the role of Eigerman, Charles Haid viewed a documentary about Klaus Barbie, the Nazi 'Butcher of Lyons', in which Barbie mentioned that 'I am the son of the Eiger' – *eiger* meaning 'rocks' in German, and thus a man of stone, a man with no heart: an Eigerman. Mark Salisbury and John Gilbert, 'A Hymn to the Monstrous', *Clive Barker's Nightbreed: The Making of the Film*. London: Fontana/Collins, 1990.

5. In *Clive Barker's The Nightbreed Chronicles*, London: Titan Books, 1990, which was developed to promote the film, Barker provides brief pseudo-biographies of the many monsters of Midian, accompanied by compelling photographs by Murray Close. The effort to establish a memorable menagerie may have been blunted by its sheer magnitude. As even a fleeting glance at *The Nightbreed Chronicles* reveals, the rich variety of the creatures is lost on screen, at least in the truncated version of the film, where only a few were characters of significance.

Chapter 23: And Death Shall Have No Dominion

1. Clive Barker, *Imajica*. New York: HarperCollins, 1991. All quotations are taken from the first edition.
2. 'Space, like time, belonged to the other tale – to the tragedy of separation they'd left behind. Stripped of his senses and their necessities, almost unborn again, he knew the mystif's comfort as it knew his, and that dissolution he'd woken in terror of so many times stood revealed as the beginning of bliss.'
3. The Imajica was named in print for the first time by the 'Fourth King' at Bethlehem: 'They were looking for the Reconciler . . .'
4. Of all his incarnations, 'he, Gentle, was probably the craziest: the lover of a creature that defied the definitions of gender, the maker of a man who had detroyed nations. The only sanity in his life – burning like a clear white light – was that which came from God: the simple purpose of a Reconciler.'
5. Julia Kristeva, *Powers of Horror: An Essay on Abjection*. Translated by Leon S Roudiez. New York: Columbia University Press, 1982, p70.
6. Clive Barker, 'Back and back we go . . .', *Imajica I: The Fifth Dominion*. New York: HarperPaperbacks, 1995.
7. Quoted in Philip Nutman and Stefan Jaworzyn, 'Meet Clive Barker', *Fangoria*, no. 51, January 1986.
8. Clive Barker, 'Back and back we go . . .'
9. *Ibid.*
10. Douglas E Winter, '*Secret* Is Horrifically Good Work from Master of Fantastic', *Washington Times*, 26 February 1990.
11. Clive Barker, 'Back and back we go . . .'

Chapter 24: The Serpent's Tail

1. Clive Barker, *The Thief of Always: A Fable*. London: HarperCollins, 1992. All quotations are taken from the first edition.
2. Clive Barker, 'The Wood on the Hill'. Unpublished. All quotations are taken from the handwritten manuscript, circa 1966. Copyright © 2001 by Clive Barker.
3. Quoted in Richard A Lupoff, 'An Interview with Clive Barker', *Science Fiction Eye*, no. 4 (August 1988).
4. Indeed, in *Weaveworld*, Shadwell's first meeting with Cal concludes with Shadwell shouting '*Stop, thief*'.
5. The choice of an American setting, which echoed Barker's recent move to the United States, underscores the poignant autobiographical element of the novel.
6. 'It was the most monstrous of the brood: its skin rotted and stretched over barbed and polished bone, its throat a nest of snaky tongues, its jaws set with hundreds of teeth.'
7. 'The idea that the lake now had something that he'd owned was somehow worse than a thief running off with his bike. A thief was warm flesh and blood; the lake was not. His possessions had gone into a nightmare place, full of monstrous things, and he felt as though a little part of himself had gone with it, down into the dark.'
8. When the spell is removed, Harvey tells Jive that the transformation was simply

a trick; but Jive demurs: 'There are those who'd disagree . . . Those who'd say that all the great powers in the world are *bloodsuckers* and *soul-stealers* at heart. And we must serve them. All of us. Serve them to our dying day.'

9. 'His eyes were made of broken mirrors, and his face of gouged stone. He had a mane of splinters, and limbs of timber. He had shattered slates for teeth, and rusty screws for fingernails, and a cloak of rotted drapes that scarcely hid the darkness of his heart from sight.'

10. Quoted in Leanne C Harper, 'Clive Barker: Renaissance Hellraiser', *The Bloomsbury Review*, September/October 1987.

11. Salvador Dalí, *Babaouo: scénario inédit précédé d'un abrége d'une histoire critique du cinéma et suivi de Guillame Tell, ballet portugais*. Paris: 1932. Dalí also noted: 'The rapid and continuous succession of images in the cinema, whose implicit neologism is in direct proportion to a particularly generalizing visual culture, prevents any attempt to reduce to the concrete and most often annuls its intentional, affective and lyrical character . . .'

12. This argument is expounded at length in Barker's 'Introduction' to *HR Giger's Necronomicon*. Beverly Hills, CA: Morpheus International, 1991.

Chapter 25: Forbidden Candy

1. Clive Barker, 'The Forbidden', *Clive Barker's Books of Blood Volume Five*. London: Sphere, 1985. All quotations are taken from the first edition.

2. The cultural phenomenon of 'urban legends' was made popular by Professor Jan Harold Brunvand in his now-classic study, *The Vanishing Hitchhiker: American Urban Legends and Their Meaning*, New York: Norton, 1981, and its sequels *The Choking Doberman and Other 'New' Urban Legends*, New York: Norton, 1984; and *Curses! Broiled Again!*, New York: Norton, 1989.

   Stories of a hook-handed killer and the lavatory mutilation of a boy are two of the more pervasive urban legends. In *The Vanishing Hitchhiker*, Brunvand describes the former myth, a mainstay of campfire lore that he calls simply 'The Hook', as a horrific cautionary tale that warns the adolescent that, as he or she grows older and moves away from home, the world's dangers (including, notably, those of sexuality) will loom closer. The story of 'The Mutilated Boy', described in *The Choking Doberman*, invokes racial or homosexual fear, proposing that members of a minority are out to 'get' our children.

   Ironically, Brunvand's *Curses! Broiled Again!* chronicled a 'Candyman murder', although it bears no resemblance to the short story or the film. In 1974, an eight-year-old boy died after trick-or-treating on Hallowe'en. Police determined that he had been given tainted candy by his father – who, Brunvand noted, is 'the only known person ever convicted of acting out an urban legend'.

3. On November 5, 1605, Guy Fawkes was discovered in the cellar of Parliament with thirty-six barrels of gunpowder, which he planned to ignite the following day during the assembly's opening. The foiling of this 'Gunpowder Plot' was celebrated throughout England with thanksgiving church services every November 5 until the late 1850s; since that time, the burning of an effigy of Guy Fawkes – the 'guy' – above a bonfire has been the centrepiece of an

increasingly secular holiday. Today, the celebration of Guy Fawkes Day has essentially merged with Hallowe'en, and most British children perceive them not as separate days, but as a single and more or less coherent series of events.

4. The Candyman's resemblance to a 'guy' – the effigy of Guy Fawkes – is obvious and no doubt intentional. The raggedy-man is a repeated icon of Clive Barker's fiction and film: from Anthony Breer, the Razor-Eater of *The Damnation Game*, to Shadwell, the cloaked salesman of *Weaveworld*, and the mysterious, unnamed derelict of *Hellraiser* to the final incarnation of the Vampire King Hood in *The Thief of Always*, he is omnipresent, a scarecrow of the soul.

5. The haunting music of *Candyman*, written by acclaimed minimalist composer Philip Glass, was probably the best motion picture score of 1992. As of this writing, it has not been released on audiocassette or compact disc. Glass's hypnotic, sequence-based music is peculiarly suited to expressionist film-making, as witness his collaborations on documentaries by Godfrey Reggio – *Koyaanisqatsi* (1983), *Powaqqatsi* (1988) and *Anima Mundi* (1993) – and Errol Morris's *The Thin Blue Line* (1989). His other scores include *Mishima* (1985) and *Hamburger Hill* (1987). Not surprisingly, that most musical of horror film-makers, Dario Argento, interspersed Glass compositions in the scores of *Phenomena* (1985) and Michele Soavi's *La Chiesa* ('The Church') (1988).

6. Attentive listeners will note a peculiar moment in the title sequence: until the Candyman speaks, only the Philip Glass soundtrack accompanies the visuals, except for a brief instant, immediately before Clive Barker's credit as executive producer, when a human voice is heard shouting.

7. Rose devised his 'urban legend' of the Candyman from oft-told stories of inattentive babysitters and hook-handed murderers (with the latter, of course, invoked in Barker's novelette), and two tales then rampant in Cabrini Green: of murderers who entered apartments through passages hidden behind medicine cabinets, and 'Bloody Mary', who would appear behind her victims if they peered into a mirror and spoke her name thirteen times.

   The notion of a killer surviving in – and striking from – a mirror was explored earlier in Ulli Lommel's *The Boogeyman* (1980). Lommel, a wayward protégé of Rainer Werner Fassbinder and director of two Andy Warhol films, proposed that the evil essence of a man would persevere in the shards of a mirror broken at the time of his death. The long-held superstition that breaking a mirror is bad luck is thus heightened to a suggestion that the broken glass would free anything that the mirror has seen.

8. 'What people fear,' Rose says, 'is graffiti-ridden buildings. It's like, if you see graffiti, you're in danger, much more so than in a graveyard. I've never really understood why more people didn't pick up on that, because that, for me, was always what was so brilliant about *The Exorcist*. It was a film that was so utterly mundane and believable; and that's what made it frightening. And that's what I liked very much about Clive's story – all of the stories in that collection, actually. They had a kind of mundane acceptance of the fantastic within very real settings. That's what struck me as being exceptional about that particular batch of stories: the jumping-off points were always so totally

recognizable, but they would always end up somewhere very peculiar – and Clive has a knack for describing that kind of stuff with a mundane elusiveness, in a way, that enables you to accept it however you best want to accept it. I never started thinking, *Well, that's just ridiculous* – but, of course, most of the stuff is . . . and that's very, very hard to do in the movies.'

9. The seduction is made complete when Helen's hand touches his chest and comes away with a clutch of bees – not special effects constructs, but live bees, newly born, since bees do not sting until they are more than forty-eight hours old. An entourage of bees then flurries out of the Candyman's mouth as he bends to kiss her (with Tony Todd bravely bearing some two-hundred bees in his mouth with the help of a prosthetic device). When, in the midst of these wonders, the Candyman announces, 'It's time for a new miracle,' the viewer quite rightly feels that he or she has just witnessed one.

10. In an American setting devoid of the lore of Guy Fawkes, the bonfire lacks mythic resonance and instead invokes less seemly thoughts about the ghetto and its occupants. Indeed, a May 1992 advance screening of *Candyman* in California was cancelled in the wake of the Los Angeles riots that followed the acquittal of four police officers in their first trial for the beating of motorist Rodney King.

11. Rose is not the only director to resort to reincarnation to 'invigorate' a film adaptation of prominent horror fiction; this is precisely the narrative conceit that Francis Ford Coppola lent to *Bram Stoker's Dracula* (1993) and that Stanley Kubrick grafted onto his version of *The Shining* (1980).

Chapter 26: Finding a Religion

1. Clive Barker, *Everville*. New York: HarperCollins, 1994. All quotations are taken from the first edition.

2. The second novel of 'The Art' thus begins farther back in time than the first, just as the third novel would begin at an even earlier time.

3. Barker names his strange town with a clever inversion of his beloved Never-Never Land.

4. Maeve is clearly the creative spirit given life: 'The instinct that had made him prick his ears that April day, hearing the name of a goddess called in a place of dust and dirt and unwashed flesh, had been good. The miraculous and the mundane lived side by side in this newfound land, and, in the person of Maeve O'Connell, were indivisible.'

5. Other characters from *The Great and Secret Show* play lesser roles. Howie and Jo-Beth, the surviving children of the warring demigods, have married, borne a baby daughter, and live in hiding in Illinois – not very happily ever after. Jo-Beth feels the pull of her father, and his son. 'He wasn't here in the flesh. At least not yet. He was in Jo-Beth's mind. And that in its way was a far more terrible place for him to be.'

6. Kissoon now wears the stolen, rotting flesh of Raul; he is the transforming prophet of the Iad: 'This chaos is no good, Tesla . . . The world needs to be put back together again . . . [W]e're not so far apart after all. You want

revelation. So do I. You want to shake your species up. So do I. You want power – you already have a little, but a little's never enough – and so do I. We've taken different paths, but are we not coming to the same spot?'

And the final revelation: Kissoon is Clayton O'Connell, offspring of Maeve and Coker Ammiano, who seeks vengeance upon the men who sought to murder him and his parents – and thus, upon the world.

7. 'I think maybe we're coming to the end of being what we are. We're going to take an evolutionary jump. And that makes this a dangerous and wonderful time ... [T]here are things out there that don't want us to take the jump. Things that'd prefer us to stay just the way we are, wandering around blindly, afraid of our own shadows, afraid of being dead and afraid of being too much alive. They want to keep us that way. But then there's people everywhere saying: I'm not going to be blind. I'm not going to be afraid. I can see invisible roads. I can hear angels' voices. I know who I was before I was born and I know what I want to be when I'm dead.'

8. Or, as one of Fletcher's acolytes announces: 'The time's come for us to *move on, up the ladder.*'

9. Thus D'Amour returns to the house on Wyckoff Street to confront his personal demon, realizing that he is no fallen angel, but a creature born on the shores of Quiddity: not the stuff of Satan, but of the imagination: 'I don't need prayers ... I don't need a crucifix. I just need the eyes in my head.'

10. 'An interesting problem for the writer of the *fantastique*,' Barker notes, 'is how to evoke paradise without it really being about doing violence to other people. How do you evoke a state of bliss? How do you evoke the excitement of Eden? I've tried it several ways. That's one of the reasons why sex is so important in my fiction, because sex is very often connected with feeling very good, thank you very much, but it's not destructive. So the adrenalin rushes, but not because somebody else is bleeding.

'In *Weaveworld*, Cal has powerful experiences – sexual at Venus Mountain, his grandfather's poetry at the orchard of Lemuel Lo; he gets to feel something very powerful without doing anything negative to anyone else to feel it. As opposed to John Carter of Mars, who gets to feel something really cool because he's beating the shit out of somebody else and he's rescuing a princess. It's an interesting problem for the writer of the *fantastique* as to how to evoke something Edenic without stooping to violence to make it more exciting. Phoebe and Joe's reunion in *Everville*, which is five-hundred pages in coming, is for me much more exciting than the violence which concludes *The Great and Secret Show*. Tesla's journey into Grillo's Reef, and encountering the leaves on the story tree, is the closest I've come to this Edenic thing, because it's about everything, then, it's about simply being alive in all the manifestations and all the strangeness of that. When Sam gets back to the Shire at the end of *The Lord of the Rings* I was faintly disappointed. *I'm home*, he says. That's the last line of the book. He's going to light his pipe, he's going to sit down, and you somehow you get the feeling that, like people who talk fondly of the Second World War, his best days are behind him.

'When Dorothy says, *There's no place like home*, it's a troubling conclusion. Barrie recognizes it most closely because in the play, one brother becomes a judge, the other a stockbroker, and they can no longer tell stories to their children. Wendy bears a child, Margaret, and Margaret holds the image of Peter Pan sacred. Wendy dies. What Barrie does, agonizingly but brilliantly, is say that you can have both of these things, but each one of them will be tragic. You can have the girl who holds on to the idea of the miraculous coming to get her, but she will eventually sink into death and she will say to her own daughter, *I can't go any longer*. So you can have that, and you can have Peter who, year after year, when he remembers, will come to the window-sill, and he will be unchanged – and there's tragedy in that, too. That seems brilliant to me. Quite brilliant. And so much more sophisticated a response to the problem than: *There's no place like home*.'

Chapter 27: Love and the Devil

1. Clive Barker, 'The Last Illusion', *Clive Barker's Books of Blood Volume Six*. London, Sphere: 1985. All quotations are taken from the first edition.
2. Perhaps the closest to such a character was that of Dr Loomis (played by the late Donald Pleasance) in the *Halloween* series – whose name is invoked in *Lord of Illusions* as the man who dispatches D'Amour to Los Angeles.
3. The Director's Version of *Lord of Illusions* contains some twelve minutes of additional footage, including twelve entire scenes excised from the theatrical release. Although hyped by MGM/UA Home Video as footage 'too sexy and terrifying for theatres', the resurrected material is instead critical to the narrative, subtext and character development. Barker compares the film that United Artists released theatrically with the film that he made: 'It was their desire that we end up making a picture which . . . they could sell as a no-holds-barred horror movie. I think we lost a lot of grace notes, we lost a lot of character work, we lost a lot of things which made the movie a little more accessible as a mainstream picture, and put the balance where the balance was always intended to be, which was between a character-driven detective picture and a scary, effects-driven horror movie. I wanted to balance those two things off. I've said several times I think the theatrical release is a horror movie with detective overtones. I would like to think that this version, the true version, is both a detective movie and a horror movie; it's those two things, fifty-fifty.'
4. With its climactic siege and the dramatic uncertainty of its characters' identities, 'The Last Illusion' resembles a host of zombie films; indeed, it was paralleled in cinema by Lamberto Bava's *Demoni* ('Demons') (1985) and *Demoni 2 . . . L'incubo ritorna* ('Demons 2') (1986), which portrayed theatregoers and apartment dwellers besieged by the minions of Hell.
5. Clive Barker, 'Lost Souls', *Time Out*, 19 December 1985–1 January 1986; reprinted in *Cutting Edge*, ed. Dennis Etchison. New York: Doubleday, 1986. All quotations are taken from the more readily available first edition of *Cutting Edge*.
6. Careful viewers will note the mysterious disappearance of the rapacious mandrill

from the scenes that follow Swann's entrance into the room. The script called for Swann to shoot the mandrill, and several takes featuring the exploding head of a mandrill puppet were made, but none of them proved satisfactory.

7. The decision to place the main action of the film specifically in 1995 rather than in something theoretical 'present' was a conscious, and difficult, one: 'I agonize about this more than I agonize about anything else in my life. In making movies, you make this thing which is a little time capsule. And I hate hipness, I hate it with such a passion – partly because I've never been hip, but partly because it seems so brittle. I like the mythological. For me, the mythological and hip are at opposite extremes, opposite positions. When a thing carries mythological weight, it carries it because it's released from the specifics of the time period or the conventions which surround it. It's really difficult to release movies from that – in fact, I think, it's impossible. Fantastic movies do it better than realistic movies.'

8. Although clearly intended to refer to the events at Wyckoff Street, viewers of the motion picture are shown only fleeting flashbacks of a demonic being that haunts D'Amour's memories.

9. In the aftermath of Quaid's death, D'Amour is interrogated by police detective Eddison, named for the author of *The Worm Ouroboros*. Later that night, Butterfield is shown looking out from a window in a composition that is virtually identical to one of Barker's more famous paintings.

10. 'Obviously, Swann's life is theatrical,' Barker says, 'but Nix's is pretty theatrical, too. This is a man who we see performing. And I wonder whether theatricality isn't the central device in all my movies . . . Pinhead is an incredibly theatrical figure. He's just completely in love with rhetoric. Helped along by Dougie's juicy performance, it has to be said, but he's very much a character who enjoys that kind of thing – you just feel like he's centre stage.

'People talk about Argento being cinematic, but he's also very theatrical, very operatic. In late Fellini pictures, like *Satyricon*, you have characters who sort of look straight at the camera, as if to say, *I know you're there. This is all being done for you. Are you happy?* And I feel as though the theatricality of what happens in my movies is an essential part of what they are.'

11. 'What I was trying for in *Lord of Illusions* is exactly what I was trying for in *Hellraiser*,' Barker says, 'which was to put this very, very weird thing into these incredibly ordinary circumstances, and see what happens. And I pushed the stuff in the normal circumstances of Los Angeles as far as I could, and then I went to a neutral space. When it got really weird, I said, *Okay, I'm never going to get away with William Nix in your local apartment. The only way I'm going to get away with this is if I go to a neutral space.*

'It's just a theory, but I feel that the notion of neutral space for imaginative eruptions in movies is important. The Ellen Burstyn character in *The Exorcist* could not have been an ordinary housewife. She had to be a movie star. She had to be removed from the context which the audience absolutely knew. If you do it the other way, you end up with *Poltergeist*, which is a comedy.

'Somehow or other, for the fantastic to really erupt in the movies, the audience has to feel comfortably distant from the environment in which it's happening. Otherwise they start to judge it, and they start to say, *That couldn't happen.* Which is a ludicrous thing to say. Isn't that why you're in the theatre in the first place?'

12. 'I don't know whether this is good box office, but *Lord of Illusions* takes these three arenas and says, *We're going to mix these things together*, and I'm going to try to find a style which coheres them – a visual style and a linguistic style – because I'm referencing some *noir* here and some horror movies here and some magic here and some pieces of stuff I just made up here. And that's why I prefer the long version, because the long version contains things which really push that further – like the cultists all leaving their murdered families, while blues music plays, it's pushing very, very hard there, and the audiences in previews hated that with a passion. And it's because the movie refuses to be one thing. It wants to be all these things, and maybe it wants to be too many things, but it wants to do all these things, like the books do. And the longer version, for me, folds in more ambition, more stuff.

'It seems to me that movies are increasingly very simple experiences. Much, much simpler than books. That you buy into one atmosphere and you stick with it. That you buy into one narrative idea, and you stick with it. What could be a more perfect example than *Seven*: this is a movie about a guy who is going to kill people by the seven deadly sins. We know that within the first ten minutes of the movie – now just watch it happen. And the tone of the movie is going to be absolutely consistent for two hours and ten minutes. The look of the picture – it's never going to stop raining – and it's a very fine aesthetic and it works really well, but it's just this self-contained thing and you buy into it while you're watching it, but then you stop and think: *Wait a minute, wait a minute, that doesn't make any sense at all.*'

Chapter 28: Extinction

1. Clive Barker, *Sacrament*. New York: HarperCollins, 1996. All quotations are taken from the first edition.

2. A reviewer has a more pejorative take on Will's art: '*Mr Rabjohns should be ashamed of himself. He has attempted to turn these documents into an irrational and self-dramatizing metaphor for the homosexual's place in America; and in doing so has demeaned his craft, his sexuality and – most unforgivably – the animals whose dying throes and rotting carcasses he has so obsessively documented.*'

3. Burnt Yarley is a fictionalized version of the Yorkshire village in which Clive's cousin Mark lived and died.

'In writing about Yorkshire in November,' Clive observed while writing *Sacrament*, 'I'm accessing a memory of seasons, which you just don't have here [in Los Angeles]. And the fact that I'm not there is making me more specific, because I'm having to work a little bit harder to grasp what these details are, as opposed to being in the midst of them. There's a kind of nostalgia in it, because I'm not there. It focuses my attention closely on what my sense memories of this place actually are. And they're good memories, although I think they're unremarkable memories.

'There are so many things tying into my childhood, going back to a place I know incredibly well in my imagination – November in Yorkshire, November in the north – I'm writing about that, and there's this weird dislocation. I write, and then I look up, and it's just bizarre. While I was writing *Weaveworld*, I was a four-hour drive from where this stuff was taking place. *Imajica* was written while I was in England, and it was very powerfully connected with how I was feeling about England, and about the fact that I was leaving: I was going to make this list of places which I knew, places which have meant a lot to me. But this is the first time that I've sat in a place and felt that I was writing about Earth from an orbit at Mars, feeling this complete dislocation, and then feeling very powerfully the connection with my childhood. With the kid who had experienced these things for the first time – Christmas. These places are just touchstones.'

4. These words came to Clive while he was drafting the novel. 'While I was writing about it, I was thinking: *Where the hell does this come from*? And I think it comes from an acute sense that I had, even as a child, that things were happening that would not come again. There was something very powerful about that.'

5. 'What had his life to date been but an extended footnote to that encounter: an attempt to make some idiot recompense for the murders he'd committed at Steep's behest, or rather for the unalloyed joy he'd taken in the thought of shaping the world that way?'

6. Thomas Simeon and Will are uncomfortably alike: 'Too gentle for this world of illusions. It made him mad, trying to find his way through this profligate Creation.'

7. Lord Fox also offers a fine and fantastic conundrum that is never resolved: 'Did you lie at the age of eleven and dream about me, coming to tell you about the man that you'd grow up to be, a man who'd one day be lying in a coma dreaming about you, lying in your bed, dreaming a fox . . . and so on. Following any of this?'

Chapter 29: Ancient of Days

1. Clive Barker, *Weaveworld*. London: Collins, 1987.
2. Clive Barker, 'Animal Life', *USA Today Weekend*, 24–26 June 1994.
3. He was then staying in a house in a small bay on the north shore of Kauai – a setting about which he would write, in the novel *Galilee* (1998): 'there's still just a chance that something . . . something *magical* might happen'.
4. Douglas E Winter, ed, *Revelations*. New York: HarperPrism, 1997. The anthology was published in the United Kingdom as *Millennium*. London: HarperCollins Voyager, 1997. All quotations are taken from the first American edition.
5. 'Genre fiction, by and large, is rather poor at that kind of ambiguity,' Barker says. 'It doesn't wish ambiguity upon itself. It plays very clearly with your here, your now. These are the moral parameters of the characters, and you

already know the resolution before you buy it. And that's just not terribly interesting anymore. It was more interesting to me when I was younger, because there is a sort of show-offy element to what you can do with understanding rules and changing them this percentage. But at a certain point, you just run out of patience.'

Chapter 30: Galilee

1. Clive Barker, *Galilee*. New York: HarperCollins, 1998. All quotations are taken from the first edition.
2. The initial draft of *Galilee* was written in the third person. 'The reason it didn't work was there was too much going on, and the point of view just shifted around so much that there was no way . . . I loved this, but I thought: *It's all over the fucking place. There's nothing that sticks this together.* And yet the story itself was really interesting. You have two families and this huge back story, and all the Civil War stuff. It just wouldn't hold; it just fell apart. And then I figured it out: *I know what I need to do. I need to put this in the first person.*

   'I had always scorned the first person for myself, because I felt it was self-indulgent. I think I get this out of the feeling that the first person can too often turn writerly, in the sense it can be about writing. It can be about the problem of actually putting the words on the page. And perhaps earlier on in my career, I would not have preferred to play that game.

   'I needed to convince myself that I could do the first person thing in a way that would be fresh, that I would feel was fresh, that I would feel confident about. I also needed to feel that the pieces *would* stick – that, at the end of the day, all the elements of the story could be legitimately told by a single person. I needed to do some fudging, a little precognitive stuff; I needed a little supernaturalism, because I didn't want to cheat – or, if I was going to cheat, I was going to cheat obviously by playing the supernatural game. I didn't want to give Maddox information he could not possibly have, so within the first thirty pages I allow him that scene with his mother in the sky room, which empowers him, opens his soul up to all kinds of knowledge that he previously would not have had.'
3. In a fine moment of self-critique, Barker writes these words: '*How shall I say what happened to me then?*' His character Rachel sees through the storyteller's gambit: 'It was a clever bluff, that sentence. The writer knew *exactly* how he was going to say what happened to him; he had the words ready. But it made those words seem more true, didn't it, if they appeared to come from a man uncertain of his own skills?'

Chapter 31: Of Gods and Monsters

1. A copy of the final shooting script was published in trade paperback 'for promotional and publicity use only' as *The Candyman Chronicles*. Los Angeles: Polygram Film Productions BV, 1995.
2. *Candyman: Farewell to the Flesh* did inspire one of the more curious items of

Clive Barker-related merchandise: a board game in which players sought to avoid a grisly fate at the hands of the mythic hook-handed killer.

Chapter 32: Stories of Our Own

1. Clive Barker, *The Essential Clive Barker*. London: HarperCollins, 1999. All quotations are taken from the first edition.
2. Information about the *Lost Souls* magazine and website is set forth in the Resources section of this book.
3. 'I tried to dramatize that when I wrote the "Afterword" to *Shadows in Eden*, which begins: *This is someone else*. I don't know who this other person is, but he's loquacious and shallow – and did he really say that?

    'It's much more important that somebody see that what I'm doing is not like anybody else's than that they like it. Being liked as an artist is lower on my list of priorities than I would sometimes like it to be. That is to say, there's a part of me that actually perceives the difficulty. To give you a petty example, in *Sacrament* there's a reference to God. I thought, *Well, I could soften this up, I could make it* : The Creator. Then I thought: *No. Right now I want it to be God, and I want it to be the patriarchal Lord of the Old Testament – because that way people will think about it afresh*. It won't be Marianne Williamson shit; it won't be some kind of soft, *I'm not here to offend anybody, I just want to talk about love*, thing. It'll be God. And if you want to argue with me about it, that'll be great, and we'll have a good argument about it; but the last thing I want is for it to be like politically correct divinity school.'
4. Clive Barker, *Clive Barker's Books of Blood: The Collector's Edition*. New York: Berkley, 1998.
5. 'I knew,' Bradley says, 'that, as fast as he was being pigeonholed as a horror writer or horror director, Clive was planning an escape from that pigeonhole. Because I knew his imaginative world well enough to know that, for him, horror was only a means to an end. It was not an end in itself. It was one way of expressing an imaginative view of the world, but what he really wanted to do was marry the whole thing together: to bring the best that horror had to offer and marry it to the best that William Blake and WB Yeats and the great mystical tradition had to offer.'

    Pete Atkins agrees. During the early days of his friendship with Clive, they were watching television with Pete's parents: 'It was a documentary about Noel Coward, who said, *I'm rather like a mole, dear, just when they've think they've got me pegged, I've popped up out of a different hole*. I remember Clive saying, *Yeah, yeah, that's very smart . . . pop up out of a different hole*. And that's precisely what Clive has done so well.'
6. Clive Barker, *Coldheart Canyon*. London: HarperCollins, 2001.
7. Clive Barker, 'Ramsey Campbell: An Appreciation', *1986 World Fantasy Convention Program Book*, 31 October – 2 November, 1986.
8. 'Images are different from words,' Barker notes, holding out hope that the fiction he wished to present in *The Scarlet Gospels* would one day see print. 'Jane said that we would use the stories in various collections, and I believe

we will. I don't believe the images will ever be published in HarperCollins. In other words, you can write about it, you just can't show it. Funny how the picture of man's finest hour can be so disturbing to people.'

For Ever More

1. Clive's grief over the loss of his father was not easily shaken. 'He spent so much of his time trying to please him, to get his approval,' David Armstrong says, 'a lot of *Why can't you be more like your brother?* When I first met him, I could tell Clive was still trying to prove himself to his dad. Clive didn't see what I saw. His father was as proud as a peacock; it was *That's my boy.* He would never say that in front of Clive, and he loved to give Clive a hard time, maybe because nobody else does; but he was so proud of him, and that meant a lot to him.'

2. To underscore the difficulty of thinking about his efforts in purely mathematical terms, Clive recounts an anecdote from art history: 'Whistler was taken to court for one of his knockdown paintings, because the purchaser didn't like it. It's a very impressionistic work; the patron doesn't like it and wants his money back, although he's not going to get it. The prosecutor says, *Mr Whistler, how long did it take you to paint this?* Whistler said, *Oh, about an hour* – I forget the exact details, it may have been a shorter time – and the prosecutor says: *And are you asking my client to pay 20,000 pounds to you for an hour of your time?* And Whistler said, *No, I'm asking him to pay 20,000 pounds for a lifetime of my knowledge.*'

3. He amplifies his delight of the ambiguities in his paintings with a singular example: 'Let's look at the picture of the grieving man. The grieving man is sitting on a stone which looks like an egg. I did not know he was sitting on an egg when I painted it. I don't know, sitting here now, whether one should think about it optimistically – whether there is something waiting underneath him which will eventually crack open and produce something better than his present state. I do know, though, that painting images like that, done with the heart, opens the opportunity to have that discussion in a way that words don't – unless you experiment with the words, which is very hard for the common reader to accept. Joyce plays that experiment, obviously. Joyce is the great example of somebody who gives you both: the possibility of the man sitting on an egg and the possibility that he is not sitting on an egg; the possibility that the egg may break, the possibility that the egg may just be a stone. In literary terms, that is plausible only if you're playing in a very intellectual space; and if you're playing in that space, you may reasonably assume that your mother and some friends will read it. While painting can be very, very ambiguous, all the time – and popular. That's an exciting prospect.'

4. Michael Marshall Smith offers his own insights into the legendary terrain of 'development hell': 'About six years ago I was contracted to write a television adaptation of *Weaveworld*, primarily for Showtime in the US – though the BBC showed some intermittent interest. After a long and very arduous process – about a year and a half, the first six months of which I worked without

payment – a convincing first draft of eight one-hour episodes was finished. There followed a hiatus of nearly a year while the English production partner (Lifetime) was extricated from the production as a result of a variety of issues between people way above my head. By the time that had all been sorted out, and they came back to me for a second draft, I was too deep in other contracted work to accept the assignment. We tried to find a compromise through a delay, but it couldn't be done – and in the end, after another long delay, in which they came back to me once more, it was given to another writer. I haven't heard anything since; and it must be over two years by now. It was the first screenwriting I ever did, and – despite some major niggles related to payment, which solely relate to the English production company – it was great fun to work on. Clive was great to work with, and Showtime showed a real commitment not just to getting it made, but to doing it well. Shame nothing's happened yet: it could make the greatest TV show of all time.'

PRIMARY BIBLIOGRAPHY

This bibliography originated with the assistance of the late James Blair Lovell, to whom it is dedicated. I also thank Jean-Daniel Brèque, David Dodds, Antonella Fulci, Agnieszka Fulinska, Stephen Jones and Hans Persson for their help in cataloguing international editions. For reasons of space, book club, foreign language and variant editions are listed only as selected examples or where there is historical or archival significance.

BOOKS (IN ALPHABETICAL ORDER)

Being Music. By Clive Barker. Produced by Ciara Nolan. London: EMI Records, Ltd/Songbook Series, 1999 (book and compact disc with illustrations by Clive Barker)

Books of Blood (Volumes One, Two and Three). Illustrated by JK Potter and Harry O Morris, with revised and corrected texts, and updated 'Introduction' by Ramsey Campbell.
- a. Santa Cruz, CA: Scream/Press, 1985 (deluxe signed limited edition hardback; 50 copies)
- b. Santa Cruz, CA: Scream/Press, 1985 (signed limited edition hardback; 250 copies)
- c. Santa Cruz, CA: Scream/Press, 1985 (hardback)
- d. London: Weidenfeld & Nicolson, 1987 (hardback)
- e. New York: Ace/Putnam, 1988 (hardback; includes original Ramsey Campbell introduction, the short story 'The Book of Blood (a postscript): On Jerusalem Street', and three illustrations by Clive Barker)
- f. New York: Dorset, 1991 (hardback; 'instant remainder' edition)

Books of Blood Volumes One to Three. 'Special Collector's Edition' with new introduction by Clive Barker.
 a. London: Sphere, 1998 (trade paperback)
 b. New York: Berkley, 1998 (trade paperback)

The Books of Blood Volumes IV & V. London: Leisure Circle, 1985 (hardback)

Cabal: The Nightbreed
 a. London: Fontana, 1988 (paperback; 'continental edition'; interior art by Clive Barker and Stephen Player; includes twelve page excerpt from *Weaveworld*)
 b. As *Cabal* (includes selected stories from *Clive Barker's Books of Blood Volume Six*). New York: Poseidon, 1988 (signed limited edition hardback, 750 copies; illustrations by Clive Barker)
 c. As *Cabal* (includes selected stories from *Clive Barker's Books of Blood Volume Six*). New York: Poseidon, 1988 (hardback)
 d. London: Fontana, 1989 (paperback)
 e. London: Collins, 1989 (hardback; excludes interior art by Stephen Player and *Weaveworld* excerpt)
 f. As *Cabal* (includes selected stories from *Clive Barker's Books of Blood Volume Six*). New York: Pocket, 1989 (paperback)
 g. New York: Pocket, 1990 (paperback; motion picture tie-in edition)
 h. London: Fontana, 1990 (paperback; motion picture tie-in edition)

Clive Barker's Books of Blood: A Portfolio. Washington, DC: Arcane, 1988 (signed and numbered limited edition of lithographs by Clive Barker)

Clive Barker's Books of Blood Volume One
 a. London: Sphere, 1984 (paperback; subsequent printings replaced cover art by John Knight with art by Clive Barker)
 b. London: Weidenfeld & Nicolson, 1985 (hardback with cover art by Clive Barker; deletes 'Introduction' by Ramsey Campbell)
 c. New York: Berkley, 1986 (paperback)

Clive Barker's Books of Blood Volume Two
 a. London: Sphere, 1984 (paperback; subsequent printings replaced cover art by John Knight with art by Clive Barker)
 b. London: Weidenfeld & Nicolson, 1985 (hardback; cover art by Clive Barker)
 c. New York: Berkley, 1986 (paperback)

Clive Barker's Books of Blood Volume Three
 a. London: Sphere, 1984 (paperback; subsequent printings replaced cover art by John Knight with art by Clive Barker)

b. London: Weidenfeld & Nicolson, 1985 (hardback; cover art by Clive Barker)

c. New York: Berkley, 1986 (paperback)

Clive Barker's Books of Blood Volume Four

a. London: Sphere, 1985 (paperback; subsequent printings replaced cover art by John Knight with art by Clive Barker)

b. London: Weidenfeld & Nicolson, 1986 (hardback; cover art by Clive Barker)

c. As *The Inhuman Condition* (story order rearranged). New York: Poseidon, 1986 (hardback)

d. As *The Inhuman Condition* (story order rearranged). Garden City, NY: Science Fiction Book Club, 1987 (hardback; book club edition)

e. As *The Inhuman Condition* (story order rearranged). New York: Pocket, 1988 (paperback)

Clive Barker's Books of Blood Volume Five

a. London: Sphere, 1985 (paperback; subsequent printings replaced cover art by John Knight with art by Clive Barker)

b. London: Weidenfeld & Nicolson, 1986 (hardback; cover art by Clive Barker)

c. As *In the Flesh* (story order rearranged). New York: Poseidon, 1986 (hardback)

d. As *In the Flesh* (story order rearranged). Garden City, NY: Science Fiction Book Club, 1987 (hardback; book club edition)

e. As *In the Flesh* (story order rearranged). New York: Pocket, 1988 (paperback)

Clive Barker's Books of Blood Volume Six

a. London: Sphere, 1985 (paperback; subsequent printings replaced cover art by by John Knight with art by Clive Barker)

b. London: Weidenfeld & Nicolson, 1986 (hardback; cover art by Clive Barker)

c. As *Cabal* (includes selected stories from *Clive Barker's Books of Blood Volume Six*). New York: Poseidon, 1988 (signed limited edition hardback, 750 copies; illustrations by Clive Barker)

d. As *Cabal* (includes selected stories from *Clive Barker's Books of Blood Volume Six*). New York: Poseidon, 1988 (hardback)

e. As *Cabal* (includes selected stories from *Clive Barker's Books of Blood Volume Six*). New York: Pocket, 1989 (paperback)

f. As *Lord of Illusions: Clive Barker's Books of Blood Volume Six*. London: Warner, 1995 (paperback; motion picture tie-in edition)

Clive Barker's Books of Blood Volumes One, Two and Three.
  a. London: Weidenfeld & Nicolson, 1985 (boxed set of signed limited edition hardbacks, with cover art by Clive Barker; 200 copies)
  b. As *Clive Barker's Books of Blood, Vols. 1–3*. London: Sphere, 1988 (trade paperback)

Clive Barker's Books of Blood Volumes Four, Five and Six
  a. London: Weidenfeld & Nicolson, 1986 (boxed set of signed limited edition hardbacks, with cover art by Clive Barker; 200 copies)
  b. As *Clive Barker's Books of Blood, Vols. 4–6*. London: Sphere, 1988 (trade paperback)

Clive Barker's Books of Blood Volumes I & II. London: Sphere, 1984 (hardback; book club edition)

Coldheart Canyon
  a. London: HarperCollins, 2001 (hardback)
  b. New York: HarperCollins, 2001 (hardback)
  c. London: HarperCollins, 2002 (paperback)
  d. New York: HarperPaperbacks, 2002 (paperback)

The Damnation Game
  a. London: Weidenfeld & Nicolson, 1985 (signed limited edition hardback; 250 copies)
  b. London: Weidenfeld & Nicolson, 1985 (hardback)
  c. London: Sphere, 1986 (paperback)
  d. New York: Ace/Putnam, 1987 (hardback)
  e. Garden City, NY: Science Fiction Book Club, 1987 (hardback; book club edition)
  f. New York: Charter, 1988 (paperback)
  g. New York: Berkley, 1996 (paperback; cover by MC Escher)

The Essential Clive Barker
  a. London: HarperCollins, 1999 (hardback)
  b. New York: HarperCollins, 2000 (hardback)
  c. London: HarperCollins, 2000 (paperback)
  d. New York: HarperPaperbacks, 2001 (paperback)

Everville ('The Second Book of the Art')
  a. London: HarperCollins, 1994 (signed limited edition hardback; with 'Introduction' by Clive Barker)
  b. London: HarperCollins, 1994 (hardback)
  c. New York: HarperCollins, 1994 (hardback)
  d. London: HarperCollins, 1995 (paperback)

   e. New York: HarperPaperbacks, 1995 (paperback)
   f. New York: HarperPerennial, 1999 (paperback; with 'Introduction' by Clive Barker)

Forms of Heaven: Three Plays (collecting *Crazyface, Paradise Street* and *Subtle Bodies*)
   a. London: HarperCollins, 1996 (hardback)
   b. New York: HarperCollins, 1996 (hardback)

Galilee ('A Romance')
   a. London: HarperCollins, 1998 (hardback)
   b. New York: HarperCollins, 1998 (hardback)
   c. London: HarperCollins, 1999 (paperback)
   d. New York: HarperPaperbacks, 1999 (paperback)

The Great and Secret Show ('The First Book of the Art')
   a. London: Collins, 1989 (signed limited edition hardback; 500 copies; interior illustrations by Clive Barker)
   b. London: Collins, 1989 (hardback)
   c. New York: Harper & Row, 1989 (hardback)
   d. London: Fontana/Collins, 1989 (paperback; 'continental edition')
   e. London: Fontana/Collins, 1990 (trade paperback)
   f. London: Fontana/Collins, 1990 (paperback)
   g. New York: HarperPaperbacks, 1990 (paperback)

The Hellbound Heart (see 'The Hellbound Heart')
   a. London: Fontana, 1991 (paperback)
   b. New York: HarperPaperbacks, 1991 (paperback)

Imajica
   a. London: HarperCollins, 1991 (hardback)
   b. New York: HarperCollins, 1991 (hardback)
   c. London: Fontana, 1992 (paperback)
   d. London: Fontana, 1992 (paperback; 'special overseas edition')
   d. New York: HarperPaperbacks, 1992 (paperback)
   e. In two volumes, as *Imajica I: The Fifth Dominion* and *Imajica II: The Reconciliation*. New York: HarperPaperbacks, 1995 (paperbacks; with 'Back and back we go . . .' by Clive Barker)

Incarnations: Three Plays (collecting *Colossus, Frankenstein in Love* and *The History of the Devil*)
   a. London: HarperCollins, 1995 (hardback)
   b. New York: HarperCollins, 1995 (hardback)

Sacrament
   a. London: HarperCollins, 1996 (hardback)

b. New York: HarperCollins, 1996 (hardback)
c. London: HarperCollins, 1997 (paperback)
d. New York: HarperPaperbacks, 1997 (paperback)

The Thief of Always: A Fable
a. London: HarperCollins, 1992 (hardback)
b. New York: HarperCollins, 1992 (hardback)
c. London: Fontana, 1993 (paperback)
d. New York: HarperPaperbacks, 1993 (paperback)
e. London: Collins, 1995 (trade paperback)

Weaveworld
a. London: Collins, 1987 (bound galley; 'special advance reader's sample: Parts 1–4'; contains 'Book One – In the Kingdom of the Cuckoo')
b. London: Collins, 1987 (bound galley; 'special advance reader's sample: Parts 1–4'; contains complete text)
c. London: Collins, 1987 (signed limited edition hardback; 500 copies for sale; 26 lettered copies for private distribution; with illustrations by Clive Barker)
d. London: Collins, 1987 (hardback)
e. London: Collins, 1987 (hardback; book club edition)
f. New York: Poseidon, 1987 (hardback)
g. New York: Poseidon, 1987 (signed limited edition hardback; 500 copies)
h. London: Fontana, 1988 (paperback; 'continental edition')
i. London: Fontana, 1988 (paperback)
j. New York: Pocket, 1988 (paperback; ABA advance edition)
k. New York: Pocket, 1988 (paperback)
l. London: HarperCollins, 1997 (paperback; 'Tenth Anniversary Edition')

Weaveworld & Cabal. London: Diamond, 1993 (hardback; 'instant remainder' edition)

SHORT FICTION AND PLAYS (IN ALPHABETICAL ORDER)

'The Age of Desire'
1. *Clive Barker's Books of Blood Volume Four*, 1985 (UK)
2. *The Inhuman Condition*, 1986 (US)
3. *Between Time and Terror.* ed. Stefan R Dziemianowicz, Martin H Greenberg and Robert H Weinberg. New York: Roc, 1995 (paperback)

'Animal Life'
1. *USA Today Weekend*, 24–26 June 1994 (magazine)

2. *Dark Terrors 2: The Gollancz Book of Horror.* ed. Stephen Jones and David Sutton
   a. London: Gollancz, 1996 (hardback)
   b. As *Dark Terrors 2.* London: Vista, 1997 (paperback)
3. As 'Hundeleben'. Translated into German by Susanne Walter. *Das Grosse Lesebuch Der Fantasy.* ed. Melissa Andersson. Munich: GSF, 1995

'Babel's Children'
1. *Clive Barker's Books of Blood Volume Four,* 1985 (UK)
2. *The Inhuman Condition,* 1986 (US)
3. *Omni,* vol. 9 no. 6, March 1987 (magazine)
4. Translated into Japanese by Jun Atsuki. *Omni,* no. 11, November 1987 (magazine)

'The Body Politic'
1. *Clive Barker's Books of Blood Volume Four,* 1985 (UK)
2. *The Inhuman Condition,* 1986 (US)

'The Book of Blood'
1. *Clive Barker's Books of Blood Volume One,* 1984 (UK)
2. *The Fantasy Sampler.* New York: Berkley, 1985 (bound galley)
3. *Clive Barker's Books of Blood Volume One,* 1985 (US)
4. *Omni,* vol. 8 no. 8, May 1986 (magazine)
5. As 'Veren kirja'. Translated into Finnish by Matti Rosvall. *Portti,* no. 1, 1988 (magazine)
6. *Night Screams.* ed. Ed Gorman and Martin H Greenberg. New York: Roc, 1996 (paperback)

'The Book of Blood (a postscript): On Jerusalem Street'
1. *Clive Barker's Books of Blood Volume Six,* 1985 (UK)
2. *Books of Blood.* New York: Ace/Putnam, 1988 (hardback; with illustrations by Clive Barker)
3. As 'Veren kirja (jalkisanat)'. Translated into Finnish by Matti Rosvall. *Portti,* no. 1, 1988 (magazine)

'Cabal'
Cabal
   a. New York: Poseidon, 1988 (signed limited edition hardback, 750 copies; illustrations by Clive Barker)
   b. New York: Poseidon, 1988 (hardback)
   c. New York: Pocket, 1989 (paperback)

'Cabal' (excerpt from *Cabal*)
Die Jumbos von Heyne. ed. Anonymous. Translated into German by Joachim Körber. Munich: Heyne Jumbo, 1989

'Candyman' (see 'The Forbidden')

'Chiliad: A Meditation' (in two parts)
Revelations. ed. Douglas E Winter.
    a. New York: HarperPrism, 1997 (hardback)
    b. As *Millennium*. London: HarperCollins, 1997 (hardback)
    c. New York: HarperPrism, 1998 (paperback)
    d. As *Millennium*. London: HarperCollins, 1998 (paperback)
    e. As 'Chiliad: Una riflessione'. Translated into Italian by Antonella Melegari. Milan: Sperling & Kupfer, 1999
    f. As 'Chiliade: Eine Meditation'. In German. *Offenbarungen*. Bergisch Gladbach: Bastei Lübbe, 1999 (trade paperback)
    g. As 'Parousie'. In French. *Douglas E Winter présente Révélations: Onze hymnes à l'Apocalypse*. Paris: J'ai Lu, 2000 (paperback)
    h. New York: HarperCollins, 2001 (trade paperback)

'A Clown's Sodom: Act I'
Dread, no. 5, 1992 (magazine)

'A Clown's Sodom: Act II'
Dread, no. 6, 1992 (magazine)

'A Clown's Sodom: Act III'
Dread, no. 7, 1992 (magazine)

'Coldheart Canyon' (excerpt)
Los Angeles Times Book Review, 16 April 2000 (newspaper)

Colossus
Incarnations: Three Plays, 1995

'Coming to Grief'
    1. *Prime Evil*. ed. Douglas E Winter.
        a. New York: New American Library, 1988 (hardback)
        b. Rhode Island: Donald M Grant, 1988 (signed limited edition hardback; print run: 1000 copies)
        c. London: Transworld/Bantam, 1988 (signed limited edition hardback; print run: 250 copies)
        d. London: Transworld/Bantam, 1988 (hardback)
        f. New York: Signet, 1989 (paperback)
        g. London: Corgi, 1989 (paperback)
        h. As 'La inminencia del desastre'. Translated into Spanish by Eduardo G Murillo. *Escalofrios*. Barcelona: Grijalbo Mondadori, 1989 (trade paperback)

    i. As 'Rouwtijd'. In Dutch. *Meesters van het Kwaad*. Amsterdam: Uitgeverij Luitingh, 1989

    j. As 'Heimkehr in Trauer'. Translated into German by Joachim Körber. *Horror vom Feinsten*. Munich: Heyne Jumbo, 1989; Stuttgart/Hamburg/ Munich: Deutscher Bücherbund, 1990; Gütersloh: Bertelsmann Lesering, 1991; Munich: HTB, 1993

    j. As 'Deuil'. Translated into French by Jean-Daniel Brèque. *13 Histoires diaboliques*. Paris: Albin Michel, 1990 (trade paperback); Paris: Grand Livre du Mois, 1990 (hardback; book club edition); Paris: Pocket, 1992 (paperback); Paris: Editions de Seine, 1995 (trade paperback; book club edition)

    k. As 'Addio al passato'. Translated into Italian by Eileen Romano. *In Principio Era il Male*. Milan: Arnoldo Mondadori Editore, 1990 (trade paperback); Milan: Arnoldo Mondadori Editore, 1994 (trade paperback)

2. *Good Housekeeping*, vol. 13 no. 4, October 1988 (magazine)

3. As 'To Pathima'. Translated into Greek by Giannis Deliolanis. *Sigchrones Istories Tromou: Skotina Oramata 1*. Athens: Epilogi, 1992

'Confessions of a (Pornographer's) Shroud'
1. *Clive Barker's Books of Blood Volume One*, 1984 (UK)
2. *Clive Barker's Books of Blood Volume One*, 1985 (US)
3. *The Mists From Beyond*. ed. Stefan R Dziemianowicz, Martin H Greenberg and Robert Weinberg.
    a. New York: Roc, 1993 (hardback)
    b. New York: Roc, 1995 (paperback)
    c. As 'Bekenntnisse eines (Pornographen-) Leichentuchs'. Translated into German by Peter Kobbe. *Nebel aus dem Jenseits*. Berlin: Aufbau Taschenbuch, 1995 (paperback)

Crazyface
Forms of Heaven: Three Plays, 1996

'The Departed' (see 'Hermione and the Moon')

'Down, Satan!'
1. *Clive Barker's Books of Blood Volume Four*, 1985 (UK)
2. *The Inhuman Condition*, 1986 (US)
3. *Twilight Zone Magazine*, June 1987 (magazine)
4. As 'Erscheine, Satan!' Translated into German by Peter Kobbe. *That's Clive*, no. 4, February 1997 (magazine)

'Dread'
1. *Clive Barker's Books of Blood Volume Two*, 1984 (UK)
2. *Clive Barker's Books of Blood Volume Two*, 1985 (US)

3. *The Dark Descent*. ed. David G Hartwell.
   a. New York: Tor, 1987 (hardback)
   b. As 'Terrore'. Translated into Italian by Grazia Alineri. *Il colore del male*. Milan: Armenia Editore, 1989

Frankenstein in Love, or The Life of Death Incarnations: Three Plays, 1995

'The Forbidden'
   1. *Clive Barker's Books of Blood Volume Four*, 1985 (UK)
   2. *Fantasy Tales*, vol. 7 no. 14, summer 1985 (magazine)
   3. *The Inhuman Condition*, 1986 (US)
   4. *The Best Horror from Fantasy Tales*. ed. Stephen Jones and David Sutton.
      a. London: Robinson, 1988 (hardback)
      b. New York: Carroll & Graf, 1990 (hardback)
      c. As *Los Mejores Relatos de Terror de Fantasy Tales*. Madrid: Grupo Libro 88, 1993 (trade paperback)
   5. As 'Candyman'. Translated into German by Peter Kobbe. *Das Grosse Horror Lesebuch II*. ed. Robert Vito. Munich: GTB, 1993 (trade paperback; in German)
   6. *The Unexplained: Stories of the Paranormal*. ed. Ric Alexander (pseudonym of Peter Haining).
      a. London: Orion, 1998 (hardback)
      b. London: Millennium, 1998 (paperback)
   7. As 'Candyman'. *The Reel Stuff*. ed. Brain M Thomsen and Martin H Greenberg. New York: DAW, 1998 (paperback)
   8. As 'Candyman'. *Vintage Science Fiction*. ed. Peter Haining. New York: Carroll & Graf, 1999 (trade paperback)

'The Hellbound Heart'
   Night Visions 3. With Ramsey Campbell and Lisa Tuttle. Introduction by George R R Martin.
      a. Niles, IL: Dark Harvest, 1986 (signed limited edition hardback; 400 copies)
      b. Niles, IL: Dark Harvest, 1986 (hardback)
      c. As *Night Visions*. London: Century Hutchison, 1987 (hardback)
      d. As *Night Visions*. London: Legend, 1987 (paperback)
      e. As *The Hellbound Heart*. New York: Berkley, 1988
      f. As *Hellehart: horrorverhalen*. Translated into Dutch by Mariëlla de Kuiper-Snel. Utrecht: Luitingh-Sijthoff, 1989

'Hell's Event'
   1. *Clive Barker's Books of Blood Volume Two*, 1984 (UK)
   2. *Clive Barker's Books of Blood Volume Two*, 1985 (US)

'Hermione and the Moon'
1. *New York Times*, 30 October 1992 (newspaper)
2. *The Year's Best Fantasy and Horror: Sixth Annual Collection*. ed. Ellen Datlow and Terri Windling.
   a. New York: St. Martin's Press, 1993 (hardback)
   b. New York: St. Martin's Press, 1993 (trade paperback)
3. As 'The Departed'. *Best New Horror 4*. ed. Stephen Jones and Ramsey Campbell.
   a. London: Robinson, 1993 (hardback; trade paperback)
   b. New York: Carroll & Graf, 1993 (hardback)
   c. As 'I defunti'. Translated into Italian by Rita Botter Pierangeli. *Horror: Il meglio*. Milan: Editrice Nord, 1994 (trade paperback)
4. As 'The Departed'. *The Giant Book of Terror*. ed. Stephen Jones and Ramsey Campbell.
   a. London: Magpie, 1994 (trade paperback)
   b. Australia: Book Company, 1994 (trade paperback)
   c. London: Parragon, 1994 (trade paperback)
5. As 'Hermione en de Maan'. Translated into Dutch by Mariëlla Snel. *Spannend Gebundeld*. ed. Nico Keulers. Amsterdam: JM Meulenhoff, 1994
6. *Das Grosse Horror Lesebuch III*. ed. Robert Vito. In German. Munich: GTB, 1994 (trade paperback)
7. *That's Clive!*, no. 1, January 1996 (magazine; in German)

The History of the Devil
Incarnations: Three Plays, 1995

'The History of the Devil: A Play in Two Acts'
Pandemonium: Further Explorations into the World of Clive Barker. ed. Michael Brown.
   a. Staten Island, NY: Eclipse, 1991 (signed limited edition hardback)
   b. Staten Island, NY: Eclipse, 1991 (hardback)
   c. Staten Island, NY: Eclipse, 1991 (trade paperback)

'How Spoilers Bleed'
1. *Clive Barker's Books of Blood Volume Six*, 1985 (UK)
2. *Cabal*, 1988 (US)
3. *The Magazine of Fantasy & Science Fiction*, October 1988 (magazine; special 39th anniversary issue)
4. As 'Wie Schänder Bluten'. In German. *Abgründe: Die Besten Horrorgeschichten*. ed. Joachim Körber. Bern/Munich/Wien: Scherz Verlag, 1996 (in German)

'Human Remains'
1. *Clive Barker's Books of Blood Volume Three*, 1984 (UK)

566

2. *Clive Barker's Books of Blood Volume Three*, 1985 (US)
3. *The Mammoth Book of Vampires.* ed. Stephen Jones.
    a. London: Robinson, 1992 (trade paperback)
    b. New York: Carroll & Graf, 1992 (trade paperback)
    c. As *The Giant Book of Vampires.* London: Magpie, 1994 (trade paperback)
    d. As *The Giant Book of Vampires.* Australia: Book Company, 1994 (trade paperback)
    e. As *The Giant Book of Vampires.* London: Parragon, 1994 (trade paperback)
    f. As *Book of Vampires.* New York: Barnes & Noble, 1997 (hardback)
    g. As 'Resti umani'. Translated into Italian by Gianni Pilo. *Vampiri!* Rome: Newton & Compton, 1997 (trade paperback)

'In the Flesh'
1. *Clive Barker's Books of Blood Volume Five*, 1985 (UK)
2. *In the Flesh*, 1986 (US)

'In the Hills, the Cities'
1. *Clive Barker's Books of Blood Volume One*, 1984 (UK)
2. *Clive Barker's Books of Blood Volume One*, 1985 (US)
3. *Masters of Darkness II.* ed. Dennis Etchison. New York: Tor, 1988 (paperback)
4. *The Complete Masters of Darkness.* ed. Dennis Etchison.
    a. Novato, CA: Underwood-Miller, 1990 (signed limited edition hardback)
    b. Novato, CA: Underwood-Miller, 1990 (hardback)
5. *Foundations of Fear, Volume 3: Visions of Fear.* ed. David G Hartwell. New York: Tor, 1994 (hardback)

'The Inhuman Condition'
1. *Clive Barker's Books of Blood Volume Four*, 1985 (UK)
2. *The Inhuman Condition*, 1986 (US)

'Jacqueline Ess: Her Will and Testament'
1. *Clive Barker's Books of Blood Volume Two*, 1984 (UK)
2. *Clive Barker's Books of Blood Volume Two*, 1985 (US)
3. As 'Jacqueline Ess: Ses Dérnieres Volontes'. Translated into French by Jean-Daniel Brèque. *Mater Tenebrarum Fantastique*, no. 2, 1985 (magazine)
4. *I Shudder At Your Touch.* ed. Michele Slung.
    a. New York: Roc, 1991 (hardback)
    b. New York: Roc, 1992 (paperback)
    c. As 'Jacqueline Ess: Ihr Wille und Ihr Vermächtnis'. In German. *Ich*

Bebe Wenn Du Mich Berührst. Bergisch Gladbach: BLP, 1992; Bergisch Gladbach: BLTB, 1996 (paperback)

d. In Swedish. *I Nod och Lust: 22 Erotiska Skracknoveller.* Stockholm: Walstroms, 1992

e. As 'Jacqueline Ess: le sue ultime volontà'. Translated into Italian by Anna Rusconi. *Se mi tocchi ho un brivido.* Milan: Longanesi, 1992; Milan: Editori Associati, 1994

'The Last Illusion'
1. *Clive Barker's Books of Blood Volume Six,* 1985 (UK)
2. *Cabal,* 1988 (US)
3. *The Mammoth Book of Terror.* ed. Stephen Jones.
   a. New York: Carroll & Graf, 1991 (trade paperback)
   b. London: Robinson, 1991 (trade paperback)
   c. As *The Anthology of Horror Stories.* London: Tiger Books, 1994 (hardback)
   d. As *The Giant Book of Horror.* Australia: Book Company, 1996 (trade paperback)
   e. As *The Giant Book of Horror.* London: Parragon, 1996 (trade paperback)
   f. As *The Giant Book of Horror.* London: Magpie, 1996 (trade paperback)
   g. As 'L'ultima illusione'. Translated into Italian by Gianni Pilo. *Terrore!* Rome: Newton & Compton, 1996 (trade paperback)

'The Life of Death'
1. *Clive Barker's Books of Blood Volume Six,* 1985 (UK)
2. *Cabal,* 1988 (US)

'Lost Souls' ('A Christmas Horror Story')
1. *Time Out,* no. 800, 19 December, 1985-1 January, 1986 (magazine)
2. *Cutting Edge.* ed. Dennis Etchison.
   a. New York: Doubleday, 1986 (hardback)
   b. New York: St. Martin's, 1987 (paperback)
   c. London: Futura, 1987 (paperback)
   d. London: Macdonald, 1988 (hardback)
   e. As 'Tamashii no yukue'. In Japanese. *Kattingu Ejji.* Tokyo : Shinchosha, 1993 (paperback)
   f. As 'Anime perdute'. Translated into Italian by Manlio Benigni. *Profondo Horror: I migliori racconti di fine millennio.* Milan: Bompiani, 1993; Milan: Fratelli Fabbri Editori, 1995
3. As 'Verlorene Seelen'. In German. *Horror vom Feinsten 2.* ed. Joachim Körber. Munich, Germany: HTB, 1993 (trade paperback)
4. *Lost Souls,* vol. 0 no. 0, 1995 (magazine; illustrations by the author)

5. *Dark Detectives: Adventures of the Supernatural Sleuths*. ed. Stephen Jones.
   a. Minneapolis, MN: Fedoghan & Bremer, 1999 (limited edition hardback)
   a. Minneapolis, MN: Fedoghan & Bremer, 1999 (hardback)
6. As 'Les âmes perdues'. Translated into French by Jean-Daniel Brèque. *Ténèbres*, no. 5, January 1999 (magazine)

'The Madonna'
1. *Clive Barker's Books of Blood Volume Four*, 1985 (UK)
2. *The Inhuman Condition*, 1986 (US)

'Mama Pus' (excerpt from *Weaveworld*)
   Time Out, 30 September – 7 October, 1987 (magazine)

'The Midnight Meat Train'
1. *Clive Barker's Books of Blood Volume One*, 1984 (UK)
2. *Clive Barker's Books of Blood Volume One*, 1985 (US)
3. *Splatterpunks: Extreme Horror*. ed. Paul M Sammon.
   a. New York: St. Martin's, 1990 (hardback)
   b. New York: St. Martin's, 1990 (trade paperback)
   c. As 'Fleischlieferung um Mitternacht'. In German. *Splatterpunk*. Munich: HTB, 1992
   d. As 'Macelleria mobile di mezzanotte'. Translated into Italian by Antonio Cecchi and Raffaela Ciampa. *Splatter Punk: Extreme horror*. Milan: Arnoldo Mondadori Editore, 1995

'New Murders in the Rue Morgue'
1. *Clive Barker's Books of Blood Volume Two*, 1984 (UK)
2. *Clive Barker's Books of Blood Volume Two*, 1985 (US)
3. As 'Nieuwe Moorden in de Rue Morgue'. Translated into Dutch by Hugo Kuipers. *Horror Factor 7*. ed. Robert-Henk Zuidinga. Utrecht: Luitingh-Sijthoff, 1988 (trade paperback)
4. As 'Neue Morde in der Rue Morgue'. In German. *Das Erste Buch des Horrors*. ed. Joachim Körber. Munich: Wilhelm Heyne, 1991 (paperback)

'On Amen's Shore'
1. *Demons and Deviants*. ed. Michael Brown. Phantom Press/Fantaco, 1992.
2. *Little Deaths: 24 Tales of Sex and Horror*. ed. Ellen Datlow.
   a. London: Millennium, 1994 (hardback)
   b. London: Millennium, 1994 (paperback)
   c. New York: Dell, 1995 (paperback)
   d. As 'An den Ufern von Amen'. In German. *Fieber*. Munich: HTB, 1996

e. As 'Sur les rives d'Amen'. Translated into French by Jean-Daniel Brèque. *La Petite Mort*. Paris: Albin Michel, 1998 (trade paperback)

Paradise Street
Forms of Heaven: Three Plays, 1996

'Pidgin and Theresa'
1. *The Time Out Book of London Short Stories*. ed. Maria Lexton. London: Penguin, 1993 (trade paperback)
2. *Secret City: Strange Tales of London*. ed. Stephen Jones and Jo Fletcher.
   a. London: 1997 World Fantasy Convention/Titan, 1997 (limited edition hardback)
   b. London: 1997 World Fantasy Convention/Titan, 1997 (trade paperback)

'Pig Blood Blues'
1. *Clive Barker's Books of Blood Volume One*, 1984 (UK)
2. *Clive Barker's Books of Blood Volume One*, 1985 (US)
3. *Nursery Crimes: Thirty Classic Tales of Horror*. ed. Stefan R Dziemianowicz, Robert Weinberg and Martin H Greenberg. New York, NY: Barnes & Noble, 1993 (hardback)

'Rawhead Rex'
1. *Clive Barker's Books of Blood Volume Three*, 1984 (UK)
2. *Clive Barker's Books of Blood Volume Three*, 1985 (US)

'Revelations'
1. *Clive Barker's Books of Blood Volume Four*, 1985 (UK)
2. *A Special Preview Tale from The Inhuman Condition*. New York: Poseidon, 1986 (bound galley; not for sale)
3. *The Inhuman Condition*, 1986 (US)

'The Rhapsodist' (Chapter 3 of *Cabal*)
Gaslight & Ghosts. ed. Stephen Jones and Jo Fletcher. London: 1988 World Fantasy Convention/Robinson, 1988 (hardback; with illustration by Clive Barker)

'Sacrament' (excerpt from *Sacrament*)
World Horror Convention 1996 Program Book. ed. Alan Burd Newcomer. Eugene, OR: World Horror Convention, 1996

'Scape-Goats'
1. *Clive Barker's Books of Blood Volume Three*, 1984 (UK)
2. *Clive Barker's Books of Blood Volume Three*, 1985 (US)

3. *Sea Cursed.* ed. T Liam McDonald, Stefan R Dziemianowicz and Martin H Greenberg. New York: Barnes & Noble, 1994 (hardback)
4. *Splatterpunks II: Over the Edge.* ed. Paul M Sammon.
   a. New York: Tor, 1995 (hardback)
   b. New York: Tor, 1995 (trade paperback)

'Sex, Death and Starshine'
1. *Clive Barker's Books of Blood Volume One*, 1984 (UK)
2. *Clive Barker's Books of Blood Volume One*, 1985 (US)
3. *The Mammoth Book of Zombies.* ed. Stephen Jones.
   a. London: Robinson, 1993 (trade paperback)
   b. New York: Carroll & Graf, 1993 (trade paperback)
   c. As 'Sesso, morte e stelle'. Translated into Italian by Paola Tomaselli. *Il ritorno degli zombi.* Milan: Arnoldo Mondadori Editore, 1994 (trade paperback)
   d.. As *The Giant Book of Zombies.* London: Magpie, 1995 (trade paperback)
   e. As *The Giant Book of Zombies.* Australia: Book Company, 1995 (trade paperback)
   f. As *The Giant Book of Zombies.* London: Parragon, 1995 (trade paperback)
4. As 'Sex, Tod und Starglanz'. In German. *Erotic Horror.* ed. Joachim Körber. Munich: HTB, 1993

'Six Commonplaces' (verse from *Weaveworld*)
Fantasy Tales, vol. 9 no. 17, summer 1987 (magazine; illustrated by Clive Barker)

'The Skins of the Fathers'
1. *Clive Barker's Books of Blood Volume Two*, 1984 (UK)
2. *Clive Barker's Books of Blood Volume Two*, 1985 (US)

'Son of Celluloid'
1. *Clive Barker's Books of Blood Volume Three*, 1984 (UK)
2. *Clive Barker's Books of Blood Volume Three*, 1985 (US)
3. *Silver Scream.* ed. David J Schow.
   a. Arlington Heights, IL: Dark Harvest, 1988 (signed limited edition hardback)
   b. Arlington Heights, IL: Dark Harvest, 1988 (hardback)
   c. New York: Tor Books, 1988 (paperback; corrected version)
   d. As 'Figlio di celluloide'. Translated into Italian by Tullio Dobner. *Lo schermo dell'incubo.* Turin: Einaudi, 1998
4. *Skeleton Crew*, no. III/IV, 1988 (magazine; special Clive Barker double issue)

5. *A Taste for Blood.* ed. Martin H Greenberg, Stefan R Dziemianowicz and Robert Weinberg. New York: Dorset, 1992 (hardback)
6. *Mondo Marilyn.* ed. Lucinda Ebersole and Richard Peabody. New York: St. Martin's Press, 1995 (paperback)

'A Story with No Title, a Street with No Name' (story fragment from which others were encouraged to write their own stories)
Kaleidospace, 1995 (now-defunct website)

Subtle Bodies
Forms of Heaven: Three Plays, 1996

'Twilight at the Towers'
1. *Clive Barker's Books of Blood Volume Six*, 1985 (UK)
2. *Cabal*, 1988 (US)
3. *The Mammoth Book of Werewolves.* ed. Stephen Jones.
   a. London: Robinson, 1994 (trade paperback)
   b. New York: Carroll & Graf, 1994 (trade paperback)
   c. As *The Giant Book of Werewolves.* London: Magpie, 1995 (trade paperback)
   d. As *The Giant Book of Werewolves.* Australia: Book Company,1995 (trade paperback)
   e. As *The Giant Book of Werewolves.* London: Parragon, 1995 (trade paperback)
   f. As 'Crepuscolo alle torri'. Translated into Italian by Gianni Pilo. *Lupi mannari!* Rome: Newton & Compton, 1997 (trade paperback)

'Die Verbannten' (excerpt from *Weaveworld*)
Heyne Jahresband 1990. ed. Anonymous. Munich: HTB, 1990

'Whose Line Is It Anyway?' (round-robin story written with Kathy Acker, Neil Bartlett, Michael Bracewell, Celia Brayfield, Jane Ellison, Neil Gaiman, Steve Grant, Lesley Grant-Adamson, Roger McGouch, Lise Mayer, John Milne, Terry Pratchett, Fiona Richmond, Dyan Sheldon and Victor Lewis Smith)
Time Out, no. 956/7, 14–28 December 1988 (magazine)

'The Yattering and Jack'
1. *Clive Barker's Books of Blood Volume One*, 1984 (UK)
2. *Clive Barker's Books of Blood Volume One*, 1985 (US)
3. As 'Teufels-Weihnacht'. Translated into German by Peter Köbbe. *Playboy*, no. 1/87, December 1986 (magazine)
4. *Iniquities*, vol. 1 no. 1, August 1990 (magazine)

SHORT NONFICTION (IN ALPHABETICAL ORDER)

'Art'
The Essential Clive Barker, 1999

'Artist's Statement for One Flesh Exhibition' (written February 11, 1997)
Hollywood, CA: La Luz de Jesus, 1997 (art exhibition essay)

'Back and back we go . . .'
1. *Imajica I: The Fifth Dominion*. New York: HarperPaperbacks, 1995 (paperback)
2. *Imajica II: The Reconciliation*. New York: HarperPaperbacks, 1995 (paperback)

'The Bare Bones: An Introduction'
1. *Scared Stiff: Tales of Sex and Death*. By Ramsey Campbell
   a. Santa Cruz, CA: Scream/Press, 1987 (signed limited edition hardback)
   b. Santa Cruz, CA: Scream/Press, 1987 (hardback)
   c. New York: Warner, 1988 (trade paperback)
   d. London: Macdonald, 1989 (hardback)
   e. As 'Introduzione'. Translated into Italian by Elisabetta Svaluto Moreolo. *Il sesso della morte*. Milan: Armenia Editore, 1992
2. As 'An Introduction: The Bare Bones'. *Clive Barker's Shadows in Eden*, 1991

'Barker's Bloody Best'
Shock Xpress, no. 3, January-February 1986 (magazine)

'Bestiary'
The Essential Clive Barker, 1999

'Big Chills'
1. *American Film*, September 1987 (magazine)
2. Revised as 'King Of Horror Picks Favourite Scary Flicks'. *Toronto Sun*, 30 October 1988 (newspaper)
3. *Clive Barker's Shadows in Eden*, 1991

'The Body'
The Essential Clive Barker, 1999

'Christopher Marlowe: *The Tragical History of Dr Faustus*'
1. *Horror: 100 Best Books*. eds. Stephen Jones and Kim Newman

   a. London: Xanadu, 1988 (signed limited edition hardback; 300 copies)
   b. London: Xanadu, 1988 (hardback)
   c. New York: Carroll & Graf, 1989 (hardback)
   d. New York: Carroll & Graf, 1990 (trade paperback)
   e. London: New English Library, 1992 (trade paperback; revised and updated edition)
   f. New York: Carroll & Graf, 1998 (trade paperback; revised and updated edition)
2. *Clive Barker's Shadows in Eden*, 1991

'Cinematic fear comes in at the ears . . .' (liner notes)
Clive Barker's Lord of Illusions: The Soundtrack of the United Artists Film. Composed, conducted and performed by Simon Boswell. United Artists/ Mute Records, 1995 (compact disc)

'Clive Barker on Stephen King, Horror and EC Comics'
1. *The Stephen King Companion.* ed. George Beahm.
   a. Kansas City, MO: Andrews McMeel, 1989 (trade paperback)
   b. Revised and updated. Kansas City, MO: Andrews McMeel, 1995 (trade paperback)
2. As 'Clive Barker über Stephen King, Horror und EC-Comics'. Translated into German by Joachim Körber. *Die Welt Des Stephen King.* Munich: Heyne Sachbuch, 1992

'Clive's Nine Big Scares'
New York Daily News, 10 September 1986 (newspaper)

'Dear Everyone'
Lost Souls, vol. 2 no. 2, September 1999 (magazine)

'Doorways'
The Essential Clive Barker, 1999

'Ectokid is a Hero of Sorts'
Ectokid, vol. 1 no. 2, New York: Marvel Razorline, October 1993 (comic book)

'Edgar Allan Poe'
1. *Independent Magazine*, 30 November 1991 (magazine)
2. *Heroes and Villains: An Anthology of Animosity and Admiration.* ed. *Independent Magazine* Staff. Introduced by John Walsh. London: Gollancz, 1994 (trade paperback)

'Footnote to *Cartoons*'
Clive Barker's Shadows in Eden, 1991

'Foreword'
1. *Clive Barker's Nightbreed: The Making of the Film*. Glasgow: Fontana/ Collins, 1990 (trade paperback)
2. As 'Introduction: *Nightbreed*'. *Clive Barker's Shadows in Eden*, 1991

'Foreword'
1. *From Dusk Till Dawn*. By Quentin Tarantino.
   a. New York: Hyperion/Miramax, 1995 (trade paperback)
   b. As 'Einleitung'. In German. Reinbek: Rororo, 1996
2. *Lost Souls*, vol. 1 no. 4, 1996 (magazine)

'Foreword'
Hellblazer, vol. 2. By Jamie Delano, John Ridgway, Alfredo Alcala. London: Titan Books, 1989 (trade paperback)

'Foreword'
Clive Barker's Hellraiser, no. 17. New York: Marvel Epic, July 1992 (comic book)

'Foreword'
Men, Makeup, and Monsters: Hollywood's Masters of Illusion and FX. By Anthony Timpone. New York: St. Martin's Griffin, 1996 (hardback)

'Foreword'
1. *Sacred Monsters: Behind the Mask of the Horror Actor*. By Doug Bradley. London: Titan, 1996 (trade paperback)
2. *Lost Souls*, vol. 1 no. 6, January 1997 (magazine)

'Foreword'
1. *Swamp Thing Volume Two*. By Alan Moore, Steve Bisette, John Totleben, Shawn McManus. London: Titan Books, 1987 (trade paperback)
2. *Clive Barker's Shadows in Eden*, 1991

'Hell Raisers' (written in collaboration with Peter Atkins)
Time Out, no. 928, 1–8 June, 1988 (magazine)

'How To Get Bloodstains Out of a Shirt'
Men's Health, vol. 11 no. 8, October 1996 (magazine)

'A Human's Guide to the Nightbreed'
Morgan Creek Productions, 1990 (pamphlet; for promotional use only; also distributed as gatefold insert in selected comic books)

'I Was Interested in Creating Mythologies . . .'
Hyperkind, vol. 1 no. 2, New York: Marvel Razorline, October 1993 (comic book)

'I've Always Been a Great Fan of Magic . . .'
Hokum & Hex, vol. 1 no. 2, New York: Marvel Razorline, October 1993 (comic book)

'Introduction'
Books of Blood Volumes One to Three ('Special Collector's Edition')
a. London: Sphere, 1998 (trade paperback)
b. New York: Berkley, 1998 (trade paperback)

'Introduction'
Clive Barker's A-Z of Horror. Compiled by Stephen Jones.
a. London: BBC Books, 1997 (hardback)
b. New York: HarperPrism, 1997 (hardback)
c. London: BBC Books, 1998 (trade paperback)
d. New York: HarperPrism, 1998 (trade paperback)

'Introduction'
Clive Barker's Book of the Damned: A Hellraiser Companion, vol. 1. New York: Marvel Epic, October 1991 (comic book)

'Introduction'
Clive Barker's Hellraiser, Book 1. By Erik Saltzgaber, John Bolton, Sholly Fisch, Dan Spiegle, Jan Strand, Bernie Wrightson, Ted McKeever. New York: Epic Comics, December 1989 (trade paperback)

'Introduction'
Everville. London: HarperCollins, 1994 (signed limited edition hardback)

'Introduction'
Everville. New York: HarperPerennial, 1999 (paperback)

'Introduction'
The Great and Secret Show. New York: HarperPerennial, 1999 (paperback)

'Introduction'
HR Giger's Necronomicon. Beverly Hills, CA: Morpheus International, 1991 (hardback)

'Introduction'
1. *Night Visions 4*.
a. Arlington Heights, IL: Dark Harvest, 1987 (signed limited edition hardback; 500 copies)
b. Arlington Heights, IL: Dark Harvest, 1987 (hardback)
c. As *Night Visions: Hardshell*. New York: Berkley, 1988 (paperback)

d. As *Night Fears*. London: Headline, 1989 (trade paperback)
e. As *Night Fears*. London: Headline, 1990 (paperback)
2. *Clive Barker's Shadows in Eden*, 1991

'Introduction'
Realms of Fantastic Fiction. London: WH Smith, 1989 (promotional flyer)

'Introduction'
'Salem's Lot: The Collector's Edition. By Stephen King. New York: Plume, 1991 (trade paperback)

'Introduction'
The Sandman: The Doll's House. By Neil Gaiman, Mike Dringenberg, Malcolm Jones III.
a. New York: DC Comics, 1990 (trade paperback)
b. London: Titan Books, 1990 (trade paperback)
c. As 'Einleitung'. In German. *Sandmann 6: Das Puppenhaus*. Munich: Feest Verlag, 1995

'Introduction'
The Shit of God. By Diamanda Galas. London: Serpent's Tail/High Risk, 1996 (hardback)

'Introduction'
1. *Taboo*, no. 1. ed. Stephen R Bissette. Wilmington, VT: SpiderBaby Grafix, Fall 1988 (trade paperback)
2. *Clive Barker's Shadows in Eden*, 1991

'Journeys'
The Essential Clive Barker, 1999

'Keeping Company with Cannibal Witches'
1. *Daily Telegraph*, 6 January 1990 (newspaper)
2. As 'Speaking from the Dark'. *Deadline*, no. 23, October 1990 (magazine)
3. As 'Speaking from the Dark.' *Pandemonium: Further Explorations into the World of Clive Barker*. ed. Michael Brown.
a. Staten Island, NY: Eclipse, 1991 (signed limited edition hardback)
b. Staten Island, NY: Eclipse, 1991 (hardback)
c. Staten Island, NY: Eclipse, 1991 (trade paperback)
4. As 'Speaking from the Dark'. *Fantasy Tales 6*. ed. Stephen Jones and David A Sutton.
a. London: Robinson, 1991 (trade paperback)
b. As *Fantasy Tales 3*. New York, 1991 (trade paperback)

577

'Knocking on Glass: The Mind's Menagerie and Other Conceits' ('A conversation between Clive Barker and Peter Atkins')
Clive Barker's Shadows in Eden, 1991

'Laughter, Love, and Chocolate: An Introduction'
1. *Forms of Heaven: Three Plays*, 1996
2. *Lost Souls*, vol. 1 no. 5, October 1996

'Life After Death'
Dancing with the Dark. ed. Stephen Jones.
   a. London: Cassell/Vista, 1997 (paperback)
   b. New York: Carroll & Graf, 1999 (trade paperback)
   c. As 'Posmrtny zivot'. Translated into Czechoslovakian by Ivan Rycovsky. *Valcík s temnotou*. Prague: Apsida/Kniznî Klub, 1998 (hardback)
   d. As 'Vita dopo la morte'. Translated into Italian by Gianni Montanari. *La danza delle tenebre*. Milan: Bompiani, 1999

'Lives'
The Essential Clive Barker, 1999

'Love'
The Essential Clive Barker, 1999

'Making and Unmaking'
The Essential Clive Barker, 1999

'The Man Who Fell to Earth' (excerpt from *The Essential Clive Barker*)
Guardian, 29 September 1999 (newspaper)

'Memory'
The Essential Clive Barker, 1999

'Notes on St Elvis'
The King is Dead: Elvis Post Mortem. ed. Paul M Sammon. New York: Delta, 1994 (trade paperback)

'Old Humanity'
The Essential Clive Barker, 1999

'On Censorship'
Clive Barker's Shadows in Eden, 1991

'Out of My Skull'
The Hellraiser Chronicles. ed. Stephen Jones. London: Titan, 1992 (trade paperback)

'The Painter, The Creature and The Father of Lies: An Introduction'
1. *Incarnations: Three Plays*, 1995
2. *Lost Souls*, vol. 1 no. 2, 1995 (magazine)

'Personal Hits'
Advocate, no. 730, 1 April 1997 (newspaper)

'Private Legends: An Introduction'
The Essential Clive Barker, 1999

'Private View: Clive Barker on His Own Early Films'
Sight and Sound, vol. 5 no. 12, 1995 (magazine)

'R.C. is a master of compression. I'm not. But damn it, I'm going to do my best . . .' (Introduction to 'Deathbed')
Dystopia: The Collected Stories of Richard Christian Matheson. By Richard Christian Matheson.
    a. Springfield, PA: Gauntlet Press, 2000 (deluxe signed and lettered limited edition hardback; 26 copies)
    b. Springfield, PA: Gauntlet Press, 2000 (deluxe signed and numbered limited edition hardback; 250 copies)
    c. Springfield, PA: Gauntlet Press, 2000 (signed and numbered limited edition hardback; 500 copies)

'Ramsey Campbell: An Appreciation'
1. *1986 World Fantasy Convention Program Book*, 31 October-2 November, 1986 (programme book)
2. *Skeleton Crew*, no. V, April 1989 (magazine)
3. *Clive Barker's Shadows in Eden*, 1991

'Shadows in Eden: An Afterword'
Clive Barker's Shadows in Eden, 1991

'The Sixties'
Graven Images: The Best of Horror, Fantasy, and Science Fiction Film Art from the Collection of Ronald V Borst. ed. Ronald V Borst, Keith Burns and Leith Adams. New York: Grove Press, 1992 (hardback)

'Speaking from the Dark' (see 'Keeping Company with Cannibal Witches')

'The Specialty of the House Introduction'
Dark Voices: The Best from the Pan Book of Horror Stories. ed. Stephen Jones and Clarence Paget.
    a. London: Pan Books, 1990 (hardback)
    b. London: Pan Books, 1990 (paperback)

579

'Stephen King: Surviving the Ride'
1. *Fantasy Review*, no. 87, January 1986 (magazine)
2. *Kingdom of Fear: The World of Stephen King*. ed. Tim Underwood and Chuck Miller
   a. Underwood-Miller, 1986 (signed limited edition hardback)
   b. Underwood-Miller, 1986 (hardback)
   c. New York: Plume, 1986 (trade paperback)
   d. London: New English Library, 1987 (paperback)
3. As 'Die Fahrt Überleben'. Translated into German by Joachim Körber. *Das Stephen King Buch*. ed. Joachim Körber. Munich: HTB, 1989
4. *Clive Barker's Shadows in Eden*, 1991
5. *Stephen King*. ed. Harold Bloom. Philadelphia, PA: Chelsea House, 1998 (hardback)

'Terrors'
The Essential Clive Barker, 1999

'A Thing Untrue'
1. *The Face*, October 1990 (magazine)
2. *Pandemonium: Further Explorations into the World of Clive Barker*. ed. Michael Brown.
   a. Staten Island, NY: Eclipse, 1991 (signed limited edition hardback)
   b. Staten Island, NY: Eclipse, 1991 (hardback)
   c. Staten Island, NY: Eclipse, 1991 (trade paperback)

'Thoughts on *Galilee*'
amazon.com, 27 July 1998 (message posting to on-line reviews of *Galilee*)

'To See or Not to See: An Introduction'
1. *Splatter: A Cautionary Tale*. By Douglas E Winter.
   a. Round Top, NY: Footsteps Press, 1987 (signed limited edition hardback: twenty-six lettered copies)
   b. Round Top, NY: Footsteps Press, 1987 (signed limited edition chapbook: 100 numbered copies)
   c. Round Top, NY: Footsteps Press, 1987 (signed limited edition chapbook: 400 unsigned copies)
2. *Clive Barker's Shadows in Eden*, 1991

'The Tomb' (book review)
Time Out, no. 787, 19–25 September 1985 (magazine)

'Trance of Innocence' (manuscript title: 'Innocence and Obsession')
Sight and Sound, vol. 5 no. 12, December 1995

'Visions and Dreams'
The Essential Clive Barker, 1999

'Want to Get Real Scared? Watch a Few Movies with a Fearmaster Filmmaker'
Orange County Register, 18 October 1987 (newspaper)

'Why Super Heroes?'
Hyperkind, vol. 1 no. 3, New York: Marvel Razorline, November 1993
(comic book)

'Worlds'
The Essential Clive Barker, 1999

STAGE PLAYS (IN ALPHABETICAL ORDER)

A Clowns' Sodom (1975) written and directed by Clive Barker; originally
performed by the Mute Pantomime Theatre

Colossus (1983) written by Clive Barker; directed by Geoff Gillham; originally
performed by the Cockpit Youth Theatre

The Comedy of Comedies (1977–1979; unproduced) written by Clive Barker

Crazyface ('A Comedy (with Lions)') (1982) written by Clive Barker; directed
by Janet Marks; originally performed by the Cockpit Youth Theatre

Dangerous Lives (1981) written by Doug Bradley and Oliver Parker; directed by
Clive Barker; originally performed by the Dog Company

The Day of the Dog ('L'Abattoir d'Amour') (1977) written and directed by
Clive Barker; originally performed by the Dog Company

Dog (1978) written and directed by Clive Barker; originally performed by the
Dog Company

A Dream (1974) unscripted mime created in ensemble collaboration; directed
by Clive Barker; originally performed by the Theatre of the Imagination

The Egg (1974) unscripted mime created in ensemble collaboration; directed by
Clive Barker; originally performed by the Theatre of the Imagination

The Fish Bride (1974) written and directed by Clive Barker; originally
performed by the Theatre of the Imagination

Frankenstein in Love, or the Life of Death (1981) written by Clive Barker;
directed by Malcolm Edwards; originally performed by the Dog Company

Grünewald's Crucifixion (1974) unscripted mime created in ensemble collaboration; directed by Clive Barker; originally performed by the Theatre of the Imagination

The History of the Devil (1980) written and directed by Clive Barker; originally performed by the Dog Company

The Holly and the Ivy (1970) written and directed by Clive Barker; originally performed by students at Quarry Bank Grammar School

Hunters in the Snow (circa 1974) written and directed by Clive Barker; originally performed by the Hydra Theatre Company

Inferno (1967) written with Phil Rimmer; directed by Clive Barker; originally performed by students at Quarry Bank Grammar School

Is There Anybody There? (1971) written with Phil Rimmer; directed by Clive Barker; originally performed by the Hydra Theatre Company

The Magician (1977) written and directed by Clive Barker; originally performed by the Dog Company

Neongonebony (1968) written and improvised with Phil Rimmer, Dave Fishel and Malcolm Sharp; originally performed by them at Quarry Bank Grammar School

Nightlives (1979) written and directed by Clive Barker; originally performed by the Dog Company

Paradise Street (1981) written and directed by Clive Barker; originally performed by the Dog Company

Poe (1974) unscripted mime created in ensemble collaboration; directed by Clive Barker; originally performed by the Theatre of the Imagination

Private Apocalypse (circa 1974) written and directed by Clive Barker; originally performed by the Theatre of the Imagination

The Sack (1978) written and directed by Clive Barker; originally performed by the Dog Company

Salomé (circa 1973) adapted in ensemble collaboration from the play by Oscar Wilde; directed by Clive Barker

The Scream of the Ape (circa 1974) written and directed by Clive Barker; originally performed by the Hydra Theatre Company

The Secret Life of Cartoons (1982) written by Clive Barker; directed by Roger Martin; originally performed by the Dog Company

The Secret Life of Cartoons (revised and expanded, 1986) written by Clive Barker and directed by Tudor Davies (West End production)

Subtle Bodies (1982) written by Clive Barker; directed by Kim Dambeck; originally performed by the Cockpit Youth Theatre

The Wolfman (1974) written and directed by Clive Barker; originally performed by the Theatre of the Imagination

The Wood on the Hill (circa 1973) written and directed by Clive Barker, based on his short story

Voodoo (1967) written with Phil Rimmer; directed by Clive Barker; originally performed by students at Quarry Bank Grammar School

MOTION PICTURE AND TELEVISION SCREENPLAYS AND SCREEN STORIES (IN ALPHABETICAL ORDER)

American Horror (2000; unproduced). A motion picture written by Clive Barker based on an original screen story

Candyman: Farewell to the Flesh (1995). A motion picture written by Rand Ravich and Mark Kruger based on an original screen story by Clive Barker; directed by Bill Condon

The Dark Tower (circa 1972; uncompleted). A short film written and directed by Clive Barker and Phil Rimmer

The Egyptian Project aka *The Mummy* (1989; unproduced). A motion picture written by Mick Garris based on an original screen story by Clive Barker

The Forbidden (1975–78; uncompleted). A short film written and directed by Clive Barker

The Great Unknown (circa 1988; unproduced). A motion picture written by Clive Barker based on his original screen story

Hellbound: Hellraiser II (1988). A motion picture written by Peter Atkins based on an original screen story by Clive Barker; directed by Tony Randel

Hellraiser (1987). A motion picture written and directed by Clive Barker based on his novel *The Hellbound Heart*

Hellraiser III: Hell on Earth (1992). A motion picture written by Peter Atkins based on an original screen story by Peter Atkins and Clive Barker; directed by Anthony Hickox

In the Flesh (1988; unproduced). A motion picture written by Mick Garris based on the Clive Barker story 'In the Flesh'

Jack O Lant (circa 1972; uncompleted). A short film written and directed by Clive Barker and Phil Rimmer

Lord of Illusions (1995). A motion picture written and directed by Clive Barker based on his short story 'The Last Illusion'

Motorhead: 'Hellraiser' (1993). A music video directed by Clive Barker

Nightbreed (1990). A motion picture written and directed by Clive Barker based on his novel *Cabal*

Rawhead Rex (1986). A motion picture written by Clive Barker based on his short story 'Rawhead Rex'; directed by George Pavlou

Salomé (circa 1972). A short film written and directed by Clive Barker and Phil Rimmer

Underworld (1985). A motion picture written by Clive Barker and James Caplin based on an original screen story by Clive Barker; directed by George Pavlou

The Yattering and Jack (1987). A television episode written by Clive Barker based on his short story 'The Yattering and Jack'; directed by David Odel

SELECTED ART EXHIBITIONS (IN CHRONOLOGICAL ORDER)

LACE (curated by Kevin Sullivan and Jam Tamlir), Los Angeles, CA, 1990: 'Frontier Tales'

Bess Cutler Gallery, New York, NY, March–May, 1993: 'Clive Barker, Paintings and Drawings 1973–1993'

Los Angeles Art Fair, Los Angeles, CA, 2–5 December 1993: 'Art/LA93'

Four Color Images, Inc, New York, NY, 1993: 'The Death Gallery'

Dallas Fantasy Fair, Dallas, TX, 1993

Bess Cutler Gallery, New York, NY, 19 November 1993 – 29 January 1994: 'An Exhibition of Original Paintings and Drawings'

The Tunnel, New York, NY, 28 January 1994

Bess Cutler Gallery, New York, NY, 1994

Bess Cutler Gallery, New York, NY, autumn 1995

Laguna Art Museum, Laguna Beach, California, 14 August – 8 October 1995: 'The Imagination of Clive Barker'

La Luz de Jesus, Hollywood, California, 7–27 April 1997: 'One Flesh Exhibition'

COMIC BOOKS AND GRAPHIC NOVEL ADAPTATIONS (IN ALPHABETICAL ORDER)

Clive Barker's Book of the Damned: A Hellraiser Companion. Created by Clive Barker. Edited by DG Chichester; written by Larry Wachowski. Vols. 1–4. New York: Marvel Epic, October 1991 – September 1993

Clive Barker's The Harrowers: Raiders of the Abyss. Created by Clive Barker. Edited by Marc McLaurin and Mike Lackey; written by Malcolm Smith and McNally Sagal. Vol. 1 nos. 1–6. New York: Marvel Epic, December 1993 – May 1994

Clive Barker's Hellraiser. Consultant: Clive Barker. Edited by Margaret Clark; consulting editors DG Chichester and Mark McLaurin; written by Neil Gaiman, Mark McLaurin, Philip Nutman, Del Stone, Jr, *et al.* Nos. 1–20. New York: Marvel Epic, 1989–1993

Clive Barker's Hellraiser Collection. Consultant: Clive Barker. Edited by Margaret Clark; consulting editors DG Chichester and Mark McLaurin. Vol. 1. New York: Marvel Epic, 1991

Clive Barker's Hellraiser Dark Holiday Special. New York: Marvel Epic, 1992

Clive Barker's Hellraiser Poster Book. Edited by Marc McLaurin. Artwork by John Bolton, Simon Bisley, Daniel Brereton, *et al.* New York: Marvel Epic, 1990

Clive Barker's Hellraiser Summer Special. New York: Marvel Epic, 1992

Clive Barker's Hellraiser Spring Slaughter. By Larry Wachowski and Mark Pacella. New York: Marvel Epic, March 1994

Clive Barker's Nightbreed. Creator/consultant: Clive Barker. Edited by Gregory Wright; consulting editor DG Chichester; written by Alan Grant, John Wagner, DG Chichester, Nicholas Vince, *et al.* Vol. 1 nos. 1–25. New York: Marvel Epic, April 1990 – March 1993

Clive Barker's Nightbreed: Genesis. Creator/consultant: Clive Barker. Edited by Gregory Wright; consulting editor DG Chichester. New York: Marvel Epic, November 1991 (collects first four issues of *Clive Barker's Nightbreed*)

Clive Barker Presents Hellraiser III: Hell on Earth. Written by Peter Atkins. New York: Marvel Epic, 1992 (motion picture tie-in)

Dread. Adapted by Fred Burke; illustrated by Dan Brereton. With *Down, Satan!* Adapted by Steve Niles; illustrated by Tim Conrad.
a. Forestville, CA: Eclipse, 1992 (hardback)
b. Forestville, CA: Eclipse, 1992 (trade paperback)
c. London: EclipseGraphicNovels, 1993 (trade paperback)
d. New York: Harper Paperbacks/EclipseGraphicNovels, 1993 (trade paperback)

Ectokid. Created by Clive Barker. Edited by Marc McLaurin; consulting editor, Malcolm Smith; written by James Robinson and Larry Wachowski. Vol. 1 nos. 1–9. New York: Marvel Razorline, September 1993 – May 1994

Ectokid Unleashed! Created by Clive Barker. Edited by Marc McLaurin; consulting editor, Malcolm Smith; written by Dan Abbott and Andy Lanning. New York: Marvel, October 1994

Epic: An Anthology (Book One and Book Two). New York: Marvel Epic, 1992 (includes selections from *Clive Barker's Hellraiser* and *Clive Barker's Nightbreed*)

Hokum & Hex. Created by Clive Barker. Edited by Marc McLaurin; consulting editor, Malcolm Smith; written by Frank Lovece. Vol. 1 nos. 1–9. New York: Marvel Razorline, September 1993 – May 1994

Hyperkind. Created by Clive Barker. Edited by Marc McLaurin; consulting editor, Malcolm Smith; written by Fred Burke. Vol. 1 nos. 1–9. New York: Marvel Razorline, September 1993 – May 1994

Hyperkind Unleashed! New York: Marvel, August 1994

Jihad. Books 1 & 2. Consultant: Clive Barker. Edited by Gregory Wright, written by DG Chichester. Illustrated by Paul Johnson. New York: Marvel Epic, 1991

The Life of Death. Adapted by Fred Burke; illustrated by Stewart Stanyard. With *New Murders in the Rue Morgue.* Adapted by Steve Niles; illustrated by Hector Gomez.
a.   Forestville, CA: Eclipse, 1993 (hardback)
b.   Forestville, CA: Eclipse, 1993 (trade paperback)

Night of the Living Dead: London (Book 1: *Bloodline* and Book 2: *End of the Line*). Written by Clive Barker and Steve Niles. Edited by Tom Skulan. Illustrated by Carlos Kastro. New York: Fantaco, 1993

Pinhead. Created by Clive Barker. Edited by Tom Daning and Dave Wohl; written by DG Chichester and Erik Saltzgaber. Vol. 1 nos. 1–6. New York: Marvel Epic, December 1993 – May 1994

Pinhead vs. Marshall Law. Nos. 1–2. New York: Marvel Epic, November – December 1993.

Primal: From the Cradle to the Grave. By Clive Barker, Erik Saltzgaber, John Van Fleet and DG Chichester. Milwaukie, OR: Dark Horse Comics, September 1992 (trade paperback)

Rawhead Rex. Adapted by Steve Niles; illustrated by Les Edwards. With *Twilight at the Towers.* Adapted by Steve Niles; illustrated by Hector Gomez.
a.   Forestville, CA: Eclipse, 1994 (hardback)
b.   Forestville, CA: Eclipse, 1994 (trade paperback)

Razorline: The First Cut. New York: Marvel, September 1993

Revelations. Adapted by Steve Niles; illustrated by Lionel Talaro.
a.   Forestville, CA: Eclipse, 1991 (hardback)
b.   Forestville, CA: Eclipse, 1991 (trade paperback)

Saint Sinner. Created by Clive Barker. Edited by Marc McLaurin; consulting editor, Malcolm Smith; written by Elaine Lee. Vol. 1 nos. 1–7. New York: Marvel Razorline, October 1993 – April 1994

Son of Celluloid. Adapted by Steve Niles; illustrated by Les Edwards.
a.   Forestville, CA: Eclipse, 1991 (hardback)
b.   Forestville, CA: Eclipse, 1991 (trade paperback)

Tapping the Vein: Book One ('Human Remains' and 'Pig Blood Blues') Forestville, CA: Eclipse, September 1989 (trade paperback)

Tapping the Vein: Book Two (In the Hills, the Cities' and 'Skins of Our Fathers')

a. Forestville, CA: Eclipse, November 1989 (trade paperback)
b. London: Titan Books, November 1989 (trade paperback)

Tapping the Vein Book Three ('Midnight Meat Train' and 'Scape-Goats')
a. Forestville, CA: Eclipse, May 1990 (trade paperback)
b. London: Titan Books, May 1990 (trade paperback)

Tapping the Vein Book Four ('The Madonna' and 'Hell's Event')
a. Forestville, CA: Eclipse, 1990 (trade paperback)
b. London: Titan Books, 1990 (trade paperback)

Tapping the Vein Book Five ('How Spoilers Bleed' and 'Down, Satan!').
Forestville, CA: Eclipse, 1992 (trade paperback)

Weaveworld. Books 1–3. Consultant: Clive Barker, with 'special thanks' to
Peter Atkins. Edited by Daniel Chichester and Tom Daning; written by Erik
Saltzgaber. New York: Epic Comics, December 1991 – February 1992

The Yattering and Jack. Adapted by Steve Niles; illustrated by John Bolton.
a. Forestville, CA: Eclipse, 1991 (hardback)
b. Forestville, CA: Eclipse, 1991 (trade paperback)

GAMES (IN ALPHABETICAL ORDER)

Candyman: Farewell to the Flesh. Gramercy Pictures Marketing Team/Jacobson
& Atkins Advertising, Inc, 1995 (board game; for promotional use only)

Clive Barker's The Undying. Redwood City, CA: Electronic Arts/DreamWorks
Interactive, 2001 (computer game)

Hellraiser Trading Cards. Forestville, CA: Eclipse, 1992 (trading cards)

Imajica. New York: HarperPrism/Zehrapushu, Inc, 1997 (collectible card game)

Nightbreed: The Interactive Movie. Ocean Software Ltd, 1990 (computer game)

SELECTED AUDIO AND VIDEO RECORDINGS (IN ALPHABETICAL ORDER)

Barker on Larry King Live – May 1987. Two-hour interview. Lion Cassette,
1987 (audiocassette)

The Body Politic in 3-D Sound. Read by Kevin Conway (unabridged). New
York: Simon & Schuster AudioWorks, 1987 (audiocassette)

Clive Barker: The Art of Horror. Directed by Christopher Holland. Narrated by Robert Russell. Hollywood, CA: Paramount Pictures, 1993 (videocassette)

Cabal: Nightbreed. Read by David Purdham (unabridged). New York: Simon & Schuster, 1990 (audiocassette)

The Damnation Game. Dramatization by Colin Fox, Graeme Malcolm, Merwin Goldsmith, Brian Murray, Bernadette Prego, Gilbert Brand; directed by Charles Potter (abridged).
a. New York: Random House/Sound Editions, 1987 (audiocassette)
b. New York: Warner Audio, 1987 (audiocassette)

Everville. Read by John Glover (abridged). New York: HarperCollins, 1994 (audiocassette)

Fear in the Dark. Produced by Paul Cowan. Directed by Dominic Murphy. Written by Mick Farren. Narrated by Christopher Lee. Features interview with Clive Barker. Los Angeles, CA: Pacific Arts Video, 1992 (videocassette)

Galilee. Read by Roger Rees (abridged). New York: Harper Audio, 1998 (audiocassette)

Galilee. Read by Paul Hecht (unabridged). Prince Frederick, MD: Recorded Books, 1999 (audiocassette)

The Great and Secret Show. Read by Stephen Lang (abridged). New York: HarperCollins, 1991 (audiocassette)

The Hellbound Heart. Read by Clive Barker (unabridged). New York: Simon & Schuster Audioworks, 1988 (audiocassette)

The History of the Devil. Dramatization by the Sci-Fi Channel's Seeing Ear Theater (unabridged). Performed by Dylan Baker, Katherine Borowitz, Simon Jones, Chip Zien, *et al.* Produced and directed by Brian Smith. Los Angeles: Dove Audio/NewStar Publishing, 1999 (audiocassette)

Imajica. Read by Peter MacNicol (abridged). New York: Harper Audio, 1991 (audiocassette)

Immortality. From the television programme 'Second Nature'. Features interviews with Clive Barker and Anne Rice. Princeton, NJ: Films for the Humanities and Sciences, 1995 (videocassette)

In the Flesh. Read by Steele Dillinger (unabridged). Santa Fe, NM: Sunset Productions, 1996 (audiocassette)

The Inhuman Condition. Dramatization. New York: Simon & Schuster Audioworks, 1988 (audiocassette)

The Inhuman Condition. Read by Steele Dillinger (unabridged). Santa Fe, NM: Sunset Productions, 1996 (audiocassette)

A Moveable Feast #77: The Inhuman Condition. Short story excerpts read by Clive Barker, with an interview by host Tom Vitale. New York: 1992 (audiocassette)

A Moveable Feast #111: Weaveworld. Novel excerpts read by Clive Barker, with an interview by host Tom Vitale. New York: 1992 (audiocassette)

Sacrament. Read by Ron Keith (unabridged). Prince Frederick, MD: Recorded Books, 1996 (audiocassette)

Sacrament. Read by Campbell Scott (abridged). New York: Harper Audio, 1996 (audiocassette)

The South Bank Show: Clive Barker. London: ITV, 1994 (videocassette)

Stephen King's World of Horror. Produced and directed by John Simmons. Features interviews with John Carpenter, Clive Barker and Frank Darabont. Edison, NJ: Baruch Television Group/Front Row Video, 1988 (videocassette)

The Thief of Always. Read by John Glover (abridged). New York: HarperCollins, 1992 (audiocassette)

SELECTED INTERNATIONAL EDITIONS (IN CHRONOLOGICAL ORDER, BY COUNTRY)

Brazil

O Jogo da Perdição (The Damnation Game). In Portuguese. Rio de Janeiro: Civilização Brasileira, 1989

Os Livros de Sangue (Clive Barker's Books of Blood Volumes One through Six). Translated into Portuguese by Fábio Fernandes. Rio de Janeiro: Civilização Brasileira, 1990 (six volumes)

A Raça da Noite (Cabal). Translated into Portuguese by Fábio Fernandes. Rio de Janeiro: Civilização Brasileira, 1994

A Trama da Maldade (Weaveworld). Translated into Portuguese by Fábio Fernandes. Rio de Janeiro: Civilização Brasileira, 1995

Sacramento (Sacrament). Translated into Portuguese by Fábio Fernandes. Rio de Janeiro: Editora Bertrand Brasil, 1998

Czechoslovakia

První Kniha Krve (Clive Barker's Books of Blood Volume One). Translated into Czechoslovakian by Ivar Tichx. Plzen: Laser, 1994

Vecné zatracení (The Damnation Game). Translated into Czechoslovakian by Lenka Sedláčková. Plzen: Mustang, 1995

Cabal: Nocní rasa (Cabal). Translated into Czechoslovakian by Karel Matásek. Plzen: Mustang, 1995

Imagika (Imagica). Translated into Czechoslovakian by Milux Kotixová.
a.   Plzen: Mustang, 1995
b.   As *Imagika I* and *Imagika II*. Plzen: Mustang, 1995 (in two volumes)

Hellraiser (The Hellbound Heart). Translated into Czechoslovakian by Pavel Dufek and Iva Harrisová. Plzen: Mustang, 1996

Zlodej duxé (The Thief of Always). Translated into Czechoslovakian by Milena Turbová. Plzen: Mustang, 1996

Druhá Kniha Krve (Clive Barker's Books of Blood Volume Two). Plzen: Laser, 1997

Velké a tajné show (The Great and Secret Show). Translated into Czechoslovakian by Lenka Sedláčková. Plzen: Mustang, 1997

Everville: 2. Kniha Umení (Everville). Translated into Czechoslovakian by Lenka Sedláčková. Plzen: Mustang, 1997

Mysterium (Sacrament). Translated into Czechoslovakian by Jirí Dejl. Prague: Neokortex, 1998

Denmark

De Verdenforviste (Weaveworld). Translated into Danish by Anders Westenholz.

a. Copenhagen: Artia, 1991
b. In two volumes. Copenhagen: Artia, 1991
c. In two volumes. Copenhagen: Danmarks Blindebibliotek, 1992

Clive Barker's Det umenneskelige: noveller (Clive Barker's Books of Blood Volume Four). Translated into Danish by Mogens Wenzel Andreasen. Introduction by Troels Møller.
a. Copenhagen: Artia, 1992
b. Copenhagen: Den grimme Ælling, 1993

Clive Barker's I kød og blod: noveller (Clive Barker's Books of Blood Volume Five). Translated into Danish by Mogens Wenzel Andreasen. Introduction by Troels Møller. Copenhagen: Artia, 1992

Clive Barker's Den levende død: noveller (Clive Barker's Books of Blood Volume Six). Translated into Danish by Mogens Wenzel Andreasen. Copenhagen: Artia, 1994

Finland

Veren kirjat 1 (Clive Barker's Books of Blood Volume One). Translated into Finnish by Ulla Selkälä & Ilkka Äärelä. Helsinki: Jalava, 1989

Veren kirjat 2 (Clive Barker's Books of Blood Volume Two). Translated into Finnish by Ulla Selkälä & Ilkka Äärelä. Helsinki: Jalava, 1990

Veren kirjat 3 (*Clive Barker's Books of Blood Volume Three*). Translated into Finnish by Ulla Selkälä & Ilkka Äärelä. Helsinki: Jalava, 1991

Veren kirjat 4 (Clive Barker's Books of Blood Volume Four). Translated into Finnish by Ilkka Äärelä. Helsinki: Jalava, 1992

Veren kirjat 5 (Clive Barker's Books of Blood Volume Five). Translated into Finnish by Ulla Selkälä & Ilkka Äärelä. Helsinki: Jalava, 1993

Veren kirjat 6 (Clive Barker's Books of Blood Volume Six). Translated into Finnish by Ilkka Äärelä. Helsinki: Jalava, 1994

Yön kansa (Cabal). Translated into Finnish by Ilkka Äärelä. Helsinki: Jalava, 1993

Kadotuksen peli (The Damnation Game). Translated into Finnish by Ulla Selkälä. Helsinki: Jalava, 1992

France

Livre de sang: Le train de l'abattoir (Clive Barker's Books of Blood Volume One). Translated into French by Jean-Daniel Brèque.
a. Paris: Albin Michel, 1987 (trade paperback)
b. Paris: J'ai Lu, 1988 (paperback)
c. Paris: France Loisirs, 1989 (hardback; book club edition)
d. Paris: Le Grand livre du mois, 1991

Livre de sang: Une course d'enfer (Clive Barker's Books of Blood Volume Two). Translated into French by Dominique Dill.
a. Paris: Albin Michel (trade paperback), 1988
b. Paris: France Loisirs, 1989 (hardback; book club edition)
c. Paris: J'ai Lu, 1994 (paperback)

Le jeu de la damnation: roman (The Damnation Game). Translated into French by Jean-Daniel Brèque.
a. Paris: Albin Michel, 1988 (trade paperback)
b. Paris: France Loisirs, 1989 (hardback; book club edition)
c. Paris: J'ai Lu, 1989 (paperback)
d. Paris: Éd. de la Seine, 1996

Le Royaume des Devins (Weaveworld). Translated into French by Jean-Daniel Brèque.
a. Paris: Albin Michel, 1988 (trade paperback)
b. Paris: France Loisirs, 1990 (hardback; book club edition)
c. Paris: Pocket, 1994 (paperback)

Cabale (Cabal). Translated into French by Jean-Daniel Brèque.
a. Paris: Albin Michel, 1990 (trade paperback)
b. Paris: J'ai Lu, 1991 (paperback)

Livre de sang: Confessions d'un linceul (Clive Barker's Books of Blood Volume Three). Translated into French by Hélène Devaux-Minié.
a. Paris: Albin Michel, 1990 (trade paperback)
b. Paris: Grand Livre du Mois, 1990 (hardback; book club edition)
c. Paris: J'ai Lu, 1994 (paperback)
d. Paris: Éd. de la Seine, 1997

Clive Barker presente Hellraiser (graphic novel adaptation by John Bolton, et al.). Grenoble: Comics USA, 1990 (trade paperback)

Cabale (graphic novel adaptation by Alan Grant and John Wagner. Illustrations by Jim Baikie. Translated into French by Jean-Daniel Brèque. Grenoble: Comics USA, 1990

Livre de sang: Apocalypses (Clive Barker's Books of Blood Volume Four). Translated into French by Hélène Devaux-Minié.
a. Paris: Albin Michel, 1991 (trade paperback)
b. Paris: Grand Livre du Mois, 1991 (hardback; book club edition)
c. Paris: J'ai Lu, 1995 (paperback)

Livre de sang: Prison de chair (Clive Barker's Books of Blood Volume Five). Translated into French by Jean-Daniel Brèque.
a. Paris: Albin Michel, 1991 (trade paperback)
b. Paris: Grand Livre du Mois, 1991 (hardback; book club edition)
c. Paris: J'ai Lu, 1995 (paperback)

Secret Show (The Great and Secret Show). Translated into French by Jean-Daniel Brèque.
a. Paris: Albin Michel, 1991 (trade paperback)
b. Paris: Grand Livre du Mois, 1991 (hardback; book club edition)
c. Paris: Pocket, 1993 (paperback)

Livre de sang: La Mort, sa vie, son oeuvre (Clive Barker's Books of Blood Volume Six). Translated into French by Jean-Daniel Brèque.
a. Paris: Albin Michel, 1992 (trade paperback)
b. Paris: J'ai Lu, 1996 (paperback)

Le Voleur d'éternité (The Thief of Always). Translated into French by Thomas Bauduret. Paris: Pocket Junior, 1993.

Imajica (Imajica). Translated into French by Jean Esch.
a. Paris: Edition Rivages, 1996
b. In two volumes, as *Imajica – Tome I* and *Imajica – Tome II*. Paris: Editions Rivages/Fantasy, 1996
c. In two volumes, as *Imajica – Tome I* and *Imajica – Tome II*. Paris: Pocket Terreur, 1997–1998 (paperback)

Everville. Translated into French by Jean-Daniel Brèque.
a. Paris: Albin Michel, 1997 (trade paperback)
b. Paris: Pocket Terreur, 1999 (paperback)

Sacrament. In French. Paris: Payot-Rivages, 1999

Galilee. Translated into French by Jean Esch. Paris: Editions Rivages, 2000 (trade paperback; in two volumes)

Germany

Das Erste Buch Des Blutes (Clive Barker's Books of Blood Volume One).
Translated into German by Peter Kobbe. Foreward by Joachim Körber:
'Horror als subversive Kunst'
a. Munich: Droemer Knaur Verlag, 1987
b. Linkenheim: Edition Phantasia, 1987 (limited edition hardback,
    illustrated by JK Potter and Harry O Morris)
c. Gütersloh: Bertelsmann Lesering, 1989
d. Munich: KHTB, 1990 (paperback)

Das Zweite Buch des Blutes (Clive Barker's Books of Blood Volume Two).
Translated into German by Peter Kobbe.
a. Munich: Droemer Knaur Verlag, 1987
b. Linkenheim: Edition Phantasia, 1987 (limited edition hardback
    illustrated by JK Potter and Harry O Morris)
c. Gütersloh: Bertelsmann Lesering, 1989
d. Munich: KHTB, 1990 (paperback)

Spiel Des Verderbens (The Damnation Game). Translated into German by
Joachim Körber.
a. Munich: KHTB, 1987 (paperback)
b. Linkenheim: Edition Phantasia, 1987 (signed limited edition hardback;
    300 copies; illustrated by Herbert Brandmeier)

Das Dritte Buch des Blutes (Clive Barker's Books of Blood Volume Three).
Translated into German by Peter Kobbe.
a. Munich 1988, Droemer Knaur Verlag, 1988
b. Linkenheim 1988, Edition Phantasia, 1988 (limited edition hardback
    illustrated by JK Potter and Harry O Morris)
c. Munich 1990, KHTB 1990 (paperback)

Das Vierte Buch des Blutes (Clive Barker's Books of Blood Volume Four).
Translated into German by Peter Kobbe.
a. Munich: Droemer Knaur Verlag, 1988
b. Linkenheim: Edition Phantasia, 1988 (limited edition hardback
    illustrated by JK Potter and Harry O Morris)
c. Munich: KHTB, 1991 (paperback

Das Fünfte Buch des Blutes (Clive Barker's Books of Blood Volume Five).
Translated into German by Peter Kobbe.
a. Munich: Droemer Knaur Verlag, 1989
b. Linkenheim: Edition Phantasia, 1989 (limited edition hardback
    illustrated by JK Potter and Harry O Morris)
c. Munich: KHTB, 1991 (paperback)

Cabal. Translated into German by Joachim Körber.
  a. Munich: Heyne Jumbo, 1989
  b. Stuttgart/Munich: Deutscher Bücherbund, 1990
  c. Munich: HTB, 1992 (paperback)

Das Sechste Buch des Blutes (Clive Barker's Books of Blood Volume Six). Translated into German by Peter Kobbe.
  a. Munich: Droemer Knaur Verlag, 1990
  b. Linkenheim: Edition Phantasia, 1991 (limited edition hardback illustrated by JK Potter and Harry O Morris)
  c. Munich: KHTB, 1991 (paperback)

Jenseits Des Bösen (The Great and Secret Show). Translated into German by Joachim Körber.
  a. Munich: Heyne Jumbo, 1990
  b. Munich: HTB, 1993 (paperback)

Das Tor zur Hölle – 'Hellraiser' (The Hellbound Heart). Translated into German by Ute Thiemann. Munich: Wilhelm Heyne, 1992

Gyre (Weaveworld). Translated into German by Joachim Körber.
  a. Munich: Heyne Jumbo, 1992
  b. Munich: HTB, 1994 (paperback)

Imagica (Imajica). Translated into German by Andreas Brandhorst.
  a. Munich: Heyne Jumbo, 1993
  b. Munich: HTB, 1994 (paperback)

Das Erste und Zweite Buch des Blutes (Clive Barker's Books of Blood Volumes One and Two). Translated into German by Peter Kobbe. Munich: KHTB, 1994 (paperback)

Der Dieb der Zeit: Ein Märchen (The Thief of Always). Translated into German by Andreas Kasprzak.
  a. Bellheim: Edition Phantasia, 1994 (limited edition hardback: 250 copies signed by the author)
  b. As *Das Haus der Verschwunden Jahre*. Translated into German by Eva L Wahser.
      1.   Munich: Wilhelm Heyne Verlag, 1995
      2.   Munich: HTB, 1998 (paperback)

Ein höllischer Gast (graphic novel adaptation of 'The Yattering and Jack'). In German.
  a. Munich: Edition Comic Speedline, Thomas Tilsner Verlag, 1994 (hardback)

b.   Munich: Edition Comic Speedline, Thomas Tilsner Verlag, 1994 (trade paperback)

Stadt Des Böse (Everville). Translated into German by Joachim Körber. Munich: HTB, 1995 (paperback)

Das Sakrament (Sacrament). Translated into German by Thomas Hag. Bellheim: Edition Phantasia, 1998 (limited edition hardback: 250 numbered copies signed by the author)

Galileo (Galilee). Translated into German by Waltraud Götting. Munich: Heyne, 2000

Greece

Ifantocosmos (Weaveworld). Translated into Greek by Elli Ekme. Athens: Bell, 1989

Ta Vivlia tou Ematos, Vol. 1 (Clive Barker's Books of Blood Volume One). Translated into Greek by Rozina Bergner. Athens: Triton, 1994

Ta Vivlia tou Ematos, Vol. 2 (Clive Barker's Books of Blood Volume Two). Translated into Greek by Rozina Bergner. Athens: Triton, 1994

Ta Vivlia tou Ematos, Vol. 3 (Clive Barker's Books of Blood Volume Three). Translated into Greek by Rozina Bergner. Athens: Triton, 1994

To Megalo Mistiko Theama (The Great and Secret Show). Translated into Greek by Gogo Arvaniti. Athens: Bell, 1995

Ta Vivlia tou Ematos, Vol. 4 (Clive Barker's Books of Blood Volume Four). Translated into Greek by Rozina Bergner. Athens: Triton, 1996

Ta Vivlia tou Ematos, Vol. 5 (Clive Barker's Books of Blood Volume Five). Translated into Greek by Rozina Bergner. Athens: Triton, 1996

Ta Vivlia tou Ematos, Vol. 6 (Clive Barker's Books of Blood Volume Six). Translated into Greek by Rozina Bergner. Athens: Triton, 1996

O Kleftis tou Pantote (The Thief of Always). Translated into Greek by Vasilis Babouris. Athens: Akti / Oxi, 1996

Aipoli (Everville). Translated into Greek by Gogo Arvaniti. Athens: Bell, 1996

To Katarameno Pehnidi (The Damnation Game). Translated into Greek by Sonia Saliba. Athens: Akti / Oxi, 1997

Hellraiser (The Hellbound Heart). Translated into Greek by Nikos Rousos. Athens: Akti / Oxi, 1999

To Arheo Mistirio (Sacrament). Translated into Greek by Michalis Makropoulos. Athens: Bell, 1999

Cabal – I Genia tis Nicthas (Cabal). Translated into Greek by Diona Moustri. Athens: Akti / Oxi, 2000

Holland

Tunnel van de Dood, en Andere Verhalen (Clive Barker's Books of Blood Volumes One and Two). Translated into Dutch by Hugo Kuipers. Utrecht: Luitingh, 1987

Prins van de Duisternis, en Andere Verhalen (Clive Barker's Books of Blood Volumes Three and Four). Translated into Dutch by JC Pasman and Mariëlla Snel. Utrecht: Luitingh, 1987

Het Boek van Bloed, en andere Verhalen (Clive Barker's Books of Blood Volumes Five and Six). Translated into Dutch by Hugo Kuipers and Hugo Timmerman. Utrecht: Luitingh-Sijthoff, 1988

Weefwereld (Weaveworld). Translated into Dutch by Mariëlla de Kuyper-Snel.
a. Utrecht: Luitingh-Sijthoff, 1988
b. Amsterdam: Poema Pocket, 1991 (paperback)
c. Amsterdam: Poema Pocket, 1996 (paperback)

Duivelsspel (The Damnation Game). Translated into Dutch by Ineke Wieberdink-Westerweel. Amsterdam: Luitingh-Sijthoff, 1989

Kabal (Cabal). Translated into Dutch by Johannes Melchior. Amsterdam: Luitingh BV, 1989

Der Grote Geheime Show (The Great and Secret Show). Translated into Dutch by Ineke Wieberdink-Westerweel. Amsterdam: Luitingh-Sijthoff, 1990

Bloed! (Graphic novel adaptations of 'Human Remains' and 'Pig Blood Blues'). Translated into Dutch by Hedy Stegge. Amsterdam: Pop Comics, 1990 (trade paperback)

De Boeken van Bloed (Clive Barker's Books of Blood Volumes One through Six). Translated into Dutch by Hugo Kuipers, JC Pasman, Mariëlla Snel and Hugo Timmerman.
a.   Amsterdam: Luitingh-Sijthoff, 1990
b.   As *Boeken van Bloed*. Amsterdam: Poema Pocket, 1994 (paperback)

De Kunst (The Great and Secret Show). In Dutch. Amsterdam: Luitingh-Sijthoff, 1990

Imagica (Imajica). Translated into Dutch by Rein van Essen, Toon van Son and Jan Smit.
a.   Amsterdam: Luitingh-Sijthoff, 1992
b.   Amsterdam: Poema Pocket, 1997 (paperback)

Seks, Dood en Stralende Sterren (Clive Barker's Books of Blood Volume One). Translated into Dutch by Hugo Kuipers. Amsterdam: Poema Pocket, 1994 (paperback)

De Helse Wedstrijd (Clive Barker's Books of Blood Volume Two). Translated into Dutch by Hugo Kuipers. Amsterdam: Poema Pocket, 1995 (paperback)

De Dief van Altijd (The Thief of Always). Translated into Dutch by Erica Feberwee.
a.   Amsterdam: Luitingh-Sijthoff, 1995
b.   Amsterdam: Poema Pocket, 2000 (paperback)

Everville. Translated into Dutch by Hugo Kuipers, *et al.* Amsterdam: Luitingh-Sijthoff, 1995

Sacrament. Translated into Dutch by Tom van Son.
a.   Amsterdam: Luitingh-Sijthoff, 1997
b.   Amsterdam: Poema Pocket, 1999 (paperback)

Galilee. Translated into Dutch by Mariëlla Snel. Amsterdam: Luitingh-Sijthoff, 1999

Hungary

Kísértetház (The Hellbound Heart). Translated into Hungarian by Dóra Puszta. Budapest: Korbacs, 1990

Korbács (Weaveworld). Translated into Hungarian by Dóra Puszta. Budapest: Maecenas Kiad, 1990

Kárhozat (The Damnation Game). Translated into Hungarian by Anna Pálos and István Turczi. Budapest: Hibiszkusz Kiad, 1991

Pokolkelto (The Hellbound Heart). Translated into Hungarian by Péter Szentmihalyi Szabó. Szeged: Szukits Kiadó, 1997

Az éjszaka gyermekei (Cabal). Translated into Hungarian by Péter Szentmihalyi Szabó. Szeged: Szukits Hydra Horror, 1998

A Hírvivő – A Tudás Elsō\ Könyve (The Great and Secret Show). Translated into Hungarian by Péter Babits. Szeged: Szukits, 1999

Végsô felvonás – A Tudás második könyve (Everville). Translated into Hungarian by Péter Babits. Szeged: Szukits Hydra Fantasy, 2000

Italy

Infernalia (Clive Barker's Books of Blood Volume One). Translated into Italian by Tullio Dobner.
  a. Milan: Sonzogno, 1988 (hardback)
  b. Milan: Bompiani, 1990 (paperback)
  c. Milan: Sonzogno, 2000

Gioco dannato (The Damnation Game). Translated into Italian by Paola Formenti.
  a. Milan: Sperling & Kupfer, 1988
  b. Milan: Sperling Paperback, 1991 (paperback)

Ectoplasm (Clive Barker's Books of Blood Volume Two). Translated into Italian by Rossana Terrone.
  a. Milan: Sonzogno, 1989 (hardback)
  b. Milan: Bompiani, 1991 (paperback)
  c. Milan: Sonzogno, 2000

Il mondo in un tappeto (Weaveworld). Translated into Italian by Roberta Rambelli.
  a. Milan: Longanesi, 1989
  b. Milan: Editori Associati, 1994
  c. Milan: Editori Associati, 2000 (paperback)

Apocalypse: il grande spettacolo segreto (The Great and Secret Show). Translated into Italian by Tullio Dobner.
  a. Milan: Sonzogno, 1990
  b. Milan: Bompiani, 1992 (paperback)

Cabal (includes Cabal and selected stories from Clive Barker's Books of Blood Volume Six). Translated into Italian by Tullio Dobner.
a.   Milan: Sonzogno, 1990
b.   Milan: Bompiani, 1994 (paperback)

Sudario (Clive Barker's Books of Blood Volume Three). Translated into Italian by Tullio Dobner.
a.   Milan: Sonzogno, 1991
b.   Milan: Bompiani, 1993 (paperback)
c.   Milan: Sonzogno, 2000

Schiavi dell'Inferno (The Hellbound Heart). Translated into Italian by Tullio Dobner.
a.   Milan: Sonzogno, 1991
b.   Milan: Bompiani, 1993 (paperback)

Imagica (Imajica). Translated into Italian by Andrea Di Gregorio.
a.   Milan: Sonzogno, 1992
b.   Milan: Bompiani, 1997 (paperback)

Libro di Sangue (Clive Barker's Books of Blood Volume Four). Translated into Italian by Tullio Dobner.
a.   Milan: Sonzogno, 1993
b.   Milan: Bompiani, 1995 (paperback)

La casa delle vacanze (The Thief of Always). Translated into Italian by Andrea Di Gregorio. Milan: Bompiani, 1994

Libro di sangue 2 (Clive Barker's Books of Blood Volume Five). Translated into Italian by Piero Spinelli.
a.   Milan: Sonzogno, 1994
b.   Milan: Bompiani, 1998 (paperback)

Everville. Translated into Italian by Tullio Dobner.
a.   Milan: Sonzogno, 1995
b.   Milan: Sonzogno, 2000

Libro di sangue 3 (Clive Barker's Books of Blood Volume Six). Translated into Italian by Fabio Zucchella.
a.   Milan: Sonzogno, 1997
b.   Milan: Bompiani, 1999 (paperback)

Sacrament. Translated into Italian by Maura Parolini and Matteo Curtoni. Milan: Sonzogno, 1998

Galilee. Translated into Italian by Matteo Curtoni and Maura Parolini.
 a.   Milan: Sonzogno, 2000
 b.   Milan: Sonzogno Best Seller, 2001

Japan

The Midnight Meat Train (Clive Barker's Books of Blood Volume One). Translated into Japanese by T Miyawaki. Tokyo: Shuesha, 1987 (paperback)

Jacqueline Ess (Clive Barker's Books of Blood Volume Two). Translated into Japanese by K Okubo. Tokyo: Shuesha, 1987 (paperback)

Son of Celluloid (Clive Barker's Books of Blood Volume Three). Translated into Japanese by K Okubo. Tokyo: Shuesha, 1987 (paperback)

The Inhuman Condition (Clive Barker's Books of Blood Volume Four). Translated into Japanese by K Okubo. Tokyo: Shuesha, 1987 (paperback)

The Madonna (Clive Barker's Books of Blood Volume Five). Translated into Japanese by T Miyawaki. Tokyo: Shuesha, 1987 (paperback)

The Last Illusion (Clive Barker's Books of Blood Volume Six). Translated into Japanese by K Yano. Tokyo: Shuesha, 1987 (paperback)

The Hellbound Heart. In Japanese. Tokyo: Shuesha, 1987 (paperback)

Wivuwarudo (Weaveworld). Translated into Japanese by Kuraivu Baka and Sakai Akinobu. Tokyo: Shuesha, 1994 (two volumes; paperback)

Mexico (see Spain)

El gran show secreto: el primer libro sobre el arte (The Great and Secret Show). In Spanish. Mexico: Edivision, 1991

Sangre (Clive Barker's Books of Blood Volume Four). Translated into Spanish by Celia Filipetto. Mexico: Ediciones Roca, 1994 (paperback)

Norway

De Fördömdas Spel (The Damnation Game). Translated into Norwegian by Tommy Schinkler. Wahlstroms, 1988 (hardback)

Poland

Ksìéga krwi, tom 1 (Clive Barker's Books of Blood Volume One). Translated into Polish by Robert Mroziûski. Gdansk: Phantom Press International, 1991

Ksìéga krwi, tom 2 (Clive Barker's Books of Blood Volume Two). Translated into Polish by Jan Pultyn. Gdansk: Phantom Press International, 1992

Ksìéga Krwi Vols. 1–3 (Clive Barker's Books of Blood Volumes One, Two, and Three). Translated into Polish by Jaroslaw Irzykowski. Lodz: Wydawnictwo Phantompress, 1991–1992

Ksìéga krwi, tom 5 (Clive Barker's Books of Blood Volume Five). Translated into Polish by Beata Jankowska-Rosadziûska. Poznaû: Rebis, 1992

Ksìéga krwi, tom 6 (Clive Barker's Books of Blood Volume Six). Translated into Polish by Robert P Lipski. Poznaû: Rebis, 1992

Potépieûcza gra (The Damnation Game). Translated into Polish by Hanna Husak. Warsaw: Amber/Novum, 1992

Powrùt z piekla (The Hellbound Heart). Translated into Polish by Pawel Kwiatkowski. Poznaû: Rebis, 1992

Kobierzec (Weaveworld). Translated into Polish by Elzbieta Wilczyłska and Urszula Zieliłska. Poznaû: Rebis, 1993

Ksìéga krwi, tom 4 (Clive Barker's Books of Blood Volume Four). Translated into Polish by Malgorzata Studziûska. Poznaû: Zysk i S-ka, 1994

Wielkie sekretne widowisko (The Great and Secret Show). Translated into Polish by Bozena Baûska. Poznaû: Rebis, 1994

Everville. Translated into Polish by Robert Lipski. Warsaw: Wydawnictwo MAG, 1998

Cabal - Nocne Plemie (Cabal). In Polish. Publisher and date unknown.

Jamajka (Imajica). In Polish. Publisher and date unknown.

Spain

Libros sangrientos, 1 (Clive Barker's Books of Blood Volume One). Translated into Spanish by Santiago Jordán Sempere.

a. Barcelona: Planeta, 1986
b. Barcelona: Ediciones Martínez Roca, 1994 (paperback)

Libros sangrientos, 2 (Clive Barker's Books of Blood Volume Two). Translated into Spanish by Santiago Jordán Sempere.
a. Barcelona: Planeta, 1987
b. Barcelona: Ediciones Martínez Roca, 1994 (paperback)

Libros sangrientos, 3 (Clive Barker's Books of Blood Volume Three). Translated into Spanish by Santiago Jordán Sempere.
a. Barcelona: Planeta, 1987
b. Barcelona: Ediciones Martínez Roca, 1995 (paperback)

Sangre (Clive Barker's Books of Blood Volume Four). Translated into Spanish by Celia Filipetto.
a. Barcelona: Ediciones Martínez Roca, 1987
b. Barcelona: Ediciones Martínez Roca, 1993 (paperback)

El juego de las maldiciones (*The Damnation Game*). Translated into Spanish by Esteban Riambau Saurí. Barcelona: Versal, 1987

Sortilegio (Weaveworld). Translated into Spanish by Roger Vazquez de Parga.
a. Barcelona: Plaza & Janés, 1988
b. Barcelona: Plaza & Janés, 1994 (paperback

Sangre 2 (Clive Barker's Books of Blood Volume Five). Translated into Spanish by Celia Filipetto.
a. Barcelona: Ediciones Martínez Roca, 1988
b. Barcelona: Ediciones Martínez Roca, 1993 (paperback)
c. Mexico: Ediciones Roca, 1994

Cabal. Translated into Spanish by Isabel Aguirre.
a. Barcelona: Plaza & Janés, 1989
b. Barcelona: Plaza & Janés, 1994 (paperback)
c. Barcelona: Círculo de Lectores, 2000

El gran espectaculo secreto (The Great and Secret Show). Translated into Spanish by Jesús Pardo.
a. Barcelona: Plaza & Janés, 1991
b. Barcelona: Plaza & Janés, 1994 (paperback)

El ladron de días (The Thief of Always). Translated into Spanish by Enric Canals. Barcelona: Grijalbo, 1993

Jack y el Diablo [and] Así sangran los expoliadores (graphic novel adaptation of 'The Yattering and Jack' and 'How Spoilers Bleed'). Translated into Spanish by Maréa Vidal Campos. Barcelona: Ediciones Junior, 1994

Sweden

Det omänskliga (Clive Barker's Books of Blood Volumes One, Two and Three). Translated into Swedish by Per Rundgren. Stockholm: Forum, 1988

De fördömdas spel (The Damnation Game). Translated into Swedish by Tommy Schinkler. Stockholm: B Wahlström, 1988

Den blodbestänkta väven (Weaveworld). Translated into Swedish by Hans Granqvist. Stockholm: Forum, 1989

Det förbjudna (Clive Barker's Books of Blood Volumes Four, Five, and Six). Translated into Swedish by Per Rundgren. Stockholm: Forum, 1990

Den stora föreställningen (The Great and Secret Show). Translated into Swedish by Tommy Schinkler. Stockholm: B Wahlström, 1991

Yugoslavia

Utkani svet: u kraljevstvu kukavice: fuga: izlazak iz prazne nastambe (Weaveworld). Translated into Croatian by Mirjana Zivkovic. Belgrade: Polaris, 1989

Pakleno Srce (The Hellbound Heart). Translated into Croatian by Mario Jovic. Zagreb: Zagrebacka naklada, 1998 (paperback)

SECONDARY BIBLIOGRAPHY

SELECTED BOOKS (ALPHABETICAL ORDER BY AUTHOR)

Badley, Linda. *Writing Horror and the Body: The Fiction of Stephen King, Clive Barker and Anne Rice.* New York: Greenwood, 1996 (hardback)

Barbieri, Suzanne. *Clive Barker: Mythmaker for the Millennium.* Foreword by Peter Atkins. Stockport, England: British Fantasy Society, 1994 (paperback)

Barker, Clive, with Mark Salisbury and John Gilbert. *Clive Barker's Nightbreed: The Making of the Film.* London: Fontana/Collins, 1990 (trade paperback)

Bell, Joseph. *The Books of Clive Barker.* Toronto: Soft Books, 1988 (limited edition paperback: 185 numbered and 15 lettered copies)

Bergal, Gilles, ed. *Phenix 34: Dossier Clive Barker.* Racour, France: Phenix, 1993 (trade paperback; in French)

Boone, Aron (pseudonym of Heiko Bender). *Raising Hell.* Nördlingen, Germany: Medien Publikations, 1997 (in German)

Brown, Michael, ed. *Pandemonium: Further Explorations into the World of Clive Barker*
   a.   Staten Island, NY: Eclipse, 1991 (signed limited edition hardback; 300 copies)
   b.   Staten Island, NY: Eclipse, 1991 (hardback)
   c.   Staten Island, NY: Eclipse, 1991 (trade paperback)

Burke, Fred. *Clive Barker Illustrator Volume II: The Art of Clive Barker*
  a. Forestville, CA: Eclipse, 1994 (hardback)
  b. Forestville, CA: Eclipse, 1994 (trade paperback)

Colombo, Maurizio, and Antonio Tentori. *Lo Schermo Insanguinato*. Chieti, Italy: Marino Solfanelli Editore, 1990

Epel, Naomi. *Writers Dreaming*
  a. New York: Carol Southern Books, 1993 (hardback)
  b. New York: Vintage Books, 1994 (trade paperback)

Hoppenstand, Gary. *Clive Barker's Short Stories: Imagination as Metaphor in the Books of Blood and Other Works*. Jefferson, NC: McFarland, 1994 (hardback)

Johansson, Annika. *Världar av ljus, världar av mörker: fantasy & skräcklitteratur* ('Worlds of Light, Worlds of Darkness: Fantasy & Horror Literature). In Swedish. Utgivning Lund: BTJ, 2000

Jones, Stephen, comp. *Clive Barker's A-Z of Horror* ('Official Companion and Guide to the Critically Acclaimed BBC Television Series')
  a. London: BBC Books, 1997 (hardback)
  b. New York: HarperPrism, 1997 (hardback)
  c. London: BBC Books, 1998 (trade paperback)
  d. New York: HarperPrism, 1998 (trade paperback)

Jones, Stephen, ed. *Clive Barker's The Nightbreed Chronicles*. London: Titan, 1990 (trade paperback)

Jones, Stephen, ed. *Clive Barker's Shadows in Eden*
  a. Lancaster, PA: Underwood-Miller, 1991 (deluxe signed limited edition hardback; 52 copies)
  b. Lancaster, PA: Underwood-Miller, 1991 (signed limited edition hardback; 500 copies)
  c. Lancaster, PA: Underwood-Miller, 1991 (hardback)
  d. Lancaster, PA: Underwood-Miller, 1994 (trade paperback)

Jones, Stephen, ed. *The Hellraiser Chronicles*. London: Titan, 1992 (trade paperback)

Kleppe, Nikolai. *Horror – taking fear literally: an introduction to the horror genre and a reading of Clive Barker's The Great And Secret Show*. Bergen, Norway: N Kleppe, 2000

Lovell, James Blair. *The Clive Barker Bibliography*. Washington, DC: James Blair Lovell, 1989 (self-published limited edition monograph; 30 copies)

Morton, Timothy, and Jennifer Wicke. *The Imagination of Clive Barker*. Laguna Beach, CA: Laguna Art Museum (exhibition guide)

Niles, Steve, ed., with text by Fred Burke. *Clive Barker Illustrator*
  a. Forestville, CA: Arcane/Eclipse Books, 1990 (deluxe signed limited edition hardback; 200 copies)
  b. Forestville, CA: Arcane/Eclipse Books, 1990 (signed limited edition hardback; 750 copies)
  c. Forestville, CA: Eclipse, 1990 (hardback)
  d. Forestville, CA: Eclipse, 1990 (trade paperback)

Proulx, Kevin E. *Fear to the World: Eleven Voices in a Chorus of Horror*
  a. Mercer Island, WA: Starmont House, 1992 (trade paperback)
  b. San Bernardino, CA: Borgo, 1992 (hardback)

Ravich, Rand, and Mark Kruger. *The Candyman Chronicles* ('Candyman: Farewell to the Flesh' screenplay). Story by Clive Barker. Los Angeles: Polygram Film Productions BV, 1995 (trade paperback; 'for promotional and publicity use only')

Rockett, Ron. *Screen Monsters # 2: The Unauthorized Clive Barker Special*. Berlin, NJ: Comic Zone, April 1993 (comic book)

Seward, Keith (Bess Cutler Gallery). *Clive Barker: Paintings and Drawings 1973–1993*. New York: Bess Cutler Gallery, 1993 (exhibition guide)

Van Hise, James. *Stephen King and Clive Barker: The Illustrated Guide to the Masters of the Macabre*. Las Vegas, NV: Pioneer Books, 1990 (trade paperback)

Van Hise, James. *The Illustrated Guide to the Masters of the Macabre II*. Las Vegas, NV: Pioneer Books, 1992 (trade paperback)

Winter, Douglas E. *Faces of Fear*
  a. New York: Berkley, 1985 (trade paperback)
  b. London: Pan, 1990 (paperback; revised edition)

Winter, Douglas E. *Darkness Absolute*. Eugene, OR: Pulphouse Press, 1991 (chapbook)

SELECTED ARTICLES, INTERVIEWS, AND REVIEWS (ALPHABETICAL ORDER BY AUTHOR)

Abbott, Spence. *'IGN for Men* Interview: Clive Barker Part 1' formen.ign.com/news/13383.html (website)

Abbott, Spence. *'IGN for Men* Interview: Clive Barker Part 2'
formen.ign.com/news/13415.html (website)

Abbott, Spence. 'IGNmovies.com Interview: Clive Barker'
movies.ign.com/news/3012.html

Affleck, Colin. 'Festival Fringe Review: *The History of the Devil'*
The Scotsman, 24 August 1981 (newspaper)

Allen, Bruce. *'Damnation Game*: Barker Beats the Devil'
USA Today, – May 1987 (newspaper)

Allen, Bruce. 'Something Wicked Comes to Oregon'
New York Times Book Review, 20 November 1994 (newspaper)

Anonymous. '$8 Million Disney Deal for Barker's Heroine Story'
Evening Standard, date unknown, 2000 (newspaper)

Anonymous. 'ALA's 1995 'Best' Lists: Recommended Books for the Reluctant
Young Adult Reader, 1995: Fiction'
Booklist, vol. 91 no. 15, 1 April 1995 (magazine)

Anonymous. 'Barker, Clive'
Contemporary Authors: New Revision Series, Volume 81. Detroit: Gale
Research, 1999 (hardback)

Anonymous. 'Barker, Clive, 1952-'
Contemporary Authors: A Bio-Bibliographical Guide, Volume 121. ed. Hal
May. Detroit, MI: Gale Research, 1987 (hardback)

Anonymous. 'Barker's Shaman'
Billboard, vol. 105 no. 27, 3 July 1993 (magazine)

Anonymous. 'Clive Barker'
Science Fiction, Fantasy and Horror Writers. ed. Marie J MacNee. New York:
UXL, 1995

Anonymous. 'Clive Barker, 1952-
Contemporary Literary Criticism. Vol. 52. Detroit, MI: Gale Research, 1989
(hardback)

Anonymous. *'Clive Barker's Shadows in Eden'*
World of Fandom, vol. 2 no. 15, Spring 1992 (magazine)

Anonymous. 'The Films of Clive Barker'
formen.ign.com/news/13258.html (website)

Anonymous. 'Heckraiser'
New York, 1 May 1995 (magazine)

Anonymous. 'The Magic Carpet Flies Into the Bestseller Lists'
Publishing News, 29 April 1988 (newspaper)

Anonymous. 'Not-So-Shocking Nudes Headlines: *The History of the Devil,* Old Rep Theatre'
Birmingham Post, Mirror Regional Newspapers, date unknown, 1998 (newspaper)

Anonymous. 'The Organic Theatre Company Announces the World Premiere of *In the Flesh*'
Dread, no. 8, 1992 (magazine)

Anonymous. *'Pandemonium: Further Explorations into the World of Clive Barker'*
World of Fandom, vol. 2 no. 15, Spring 1992 (magazine)

Anonymous. 'A Piece of My Mind: A Conversation with Clive Barker'
Diamond Dialogue, January 1993 (magazine)

Anonymous. 'A Pilgrim's Progress Through the Worlds of *Imajica*'
World of Fandom, vol. 2 no. 15, Spring 1992 (magazine)

Anonymous. 'A Prince of Horror Faces the Camera'
Maclean's, 27 February 1989 (magazine)

Anonymous. '75 Star Players'
The Advocate, 30 March 1999 (newspaper)

Anonymous. 'Talk Mit Clive Barker Im 'Alhambra''
That's Clive!, no. 3, October 1996 (magazine; in German)

Anonymous. *'Weaveworld'*
Kirkus Reviews, 1 August 1987 (magazine)

Anonymous. 'USAToday.com Talk Today: Horror in Books and Movies: Clive Barker'
www.usatoday.com/community/chat/1031barker.htm (website)

Armstrong, Mark. *'Undying:* Clive Barker Turns Gaming Geek'
www.eonline.com/News/Items/0,1,7835,00.html, 17 February 2001 (website)

Arnold, Gary. 'Trite Fright Makes *Nightbreed* a Big Dud'
Washington Times, 19 February 1990 (newspaper)

Astic, Guy. 'Clive Barker: Portrait'
  Ténèbres, no. 5, January 1999 (magazine; in French)

Athanas, Charlie, with Stephanie Farrell. *'Burning Chrome* Live: Clive Barker
  Interviews William Gibson'
  burningcity.com/CBWGP1.html (website)

Atkins, Peter. 'A Brief History of *A Clown's Sodom*'
  Dread, no. 5, 1992 (magazine)

Atkins, Peter. 'Children of Fire'
  Dread Summer Special, 1992 (magazine)

Atkins, Peter. 'A Dog's Tale'
  Clive Barker's Shadows in Eden, 1991

Atkins, Peter. 'Hellbound: Bringing It to Light'
  Clive Barker's Shadows in Eden, 1991

Atkins, Peter. 'Other Selves, Other Shadows: A Conversation with Clive Barker'
  Cut! Horror Writers on Horror Film, ed. Christopher Golden. New York:
  Berkley, 1982 (trade paperback)

Atkins, Peter. 'A Reader's Guide to the *History of the Devil*: Peter Atkins Talks
  to Clive Barker'
  Pandemonium: Further Explorations into the World of Clive Barker, 1991

Atkins, Peter, and Clive Barker. 'Knocking on Glass: The Mind's Menagerie
  and Other Conceits' ('A conversation between Clive Barker and Peter
  Atkins')
  Clive Barker's Shadows in Eden, 1991

Bacal, Simon. 'Clive Barker's Triple Threat: *Lord of Illusions*, A Fable of Death
  and Resurrection'
  Sci Fi Entertainment, February 1995 (magazine)

Bacal, Simon. 'Sweet Talking Guy'
  Shivers, no. 4, December 1992 (magazine)

Barron, Neil. 'Barker, Clive'
  Horror Literature: A Reader's Guide. ed. Neil Barron. New York: Garland,
  1990 (hardback)

Battista, Bobby. 'CNN: Clive Barker returns with *Galilee* – June 2, 1998'
  www.cnn.com/books/dialogue/9806/clive.barker (website)

Beeler, Michael. 'Barker: Producing Horror in Hollywood'
Cinefantastique, vol. 26 no. 3, April 1995 (magazine)

Beeler, Michael. 'Barker: *The Thief of Always*'
Cinefantastique, vol. 26 no. 3, April 1995 (magazine)

Beeler, Michael. 'Clive Barker: Horror Visionary'
Cinefantastique, vol. 26 no. 3, April 1995 (magazine)

Beeler, Michael. 'Clive Barker's *Lord of Illusions*'
Cinefantastique, vol. 26 no. 3, April 1995 (magazine)

Beeler, Michael. 'Filming the *Books of Blood*: Clive Barker's *Lord of Illusions*'
Cinefantastique, vol. 26 no. 2, February 1995 (magazine)

Beeler, Michael. '*Lord of Illusions*'
Cinefantastique, vol. 26 no. 6, October 1995 (magazine)

Beeler, Michael. '*Lord of Illusions*: Writer-Director Clive Barker on Fine-Tuning the Horror Magic Act During Post-Production'
Cinefantastique, vol. 26 no. 5, August 1995 (magazine)

Bentzen, Cheryl, and Stephen Dressler. 'Clive Barker Talks About *Lord of Illusions*'
Lost Souls, vol. 1 no. 2, 1995 (magazine)

Bentzen, Cheryl, and Stephen Dressler. 'Doug Bradley: The Man Behind the Mask'
Lost Souls, vol. 1 no. 7, April, 1997 (magazine)

Bentzen, Cheryl, and Stephen Dressler. 'From the Dog Days to *Bloodlines*: A Chat with Pete Atkins'
Lost Souls, vol. 1 no. 3, 1996 (magazine)

Bentzen, Cheryl, and Stephen Dressler. 'Hell's Event'
Lost Souls, vol. 1 no. 2, 1995 (magazine)

Bentzen, Cheryl, and Stephen Dressler. 'Light, Wisdom and Sound'
Dread, no. 11 1992 (magazine)

Bentzen, Cheryl, and Stephen Dressler. '*Lost Souls* Catches Up with Scott Bakula'
Lost Souls, vol. 1, no. 2, 1995 (magazine)

Bernstein, Abbie. 'Carving Out a Niche'
Fangoria, no. 140, March 1995 (magazine)

Bernstein, Abbie. 'Hooked on *Candyman*'
Fangoria, no. 139, January 1995 (magazine)

Bhose, Indra. 'Clive Barker, créatur de monstres II'
L'Ecran Fantastique, no. 76, January 1987 (magazine; in French)

Billson, Anne. 'Hell Hound'
1. *Time Out*, 15–22 October 1986 (magazine)
2. *Clive Barker's Shadows in Eden*, 1991
3. As 'Clive Barker – Der Höllenhund'. *Der Horror Film II*. ed. Willy Loderhose. In German. Hamburg: Cinema Verlag, 1991

Blackmore, Leigh. 'Weaving Words with Clive Barker'
Terror Australis, no. 1, Autumn 1988 (magazine)

Blake, Julie. 'Beginnings'
Unpublished manuscript, April 1996

Bleiler, E. F. 'Clive Barker's Magic Carpet'
Washington Post, 27 September 1987 (newspaper)

Blevins, Tal. *'Clive Barker's Undying'*
pc.ign.com/reviews/14693.html (website)

Bloom, John (writing as Joe Bob Briggs). 'Sex in the Attic with Devilhead Slime'
1. *Datebook*, 4 October 1987 (magazine)
2. *Clive Barker's Shadows in Eden*, 1991

Blue, Tyson. 'A Conversation with Clive Barker'
Cemetery Dance, Winter 1992 (magazine)

Bradley, Doug. 'Pinhead's Progress'
1. *Fangoria*, no. 112, May 1992 (magazine)
2. In *Fangoria's Best Horror Films*. ed. Anthony Timpone. New York: Crescent, 1994 (hardback)

Braun, Liz. 'His *Weaveworld* Has Us in Knots'
Toronto Sun, 28 October 1987 (newspaper)

Brigg, Peter. *'Weaveworld'*
Magill's Guide to Science Fiction and Fantasy Literature: Volume 4. ed. TA Shippey. Pasadena, CA: Salem Press, 1996

Brodsky, Sascha. 'Clive Barker, Horror Novelist, Brings His Art to Soho'
The Villager, 17 February 1993 (newspaper)

Brosnan, John. 'Terror Tactics'
1. *Time Out*, 16–23 March 1988 (magazine)
2. *Clive Barker's Shadows in Eden*, 1991

Brown, Charles N. 'Clive Barker: Love, Death & the Whole Damned Thing'
Locus, vol. 34 no. 4, April 1995 (magazine)

Brown, Michael. 'Clive Barker: The Creator'
Dread, no. 6, 1992 (magazine)

Brown, Michael. 'Clive Barker: Yesterday, Today and Tomorrow'
Dread, no. 11, 1992 (magazine)

Brown, Michael. 'Dan Chichester Co-Creator of the *Hellraiser* Comic Series
Tells of Pinhead's Upcoming Series'
Dread, no. 10, 1992 (magazine)

Brown, Michael. '*Dread* Goes to Hell with Doug Bradley'
Dread, no. 3, 1992 (magazine)

Brown, Michael. '*Dread* Goes to Hell with Doug Bradley – Part Two'
Dread, no. 4, 1992 (magazine)

Brown, Michael. '*Dread* Speaks with Clive Barker'
Dread, no. 3, 1992 (magazine)

Brown, Michael. '*Dread* Speaks with Dan Chichester'
Dread, no. 1, 1991 (magazine)

Brown, Michael. 'Hell on Earth'
Dread, no. 1, 1991 (magazine)

Brown, Michael. 'Introduction'
Pandemonium: Further Explorations into the World of Clive Barker, 1991

Brown, Michael. 'John Bolton: Artist of the Macabre Shrieks Out'
Dread, no. 10, 1992 (magazine)

Brown, Michael. 'The Making of a Cenobite'
Dread, no. 4, 1992 (magazine)

Brown, Michael. 'Malcolm Smith Continued'
Dread, no. 12, 1993 (magazine)

Brown, Michael. 'Malcolm Smith, Gene Colan and Clive Barker . . . *The Harrowers: Raiders of the Abyss*'
Dread, no. 11, 1992 (magazine)

Brown, Michael. 'Marvel Comics Barkerverse: A Special Preview!'
Dread, no. 9, 1992 (magazine)

Brown, Michael. 'Nick Vince Talks About Writing *Nightbreed* for Comics'
Dread, no. 8, 1992 (magazine)

Brown, Michael. 'Peter Atkins and the Upcoming *Hellraiser 4*'
Dread, no. 12, 1992 (magazine)

Brown, Michael. 'Raising Hell with Peter Atkins'
Pandemonium: Further Explorations into the World of Clive Barker, 1991

Brown, Michael. 'Ready for Hell?'
Dread, no. 4, 1992 (magazine)

Brown, Michael. 'So Many Monsters, So Little Time'
Pandemonium: Further Explorations into the World of Clive Barker, 1991

Brown, Michael. 'Theatre of Pain'
Pandemonium: Further Explorations into the World of Clive Barker, 1991

Bryant, Edward. '*Clive Barker Illustrator*, Clive Barker & Fred Burke'
Locus, no. 363, April 1991 (magazine)

Bryant, Edward. '*Everville*'
Locus, no. 408, January 1995 (magazine)

Bryant, Edward. '*Galilee*'
Locus, no. 454, November 1998 (magazine)

Bryant, Edward. '*The Great and Secret Show*'
Locus, no. 346, November 1989 (magazine)

Bryant, Edward. '*Imajica*'
Locus, no. 370, November 1991 (magazine)

Bryant, Edward. '*Sacrament*'
Locus, no. 427, November 1996 (magazine)

Bryant, Edward. '*Tapping the Vein: Book One*'
Locus, no. 345, October 1989 (magazine)

Bryant, Edward. 'Tapping the Vein: Book Two'
Locus, no. 348, January 1990 (magazine)

Bryant, Edward. 'The Thief of Always'
Locus, no. 384, January 1993 (magazine)

Budrys, Algis. 'What Evil Is Lurking Beneath Your Bed?'
Chicago Sun-Times, 3 May 1987 (newspaper)

Burbeck, Rodney. 'Some Harsh Words for the Critics from Ballard
and Barker'
1. Publishing News, 24 July 1987 (magazine)
2. Clive Barker's Shadows in Eden, 1991

Burden, Martin. 'Top of the Horror Heap'
New York Post, 30 December 1988 (newspaper)

Burnett, Thane. 'What Scares Clive Barker?'
New York Daily News, 6 November 1987 (newspaper)

Burns, Craig William. 'It's That Time of the Month: Representations of the
Goddess in the Work of Clive Barker'
Journal of Popular Culture, vol. 27 no. 3, Winter 1993 (journal)

Burton, Peter. 'The Candyman Cometh (Out)'
Gay Times, July 1995 (magazine)

Campbell, Ramsey. 'Introduction'
1. Clive Barker's Books of Blood, Volume 1, 1984 (UK)
2. Clive Barker's Books of Blood, Volume 1, 1985 (US)

Campbell, Ramsey. 'Weaver of Wonders'
Clive Barker's Shadows in Eden, 1991

Casebeer, Edwin F. 'Clive Barker (5 October 1952-)'
Dictionary of Literary Biography: British Science-Fiction and Fantasy Writers.
Detroit: Gale Research, 1994 (hardback)

Chambers, Andrea, and Jonathan Cooper. 'Meet the New (Stephen) King of
Horror, Briton Clive Barker'
People, 15 June 1987 (magazine)

Cherry, Brigid SG. 'Straight for the Jugular'
Fear, December 1989/January 1990 (magazine)

Cherry, Brigid, and Brian J Robb. 'The Final Cut: Editing *Hellbound*'
Fear, no. 7, July 1989 (magazine)

Chichester, DG. 'Afterword'
Clive Barker's Nightbreed: Genesis. New York: Epic Comics, November 1991
(graphic novel)

Chick, Tom. 'CNET.com Game News: Clive Barker Talks About *Undying*'
digitalcity.gamecenter.com/News/Item/0,3,0–5102,00.html (website)

Christy, George. 'The Great Life'
The Hollywood Reporter, 17 November 1987 (magazine)

Clarke, Dan. 'Pinhead and the Human Condition'
Inklings, December 1998 (magazine)

Conrad, Daniel, and Benoît Domis. 'Clive Barker'
Ténèbres, no. 5, January 1999 (magazine; in French)

Costello, Matthew J. 'Conversation with Clive Barker'
Fantasy Review, no. 100, April 1987 (magazine)

Coven, Lawrence. 'Realms of Horror'
Los Angeles Daily News, 13 October 1991 (newspaper)

Coveney, Michael. 'The Secret Life of Cartoons'
Financial Times, 16 October 1986 (newspaper)

Cox, Murray. '*Books*: The Arts'
Omni, vol. 9 no. 1 October 1986 (magazine)

Crane, Jonathan L. 'Nothing Matters and So What If It Did: Clive Barker and
Splatterpunk'
1. *The Image of Violence in Literature, the Media, and Society.* ed. Will
    Wright and Steven Kaplan. Pueblo, CO: Society for the
    Interdisciplinary Study of Social Imagery, University of Southern
    Colorado, 1995
2. Selected Papers, 1995 Conference, Society for the Interdisciplinary
    Study of Social Imagery, Colorado Springs, Colorado, 1995

Cunningham, Carl. '*Nightbreed*: From Midian to Obscurity?'
Dread, no. 8, 1992 (magazine)

Cunningham, Carl. 'Sweets to the Sweet'
Dread, no. 7, 1992 (magazine)

Curci, Loris. 'Peter Atkins'
Shock Masters of the Cinema. By Loris Curci. Key West, FL: Fantasma, 1996 (trade paperback)

Czech, Winfried, Gero Reimann and Norbert Tass. 'Interview: Clive Barker'
Phantastische Zeiten, no. 2, 1988 (magazine; in German)

Dair, G. 'Eroticizing the World'
1. *Cut*, vol. 2 no. 10, October 1987 (magazine)
2. *Clive Barker's Shadows in Eden*, 1991

Daoust, Phil. 'Arts: I Sound Like a Pervert? Whoopee!'
Guardian, 12 November 1998 (newspaper)

Darvell, Michael. 'Outboards'
What's On, 30 April 1982 (magazine)

Darvell, Michael. 'Tap-Dancing Ducks and Hammer Murders'
What's On, 30 October 1986 (magazine)

Dauphin, Gary. 'Clan Destiny'
Village Voice, 14 July 1998 (newspaper)

Della Flora, Anthony. 'Horror Master Tempts Audiences with *Devil*'
Albuquerque Journal, 6 October 2000 (newspaper)

Dery, Mark. 'Clive Barker'
Carpe Noctem, no. 13, 1998 (magazine)

Douglas, Janice. 'Backtalk'
Emergency Librarian, vol. 20 no. 5, May/June 1993 (journal)

Dressler, Stephen. 'Confessions: A Question and Answer with Clive Barker' (an irregular series of interviews)
Lost Souls, vol. 1 no. 1, 1995 (magazine)
Lost Souls, vol. 1 no. 2, 1995 (magazine)
Lost Souls, vol. 1 no. 3, 1996 (magazine)
Lost Souls, vol. 1 no. 4, 1996 (magazine)
Lost Souls, vol. 1 no. 5, October 1996 (magazine)
Lost Souls, vol. 1 no. 6, January 1997 (magazine)
Lost Souls, vol. 1 no. 7, April 1997 (magazine)
Lost Souls, vol. 1 no. 11, September 1998 (magazine)
Lost Souls, vol. 1 no. 12, January 1999 (magazine)
Lost Souls, vol. 2 no. 1, April 1999 (magazine)

Dressler, Stephen. 'Nights of Blood and Wine'
Lost Souls, vol. 1 no. 3, 1996 (magazine)

Dubin, Zan. 'Dr. Jekyll and Mr. Clive'
Los Angeles Times, 12 August 1995 (newspaper)

Dubin, Zan. 'Horrormeister Barker Turns Imagination Loose on Canvas'
Los Angeles Times, 22 August 1995 (newspaper)

Duniday, Cathy. 'Barker Paints a Dis Franchise'
Hollywood Reporter, 17 April 2000 (magazine)

DuPree, Robert. *'Lord of Illusions*: Robert DuPree Interviews Clive Barker'
Subliminal Tattoos, 1995 (magazine)

Dziemianowicz, Stefan R. 'Barker, Clive. *Cabal'*
Science Fiction and Fantasy Book Review Annual 1989. ed. Robert A Collins
and Robert Latham. Westport, CT: Meckler, 1990 (hardback)

Dziemianowicz, Stefan R. 'Barker, Clive. *In The Flesh'*
Science Fiction and Fantasy Book Review Annual 1988. ed. Robert A Collins
and Robert Latham. Westport, CT: Meckler, 1989 (hardback)

Dziemianowicz, Stefan R. 'Barker, Clive. *Weaveworld'*
Science Fiction and Fantasy Book Review Annual 1988. ed. Robert A Collins
and Robert Latham. Westport, CT: Meckler, 1989 (hardback)

Dziemianowicz, Stefan. 'Contemporary Horror Fiction, 1950–1998'
*Fantasy and Horror: A Critical and Historical Guide to Literature, Illustration,
Film, TV, Radio, and the Internet*. ed. Neil Barron. Lanham, MD: Scarecrow
Press, 1999 (hardback)

Dziemianowicz, Stefan. 'Other Voices, Other Realms'
Washington Post, 27 October 1991 (newspaper)

Dziemianowicz, Stefan R, and Michael A Morrison. 'The Year in Horror, 1988'
Science Fiction and Fantasy Book Review Annual 1989. ed. Robert A Collins
and Robert Latham. Westport, CT: Meckler, 1990 (hardback)

Eggar, Robin. 'L'Enfant Horrible'
Sunday Express Colour Supplement, 1 February 1987 (newspaper)

Eller, Claudia. 'Disney to Pay $8 Million for Fantasy Series'
Los Angeles Times, 15 April 2000 (newspaper)

Ellison, Harlan. 'Can We Talk?'
Midnight Graffiti Special, no. 1, 1994 (magazine)

Ellsworth, Robert. 'Black & White'
Detour, December 1993 (magazine)

Etchison, Dennis, and Clive Barker. 'A Little Bit of Hamlet' ('A Conversation Between Clive Barker and Dennis Etchison')
Clive Barker's Shadows in Eden, 1991

Evans, Everett. '*Frankenstein* a real Frankenstein'
Houston Chronicle, 15 October 1998 (newspaper)

Farrell, John M. 'World Weaver'
Hot Press, no. 13951, 1995 (magazine)

Ferrante, Anthony C. 'The Conjuring of *Lord of Illusions*: Part One'
Fangoria, no. 138, November 1994 (magazine)

Ferrante, Anthony C. 'The Conjuring of *Lord of Illusions*: Part Two: Principal Photography – The First Half'
Fangoria, no. 139, January 1995 (magazine)

Ferrante, Anthony C. 'The Conjuring of *Lord of Illusions*: Part Three: Principal Photography – The Second Half'
Fangoria, no. 140, March 1995 (magazine)

Ferrante, Anthony C. 'The Conjuring of *Lord of Illusions*: Part Four: Postproduction'
Fangoria, no. 141, April 1995 (magazine)

Ferrante, Anthony C. 'The Conjuring of *Lord of Illusions*: Part Five: The Last Interview'
Fangoria, no. 146, September 1995 (magazine)

Ferrante, Anthony C. '*Hellraiser IV: Bloodline* – To Hell and Back'
Fangoria, no. 141, April 1995 (magazine)

Ferrante, Anthony C. '*Monster Invasion: Hellraiser IV: Bloodline*'
Fangoria, no. 140, March 1995 (magazine)

Ferrante, Anthony C. '*Monster Invasion: Illusions* Update'
Fangoria, no. 143, June 1995 (magazine)

Fielder, Words Miles. 'Renaissance Man'
The Scotsman, 18 September 1999 (newspaper)

Fisher, Mark. 'Theatre: the *Books of Blood*, Citizens' Theatre, Glasgow'
The Herald, date unknown 1999 (newspaper)

Flippo, Chet. 'Omigod!! Meet Clive Barker, the Man Who Can Scare Stephen King'
New York Daily News, 3 August 1986 (newspaper)

Floyd, Nigel. 'Frights of Fancy'
1. *20/20*, no. 2, May 1989 (magazine)
2. [revised version] *Clive Barker's Shadows in Eden*, 1991

Floyd, Nigel. 'Slime Time'
1. *Time Out*, no. 889, 2–9 September 1987 (magazine)
2. As 'Clive Barker: *Hellraiser*': *Clive Barker's Shadows in Eden*, 1991

Flynn, Bob. 'Intro: *Hellraiser*'
The Face, August 1987 (magazine)

French, Todd. '*Candyman*: Interview with the Monster'
Cinefantastique, vol. 26 no. 3, April 1995 (magazine)

French, Todd. 'Clive Barker's *Candyman 2*'
Cinefantastique, vol. 26 no. 3, April 1995 (magazine)

Fritz, Steve. 'Clive Barker: In Divine Territory'
www.fandomshop.com/movies/features/clivebarker062698.html (website)

Fröhder, Hans Georg, and Oliver Schätzlein. 'Fragen und Antworten – Das Clive Barker Interview in Amsterdam'
That's Clive!, no. 3, October 1996 (translated into German by Hans Georg Fröhder)

Gaiman, Neil. 'Clive Barker'
Penthouse, May 1985 (magazine)

Gaiman, Neil. 'Flame On!'
Clive Barker's Shadows in Eden, 1991

Gaiman, Neil. 'King of the Gory Tellers'
1. *Today*, 19 October 1986 (newpaper)
2. *Clive Barker's Shadows in Eden*, 1991

Gainor, Dan. 'A Bloody Good Scare for '80s'
Washington Times, 29 October 1986 (newspaper)

Ganahl, Jane. '*Hellraiser* Barker on a Spiritual Quest'
San Francisco Chronicle, 11 August 1996 (newspaper)

Ganahl, Jane. 'Mining the Dark Side'
San Francisco Examiner, 21 August 1995 (newspaper)

Garcia, Nancy & Robert T Garcia. 'Clive Barker: Interview'
American Fantasy, Winter 1987 (magazine)

Gates, Rob. 'A Bloody Sham'
Lambda Book Report, vol. 8 no. 8, March 2000 (magazine)

Gerard, Morgan. 'Clive Barker The Horror!'
Graffiti, vol. 4 no. 1, January 1988 (magazine)

Gilmore, Mikal. 'Hell Raisers'
Rolling Stone, 11 February 1988 (magazine)

Gire, Dann. 'Clive Barker on *Hellraiser*'
Cinefantastique, vol. 18 no. 2/3, March 1988 (magazine)

Glaberson, Cory, and Stephen Jones. '*Hellraiser* Movie Preview'
American Fantasy, Winter 1987 (magazine)

Goddard, Peter. 'Guru of Gore'
Toronto Star, 31 October 1987 (newspaper)

Goldstein, Patrick. '*Hellbound's* Horror-Fiction Lion'
Los Angeles Times, 28 December 1988 (newspaper)

Golini, Marisa. 'Let's Talk Lesbian Bondage'
Boing Boing, no. 14, 1995 (magazine)

Gore, Christian. 'The Interview from Hell: Clive Barker'
Film Threat, no. 5, August 1992 (magazine)

Grabowski, William J. 'Clive Barker'
The Horror Show, Spring 1986 (magazine)

Gracey-Whitman, Lionel, and Don Melia. 'Beneath the Blanket of Banality'
1. *Heartbreak Hotel*, no. 4, July/August 1988 (magazine)
2. *Clive Barker's Shadows in Eden*, 1991

Graham, Bob. 'A Demon For Work / Busy Horror Auteur Clive Barker Branches Out Into Erotica'
San Francisco Chronicle, 22 February 1999 (newspaper)

SECONDARY BIBLIOGRAPHY

Graham, Bob. 'On Obsession, Failure and Art'
San Francisco Chronicle, 22 February 1999 (newspaper)

Grassman, Preston. *'Galilee'*
Locus, no. 451, August 1998 (magazine)

Green, Tom. 'Barker, More Than Just a Hellraiser"
USA Today, 24 September 1992 (newspaper)

Gregory, Jon. *'Cabal*: The Nightbreed/Clive Barker's *Nightbreed'*
Hellraiser, no. 1, 1991 (magazine)

Gregory, Jon. 'Clive Barker Interview'
Hellraiser, no. 1, 1991 (magazine)

Gregory, Jon. 'Doug Bradley Interview: Angel to Some, Demon to All'
Hellraiser, no. 1, 1991 (magazine)

Gregory, Jon. 'Review: *Underworld* aka *Transmutations'*
Hellraiser, no. 1, 1991 (magazine)

Guzman, Vince. 'Clive Barker'
Underscope, August 1995 (magazine)

Hacker, Kathy. 'He Delights in Horror'
Philadelphia Inquirer, 22 September 1987 (newspaper)

Haff, Stephen. 'Clive Barker: Spokesman for the Strange'
Other Dimensions, no. 1, Summer 1993 (journal)

Hand, Elizabeth. 'The City on the Borderlands'
Washington Post Book World, 18 December 1994 (newspaper)

Harley, Kevin. 'Carry On Screaming'
New Statesman & Society, 22 March 1996 (newspaper)

Harper, Leanne C. 'Clive Barker: Renaissance *Hellraiser'*
 1. *Bloomsbury Review*, vol. 7 no. 5 September/October 1987 (journal)
 2. *Clive Barker's Shadows in Eden*, 1991

Harrington, Richard. *'Candyman*: Risky Beeswax'
Washington Post, 19 October 1992 (newspaper)

Harrington, Richard. 'Clive Barker and the Horror of It All'
Washington Post, 11 September 1992 (newspaper)

Harrington, Richard. 'Clive Barker's Sleight of Bland'
Washington Post, 25 August 1995 (newspaper)

Harrington, Richard. 'The Horrors of *Hellraiser*'
Washington Post, 19 September 1987 (newspaper)

Higgins, Bill. 'Barker Takes Disney to New Fantasyland'
Variety, 17–23 April 2000 (magazine)

Higgins, Bill. 'Mouse Catches Barker'
Daily Variety, 17 April 2000 (newspaper)

Hoppenstand, Gary. 'From Here to Quiddity: Clive Barker's *The Great and Secret Show*'
Clive Barker's Shadows in Eden, 1991

Hoppenstand, Gary. 'The Secret Self in Clive Barker's Imaginative Fiction'
Pandemonium: Further Explorations into the World of Clive Barker, 1991

Hughes, Dave. 'Clive Barker: In the Flesh'
Skeleton Crew, no. 3/4, 1988 (magazine)

Huisman, Mark. 'Force of Nature'
The Advocate, 23 July 1996 (newspaper)

Hurren, Kenneth. 'Cartoon Comedy of Errors'
The Mail on Sunday, 19 October 1986 (newspaper)

Isherwood, Charles. 'Lord of Illusion'
The Advocate, 21 February 1995 (magazine)

Jackson, Shannon. 'Clive Barker: Using Art As a Literary Tool'
www.geocities.com/Paris/Metro/3429/clive2.html (website)

Jackson, Henry. 'Horror Hotel'
Jamming, November 1985 (magazine)

Jenison, David. 'Clive Barker: Lord of Storytellers'
Hypno, vol. 4 no. 2, 1995 (magazine)

Jones, Alan. 'Blood and Cheap Thrills'
1. *Cinefantastique*, vol. 17 no. 2, March 1987 (magazine)
2. [revised version] *Clive Barker's Shadows in Eden*, 1991

624

Jones, Alan. 'Clive Barker's *Nightbread*'
Cinefantastique, vol. 20 no. 4, November 1989 (magazine)

Jones, Alan. '*Hellbound: Hellraiser II*'
1. *Cinefantastique*, vol. 19 no. 1/2, January 1989 (magazine)
2. As 'See You In Hell, Darling': *Clive Barker's Shadows in Eden*, 1991

Jones, Alan. 'How Fox Bungled *Nightbreed* Per Clive Barker'
Cinefantastique, vol. 21 no. 1, July 1990 (magazine)

Jones, Chris. '*Crazyface* a Juvenile Embarrassment'
Chicago Tribune, 26 August 1998 (newspaper)

Jones, Stephen. 'Celui qui vint diner'
Phenix, no. 34, March 1993 (magazine, in French; special Clive Barker issue)

Jones, Stephen. 'Clive Barker'
Locus, no. 327, April 1988 (magazine)

Jones, Stephen. 'Clive Barker: Anarchic Prince of Horror'
1. *Knave*, vol. 19 no. 5, 1987 (magazine)
2. *Clive Barker's Shadows in Eden*, 1991

Joshi, ST. 'Clive Barker: Sex, Death, and Fantasy'
Studies in Weird Fiction, no. 9, Spring 1991 (magazine)

Jüdell, Brandon. 'Devil Doll'
10 Percent, March/April 1995 (magazine)

Jüdell, Brandon. 'The Future of Horror Is Queer'
Etcetera, 25 August 1995 (magazine)

Kaveney, Roz. (Untitled)
Times Literary Supplement, 11 October 1991 (newspaper)

Kay, Laura Smith. '*People* Online: Clive Barker 7/27/98'
people.aol.com/people/sp/clive (website)

Kay, Laurie. 'Power Play: Q&A with Clive Barker'
www.prideisp.com/onlinepowerplay/barker.html (website)

Kean, Barbara. 'Nightmares for Real'
Boston Herald, 4 February 1990 (newspaper)

Kelleghan, Fiona. 'Barker, Clive. 12–7. Jones, Stephen, ed. *Clive Barker's Shadows in Eden.* Underwood-Miller, 1991.'
Fantasy and Horror: A Critical and Historical Guide to Literature, Illustration, Film, TV, Radio, and the Internet. ed. Neil Barron. Lanham, MD: Scarecrow Press, 1999

Kennedy, Dana. 'Can Gay Stars Shine?'
Entertainment Weekly, 8 September 1995 (magazine)

Kermode, Mark. 'Ghoul School'
Sight and Sound, vol. 3 no. 6, June 1993 (magazine)

Kermode, Mark, with Lizzie Francke. 'Terror Master'
Sight and Sound, vol. 3 no. 6, June 1993 (magazine)

Kilday, Gregg. 'Clive Barker Raises Hell'
Out, March 1995 (magazine)

Kilgore, Charles. 'Is Clive Barker a Whore?'
Ecco, vol. 1 no. 3, May/June 1988 (magazine)

Killheffer, Robert KJ. 'Fantasy Charts New Realms'
Publishers Weekly, 16 June 1997 (magazine)

Kuntzman, Gersh. 'Clive Paints It Black'
New York Post, 20 November 1993 (newspaper)

Lacey, Liam. 'In World of Skinless Bodies, 'Weird' Means Really Macabre'
Toronto Globe & Mail, 31 October 1987 (newspaper)

Lackey, Mike. 'The Clive Barker Interview'
Marvel Age, no. 107, December 1991 (comic book)

Lammana, Dan. 'Clive Barker's Lurid Fascination'
Cinescape, vol. 4 no. 1, January 1995 (magazine)

Lannon, Linnea. 'A Man and His Monsters'
Detroit Free Press, 7 February 1990 (newspaper)

Larson, Susan. 'Bless the Beasts'
New Orleans Times-Picayune, 21 July 1996 (newspaper)

Larson, Susan. 'Dark Fantasy'
New Orleans Times-Picayune, 23 July 1996 (newspaper)

Leland, John. 'Clive Barker: The Horror, the Horror'
Spin, vol. 4 no. 12, December 1988 (magazine)

Lemons, Stephen. '*Salon* People: King of Pain'
www.salon.com/people/feature/2000/02/04/barker (website)

Levine, Beth. 'Ready or Not, Here Comes Clive Barker'
Publishers Weekly, 4 July 1986 (magazine)

Levine, Bettijane. 'Horror's New King'
Los Angeles Times, 31 January 1990 (newspaper)

Leydon, Joe. 'Director Horrified by *Nightbreed* Publicity'
Houston Post, 23 February 1990 (newspaper)

Leydon, Joe. 'The Man and the Myth'
Houston Post, 10 September 1992 (newspaper)

Liberatore, Karen. 'Clive Barker, Horror Heir Apparent'
San Francisco Chronicle, 31 October 1988 (newspaper)

Liberatore, Karen. 'Fantastical Horror Show To End All Horror Shows'
San Francisco Chronicle, 15 January 1990 (newspaper)

Lovece, Frank. 'Just a Couple'a Comic Guys, Sittin' Around Talkin'
Hokum & Hex, vol. 1 no. 2, New York: Marvel Razorline, October 1993
(comic book)

Lovell, James Blair. 'Adams-Morgan House Shelters Tales of Horror'
Washington Times, 29 December 1987 (newspaper)

Lovell, James Blair. 'Area 'Horror' Fans Get Look at Barker Film'
Washington Times, 18 September 1987 (newspaper)

Lovell, James Blair. 'Clive Barker, Vision of the Fantastique'
Fly in My Eye: An Anthology of Unparalleled Confusion (no. 2). ed. Steve
Niles. Washington, DC: Arcane, 1988 (trade paperback)

Lovell, James Blair. 'Introduction'
Clive Barker's Books of Blood: A Portfolio. Washington, DC: Arcane, 1988

Lowman, Rob. '*Freakz* Alive, Clive! – His 'Living Movie' An A-Maze-Ing
Experience'
Los Angeles Daily News, 14 October 1998 (newspaper)

Lupoff, Richard A. 'An Interview with Clive Barker'
Science Fiction Eye, vol. 1 no. 4, August 1988 (magazine)

Macabre, JB. 'Author's POV: Clive Barker Interview'
Tekeli-li!, no. 3, 1991 (magazine)

Macabre, JB. 'Doug Bradley: JB. Macabre's Conversations with the Man, the Actor Pinhead and Lylesburg'
World of Fandom, vol. 2 no. 15, Spring 1992 (magazine)

Macabre, JB. 'JB Macabre Sits Down with Special Effects Master Bob Keen'
World of Fandom, vol. 2 no. 15, Spring 1992 (magazine)

Macabre, JB. 'JB Macabre Takes a Walking Tour of Hell with the Scribe of Hades Peter Atkins'
World of Fandom, vol. 2 no. 15, Spring 1992 (magazine)

Macabre, JB, and Michael Brown. '*Hellraiser III: Hell on Earth* – JB Macabre and Michael Brown Interview Director Anthony Hickox'
World of Fandom, vol. 2 no. 15, Spring 1992 (magazine)

MacKenzie, Angus. 'Brush Strokes in Blood: An Exclusive Interview with Alan Plent'
Pandemonium: Further Explorations into the World of Clive Barker, 1991

Malcolm, Derek. 'The Angel Who Fell to Earth'
Guardian, 27 September 1990 (newspaper)

Marino, Frank P. 'Sex, Death and Comics: Clive Barker in Comics'
Pandemonium: Further Explorations into the World of Clive Barker, 1991

Mauceri, JB. 'JB Mauceri-Macabre Talks with Clive Barker, the True *Lord of Illusions* on the Set of His New Film'
1. *World of Fandom*, vol. 2 no. 22, 1995 (magazine)
2. As 'Andere Reden Über den Film Wir Reden Mit Dem Regisseur: *Lord of Illusions*. Doom Im Gespräch Mit Clive Barker Auf Dem Set Seines Neuen Films': *Doom*, no. 0, June 1995 (magazine; in German)

Maupin, Armistead. 'Foreword'
The Essential Clive Barker, 1999

McCormick, Carlo. 'Meet Pinhead's Daddy'
Paper, April 1993 (magazine)

McDonagh, Maitland. 'Clive Barker and William Gibson: Future Shockers'
Film Comment, vol. 26 no. 1, January-February 1990 (magazine)

McDonagh, Maitland. 'A Kind of Magic'
The Dark Side, no. 45, April/May 1995 (magazine)

McDonald, T Liam. 'A Conversation with Clive Barker'
Cemetery Dance, no. 15, Winter 1993 (magazine)

McIntyre, Gina. 'Dream Catcher'
Wicked, vol. 2 no. 1, Spring 2000 (magazine)

McLaurin, Mark. 'The Clive Barker Interview'
Marvel Age, no. 107, December 1991 (comic book)

McLeod, Donald J. 'Festival Fringe Review: Dangerous World'
The Scotsman, 31 August 1981 (newspaper)

Mietkiewicz, Henry. 'Gloom with Room for Redemption'
Toronto Star, 31 October 1987 (newspaper)

Miller, Charles V. 'Introduction'
Illustrator Volume II: The Art of Clive Barker, 1993

Miller, Faren C. 'Cabal'
Locus, no. 333, October 1988 (magazine)

Miller, Faren C. 'Clive Barker's Books of Blood, Vols. 1–3'
Locus, no. 288, January 1985 (magazine)

Miller, Faren C. 'Clive Barker's Books of Blood, Vols. 4, 5 & 6'
Locus, no. 295, August 1985 (magazine)

Miller, Faren C. 'The Damnation Game'
Locus, no. 297, October 1985 (magazine)

Miller, Faren C. 'Everville'
Locus, no. 406, November 1994 (magazine)

Miller, Faren C. 'The Great and Secret Show'
Locus, no. 346, November 1989 (magazine)

Miller, Faren C. 'Sacrament'
Locus, no. 427, August 1996 (magazine)

Miller, Faren C. 'The Thief of Always'
Locus, no. 383, December 1992 (magazine)

Miller, Faren C. *'Weaveworld'*
Locus, no. 319, August 1987 (magazine)

Mittelmark, Howard. *'Cabal'*
New York Times Book Review, 18 December 1988 (newspaper)

Moore, JT. 'Barker, Clive. *The Great and Secret Show'*
Science Fiction and Fantasy Book Review Annual 1990. ed. Robert A Collins
and Robert Latham. New York: Greenwood, 1991 (hardback)

Moore, Jim. 'A Graveside Chat with Clive Barker'
Deathrealm, no. 29, Fall 1996 (magazine)

Morgan, Chris. 'Brilliant First Novel'
Fantasy Review, vol. 8 no. 9, September 1985 (magazine)

Morris, Chris. 'Clive Barker: The *Well-Rounded* Interview'
www.well-rounded.com/games/reviews/cliveint.html (website)

Morrish, Robert. *'Weird Tales* Talks with Clive Barker'
Weird Tales, no. 292, Fall 1988 (magazine)

Morrison, Benjamin. 'Barbarossas at the Gate'
New Orleans Times-Picayune, 7 June 1998 (newspaper)

Morrison, Benjamin. 'Voice of the Narrator'
New Orleans Times-Picayune, 7 June 1998 (newspaper)

Morrison, Michael A. 'Blood Without End'
Fantasy Review, vol. 8 no. 6, June 1985 (magazine)

Morrison, Michael A, 'Clive Barker: The Delights of Dread'
    1. *Fantasy Review*, vol. 8 no. 2, February 1985 (magazine)
    2. *Clive Barker's Shadows in Eden*, 1991

Morrison, Michael A. 'Monsters, Miracles and Revelations'
Clive Barker's Shadows in Eden, 1991

Morrison, Michael A. 'Visions of the Joyous Apocalypse'
Fantasy Review, no. 95, October 1986 (magazine)

Morrison, Michael A. 'The Year in Horror, 1987'
Science Fiction and Fantasy Book Review Annual 1988. ed. Robert A Collins
and Robert Latham. Westport, CT: Meckler, 1989 (hardback)

Morrison, Michael A, and Stefan Dziemianowicz. 'The Year in Horror, 1989'
Science Fiction and Fantasy Book Review Annual 1990. ed. Robert A Collins
and Robert Latham. New York: Greenwood, 1991 (hardback)

Mungo, Paul. 'LA Gore'
GQ, December 1992 (magazine)

Murray, Steve. 'Embargoed Until December 20 *Gods* Willing, Director To Stay
In Best Picture Heaven', Cox News Service, 1998

Musto, Michael. 'Clive Barker's Brush with Horror'
New York Daily News, 19 November 1993 (newspaper)

Myerson, Jeremy. 'Play Reviews'
The Stage & Television Today, 23 July 1981 (magazine)

Nash, Jesse. 'He Knows What Evil Lurks'
New Orleans Times-Picayune, 28 January 1990 (newspaper)

Nasson, Timothy. (title unknown)
In Step Magazine, vol. 13 no. 14, 25 July – 6 August 1996 (magazine)

Neilson, Robert and Des Doyle. 'Clive Barker Interviewed'
Albedo One, no. 3, 1993 (magazine)

Newman, Kim. 'Clive Barker at the UCA: Imagining the Horrific' (in three
parts; translated into German by Nikki Iskra)
1. *That's Clive!*, no. 0, August 1995 (magazine)
2. *That's Clive!*, no. 1, January 1996 (magazine)
3. *That's Clive!*, no. 2, May 1996 (magazine)

Newman, Kim. 'Clive Barker Interview'
1. *Interzone*, no. 14, Winter 1985–86 (magazine)
2. As 'Interview Mit Clive Barker: Der Neue Altmeister Des Horrors?':
    Science Fiction Media, No. 34, March 1987 (magazine; translated into
    German by Joachim Körber)

Newman, Kim. 'Direct to Hell with Clive Barker'
AIP&CO, no. 79, November-December 1986 (magazine)

Newman, Kim. 'Hell on Earth'
City Limits, no. 398, 18 May 1989 (magazine)

Newman, Kim. 'Hellbound: Hellraiser II'
Monthly Film Bulletin, no. 666, July 1989 (magazine)

Newman, Kim. 'Hellraiser'
Monthly Film Bulletin, no. 644, September 1987 (magazine)

Newman, Kim. 'Hellraiser: From Horror Fiction to Horror Movies'
Sight and Sound, vol. 56 no. 4, Autumn 1987 (magazine)

Newman, Kim. 'Hellraiser 3: Hell on Earth'
Sight and Sound, February 1993 (magazine)

Newman, Kim. 'The Man Who Collected Barker' (fiction)
Fantasy Tales, vol. 1 no. 1, Spring 1990 (magazine)

Newman, Kim. 'Nightbreed'
Monthly Film Bulletin, no. 681, October 1990 (magazine)

Newman, Kim. 'Slime Time'
Clive Barker's Shadows in Eden, 1991

Nicholls, Stan. 'Clive Barker Pulls Away the Veils'
Wordsmiths of Wonder: Fifty Interviews with Writers of the Fantastic.
London: Orbit, 1993 (hardback)

Nicholls, Stan. 'A Strange Kind of Believer'
Million, no. 13, January/February 1993 (magazine)

Nicoll, Gregory. 'The Comic *Books of Blood*'
Fangoria, no. 82, May 1989 (magazine)

Niles, Steve. 'Triple Threat: The Blood-Soaked Brushwork of Writer/Director
Clive Barker'
Greed, no. 5, 1988 (magazine; with illustrations by Clive Barker)

North, Kate. 'Collected Works: Review of Science-Sprung Fiction'
New Scientist, vol. 151, 6 July 1996 (journal)

Nutman, Philip. 'Birth of the *Nightbreed*'
Fangoria, no. 86, September 1989 (magazine)

Nutman, Philip. 'Breaking The Last Taboo'
Fangoria, no. 76, August 1988 (magazine)

Nutman, Philip. 'Breed Magic'
Fangoria, no. 92, May 1990 (magazine)

Nutman, Philip. 'Bring On The Monsters, Part One'
Fangoria, no. 87, October 1989 (magazine)

Nutman, Philip. 'Clive Barker: 1995 World Horror Convention Grandmaster'
1. *World Horror Convention 1995.* ed. Edward E. Kramer. Atlanta: World Horror Convention, 2–5 March 1995 (program book)
2. *Lost Souls*, vol. 1 no. 1, 1995 (magazine)

Nutman, Philip. 'Clive Barker – Lord of the Breed'
Fangoria, no. 91, April 1990 (magazine)

Nutman, Philip. 'Clive Barker Raises Hell'
Fangoria, no. 60, January 1987 (magazine)

Nutman, Philip. 'Cronenberg Cuts Up'
Fangoria, no. 90, February 1990 (magazine)

Nutman, Philip. 'The *Fangoria* Hall Of Fame: Clive Barker'
Fangoria, no. 100, March 1991 (magazine)

Nutman, Philip. 'Gangsters vs. Mutants!'
1. *Fangoria*, no. 50, January 1986 (magazine)
2. *L'Ecran Fantastique*, 1986 (magazine; in French)
3. [revised version] *Clive Barker's Shadows in Eden*, 1991

Nutman, Philip. 'Hammering Out *Hellraiser*'
Fangoria, no. 65, July 1987 (magazine)

Nutman, Philip. '*Hellbound* Heartthrob'
Fangoria, no. 80, February 1989 (magazine)

Nutman, Philip. '*Hellraiser* Update'
Fangoria, no. 67, September 1987 (magazine)

Nutman, Philip. '*Hellraiser II: Hellbound*'
Fangoria, no. 75, July 1988 (magazine)

Nutman, Philip. 'If You Knew Clive Like We Know Clive . . .'
Fangoria, no. 78, October 1988 (magazine)

Nutman, Philip. '*Nightbreed*'
Fangoria, no. 83, June 1989 (magazine)

Nutman, Philip. '*Nightbreed*'
Fangoria, no. 91, April 1990 (magazine)

Nutman, Philip. 'Peter Atkins: The Long Road to Hell'
Gorezone, no. 22, Spring 1992 (magazine)

Nutman, Philip. 'The Pride of Pinhead'
Fangoria, no. 82, May 1989 (magazine)

Nutman, Philip. 'Putting the Hell in *Hellraiser*'
Fangoria, no. 66, August 1987 (magazine)

Nutman, Philip. 'Rampaging with *Rawhead Rex*'
Fangoria, no. 61, February 1987 (magazine)

Nutman, Philip. 'Scorpio Goes to Hell'
Fangoria, no. 67, September 1987 (magazine)

Nutman, Philip. '*Hellraiser III: Hell on Earth* - Welcome to Club Dead'
Fangoria, no. 110, March 1992 (magazine)

Nutman, Philip, and Stefan Jaworzyn. 'Meet Clive Barker'
1. *Fangoria*, no. 51, February 1986 (magazine)
2. As 'Clive Barker, créateur de monstres': *L'Ecran Fantastique*, no. 69, June 1986 (magazine; in French)
3. 'Das *Tales*-Interview, Teil 1': *Tales*, no. 3, April 1987 (magazine; translated into German by Tina Hess)
4. *Clive Barker's Shadows in Eden*, 1991

O'Gorman, Rochelle. 'Audio Books: An Unholy Terror Resurfaces on Tape'
Los Angeles Times, 27 October 1999 (newspaper)

Oakes, David A. 'Holy Terror or Gentle Redeemer: The Depiction of God in Clive Barker's *Imajica* and Stephen King's *The Stand*'
Paper presented to the International Conference on the Fantastic in the Arts, Fort Lauderdale, Florida, March 1998

Oakes, David A. '*Imajica*'
Magill's Guide to Science Fiction and Fantasy Literature: Volume 2. ed. TA Shippey. Pasadena, CA: Salem Press, 1996

Olley, Michelle. 'The *Skin Two* Interview: Cult, Novelist and Film-Maker Clive Barker'
Skin Two, no. 10, 1991 (magazine)

Olson, Ray. 'Upfront: Advance Reviews'
Booklist, vol. 92 nos. 19–20, 1–15 June 1996 (magazine)

Outerbridge, Laura. 'King of Gore Clive Barker Haunts DC'
Washington Times, 18 October 1987 (newspaper)

Outland, Orland. '*Lord of Illusions*' Clive Barker: Gay Heroism, Tales of Transcendence'
Frontiers, 8 September 1995 (magazine)

Owen, Nick. 'Clive in London'
Lost Souls, vol. 1 no. 1, 1995 (magazine)

Pener, Degen. 'Egos & Ids'
New York Times, 24 January 1993 (newspaper)

Penfield III, Wilder. 'Coming Out No Horror for Barker'
Toronto Sun, 17 August 1996 (newspaper)

Perry, Vern. 'Prince of Horror: Just Who Is Clive Barker and Why Is He Trying to Scare Us?'
Orange County Register, 18 October 1987 (newspaper)

Perry, Vern. '*Weaveworld* Spins a Fine Web of Fantasy'
Orange County Register, 18 October 1987 (newspaper)

Petrucci, Lisa. 'Drawing upon the Imagination'
Gauntlet, vol. II, 1993 (magazine)

Piccoli, Sean. 'Horror Titan Clive Barker Unleashes a Children's Fable'
Washington Times, 16 December 1992 (newspaper)

Pooley, Eric. 'Horrors!'
New York, 26 May 1986 (magazine)

Pouncey, Edwin. 'Go Straight to Hell'
1. *New Musical Express*, 2 April 1988 (magazine)
2. *Clive Barker's Shadows in Eden*, 1991

Proposch, Stephen. 'Clive Barker: The Illusion Revealed'
Bloodsongs, no. 6, Spring 1995 (magazine)

Provenzano, Tom. 'Great Scott'
The Advocate, 27 August 1995 (magazine)

Rahier, Francois. 'Imagica'
Keep Watching the Skies, no. 19, May 1996 (magazine; in French)

Rahlmann, Reed Kirk. 'Tortured Artist'
Contra Costa Times, 24 August 1995 (newspaper)

Reial, Sandy. '1993: A Year of Clive – A Fan's Dream Come True'
Dread, no. 12, 1993 (magazine)

Ricapito, Maria. 'Creeping Back into Vogue'
New York Times, 13 August 1995 (newspaper)

Rice, Carole Anne. 'Master of Macabre Is Sweetness and Light'
Birmingham Post Style, 26 April 1995 (newspaper magazine insert)

Richards, Linda. 'Clive Barker Comes Out: An Intimate Visit with One of the Masters of Scary Stuff'
www.januarymagazine.com/barker.html (website)

Riddle, Timothy L. 'Ecstasies and Abominations: Religious Tradition as Terror in Selected Works of Clive Barker'
Thesis (MA), Bowling Green State University, 1998

Ringgenberg, SC. 'Clive Barker: A Man for All Seasons'
Comics Journal, no. 171, September 1994 (magazine)

Rose, Bernard. 'More Things in Heaven and Earth'
Sight and Sound, March 1993 (magazine)

Ross, Jean W. 'Contemporary Authors Interview'
Contemporary Authors, Volume 129. Detroit: Gale Research, 1990 (hardback)

Roush, Matt. 'Barker vs. The King'
USA Today, 22 August 1986 (newspaper)

Roush, Matt. 'Meet Horror's Heir Apparent'
USA Today, 22 August 1986 (newspaper)

Russo, Michelle. 'Clive Barker: An Interview'
Lost Souls, vol. 1 no. 12, January 1999 (magazine)

Salisbury, Mark. 'Babel's Child'
Fear, September/October 1988 (magazine)

Salisbury, Mark. 'Chains of Love'
Fear, November/December 1988 (magazine)

Salisbury, Mark. 'Die Laughing! Clive Barker in Conversation with Tim Burton'
1. *Fear*, no. 5, March/April 1989 (magazine)
2. *Clive Barker's Shadows in Eden*, 1991

Salisbury, Mark. 'Don't Hammer the Horror'
Guardian, 4 October 1990 (newspaper)

Salisbury, Mark. 'Flesh and Fury'
Fear, October 1990 (magazine)

Salisbury, Mark. '*Monster Invasion*: Barker's Latest'
Fangoria, no. 133, June 1994 (magazine)

Salisbury, Mark, and John Gilbert. 'A Hymn to the Monstrous'
Clive Barker's Nightbreed: The Making of the Film. Glasgow: Fontana/
Collins, 1990 (trade paperback)

Schechter, Barry. 'Warring Gods of the Imagination'
Chicago Tribune, 5 February 1990 (newspaper)

Schenden, Laurie K. 'Dream Weaver'
The Advocate, 23 June 1998 (newspaper)

Schenden, Laurie K. 'Frights of Fancy: Universal Studios Asked Creepy
Creative Souls to Mastermind Mazes for Halloween'
Los Angeles Times, 14 October 1999 (newspaper)

Schleier, Curt. 'The Future of Horror Is Here: His Name Is Clive Barker'
Inside Books, November 1988 (magazine)

Schow, David J. '*Raving and Drooling*: Insert Blurb Here'
Fangoria, no. 142, May 1995 (magazine)

Schramm, Joan C. 'The Face of Horror: An Evening with Clive Barker'
House Carfax, Fall 1990 (magazine)

Schweiger, Daniel. 'Bernard Rose's Demons of the Mind'
1. *Fangoria*, no. 118, November 1992 (magazine)
2. In *Fangoria's Best Horror Films*. ed. Anthony Timpone. New York:
   Crescent, 1994 (hardback)

Semel, Paul. 'GameSpy.com Interviews: Clive Barker Interview'
www.gamespy.com/interviews/december00/clive (website)

Seward, Keith, and Lisa Petrucci. 'Hellraiser in SoHo: An Interview with Clive
Barker'
Clive Barker: Metaphysics & Aliens, March 1993 (promotional flier published
by Bess Cutler Gallery)

Sheehan, Bill. 'A Look Within'
Lost Souls, vol. 1 no. 6, January 1997 (magazine)

Sheehan, Bill. 'Reflections on Jacqueline Ess'
Lost Souls, vol. 1 no. 7, April 1997 (magazine)

Sheehan, Bill. *'Revelations'*
The New York Review of Science Fiction, no. 106, June 1997 (magazine)

Sheehan, Bill. *'Sacrament'*
Lost Souls, vol. 1 no. 5, October 1996 (magazine)

Sheehan, Harry. 'Clive Barker and His Visions of Horror'
Orange County Register, 14 August 1995 (newspaper)

Sherman, David. 'Nightmare Library: *Clive Barker's Books of Blood*'
Fangoria, no. 48, October 1985 (magazine)

Sherman, Steve. 'Horror Spreads Across the Country'
Publishers Weekly, 4 December 1987 (magazine)

Shulman, Milton. 'Anyone for Rabbit Stew?'
London Standard, 16 October 1986 (newspaper)

Skipp, John, and Craig Spector. *'Clive Barker's Nightbreed*: Skipp & Spector Get Killed' (in two parts)
1. *Gorezone*, no. 10, November 1989 (magazine)
2. *Gorezone*, no. 11, Januaruy 1990 (magazine)

Smith, Andrew. 'Worlds That Creep Up On You: Postmodern Illusions in the Work of Clive Barker'
Creepers: British Horror and Fantasy in the Twentieth Century. ed. Clive Bloom. London: Pluto, 1993 (trade paperback)

Smith, Malcolm. 'From Doodles to Decamundi'
1. *Hokum & Hex*, vol. 1 no. 6, New York: Marvel Razorline, February 1994 (comic book)
2. *Hyperkind*, vol. 1 no. 6, New York: Marvel Razorline, February 1994 (comic book)

Smith, Malcolm. 'Introduction.'
Clive Barker's Nightbreed: Genesis. New York: Marvel Epic, November 1991 (graphic novel)

Smith, Peter. *'Devil* Is Strong Theater in More Ways Than One'
St. Petersburg Times, date unknown, 1999 (newspaper)

SECONDARY BIBLIOGRAPHY

Smith, Sean K. 'Imp of the Perverse'
LA Village View, 25 August 1995 (newspaper)

Smith, Sid. 'Horror's Roots'
Chicago Tribune, 23 May 1993 (newspaper)

Stevenson, Jay. 'Clive Barker Hellraiser'
Imagi-Movies, vol. 1 no. 2, Winter 1993/1994 (magazine)

Strauss, Bob. 'Barker's Searching for a Higher Plane'
Fresno Bee, 25 October 1987 (newspaper)

Streitfeld, David. 'Who's Afraid of Clive Barker? The Titan of Terror and His Studies in Dread Reckoning'
1. *Washington Post*, 30 September 1987 (newspaper)
2. [revised version] *Clive Barker's Shadows in Eden*, 1991

Stroby, WC. 'Clive Barker's Boundless Imajination'
1. *Fangoria*, no. 109, January 1992 (magazine)
2. In *Fangoria's Best Horror Films*. ed. Anthony Timpone. New York: Crescent, 1994 (hardback)

Stroby, WC. 'Clive Barker: Trust Your Vision'
Writer's Digest, vol. 71 no. 3, March 1991 (magazine)

Stroby, WC. '*Imajica* by Clive Barker'
Fangoria, no. 109, January 1992 (magazine)

Sullivan, Jack. 'Clive Barker and the End of the Horror Boom'
Studies in Weird Fiction, no. 14, Winter 1994 (journal)

Talbot, Linda. 'Linda Talbot at the York and Albany'
Hampstead and Highgate Express, 10 July 1981 (newspaper)

Thomas, Kevin. 'Barker Proves a Master with *Illusions*'
Los Angeles Times, 25 August 1995 (newspaper)

Tinker, Jack. 'What's Up, Doc, with All This?'
Daily Mail, 16 October 1986 (newspaper)

Tookey, Christopher. 'Enfant Terrible'
Books and Bookmen, July 1985 (magazine)

Tucker, Ken. 'One Universe at a Time, Please'
New York Times Book Review, 11 February 1990 (newspaper)

Tuttle, Lisa. 'Every Fear Is a Desire'
Clive Barker's Shadows in Eden, 1991

Villegas, Rubén Sosa. 'Clive Barker Interview'
The Blood Review, April 1990 (magazine)

Villegas, Rubén Sosa. 'For Clive Barker, a Good Story Is More Than a Scare'
Rocky Mountain News, 27 October 1991 (newspaper)

Vince, Nick. 'Clive Barker: The Magic Show'
Clive Barker's Hellbreed, no. 1, May 1995 (comic magazine)

Vince, Nick. 'Doug Bradley'
Pandemonium: Further Explorations into the World of Clive Barker, 1991

Vince, Nick. 'Doug Bradley: Pinned Down'
Clive Barker's Hellbreed, no. 2, June 1995 (comic magazine)

Vince, Nick. 'Doug Bradley: Pin Points'
Clive Barker's Hellbreed, no. 3, July 1995 (comic magazine)

Vince, Nick. 'The Luggage in the Crypt: A Candid Interview with Clive Barker'
Pandemonium: Further Explorations into the World of Clive Barker, 1991

Vince, Nick. 'More than a Face: An Actor's View of Prosthetic Make-Up'
Pandemonium: Further Explorations into the World of Clive Barker, 1991

Vince, Nick. 'Simon Bamford'
Pandemonium: Further Explorations into the World of Clive Barker, 1991

Wallace, Amy. 'It's Showtime for Projects Heading to the Big Screen'
Los Angeles Times, 3 March 1999 (newspaper)

Wardle, Irving. 'A Disgraceful Cartoon Comedy'
Times of London, 16 October 1986 (newspaper)

Warman, Juliet. 'Little House of Horrors: Master of Gore Lives It Up On Blood Money'
1. *Today*, 3 September 1988
2. *Clive Barker's Shadows in Eden*, 1991

Warren, Steve. 'Clive Barker A Lord of Illusion'
Center Stage, September 1995 (magazine)

Warren, Steve. 'Movies: Clive Barker, Happy Homo Horror Hero'
1. *San Francisco Sentinel*, 23 August 1995 (newspaper)
2. As 'Queen of Horror': *TWN News Magazine*, 30 August 1995 (newspaper)

Watts, Mordecai. 'Clive Barker: Beyond Good and Evil'
Axcess, vol. 3 no. 5, 1995 (magazine)

Weightman, Sharon. 'Play's the Thing for Terror King'
Jacksonville Times-Union, 21 November 1997 (newspaper)

Welch, Frances. 'Horror Stories with a Walk-On Part for Jesus'
Sunday Telegraph, 13 December 1998 (newspaper)

Welkos, Robert W. 'A Spinner of (Horrorific) Tales'
Los Angeles Times, 11 October 1993 (newspaper)

Westbrook, Bruce. 'Barker's Superheroes'
Houston Chronicle, 24 October 1993 (newspaper)

Wiater, Stanley. 'Assorted Interview Quotes'
Dark Thought On Writing: Advice and Commentary from Fifty Masters of Fear and Suspense. Lancaster, PA: Underwood, 1997 (trade paperback)

Wiater, Stanley. 'Catching Up With Clive Barker: Part Two"
1. *Fangoria*, no. 55, July 1986 (magazine)
2. As 'Das *Tales*-Interview, Teil 2': *Tales*, no. 3, April 1987 (translated into German by Tina Hess)
3. *Clive Barker's Shadows in Eden*, 1991
4. As 'Catching Up with Clive Barker': *Fangoria: Masters of the Dark*. ed. Anthony Timpone.
   a. New York: HarperCollins, 1997 (paperback)
   b. As *Stephen King – Clive Barker: Les maîtres de la Terreur*. Pantin: Editions Naturellement, 1999 (in French)

Wiater, Stanley. 'Clive Barker'
Dark Dreamers: Conversations with the Masters of Horror.
   a. Lancaster, PA : Underwood-Miller, 1990 (limited edition hardback)
   b. New York: Avon, 1990 (trade paperback)
   c. As 'Interview Mit Clive Barker': *Phantasia Almanach*, no. 1, November 1994 (magazine; translated into German by Hans Schuld)

Wiater, Stanley. 'Clive Barker'
Dark Visions: Conversations with the Masters of the Horror Film. New York: Avon Books, 1992 (trade paperback)

Wiater, Stanley. 'Clive Barker: Master of the Fantastique'
amazon.com, June 1998.

Wiater, Stanley. 'An Interview with Clive Barker'
barnesandnoble.com, May 1998

Williams, Ian. 'From Spook City'
New Statesman, 25 September 1987 (magazine)

Wilson, Andrew J. 'Visions Presents Clive Barker'
Visions, Fall 1991 (magazine)

Wilson, Kristi M. 'Cross-Cultural Othering Through Metamorphosis'
Paroles Gelees: UCLA French Studies, vol. 14 no. 2, 1996 (journal)

Winter, Douglas E. 'An Artistic Escape'
Lost Souls, vol. 1 no. 8, July 1997 (magazine)

Winter, Douglas E. 'And Death Shall Have No Dominion'
Necrofile, no. 3, Winter 1992 (magazine)

Winter, Douglas E. 'Barker tours the fantastic pursuing the (im)possible'
Washington Times, 9 October 1991 (newspaper)

Winter, Douglas E. 'A Breed Apart: Clive Barker'
Gallery, September 1990 (magazine)

Winter, Douglas E. 'The Class of '79'
Fangoria, no. 150, March 1996 (magazine)

Winter, Douglas E. 'Clive Barker'
Faces of Fear. By Douglas E. Winter
  a. New York: Berkley, 1985 (trade paperback)
  b. London: Pan, 1988 (revised version; paperback)

Winter, Douglas E. 'Clive Barker: Britain's New Master of Horror'
Washington Post Book World, 24 August 1986 (newspaper)

Winter, Douglas E. 'The Dark Chamber: By Any Other Name'
Necrofile, no. 13, Summer 1994 (magazine)

Winter, Douglas E. 'Forbidden Candy'
Other Dimensions, no. 2, Fall 1994 (journal)

Winter, Douglas E. 'Foreword'

The Worm Ouroboros. By ER Eddison. New York: Dell, 1991 (trade paperback)

Winter, Douglas E. 'Foreword'
Zimiamvia. By ER Eddison. New York: Dell, 1992 (trade paperback)

Winter, Douglas E. 'The Fun House of Fear'
1. *Harper's Bazaar,* October 1985 (magazine)
2. *Fantasy Review,* no. 95, October 1986 (magazine; revised version)

Winter, Douglas E. 'Give Me B Movies or Give Me Death!'
1. *Faces of Fear.* By Douglas E. Winter.
   a. New York: Berkley, 1985 (trade paperback)
   b. London: Pan, 1990 (paperback; revised edition)
2. Clive Barker's *Shadows in Eden,* 1991

Winter, Douglas E. *'The Great and Secret Show'*
Pandemonium: Further Explorations into the World of Clive Barker, 1991

Winter, Douglas E. 'The Heights and Depths of *Hellraiser*'
1. *Fangoria,* December 1992 (magazine)
2. As 'Les chroniques d'Hellraiser': *Phenix 34: Dossier Clive Barker.* ed. Gilles Bergal. Racour, France: Phenix, March 1993 (trade paperback; in French)
3. *The Bloody Best of Fangoria,* no. 7, 1998 (magazine)

Winter, Douglas E. *'Hellraiser:* A Discussion with Writer/Director Clive Barker'
Touch of Evil Film Festival Program Book. ed. Brian Tate. Washington, DC: Satellite Foundation, 1987 (booklet)

Winter, Douglas E. 'The Literary Life of Harry D'Amour'
Fangoria, no. 141, April 1995 (magazine)

Winter, Douglas E. 'Nowhere Land: Clive Barker and *The Damnation Game*'
SPG Quarterly, 2001 (journal)

Winter, Douglas E. 'Opera of Violence: The Films of Dario Argento'
1. *Cut! Horror Writers on Horror Film.* ed. Christopher Golden.
   a. Baltimore, MD: Borderlands, 1992 (signed limited edition hardback)
   b. New York: Berkley, 1992 (trade paperback)
2. In *The Horror Film in World Cinema.* ed. Steven J Schneider. Woburn, MA: Tufts University/booktech.com, 2000 (course materials)

Winter, Douglas E. 'Over the Threshold of Dreams'
Necrofile, no. 17, Summer 1995 (magazine)

Winter, Douglas E. 'The Play's the Thing (Part One)'
Cemetery Dance, vol. 7 no. 1, Spring 1996 (magazine)

Winter, Douglas E. 'The Play's the Thing (Part Two)'
Cemetery Dance, vol. 7 no. 2, Summer 1996 (magazine)

Winter, Douglas E. 'Raising Hell with Clive Barker'
1. *Twilight Zone Magazine*, December 1987 (magazine)
2. *Clive Barker's Shadows in Eden*, 1991

Winter, Douglas E. '*Secret* Is Horrifically Good Work from Master of Fantastic'
Washington Times, 26 February 1990 (newspaper)

Winter, Douglas E. '*Shadowings*: Finding My Religion'
Worlds of Fantasy & Horror, no. 3, Summer 1996 (magazine)

Winter, Douglas E. '*Shadowings*: Nowhere Land'
Weird Tales, no. 323, Spring 2001 (magazine)

Winter, Douglas E. '*Shadowings*: Of Gods and Monsters'
Weird Tales, no. 321, Fall 2000 (magazine)

Winter, Douglas E. '*Shadowings*: Sacrament'
Weird Tales, no. 313, Summer 1998 (magazine)

Winter, Douglas E. '*Shadowings*: Stories of Our Own'
Weird Tales, no. 319, Spring 2000 (magazine)

Winter, Douglas E. 'Talking Terror with Clive Barker'
1. *Twilight Zone Magazine*, June 1987 (magazine)
2. *Clive Barker's Shadows in Eden*, 1991

Winter, Douglas E. 'Words That Haunted You'
Fangoria, no. 100, March 1991 (magazine)

Wyrick, Laura. 'Summoning *Candyman*: The Cultural Production of History'
Arizona Quarterly: A Journal of American Literature, Culture, and Theory,
vol. 54 no. 3, Autumn 1998 (journal)

Yablonsky, Linda. (Exhibition Review)
Artforum International, vol. 32 no. 8, April 1994 (journal)

Ziegler, Robert. 'Fantasy's Timeless Humor in Clive Barker's *The Thief of
Always*'
Notes on Contemporary Literature, vol. 24 no. 5, November 1994 (journal)

SELECTED MUSIC INSPIRED BY CLIVE BARKER

Bolus, Andy. *Evil Moisture*. Performed by Commode Minstrels in Bullface, with Bolus on 'toy sampler, Realistic TR882 8-track recorder, broken PAL VCR, Fisher-Price tape recorder, reel to reel, guitar amp, splice tape, razors, finger resistance, and hiss.' New York: Birdman, 1996 (BMR004; 33 1/3 rpm vinyl single). Musique concrete packaged with a copy of the graphic novel *Hellraiser*, no. 17 (Epic Comics).

Pape, Gerard. *Electroacoustic Chamber Works*. Performed by Ensemble Vox Nova, with Pape on tape. New York: Mode, 1998 (compact disc). Of five works, the fourth is for two sopranos, tenor, bass, and tape, 'from Clive Barker's novel *Weaveworld*'.

RESOURCES

Lost Souls: The Official World of Clive Barker
www.clivebarker.com

Fan Magazines
Clive Barker's Hellbreed, nos. 1–3, 1995
Coenobium: Explorations in the Further Regions of Hellraiser, nos. 1–12, 1990–1994
Dread, nos. 1–12, 1991–1993
Lost Souls, vol. 1 no. 1, 1995-present

Internet Newsgroups and Websites
Clive Barker Usenet Newsgroup
  alt.books.clive-barker
Clive Barker: Creator of the Fantastique
  www.lib.uconn.edu/klaity/clive.html
Clive Barker: Director and Writer
  www.angelfire.com/nb/djinn1928/barker.html
Clive Barker: Mythmaker for the Millennium
  members.aol.com/alba269068/cb1a.htm
Clive Barker: Revelations
  www.btinternet.com/revelations/
Candyman
  website.lineone.net/djinn/candy.html
Fantastic Fiction: Clive Barker Bibliography
  www.fantasticfiction.com/authors/CliveBarker.htm

Frequently Asked Questions on alt.books.clive-barker
www.bloodletters.com/Barker/
Gods and Monsters – Official Website
www.godsandmonsters.net
HarperCollinsPublishers
www.**fire**and**water**.com
The Hellbound Web – The Shoppe – The Amazon
www.rexer.com/hell/amazon.html
Hellraiser: The Hellbound Web
www.cenobite.com/
Hellraiser 'We Will Tear Your Soul Apart'
website.lineone.net/djinn/candy.html
Horror Usenet Newsgroup
alt.horror
Internet Movie Data Base
us.imdb.com/Name?Barker,+Clive
us.imdb.com/Name?Atkins,+Peter
us.imdb.com/Name?Bradley,+Doug
us.imdb.com/Name?Condon,+Bill
us.imdb.com/Name?Garris,+Mick
us.imdb.com/Name?Parker,+Oliver
us.imdb.com/Name?Pavlou,+George
us.imdb.com/Name?Rose,+Bernard
The Lament Configuration - Clive Barker Webring
nav.webring.yahoo.com/hub?ring=barker&id=5&next5
Nightbreed: Children of Midian Webring
www.geocities.com/Area51/Hollow/4621/breed.htm
nav.webring.yahoo.com/hub?ring=nightbreed&list
Red Zone: Clive Barker
www.webcom.com/tby/cbarker.html
Sniper's Clive Barker Web Page
www.geocities.com:80/SunsetStrip/Stage/1883/
Souls at Zero
www.geocities.com/Area51/Corridor/5758/soulsatzero.html
Webcom
www.webcom.com/tby/cbarker.html
A Whisper from Beyond
www.geocities.com/Area51/Cavern/2762/

INDEX